Tarr's sprightly employmen
gift of a gifted communicator—
to a wide range of people, both to the scholarly-inclined and to the general public. The central thesis is to arrest attention to the surprising ways God addresses His creation and challenge readers to allow God to operate outside of one's own little box! Both Pentecostals and non-Pentecostals will profit from a careful reading of this book.

Dr. William Menzies
President-Emeritus, Asia Pacific Theological Seminary

Del Tarr's *The Foolishness of God: a Communicologist looks at Glossolalia* is a new approach to the troubling questions surrounding speaking in tongues. In this scholarly but polemic work, Tarr looks at the critics and defenders of the current Pentecostal emphasis on speaking in tongues while addressing the subject with the eye of a professional in modern communications theory. I highly recommend this book to scholars and general readers alike.

Vinson Synan
Professor of Church History
Dean Emeritus, School of Divinity, Regent University

The Foolishness of God is a fresh analysis of the nature and power of speaking in tongues. Rejecting a rationalistic and stultifying approach to Christian spirituality, Dr. Tarr calls for a return to the more oral roots of early Christianity and a new sense of immediacy with God in the practice of glossolalia. He charts a course of radical dependence upon the Spirit and return to effective Spirit-empowered witness.

Randy Hurst
Assemblies of God Commissioner of Evangelism
Former student of Dr. Del Tarr

"TONGUES IS GOD'S JOKE
ON HUMAN REASON."

—ISAAC CANALES

The Foolishness *of* God

Published by The Access Group
Springfield, MO 65802
417-831-7000

ISBN: 978 0 9844470 0 8

Printed in the United States of America

Preceeding Page: The traditional Upper Room in Jerusalem, believed by some to be the site of the Last Supper. Seven weeks later at the celebration of Pentecost, the apostles and other disciples were filled with the Holy Spirit.

Photo: ThinkStock

THE FOOLISHNESS *of* GOD

A Linguist Looks *at the* Mystery *of* Tongues

AN UNPRECEDENTED REVIVAL HAS SWEPT THE WORLD IN THE LAST 100 YEARS. AS LATE AS THE MID-TWENTIETH CENTURY—FIFTY YEARS INTO THIS MOVE OF GOD—ALMOST NO ONE ANTICIPATED IT WOULD BE CALLED BY SOME THE "CENTURY OF THE PENTECOSTALS." AT THIS WRITING AT LEAST 650 MILLION LIVING BELIEVERS SUBSCRIBE TO THIS DOCTRINAL POSITION OF GLOSSOLALIA. "STATISTICIANS TELL US THAT MORE THAN 1.5 BILLION PEOPLE ASSOCIATE THEMSELVES WITH THIS GLOBAL REVIVAL."[1]

KJV indicates the King James Version of the Bible.

TABLE OF CONTENTS

Acknowledgments

This writer is grateful for a personal family environment of Christian ministers whose parents taught us a strict moral code but did not model for us a small sectarian view of the Church of Jesus Christ. In that "broad view of the Kingdom," I soon perceived that conformity to much of the church world's expectations about faith (as well as the secular population's opinions of the "ought" of Christian belief) was not the model the Scriptures seem to suggest. I began to understand early that, in fact, *God is a rebel* if judged by the measure of human reason. I'm indebted to a familial climate of diversity which permitted innovative thought.

Now, more specifically, I acknowledge the help of the following persons and/or their literature on the topic of glossolalia and the Holy Spirit's empowerment.

To my wife Dolly—who is my married companion for over 50 years: my lover, counselor, encourager, faithful mother of our three children, fellow teacher and international traveler, besides patient confidant while I am emotionally absent preparing manuscripts—goes my deep and everlasting love and gratitude.

I acknowledge the editorial assistance and advice of Dr. Barbara Liddle Cavaness and Ms. Ginger Niemeyer. As a communication "oralist," the writer is dependant on the literary help of such gifted people.

From the substantial bibliography at the end of the book must come special notice to specific sources of inspiration on which I drew generously:

David Lim, *Spiritual Gifts: A Fresh Look.*

Gordon Fee, *God's Empowering Presence: The Holy Spirit in the Letters of Paul*

__________ *Corinthians; A Study Guide, 3rd Edition.*

Morton Kelsey, *Tongues Speaking: An Experiment in Spiritual Experience.*

Wade Horton, ed., *The Glossolalia Phenomenon.*

Larry Christenson, *Speaking in Tongues, Its Significance for the Church.*

Murray Dempster, et. al. eds., *The Globalization of Pentecostalism, A Religion Made to Travel.*

Harvey Cox, *Fire From Heaven*

Gary McGee, ed., *Initial Evidence, Historical and Biblical Perspectives on the Pentecostal Doctrine of Spirit Baptism.*

Edmund Rybarczyk, "Expressing the Inexpressible: Tongues as Apophatic Speech."

Robert K. Greenleaf, *Servant Leadership*

Special thanks to Pastor Rick Cole and Capital Christian Center, Sacramento, CA, for their investment in our lives toward the termination of this project during a time of personal stress. This congregation's faith in us assures a positive outcome.

Foreword

Since the author has given me the first word—to precede his brilliant treatise with a "foreword," may I beg the reader's patience if my words here become too forward. But first...

This is a communicator's book about communication—an exploratory work examining matters too often thought unthinkable to the thoughtful, but only because we have so often been presented so shallow or lopsided a view of so deep and enriching and actually balanced a practice as the one discussed here. The "communicator"—indeed, the professorial presenter here—is Del Tarr, a man of accomplished scholarship, respected leadership, and broad cultural exposure. These descriptions apply to his work both within and without the ecclesiastical world, as well as both here and beyond the cultures of the Western world. Del is a creative educator, an insightful anthropologist, a capable speaker, a lucid writer, and a trustworthy churchman; in each of those regards, one who has given decades to bettering the lives of the innumerable host of people, his influence has touched.

Add to the above that Dr. Tarr is a forthright researcher, whose risk in writing on the subject of "glossolalia" (the academically respectable word for "speaking with tongues") indicates something of that pioneer spirit that has caused so many "insightful-before-their-time" people to be branded naïve at best and fools at the inception of a longer list of worse epithets. So ask, "Why?" Why would a man of acknowledged attainment risk the broad esteem given his lifetime of labors? Why would he write on this theme now? And that answer is in the second paragraph above: because Del Tarr is all about seeking to "better the lives" of people he touches. And as peculiar as it may doubtless seem to many, he has found (and admittedly, I side with his findings) that glossolalia is a part of "a better way" for us all. However, like all things beneficial, there are terms for the healthy adoption and application of things by which we might advantage ourselves; terms which some refuse under the guise of supposed superior "reason." Which brings me to my forewarning of becoming "too forward" in this foreword. Here's the reason.

It concerns those thought habits so common to our contemporary mindset which presume "God" is (a) a rationally untenable idea; or (b) if He does exist, He is coldly impersonal or mildly impractical; and thereby (c) even granting His actual being and pragmatic wisdom, in reference to this book's propositions, He surely wouldn't seriously expose Himself to expect serious thinkers to have anything to do with so ludicrous a proposition that "speaking in tongues" might have a sane, sensible, scholarly, or even scientifically significant place in intelligent society.

So my "forward" is on the table—to challenge our human arrogance, not as an abrasive insult, but in the light of practical discovery myself, as one who has moved among the socially sophisticated for decades. At the same time, I have also served among the society's simplest as a shepherd of souls—as a pastor, a teacher, and a leader who found at every point on the spectrum, beginning with atheists-turned-to-faith, to very simple folk at the baseline of normal skills or intelligence, the evidence of the effectiveness of "glossolalia" as a practical contributor to increased life-effectiveness. Those participating in this oft-discarded as "transcendent" or "ecstatic" form of "dubious" communication have too often enhanced too many features of individual lives, homes, and relationships (including their intellectual sharpness) to too easily dispense with it as merely "mystical" or solely "emotionalistic." In fact, applied on the terms revealed in the Holy Bible, has produced the conviction that "even speaking in tongues" is a stroke of Divine brilliance offered to humankind. Though, it must be added—as with many things God offers, including forgiveness via His terms of "grace and mercy"—this gift is still sometimes scorned, mocked, or trivialized even by professed believers in the Bible or in Christ, God's Son.

Still, herewith, in glossolalia, is a profound communications resource; one I predict to be among many that at some point in the future will be discovered to be yet another of those abounding and benevolent "intentioned resources" offered by God, our Creator. And when that happens, I believe it doubtless that we will be humbled to find how such "abundances and benevolences" were awaiting us all the time, filled with potential to pragmatically enrich all lives, help address all problems, and assist in resolving all matters that concern our race. And with direct reference to "speaking in tongues," given the fact that most observers of our world at large openly admit that the absence of "clear communication" may be the greatest obstacle to human understanding, we might do well to pause around this theme and ask the help of the Helper who alone can enable our entry into accessing the dynamic inherent in this gift.

The writer of the First Epistle to the Corinthians forthrightly spoke of "the foolishness of God" in addressing his readers in that ancient, philosophy-and-sensuality-enthralled culture. Among those things he wrote about, thought foolish to this day, St. Paul—acknowledged by millions as among the ancient world's most accomplished thinkers—described and encouraged believers toward receiving a divinely imparted linguistic capacity exceeding human learning. His instruction, rooted in his own experience, opens the pathway to a God-given possibility in communication that could provide everything from insight beyond one's usual perceptions to therapeutic healing transcending one's internal pain or torments. Those words still point us in a very pragmatic way to open to the wonders available in communicating with our Creator; wonders that await our being humble enough to receive from Him, and which begin with our becoming reasonable enough to believe in Him.

With that, I welcome to the "believable"—to that availability when our child-ish-ness in describing as "foolish" those gifts God offers, turns to a child-like-ness that is ready to welcome wisdom from the most practical Source in the universe; the One who invented it all.

Jack W. Hayford
Chancellor, The King's Seminary (Los Angeles)
President, The International Foursquare Churches
Founder, The Church On The Way (Van Nuys, CA)

PREFACE

The New Testament world of the apostle Paul breathed the atmosphere of pride in human wisdom and the philosophy of the Greeks. To those who epitomized worshipers of human wisdom, the cross of Christ was mere foolishness.[1] Our world in the West of the twenty-first century is no different. What the "wise" person of today's world cannot understand, he or she tends to dismiss as foolishness too. Two thousand years of elapsed time have not improved this characteristic of the human mind to quickly deprecate what it cannot reasonably perceive. This may be especially true of many of the faithful believers in the Church, despite the fact that they should be better equipped to appreciate God's ways of ambiguity and enigma.

God makes plain in His Word by hundreds of examples and some direct address that mankind should anticipate His acting "outside the box" of human expectations. This book will discuss many of those passages for the researcher as well as the layperson who might be trying to understand the connection between what God did thousands of years ago and what He is doing today. An unprecedented revival has swept the world in the last 100 years. As late as the mid-twentieth century—50 years into this move of God—almost no one anticipated it would be called by some the "Century of the Pentecostals." At this writing, at least 650,000,000 living believers have experienced *glossolalia* (speaking in tongues). "Statisticians tell us that more than 1.5 billion people associate themselves with this worldwide revival."[2]

God makes plain in His Word...that mankind should expect His acting "outside the box" of human expectations.

No one component of the Church can lay claim to this advance. That group, representing many denominations and independent churches across the ethnic diversity of our "global village," now represents the second largest theological segment of Christianity—second only to the Roman Catholic Church (who themselves count over 75,000,000 Charismatics among their number).[3] Early Pentecostals moved from what was considered *normal* in ecclesial circles concerning the role the Holy Spirit plays in church and personal life, to that which was considered *abnormal* by the churches they were a part of when they experienced the Baptism in the Holy Spirit. For this experience many paid the high price of excommunication from the traditional denominations.

This work will attempt to challenge and invite the true seeker of Charismatic revival to encounter the joy and power of glossolalia. In addition, it will warn the present holders of the title *Pentecostal/Charismatic* of the dangers of any attempt to make God's dealing with humanity through the cross of Christ or His baptism of fire a "reasonable" one. Pentecostals are not meant to be "mainstream," and God help us if we get there. We have made great social strides from the tent revivals and storefront churches of the past, which may be good. But if God doesn't show up in our robed choirs, tuned orchestras, and timed services, we will have left God's "foolish" biblical pattern and have become another run-of-the-mill clergy-dominated organization. However, nowhere in this book will one find an invitation to be a fanatical freak exercising the excessive freedom of egomania (though some would describe any and all who practice glossolalia as such, or worse). The reader is asked to try to accept this truth: The Holy Spirit will always burst out of the corked bottle where churches have traditionally tried to keep Him.

A recent book by Ernest Gentile on a related topic, *The Glorious Disturbance,* starts like this:

> For sixty years I have been speaking in tongues—and listening to the theological debates about whether this is done by some mental gymnastics, the power of the devil or the power of the Holy Spirit. Rarely has a subject so divided sincere followers of Christ. The Holy Spirit, our greatest Helper, has been our biggest battleground! ... Throughout the history of the early Church, people continued to experience that outpouring—and it continues today as people all over the world enjoy this amazing miracle and have a wonderful new appreciation of their Savior Jesus Christ because of it. I have now lived long enough to see this appreciation grow in regard to Holy Spirit activity. Take seminaries, for example. Back in my early days, not very many Pentecostals attended seminaries. They were not particularly welcome. Since professors invariably had not had the experience, they were usually outspoken against it.
>
> Today, so many seminary students are Pentecostal or charismatic that if they were removed, some schools would be out of business! Some well-known professors speak in tongues. More Ph.D. dissertations have been written on the baptism of the Holy Spirit and the Pentecostal movement and charismatic renewal than we could imagine.[4]

I hope to stimulate new thinking by a rather unorthodox look at this baffling issue of speaking in tongues. How could one-fourth of all Christendom today be made up of these "tongues talkers"? How could their numbers have grown so fast in the space of 100 years? The kingdom of God, as announced by Jesus, was seen as unorthodox in the midst of Palestinian culture in the first century. God's kingdom—as seen through the lens of secular (and some religious) circles—still seems anomalous. Yet as witnesses and communicators we must face the dilemma, accept the ambiguous "upside-down" nature of the gospel, resist the attempt to make it reasonable, and still present it as relevant.[5] Does that sound antithetical—even impossible? I would assert this:

A good communicator of the gospel today must make the language understood to his immediate audience, allowing how unreasonable the gospel is, while still showing how desperately it remains mankind's only hope for life and happiness and future security.

Christ's upside-down response to Paul's requests for healing marks the very *summit* of his epistle to the Corinthians. Paul had prayed repeatedly for deliverance from his 'thorn in the flesh' (probably some physical infirmity). But the Lord revealed to him: *"My grace is sufficient for you, for my power is made perfect in weakness"* (2 Cor. 12:9). Following this the apostle concludes that he must boast and delight in his weaknesses, *"For when I am weak, then I am strong"* (v. 10). Just try to justify that ridiculous speech to our twenty-first-century's mentality of ego-enhancing mania and grasping for prideful power. Mankind hates to admit it, but the abject weakness of the human instrument serves only to magnify the perfection of divine power and truth and all-sufficiency. Two thousand years of Christianity have not been enough, it seems, for some of the bearers of its banners to have learned this truth well. But one should not despair. It's a new day! Growing up as a young man, hearing the snide remarks and being marginalized for being a Pentecostal, I would have never believed, then, the current changes in opinion about this Spirit-led renewal. I intend to celebrate the joy and power of glossolalia through human instruments (seemingly unreasonable?) as we seek to obey Christ's ascension mandate to build His Church ("Go and make disciples of all nations..." [Matt 28:19]), as He promised the Paraclete—the one called alongside to help.

ENDNOTES:

1. Philip E. Hughes, International Commentary of the New Testament: The Second Epistle of Corinthians (1962), 352.
2. Thomas Trask, "Pentecost: Empowerment for Life-changing Ministry," Enrichment 10 (Winter 2005): 144.

3. John A. Radano, Annual Statistics from the Pontifical Council for Promoting Christian Unity (2005), 47.

4. Ernest B. Gentile, The Glorious Disturbance (2004), 11.

5. At least four sources very helpful in this area of "upside-down" thinking are: Donald B. Kraybill, The Upside-Down Kingdom (1990); Paul G. Bretscher, The World Upside-Down or Right Side Up? (1964); Edmund Rybarczyk, "Expressing the Inexpressible: Tongues as Apophatic Speech," Presentation at the 31st Annual Meeting of the Society for Pentecostal Studies (2002); and one other specifically focused on our topic, Ernest B. Gentile, The Glorious Disturbance (2004).

CHAPTER 1

SQUARE ONE

The history of the Church hinges heavily on the humble background of the original apostles charged with the propagation of Yahweh's new covenant. *Jesus' choice of these individuals, which seemed so unreasonable then, is an example pro forma of the tack of this book, which intends to speak to ordinary people about a similar encounter with the Holy Spirit today.* Looking at the historically significant Azusa Street revival of 1906-1909, Harvey Cox asks: "What kind of a buffoonish God would entrust a revival of religion to such people?"[1]

How could mainline Protestant churches have been so wrong in the early 1900s when almost everyone receiving the baptism of the Holy Spirit (with speaking in tongues as Acts 2 records) was "excommunicated"—or at the least made unwelcome? Why was it so easy, then, for many of these ecclesiastical bodies to act so vigorously against the biblical record and, now lately, to have a much more receptive attitude? Does it not demand that we examine the phenomenon of God's seeming unreasonableness in the way He directed the events of the first century?

THE SURPRISING CHOICE OF THE TWELVE APOSTLES

The Lord's assessment of leadership shocks us. He cut straight across our lists of who would make a good leader—whether in His day or our own. Who would have guessed He was forming a first-class cadre of *world changers* by such an unprepossessing group of seemingly ragtag, untrained, and obscure men? And the Master's positioning of women as learners, helpers, and confidantes was almost blasphemy for His era. You would have thought Jesus, the Omniscient, would have chosen at least one statesman, a member of the priesthood or two, a successful businessman (other than a hated tax collector), a university professor, a financier, an athletic star who had won a laurel in the Roman games, a published scholar, or a craftsman like a boat builder or creator of musical instruments. He chose none of these. The disciples were all from the lower class of "nonprofessionals." Of course, Christ did finally choose one of a different sort, Saul/Paul, for a super special mission. But He had to invest a lot of faith in the original twelve!

Faith is not so much a comfort as a challenge! God has designed it that way. Yes, it can be a comfort; but to really please God, one must accept the fact that we can't figure Him out with analysis or reason. Literalists and many exegetes exhibit this great weakness. To really please God, one must accept His DARE. He dares us to believe, to trust. The more literate and technological we become in the modern world, the further away we get from accepting why He chose something as foolish and, at the same time, as wise as glossolalia or a Roman cross as the symbols of His interaction with humankind. Further, why did He reveal this wisdom to those who, either from the epoch of the disciples or from our modern world, would never have been chosen by selective profiling methods or pre-selection?

Philip Yancey believes Jesus prefers working with unpromising recruits.[2] These men were ordinary people who misunderstood Him, didn't demonstrate much spiritual power, and often behaved like school children in their jealousy and ignorance. However, when they did get ministry and attitudes right, Jesus showed great joy. Luke 10:21 tells us: *"At that time Jesus, full of joy through the Holy Spirit, said, 'I praise you, Father, Lord of heaven and earth, because you have hidden these things from the wise and learned, and revealed them to little children. Yes, Father, for this was your good pleasure.'"* One of those recruits—Paul, the last one—came to understand this hiding and revealing. In his two letters to the Corinthians, Paul spoke of God's unusual wisdom and called it a "mystery." The foolishness of God (Paul's words in 1 Cor. 1:25) will be a recurring theme here and the source of the title of this work. Jesus showed the most joy recorded in the Gospels on this topic of "upside-down" wisdom, hidden from those who would have been expected to understand it and given to those whom no one would have chosen. In the true meaning of the word: wonderful!

Perhaps no other small book has impacted my thinking and preaching like the work of Paul Bretscher, a Lutheran professor at Concordia Seminary in St. Louis, Missouri. He gives us a seminal and revolutionary look at the Beatitudes of Matthew 5. For the oft-recited and rather perplexing saying of Jesus in verse 8, *"Blessed are the pure in heart for they shall see God,"* Bretscher gives the *world's* substitute: "No! Rather, blessed are the sharp of mind, for they 'can't see' God."[3] Bretscher titles his comments on this Beatitude: "Wisdom." For each of these sayings of Jesus, he separates the wisdom of the "right-side-up" thinkers and the "upside-down" thinkers. This vital concentrated passage of

Scripture gives great insight to the mind of the Master. The following few lines reflect Bretscher's thesis on the verse, which I have chosen as the title of this book. He agrees that the secular world and a large portion of the modern (but shrinking) Church world sees the wisdom of God as foolish.

"The foolishness of God is wiser than the wisdom of men" (1 Cor. 1:25). This verse on the front cover reflects the Beatitudes, as do many other passages in the Bible. The wisdom of Jesus in Matthew's gospel is radically new, built on an altogether different understanding of God and man. It does not focus on man's mind or communication skills but goes directly to the heart of his motives—the "boiler room" of what mankind really is. God made us with this capacity to choose. Bretscher says God demands man be turned right side up: *"Blessed are the pure in heart, for they shall see God."* People "can't see God," not because they are dull of mind NOR because they are sharp of mind, but because they are impure, dishonest of heart, and basically prideful.

We imagine our mind is supreme, and in this we all delude ourselves. We use our minds as we want to. When Adam and Eve sinned, they couldn't see God either. They didn't want to! How amazing God made them to have that ability—to not see Him—when He might have made them like automatons with no chance for error! God's design made possible mankind's great *declaration of independence,* which has become both our greatest boon as well as our bane. Our intelligence became the means of "not seeing." We use our minds (superior among all God's creatures) to justify our grand rebellion against God and His ways, by recreating God in OUR own image. Similarly, in mankind's upside-down thinking, the secular world took Darwin's theory as their gospel because it allowed mankind to get rid of the judge.[4]

Donald Kraybill calls Jesus the "Upside-down Messiah" because He rejected embracing the religion of the Jews, which had been so distorted by power-hungry tyrants (the teachers of the law). They had created and exalted their own traditions to replace the intention of the Father. The devil tempted Jesus in the wilderness (Matt. 4) and offered Him a certification of the Messiah's miraculous arrival with a "spectacular display" in the temple.

> The scribes, the Sanhedrin, the high priests—all the religious heavyweights—would be sacred witnesses. They would accredit the Messiah's arrival...the Jerusalem aristocracy would welcome the new miracle worker. Jesus could avoid wandering among poor peasants in Galilee. There could be no doubt—no question about it. Jesus the Messiah had arrived! ...
>
> But he turned away.... Jesus rejected the temptation for spectacular

> display. He preferred the messianic secret.... This was no arrogant, horn-blowing Messiah.... Care for the lost, compassion for the poor, love for all. These were the messianic signs.
>
> The new heroes were the throwaways of institutionalized religion. They were the repentant sinners and publicans, the tax collectors and harlots. And what of the old heroes, the scribes and the priests, the Pharisees and Sadducees, the guardians of the old sacred way? They now were the villains, dethroned, brought low. No wonder they killed him.[5]

ABOUT THEOLOGY AND COMMUNICATIONS

An important statement by this author needs to be clear at the beginning of the reader's journey into these pages. It will be impossible to speak of the material herein concerning glossolalia without using the tools (word symbols) of the theologian. The reader may be led to believe the author intends this book to be a theological discourse on "tongues" from the same framework as hundreds of other books by men and women of considerable theological expertise (and some not so expert as well). The author has studied theology, both formally and informally, in three living languages for over 50 years and has taught theology in the 2/3rd World in two African vernaculars. His main professional formation, however, has been in the social and behavioral sciences (Communications, Sociology, Psychology, and Cultural Anthropology). This book discusses a very controversial theological concept, but will be written by someone wishing to look at the topic from a different vantage point than the usual theological perspective. (Of course, professional theologians don't agree among themselves any more than those of the "hard" sciences see eye to eye, so disagreements are inevitable. That fact, however, does not give one the license to be cavalier about such things.)

I will speak as a *communicologist* discussing a theological topic, which is much written about but not normally treated by a social scientist who has not been trained as rigorously (or exclusively) as some professionals in the discipline of theology. (I am prepared for eventual criticism from theologians for lacking a terminal degree in theological studies.) Theologians use my field of expertise, however, as the medium to speak/write of *their* specialization, though they have studied very little of communications theory, linguistics, or social semantics. These are not their professional strengths. Generally speaking, social scientists are more generous about this crossover than are theologians, but they too generally reject the very idea of theological concepts being integrated with their own, especially those about the supernatural. Because of my cross-disciplinary approach, I realize the road will be quite precarious. As one moves between the disciplines of theology and communications, one is bound to annoy the guardians of both traditions. While that is not my aim, I'll accept the risk, nonetheless.

Thus, I am not writing for the professional in either theology or the social sciences. However, a thorough academic research model with proper authentication will be observed. I will attempt to blend a useful everyday speech style with scholarship. To keep the flow of the book moving, endnotes after each chapter will be used instead of the heavy academic mode of footnoting on each page—with only a few exceptions.

I must acknowledge that academic analysis is seldom neutral and almost never free from presuppositions. A degree of advocacy is unavoidable. Although it is impossible to bracket biases completely, I will attempt to do so, no doubt with less success than I would wish.

I strive to write about this complex topic in an emotional climate of peace and love, with compassion and earnestness, and without defensiveness or triumphalism. This is difficult, in spite of my announced goals. The topic has traditionally raised such "heat" that often little "light" can penetrate. It resembles trying to move a hornet's nest from one place to another pacifically.

Early in my youth, Pentecostal scholars and apologists were relatively rare. Persons in opposition to glossolalia, highly convinced of its condemnation, went unchallenged. Now, 60 years later, the literature about this worldwide phenomenon has changed drastically, even done an about-face in some instances. It is amazing to see the inclusion of pneumatological elements in confessionals and doctrinal materials where once there was almost no mention of them. Still, there are enough "weird" Pentecostals and Charismatics in the movement to justify people who cite their existence as evidence supporting an unchanging negative attitude toward this religious force. On the other hand, Pentecostals and Charismatics cite their numbers in the world as proof of doctrinal orthodoxy and thus claim exoneration from earlier over-generalized criticism and rejection. In my opinion, neither side represents wisdom or truth, but clarifying that will not be easy.

IRRATIONAL BY DESIGN

From the broad matrix of Communications Theory (humans as meaning makers), I will discuss this theological issue—the use of tongues—as related to human speech. I do not intend to debate the rationale of glossolalia, either from the perception of those who oppose it or support it. I propose the phenomenon of glossolalia is *irrational by design*. This approach will be quite different from the voluminous bibliographical material by the proponents and defenders of "tongues" available to the reader.[6] A great many of the authors of sources compiled by Watson Mills defend glossolalia, using constructs of modern reasoned discourse and logical systems, hoping to make this misunderstood phenomenon acceptable.[7] I would boldly insist one can often be more effective by stepping away from the expected.

I will attempt to show that if God has expressly chosen that which secular man and a good portion of the church world deem to be foolishness, any attempt to make God look less foolish is aimless.

COMMUNICATIONS INSIGHT:

"MEANING IS PERCEPTION"

A CHINESE STUDENT in Canada returned home after spending a semester in a university there. She was asked by her friends in Shanghai, "What is the most unusual thing you noticed about Canadians?" She responded that it was the unusual slant of their eyes. That may be a crude example, but meaning is tied to individual perception.

If you hear the word "dog," and you have a three-pound poodle for a pet, you will probably see a very different creature in your mind than a person who owns a 120-pound slobbering Saint Bernard!

In the US the word "temperance" had an earlier use and generic meaning of "moderation," for instance, in reference to drinking alcoholic drinks. But the Women's Christian Temperance Union intended the word to mean that you don't touch the stuff!

The great diversity of understanding (perception) about glossolalia is just as varied.

ELEMENTS THIS STUDY DOES NOT INCLUDE

Having clarified my approach to this subject, I need to further delimit the content of this study. I acknowledge, as do many other authors, the topic of glossolalia is extremely complex. Some writers with empirical experience of "tongues speech" tend to oversimplify this complexity. They leave the impression the topic of tongues in the Bible is straightforward and leaves no room for questions or caution in interpretation. I don't hold to that simplistic view. Did not glossolalia in the New Testament take several forms? Are we sure tongues as practiced by the majority today (with variations and disagreements even

Dear reader: The final editors switched two important words in the Initial Evidence paragraph (3) below. Please substitute the word ***normal*** for ***normative*** on line 4. AND the word ***normative*** for the word ***normal*** on line 6. AGAIN on line 9, please put ***normative*** for ***normal***. Thanks!

among Pentecostals and Charismatics) are exactly as the disciples of Christ and Paul described them?[8] In my understanding, all the expressions of glossolalia in the New Testament are of the same essence, but have six different functions as described by Scripture.[9] A descriptive comparative study of the breadth and heighth of glossolalia, however, is not the topic of this book—as interesting as some might find such a discourse.

Subsequence

This study will not consider the issue of "subsequence" (i.e., whether or not a believer receives the endowment of power to witness [Acts 1:8] by the Holy Spirit at the moment of salvation OR in a separate experience *subsequent* to regeneration—and that being a few minutes or a few weeks/months/years later). Though this study will show the author's position to be one of embracing the scriptural examples of subsequence, no attempt will be made here to argue or prove that doctrinal point.[10]

Initial Evidence

This study will not attempt to discuss, apologetically, the doctrinal points of whether or not tongues is the "initial evidence" of the Baptism in the Holy Spirit as held by most traditional Pentecostal churches and many Charismatic believers. The words scholars use in this regard are "normative" (for those who say tongues *normally*, but not always or inevitably, are the sign of Holy Spirit's baptism) and the word "normal" signifying the belief that tongues are the *only* and *inevitable* initial physical sign of the Spirit's baptism as witnessed in the Acts 2:4 account and other references. Again, the reader will discover the author firmly believes the best term is "normal" after studying many of the scholarly works available on this topic. In addition, I have witnessed literally thousands of believers on four continents who have experienced this physical sign. This is a critical issue and needs to come under the careful scrutiny of the best scholars on the subject—especially with the increase of quasi-Pentecostal churches which may not hold the traditional Pentecostal distinctive. More specifically trained theologians need to carry on that dialogue.[11]

Linguistic Description

Nor is it my intention here to carry on the dialogue and argument as to whether tongues are actual languages potentially identifiable on earth, ecstatic speech, gibberish, or "tongues of angels" as described by the apostle Paul in First Corinthians (13:1). While this book will show my opinion to be that an ideal or highest expression of utterance of Spirit-enabling speech is attainable (being one or more of the elements above), I also believe one must learn to yield to the Spirit in a process until "the ideal" is attained. While I agree this dialogue is important and even vital, it will not be included in this study. My opinion is the apostle Paul believed tongues were actual languages. David Lim says the text will allow no other interpretation.[12] Yet for my thesis, it does not really make that much difference. Let others state their cases.

A recent scholarly book, yet one easy to understand, is that of Bill and Bob Menzies.[13] The authors bring a great array of scholarship, plus an irenic spirit to these arguments with the most skill to date, in my opinion. They are especially generous in their gratitude to the opponents of the traditional Pentecostal doctrines for forcing Pentecostals to dialogue—in order that they may grow to understand each other, as well as their Evangelical brothers, to whom Pentecostals owe so much.

ELEMENTS THIS STUDY DOES INCLUDE

"For the foolishness of God is wiser than man's wisdom, and the weakness of God is stronger than man's strength.... The man without the Spirit does not accept the things that come from the Spirit of God, for they are foolishness to him, and he cannot understand them, because they are spiritually discerned...'For who has known the mind of the Lord that he may instruct him?' But we have the mind of Christ" (1 Cor. 1:25; 2:14, 16).

In many ways tongues speech defies normal explanation. Attempts to define it in logical terms often only complicate the issue and prove counter-productive. Looking at this growing religious phenomenon from the view-point of a communicator and *communications theory* may help one to see that perhaps God delights in communicating to us in surprising ways. Of course, that does not mean God can *only* communicate in unexpected ways, but this study will illustrate how illogical and non-linear the Bible is when God desires to talk to us. He doesn't seem to be much concerned that He fit neatly into the Church's or secular society's agenda! I will readily admit to the theory that God generally laughs at scholars' "truth" about Him. They so often fall into the trap of "reification"[14]—a subtle blinding force of circular reasoning, propelled by the weight of their own bibliographies. I will attempt to avoid that trap myself!

THE CLASH OF THEORIES

For this reason I have chosen to introduce this topic from the matrix of a *clash of theories* about truth and wisdom that the apostle Paul speaks about in the first three chapters of First Corinthians. This passage considers two ways of knowing. One seems reasonable, acceptable, logical, and desirable because it is *inside* the arena of man's control. It is espoused by the intellectuals; it has been won by conquest and possessed by the "rulers of the age." It is the current political and social power brokers' ideological *raison d'etre* (reason for being). Most of the people who really *know* (cognitively) were totally convinced there was no other way to know. The other "wisdom" seemed to the proponents of the first way of knowing to be unreasonable, foolish, and even absurd.

The Greek mind saw Jesus a loser who, from a backward country and obscure family, lost his life in a shameful manner in defense of this ideological foolishness.

For the Greek mind (which the Corinthians embraced) this new way of thinking was based on a "loser" who, from a backward country and an obscure family, lost his own life in a shameful manner in defense of this ideological foolishness. Two wisdoms: One accepted by the popular masses and opinion makers of current culture; the other (according to the latest polls) seen as foolish, ridiculous, and idiotic. I submit it should surprise no one that this unenviable ideology was chosen *on purpose* by He who is the source of all wisdom. Jon Ruthven suggests the world looked on Christ the Messiah's wisdom-system with total misunderstanding—even to the point of killing Him. The world's wisdom, both then and now, is the sort that Adam and Eve chose and Jesus rejected.[15]

This project seeks to examine how the old "wisdom of this world" has invaded the Christian world so extensively and so undetected. Until the beginning of the last century, believers could be described as ignorant of Paul's thesis about the two wisdoms in First Corinthians. The Church had so abandoned the life and power of the Spirit that it could better be described as knowing the Greek world better than the New Testament Christian world.

It had all happened before. The mandate of influencing the nations with the knowledge of Yahweh was clearly the intention of the promises and instructions given to the Old Testament patriarchs. But they largely failed. If ever a people were prepared and destined to bless the world, it was Israel. They were given transcendent truth and power to make the worship of Jehovah a new force for mankind in the world. Theirs was an ethical plane, truer than had ever been conceived, a new conception of God and man in which the world was all sacred and not secular. But did they recognize this? Hardly. J. D. Pentecost speaks of the decline of Israel's religion in these terms:

> The nation in its collective being was meant to be the vehicle and master of the Divine Will. Worship was, while individual, national, the homage of the people to their invisible King. While the nation by its worship and through its priests spoke to God, God by His prophets spoke to the nation. They were, indeed, the voices of God, speakers for Him, revealing His truths, enforcing His will. But a recognized is not always an obeyed authority. The notion of religion was sublimer than the people had mind to appreciate or will to incorporate and adequately actualize. Worship is easier than obedience. Men are ever readier to serve the priest than to obey the prophet, and sacerdotalism flourished in Israel while prophecy decayed and died. And so while the prophets created a literature embodying an unrealized religion, the priests created a nation, a people devoted to the worship they administered, the symbols and ceremonies they had instituted.[16]

Is this not the same progressive picture after the first 1500 years of the Church? Priests were indeed easier to accept than the prophets who always confront us with the Cross. Priests often present a way which is less costly than the way of the cross. Worship is easier than obedience. Prophets are never on the payroll!

But this picture is being repeated again after the Reformation. Are we always doomed to repeat the same institutionalization of God's purpose, and then defend it against any renewal the Spirit of God brings? Are not traditional Pentecostals, at this writing, in the photographic darkroom trying to develop the same picture yet again? For the reader newly entering the jargon of the religious world of this book, a couple basic definitions will help.

BASIC DEFINITIONS

Pentecostals: Jim Hernando defines us well. Pentecostals are:

> Christians who believe that there is a post-conversion experience called the BAPTISM IN THE HOLY SPIRIT available to every believer. Taking their cue from the Book of Acts, Pentecostals contend that this experience provides spiritual empowerment for Christian service and gospel witness (1:8), which included all the spiritual gifts (Gk. *charismata* [1 Cor. 12]) mentioned in the Pauline epistles, including miraculous signs and wonders necessary to fully preach the gospel to the world (Rom. 15:19). The underlying theological assumption is that the same experience of Spirit-baptism that

empowered the disciples on the Day of Pentecost is a "gift" available to believers of every age (Acts 2:38).[17]

Speaking in tongues, or glossolalia: "Usually, but not exclusively, the religious phenomenon of making sounds that constitute, or resemble, a language not known to the speaker. It is often accompanied by an excited religious psychological state, and in the Pentecostal and charismatic movements it is widely and distinctively (but not universally) viewed as the certifying consequence of the Baptism in the Holy Spirit."[18]

I will here, briefly, extract a few cogent remarks by the writer of the above paragraph, Russ Spittler, whose succinct overview of the topic of glossolalia is included in the *Dictionary of Pentecostal and Charismatic Movements*.

- The term "glossolalia" was not used in English before 1879. It derives from a Greek phrase *glossais lalein*—"to speak in or with tongues."
- It is not limited to Christianity or even to religious expression, but much studied in psychology and medicine. Some ancient oracles related to this phenomenon.
- In the biblical data, it is referenced 35 times (Mark, Acts, and 1 Corinthians).
- In Luke's account in Acts, he marks the movement of the gospel westward by stages, each characterized by the descent of the Holy Spirit—first Jerusalem (Jews alone); then Caesarea (Gentiles on Jewish soil); then Ephesus (Gentiles in Greek territory). At each step, the Holy Spirit falls, and glossolalia is an accompanying feature.
- It is the apostle Paul's first letter to the Corinthians that most speaks of glossolalia. This church had distorted the nature of the gift, using it as a sign of higher spirituality.
- Paul's admonition to the Corinthians was not to end the use of the gift, but to govern its use by three criteria:
    a. The diversity of the charismata from God
    b. The supremacy of love, without which no charismata count
    c. The priority of congregational edification over personal benefit
- Nearly all classical Pentecostal groups adhere to the doctrine that speaking in tongues certifies the personal experience of the Baptism in the Holy Spirit. Representative is the doctrinal formulation of the US Assemblies of God: "The baptism of believers in the Holy Spirit is witnessed by the initial physical sign of speaking with other tongues as the Spirit of God gives them utterance (Acts 2:4). The speaking of

tongues in this instance is the same in essence as the gift of tongues (1 Cor. 12:4-10, 28), but different in purpose and use."[19]

- Many Christians believe the charismata ended with the days of the apostles. Pentecostals and Charismatics disagree and take the apostle Peter's words on the day of Pentecost in Jerusalem at face value: *"The promise is for you and your children and for all who are far off—for all whom the Lord our God will call"* (Acts 2: 38-39). Viewing this promise extended to all generations and peoples as the gift of the Holy Spirit, Pentecostals claim that they too have received this gift.[20]

TONGUES SPEECH AND THE SOCIAL SCIENCES

This author's aim is to show the relationships between the study and science of human speech and "meaning making" (which some believe is mankind's exclusive domain) to tongues speech. This religious phenomenon is embraced by a group with a theological point of view and experience, which represents the fastest-growing religious movement since recorded history. Adherents are now estimated at 650 million and have come to constitute almost one-third of all Christians in the century since their inception. David Barrett projects that the present growth of this phenomenon worldwide will augment the figure to 811 million by 2020.[21]

> **Strangers hearing "tongues" spoken in church for the first time may believe it contributes to utter confusion.**

I will then advance my theory of why God may have *intentionally chosen* a seemingly undesirable sign/evidence/consequence of the Holy Spirit's presence in an individual (speaking in tongues having been judged as foolish, nonsensical, psychologically aberrant, or even demonic). The belief and doctrine of glossolalia has been misunderstood and often rejected by a large part of Christendom, even though many denominations see its existence in the New Testament and in the Early Church. The secular or unchurched world generally has been even less accepting of glossolalia, while remaining in their state of uncaring and/or ignorance about it. Strangely, some unchurched folk have shown a greater willingness to examine the phenomenon than some Evangelicals.

"Even though it is mentioned in the Bible and practiced regularly by a growing group of Christians, many Christians of the older churches look with suspicion on this phenomenon and believe that there is no place for it in the modern church. Looking at it from the outside, they conclude that tongues speaking is only what it appears on the outside, a meaningless gibberish, with no value or purpose. It is merely emotional indulgence in sheer irrationality in the name of religion, a return to a more primitive kind of religion."[22]

When uninitiated people hear "tongues" spoken unexpectedly for the first time in church, they may believe it intrudes on their devotion and contributes to utter bedlam and confusion. It is seen as irrational at best and evil at worst. Others, however, are very attracted to it. Tongues speaking strikes at the very center of our culture's rational understanding of meaning, as the opposite of the "method of science" that has set Western society apart from the chaos of the superstitious ignorant past. To give one's self to the unknown, the mysterious, is highly risk-ridden for the modern rational mind. This book seeks to ask the question: **Does the God of the Christian Bible know all about man's struggle with this issue, and has He chosen glossolalia on purpose and for that very reason?** There are multiplied millions now who hold this conviction. How and why is this group growing so fast?

COMMUNICATIONS INSIGHT

LET ME GIVE YOU THE analogy of dance. We have all seen television accounts of someone winning an unexpected prize of money or a product, like a new car. Some folk cannot keep their feet still at such a moment and dance a jig of joy. The action of the body expresses an emotion that their words would probably never be able to produce.

There is another kind of dance too, the professional artistic medium of expression called ballet. Like the true arts of painting, sculpture, music, and great photography, there is a time when dancing takes over for the feelings and words are no longer necessary.

In a sense, words are our prison because they demand intentional selection and sorting from the cognitive processes of the mind. And yet words are our salvation and freedom, because salvation demands a conscious choice of the will. So here, living inside us, is the paradox of prison and freedom cohabiting together! But words are not the only, and sometimes not the best, way to express the soul.

Glossolalia is like that—pure freedom like extemporaneous dance!

GROWTH AND SCOPE OF THE MOVEMENT

"Amazingly, just one hundred years ago not one Pentecostal/ Charismatic congregation, as we understand the term today, existed.

> Now such churches and denominations dot the religious landscape and constitute the most dynamic and fastest-growing segment of Christendom.... "A 1980 Gallup Poll published in *Christianity Today* ... indicated that 19 percent of the total population of the United States, or about 50 million people, identified themselves as Pentecostal or Charismatic Christians. In a more recent 1998 *Newsweek* poll, 47 percent of the Christians surveyed said they had 'personally experienced the Holy Spirit.'... This phenomenal growth is one of the main reasons that well-known Harvard theologian Harvey Cox is willing to say that Pentecostalism is 'reshaping religion in the twenty-first century.'"[23]

It is a history long known, but little researched until recent Pentecostal scholarship came into its own.[24] Various revival and renewal movements have appeared throughout the history of the Christian church. These renewals were often Charismatic in nature, but because the Holy Spirit's "in-breaking" into an organized church seems to threaten the power structure of ecclesiastical control, these revivals were often condemned and marginalized by the institutional church. The historical record of such renewals generally only appears as the church officially judged and condemned them as heretical. Eddie Hyatt writes "that the Pentecostal/Charismatic revival of this century is orthodox Christianity is confirmed not only by the New Testament itself, but also by the existence of two thousand years of charismatic Christianity."[25]

AUDIENCE OF SPECIAL CONCERN FOR THIS BOOK

Many readers will already have some knowledge of the Pentecostal Movement. Others will come to these pages out of curiosity and have little knowledge of Pentecostals or Charismatics. Yet others read to reaffirm what they already believe, or want to believe. Few will pick up this book from skepticism. Most skeptics have already made up their minds about Pentecostals/Charismatics and tongues and don't want to entertain competing ideas. Trying to change their minds is not high on my lists of goals for this work. Many of them, sadly, are beyond changing. It would be like beating on cold iron. Jack Deere, speaking of a time when he opposed all the gifts from a dispensational bias, says: "When you go with a closed mind, it is rare for God to violate your prejudices."[26] But there are folks who ARE important for this writer.

True Seekers

I speak to those who are true searchers and may not know much about this religious phenomenon sweeping the religious world—especially in the last three decades—but have heard of it.

The book also addresses true seekers, who have been raised in other theological communities which have been recently influenced by laypersons (and many times clergy too) from their midst, who have experienced glossolalia in their spiritual lives.

Starters Who Stopped

To those who may have had an initial experience, and have spoken in tongues, but didn't continue to progress because of a lack of teaching or poor instruction about the baptism of the Holy Spirit, I say read on. Someone may have, early on after this initial experience, dissuaded them from its reality, saying it was pure emotionalism, or worse. But they can't forget the overwhelming love of God that flooded their hearts, and they are still searching for answers.

Negatively Influenced Seekers

Let me speak directly to you who have good friends or close family members who have told you about speaking in tongues. You may be skeptical because of negative opinions held by people you respect. There are hosts of wonderful, sincere, and godly persons who are really ignorant about these things, even though they make themselves out to be experts because they are experts on many other biblical truths.

Those with Experience but Little Teaching

You exercise glossolalia and perhaps other gifts of the Spirit, but find it difficult to explain to others because you have not studied much about these phenomena. You are looking for ways to better explain that which you hold dear.

My desire is *less* to defend tongues than to show how this humbling experience can open the door to God's empowerment. I wish the reader to come to maximize God's intention in a world obsessed with power. But God's power, however, is upside down! In the automotive world of persuasive commercials, we are enticed to buy bigger and bigger engines that will literally drain the blood from our faces when these gas-guzzling behemoths roar away from a stop sign! We are dazzled with spiraling statistics of cubic centimeters of piston displacement of a V8 or V12 engine. God's power comes not with an augmentation of our displacement (inner space), but with a person's *diminished* space. In direct proportion to our "space" getting smaller, His "space" in us gets larger. How *unreal* this paradox seems!

In general, this writer hopes to write clearly without being heavy with "academics." (Sometimes, however, the reader may feel I have forgotten that last sentence because the nature of the subject at hand will require using some strange sounding words.) The academic world calls that heavy style of writing "pedantic" when excessive. But my deepest desire is to give a fresh rationale for what the secular and some in the religious world call foolishness. You will note, however, the careful footnoting of the sources that have helped the writer by their opinions and research—whether for or against tongues—available at the end of each chapter for those who need authentication as an expected element of reasoned discourse.

For those to whom I am directing this writing, who may lack a historical backdrop, I wish to give a quick overview of the movement's history and why Pentecostals believe we have a mission to fulfill. But first, a suggestion from Philip Yancey: "The church has too often jumped up too quickly to defend what it thought was unfair criticism of scripture or its dogma." He writes about the attempt to reach those who are living on the edge of belief. They are asking legitimate questions that are often not welcome inside the church. They are honest questions by honest folks. He goes on, saying "the church should be a place that rewards that kind of honesty because Borderlanders [Yancey's term for those on the "edge of belief"] who are allowed and encouraged to vocalize their doubts about God are on their way toward being open to hearing responses to those doubts."[27] I resonate with that bold suggestion.

COMING TO BELIEVE LIKE THE APOSTOLIC CHURCH

Let me start with "why" people are coming to believe like the first Christians in the apostolic age. Unlike what the media or preachers from traditional churches may say, the "tongues movement" has almost nothing to do with *style* (even though Charismatics and Pentecostals may indeed share or possess a style of worship or speaking). But style is not the essence of what Pentecostals are. Besides, the worldwide Pentecostal Movement is so varied with literally hundreds of "styles" that are more cultural than biblical or theological that looking at style in any one culture and labeling the Movement by it would be limiting and incorrect. Observers from the outside are attracted to the externals—the things most evident or observable—but that doesn't make them the most important part. You can understand that.

Tongues speaking is only one part of a complex and meaningful accommodation God has provided for His church. Because it is a doctrine Pentecostals see as distinctive of their theology, it seems good to show the role this small but vital part plays in God's dealing with humankind.

People are attracted to "speaking in tongues" for both positive and negative reasons. It is a small part of the experience, but has been the "noticeable part" from the observer's vantage point. Besides this, some who believe it is

God's sign, like the believers in Corinth in Paul's day, use it improperly. They thus give tongues undue importance in the whole scheme of the larger picture of being empowered for the winning of souls for Christ. So for me, Pentecost is not merely a stylistic thing. It's a way of looking at Scripture and interpreting and experiencing it. The theological world calls that *hermeneutics*.

Cook's Three-stage Progression

The same apostle, when writing to the Colossians and wanting to explain that God was doing something new in this regard, says the great secret God has kept hidden over the ages but now is making clear is, "*Christ in you, the hope of glory*" (Col. 1:26). Jerry Cook says this is not a simile, but a direct statement. "Christ (God) lives in you, and because of that, there is hope. This is stunning because, if it is true, it involves a radical relocation of God from 'out there' to 'in us.'"[28]

Cook explains that in the Old Testament times, God was more "out there" (he calls this stage one), who had to be approached with sacrificial animals. One dared not pronounce His name. If you wrote it (like the scribes who copied manuscripts), you had to wash your garments and take a bath every time His name was to be copied on a manuscript. He was austere and far away. God was "out there," but was to be feared. He gave the Ten Commandments, which are basic, but very hard to keep. Paul, the apostle, said it was impossible to be justified by the law alone (Rom. 3:20).

Then Jesus, the Son of God, came (stage two—*God with us*) and lived on the earth as a person. When this staggering event was to take place, the name used to describe Him was Immanuel, meaning "*God with us*." He was an impressive teacher and chose twelve men to be His close disciples. For three years they lived together, walked together, and ate together, the twelve listening to what He said and watching what He did. As they stayed with Jesus, they realized He was not an ordinary human being. The man they called "teacher," and were amazed at His teaching, caused them to discover He was the God who created the universe but chose to come in human form so He could relate to mankind. He did this to demonstrate what He and the Father were really like, and in a manner which the disciples could understand. That discovery forever changed them and will change anyone who will make this Jesus the Lord of his or her life.

But after He was killed by crucifixion, the fact He had been *with them* for three years didn't make them into the witnesses He needed them to be. Yes, even after He rose from the dead and appeared to them many times, they still needed something. After the Resurrection the disciples were still cowering behind closed doors. It was going to take more than Jesus' coming back to life and ascending to His father to propel His followers to be witnesses into all the world to bring the deliverance of God to man's depraved and needy heart. So He told them not to disperse but to stay in Jerusalem until the third stage happened. First stage—God "*out there,*" second stage—God "*with them,*" and finally, third stage—God "*in them.*" Astonishing! Stage three came with fire and wind (Acts 2), and it came with the physical sign of speaking in "other tongues." It was not a subjective internal sign which could be pretended or falsely claimed and which no one could verify. This sign was not just a subjective experience, but an objective one that any observer could examine! **And it has been seen as foolish and ridiculous and even called demonic, starting with the first day when those who spoke in tongues were accused of being drunk. The epithets have never stopped—right up to our day. COULD GOD REALLY BE THAT FOOLISH?** This is the sign/evidence which has been so maligned throughout history (Acts 2:13).

First stage – God "out there", second stage – God "with us", and finally, third stage – God "in them". Astonishing!

From the dawning of the last century, when a new effusion of Pentecost broke onto the religious world, the phenomenon of speaking in tongues has stimulated criticism, wonder, and rejection—but not by all. At this writing, hundreds of millions of living souls have experienced glossolalia. This theological persuasion has found resistance at every point in history, a tempest of debate evoking curious interest, some acceptance, careful censure, and frequent caustic derogation. "It is regrettable that those who are so militant in protecting the Christian faith against Pentecostals do not spend sufficient time discovering precisely what the traditional Pentecostals believe and teach."[29]

The Frightful Word "Experience"

The religious world and the world of scientific research are quite skeptical of personal experience (unless, of course, it is a cultural anthropologist who MUST write her thesis from the experience of living with the people she's researching). Yet the Bible is so dependent on man's experience with God, upon which the major doctrines of the Church are founded. With good reason *experience* is to be feared, because it is related to a person's perception and individual meaning. William Howell, an expert on persuasion, says that "meaning IS perception."[30] But as risky as it is to take experience seriously, to *ignore* experience and one's perception of its significance in human dialogue, in literature, and in religion is to be as unbalanced as walking on only one leg. What a person experiences in the spiritual realm cannot be ignored, nor can it escape close scrutiny—as unscientific as that exercise may be. Many totally ignore the element of perceived experience because of its intangible properties. Below, I will illustrate how the reformers of the great Reformation generally obviated the supernatural experiences the Bible records. They claimed, against their Roman Catholic critics, that all miracles ceased with the apostles. The inheritors of the Reformed tradition still continue to do the same today. L. T. Johnson, although not a proponent or practitioner of glossolalia, speaks to this issue of the preponderance of experience in the biblical record: "Indeed the New Testament is remarkable among ancient religious texts for its high proportion of first-order discourse about experience ... that seems to express fundamental convictions, that demand some kind of account, but that all of our learning does not touch."[31]

So why does "all our learning" not touch this element in our informed and modern world? Is it because "experience" is dangerous, risky, not convenient to put through the matrix/taxonomy of the scientific method? Is it because no two people experience the same event alike? At a football game two folks sitting together may react to a goal/touchdown very differently. Human nonverbal reactions are misleading by their personal individuality. At a concert, closed eyes may mean boredom or intense appreciation. Ideas have always been attacked by opponents, but physical reactions (to experiences) evoke much more virulent criticism. (In fact, most of the criticism of glossolalic individuals relates to their physical reactions to the experience of speaking in tongues or prophesying.) The individual psychological nature of experience makes analysis a guessing game at best.[32]

To add to this complexity, the way an individual interprets a given experience is largely a product of his or her world of perception. As such, meaning (through language) is part of the happening's reality for the participant as well as for the one listening to the participant's explanation of what happened. The old Sapir-Whorf theory of how language is a factor in *forming* certain experiences and definitions of "reality"—contrary to the older theory that culture determines language—must also be seen as an important variable.[33] Actually, this street runs both ways. Language forms culture and culture forms language. Each participant in a Charismatic prayer meeting has a distinct personal experience and will relate such through their own sub-cultural grid which has formed their language ability and perceptive capacity.

The listener will interpret that related tale from his own "database" of perception. I add a word of caution, even to myself. A religious person must not believe that a given religious experience is so different (transcendent) from any other type of nonreligious experience that it is exempt from any examination by others.

Religious experiences, like speaking in tongues, are not totally unique! On the other hand, neither should social scientists believe that all religious experiences can be completely evaluated by their social-scientific categories of Behaviorism or even Socio-Linguistics. Here lie two extremes to be avoided. The Charismatic wants to place "transcendent power" in an untouchable category, and the social scientist wants to exercise reductionism equating all religious experience as unscientific and untrustworthy—even spurious, delusionary, or evil.

If God wanted to hide something from those who insist on leaning too hard on the intellectual, analytical; rationalistic side of knowledge, might He not choose something they would ignore, on purpose and from justifiable reason? Ah yes, reason. What a wonderful concept! I submit He might have done just that.

But you can see, God was wise enough to have leaped from the promises of history with a sign (experience) to which even the children could attest. And in subsequent chapters you'll read my reasons for why God chose a seemingly foolish sign, but a sign which, when examined closely, is almost impregnable to human logic and/or serious attack. (Do not read this last statement to mean that the attacks are not serious in the mind of the attackers!)

On the day of Pentecost, at Jerusalem, God made some historical changes in His plan. He fulfilled the prophet Joel's words by putting His power *in* the recipients, without discrimination (Joel 2:28). Up to that time, only select people could know God's mind and speak for Him. But at Pentecost God broke all the old molds! Now no one—men, women, young, old, slave, or free—was to be left out. It's beyond belief! He's *in* all of those who surrender themselves to His direction. No one is preferred above another. Gone are the restrictions of *who* can be His emissaries of salvation. Now, anyone can call on the name of the Lord and be saved. All can become God's chosen people and priests—even those whom the religious leaders of long ago said must be excluded.

Many religious leaders are saying the same today! They resent the fact that a person doesn't need to be a member of the "cloth" to pray for a sick person's healing or to give a powerful testimony. Religious leaders are very jealous of their ecclesiastical power and resent anyone whose actions encroach on their turf. This is, of course, contrary to the words of the Master, who would call us all to servanthood (Matt. 20:26). Jon Ruthven writes: "Hadn't I just overheard a faculty member from my seminary (in Illinois) heatedly insist that, along with Mormons and Jehovah's Witnesses, Pentecostals should not be allowed to matriculate here? Another professor demurred, who, in Christian charity, clung to the hope that Pentecostal students might be salvageable." Ruthven adds, "The movement, originally dismissed as 'the last great vomit of Satan,' has become now the largest active group in Christianity."[34]

GET BACK WHERE YOU BELONG!

A great portion of my growing-up years took place in Slayton, Minnesota, where my father planted a new church during the Second World War. In junior and senior high school, I participated in all the sporting activities offered (except football—because of a physical limitation). My favorite sport was basketball. Seventh and eighth and even some ninth graders practiced in the "old gym" until they were chosen one at a time to move up to the "new gym," where the varsity practiced and played its games. This was the great "dream," to be called up to the big gym and be a part of the "B" squad that played an exhibition game prior to the varsity's main event. The day I was called up was one of the most memorable days of my life! I made my "grand entrance" (unnoticed by anyone but me) coming onto the main gym floor. It was during the practice of free throws. (When in this sport a player is "fouled" by an opposing team's player, he/she gets to attempt to make a basket uninhibited from a line on the floor.) I didn't notice that the "lesser" players (younger and on the "B" squad) practiced on one end of the gym, while the "A" squad practiced on the other. I thought that once someone was called up to play with the "big boys," one could have access to the whole gym. Was I wrong! "Get back where you belong" was the first complete sentence I understood—stated by one of the "big boys." Growing up a Pentecostal, I often heard the same command from clergy of the "accepted" churches. We were marginalized by fellow pastors and leaders of the "big boys." This is now changing fast as the burgeoning revival continues to accelerate and as many Pentecostal ministers are becoming as well trained as the others. But many Evangelicals and Mainline denominations still want nothing to do with the relatively new Spirit-renewal movement.

Frequently people ask, "Can one be an instrument of the Holy Spirit without being baptized in the Holy Spirit and speaking in tongues?" I think the answer is clearly yes! But it's like asking if there is any advantage in having a motorcycle over a bicycle. Both are a means of transportation; one has much more power. But, more power of the Spirit doesn't make one necessarily more holy or a better person in God's evaluation—just more useful in His design of using humans (and not angels) to announce the gospel to all peoples (Matt. 28:19).

A. J. Gordon, in his book *Ministry of the Spirit,* shows clearly this was the case with believers in Ephesus. They were disciples, but had not yet been recipients of the Baptism in the Holy Spirit. They received this gift 20 years after the Jerusalem outpouring. Gordon's words: "This passage seems decisive as showing that one may be a disciple without having entered into possession of the Spirit as God's gift to believers. ... In other words, these Ephesian disciples on receiving the Holy Ghost exhibited the traits of the Spirit common to the other disciples of the apostolic age.[35]

Pentecost takes any believer and makes her or him to be a part of the prophetic community that brings healing and hope to a sin-sick world—a community that has the maturity to stand against the criticism and the hate the enemy would inspire against them. They know they are accepted because they have confessed their sins and have been born of God's Spirit. Now, in the yielding of their mother tongue (or any other acquired language) to God's Spirit, they hear themselves speak a prayer language they never learned, nor one they can understand. They do not wonder if it's real or not. Someone else may wonder, but participants instinctively know if they are faking it or not. This realization that God is *within* them is empowering. They have new self-confidence to march out into the devil's fields and plant the seeds of the gospel that bring life and yield a harvest for the Kingdom, in direct response to Christ's mandate.

NOTE: Many other signs give evidence that the Holy Spirit has clothed people with His presence. Other attributes are seen over time, like spiritual dedication, increased effectiveness in interpersonal relations, increased boldness to witness for Christ, and greater insight into the Bible. The New Testament also speaks of the fruit of the Spirit in Galatians 4. The Spirit of God certainly is given to develop these attributes in the life of the believer. These evidences require time to come to fruition, whereas speaking in tongues gives immediate witness to the Spirit's presence. Obedience and submission are two items we will return to while explaining our thesis.

You see why I say this isn't just a **style**, unless it's a **lifestyle**.

Pentecostals have clergymen and women ministers. The Scriptures are clear that the true Church needs leaders. But these leaders do not insist they are the only ones to have ministry or to possess the power of God to bless others.

Gone are the old classifications of only a select group of prophets who could hear from God and do His bidding. Now any man or woman can be a witness or a prophet. But there's no room for "lone rangers" in the Body.[36] Thus Spirit-filled persons must be in subjection to one another in the unity of the Spirit, so as to work together with much more power and influence in a world needing a relationship with its Creator. Yes, anyone who makes God the Lord of his/her life, and seeks God's power through His Spirit, can see, hear, and speak from God's perspective. It's not at all a "putting on of personal power," but rather "submitting to His power in surrender." God has put in place controls and boundaries so order can be maintained. Yes, a veritable paradox!

SOME QUALIFICATIONS

An important point needs to be made here for those who are seeking clarification of this much-publicized phenomenon. The Baptism in the Holy Spirit is not given, or available for the individual who is not a believer in Christ. One becomes a "Christian" by accepting God's love, by repentance of sin, and by believing in the redemptive work of Jesus as the Son of God who gave His life on the cross so that anyone who believes on Him might be saved (John 3:16). One must exercise faith in the death of Jesus as God's substitute for his/her sins in order for the miracle of salvation to be effective.

When Jesus was about to leave His disciples and go back to the Father, He promised them this empowerment of the Spirit: *"If you love me, you will obey what I command. And I will ask the Father, and He will give you another Counselor to be with you forever—the Spirit of truth. The world cannot accept Him, because it neither sees Him nor knows Him. But you know Him, for He lives with you and will be in you"* (John 14:15-17).

Here the statement is clearly made. The unbeliever cannot expect to be a recipient of God's power to witness without preconditions. The disciples were already influenced by the Spirit ("you know Him, He lives with you," v. 17). In the near future, the Holy Spirit would not only be *with* them but be *in* them. This is the infilling of the Holy Spirit that folks refer to as the Baptism in the Holy Spirit. It's the "stage three" referred to above, and it is related to obedience. *"We are witnesses of these things, and so is the Holy Spirit, whom God has given to those who obey Him"* (Acts 5:32).

R. A. Torrey makes a further distinction about the baptism in the Holy Spirit, which is a truth/concept that has been greatly misunderstood by the larger Evangelical community. They have failed to see that the biblical author Luke speaks of the Holy Spirit in a clearly different way than does the apostle Paul in his many references. Luke makes a clear distinction as to the role of the Holy Spirit in a person's life. "In every passage in the Bible in which the results of the baptism with the Holy Spirit are mentioned they are related to testimony and service. The baptism with the Holy Spirit has no direct reference to cleansing from sin [in Luke's writings]. It has to do with gifts for service rather than with graces of character."[37]

These gifts are an incredible provision God is making available in this age of the Spirit. He, the third person of the Trinity, gives gifts to ordinary folks to help them with this task of being a witness. These gifts (1 Cor. 12; Rom. 12; Eph. 4) are tools to use as a witness to produce fruit (personal characteristics) for the weary traveler. They are not badges of holiness or signs of achievement. They are simple tools to counter the powers of the evil one and bring healing, knowledge, wisdom, supernatural miracles, and an unusual measure of faith to bear on the chains that bind unbelievers—to release them to come to the light of the gospel.

DO ONLY SPIRIT-BAPTIZED FOLK HAVE POWER WITH GOD?

As early as 1907 A. G. Garr, missionary to India who had been baptized in the Holy Spirit in 1906 at Azusa Street, refused the narrow view of some that no one but a Pentecostal had power with God to witness. "Of course, men have been and are now greatly used of God without the baptism of the Holy Ghost. The power of God was manifested in the lives of the disciples before Pentecost; for they healed the sick, cast out demons, and even raised the dead. When we say that the Holy Ghost baptism is invariably witnessed by speaking in tongues, we do not depreciate the fact that men may have Holy Ghost power who have not been baptized."[38] I'm sorry that some Pentecostals would like to "franchise" God's power as their exclusive domain. This is neither generous nor biblical.

The gifts of the Holy Spirit (*charismata*) are tools to help work in the orchard to grow fruit. Gifts are given; fruit is grown. The fruit of the Spirit is as powerful a witnessing tool as are the gifts of the Spirit. Ideally they should both complement each other. I like to call this enabling *gift-wrapped fruit.* A Pentecostal (or anyone who has been baptized in the Holy Spirit) has the potential to be fully equipped to respond to those calling out to be rescued, to be saved. This is Pentecost. (This is the ideal, of course. There are many who call themselves Pentecostals who have none of these attributes. Others show wonderful fruit, but have failed to avail themselves of the power available to witness.)

Millions have accepted this challenge and have become an empowered people to bring about change in the lives of loved ones and strangers, no matter where they are found on the world's stage. In fact, one of the most marked signs of a Pentecostal is someone who either goes to a mission site or makes it possible for someone else to go. No recent theological group has made, per capita, greater sacrifices or sent more volunteers to the less fortunate and underprivileged than those of this theological persuasion. You haven't seen a genuine Pentecostal unless that person is a missionary at heart. No view of Pentecost and its purpose is complete which does not see its matrix and *raison d'etre* as the work Jesus came to accomplish and the call to the ripened harvest fields (see John 4:34).

Pentecost has fueled a missionary zeal like no other group of believers.

THE FUEL OF MISSIONARY ZEAL

Pentecost has fueled a missionary zeal like no other group of believers. Pentecostals are passing on the torch to Two-thirds World people. These Spirit-filled converts say, "Even in relative poverty, we can and must advance the gospel message to the target (all the world) that Jesus requested." Pentecostals believe we can make a difference and always have believed it. We believed in this optimistic projection of energy and funds and results—long before the present burgeoning statistics. It has little to do with our methods or our goodness, and certainly nothing to do with our name, but much to do with obedience to the Ascension Mandate (Mark 16:15-18; Acts 1:8) and faith in its charter.

Jesus used common folk, because others would not take that leap of faith from their traditionalism and stations of power in it. Pentecostals haven't traditionally sought or rationalized the need to be powerful in worldly (or even church worldly) terms because we were considered unqualified. (There are now, however, starting to be exceptions to this statement about power, sorry to say, as we become more "qualified" in the eyes of the world and Christendom.) What is the equation for missionary effectiveness, social influence, and political power? Might this be a good topic for an academic dissertation?

The late David du Plessis was a noted Pentecostal ecumenist and author of *A Man Called Mr. Pentecost*. As quoted in Grant McClung's book, here is a dialogue du Plessis had in an ecumenical meeting with religious leaders from across the nation. "Please tell us," asked one of the churchmen, "what is the difference between you and us? We quote the same Scriptures as you do, and yet when you say those words they sound so different....You have said nothing with which we want to differ and yet there seems to be a distinct difference somewhere."

McClung finds that the 'distinct difference' was revealed in du Plessis' answer: "Gentlemen, comparisons are odious, and I do not wish to injure anyone's feelings or hurt your pride. But the truth as I see it is this: You have truth on ice, and I have it on fire." [39]

McClung adds:

> This "on fire" pentecostal mission theology has tended to be a "theology on the move." Its character has been more experiential than cognitive, more activist than reflective. Pentecostals have often acted now and theologized later.... Only recently have pentecostal missiologists begun to solidify a more formalized "pentecostal missions theology." ... The accessibility of God and His power has been understood by pentecostals due to their literal acceptance of "thus saith the Lord." "This," said missions strategist David A Womack "was one of the major causes for the rise of the Pentecostal Movement; for, as people read their Bibles with renewed interest and better understanding, they found the description of a kind of Christianity very different from that of their own churches. Once the new approach to Bible interpretation was established, it was inevitable that some group would call for a return to the full gospel of the apostles."[40]

TO TASTE OR NOT TO TASTE

In all parts of the world today, people have a widespread interest in the baptism in the Holy Spirit, especially in the phenomenon that accompanies it—the manifestation of speaking in tongues. There is also a great need for clarifications about speaking in tongues, so that those interested in the subject may understand the viewpoint from those who *have* and maintain this experience, instead of the volumes of material by those standing on the outside. *These folks are not just wondering, but deciding if "the orange is sweet or sour"* **without tasting it**. Over one hundred years ago, H. Gunkel said it right, in my opinion: "It is tempting to conceive of the Spirit in Paul as a 'concept' that merely needs defining in order to be mastered. But to this concept belong very concrete views and deep inner experiences in which we must imitate the Apostle in order to understand his dogmatic statements."[41] Pentecostals and Charismatics are now increasingly beginning to write authoritative academic and practical illumination on the subject. I wish to do that in this book, and from a different vantage point—that of a student and teacher of communications so as to illustrate a side of the "tongues" question that perhaps has been neglected heretofore.

Too often, great mistakes have been made by those who brazenly write about this topic, but with a deplorable lack of understanding about either the baptism in the Holy Spirit or the gifts of the Holy Spirit. No one would question their rights to do so. Also, and rightfully so, folks have been quick to criticize others who have some experience of this gift of God to the Church, but little knowledge about it theologically. One of the great perplexing truths is that God doesn't require a candidate for the infilling of the Spirit to be able to exegete perfectly all the Scriptures about God's empowerment to be able to testify of Him. The same is true for the gift of salvation! And thank God for both truths. But those who speak in tongues should indeed strive to bring clarity about the subject to earnest seekers.

Sometimes when well-trained theologians read or hear someone who witnesses to this experience, but in terms betrays his or her unprofessional training in biblical theology, the "expert" may make pejorative statements about that person's mental stability or theological naiveté. One does not question these critics' right to self-expression. However, it is difficult to understand how they can set themselves in a position of authority or judgment.

Perhaps there are some who would refute the baptism in the Spirit on the basis that experience plays a too important role in the formulation of the doctrines of Pentecostals and Charismatics. I want to demonstrate the Scriptures' studied conclusions, confirmed by experience, that form solid grounds for the twentieth century's revival. It has not been based on experience alone.

Wouldn't it be an act of charity for these critics to examine their own argumentation, *also* based on experience, but in their case, a lack of experience? "Evangelicals, many of whom had been led to believe that Pentecostals should be classified as a cult, had come to recognize that apart from the Pentecostal teaching about the baptism in the Spirit with the accompanying sign of speaking in tongues, Pentecostal teaching was squarely in line with orthodox Christian theology."[42] Theologians are similar to historians, in my opinion. Both are searching for truth, even though theologians do so in a broader context than that employed by secular historians. Individual theologians, surely, can be ignorant, narrow-minded, or quickly dismissive of others' viewpoints. Journalists too often fall into this trap as any national political season will attest. This author must make a decided effort to refrain from "dismissiveness" toward those who, past or present, still relegate the unprecedented growth and vitality of the Charismatic movement in the world to the ash heap of religious experience.

> There is one basic reason why Bible-believing Christians do not believe in the miraculous gifts of the Spirit. It is simply this: *They have not seen them.* Their tradition, of course, supports their lack of belief, but their tradition would have no chance of success if it were not coupled with their lack of *experience* of the miraculous.... It often goes unnoticed that this appeal to history, either past or present, is actually an argument from *experience,* or better, an argument from the *lack of experience.*[43]

Gordon Fee, in an article for the *Bulletin for Biblical Research*, addresses the pain and sometimes the consternation of Pentecostals on this issue. His article centers on this interesting separation (dividing wall) between the words of the text and any of the interpreter's experience, and also any emotive content or intention of the biblical author. Fee's thesis is that everything is being imprisoned by the Germanic rules of historical critical methodology. This he faced when he "fell into scholarship." These rules imposed on a given text, to him, had nothing to do with what God may have intended spiritually for the audience the text was written for. All this was to be neutralized by the academy. Further, the meaning of scripture could only reach the people by way of the academy—who had a decided non-supernatural bias (even anti-supernatural) about a decidedly supernatural book! What Fee considered to be the first tasks of exegesis (spirituality, doxology, discipleship) were all disallowed by the present rules of the game.[44]

No doubt Pentecostals have been at fault for not writing clearly or charitably themselves, and not enough on the subject of glossolalia. Happily, as most Pentecostals have lately learned that one could be both educated and spiritual, they are now starting to correct that neglect. Many recent sources will be cited in this book. One of these, Morton T. Kelsey, serves as Rector of St. Luke's Church, with a group of members who are glossolalic and to which the parish church is also related in a psychological clinic. These two elements gave the rector the occasion to observe the practical results of glossolalia in his own parish, from both the theoretical/clinical side as well as the experiential component. He describes the plethora of material written by folks who have no experience of the subject: "A growing collection of research is being compiled, by both religious and secular writers, of the primary data which makes necessary the postulating of the collective unconscious about which we have not fully understood. This body of data is not just someone's rational criticism of the human psyche based on his own limited personal knowledge of what should happen."[45] Kelsey makes a startlingly true assertion about what the modern scientific world ignores about the Scriptures relative to non-physical realities in the New Testament alone.

The Church today almost totally ignores the issues of angels, devils/demons, being demonized, and similar talk of Satan. Kelsey has listed over 300 New Testament references to Jesus' and the apostles' belief and description of these nonphysical phenomena in the New Testament. The "rational" world of today's Church tends to ignore, deny, or explain away these passages in scientific terms.[46]

THINK ABOUT A SHOE

As strange as it may seem, writing about tongues is writing about a rather inconsequential ingredient in the whole spiritual experience that sets Pentecostals apart from other denominations and theological persuasions. It's just the most controversial, unusual, and bewildering aspect. I think a good analogy to this dilemma is the shoe. A traditional shoe contains a tongue, but it would be incorrect to overemphasize its importance in the role and function of the product. The phenomenon of glossolalia is a valid one in the Christian experience, but it is not the ultimate goal and should not be sought for its own sake. All serious Pentecostals believe that in addition to the initial evidence of God's "clothing them in His Spirit" (authenticated by speaking in tongues), there are other evidences that relate to the *walk in the Spirit.* The Holy Spirit is the "Paraclete" (one called alongside to help)—known as the Comforter (John 14:16; 15:26). He empowers for witness (Acts 1:8). Jesus said He would be a Teacher (John 14:26; Luke 12:12). The Lord also said the Holy Spirit would testify/witness of Him, Jesus, and those called to be a disciple must do the same (John 15:26-27).

The phenomenon of glossolalia is a valid one in the Christian experience, but it is not the ultimate goal and should not be sought for its own sake.

> Tongues are not the only evidence of a Spirit-filled life, but they are always the initial or first evidence that one has been baptized in the Holy Spirit as the entrance into a Spirit-filled life. One purpose of baptism in the Spirit is to empower the believer for witness; therefore, enthusiasm and boldness in witnessing, divine guidance and enabling in the presentation of the gospel, and miraculous manifestations of God's power before unbelievers all may serve as additional

> evidences of baptism in the Holy Spirit, though not as substitutions for speaking in tongues.[47]

Can Pentecostalism be discussed, researched, and examined without a strong emphasis on glossolalia? Yes! Because it is so much more than a "tongues movement." For example, the recent "continent-reaching" revival at the Brownsville Assembly in Pensacola, Florida (Pastor John Kilpatrick), stopped counting after over 200,000 first-time conversions at the altars of the church were duly registered over a three-year period. People lined up outside the church in rain or shine for up to six hours, five nights a week during that time, to get a seat in the sanctuary that could accommodate 2,000. The media hardly reported this phenomenon of conversions which, by any account, was the defining element of this revival. What they did report was the force of gravity on those surrendered to the Holy Spirit's wooing! The same is true with glossolalia related to Pentecostal theology. Human nature is attracted to what seems weird. Theologians are part of that humanity. Again, the tongue is just a small part of the shoe.

Because Western theology has been so influenced by the philosophical thinking patterns of the Greco-Roman world, it has been seconded by logic. Emil Brunner talks of the Holy Spirit as the "stepchild" of theology. Frank Macchia says, "This is because theology has accented the *logica* of faith and thus has been ill-equipped to respond to the kind of dynamic pneumatic experience that borders on the non-rational. Theology has served only to shun and stifle the creative manifestations of the Spirit, which continue to be a 'bugbear' for theologians."[48] Macchia continues and also quotes Hendrikus Berkoff who referred to the "water-tight" wall of partition between Charismatic experience and academic theology, which he wishes could be removed: "Although Pentecostalism is a great deal more than a 'tongues movement,' it is the first movement to focus attention on this gift as being of crucial importance for understanding the nature of the divine-human encounter."[49]

There are many in the world today who accept the fact of "tongues" as being the biblical sign of the baptism in the Holy Spirit. But they wish to avoid any human emotion related to the experience. This group wants to be sure that the multitudes are not confused or perplexed by their actions. They wish to deny any stigma or unfavorable reputation often attached to the experience by their friends and acquaintances or on-looking strangers. This is partly due to the perception that "tongues talkers" were uneducated or unstable folk. Some of this criticism is justified. There certainly have been people who have misused the gift of God and others who have abused it, while some bearing the name of Pentecostal or Charismatic have truly been poor representatives of the majority.[50] I would guess, however, that much criticism might turn out to be a simple matter of ignorance about the doctrines of Pneumatology and could come under the heading of "amazed and perplexed" as were the first observers in Jerusalem. What is the biblical account of that day in Jerusalem, at the birth of the Church?

> All of them were filled with the Holy Spirit and began to speak in other tongues as the Spirit enabled them. Now there were staying in Jerusalem God-fearing Jews from every nation under heaven. When they heard this sound, a crowd came together in bewilderment, because each one heard them speaking in his own language.... Amazed and perplexed, they asked one another, "What does this mean?" Some, however, made fun of them and said, "They have had too much wine" (Acts 2:4, 5, 12, 13).

AVERSION TO SIDE EFFECTS

One of the pivotal points of the thesis of this book on the phenomenon of tongues focuses on this aversion to the "side effects" of God's gift. **Why did God choose a sign related to human speech/communications that would be so ridiculed, maligned, resisted, and rejected?** He is all knowing. There must be reasons. We know He has a great sense of humor (thankfully), but is that the only motivation? This is what I wish to explore through the understanding of current communications theory and speech mannerisms.

The reader should be aware that in this endeavor, the author is a confirmed Pentecostal who had the initial experience of "speaking in tongues" when he was a lad of eleven years old. That experience was the launching point of a missionary career spanning over 40 years in Africa and Asia, once he was ordained and certified by his church. During this adventure, he communicated in four languages he had to *learn*. In the process of preparation and equipping for the ongoing task of training national ministers, he obtained two graduate degrees (including the Ph.D.) from the University of Minnesota in Speech Communications and Cross-Cultural Communications/Cultural Anthropology. I hesitate to mention these achievements for fear of sounding prideful. However, I have mentioned this issue as analogous to a medical doctor who frames and hangs his medical certifications on the office wall when you visit him/her, as reassurance for the patients. As a disclaimer, I agree with those who state that degrees don't necessarily mean one is "educated." My father, who was born in 1908, used to tell me: "Son, it's all right to have degrees as long as there is temperature!"

William Menzies and his son Robert, in their recent book, have an especially enlightening chapter entitled: "Evidential Tongues." These authors have traveled and worked in Asia for 20 years. They mention that in those travels, they can always count on the same question being asked, and that concerns tongues. "The fact that the question is asked so frequently and in a variety of settings indicates that Pentecostals have not effectively dealt with this issue.... We have failed to speak to this issue in a manner that makes sense in today's hermeneutical context."[51]

This Menzies' volume represents a watershed on the issue of Pentecostal theology. It builds on the seminal breakthrough work of Roger Stronstad, who demonstrates that the Spirit came upon the disciples at Pentecost, not as a source of new covenant existence, but as the source of power for effective witness.[52] In clearer accents, the Menzies "softly" SHOUT to the Evangelical world that a true exegete must stop looking at Lukan theology through the lens of the apostle Paul. While Paul's and Luke's theologies relative to the Holy Spirit are *complementary*, they each have a *distinct* focus and purpose.[53] The theology of Paul is largely soteriological (relating to salvation), and that of Luke is exclusively Charismatic and missiological (the science of missionary activity) for gospel witness.

Another clear voice, Jon Ruthven, a professor of Systematic Theology (Regent University), sees a definite paradigm shift ahead, as the growing worldwide church needs to be a great deal more informed theologically by the Charismatic power of God which the New Testament so clearly demonstrates. (Ruthven suggests that the 2/3rd World churches are already there in praxis, but their Western-dominated theology is lagging far behind.)[54] Traditional Protestant hermeneutics, translated and transported around the world by missionaries, has shown a conscious denial or ignorance of the Charismatic themes in the New Testament. Pentecostal missionaries, often more interested in evangelizing than internalizing and writing about theology, simply adopted the traditional view of miracles to serve as "evidence" or "sign" of invisible divine actions. Needed: A conceptual shift in understanding the experience of the Spirit—from these old "wine skins" into newer, more useful, and more biblical models.

"Recent statistical methods show that the OT and NT share essentially the same profile of emphases about the Spirit that is overwhelmingly active in charismatic expression. It is this charismatic Spirit, not simply the protestant Spirit of regeneration and sanctification, that is normative for all Christians."[55] Ruthven suggests, with reason, that a reprioritizing is needed for a whole list of the doctrines of the Holy Spirit, Kingdom of God, the New

Covenant, the Human Condition, Salvation, Miracles, Christology, Discipleship, Faith, Prayer, and Ecclesiology, and so on. No Evangelical (including Pentecostals/Charismatics) should abandon their Reformational grounding on *sola gratia, sola fidei,* and *sola scriptura.* But we need rather to be bold in separating the historically conditioned traditions of men from our allegiance to the Word of God shown plainly in its Charismatic emphasis. The following two excerpts, one from a Lutheran and the other from a Roman Catholic, will exemplify this move of God from a new perspective.

THE REVIVAL TOUCHED LUTHERANS

Our first pastorate was in Hopkins, Minnesota, a suburb of Minneapolis, from 1956 to 1958. Can you imagine my joy at hearing that this Lutheran-dominated state (many of whom had suppressed Pentecost and disparaged the gift of tongues) was beginning to see Lutheran pastors and laity desire and experience glossolalia in their search for God's renewal! Only a few came to my attention before we left for our first assignment to West Africa in 1959. Upon our return (1963) many scores testified of this revival in certain Lutheran communities. One of the most thrilling was that of the Lutheran pastor Larry Christenson who began to write about this experience, encouraging his fellow Lutherans to jump in this spiritual river with him.

> The Bible tells us that speaking in tongues is a manifestation of the Holy Spirit (Acts 2:4, 10:46, 19:6; 1 Cor. 12:10). Paul warns that the tongue can have a false note—like a noisy gong or a clanging cymbal—if the speaker does not manifest the gift in love (1 Cor. 13:1); it may be used out of turn (1 Cor. 14:27), or at the wrong time (1 Cor. 14:28). But not even in Corinth, where tongues were greatly abused, does St. Paul suggest that it has degenerated into a purely human phenomenon, the product of excess emotionalism. His plea, rather, is that precisely because this is a manifestation of the Holy Spirit, it should be manifested "decently and in order" (1 Cor. 14:40), for "God is not a God of confusion but of peace" (1 Cor. 14:33). He does not tell them to *stop* manifesting this gift. On the contrary, he tells them to *continue manifesting the gift* (1 Cor. 14:5a), but in a proper way (1 Cor. 14:13, 28), and with the proper regard for the other manifestations of the Spirit as well (1 Cor. 14:5b).... We miss St. Paul's point altogether if we begin to search out reasons why we should *not* speak in tongues, why we *don't* need this gift in the churches today, how much better we can do *without* it, and so on. It is well to be alert to the dangers of abuse which St. Paul points out,

> but we cannot depreciate the gift as such, for it is of the Holy Spirit. Scripture simply does not support an argument *against* speaking in tongues—only against its abuse. When once we grasp this basic truth, our whole discussion of tongues is cast in the positive framework which St. Paul himself reflects when he says. "I thank God that I speak in tongues more than you all" (1 Cor. 14:18). The cure for abuse is not *disuse* but *proper* use.[56]

Next Pastor Christenson explains for fellow Lutherans, who have doubted God's provision, with tones so purely simple and with understatement:

> What is speaking in tongues? Why has it begun to appear in many historic Christian denominations?...However we may analyze or explain it, we cannot escape the fact that traditional church people now numbering in the thousands and perhaps millions—Episcopalians, Presbyterians. Roman Catholics, Lutherans, Baptists, Methodists, to *name* a few—witness to having experienced this New Testament phenomenon.[57]

> In a day when serious historians are beginning to characterize our times as the "post-Christian era" we see this strange counter-phenomenon: The return of the *charismata.... It involves a supernatural manifestation of the Holy Spirit which is clearly spoken of in the Bible.* [Emphasis Christenson] This is holy ground, where snap judgment or an ill-informed opinion could truly grieve the Spirit. One even writes about it with some qualms. But where silence runs the danger of conceding the day to fear and uniformed prejudice, one should speak.[58]

I should learn better how to express this wonderful experience, take my cue from this Lutheran, and write of this personal experience in hushed tones—not bombastic triumphalism.

ROMAN CATHOLICS ARE "AGAIN" EXPERIENCING GLOSSOLALIA

Ever since Vatican II (1963-65), Roman Catholics have been on a renewed mission to reestablish contact with their "separated brethren" (formerly called heretics) in genuine attempts to close the theological breach of misunderstanding between themselves and Protestants. It is not my purpose, nor am I qualified, to fully evaluate or justify this initiative that did not come from the Protestant side, but from the Catholic side. The reason for mentioning it here is that I was privileged to participate in the International Roman

Catholic/Pentecostal Dialogue for eight years over a twelve-year period, as an invited participant representing one of the classical Pentecostal churches in this dialogue. This interchange had as its goal neither ecclesiastical unity nor administrative rapprochement, but rather an attempt at mutual understanding and a diminishing of certain myths held about each other in the true spirit of ecumenicity. I here include, similar to the above material by a prominent Lutheran, astonishing words by two prominent Catholic theologians and scholars who are reflecting on the Charismatic renewal movement in the Catholic Church since the mid-1960s.

> Classical Pentecostals (Protestant Pentecostals) did not invent the baptism in the Holy Spirit. Rather it belongs to the integrity of Christian initiation as witnessed by the New Testament and the early post-biblical teachers of the church. Peter describes the essential elements of Christian initiation in these words: "Repent and be baptized ... in the name of Jesus Christ for the forgiveness of your sins; and you will receive the gift of the Holy Spirit" (Acts 2:38).[59]

McDonnell and Montague then examine an impressive list of eleven post-biblical early church fathers such as Tertullian, Hilary of Poitiers, Cyril of Jerusalem, Basil, Chrysostom, Philoxenus, and others, representing Latin, Greek, and Syrian cultures. These writings show that the biblical evidence of baptism in the Holy Spirit existed hundreds of years after the resurrection of Jesus and the death of the apostles.

> John Chrystosom (c. 347-407) represents the Syrian liturgy in Antioch, though he himself, like Cyril, was Greek-speaking. According to him, the model of the apostolic church had the reception of charisms with the initiatory liturgy: "whoever was baptized at once spoke in tongues, and not only in tongues, but many prophesied: some performed many other wonderful works."[60]

The authors then speak of an element very close to the central thesis of this book by citing the point of the church father Philoxenus, who (of course justifying the interval of time between infant baptism in the Roman tradition and the fact that a child could not exercise his/her will at that age) speaks to the need for the recipient to make a conscious act of the will. "Accepting the gift is required on the part of the recipient, if he is to experience properly the benefits that result from the gift. This acceptance involves the self-emptying that Christ himself underwent (Phil 2:7); *only once the ego has been stripped away can the gift of the Spirit be fully experienced.*"[61] (Emphasis mine)

Few authors, in my research, have better plumbed the core of that which I hope to illustrate here than the above statement. The gift of the baptism in the Holy Spirit is, in my opinion, anchored here at the crux of three elements: *Accepting, self-emptying,* and *subordinating* the 'meaning making' skills (mother-tongue speech) in which humanity excels.

AN INITIAL LIST OF THE STEPS OF THE WORK OF THE HOLY SPIRIT

The Holy Spirit:

1. Convicts and convinces men of sin: John 16:8-11.
2. Is the agent in regeneration of the soul—to a restored position with the Creator (Eph. 2:1)—which soul is thus baptized into the body of Christ: 1 Cor. 12:13; Gal. 3:27.
3. Is the "helper" (Paraclete) for progressive sanctification and growth of fruit of the Spirit with the volition of the believer: John 15:5; Rom. 5:5; 2 Thes. 2:13.
4. Baptizes in the Holy Spirit, through Jesus the agent: Acts 2:4; 10:46.

Summary

The believer is convicted of sin, comes to repentance, abides in Christ, produces the fruit of the Spirit, and progresses in sanctification, then seeks and receives the baptism in the Holy Spirit. **NOTE** that there can be many other scenarios here. Few follow these steps in progression sequentially. The baptism in the Holy Spirit can help produce the fruit of the Spirit besides equipping the believer for witnessing (Acts 1:8). To our astonishment, some receive the baptism in the Holy Spirit without demonstrating ANY of the fruit of the Spirit or having been baptized in water (Acts 10).

A brief overview of certain aspects of this study quickly acknowledges that the depth and complexity of this topic obviates any further exposition of this vast doctrine in the space available here. Now, let us look at some of the objections and denials of the general topic of Pentecostalism's belief concerning the baptism in the Holy Spirit and the supernatural gifts of the Spirit.

ENDNOTES:

1. Harvey Cox, Fire From Heaven: *The Rise of Pentecostal Spirituality and the Reshaping of Religion in the Twenty-First Century* (1995), 47.
2. Philip Yancey, *The Jesus I Never Knew* (1995), 99-100.
3. Paul G. Bretscher, *The World Upside-Down or Right-Side Up?* (1964), 82.
4. Ibid., 91-92.

5. Donald B. Kraybill, *The Upside-Down Kingdom* (1990), 70-72.
6. I will not list even a small portion of them here, but the reader will find scores in the ongoing bibliographical data in bibliography.
7. For a remarkably complete bibliography see: Watson E. Mills, *Glossolalia: A Bibliography* (1985) and Watson E. Mills, *A Guide to Research on Glossolalia* (1986).
8. L. T. Johnson, *Religious Experiences in Early Christianity* (1999), 107.
9. See chapter following on "The Case for Glossolalia in the Bible."
10. For instance, see: Gordon Fee, *Gospel and Spirit: Issues in N.T. Hermeneutics* (1991) on the issue of subsequence.
11. See: Gary B. McGee, ed., *Initial Evidence, Historical and Biblical Perspectives on the Pentecostal Doctrine of Spirit Baptism* (1991) and Max Turner, *The Holy Spirit and Spiritual Gifts: Then and Now* (1996).
12. David Lim, *Spiritual Gifts: A Fresh Look* (1999), 141.
13. Robert P. Menzies and William W. Menzies, *Spirit and Power* (2000).
14. The process of regarding something abstract (spiritual) as a material or concrete thing (e.g., a teacher who gives too much weight to the IQ test).
15. Jon Ruthven, *On the Cessation of the Charismata: The Protestant Polemic on Post-biblical Miracles* (1993).
16. J. D. Pentecost, *The Words and Works of Jesus Christ* (1981), 538.
17. James D. Hernando, *Dictionary of Hermeneutics* (2005), 170.
18. R. P. Spittler, "Glossolalia," in *Dictionary of Pentecostal and Charismatic Movements,* ed. Stanley M. Burgess and Gary B. McGee (1992), 335-341.
19. *Constitution and Bylaws of the General Council of the Assemblies of God* (2005), 84.
20. Spittler, 335-341.
21. David B. Barrett, *The Encyclopedia of Christianity* (2002).
22. Morton T. Kelsey, *Tongues Speaking: An Experiment in Spiritual Experience* (1968), 4.
23. Eddie Hyatt, *2000 Years of Charismatic Christianity* (2002), 3. See also Cox.
24. See Ronald A. Kydd, *Charismatic Gifts in the Early Church* (1984) and Cecil M. Robeck, Jr., ed., *Charismatic Experiences in History* (1985).
25. Hyatt (2002), 5.
26. Jack Deere, *Surprised by the Power of the Spirit* (1993), 78.
27. Philip Yancey, "Letters from the Borderlands," *Outreach* (September/October, 2003): 34-36.
28. Jerry Cook, "Why I'm a Pentecostal," *Foursquare World Advance* (July-August, 2002): 10-11. I'm indebted to Jerry Cook for the three-phase idea. See also Charles W. Conn, "Glossolalia and the Scriptures" in *The Glossolalia Phenomenon* (1966), 28-29.
29. Lewis J. Willis, "Glossolalia in Perspective," in *The Glossolalia Phenomenon* (1966), 249.
30. Classroom lectures, University of Minnesota, 1967-1968. Subsequent chapters will explain this concept in detail.
31. L. T. Johnson, *Religious Experience in Earliest Christianity* (1998), 4.
32. Ibid., 46-50.
33. See Edward Sapir, *Language, Culture, and Personality* (1957) and Benjamin Whorf, Language, *Thought and Reality, John B Carroll,* ed. (1956).
34. Jon Ruthven, "Back to the Future for Pentecostal/Charismatic Evangelicals in North America and World Wide: Radicalizing Evangelical Theology and Practice," forthcoming. Ruthven states this characterization of Pentecostals is widely attributed to G. Campbell Morgan, *The Phenomenon of Pentecost,* ed. Frank J Ewart, rev. ed. (1975),

38-39. This epithet is also cited in Vinson Synan, *Holiness-Pentecostal Movement* (1971), 144.

35. A. J. Gordon, *Ministry of the Spirit (1950),* 71-72.
36. Because the traditional churches have rejected the New Testament model of the gifts of the Spirit and "put out" those who seemed to challenge the authorities by the use of these gifts, the Pentecostal Movement has always been plagued by the existence of many "lone rangers." Such persons were attracted to the potential of personal power and, by so doing, contradicted the very ethic they proclaimed. Christ's whole Church is poorer because of these who refuse to be "matured" (i.e., corrected and/or encouraged) by the body of Christ in the assembly.
37. Quoted in W. Horton, 33. Also see: Robert and William Menzies, *Spirit and Power* (2000); Roger Stronstad, *The Charismatic Theology of St. Luke,* (1984); and Strondstad, *Spirit, Scripture and Theology* (1995).
38. A. G. Garr, "Tongues: The Bible Evidence to the Baptism with the Holy Ghost," *Pentecostal Power* (March 1907): 40.
39. David J. du Plessis, *A Man Called Mr. Pentecost* (1977), 181-182.
40. L. Grant McClung, ed., *Azusa Street and Beyond: Pentecostal Missions and Church Growth in the Twentieth Century* (1986), 47-48; quoting David Womack, *The Wellsprings of the Pentecostal Movement* (1968), 84. For additional emphasis see J. M. Thoburn, *The Church of Pentecost* (1899), 31.
41. H. Gunkel, *The Influence of the Holy Spirit: A View of the Apostolic Age and the Teaching of the Apostle Paul: A Biblical-Theological Study,* trans. R.A. Harrisville and P.A. Quanbeck, ([1888] 1979), 75.
42. W. and R. Menzies, *Spirit and Power* (2000), 29.
43. Jack Deere, *Surprised by the Power of the Spirit* (1993), 55.
44. Gordon Fee, "To What End Exegesis?" *Bulletin for Biblical Research 8* (1998): 75-88.
45. Morton T. Kelsey, *Tongues Speaking: An Experiment in Spiritual Experience* (1968), 213.
46. Ibid., 234-241. See also Jon Ruthven, "Are Pentecostal Seminaries a Good Idea?" *Pneuma,* Vol. 26, No. 2 (Fall, 2004): 339-345. In this article Ruthven highlights the need of Pentecostal seminaries to abandon attempts to look like all the other seminaries and obey the apostle Paul's admonition in 1 Cor. 2:5 "*that your faith might not rest on men's wisdom, but on God's [miracle] power.*" Ruthven writes, "If we examine the programmatic and summary statements of Jesus' ministry, the Gospels' emphases upon healing, exorcism and revelation in the public expression of that ministry, the explicit commissions he made to his disciples (who were to replicate his life and ministry closely, Mt. 9; Mk. 3:14-15; 2 Cor. 12:12; 1 Th. 1:5) and finally, to observe what it is they actually did in the Book of Acts, 27.2% of which is miracle story—more than all the sermons and speeches—not to mention the highly charismatic summary statements of Paul's ministry (Acts 15; Rom.15:19; 2 Cor. 12:12; 1 Th. 1:5), we find a profile of activities that is breathtakingly far removed from modern seminary curricula. The central training of Jesus to his disciples, and they to theirs, in faith, prayer, exorcism, and healing, rarely find a place in a seminary graduate's transcript, much less as core educational experiences."
47. *The Baptism in the Holy Spirit.* An official statement by the General Presbytery of the Assemblies of God (2000).
48. Frank D. Macchia, "Sighs Too Deep for Words: Toward a Theology of Glossolalia," *Journal of Pentecostal Theology* 1 (1992): 47-73. See also: E. Brunner, Misverstandnis der Kirch (1988), ch. 5; H. Berkoff, *The Doctrine of the Holy Spirit* (1964), 87-89.
49. Ibid., 50.

50. See below the chapter on criticism and self-criticism.
51. W. and R. Menzies (2000), 121.
52. Roger Stronstad, *The Charismatic Theology of St. Luke* (1984). See earlier writers with similar leanings: H. Gunkel, *The Influence of the Holy Spirit* (1979) and D. Hill, *Greek Words and Hebrew Meanings* (1967).
53. W. and R. Menzies (2000), 51, 113-114.
54. Ruthven, "Back to the Future," (2003), 4.
55. Ibid.
56. Larry Christenson, *Speaking in Tongues, Its Significance for the Church* (1968), 18-19.
57. Ibid., 15.
58. Ibid., 18.
59. Killian McDonnell and George Montague, *Fanning the Flame* (1991), 14.
60. Ibid., 18.
61. Ibid., 21.

CHAPTER 2

WHAT CRITICS SAY

Tongues have always been an issue, even in the first 100 years of the early apostolic churches themselves. Many of their founders had witnessed the message of the Messiah, His cross, and His resurrection. The Early Church was at home with and practiced the Charismatic reality of the gifts of the Spirit. We know this because the apostle Paul wrote most pointedly to the excesses in using the gifts in his first letter to the Corinthians (chapters 12-14). Some of the opposition to tongues after the third century will be discussed below—its occurrence in the maturing and changing Christian church was often documented centuries apart. These historical data most generally are records of the negative evaluation of the charismata seen through the actions of the Roman Catholic Church to restrain or prohibit any renewal movement it deemed spurious. More important for my purposes are the writings of critics *since* the great renewal of the "charismata" (gifts of the Spirit listed in 1 Cor. 12, Rom. 12, and Eph. 4) around the beginning of the last century.

WHY LOOK AT CRITICISM?

It is this writer's opinion that an apologetic for the wisdom of God (seen as foolish by so many) in offering the gift of the Spirit to individuals—manifested by tongues/glossolalia—for the edification of the Church and the power of witness to build that Church, only has validity if it considers the many critics, both gentle and severe, of this phenomenon. The strongest criticism and most voluminous has come from the more recent observers of the Pentecostal (and lately Charismatic) renewal movement's rapid growth, beginning in the early 1900s. What today is called Evangelical Christianity is a broadly defined multi-denominational group of churches, in which those who practice glossolalia are generally included. Evangelicalism is *itself* a renewal movement that sought distinction from "Reformed Theology" which had been much impacted by the age of Enlightenment and scholastic

Protestantism—which was *in its time also* only one renewal movement away from the original dissenters with Roman Catholicism (e.g., the likes of Luther and Calvin, whom we call the fathers of the Great Reformation of the sixteenth century). Each renewal movement was heavily opposed (sometimes persecuted) by the older churches the revivalists felt needed renewing and were generally "shown the door" (given the right foot of fellowship!) by the older established organizations.

Pentecostals are the latest major "renewers" in this recurring phenomenon. It was the Evangelical Churches the Pentecostals most sought to revive. Thus, they are the loudest source of criticism in the latest round of opposition to the idea that the New Testament gifts of the Spirit are currently valid and available to all believers including, of course, the fact of glossolalia.

For critics of Pentecostal theology and/or Charismatic belief one does not have to search very deeply. Like any renewal movement, the act of changing the status quo of tradition invites criticism. And like any new "movement" some criticism is certainly justified. Many early and current believers who classify themselves as Pentecostal or Charismatic sincerely need teaching or humility or both. So it was and is with the Reformers and the birth of Protestantism in the Roman Catholic Church, AND the Anglicans/Episcopalians who criticized the Methodist movement when they found them growing cold, AND the Presbyterians about the revivals in Scotland AND the renewal of the Wesleyans inside the Methodist church AND the reformed movement seeking to reform the churches formed by the original Reformation!

Gary McGee gives genuine wisdom and perspective here. He draws from Peter Toon, Eugene Klug, and Otto Stahkle:

> In the history of Christianity, the blueprints of doctrinal development have not been left in the sole possession of the professional schools of theological architecture. The New Testament itself, far from including a systematic theology by modern criteria, contains gospels and letters, which address issues of faith and practice as they arose in the churches. Growth in doctrinal insight has characterized all Christian movements since the time of the early church and has been shaped by theological questions, new insights arising from revival movements and a myriad of cultural and historical factors. For example after the death of Martin Luther in 1546, Lutheranism almost foundered from differences of opinion over the correct interpretation of his theology; eventually they were resolved and unity was restored.[1]

There are now those wanting to renew the Pentecostals—who date their beginnings from the turn of the last century. And for many Pentecostals, renewal is desperately needed!

I do not wish to diminish the need or value of either *reform* or *criticism.* Critics are often our best friends. They are sometimes only trying to defend the status quo of strongly-held beliefs and tenets they would die for. Biblical truth is subject to interpretation. There are cultural and political forces that have always and will always impact what people write down in creeds and bylaws. Like old coins in circulation, they are worn thin and sometimes need to be "reminted" to meet the new circumstances of change. Not unimportantly, doctrines need to accept progressive revelation of the Holy Spirit as a sovereign God works through time and governments of mankind to fulfill His ultimate intention.

INSIGHT INTO THE CRITICS OF GLOSSOLALIA

Morton Kelsey gives a broad overview of four general categories of people's attitudes about tongues in current thought:

1. People think tongues has little value or meaning, because they judge it to simply result from an up thrust of primitive mentality or from psychological abnormality or, as some people see it, from demon possession.
2. Others see it as happening so long ago that current understanding and definition must be wrong and different from that described in the Bible.
3. Some believe it was useful for the establishment of the Church but is no longer of any value. The "tongues" of Acts 2 could not have been anything but solemn speech—not ecstatic utterance—and all tongues of the New Testament must have been the same.[2]
4. Finally, many believe speaking in tongues is a valuable experience in which the Holy Spirit gives the ability to speak a language other than one's own.[3]

Kelsey substantiates my contention that much of the opposition to the "tongues movement" can be viewed as old-fashioned protectionism. "There is always tension between those who stand for individual experience and those who stand for ecclesiastical authority ... This same tension accounts for much of the modern rejection of tongues."[4] In the third category of Kelsey (listed above) would come the most caustic and serious invective writing of B. B. Warfield in *Counterfeit Miracles*, who contends that the gifts of the Spirit were uniquely associated with the twelve Apostles—authenticating their ministry—and "ceased" when they died.[5] See also Merrill Unger for a similar theme.[6] In this same category is the author Robert Gromacki. He says that today's tongues speaking is not biblical because it is not actual foreign languages and maintains that tongues ceased shortly after the apostolic era. (He, like Warfield, is a classic cessationist.) Gromacki errs from inadequate research and makes statements such as: "Tongues did cease" and "No genuine occurrences of tongues were seen in the post-apostolic period through the Protestant Reformation." Latter scholarship shows his research as being premature and inadequate.[7]

It seems almost humorous to me when some disparage tongues because, as they claim, they were absent so long (which turns out not to be true). They must have forgotten that the doctrine of "Justification by Faith" was absent for over 1,000 years!

Another well-known critic and protagonist is John MacArthur, who basically denies current supernatural miracles. In his thesis, one of his points of contention is: "According to Scripture those who possess miraculous gifts could use them at will." He says this in the face of at least two instances when the Lord himself was inhibited from the miraculous by the unbelief and rejection of His hearers. MacArthur seems to use "selective research" to make the point that the majority of Charismatics practice abuses in their ministry.[8] A former critic of Pentecostals and this global revival, Jack Deere, rejects that claim and feels MacArthur seizes on the bizarre in his research (studying mainly the religious television channels) while his own research, much more extensive and over a longer period, shows the vast majority of Charismatics, even on the international scene, acknowledged there are those who hold to some bizarre doctrines but are a small minority. He observes that responsible leaders in the movement speak out against such abuses.

> The author [MacArthur] carefully, but persistently recorded only the most spectacular and unusual/weird physical manifestations represented by those who described their own feelings, sensations and impressions while receiving the initial baptism in the Holy Spirit. This gives the impression that only the unusual is the norm. 2. He rightfully records the false initial reasoning for tongues as "missionary tongues" at the turn of the century, (so study and time not needed to minister overseas in foreign cultures). 3. As for the conclusion of tongues origin, he settles on a psychological definition called "functional disassociation" of the speech process and the "evangelical culture" that gave the appropriate cues for the initiates. Perhaps a

more thorough study would have revealed that his research is on a small minority in North America and ignores the millions in the 2/3rd World that have no such "culture" and are part of the explanation or model of Acts 8 and the house of Cornelius.[9]

In his recent book, Harvey Cox lists the most virulent critics of the "tongues phenomenon":

> If the mainline churches merely disliked the Pentecostals, it is not an exaggeration to say that the fundamentalists loathed them. The staunch Presbyterian and unyielding fundamentalist Benjamin B. Warfield condemned the Pentecostals by lumping them together with Roman Catholics and others who believed that miracles still took place today. The Lord, insisted this professor at Princeton Theological Seminary, had not performed a single miracle since the days of Peter and Paul. Another conservative theologian, H. A. Ironside, fired off the most influential anti-Pentecostal barrage in 1912. In a book, *Holiness, the False and the True*, he asserted of the Pentecostals that "superstition and fanaticism of the grossest character find a hotbed in their midst." Still another fundamentalist, G. Campbell Morgan, trumped all the others by declaring that Pentecostalism was the "last vomit of Satan."[10]
>
> I also learned that it is a serious mistake to equate Pentecostals with Fundamentalists. They are not the same. Fundamentalists attach such unique authority to the letter of the verbally inspired Scripture that they are suspicious of the Pentecostals' stress on the immediate experience of the Spirit of God. This should not be surprising. Text-oriented believers in any religion tend to be wary of mystics. However, this does not mean that Pentecostalism does not embody a complex of religious ideas and insights. It does. The difference is that while the beliefs of the fundamentalists, and of many other religious groups, are enshrined in formal theological systems, those of Pentecostalism are imbedded in testimonies, ecstatic speech, and bodily movement. But it is a theology, a full-blown religious cosmos, an intricate system of symbols that respond to the perennial questions of human meaning and value. The difference is that, historically, Pentecostals have felt more at home singing their theology, or putting it in pamphlets for distribution on street corners. Only recently have they begun writing books about it.[11]

By far the most-repeated criticism goes like this: "Tongues served their purpose, but now their time is finished."

> The traditional answer given to this question is that glossolalia is the permanent and supernaturally given ability to speak a foreign language that one has not previously learned. This gift was given so that the gospel could be preached to all nations and language groups and was a useful tool for converting the Mediterranean world from paganism to Christianity. Once the entire known world had converted to Christianity the gift was withdrawn because there was no longer any need for it. This explanation of the nature and purpose of tongues was used by both Chrysostom and Augustine to explain why the gift of tongues was no longer found in the church.[12]

Many recent scholars have refuted this unfounded stance. One of the chief of these would be Ronald A. N. Kydd, who finds that Warfield's research overlooked the vast material available about the operation of the gifts through the second century.[13]

EARLIER CRITICS

Of the early Pentecostal revival in India came immediate critics like Fredrick Price in *Indian Witness*, a Calcutta-based Methodist publication, who dismissed speaking in tongues as "barnyard cackle."[14] "Another critic from this revival period in India relegated all such emotional display as 'heated brain ... common with insane patients or those whose nervous system is abnormally excited,' quite apart from any devout habits."[15]

Of Satanic Origin

A 1936 writer from Minneapolis, Minnesota—a teacher in the Lutheran Bible Institute—articulates an accusation often heard in my youth. Most later writers with more scholarly research, however, take a milder view: "We want to remind ourselves that the power and methods of Pentecostalism are more subtle than mysterious. Much of its mystery disappears when we consider one of its sources, that which is the real source of all error and confusion among men. This movement is subtle because it is satanic. That is the verdict of the Scriptures. It is verified by the horrid trail of schism, immorality and insanity that everywhere has marked its inroads into the Church."[16] There are many sources for this accusation, but most of them, like Stolee, are old. Little by little, the Pentecostal Movement began to be seen as more orthodox as time went by—as is attested by later authors.

Tongues and Psychology

One can count on psychologists to show up in any public meeting where tongues is discussed! In one article Janet Powers, a Pentecostal scholar, cites two psychological works on tongues which state that "Glossolalic utterances cannot be proven linguistically."[17] First, she cites authors H. Newton Maloney and Adams Lovekin, who quote still others who categorize glossolalics as weak mentally, low in education, and emotionally excitable; though they themselves hold a more balanced view. Lovekin himself is glossolalic.[18]

For a generally well-balanced view see John Kildahl.[19] This author finds no significant difference between glossolalics and non-tongues speakers for personality type, economic level, mental health differences, and so on. He advises both critics and proponents to be modest in their claims for it.

One of the most reasonable sources to debunk most of the criticism about the pathological nature of people who speak in tongues is the Roman Catholic author Killian McDonnell, who is the founder and president of the Center for Ecumenical and Cultural Research, Collegeville, Minnesota, and professor of theology at St. John's University. In his book, *Charismatic Renewal and the Churches*, McDonnell draws from history, sociology, cultural anthropology, psychology, and theology over a two-decade study. In it he found professional prejudice towards people who speak in tongues.

> A basic assumption is that a person or persons are to be considered psychologically normal until otherwise demonstrated. Psychologists will generally agree that the outward boundaries of normality are ample and wide rather than restrictive and narrow. These assumptions were not always granted when dealing with persons who speak in tongues. Not only religious leaders, who may be forgiven a certain ineptness in the more scientific aspects of psychology but also those trained in the behavioral sciences, who are not so easily absolved from guilt in the matter which belongs to the first principles of their science, have at times failed to grant these assumptions to glossolalics. The author knows of a team of anthropologists and psychologists, professors and graduate students at a well-known university in the United States ... They assumed without adequate knowledge of the persons involved that glossolalics were psychologically deprived *because* they spoke in tongues (emphasis McDonnell's).[20]

Virginia Hine also comes to the conclusion that "available evidence requires that an explanation of glossolalia as pathological must be discarded."[21]

For additional bibliographical sources on the psychological study of tongues, many as prejudiced as described by McDonnell, see Everett Wilson, in *The Globalization of Pentecostalism.*[22] In addition, see George Cutten[23] and Felicitas Goodman.[24]

The Seventh Day Adventist writer, Gerhard F. Hasel, questions the legitimacy of tongues because the "tongues movement" is not unified and is composed of a wide variety of beliefs such as Roman Catholics, liberal and conservative Protestants, a-millennialists and pre-millennalists, Calvinists, Armenians, and rank liberals. He asks the question: "Would the Holy Spirit not be concerned to teach anyone among those who engage in glossolalia any truth that would correct any and all of these differences? ... *Should the Holy Spirit not have taught them by now that the seventh day of the week is binding upon all believers?"* (emphasis mine).[25]

In *The Interpreter's Dictionary of the Bible*, E. Anderson makes a quick judgment of those who speak in tongues by his contention that "the psychological aspects are patent."[26] Some severe criticism comes from I. M. Lewis, who links glossolalia to shamanism.[27] Tongues are thought to be "psychological dissociation" according to F. Goodman.[28]

There is a growing field of data, however, which rejects earlier conclusions that glossolalia is intrinsically connected to psychopathology.[29] Morton Kelsey describes a meeting of psychiatrists, analysts, and clergy in New York city in 1962 where some told of the physical and emotional *benefits* that tongues brought to their patients.[30] In this vein, there is an interesting quote by C. S. Lewis in which he describes how a "transposition" occurs whenever a higher medium reproduces itself in a lower. If viewed merely from the perspective of the lower, the higher may be completely missed. Concerning glossolalia Lewis says "all non-Christian opinion would regard it as a kind of hysteria, and involuntary discharge of nervous excitement." However, "the very same phenomenon which is sometimes not only not natural but even pathological, is at other times ... the organ of the Holy Ghost.... Those who spoke with tongues as St. Paul did, can well understand how that holy phenomenon differed from the hysterical phenomenon—although ... they were in a sense exactly the same phenomenon."[31] Lewis later speaks about "the inevitableness of the error made about every transposition by one who approaches it from the lower medium only.... Transposition, accordingly, is an excellent term to express what happens when the Holy Spirit, the higher medium, is expressed in the lower, the human spirit. For the vehicle of expression, human language, becomes transposed into a new dimension of utterance."[32]

Tongues Speakers Are Schizophrenic

Many critics of tongues would place the personality of anyone who exercises glossolalia in a psychotic frame, especially that of schizophrenia. E. M. Patterson so labels glossolalics and attributes their behavior to "regression."[33] Morton Kelsey disagrees with this view and cites the works of C. G. Jung:

> Jung's conclusions were based upon the empirical evidence which thousands of patients presented him over fifty years of psychiatric practice. Speaking in tongues, Jung found, is one evidence of a break-through of this objective psyche or deep, collective level of the unconscious. Jung believes that there are levels of the unconscious beyond the personal, the buried memories, and the primitive impulses of the id, ... that man is in touch with an objective realm of psychic reality containing elements both inferior and superior to human consciousness."[34]

Kelsey strongly refutes the criticism that people who speak in tongues are schizophrenic. He does this from statistical reason and from psychiatrist's reports. Apparently there has been little evidence to suggest a correlation between the phenomena (speaking in tongues and psychotic behavior). Indeed if any large number of the two million Pentecostals in this country who have spoken in tongues were schizophrenic, one would hear from them in public, because lack of control is one characteristic of this disease.[35] Kelsey cites cases where: "Tongues speaking may well be an unconscious resolution to neurosis ... the number of persons who tell of being healed, both of physical illness and emotional or psychological difficulties along with the experience of glossolalia."[36]

EARLY DENUNCIATION BY EVANGELICALS

The following paragraphs come from the struggle between the Pentecostals and the Fundamentalists that came to an open breach in 1928 at the Chicago conference where the Fundamentalists denounced the Pentecostals. In fairness, one must say that voices have moderated and would not go on record today with such language. In fact, some of the major Pentecostal churches later were invited to join the latter organization, known as the National Association of Evangelicals, with Pentecostals eventually becoming the president of the body![37]

> Whereas the present wave of Modern Pentecostalism often referred to as the "tongues movement" and the present wave of fanatical and unscriptural healing which is sweeping over the country today, has

> become a menace in many churches and a real injury to sane testimony of Fundamental Christians,
>
> Be it resolved that this convention go on record as unreservedly opposed to Modern Pentecostalism, including the speaking in unknown tongues, and the fanatical healing known as general healing in the atonement, and the perpetuation of the miraculous sign-healing of Jesus and His apostles, wherein they claim the only reason the church cannot perform these miracles is because of unbelief.[38]

Another source of early virulent criticism is by C. W. Naylor who describes Pentecostalism as "the very scum of sectism."[39]

Grant Wacker, in *Heaven Below,* would like to pose as a friend to those who support the Charismatic renewal movement. But, like many others whose premise is to argue against the theological center of the twentieth century's revival, Wacker does so under what appears to be the cover of good scholarship. Chapter two in his book, titled "Tongues," is a compilation of some hard but very selective research. Like many current journalists who are "crises junkies," he quotes only the obtuse, dramatic, even extreme experiences of early writers who described their experience of glossolalia. I would have appreciated more balance—if he had also included early testimonies of more moderate accounts. Wacker suggests, finally that some form of dissociation, heavily impacted by the cultural environment, is that which determined the appropriateness of the experience and is the source of glossolalia.[40] One must be generous of heart and hesitant to quickly "write off' our critics, acknowledging that the temptation to primarily record the sensational is an ever-present one for those of us who write or document.

Tongues can occur in a highly charged atmosphere... or in quiet surroundings... emotionalism is not a necessary part of speaking in tongues.

It's true that when the Pentecostal Movement was small, the criticism was certainly more virulent. After the Charismatic move amongst the mainline churches broke in the 1960s, a more balanced and moderate spirit began to be seen. Pastors and writers like Lutheran Larry Christenson or Episcopalian Dennis Bennett or Presbyterian James Brown or Baptist Jack Deere added a new dimension to criticism. These later pastors and scholars are extremely important for our consideration because they are from older and more traditional denominations, who may at one time have spoken against the tongues movement. They later have tasted glossolalia themselves and have become partisans, after having joined what is now the second largest single theological persuasion in the Christian world.

LET'S EVALUATE/CRITIQUE THE CRITICS

Larry Christenson talks about the critics in a defense of tongues.

> Another common misconception is that speaking in tongues is a highly emotional or "ecstatic" utterance. The terms "ecstatic utterance" or "tongues of ecstasy" are *never* used in the Bible in reference to a speaker in tongues. Those who *hear* a speaker in tongues are sometimes described as "ecstatic" or "amazed" (*existanto, Acts 2:7; exestesan, Acts 10:45)* but the speaker himself is *never* described in this way. These misleading terms occur frequently in commentaries, and even turn up in translations of the Bible. The original text of the Bible gives no basis for such a translation. It seems to stem from an assumption on the part of the commentators and translators, who perhaps have not experienced this gift.[41]

Morton Kelsey joins Christenson at this point: "Tongues can occur in a highly charged atmosphere, but it can also occur in quiet surroundings, and the unleashing of emotionalism is simply not a necessary part of speaking in tongues...on a news program on KTTV, Los Angeles, Father Bennett demonstrated that one does not have to turn an emotional hair in order to speak in tongues...yet this prejudice, which obscures the real meaning of the experience, is hard to dislodge."[42]

COMMUNICATIONS INSIGHT

IN THE COMMUNICATIVE ART of persuasion there is a term really apropos at this juncture. It is called "the will to believe." This phrase is sometimes related to the rampant conspiracy theories that folks will not abandon, even in the face of overwhelming evidence. Perhaps they *want* to believe because it supports another agenda they find too painful to change or drop. Kenneth Christian has a great line here: "To label something is not to understand it. Too often inquiry and understanding stop once the label ... has been applied. Furthermore, the label sounds like a diagnosis when it is only a description.... All labels are problematic for the value judgments they imply."

[Quote from: Kenneth W. Christian, *Your Own Worst Enemy* (New York: Harper Collins, 2002), xvii.]

Judging the Orange Without Tasting It

How in the name of reason and/or academic integrity can such a plethora of books and articles on this subject (a fair number referenced here), from many different levels of criticism or evaluation, be written by authors who have never spoken in tongues and still gain the approval of publishers? Would an anthropologist be publishable if he/she had never lived in the target culture or learned the local language? What medical journal would publish an article about a certain surgical procedure by a non-surgeon? Is not the criticism of this topic by "non-practitioners" more a commentary on their own level of bias or ignorance than their competence in the subject matter? Shouldn't they at least, up front, acknowledge this lack of empirical experience? Would not this near-century long exercise of invective and speculative nonsense be tantamount to asking a Roman soldier at Calvary to explain the salvific expiatory significance of the death of Jesus? (At least *one* of *them* got part of it *right* when he said, "*Surely this was a righteous man*" [Luke 23:47].)

I admire the literary acumen of L. T. Johnson when he addresses, quite fairly for a non-participant, this topic of tongues speech. In a footnote he quotes J. M. Ford's dismissal that tongues are ecstatic utterance, when Ford criticizes glossolalics for assuming today's tongues speech is equivalent to that addressed by the apostle Paul. Johnson himself says, however, "It must be noted that no one who has ever heard the exquisitely beautiful choral singing in tongues at a quiet prayer meeting could ever declare this to be 'bedlam'... all these articles appear to speak from the standpoint of persons who have no empirical experience of the phenomenon which they wish to evaluate."[43]

"It's Not Reasonable"

"From the age of Enlightenment, scholastic Protestantism has extended its influence on modern evangelicalism. This influence is disclosed in an uneasiness with the supernatural manifestations of God's power, in an eagerness to ascribe as 'superstition' a serious belief in the demonic. Pentecostals, conscious of God's power to take authority over evil spirits and satanic power, at this point are not quite equal to their evangelical 'cousins.'"[44] Thus writes Bill Menzies about Evangelicalism's general tendency to marginalize Pentecostals over the doctrine of the Holy Spirit. The early Enlightenment led the reformers of early Protestant doctrine to the notion that grasping the whole counsel of God consisted mainly in arranging the "facts" of Scripture into their prearranged categories of systematic theology. To them Christianity was a religion of reason. Benjamin Warfield, a leader of the "twentieth century Princetonian Presbyterians" writes: "It is the distinction of Christianity that it has come into the world clothed with the mission to reason its way to its dominion. It is solely by reasoning that it has come thus far on its way to its kingship. And it is solely by reasoning that it will put all its enemies under its feet."[45]

So personally painful for me is a critic such as John Stott. He suggests God is a *rational* God and does not delight in *irrationality*. Tongues are not for today. It was a unique, one-time, historical event—finished.[46] Stott is a giant in biblical exegesis, but I wonder if he would classify the cross of Christ as a rational act, or the whole issue of the Incarnation and the circumstances surrounding the almost total unexpected nature of the Messiah's birth and life as examples of God's rationality. Interesting! But also sad. (See below chapter seven on God's risky, ambiguous dealings with mankind.)

The non-logical, non-analytical nature of God's working in our lives through His Spirit makes it very difficult for many academically-oriented people to be able to articulate or sometimes internalize or experience the ambivalent, yet sovereign, move of God on a person's life. The Bible is literally full of such unexpected phenomena. I admire Stott's great works and useful theological contributions to Evangelical thought, but to imply that God is a "reasonable" or "rational" God from a Northern European Germanic grid perception is more than a little humorous, and it's regrettable. If a person has a trained mind and he or she has been rewarded positively for many years for that particular acumen, that person will often be unable to accommodate the opposite poles of an intellectual specialty needed for the ambiguity of God's sovereign paradoxes. Jesus compared the sensitivity needed for this "stretching" before the Spirit to experiencing the wind: *"The wind blows ... you cannot tell where it comes from or where it is going"* (John 3:8). If Jesus was trying to tell us the Spirit's ways are "rational," might He not have used another metaphor? Let the "fighting fundy" Evangelical who opposes the Charismatic renewal sweeping the world ask himself: "What am I willing to 'trade away' to retain the certainty of control and predictability of the Aristotelian paradigm in the name of reason?" I'm grateful this does not describe all "Evangelicals."

Many academically-oriented folk stumble over the non-logical, non-analytical nature of God. They can't internalize that he is both ambivalent and sovereign.

The Miracle Was One of HEARING in Acts 2

A very interesting, if not bizarre, argument against modern glossolalia is that the 120 people at Jerusalem who spoke in tongues **didn't!** They spoke their own Galilean dialect, but the listeners who gathered because of the noise *actually heard them in their own languages,* ***not in the languages orally being spoken as listed in this chapter of Acts.*** "It was the crowd who are empowered, each to *hear* in his own tongue what the Galileans voiced in ordinary words ... This is an explanation frequently used among fundamentalists who do not believe in the experience of tongues and yet must account for it in the N. T.... it is hard to see why the crowd should mock the disciples as being drunk with new wine if nothing more was being experienced than hearing a voice speak one's own language."[47]

The Acts 2 Account Was for Salvation

Much scholarly argument has ensued since James Dunn advanced the thesis that the disciples were not really converted until baptized in the Holy Spirit—which incorporated them into the Body of Christ (salvation).[48] Many Evangelicals and Pentecostals have written effectively to counter Dunn's thesis including Turner, Barth, Ervin, Horton, Stronstad, and Menzies, among others.

MARGINALIZATION BY EXCLUSION

When first drafting this chapter for the manuscript, I experienced great sadness thinking about the earlier years when Pentecostals were fair game of criticism, marginalization, and exclusion by those I see as brethren in Christ. Even sadder, perhaps, are modern examples of Evangelical exclusion.

In a recent article Gary McGee wrote for the *International Bulletin of Missionary Research* on the legacy of Melvin Hodges, he points out a very revealing incident when Moody Press gained permission to print Hodges' seminal work on *The Indigenous Church.* At the time, Hodges' book was common text material in virtually all Evangelical seminaries in the US. Moody wanted to print the book as part of its Colportage Library, albeit with an important abridgment. In the chapter "Pentecost and Indigenous Methods," the editors removed the following statement, among others, in order to de-emphasize the *charismata* which Hodges knew to be indispensable for powerful and effective evangelism:

> On the mission field, the emphasis which Pentecostal people place on the necessity of each individual believer receiving a personal in filling of the Holy Spirit has produced believers and workers of unusual zeal and power. Again, the emphasis on the present-day working of miracles and the healing of the sick has been the means

> in the hand of God of awakening whole communities and convincing unbelievers of the power of God. These have seen a Power at work superior to that of their own witch doctors and priests. The faith which Pentecostal people have in the ability of the Holy Spirit to give spiritual gifts and supernatural abilities to the common people, even to those who might be termed "ignorant and unlearned" has raised up a host of lay preachers and leaders of unusual spiritual ability—not unlike the rugged fishermen who first followed the Lord.[49]

In fact, THIS DISTINCTIVE is probably the genius of Assemblies of God world missions—along with a truly indigenous missiology. Where it is employed, as it is in most countries, it is very effective.[50]

And for another example, what should be a Pentecostal's response to *recent* missions historians who IGNORE the unprecedented growth and vitality of the Pentecostal/Charismatic movement. How can I accept this with grace and Christian love and with an irenic spirit? John York points out such an omission in one of his footnotes in the chapter "Approaching Missions History" in his book: *Missions in the Age of the Spirit.* He comments on David Bosch's recent work, *Transforming Mission.* York actually follows Bosch's paradigm for looking at missions through the ages, but questions how Bosch could have missed the greatest missions movement in the last 50 years! York states: "Note with respect to his sixth paradigm, that Bosch ignores conservative evangelical and Pentecostal resistance to ecumenism, the relative ineffectiveness of the Liberal ecumenical movement, and the growth of Pentecostal missions in recent times."[51]

I wonder how this happens with good and effective writers such as Ruth Tucker, *From Jerusalem to Irian Jaya* (I use this book in teaching), who describes at last the great role women have played in the long history of Protestant missions, yet she has all but ignored the Pentecostal movement which has always employed women in unprecedented numbers in missions, especially during the epochs of which she writes.[52] They ministered, not just as wives, but as single women who have gone where men dared not go to plant the Church. This data is not a new phenomenon, as is evidenced by Barbara Cavaness in her recent dissertation for Fuller Theological Seminary on the role of women in Assemblies of God missions.[53] I doubt Tucker (1983) or Bosch (1991) can plead ignorance to this growth that at times astounds the statisticians! Shall we seek another motive for this marginalization? Can it be justified from statistical, analytical, methodological, or other academic research reasons? I must extend grace and continue to pretend they just didn't know.

Think of the power of experience—deriving true objectivity from sense perception of the actual phenomena. It reminds me of going to Europe the first time in 1959 and observing so many Europeans who had become "experts" on the US, having never visited much less lived there. Think of the amazing courage it must take for a person to pretend to be an "expert authority" about something, which is only an abstraction to him/her. Isn't this a good example of the human mind's ability to project on an idea, even if it's only by imagination? Some theologians would even argue they are in a better position (more "objective") to write about the tongues issue NOT ever having spoken in tongues! How convenient! Happily they do not take this surrogate reality (lack of experience) as a surgeon into the operating room in the local hospital!

True maturity has the ability to be self-critical without being self-demeaning or destructive.

Are critics' words valid only because they are articulate? George Tunks observes the marriage ceremony may be performed in all solemnity and decorum of the church but the ceremony of marriage is not recognized by the law of the land unless it is consummated in experience. Without the consummation the wedding may be declared null and void—without effect—as though it never took place. Laying on of hands, or any ceremony, is not sufficient unless validated by personal experience. Simple criticism does not make one an authority![54] Though we can criticize the critics, they are still valuable for two main reasons. One, they force us to do what the great apostle Paul (in 2 Cor. 12-14 and 1 Thes. 2:1-4) did in the face of his critics in defending his faith. Paul addressed the issues of impure motives and trickery. Two, there is much criticism of Pentecostals and Charismatics that is justified, for we are subject to human weaknesses. We must always be ready to identify, in love, those who by their ignorance or malfeasance embarrass us all and who don't represent the way of the cross that all true believers, whatever their theological position, must accept and gladly embrace.

SELF-CRITICISM: DIFFERENT LEVELS

One of the measures of a person's or of a family's or of a movement's maturation is the ability to be self-critical without being self-demeaning or destructive. By self-criticism I do not mean a negative neurotic attitude, which can see no positive side—only pessimism and worthlessness. Self-criticism has a good side, and often a critic well attended (if one can heed the counsel) is one's best friend. So it is in the religious realm. In this space I wish to show openly the weaknesses and failings of some who profess to speak in tongues, but whose lives come short of the ethics and piety of some who have never submitted themselves to the power of the Holy Spirit in glossolalia. Nothing is as disheartening as those who profess so strongly and produce so weakly. Jesus called them hypocrites.

Finding Balance

Everett Wilson, missionary, author, and administrator, coolly looks at faults and strengths at the same time:

> From its beginning Pentecostalism has tended to fascinate—or spawn—extremists. For almost a half century, while the movement did not draw impressive numbers of adherents, it was always an option for individuals who went beyond the conventional. It became home to some persons who believed that they had special but elsewhere unappreciated gifts. It also made room for individuals who found in the freedom of Pentecostal meetings the opportunity for self-expression or the assumption of leadership roles, not to mention personalities whose persecution complex made them enjoy being among the "Lord's despised few." Probably only a small proportion of adherents were psychopathic, but the sectarian splintering, the sometimes mean-spirited legalism and vitriolic denunciation of everyone who did agree with some leader's opinions demonstrated that a fair number were obsessive, self-absorbed types. So the spectrum includes not only the passive adherents at one extreme and the eccentric activists at the other, but also a range of activists, most of whom were not eccentrics, exhibitionists or megalomaniacs. The stability and growth of the movement points to the probability that there were proportionately many more men and women than has been recognized who were earnest, enlightened and committed and whose "fanaticism" was manageable and channeled. The movement collectively would hardly have had the leadership, staying power and confidence necessary to stabilize and develop it had there not been a considerable number of these inspired and inspiring men and women. The self-sacrifice of generous, sincere local leaders stand out, perhaps simply because they were exceptional, but not without

their having made an extraordinary collective impact on the emerging movement.[55]

Ray H. Hughes, administrator of the Church of God, Cleveland, Tennessee, also comments on the faults of some Pentecostals: "Pentecostals do not deny the fact that there have been spiritual excesses and fleshly extravagances among those who profess the operation of the spiritual gifts. By the same token, there are many who profess other religious experiences who do not measure up to requirements. This does not, however, negate the experience. While some err, countless thousands bear witness to the true testimony."[56]

Hughes further quotes a British scholar/writer who acknowledges errors but suggests a balanced judgment of the movement: "After all allowances have been made for the admitted fanaticism and extremes of those zealous early Pentecostals, it still has to be said that the responsibility for the creation of yet another group of denominations (the Pentecostals) rested squarely on the shoulders of the older churches that rejected them, demanded the resignation of missionaries who testified to their new-found blessing, and did not hesitate to publish the literature stating that the Pentecostal Movement was of satanic inspiration."[57]

Just as Simon, the sorcerer, sought to profit from what seemed to be an emotional experience in Acts 8, there are those who from their own carnal need for personal power will "counterfeit" a spiritual gift for their own profit—not the profit of Christ's Kingdom. For this reason, in writing his first letter to the Corinthians, Paul included chapter 13 in his discussion of the abuse of spiritual gifts. Again, Donald Gee writes, "Quite reputable writers use it (the term Pentecost) without any discrimination. We who are standing and struggling with the Movement for a clean, sane, and scriptural Pentecostal testimony often blush with shame at even nominal association with certain things laid at our door."[58]

Donald Gee, early Pentecostal author, was known for his conservative advice to those who tended toward fanaticism:

> May we be allowed, after long experience, to respectfully offer a word of brotherly counsel? Do not allow the first rush of novelty where prophetic gifts are concerned to sweep you off your feet. It is all so wonderful, and is such a liberation of spirit, that it is easy to become unbalanced, with speedy disaster.... Beware of making too much of "messages," whether through tongues and interpretation, or in any other way.... May we, with great humility of mind, offer another word of advice. Many of you are trained theologians with

> good academic background. Do not, now that you have tasted spiritual gifts, become fanatical in your repudiation of consecrated scholarship. Let the Holy Spirit of truth set it on fire and use it for the glory of God. Some of us in our early folly set a premium on ignorance."[59]

EARLY RACISM

Save for a few scholars in the Pentecostal Movement, what is not well known is that W. J. Seymour modified his belief about the role of tongues as evidence to the baptism in the Holy Spirit. In the beginning of his ministry in California, he espoused the position of his mentor Charles Parham who, like most Pentecostals today, held that tongues is the *initial evidence* of Spirit baptism. But as the revival at Azusa Street progressed, the issue of racism emerged. This greatly distressed Seymour.

> Seymour adopted a position which rejected speaking in tongues as "the Bible evidence" of baptism with the Spirit. To be sure it could serve as a sign, but baptism in the Spirit would have to come first. In short, Seymour would not be acceptable as a Pentecostal today, if the normative standards of the Pentecostal Fellowship of North America were imposed upon him.... [He] would remain more faithful to the Wesleyan-holiness tradition out of which the Pentecostal movement emerged, including a more profound commitment to the ethical dimension of the Christian faith....
>
> Seymour came to reject the theory because he could not find consistency in the ethical dimension of those who claimed to have experienced it: the inability of whites to maintain a supportive role in relationship to a black pastor and the ugly spectacle of underlying or incipient racism played a role in the formation of his thought.[60]

Improper Emphasis on Tongues

Some early Pentecostals (and some Chrismatics today) consider the First Corinthians 12:11 "sovereignly" dispensed gifts of the Holy Spirit to disallow the doctrine that ALL who are filled with the Spirit MUST speak in tongues as the essential evidence. Among those who held this position was Minnie Abrams, a holiness missionary to India who participated in Pandita Ramabai's Mukti Mission revival. She wrote: "We have not received the full Pentecostal baptism of the Holy Ghost until we are able not only to bear the fruit of the Spirit, but to exercise the gifts of the Spirit." McGee notes she does not discount the value and need of tongues but, like Seymour's later stance, remained more consistent with her Wesleyanism than Parham. She further explained her position: "Now I want to say that I believe it is God's rule to give speaking in tongues at the time or sometime after one's baptism, but I think I see from the Word of God that He has exceptions, and I do not like to strain a point to bring it to my ideas, and when I see anybody seeking to speak in tongues rather than seeking power to save souls I am grieved."[61]

Some Charismatics object to the doctrine of "Initial Evidence"

Few Charismatics accept that glossolalia is the condition *sine qua non* for Spirit baptism. Cessationists and some Charismatics refuse the doctrine of "Initial Evidence," citing the existence of tongues speech in Spiritist and non-Christian circles.[62] Others took an even stronger resistance. A. B. Simpson's "Seek not, Forbid not" conclusion advised:

> We believe the scriptural teaching to be that the gift of tongues is one of the gifts of the Spirit, and that it may be present in the normal Christian assembly as a sovereign bestowal of the Holy Spirit upon such as He wills. We do not believe that there is any scriptural evidence for teaching that speaking in tongues is a sign of having been filled with the Holy Spirit, nor do we believe that it is the plan of God that all Christians should possess the gift of tongues. This gift is one of the many and is given to some for the benefit of all. The attitude toward the gift of tongues held by pastor and people should be "Seek not, forbid not." This we hold to be part of wisdom for this hour.[63]

The Concept of Reification

Some Charismatics object to the doctrine of "Initial Evidence" because it tempts one to formalize or reify the belief in the same mode that some Lutheran and Reformed traditions reify *confessionalism.*[64] The danger seen here is that the issue of tongues as the only proof of the indwelling Spirit of God can become a reified idol instead of only being a distinction. To clarify: the Binet IQ test is now quite universal in Western education. It's relatively easy for teachers who use this test to allow the *number* to become reality. "Johnny, you are a 105, definitely not a 115." Rightfully so, minorities in the US are objecting to this oversimplification of intellectual evaluation, citing the failure of the IQ test's makers to account for sub-cultural differences inside any given society.[65]

COMMUNICATIONS INSIGHT

WHAT PLACE DOES a reluctance to communicate have in the receptivity of glossolalia? As the reader can see, there is much discussion and many divergent interpretations even among those who practice glossolalia. This actually is good. Self-criticism is vital for the life and health of any concept or doctrine.

I wish here, however, to make an observation after much distillation of many factors, that might be a contributing factor for the reasoning some give for rejecting glossolalia. I have been a participant observer of this Movement, on four continents, from my teenage years.

I was very young when the initial experience of seeking God for months for His blessing and power resulted in my personal baptism in the Holy Spirit. The issue of "tongues" was a very small part of that "pressing into God" for me. (This will be described in another section in more detail.)

On the 4th of July, 1945, I heard the voice of God calling the name my parents lovingly called me, Sonny, and accepted a life's work in Africa. I struggled then—not to speak in tongues, but because I was afraid of the emotion—but I did want God to take control of my life and make me a useful vessel for Him. I call this resistance the Spirit of Michal (1 Chron. 15:29).

THE SPIRIT OF MICHAL: DON'T DANCE

"As the ark of the covenant of the Lord was entering the City of David, Michal daughter of Saul watched from a window. And when she saw King David dancing and celebrating, she despised him in her heart" (1 Chronicles 15: 29).

This is the spirit that says, whoa! We can't trust this much emotion. Don't dance! Don't demonstrate your joy or emotions. Maintain dignity, because that's what society says is "politically correct"—in *church* or *about God.* You can act like an imbecile at the ball game! For me, two things have come to us from the Middle Ages about which we hardly ask questions or challenge. They are the academic attire (the penguin suit) at graduation time and the "holy hush" in church. Of course, you may have your own list, but those two always impact my life.

This Michal attitude has squelched the Spirit down through the ages. *"Don't quench the Spirit"* (KJV), *"Do not put out the Spirit's fire"* (NIV), says the apostle Paul in First Thessalonians 5:19. Paul spoke so clearly because the

Holy Spirit knew at this very juncture the Church would fail—again and again. All traditional Pentecostal denominations (some now approaching 100 years of existence) are facing the same temptation today. During the Middle Ages, the transformation of the Early Apostolic Church into the medieval Roman Catholic Church was complete. Once this was accomplished and the institutional church became both the political and religious powers together, about the only arena of spiritual gifts in operation was found in monastic circles. But an amazing dichotomy emerged. Due to the power/control the Church now wielded, a sharp distinction emerged between those who performed acts of the supernatural and those who didn't. The clerics and monks were allowed these gifts, but the common people were not. "This bias was clearly demonstrated by the Roman Catholic Church's publication of the Roman Ritual around the year A.D. 1000. It declared, among other things, that speaking in tongues among the common people was to be considered prima facie evidence of demon possession. Among the monastics and church hierarchy, however, it could be considered the essence of sainthood!"[66]

Some glossolalics struggle with talking about their gifts without inferring that others are inferior.

Don't dance, but if you must, let it be done by those we can control! Let's not trust the Holy Spirit to the lay people. After all, if the laity can do what we do, why all this study and preparation for the ministry?

The *Spirit of Michal* has been at work to throttle almost every period of spiritual renewal since the apostles. Consider the Cathari and others willing to "come out," whose history can most readily be read by biased unfriendly testimony of their enemies. They no doubt paved the way for the Protestant Reformation. Add to this list the excommunication of the Waldenses by Pope Innocent III in 1184.[67]

DON'T DANCE, Martin Luther. You have suffered Michal's sharp tongue from both the Catholics AND the church you founded. In the first instance you dared to invoke the priesthood of all believers. In the second the prophethood of common believers, and this belief and practice of a prophetic and healing ministry has scarcely made the pages of Lutheran history.[68]

Careful historians have expunged any tendency of "excessive emotion" from the Great Awakening or of the Methodist revivals. More current scholars, however, who are not unfamiliar with the physical expressions by those seeking the baptism in the Holy Spirit that Jesus gives have uncovered the original diaries of Jonathan Edwards and the Wesleys that explain in detail how some folk simply must "dance" when the joy and power of God surges through them.[69]

The comforting words of Jose Bonino address the issues of the oft-mentioned fear of "getting something one wasn't seeking for" when asking God for a more New Testament expression of Christianity. He would encourage any serious, but hesitant, reader who seeks God's power and guidance, to consider the following:

> "As I see it, Pentecostalism has at least 3 powerful defenses against these threats. ...
>
> > [1] Biblical Rootage. While its interpretation may be 'spiritual,' still there is the reverence for a 'text' in which God speaks to us.... [Respect for the canon = a referent for experience.]
> > [2] The communal nature of Pentecostalism, which conditions and directs the individual. Praying, singing, and witnessing in and with the community establishes parameters, even 'formulae,' that internalize a certain 'shape' of the faith 'event'....
> > [3] 'Eschatological spirituality,' an expectation that mobilizes for mission [aimed at the future in activity and sacrifice], but at the same time establishes a provisionality of the present time and therefore a distance that cannot be collapsed simply into experience....[70]

The three powerful defenses can be summarized thus:

Scripture: (Memory)
Community: (Discernment)
Eschatology: (The foretaste and the fullness)[71]

True seeker: Let Bonino's outline above help you to open up your heart to what the Holy Spirit is doing in the world today.

Some glossolalics struggle with the way to balance the exuberance, joy, and empowering sense of God's presence they feel personally when exercising the gift of tongues and the method of communicating this without making others feel inferior unless they are like them. They resist the "us and them" insinuation. Nationally-known pastor and conference speaker Jack Hayford addresses the topic by fully affirming the role of tongues relating to the baptism in the Holy Spirit, but refusing to be the judge of whether or not someone has received the "fullness" of the Spirit.

> God hasn't called me to tell people whether or not the Lord Jesus Christ has baptized them with the Holy Spirit. What a relief! ... I believe the simple evidence in God's Word is that He never intended spiritual language as a proof, but that He has offered it as a provision—a resource for readiness in prayer and praise.
>
> Finding this liberating perspective, I made a pastoral choice within our own congregation. We chose to continue urging those to whom we ministered to *expect* to speak with tongues when they receive the fullness of the Spirit.... But it is (1) always encouraged in an environment of faith, and (2) never pressured as a requirement for spiritual acceptance of one's experience with God ... [ministry] borne of the simple conviction that since the church was given this birthright at its inception, it is verifiably available today, and that in God's own time everyone may expect this blessed prayer and praise resource.... There's a reason that we see so many who do enter into spiritual language. It's not that they're coerced, nor are they made to feel inferior if they do not speak with tongues. But in time, virtually all to whom we minister do, for the simple reason that *they believe this potential belongs to every believer* (Hayford's emphasis). This is the viewpoint we foster, and we believe there is strong biblical basis for such a peace-filled, confident expectancy ... (1) Jesus Himself initiated the subject of spiritual language; and (2) the Father Himself designed for the church to be born with it as a birthright.[72]

While president of AGTS in Missouri, we invited Jack to speak at two national conferences on the Holy Spirit. I had been privileged to collaborate with him on previous occasions at his annual pastors' conferences. In the light of that friendship, I quizzed him: "Jack, about how many people, in a quick estimate, have received the Holy Spirit baptism with the traditional evidence in your church?" His answer: "Oh, about 20,000."[73] Of course, the central theme of his book is an apologetic *for* tongues, but many others hold it to be erroneous on this point because of the above quote. This argument will be with our growing movement for some time!

Many Pentecostals have long struggled with Hayford's burden of sharing his joy, yet finding a way to avoid a "holier than thou" attitude and still maintain their traditional insistence that without speaking in tongues one has not received the gift. John Koenig takes issue with that traditional stance and terms it an "over-interpretation": "Pentecostally oriented believers within a traditional congregation 'invite' non-Pentecostals to share in their newfound spiritual riches. In itself this is a fine practice, well documented in the New Testament (Rom. 1:11f; 1 Peter 4:9-11). Often however, the invitation carries a hidden clause. It reads not, 'Come as you are and enjoy the treasure I have been granted,' but 'Come and become like me, since only then will you enjoy God's higher blessings.'"[74]

Most traditional Pentecostal denominations retain the hard line for fear of weakening their distinctive. Many Charismatics have long taken a softer stance similar to Hayford's explanation above. This is one of the most debated issues in the Pentecostal world—but mainly in North America.

PENTECOSTALS: A PROBLEM FOR THE CHURCH

Everett Wilson, a Pentecostal administrator, talks about the problem the Church at large has had with the supernatural.

> Pentecostalism has usually carried a stigma based in large part on its admission of the mystical, the 'supernatural' and the allegedly miraculous, all of which carry with them considerable implication for one's world-view. Undeniably, the transcendental, mystical and ineffable have always been inherent in the Christian faith, but to avow that such practices are the spiritual legacy of all believers which should be routinely practiced—and especially to give place to their spontaneous expression in public services—gravely tests orderliness, predictability and established institutional authority. It has to be admitted that Pentecostals from the beginning have often been a pain for the ecclesiastical establishment—including their own, and the movement is still suspect in some quarters where it has never entirely escaped suspicion of being nothing more than a modern recurrence of the ancient Montanist heresy.[75]

COMMUNICATIONS INSIGHT:

SELF-CRITICISM ABOUT EARLY MISINTERPRETATION

IT MUST HAVE BEEN with some embarrassment that the first American Pentecostals (at the beginning of the twentieth century) had to modify their belief that the Holy Spirit gave the gift of tongues so missionaries going abroad wouldn't have to struggle to learn a new language—to be the witness promised by this new endowment of power. It had been one of the earliest formulated Pentecostal doctrines.

Charles F. Parham witnessed one of the first recorded incidences of tongues speaking while directing a Bible School in Topeka, Kansas. He was in turn the teacher of William J. Seymour, later of the Azusa Street mission in Los Angeles. He and Parham introduced in their periodical *Apostolic Faith* ("The Pentecostal Baptism Restored, October 1906) the belief that a great new linguistic aid to new missionaries was one of the designs of the Holy Spirit.

Charles Parham wrote in his book, *A Voice Crying in the Wilderness*: "How much better it would be for our modern missionaries to obey the injunction of Jesus to tarry for the same power—instead of wasting thousands of dollars, and often their lives in the vain attempt to become conversant in almost impossible [languages] which the Holy Ghost could so freely give."[76] It is Gary McGee who has faithfully chronicled for our day the great revival of the Holy Spirit in India starting in 1906, and the writings of A.G. Garr, early missionary to India, who went with the hope he could speak in the language of the native East Indians. Garr found, to his dismay, that no one could understand him.

> This left him with no alternative but to reexamine the doctrine, amid the swirl of controversy that engulfed it. Given the mission ethos of the Pentecostal movement, it should come as no surprise that the "flaw" in Parham's doctrine—the theoretical belief that one could preach in tongues at will—would be corrected in a mission context in the actual practice of ministry. To present his views in print, Garr published the periodical *Pentecostal Power* in March 1907.... With the disappointment in tongues for preaching, Pentecostals might have been tempted to discard the phenomenon altogether, but that did not happen due to the transforming nature of the experience. In the context of Bible study and seeking empowerment for world evangelization, Garr demonstrated the close relationship between the intense restorationism of the Pentecostal movement and pragmatism. Simply put, when the application of tongues for preaching failed, he went back to the New Testament to gain a more accurate understanding, but without questioning the fundamental integrity of the doctrine.[77]

Jenny E. Powers sums it up well.

> Tongues remained as an enduring aspect of the charismatic life of the Pentecostal churches because Pentecostals abandoned a utilitarian view of tongues as simply a tool necessary to communicate miracu-

> lously to foreign people.... However, though the mistaken notion of tongues as divinely given human languages as an evangelistic tool was abandoned, the vision of dynamic empowerment for the global witness of the people of God that originally cradled this notion remains fundamental to a Pentecostal understanding of tongues.[78]

The Abuse of Tongues

Jack Deere, former Dallas Theological Seminary professor and pastor, tells that his revulsion to tongues early in his ministry and teaching was due primarily to the abuse of tongues in Charismatic and Pentecostal churches.[79]

Early critics of Pentecostals, before 1960 when there were no "Charismatics" from the more traditional churches on the scene, tended to classify Pentecostals with the lower and lower-middle classes of economic and educational levels in US society. As shown in the work of Eric Hoffer, *The True Believer*, those engaging in glossolalia were seen as people yearning for change from their position of powerlessness and being disenfranchised from society.[80] Few Pentecostal scholars today would contradict that assertion as being true for the first 40 years of the Movement. To the degree that this is true (though there have always been some middle and upper class Pentecostals), a few of those dissatisfied with their lot in life and aggressively upwardly mobile became problem individuals—whether in church or society. When people believe they have direct access to spiritual reality, they can become a problem. Prideful of their spiritual experience, some—in the past as well as present—have become inflated with the inner witness that God did a work in them, and they are no longer humble members of their churches or social groups. This does not make for a tidy assembly or a docile social group.[81] Any attempt to exploit God's gifts for personal aggrandizement or profit is a messy business. Learning humility with the gifts of the Holy Spirit is like the Ashanti proverb: *Whether a leader, parent, or boss, learning humility is like learning to hold an egg. Hold it too loosely and it will fall and break. Hold it too tightly and you'll have yolk running off your elbow—so hold it lightly.*

Today, Pentecostal historians and scholars are quick to write about the weaknesses and faults of their own members, in the spirit of constructive criticism. "The rapid growth of the Church of God and other Pentecostal movements has been at times imperiled by false teachers, erroneous doctrines promulgated by zealots not sufficiently instructed in Biblical truths, and by dissensions within their own ranks."[82]

> The third most common reason for disbelieving in the gifts of the Spirit is the revulsion caused by the misuse, or the perceived misuse,

> of the gifts in contemporary churches and healing movements.
>
> None of these reasons are ultimately founded on *Scripture*. They are based on *personal experience*....
>
> It is common for charismatics to be accused of building their theology on experience. However, all cessationists ultimately build their theology of the miraculous gifts on their lack of experience.[83]

Excesses and Abuse of Power

One of the first Episcopalians to embrace the current Charismatic revival among the traditional churches was Dennis Bennett. He resigned as rector of his parish in Van Nuys, California, when his church split over this issue. "It is easy to point to the conflict and division which have been caused by this irrational practice.... The practice of speaking in tongues (glossolalia) is divisive, often leading to overzealous claims for power.... The experience is so meaningful for them that they assume it should be experienced by everyone else." Kelsey himself says: "Some persons who speak in tongues suddenly find themselves getting God by the tail and receiving messages that 'God told me this about you' ... or 'God wants you to do this'... and these are the very people who receive messages for everyone but themselves."[84]

When tongues become the central experience of the Christian life, it then takes a precedence that is out of balance. It makes the *door* of the house the most important part of the building, instead of only the entryway to the fullness of the house and the rooms of growth and maturity and power for witness God intended. An overemphasis on tongues then becomes a substitute for the patience, and the suffering, of growth into all the fruit of the Spirit (which must be *grown*)—plus some other "gifts" as the Spirit determines.

Incarnational View Invites Criticism

In this writer's opinion, following the explanation of David Lim, the gifts of the Spirit are **incarnational.**[85] This means they are neither all human nor all supernatural. The best model for this stance is the Bible itself, which is both a divine book and a human book. Men wrote it with their own cultural backgrounds, their own language usage style, and particular historical contexts influencing the words employed, BUT it is also God's book, inspired (breathed) by His Spirit using human instruments. This was His choice. He might have used angels, taking over the total package of communicative instrumentation. As the chapter on Communications will show, each one of the 44 human biblical authors' "perceptual fields" were both employed **and** superceded!

Not all Pentecostals/Charismatics are (were) lily-white in character, nor have all our churches been free from evil. However poorly these current New Testament believers have followed their ideals, they are distinct from the pagan world around them and even other brothers and sisters in the body of Christ—measured by the results of church growth and zeal for personal witness.

Experiential Spirituality Substituted for Theology

Many theologians today still consider glossolalia to be a language of experiential spirituality rather than theology. Only in the last 25 years have Pentecostal beliefs and theology begun to be developed and written about extensively, and they do not fit well within the rationalistic limits of much of Evangelical spirituality and theological boundaries. This is exacerbated by Pentecostals having left theological exposition to Evangelical scholars, the very ones who opposed them the most, naively trusting that Pentecostal doctrines could be easily incorporated into Evangelical theology without distortion. "Even more injuriously, by neglecting reflection and research and by continuing to emphasize personal experience above academic inquiry, Pentecostals allow an underlying anti-intellectualism to continue to pervade the movement."[86]

McGee continues, even more pointedly, about how the neglect of arriving at doctrinal certitude through inquiry and response to honest and open questions can lead to one's *distinctive* becoming one's *idol*. His words: "Ironically, doctrines may then change from being signposts of spiritual and theological vitality to 'shibboleths' of acceptance, serving new and potentially divisive functions within the body of Christ."[87]

A BADGE OF HOLINESS

Just like the Corinthians in the first century of the Church, some Pentecostals and Charismatics today believe the gift of speaking in tongues is a "badge of holiness" which makes them superior to all others. This is clearly an *elitist* stance. David Lim correctly states this belief is the same as that of the excesses of the Second-century Church, which led to an organizational "sacerdotalism." Pentecostals who claim to be able to impart gifts to others at will, have—just as the Roman Church—created a hierarchical system which makes experience an authority equal to Scripture.[88]

Donald Gee joins in this self-criticism:

> A view of the gifts contained in the slogan that they are 'a hundred percent miraculous' has obtained considerable acceptance in some quarters. We are told that 'there is no element of the natural in them

> at all.' This is a pardonable language of enthusiasm for enforcing the truth that a supernatural element in spiritual gifts does exist, and we can respect the statement as such. But it will not do as a statement covering all the facts. We need a more balanced view. If we do not achieve it, we shall perpetuate the extremes that have marred the Pentecostal testimony from its beginning. Indeed, in that way lies considerable danger.[89]

The Heresy Itch

In the January 2004 issue of *Christianity Today*, Sarah Wilson (then a doctoral student at Princeton Theological Seminary) reminds us that folk will always chase after heresy, seek out cults, and experiment with wacky rituals. She gives the following rationale: "Nine times out of ten it isn't because of a profound and intellectual departure from the traditional doctrine of the church. It's because the heretical thing fills some need, and the orthodox thing touches some weakness or pain." She suggests some folk get tripped up by the lust for "gnosis," the spawning ground for heresies old and new. Gnosis, the secret knowledge hidden from the ordinary folk, sets the bearer apart and above. It's an infatuation with mystery taken to a prideful extreme.[90]

The Pentecostal/Charismatic movement has certainly had its share of those with this "heresy itch" (as have all other communions). In its infancy, the whole Pentecostal Movement was considered heretical, since it was small, innovative, and disruptive. No one believed at the turn of the last century that it would become the largest Christian theological block, apart from the Roman Catholics. But its size and growing theological sophistication should not blind its followers of this constant danger: the "heresy itch."

Labelism, a False Holiness

Related to the above "badge of holiness" carnality is the perversion of the pride of ownership for having the "right" religion. Many Pentecostals have in the past, and still today, are like the New Testament Jewish Christians who saw their commitment to the laws of food preparation and circumcision as a badge of ownership, a symbol of the covenant between them and God. (See Galatians 1:6-7.) This gave them a superior attitude towards others (especially the Gentile "dogs") based on their correctness of performance before God. Pentecostals and Charismatics sometimes hold a superior self-esteem because of the gifts of the Spirit. "Some Christians display this same love for having the 'right' label, identifying with the right church, pastor, denomination, or religious viewpoint. Often their only identity as believers is a stance taken quite proudly over a single issue. By comparing themselves spiritually, they demean others who don't hold their view."[91]

TIME OUT! YOU SAY, ENOUGH ALREADY. ISN'T THAT ENOUGH SELF CRITICISM?

VALUE OF SELF CRITICISM

Self-criticism is always healthy, as is a serious look at outside critics. The greatest danger, in my opinion, is not the criticism from without that would weaken the evangelical and missionary thrust of Pentecostals, but rather the weakening of our willingness to tolerate God's "foolishness" in a seemingly unreasonable process whereby the Holy Spirit endues the submissive with His power and enablement. Morton Kelsey defends the early apostolic church leaders concerning the reasons they didn't speak much about tongues—when the practice of the gifts, including tongues, can now be demonstrated as having been present all during the first few hundred years. His thesis for their reticence is related to the same issue confronting modern Pentecostals and Charismatics today and represents, for me, a self-criticism we would do well to heed.

The basic fact is that the church was hard-pressed, first from without and then later from within, and the church fathers were writing to gain acceptance from a hostile Gentile world.... But since most people were already irrational enough about Christianity, describing glossolalia would have been to magnify this sign into wild rumor.... They had to show that Christianity was a reasonable faith and adaptable to the world.[92]

AUTHOR'S CONFESSION

This writer has joined ranks in the past with those who try to make Pentecostal Christianity look acceptable and reasonable to the world. I have participated in this from two motives: one, from the sadness of being marginalized by other Christian brothers and sisters; and two, from joy at the empirical evidence of the growth curve of the success of the missionary efforts and methods of those enlightened and equipped with the New Testament gift. But I see that this exercise of self-justification, to make us more palatable to our critics, if pursued with much vigor will soon become counterproductive. Should not the Pentecostal world be prepared to spend less time trying to make its doctrinal and methodological tenets understandable inside the perceptual fields of others and better use that energy to accept God's unusual, irrational plan? We must come to grips with it, get used to it, get over it, "come to own" it, and be content with His will for us in recognition of First Corinthians 1: 20-31!

Let me say it flat out: *Make tongues acceptable, make the "foolishness" of God wise (in the eyes of critics and skeptics) and as a result you risk a denial of its reality and its power for witness and deliverance.* It's a little like books written about humor; they tend to "get it down and break its arm"! Should not we spend less time defending our quantifiable reasoned quest for acceptability among those who oppose us? Where in this book should this writer's desire to appeal to the sincere seeker back off from making the experience of the baptism in the Holy Spirit a "commercially desirable commodity," and let it be—in all its unreasonableness—fully exposed, its naked self, as shown in Scripture and practiced by those convinced of its reality? The rationalistic materialism of our age, which is certainly the dominant philosophy of our time, can find no place for such an experience. How far should I defend glossolalia? Should I defend it all? Let me attempt to find the balance between reasonable explanation and too much defensive rhetoric. Hear Edmund Rybarczyk say "that God delights in communicating to us in surprising ways." Obviously, this does not mean God can only communicate in less-than-expected ways. But it should make Pentecostals once again aware that perhaps God is not overly concerned to fit neatly into the agenda of commitments of modernism.[93]

Rationalizing tongues as acceptable, or reasonable (in the eyes of the critics and skeptics) risks a denial of its reality and its power for witness and deliverance.

Every vital and dynamic religious movement is constantly threatened by excesses and imbalances on the part of its followers. This may be especially true of the Pentecostal and later Charismatic Movements who traditionally have resisted the authority of synods and counsels as their *only* authority, and prefer to believe that God the Holy Spirit talks to them through His Word, through His Church, and also in the direct manner of prophetic manifestations by His Spirit to the assembled church. Imbalance comes when this latter category becomes their *exclusive* authority, to the neglect of theological truths held for centuries by the Church.

PROGRESSIVE HOLINESS

One of the origins of the Pentecostal Movement was the Holiness Movement of the nineteenth century, that embraced the doctrine of entire sanctification as the believers' possession. Few Pentecostals or Charismatics would hold that position today, believing rather that one matures into the knowledge and likeness of Christ as was the apostle Paul's prayer in Philippians 3:10-14 (this doctrine known as progressive sanctification). This "pressing toward the mark," however, also demands responsible stability.

If the believer increases in holiness until he/she *qualifies* for a special gift of the Spirit, does this not make faith itself a sort of stairway of works—a superhuman effort—rather than a despair of all effort? No doubt many well-meaning teachers fail to adequately address this danger when admonishing those who seek to be "filled with the Spirit" to grasp the true nature of faith in the reception of all of God's gifts. The charismata, after all, are "gifts of grace" not *earned* by works. Would not sound teaching on this matter help balance the need for spiritual maturity and holy living while seeking the Spirit's fullness? Herein lies the positive relation of faith and obedience to spiritual growth resulting in a powerful witness for Christ's kingdom.[94]

SECULARISM

Much of the traditional Church, in the view of Pentecostals, fails to appropriate the power of God and His provision for the health and daily needs of the believer by denying the supernatural works of God as witnessed in the New Testament. But, there is a down side to an overemphasis on that provision and power of God as well. It is the unscriptural teaching of the "prosperity gospel," which can easily become crass materialism and secularism. Abandoning the harsh truth of the way of the cross as the central pillar of Christianity, the believer is taught that the way of health and wealth, gaining the goods of the secular world, is the inevitable fruit of faith (and conversely, suffering unequivocally indicates a lack of or failure of faith). Also left behind is the doctrine of the parabolic powerlessness of the cross. God continually shows us we can win by losing. This is totally upside down to the value systems of the world, yet it is preeminent in the Bible. When Pentecostals buy into that secular value, they miss God's better plan and weaken their true potential for power to witness.

Some folks think that all criticism is bad criticism. I don't agree because Scripture admonishes us to be self-critical and to judge ourselves—so God doesn't have to. Jesus talked about first removing the impediment in our own eyes so we can see clearly to identify what is wrong with our brother's eye (Matt. 7:1-5). In spite of our imperfections as a church and as individuals in it, constructive criticism is a positive thing and should be distinguished from destructive criticism.

ENDNOTES:

1. Gary B. McGee, "The Calcutta Revival of 1907," AJPS Vol. 6, No. 1 (2003): 113; quoting from Peter Toon, The Development of Doctrine in the Church (1979), xi; and Eugene F. Klug and Otto F. Stahlke, Getting into the Formula of Concord: A History and Digest of the Formula (1977), 9-15.
2. Barclay M. Newman and Eugene A. Nida, A Translator's Handbook on the Acts of the Apostles, (1972), 35.
3. Morton T. Kelsey, Tongues Speaking: An Experiment in Spiritual Experience (1968), 137. See also Charles F. Potter, The Faiths Men Live By (1954), 301f; see also in The Interpreter's Bible, Vol. X (1951-55),155. Potter's definition is "primitive religious ecstasy." And see Ichamenes Weiss, The History of Primitive Christianity (1937), 626. His assessment is that primitive religion was soon overcome by the Early Church.
4. Ibid., 159.
5. Benjamin B. Warfield,
Counterfeit Miracles (1976), 3-31.
6. Merrill F. Unger, The Baptism and Gifts of the Holy Spirit (1974), 60-68.
7. Robert G. Gromacki, The Modern Tongues Movement (1967), 139-141.
8. John MacArthur, Charismatic Chaos (1992).
9. Jack Deere, Surprised by the Power of the Spirit (1993), 80, 274.
10. Harvey Cox, Fire from Heaven (1995), 75.
11. Ibid., 15.
12. M. Kelsey (1968), 151.
13. Ronald A. Kydd, Charismatic Gifts in the Early Church (1984). See also Cecil M. Robeck, Jr., ed., Charismatic Experiences in History (1985).
14. Fredrick Price, "Manifestations," Indian Witness (1907): 251-2. Cited in Gary B. McGee, "The Calcutta Revival of 1907," AJPS Vol. 6, No.1 (2003): 123.
15. Arthur T. Pierson, "Speaking in Tongues," Missionary Review of the World XX (September 1907): 683.
16. H. J. Stolee, Pentecostalism: The Problem of the Modern Tongues Movement (1936), 112.
17. Janet Evert Powers, "Missionary Tongues?" Journal of Pentecostal Theology 17 (2002).
18. H. Newton Maloney and A. Adams Lovekin, Glossolalia: Behavioral Science Perspectives on Speaking in Tongues (1985), 22-38. See also The second source Powers cites is by William Samarin, Tongues of Men and Angels: The Religious Language of Pentecostalism (1972), 73-128.
19. Kildahl, John P. The Psychology of Speaking in Tongues (1972), 86.
20. Killian McDonnell, Charismatic Renewal and the Churches (1976), 13.
21. Virginia Hine, "Pentecostal Glossolalia: Toward a Functional Interpretation," Journal for the Scientific Study of Religion 8 (1969): 217.
22. Everett Wilson, "They Crossed the Red Sea, Didn't They?" in The Globalization of Pentecostalism: A Religion Made to Travel, ed. Murray W. Dempster, Byron D. Klaus, and Douglas Peterson (1999), note 25, 114.
23. George B. Cutten, Speaking in Tongues: Historically and Psychologically Considered (1927), 25-27.
24. Felicitas D. Goodman, Speaking in Tongues: A Cross-Cultural Study of Glossolalia (1972).

25. Gerhard F. Hasel, Speaking in Tongues (1986).
26. E. Andrews, "Gift of Tongues," The Interpreter's Dictionary of the Bible, George Buttrick, ed. (1976), 672.
27. I. M. Lewis, Ecstatic Religion (1971).
28. F. Goodman, Speaking in Tongues: A Cross-Cultural Study of Glossolalia (1972), 124.
29. J. T. Richardson, "Psychological Interpretations of Glossolalia: A Re-examination of Research," Journal for the Scientific Study of Religion 12 (1973): 199-207.
30. M. Kelsey, 200, citing William Sargant, "Some Cultural Group Aberactive Techniques and Their Relation to Modern Treatments," Proceedings of the Royal Society of Medicine (1949), 367ff.
31. J. Rodman Williams, Renewal Theology II (1990), 221.
32. Ibid.
33. See E.M. Patterson, "Behavioral Science Research on the Nature of Glossolalia," in Journal of American Scientific Affiliation (1968), 20, 78-86. See also: Alexander Mackie, The Gift of Tongues: A Study in Pathological Aspects of Christianity (1921).
34. M. Kelsey, 7-8.
35. Ibid., 208.
36. Ibid., 207.
37. Thomas F. Zimmerman, Ray H. Hughes and, most recently, Donald Argue, currently president of Northwest University in Kirkland, Washington.
38. H. V. Synan, "Fundamentalism," in Dictionary of Pentecostal and Charismatic Movements, ed. Stanley M. Burgess and Gary B. McGee and P.H. Alexander (1988), 326.
39. See Grant Wacker, "Travail of a Broken Family: Radical Evangelical Responses to the Emergence of Pentecostalism in America, 1906-16," in Pentecostal Currents in American Protestantism, ed. E. L. Blumhofer, et al. (1999), 30.
40. Grant Wacker, Heaven Below (2001), 56.
41. Larry Christenson, Speaking in Tongues: Its Significance for the Church (1968), 24.
42. M. Kelsey, 145.
43. L.T. Johnson, Religious Experience in Earliest Christianity (1999), 108; citing J.
M. Ford, "Towards a Theology of Speaking in Tongues," Theological Studies 32 (1972): 3-29.
44. William Menzies, foreward to The Third Force in Missions by Paul Pomerville, (1985).
45. John E. Meeter, ed., Selected Shorter Works of B.B. Warfield (1973), 98.
46. John R. W. Stott, Baptism and Fullness: The Work of the Holy Spirit Today, (1975), 113.
47. M. Kelsey, 150.
48. James D. Dunn, Baptism in the Holy Spirit (1970).
49. Melvin L. Hodges, The Indigenous Church (1953),132. The Moody Edition was entitled On The Mission Field: The Indigenous Church (1953).
50. Del Tarr, From "Transcendence/Immanence and the Emerging Pentecostal Academy," Paper presented at The 9th William Menzies Annual Lectureship, APTS, January, 2001, Baguio City, Philippines.
51. John V. York, Missions in the Age of the Spirit (2000), 105; commenting on David J. Bosch, Transforming Mission: Paradigm Shifts in Theology of Mission (1991).
52. Ruth A. Tucker, From Jerusalem to Irian Jaya (1983).

53. Barbara Liddle Cavaness, "Factors Influencing the Decrease in the Number of Single Women in Assemblies of God World Missions"(Ph.D. diss., Fuller Theological Seminary, 2002).
54. Tunks, George, "I Believe in the Holy Ghost," The Pentecostal Evangel (June 2, 1963), 7.
55. Everett Wilson, The Globalization of Pentecostalism, A Religion Made to Travel, Murray W. Dempster, Byron D. Klaus, Douglas Peterson, eds. (1999), 101-102.
56. Ray H. Hughes, "Glossolalia in Contemporary Times," in The Glossolalia Phenomenon, ed. Wade H. Horton (1966), 160.
57. Ibid., 42; quoting Donald Gee, "Don't Spill the Wine," Pentecost No. 61 (September-November, 1962): 17.
58. Ibid., 169; quoting Donald Gee, "Editorial," Pentecost, No. 35 (March, 1956): 17.
59. Donald Gee, "Editorial" Pentecost, No. 58 (Dec. 1961).
60. Cecil M. Robeck, Jr., "William J. Seymour and the 'Bible Evidence,'" in Initial Evidence, ed. Gary B.McGee (1991), 88-89.
61. Minnie F. Abrams, "The Object of the Baptism in the Holy Spirit," The Latter Rain Evangel (May 1911): 10, quoted in McGee, 1991, 107-108.
62. See L.C. May, "A Survey of Glossolalia and Related Phenomena in Non-Christian Religions," in Watson E. Mills, Speaking in Tongues: A Guide to Research on Glossolalia (1986), 53-82.
63. A. B. Simpson, The Alliance Witness, Vol. 98, No. 9 (May 1, 1963): 19.
64. Henry Lederle, "Initial Evidence and the Charismatic Movement," in McGee, (1991), 135.
65. For more on the concept of reification see: Neil Postman, Teaching As An Affirming Activity (1979), 89-91.
66. Eddie Hyatt, 2000 Years of Charismatic Christianity (2002), 55.
67. J. D. Douglas, ed., The New International Dictionary of the Christian Church (1974), 1026.
68. See John S. Oyer, Lutheran Reformers Against the Anabaptists (1964) 231; and John Horsch, "The Faith of the Swiss Brethren, II," Mennonite Quarterly Review 5, No. 1(1931): 16.
69. Hyatt, chapters 12-16.
70. Jose Miguez Bonino, "Changing Paradigms: A Response" in The Globalization of Pentecostalism (1999), 122. Bonino gives credit for these thoughts to Steven Land, Pentecostal Spirituality, A Passion for the Kingdom (1993).
71. Ibid., 123.
72. Jack Hayford, The Beauty of Spiritual Language: A Journey Toward the Heart of God (1992), 98-99.
73. Jack Hayford, personal interview by Del Tarr, March 1997, Springfield, MO.
74. John Koenig, Charismata: God's Gifts For God's People (1978), 171.
75. E. Wilson, "They Crossed the Red Sea, Didn't They?" (1999), 89.
76. Charles Parham, A Voice Crying in the Wilderness, 2nd ed. (n.d.), 28.
77. Gary B. McGee, Asian Journal of Pentecostal Studies Vol. 6, No.1 (2006): 130, 133. See also Grant Wacker, Heaven Below: Early Pentecostals and American Culture (2001), 10, 35-37.
78. Janet Evert Powers (2000), 17ff.
79. Jack Deere, Surprised by the Power of the Spirit (1993), 23.
80. Eric Hoffer, The True Believer: Thoughts on the Nature of Mass Movements (1951).

81. M. Kelsey, 183.
82. James A. Cross, "Glossolalia: Its Value to the Church" in The Glossolalia Phenomenon, ed. Wade H. Horton (1966), 200.
83. Deere, Surprised by the Power of the Spirit, 56.
84. M. Kelsey, 223.
85. Lim, Spiritual Gifts: A Fresh Look (1999), 43.
86. Gary B. McGee, ed., Initial Evidence, Historical and Biblical Perspectives on the Pentecostal Doctrine of Spirit Baptism (1991), xvi.
87. Ibid., xvii.
88. Lim, 42.
89. Donald Gee, Spiritual Gifts in the Work of the Ministry Today (1963), 10.
90. Sarah H. Wilson, "Guest Column," Christianity Today (Jan. 2004).
91. Life Application Bible Commentary: Galatians, Philip Comfort, gen. ed. (1994), 2.
92. M. Kelsey, 33.
93. Edmund Rybarczyk, "Expressing the Inexpressible: Tongues as Apophatic Speech," Presented at the 31st Annual Meeting of the Society for Pentecostal Studies, 2002, 16.
94. See Donald Bloesh, The Holy Spirit: Works and Gifts (2000), 197.

CHAPTER 3

HISTORY OF EARLY BELIEFS AND WRITING ON TONGUES

Now, let's do a very brief history for our true seeker or inquirer. We'll start with some very recent history as it was the year of VJ Day (victory in Japan), 1945. Subsequently, we'll go on to compare two segments of 100-year intervals that let us reflect on history 2000 years ago with history quite a bit closer.

RECENT HISTORY IN ONE MAN'S STORY

When just a boy of eleven years of age, the year WWII ended, Sonny became hungry for the Baptism in the Holy Spirit he witnessed others receiving in the church pastored by his father. This congregation was growing in a small town in Minnesota where the boy's father had founded the church by holding a two-month tent revival on the main street of the town in a vacant lot right next to the Methodist church. (The Methodists didn't mind; it recalled the days when many a Methodist congregation started the same way.) The new congregation established by the converts from the tent revival grew and built their own sanctuary about a mile away, with a loan for a small part of the needed funds from a Mennonite brother in a nearby town. The lad's father preached that the biblical way to receive this endowment of power and an enhanced ability to testify of Christ's redeeming love was to "tarry" the way the disciples and others did in the Acts account. The boy did, sometimes alone in the house when his parents were away doing pastoral duties and sometimes in special church services and at altar times after the Sunday night services. He became earnest in this pursuit of God's promised blessing. He wondered why his prayer was not immediately answered.

Each summer the family journeyed to Alexandria, MN where existed an old time revival "camp meeting." It was here that many congregations converged, always over the fourth of July holiday, to hear rousing preaching, attend tarrying meetings and pray for the sick. Sonny wondered if this special time of seeking God in sanctification was the time he was waiting for. It was! During a two-hour session of prayer, praise, singing and (yes) laughing in the Spirit, Sonny spoke in a new language he had never learned, but far more importantly tells of how God "spoke" to him about the future. "Sonny, you will serve me in Africa when you are grown. You should start preparing now." He told of this experience and interior voice to his parents—who had witnessed this son while he prayed. They were joyful and encouraging.

He studied the only language courses his high school offered: Latin. Other electives were chosen, not for their ease of credit but with Africa in mind. Few fellow students related to his plans, nor did his instructors who encouraged him to take extra curricular events like competitive speaking events and oratory competitions. He had some of his father's speaking gifts and earned better than average grades. His teachers encouraged him to become a professional musician or a lawyer. But his face was set. Bible Institute in the big Twin Cities was his choice where he majored in Bible and Missions. He maintained his prayer language and often told others of his special "call." North Central Bible Institute (later to become College and today University) DID encourage his goals. Marrying his college sweetheart who also was "called" to missions, they pastored in the area and received appointment to Africa soon after ordination. Sonny's missionary journey began with this controversial, often despised and criticized, experience of "tongues." He says it's related to the word *submission*. He's sorry for the need to defend the theological concept. He's sad that such a wonderful experience for him is doubted, and even reviled, by so many wonderful brothers and sisters in the family of God. He's delighted to see the unbelievable reversal of opinion and praxis of so many former doubters over the last six decades. "I never thought I'd see such a day," he says. He believes this experience is available to all laypersons and clergy who seek it—not for their personal benefit or profit, but as a gateway to the *loss of all things that one might wish to save much*. Now after 55-plus years of the journey, he still believes the paradoxical promise that he will eventually save in losing, but knows it's carnal and really un-Christian to have that as his motive. Sonny came to be called by that name because he was a "junior" (having the exact same name as his father who died at age 92). His other name is on the jacket of this book.

SPEAKING IN TONGUES THROUGH HISTORY

Glossolalia is not a new or even recent phenomenon in the long history of Christianity. What follows, however, will largely be the relatively recent history of the last 100 years. I will now give you brief "snapshots" from different authors about the same event and its results, its failures, its joys, and its challenges. There are literally hundreds of books about the subject, most of them written from the historical perspective.

Recent research has shown there never has been a time in the history of the Christian Church but that there were those who possessed the gifts of the Spirit including speaking in tongues; however rare, these folks existed even in the "dark ages" when the Church was highly apostate and syncretistic.[1] Many authors have now shown that the Spirit's activity was not missing from the church's past, but a prevailing bias against Charismatic gifts often led modern historians to ignore the role of the Holy Spirit, or to speak of those gifts and people disparagingly. This was compounded by the fact that early Pentecostals were reluctant to do research and relied on the histories of others. It is only recently, in the last 20 years, that Pentecostals/Charismatics have seen the need of doing their own research of the past, which led them to ultimately reject the non-Charismatic judgment of those historians. This writer subscribes to the old dictums that say: "*There is no such thing as history—only histories.*" It's related to the similar phrase: *There is no such thing as objectivity—only degrees of subjectivity.*" I doubt anyone of us can escape this human tendency. We can only strive for objectivity.[2] It took Pentecostal scholars to research the exact words of John Wesley about the subject of human emotion relating to religion because more recent historians had excised his words about emotions:

> Man recognizes the desirability of manifest emotion in every realm except the religious. It is accepted as a vital part of human existence and is appealed to by all who deal with men, and it seems that the children of this world are wiser than the children of light in their recognition and use of the emotional element. They would not dare to remove it from the stage, or screen, or radio, because they know that the public would shun unemotional entertainment, even as it shuns the dry, unimaginative services of the average church today.[3]

A sane and sensible attitude toward bodily demonstrations has been expressed by John Wesley in his Journal, Sunday, November 25, 1759:

> The danger was to regard extraordinary circumstances too much, such as outcries, convulsions, visions, trances, as if they were essential to the inward work, so that it could not go on without them. Perhaps the danger is to regard them too little: to condemn them altogether; to imagine they had nothing of God in them, and were a hindrance to His work. Whereas the truth is: (1) God suddenly and strongly convinced many that they were lost sinners, the natural consequences

> whereof were sudden outcries and strong bodily convulsions; (2) to strengthen and encourage them that believe, and to make His work more apparent, He favored several of them with divine dreams, others with trances and visions; (3) in some of these instances, after a time, nature mixed with grace: (4) Satan likewise mimicked this work of God in order to discredit the whole work; and yet it is not wise to give up this part any more than to give up the whole.[4]

Brembeck adds: Thus, from the pen of the eminent founder of Methodism we can deduce these two facts: (1) bodily demonstrations must not be magnified beyond their rightful sphere; (2) nor must they be rejected because of irregularities. He then quotes Wesley again: *"The shadow is not disparagement of the substance nor the counterfeit of the real diamond."*[5]

TWO ONE HUNDREDS—1900 YEARS APART

There are interesting and remarkable parallels between the first 100 years of the Apostolic Church and the first 100 years of the most recent Pentecostal beginnings of our times. Both "beginnings" were marked by our topic of glossolalia. While in dialogue with Roman Catholics in the International Roman Catholic/Pentecostal Dialogue in Switzerland, I wrote down Father Killian McDonnell's quotation of the early church father Chrysostom's comments about the Early Church : "Whoever was baptized in apostolic days, he straightway spake with tongues; they at once received the Spirit; not that they saw the Spirit, for He is invisible, but God's grace bestowed some sensible proof of His energy. It thus made manifest to them that were without that it was the Spirit in the very person speaking."[6]

It thus made manifest to them that were without that it was the Spirit in the very person speaking.

April 2006 was the month those in the Pentecostal tradition remembered as the most storied of dates in last century's explosive events at the Azusa Street Mission in Los Angeles, California. The centennial celebration (April 24-29, 2006) brought visitors from 45 countries to remember and reflect on the unassuming beginnings of a spiritual awakening that has changed the theological landscape of the Christian church in the world.

> I spent the better part of this spring exploring another side of the Azusa Street story and that is the composition of the folks that

> attended the Azusa Street episode. Clearly this was a church that ran counter to the separate worlds of existence that the U.S., in general, and Los Angeles, in particular, were experiencing in the early part of the 20th century. The early news reports of the events of the Azusa Street awakening are rife with pejorative descriptions and critical characterizations of the participants. The fact that multiple immigrant groups were represented, that blacks were in leadership and women served beside men in the forefront of this incipient religious paradigm shift is met with the poor investigation and shallow understanding that 100 years later still typifies the media and religion.[7]

Byron Klaus then reports on the term "Full Gospel" and what it meant in Jerusalem on the day of Pentecost and what it meant in the Azusa Street Mission in 1906.

> It is understandable why the term Full Gospel might be employed as a descriptor of revitalization and the getting back to the basics of the Bible that this movement represented. These dual elements of the legacy of Azusa Street (i.e. the miraculous and the empowered missionary service) have long been the heritage I have been nurtured on and value deeply...This "miraculous sign" is the reconciliation of people who have been taught to avoid and even hate one another, now experiencing life-changing spiritual encounters together in this humble place...If we Pentecostals wish to celebrate the book of Acts we need to move with the Spirit from Jerusalem to Antioch. It is at Antioch that Full Gospel finally plays itself out in the creation of a church where transformed people don't look alike nor come from the same roots. It is that church that Acts 13 records is the model that the Spirit anoints for church planting efforts that will replicate this New Testament version of the "great world house" all over the Mediterranean world.[8]

There are literally scores and scores of good volumes written about the historical nature of this seemingly foolish phenomenon of glossolalia that is only the symbol of the submission God seeks to make us into the effective instruments He desires—and about the churches and denominations and movements born out of this "second 100 years" of unusual events and people. It's not all joyful reading where ethnocentricity and racism and egocentrism needed to be purged out by the fire of the Spirit. All can be found in any true attempt to show what was and is. Wm. and Robert Menzies give us their snapshot of the beginnings of the "second hundred."

> Between 1906 and 1909, meetings were conducted at the Azusa Street hall continuously. Striking during the Jim Crow era in American social history is the mixed-race character of the Azusa Street meetings. Blacks and whites worshiped together, united by the power of the Holy Spirit. Because of the strategic location of Los Angeles for international travel and because of publication in the local papers about the sensational happenings at Azusa Street, travelers from various nations gravitated there. Some of the visitors were missionaries attached to various sending agencies. Many of these curious seekers received the Pentecostal experience. On fire for God, these new Pentecostals, often ostracized from parent bodies, scattered to spread the gospel, sometimes with no credentials and no visible means of support. They had little except the joy of the Lord and a great sense of God's providential care. These were the Pentecostal pioneers.[9]

These pioneers gave little thought about writing of the deep theological significance of what had happened to them, apart from small historical accounts and inspirational tracts. In like manner, as a missionary in my youth (26 years old) after pastoring my first church in Minnesota, I didn't feel the need of graduate education until after serving two four-year terms in Africa. I then knew I needed the additional training. My heart was still full of the zeal and call of God to missions at age 11, as recounted above. I've often wondered what I might have done differently had I gone to Africa with more than a BA and the experience of being raised in a pastor's home and pioneering a church before sailing to my early calling. Did I need the zeal of calling and youth to help make the serious attitude change allowing learning two languages well enough to teach and preach in them, besides learning to eat strange food and learn vital inter-relational communication habits? Would I have been flexible enough to do these things had I stayed in university or seminary until graduate degrees were earned, mortgages encumbered, and a house full of furniture acquired to then leave the US with three teenage children? Maybe not! Some people do. While in retrospect, I can see the advantages and disadvantages of each of these scenarios, I can't advocate either as the best way for anyone else.

Back to the first 100 years:

"The church struggled toward stability and permanence, although the people who were playing out the roles did not realize that this was what they were doing." Thus wrote Ronald Kydd of the Early Church.[10] He might as well have described the beginnings of the "Twentieth Century Revival" of which the whole religious world today, decades after its beginnings, has become aware. We have just celebrated one hundred years since what is broadly accepted as the beginning of the "Pentecostal Century." Early in that century, and as late as the 1950s, almost no one on the religious scene saw the Pentecostal revival coming. With the passing of time, organizations were formed, the Spirit-filled believers began to reflect on what they believed and record it in print and the electronic media. Even the revivalists' own scholars began to emerge to research the past and its significance to the new steady growth. Secular journals and the news media noted the rapid growth of the "tongues" people, but the established churches hardly believed they would ever amount to the burgeoning revival and gigantic growth now apparent.

...the established churches hardly believed they would ever amount to the burgeoning revival and gigantic growth now apparent.

One of the reasons for this skepticism was a matter of theological belief as exemplified by author C. Peter Wagner. He writes of his early life committed to Christ and being sold out to obeying the call of Jesus in the great commission (Matt. 28:18-20) to "make disciples of all nations." He then spent 16 years as a missionary in Latin America rather ignoring the promises of God's power to equip folks like missionaries to chase demons, heal the sick, and see miraculous works of God while announcing the gospel of the Kingdom. He came to this sense of powerlessness when reading again of what Jesus promised the "sent ones" should expect. How could this be, he asked, since he was a Bible-believing evangelical minister? The conclusion was that the pervasive influences of secular humanism in American culture in public schools and universities and even in churches, Bible schools, and seminaries resulted in the belief that while the disciples of Jesus did such things, we in our sophisticated age were not supposed to do such things. He was taught in seminary that now that we had the Word of God in Scripture, the miraculous power in the ministry of the first century was no longer available or needed.

> A recent research project turned up the fact that of 87,000 pages of theological reference works in the library of a prominent evangelical seminary, only 288 touched on divine power. That is about one third of one percent. No wonder entire generations of ministers go out relatively powerless.[11]

Wagner is quite hard on himself (but probably honest) when he says:

"This secular humanism, I am ashamed to admit, actually caused me to be a secularizing force when I went to Bolivia."[12]

Wagner's early experience (he has now become a "Third Waver" embracing the work and intentions of the Holy Spirit in ministry) was not a recent development in the theology held by Westerners. It has been of long standing by the majority of theologians and ministers, actually from the start of the Protestant Reformation. So when Kydd compares the forces of thought and faith existing in the early church that began to resist the Apostolic era with the forces encountered by the Charismatic renewal movement of the last 100 years, he sees many similarities.

Kydd marshals his arguments with excellent research on the first 200 years of the Early Church and the existence and maintenance of the charismata. He searches the writings of the Didache (teachings of the 12 apostles to Gentile churches), to Clement of Rome, Ignatius, Justin Martyr, of Montanism, on to Bishop Irenaeus. In summary of this period he states:

> Up to this point in our study of the gifts of the Spirit in the Church in the second half of the second century we have looked at a poet, a philosopher, a group of so-called heretics and an archbishop of Christianity...what they have done is add significantly to the body of evidence which supports the idea that Christians of that time continued to be charismatic.[13]

Many have advanced the theory that the gifts of the Spirit as seen in the New Testament ceased with the establishment of the Canon of Scripture. This has now been proven totally false. As Ash says: "The bishops, not the Canon expelled prophecy."[14]

Morton Kelsey[15] notes the two streams of Christianity, Eastern Roman Empire (Orthodox—Greek) and Western Roman Empire (Catholic—Roman) retained very different understanding and expressions about the Charismatic gifts including tongues speaking.[16] He explains the difference by both cultural forces and political and practical forces.

When visiting the Greek Orthodox monasteries on top of the large granite protrusions in central Greece (the Meteores), I visited with monks in two different monasteries who were much more conversant with the modern worldwide Pentecostal revival. They were surprised I didn't know how different they teach Pneumatology than the Roman Church in the West. According to them, there have always been Greek and Russian Orthodox Christians who have spoken in tongues, even though it is generally confined to the orders (religious groups) in the church.[17]

At the turn of the last century, a sudden upsurge of this phenomenon broke into the religious world growing out of the "holiness movement" of the 1850s. At the close of the nineteenth century, frequent records of speaking in tongues can be traced to several states of the US: North Carolina, Tennessee, Georgia and Kentucky. However, a few years later, the beginning of the twentieth century (and simultaneously from Kansas, California, Texas and overseas in India, Sweden, Korea, Chile, and South Africa) came reports of a renewal of the apostolic phenomenon of those who sought a deeper life with God were speaking, in prayer, in a language they had not learned.

The twentieth century may well be known as the most significant period of church history since the first-century church. Incredible church growth has occurred throughout the world in the last 100 years. There are hundreds of denominations and church fellowships which are ardently seeking to obey Jesus' last words known as the Great Commission. One of those sparks of revival started in a Bible School in Kansas in 1901 when the director (Charles Parham) challenged his students to find the biblical evidence for reception of the baptism with the Holy Spirit. They all agreed that it was glossolalia. Soon many had received God's gift as in Acts 2 with the same sign. It was later a student of Parham's, Wm. Seymour, however, who was to have the greatest influence on the revival storm to follow. He was the leader of the Asuza Street Mission in Los Angles where he conducted services night and day while thousands came from all over the US and foreign countries during a four-year period to seek God. There was no question that unique things were happening at Azusa Street.[18] While writing these pages, a new book has just surfaced by scholar Cecil M. Robeck. The book: *Azusa Street: Mission and Revival* surfaced just in time for the centennial celebration of that historic renewal of the Church in Los Angeles where the revival centered.[19] His words:

> There are several reasons this African American mission received so much coverage and why the story bears retelling today. First, it grew with unparalleled speed. The Azusa Street Mission was aggressively evangelistic. In a day of "church growth" schemes, burgeoning "mega churches" and "emergent" churches on the one hand, and declining church membership in many historic congregations on the other, it is important for us to hear once again how a small prayer meeting of some fifteen people, including children, grew into an internationally acclaimed congregation of hundreds in just three months...By September 1906, the mission had sent a score of evangelists up and down the west coast of the United States to places such as Portland,

> Oregon, and to Spokane and Seattle, Washington. By December 1906 they were in Denver and Colorado Springs, in Indianapolis and Minneapolis, in Akron, Alliance, and Cleveland, Ohio, in Chattanooga, Tennessee, in Norfolk, Virginia and even in New York City. By December 1906 the mission had commissioned and sent at least thirteen missionaries to Africa. Four of them were white; they all went to Angola. Nine of them were African American who, in their travels across the United States, recruited three more people to join them for ministry in Liberia...By early 1907, missionaries from the Azusa Street Mission had entered Mexico, Canada, Western Europe, the Middle East, West Africa, and several countries in Asia. By 1908, the movement has spread to South Africa, Central and Eastern Europe, and even Northern Russia. It is because of the singular success of Azusa Street's Missionary program, before others were in place, that I have chosen to claim that its story is unique to the birth of global Pentecostalism.[20]

The people who came into that humble building were hungry for God. Often a mid-day service found folks staying in prayer until the next morning as they sought God for the Spirit's power. This revival spread nationally and transformed many congregations and started new ones. People who were filled with the Baptism in the Holy Spirit went back to their home countries. Soon the revival was continuing in Europe, China, the Philippines, Japan, India, South Africa, Egypt, Liberia and Canada.[21] Harvey Cox describes the humble former horse stable and the revival that followed like this:

> They swept it out and moved their daily meetings there on April 14, 1906. It was no White City, but from that nondescript storehouse where on a rainy day one could still detect the scent of horses, a spiritual fire roared forth that was to race around the world and touch hundreds of millions of people with its warmth and power.[22]

Nearly every Pentecostal denomination in the United States and many foreign countries trace their roots to Azusa Street. The Azusa Street revival was marked by its multi-racial beginnings and within two years had sent missionaries to 25 countries. By mid-century, both Protestants (who initially expelled their clergy and members having received this gift) and Roman Catholics began to embrace the Charismatic renewal movements in their own churches. Many, however, have consistently resisted this revival—some even calling it Satanic.

COMMUNICATIONS INSIGHT

IT REVEALS THE PERSONALITY OF THE SPIRIT

THE PHILOSOPHY of speech is given to us by Paul in 1 Corinthians 13:11, where in describing his childhood, he says, *"I spake as a child, I understood as a child, I thought as a child."* By reversing the order of these verbs, we can see the manner in which speech works. First is the thought, second the understanding, and third speech. We think various thoughts on a subject; then, by a process of analysis and summary, we come to an understanding or comprehension; and then, we speak. One thing is absolutely necessary in this process, however: our thinking, understanding, and speaking must be in a familiar tongue. But at Pentecost, and in every similar experience, the disciples were speaking in unfamiliar tongues. The words which poured forth from their lips had not been previously in their thoughts and understanding. Since intelligent speech demands an intelligent speaker, we know that in back of their speech there must have been someone else who was thinking and understanding in those other tongues. That Someone was the Spirit of God.[23]

Harvey Cox continues a look at what has become known as the Twentieth Century's Revival.

> When the fire finally did fall, shouts of joy and rapturous dancing before the Spirit resounded throughout the neighborhood. The word got out. Night after night people crowded into the little house, stood on the porch, and stopped in the street to listen and catch a glimpse. White people began to come, and Mexicans. Soon the crowds grew too large, so Seymour and his friends rented a small abandoned church on nearby Azusa Street which had recently done service as a warehouse and then as a livery stable... The Azusa Street revival itself continued day after day, month after month for three years...What kind of buffoonish God would entrust a revival of religion to such people? But despite ridicule and opposition, the conflagration continued to expand as the sparks blew from ghetto to slum to rural hamlet, to St. Louis and New York, and then across the oceans to Europe and Asia, Africa and South America. As the world approached the cusp of a new millennium, the fire was still spreading.[24]

Today nearly 650 million people call themselves Pentecostal or Charismatic. Pentecostals alone outnumber Anglicans, Baptists, Lutherans, and Presbyterians combined. Two thousand years ago, Jesus gave His followers a seemingly impossible task. He asked them to become witnesses to the world. He told them to stay put a few days until they received the power to do what must have seemed unreasonable. They were to wait for God to manifest Himself *in* them so as to make them to become a part of His new power package for the task. They took the claims of Jesus and their baptism experience to the Roman Empire and brought it to its knees.[25]

For those early converts, the baptism of the Spirit did not just change their religious affiliation or their way of worship. It changed everything.

A few simple folks, at the turn of the last century, again waited on God for this power. Not to build something for themselves, but to rekindle the original flame to witness what Christendom had seemingly lost.

The original intent of those who received the baptism in the Holy Spirit was to bring a renewal to their own churches, not to start a new denomination. This is similar to the intent of earlier leaders such as Martin Luther and John Wesley. But as Lutheranism was considered incompatible with the Catholic Church in the sixteenth century, and as Methodism was considered incompatible with the Anglican Church in the eighteenth century, so Pentecostalism was considered incompatible with the mainline denominations in America and Europe in the twentieth century.[26]

Harvey Cox tells us why the newly baptized believers who experienced glossolalia were not content to just quiet themselves and stay in their old churches:

> As I pored over these archaic accounts, it became clear to me that for those early converts, the baptism of the Spirit did not just change their religious affiliation or their way of worship. It changed everything. They literally saw the whole world in a new light. Spirit baptism was not just an initiation rite, it was a mystical encounter.[27]

These early Pentecostals feared "creeds." Creeds, according to them, were designed to keep people out, to divide believers and to say what God could and could not do. They seemed to shut down the sovereignty of the Spirit and to frustrate the desire of Pentecostals to have a church unified in the Spirit for the last-days' mission. Land[28] says: "Creeds tended to be exalted to the place of Scripture and that would not do. The Spirit was over the church. The Spirit was prior to Scripture so the order of authority was: Spirit, Scripture, Church. Without the Spirit there would have been no Word, incarnate or written; without the Word, no church."[29] The struggle to maintain integrity, however, soon drove the first movements to their own "creeds"! (We call them Fundamental Truths!) It remains to be seen if Pentecostal Movements (denominations) can resist the inexorable slide to hierarchical bureaucracies. Some say we are already there.

COMMUNICATIONS INSIGHT:

I WILL RETURN to this seminal thought in a variety of fashions. Leaders, who are almost always the top communicators in their own community, tend to gravitate to power that resists outside influences (read laity) to cope with stress and decision-making. When the church loses its stomach for the constant wrestling to maintain the relationship and balance of these priorities (Word, Spirit, Church), she will abandon the risky part (prophesy, gifts, supernatural) and hold ever more tightly to that which is predictable and visible. ("Aaron, make us a calf! Moses is up doing the spooky part; it is too ambiguous for us. We need something more concrete—more Aristotelian.")

Facing the "right foot of fellowship" Pentecostal leaders turned to the regrettable task of establishing new Movements (they didn't call them denominations—bad word back then) where they could live a new lifestyle, organize legal entities, send missionaries and establish defining doctrinal charters to protect against spurious fanatics and destructive independent doctrinal issues. So they sought mutual support in an atmosphere of holiness to biblical principles. From this era (the turn of last century) many denominations (its safe to use the word now) such as Assemblies of God, Church of God (Tennessee), Church of the Foursquare Gospel, Pentecostal Holiness, Pentecostal Church of God, Church of the Open Bible Standard, and many others were formed.

Most of the religious world of the 1900s thought they were crazy. Some still do. Many others, however, are beginning to change their minds. The main reason for this is the second phase of the movement, which began after the 1940s when the growth and biblical orthodoxy of these revivalist churches began to be recognized and included in ecumenical gatherings. Also, the missionary fervor and success was immediately apparent.

COMMUNICATION INSIGHT:

STEVEN LAND, joins W.J. Hollenweger for some of the sociological reasons why this Movement has such appeal around the world. What Hollenweger attributes to African Americans in the USA can be, in large measure, equated to much of the 2/3rd world's worship expression also:

Orality of liturgy
Narrativity of theology and witness
Maximum participation—reflection- prayer- community
Inclusion of dreams and visions into public worship
An understanding of body/mind relationship

Unlike much of reformed theology which interpreted the "finished work" of Calvary as an accomplished fact with which to be identified only mentally, Pentecostals rather saw "movement" into God instead of a "standing." Not only the need to "identify with" Christ but to a more visceral "conformity" to Him. Less of a "position" than a "participation." C.E. Jones sees this as "The journey toward God was a journey into God."[30]

The 1960s in America saw a Neo-Pentecostal movement take fire in older denominations, many who had earlier opposed the manifestations of the Holy Spirit. Such were the "out breakings" amongst Anglican and Roman Catholic churches first and then in other Confessional bodies and even some Evangelical church bodies.

Why does the Church of Jesus Christ through history always need renewing and rejuvenation by the Holy Spirit? Why does it seem that the first sign of the cooling of the fervor of the Great Commission of our Lord involve the obviation of the role of the Holy Spirit in the Church? Surely we can learn something about this fact from the historic record of the first years of the Apostolic Church.

Related to our brief "history lesson" here, one should take a quick look at the Primitive Church soon after the Apostles.

THE EARLY FIGHT FOR CHARISMATA IN THE APOSTOLIC CHURCH

The first three centuries show a continued desire for Charismatic manifestation.[31]

Ron Kydd, in the conclusion of his work, states:

We have been able to come to a fairly clear conclusion, I think.

> Throughout the first and second centuries, the gifts remained very important to the Church. We have looked at material from all parts of this period, and we have drawn from virtually every kind of person in the Church. We have heard from bishops and heretics, philosophers and poets, storytellers and theologians. Generally speaking, and of course there must have been exceptions at specific places and times, the Church prior to A.D. 200 was charismatic. However, in the first half of the third century, things change...It is clear that the importance granted to the gifts was passing... These three centuries saw dramatic changes in the Christian Church.[32]

In retrospect, it becomes clearer why the gifts of the Holy Spirit were soon banished by the now organized Church and its hierarchy. Following the example of Jesus in John 13, where He modeled the attitude of a servant, Jesus warned His followers/disciples against seeking position over others (Mark 10:35-45 and Matthew 23:1-12). Here are some of the most neglected words of Jesus in my organization as well as others. In the meetings of the early Church, all were free to exercise their gifts (I Cor. 14:26ff). No ranking among members was predicted. This sense of equality through *interdependence* was clearly stated in I Cor. 12:24-25.[33]

Spiritual Maturity the "Sine Qua Non" of Healthy Spiritual Gifts

Is it any wonder that the organizing and status seeking church of the third and fourth centuries soon "shut down" any voices that challenged their supreme authority? Besides, to operate the gifts in the assembly, properly and healthfully, requires much teaching and a process of maturing the practitioners that few pastors and leaders are willing to do. It's much easier to "take control" of this "messy" and "risk prone" behavior for the sake of order and predictability, to say nothing of squashing the all-seeing eye of the prophetic which would uncover the sins of any and all—including the leaders! No wonder Paul said in I Cor: 14:39, *"Therefore my brothers, be eager to prophecy, and do not forbid speaking in tongues."* (And then he added in verse 40:)—*"But everything should be done in a fitting and orderly way."* The Church **then** and **now** is still emphasizing verse 40 to the neglect of verse 39! Sorry to say, this is also true of many "Pentecostal" churches. It's a lot cleaner and neater and free from the hard work of "maturing the saints."

The church then and now is still emphasizing verse 40 to the neglect of verse 39!

Add to this the fact that if pastors themselves are not comfortable with the gifts in operation in the assembly (many times because they have not taken authority in the gifts themselves), why let a non-title holder be seen as an important instrument in the body?[34]

York identifies three major factors in the growth of the Church during this period: the effectiveness of the early prophets, the effectiveness of teachers, and the changed lives and testimony of women.[35] Bosch (1991) even notes the historical record of the early church as Charismatic. "The significance for the early Christian mission up to the third century of charismatic healer-missionaries, miracle workers, and itinerant preachers should not be underestimated.[36] The Didache (the teaching of the Lord to the Gentiles through the Twelve Apostles) notes that enough of these prophets were itinerant to require regulation of their activities at the time of the second century.[37]

From the preface of Eddie Hyatt:

> As I began a serious search, I discovered that the charismatic dimension of the Spirit's activity was not missing from the church's past. Instead, a prevailing bias against charismatic gifts often influenced modern historians either to ignore the gifts of the Holy Spirit or to speak of them disparagingly. Further, I discovered that Pentecostals and Charismatics, because of a lack of scholarly research, often accepted the determinations of non-Charismatic historians.
>
> As my search continued, I discovered the perennial conflict between the spontaneity of the Spirit and the rigid structures of the institution. This often resulted in the institutional church labeling as heretics those who championed the freedom of the Spirit and suppressing or destroying their writings. This of course, contributed to the lack of data about the Holy Spirit's activity in history. The purpose of this study is to show that Pentecostals/Charismatics do have a legitimate history. It also suggests that instead of being on the fringes of orthodox Christianity, Pentecostals/Charismatic Christianity is in the mainstream of both biblical and historic Christianity.[38]

It's one thing to write in retrospect of the beginnings of the Pentecostal/Charismatic movement by quoting recent historians; but now let's look at some of the actual words of the early recipients of the "blessing" in the "last" 100 years.

HISTORY: EARLY BELIEFS (WRITINGS) ON TONGUES

Early writings about glossolalia (the word wasn't used then) helps us cast the proper light on the thoughts, doubts, beliefs, joys and challenges of those who went before.

One should not seek Tongues—rather seek the Baptism of the Holy Spirit.

In Amsterdam we don't say much about speaking in tongues. More and more we are seeking to glorify Jesus, and when we speak of Tongues we are only seeking His glory, and for the edification and the building up of the Church of God, that she may glorify more and more our blessed Jesus, or Savior. In Amsterdam it is generally believed that the Tongues is the evidence of the Pentecostal Baptism, but we are seeking only the Baptism of the Holy Spirit. We have not to seek for Tongues; Tongues are rather seeking us. When the Holy Spirit has come in, He will control our tongues.[39]

The Baptism of the Holy Spirit is possible without Tongues—temporarily. (-Rev. Polman, 1911)

We can easily hinder the worship of the Holy Spirit. I believe there are dear people who have received the Baptism of the Holy Spirit, but have not spoken with new tongues. I don't know why, I will not discuss the hindrance, I leave it to the Lord. I also believe that all who speak with tongues cannot truly say they have received the Holy Spirit. Right from the beginning I have taken this stand—those who have received the Pentecostal Baptisms as the first disciples will speak in tongues, but all who speak in tongues cannot say that they have received the Pentecostal Baptism....We are all longing for a further Pentecostal blessing, and I believe when that comes our cup will run over.... As a dear old mother in Amsterdam said when she received the blessing, "OH, I CAN'T RULE MY OWN TONGUE." It is glorious when we cannot thus control or rule our own tongue, the Lord fills his temple with glory....My heart is rejoicing in the Lord, and I pray that everyone will get such a baptism in the Holy Ghost, that you will say, "Oh, I cannot rule my tongue, I must glorify Him in tongues." Hallelujah![40]

W. T. Gaston in 1913 writes about the controversial nature of glossolalia.

In these last days when God is bringing to pass His STRANGE ACTS. Nothing He does seems to excite more comment, stumbling or opposition than the miraculous speaking with other tongues. In every place we find those who are stumbling over tongues, they say,

"We admire your zeal, your love, your faith, your self-sacrificing spirit, etc., etc.; but we don't understand about these UNKNOWN TONGUES.

Why do people err about the things of God? Jesus answers, "Ye do err greatly, not knowing the scriptures or the power of God." It is unfair to yourself and to God to remain in ignorance on anything already revealed in the Word and still claim to want to know the truth. We should first know the scripture, then the power of God; for "Faith cometh by hearing and hearing by the word of God." And no word of God shall be void of power. The Bereans set a noble example by "searching the scriptures daily" as Jesus commanded. Let us see then what our "guide book" says on tongues:

"For with stammering lips and another tongue will He speak unto this people" (Isaiah 28:11). Paul quotes this as thus "Saith the Lord." See 1 Corinthians 14:21.

W. T. Gaston continues by listing the traditional New Testament references for the instances when tongues is mentioned in connection with the initial receiving of the Holy Spirit Baptism.

—Jesus said simply "they shall speak with new tongues" Mark 16:17
—Luke records that all 120 in the upper room spoke with tongues as the Spirit gave them utterance.
—The Roman gentiles in the House of Cornelius were heard to speak with tongues. Acts 10:45, 46. The Jews who accompanied Peter "were astonished because on the Gentiles also (as well as on the Jews) was poured out the gift of the Holy Ghost."
—The Greek Gentiles at Ephesus "spoke with tongues and prophesied when the Holy Ghost came upon them." Acts 19:6[41] [a]

---

[a]For good sources on early writings on the Pentecostal movement and tongues, see the following: *Cloud of Witnesses to Pentecost in India*, Max Wood Morehead, ed. (Sept. 1907), 55, and *Cloud of Witnesses II* (1907); also by Morehead, "The Latter Rain in Calcutta, India," *Pentecostal Evangel* (April 17, 1920); and Etta Costellow, "After Two Years," *Cloud of Witnesses to Pentecost in India* (August 1909). See Gary McGee, "Minnie F. Abrams: Another Context, Another Founder" in *Portaits of the First Generation*, eds. James R. Goff and Grant Wacker (2002), 89; A.C. George,"Pentecostal Beginnings in Travancore, South India" in *Asian Journal of Pentecostal Studies 4,* (July 2001), 215-237; James R. Goff, Jr., *Fields White Unto Harvest: Charles Parham and the Missionary Origins of Pentecostalism* (1988); Minnie F. Abrams, "How the Recent Revival Was Brought About in India" in *The Latter Rain Evangel* (July, 1909); also by Abrams, "The Object of the Baptism in the Holy Spirit" in *The Latter Rain Evangel* (May, 1911); A.G. Garr, "Tongues: The Bible Evidence to the Baptism with the Holy Ghost" in *Pentecostal Power* (March, 1907).

David W. Dorries writes about a revival in the Presbyterian world of Scotland with Edward Irving.[42] Speaking for Irving: "we find it always to have been the gift first bestowed upon the baptized...is the root and the stem of them all, out of which they all grow, and by which they are all nourished."[43]

> Irving's perspective was the level of communication established by the Holy Spirit with the human spirit of the recipient. This deep level of personal edification enables the believer to become increasingly familiar with the supernatural realm of the Spirit. This is in preparation for heightened availability to other spiritual gifts whereby the entire church may be edified.[44]

Quoting Irving himself:

> Therefore it is nothing to be doubted, that tongues are a great instrument for personal edification, however mysterious it may seem to us: and they are on that account greatly to be desired, altogether independently of their being a sign unto others. And to me it seemeth reasonable to believe, that they will be conferred in private exercises of devotion, and earnest longings after edification; and being given, ought especially to be occupied in secret actings of the soul towards God... But, withal, there is an ultimate end to be aimed at, beyond present enjoyment and personal edification, which is that they may prophesy and edify the church when they shall themselves have been edified.[45]

WHO WOULD HAVE BELIEVED IT?

Our brief look at some history of the Twentieth Century's Revival and of some of its early pioneers who helped articulate why they were so disavowed and persecuted helps us appreciate even more what the Holy Spirit is doing across the world today and the debt we owe to the stalwart believers who dared to believe the scriptures against much opposition. Thank God most of them had pure motives and were men and women of biblical values and the perseverance of the prophet Daniel of the hymn by Philip Bliss:

Dare to be a Daniel,
Dare to stand alone!
Dare to have a purpose firm!
Dare to make it known.
— Philip P. Bliss, 1873

We now turn our attention away from [the] setting of the goal of the book and away from the major critics of glossolalia and a brief history of the "tongues" movement to the philosophical setting (matrix) from which our subsequent thesis springs: *Glossolalia* from the perspective of *communications theory.*

ENDNOTES

1. Eddie L. Hyatt, *2000 Years of Charismatic Christianity* (2002), 9-24.
2. Both of these sayings are credited to Neil Postman and Charles Weingartner in *Teaching as a Subversive Activity* (1969), 115.
3. John Wesley, as quoted in Carl Bremback, *What Meaneth This*? (1947), 105.
4. Ibid., 109.
5. Ibid., 109.
6. International Roman Catholic/Pentecostal Dialogue, 1992.
7. Klaus, Byron, "Prez Report," An eNewsletter to AGTS friends, April, 2006.
8. Ibid.
9. William and Robert Menzies, *Spirit and Power, Foundations of Pentecostal Experience* (2000), 17.
10. Ron Kydd, *Charismatic Gifts in the Early Church* (1984), 6.
11. C. Peter Wagner, *The Third Wave of the Holy Spirit* (1988), 20-21.
12. Ibid, p.21.
13. Ron Kydd (1984), 48.
14. James L. Ash, "The Decline of Ecstatic Prophecy in The Early Church," *Theological Studies* 37 (1976), 227.
15. M. Kelsey, 41-2.
16. Ibid.
17. See for example: S.M. Burgess, *The Spirit and the Church: Antiquity.* (1984).
18. For a detailed history of Pentecostals during this period see Vinson Synan *The Century of the Holy Spirit* (2001).
19. Cecil M. Robeck, Jr., *Azusa Street, Mission and Revival, The Birth of the Pentecostal Movement* (2006).
20. Ibid., 6-8.
21. Wade and Rosalyn Goodall, eds., *By My Spirit; The Assemblies of God, 1914 to 2000:* (2000), 11-12; 17, 19.
22. Harvey Cox, *Fire From Heaven The Rise of Pentecostal Spirituality and the Reshaping of Religion in the Twenty-first Century* (1995), 46.
23. Carl Bremback, 240.
24. Ibid., 46-47.

25. Wade and Rosalyn Goodall, eds., (2000), 195-6.

26. C. Peter Wagner, *Your Spiritual Gifts Can Help Your Church* (1979), 20-21.

27. Harvey Cox (1995), 71.

28. S.M. Burgess, et. al., *Dictionary of Pentecostal and Charismatic Movements* (1988), 106-108.

29. Ibid.

30. C. E. Jones, "Perfectionist Persuasion: the Holiness Movement and American Methodism," reviewed in *Dictionary of Pentecostal and Charismatic Movements*, Stanley M. Burgess and Gary B., eds. (1988), 406-409.

31. Besides Kydd and Hyatt, see writers like V. Raymond Edman, *The Light in Dark Ages* (1949), 34-35.

32. Kydd, (1984), 87.

33. See Merrill Tenney, *New Testament Survey,* (1985), 124.

34. Every pastor should read *The Territorial Imperative* by Robert Ardrey (1997), who is concerned about one's tendency to 'divide and conquer or play king of the hill' (which is so un Christ-like).

35. York (2000), 114.

36. David J. Bosch, *Transforming Mission; Paradigm Shifts in Theology of Mission* (1991), 191.

37. See York, 114. Also, see Hyatt (2002), back cover, for good documentation of early church fathers.

E. Hyatt (2002), XII.

39. From an early periodical: *Confidence,* Vol. IV, No. 8, 176-179, contributed by A.A. Boddy, August 1911.

40. From Rev. Mrs. Polman (no first name) in *Confidence*, Vol. IV, no. 8, 179. Some would say of the last paragraph ("I can't rule my own tongue") that the dear sister is speaking of uncontrollable ecstasy. Another, perhaps a better understanding is that she found her mother tongue inadequate and could not rule (will) it to accomplish the deep need to extol the Lord in a manner appropriate with her deep yearnings.

41. W. T. Gaston in *Word and Witness* (March 20, 1913) 4.

42. Edward Irving and the "Standing Sign" of Spirit Baptism in Gary McGee, *Initial Evidence* (1991) 49.

43. "Facts Connected with Recent Manifestations of Spiritual Gifts," *Frazer's Magazine* (March, 1832), 204, quoted in *Initial Evidence*(1991).

44. Dorries in McGee (1991), 51.

45. From: "On the Gifts of the Holy Ghost, Commonly Called Supernatural" in *The Collective Writings of Edward Irving in Five Volumes,* ed. rev. G. Carlyle (1864), 548.

CHAPTER 4

COMMUNICATIONS THEORY AND GLOSSOLALIA

The most powerful force man has is his power of communication. It is the form and function of our reason. It is the connection to the most sophisticated philosophies of mankind. Even a tiny infant attempts to reach out with its cry and nonverbal gestures. Humans have more complex facial muscles for expression than other species. Body language is as important for a baby as its voice. As adults our paralanguage becomes very sophisticated, though much of this activity is outside of the awareness of the user. We never used to place telephones in the bathroom or even the bedroom, but on the wall in the hall. Now the cell phone has become an extension of our bodies. They are also used as cameras and can be connected to the Internet, and that has totally revolutionized how we perceive communications. It is marvelous and frightening at the same time (especially for us older ones who are rather in a daze).

Our family lived for many years in a small village in West Africa that had one phone for the whole community of 700 square miles. It was in the post office, but the lines were down half the year due to brush fires, so it wasn't very convenient. We would tell our friends, jokingly, "If you call, please let it ring a few times because we're two miles away and someone would have to come running to tell us!"

Electronic communication has rearranged geography. It has become the nerve system of the world with over 700 million phones at this writing, and growing quickly every day. In the year A. D. 1000, only about five percent of the world was "literate." In 2000 (slightly over 50 percent literate) the electronic age was upon us and collective knowledge was born. But as a young boy I remember my grandmother shouting over the phone. After all, when talking to someone in town (we were on a farm in Minnesota) or to a neighbor on the party line, there were miles between her and the person on the other end of the line. So she thought shouting must be necessary! People used to travel long distances to hear an important person's words; now that's all changed. Morse's invention required wires, but in 1901 Marconi freed man's knowledge from wires. It took many decades, however, for technology to catch up. Now a single person's voice can be heard in every home worldwide.[1]

People thought the first television system would never be widespread because it could not be made cheap enough for common use. We are far past that hurdle today with TV sets in almost every room. But humans have always sought interaction, and we resent just watching TV. Some think we are on the dying edge of TV as it now used. Is Internet TV next, where people control it, instead of it controlling the viewer?

In the year 1000 mankind could only talk to those physically close. By the year 2000 we could communicate at the speed of light to great distances with words and pictures. Will we incorporate a system inside our bodies with thought and holographs by 3000? Look at the difference in *frequencies* of message transmission in this march forward. Is there also a "spiritual frequency" available for the person of faith to communicate with his Maker that God has prepared for those who dare to risk the unusual?

In the year 1000 mankind could only talk to those physically close. By the year 2000 we could communicate at the speed of light to great distances with words and pictures.

If you have studied Communications Theory, you'll remember that a considerable emphasis in this discipline concerns how words influence attitude change. The topic of persuasion is a subsection in Communications Theory and a brief review here will be useful.

A few hundred years before Christ, Aristotle wrote his *Rhetoric*, in which he described some of the basic elements of human communication. His writing has vastly affected the world's understanding of the process by which humans communicate to each other. According to Aristotle the three most significant elements related to one person's desire to influence another (today we name this university discipline: *persuasion*), are:

Ethos: the perceived personal character of the speaker, or credibility—always given by others to the speaker or source of the communication;

Pathos: the emotional state of the speaker, and the emotions he/she may evoke in the hearer;

Logos: or the words/speech/content itself of the communication event.[2]

The third element, *logos,* has received much study and was considered, in most quarters, to have been of greater importance. This is especially true concerning the vast topic of literacy and the inordinate power literacy can command in the parts of the world where *print* literacy is valued. "Print" is the indispensable element of formal education in all cultures and languages. *Logos* also has special significance to theologians because of the influence of the Jewish and Christian Bibles—called the Holy *Word* of God. Those who place importance on *logos* generally are preparing intentional messages to give to others. This is not to deny the power of the spoken word (another form of *logos*), however, as the following event illustrates.

The National Geographic Channel on the West Coast aired a debate with nationally-known animal rights proponents, who argued in a public forum with natural and medical scientists about the strong opposition by the animal rights people to the use of animals in scientific and medical research. The forum encompassed 90 minutes of intense debate and accusations involving some of the most eminent medical research specialists and animal research personnel in the nation.[3]

I was drawn to the debate by the almost exclusive use of *communication* by *speech/cognition* as the defining element to justify BOTH sides of the argument. From the medical research people came statements such as: "You are using one of the most preposterous overstatements of cognitive capacity to justify a move to give certain animals 'human rights' (e.g., elephants, whales, dolphins, African gray parrots, great apes, etc.)." "Where would our great advances in medicine in the last decade be if animals could not be used in experimentation?" was the question posed to the opposing side. The animal rights people made statements such as: "These are not dumb animals; they have communication/cognition capacities similar to human beings. Why not experiment on humans themselves instead of defenseless animals?" The animal rights side used the now deplorable historical event of the capture and display of a Pygmy from the Congo. He was displayed in a cage with a chimpanzee at the 1912 Chicago World's Fair because of his "perceived lack of capacity for reason and language skills." In my opinion and experience, the only lack of capacity was with his captors! They used this example to illustrate how scientists misjudged the Pygmy's language skills at that time, and how science is making similar mistakes about some animals today. Indeed, animal rights folks are understanding more and more about the communication abilities of our furry and feathered friends. "Communication is the glue of animal societies. Without a means of communicating, no life, including the simplest single-celled organisms, could exist. Communication, like the tango, takes two. And it requires a signal, which can be anything from the release of chemicals between colonizing bacteria, the 'come-hither' flashes between male and female fireflies in the backyard, the 'let's go' rumble of

African elephants, the 'signature' whistles of dolphins, to a dog barking simply to be let outside."[4]

Two-thousand years ago, Aristotle said only humans were "endowed with the gift of speech." Humans are not the only ones to vocalize or even use symbols to communicate, "but humans seem to be the only animals capable of fusing vocalized sounds with symbolic language.... The differences (with lower animals) are in the capacity of the human brain for fusing, monitoring, and controlling the coordination of the sound-production equipment with the linguistic symbols."[5]

For many scholars, the uniquely human ability to fuse vocalized sounds with symbolic language is significant because it results in a phenomenon quite different from either process alone. As anyone who has ever practiced speech aloud knows, we perceive and react to spoken language much differently than when we "say" the same message to ourselves silently.[6]

Wherever the reader is positioned on this issue, the element to note is the criterion of meaning making/language capacity as the *sine qua non* of both sides of the debate. Not physiology—similarity of body appearance or size of any particular organ (like the brain) or its function—but the issue of cognition and the animal's capacity for speech communication. This was front and center in all the argumentation. Yet, "communication" is difficult to define. There are 126 definitions of communication listed in the text by Frank Dance and Carl Larson.[7] (For more sources for those seeking an academic approach to Communications, see Appendix 1.) A more recent scholar studying the importance of diverse theories of communications is Robert Craig.[8]

Raymond Ross is the inspiration for the graphic illustrations of human communications to follow,[9] even though there are many more recent models of human interaction.[10] Ross's text is my personal choice because of its simple, yet comprehensive, coverage of the elements of human communications for our intention in this chapter—which will serve as the background of the Theory of Communications relating to glossolalia. One must recognize that much of human communications is *unintentional*—widely called nonverbal communications. Intentional communication, the aspect of this vast subject we are most interested in for this study, is described carefully here: "*Intentional communication is a transactional process involving a cognitive sorting, selecting, and sharing of symbols in such a way as to help another elicit from his own experience a meaning or response similar to that intended by the source.*"[11]

The nature of man, the very definition of what it means to be "human" is directly related to his ability to communicate and express himself. In comparison to other creatures, this ability represents a physical and psychological need of overwhelming proportions. In many ways, humankind is unique in communicative skills. Littlejohn, like Ross, speaks of humans' need always to represent reality symbolically.[12] Think, for example, of man's skills at rationality and his very sophisticated systems of communication. No other creature, it seems evident, can use words to talk about words!

Though man has recently studied the communication systems of animals such as whales, dolphins, chimpanzees, elephants, and others, we doubt any of these non-human creatures can abstractly speak of the future (for example, "in six weeks we will have achieved an objective"). The animal kingdom can pass on certain genetic evolutionary mutations and thus benefit current species from the "learning" of the past generations over thousands of years, but they can't talk about it. Bees communicate to each other the direction of and distance to the place where nectar can be found to make honey. Dogs communicate by intense sensitivity to smell, and they can communicate to man to warn of burglars, impending seizure, or fire. We have even made machines that can communicate to each other and program computers to fly airplanes. The aim of all these levels and differing complexities of communication is to bring about change. Only humans can "capture or bind" time by preserving it in symbolic writing or electronic preservation and thus exploit the past and its knowledge for the immediate and future generations.

No other creature, it seems evident, can use words to talk about words or "capture or bind" time by preserving it in symbols.

Others see our uniqueness by other means. Sara King says: "We are the only animals who can haggle about the definition of ourselves and therefore can be, within limits, whatever we choose to define ourselves as being."[13]

According to George Miller, "The human capacity for language made human culture possible, and culture, with all its social, artistic, technological and scientific innovations, set *homo sapiens* apart from all other animals.... Little wonder that the gift of language has so often been seen as nothing less than a divine miracle."[14] In all societies, the person who can communicate well is often advantaged and advanced to leadership. "I'll pay more for a man's ability to express himself than for any other quality he might possess," says a modern entrepreneur.[15]

WHY LINK COMMUNICATIONS THEORY TO GLOSSOLALIA?

This author's purpose is to explore one or more of the reasons God has chosen the medium of interpersonal communication to make Himself known to mankind, and why He chose to use a certain medium that is perceived as illogical and unreasonable to many serious thinking people. Glossolalia (speaking in tongues) is oral communication as first seen in the New Testament and repeated all through the age of the Church in isolated events, until the last century when a renewal of apostolic use of this form of *logos* again became common. By then, written communication, principally printing, had become the prominent form of using words as symbols. Once humans developed and perfected writing, they came to value it the most, even to the exclusion of older systems that were based mainly on oral/aural systems. Symbols and more symbols—representing significance to their makers and interpreters—have become indispensable necessities in our lives. One may safely say that only humans can communicate in the form of symbols with no relationship to their referents.

THE SIGNIFICANCE OF SPEECH IN THE BIBLE

"In the past God spoke to our forefathers through the prophets at many times and in various ways, but in these last days he has spoken to us by His Son" (Heb. 1:1-2).

Lips are the most visible part of speaking. In Isaiah 6:1-8 "lips" are used as the symbol for the many elements of speech: the actual verbalization, the voice, the thoughts, and the *heart/emotions* of human communication. Lips, like the tongue and the mouth, are highly symbolic of speech in the Bible. Jesus said of this symbolism, *"Out of the overflow of the heart the mouth speaks"* (Matt. 12:34), relating the feelings, emotions, and thoughts to the mechanics of speech. Hence, lips and tongues and mouths become the embodiment of speech, the measurable gauge of the state of the human heart/attitude/belief. Jesus also indicated the gravity of speech (thoughts, intentions) by the statement: *"For by your words you will be acquitted, and by your words you will be condemned"* (Matt. 12:37).

When Tony Schwartz writes of the current media and how it is focused on the 500 year-old tyranny of print,[16] I can easily see how this electronic/technological era disadvantages us (literate people) to an important aspect of God's major communication style—oral/aural. We can be thankful much of His "speaking" was eventually written down. What is written is surely more permanent. We like what can be researched because someone took pen and ink and preserved it. In fact, there are hundreds of references where God Himself commanded someone to "write the words" He was speaking (e.g., Ex. 17:14). But the "permanency factor" does not mean mankind always *sys-*

tematizes written words without personal bias. Even in using the written Word of God there is a tendency for us to manipulate its organization.

Unity at the Expense of Diversity

Roger Stronstad stresses the unity and diversity of the ways God has spoken to mankind in His ultimate intention to redeem His creation. In so doing, He not only used prophets, but also His Son. This diversity continues into the New Testament. God spoke through the coming of Jesus, the Messiah of the Jews (few of whom accepted Him as such), and those who believed on Him while He was living on the earth. Subsequently, God spoke through prophets and writers who had been Christ's disciples in the gospels and the epistles.

Stronstad pointedly suggests that the human tendency for "closure" (make similar things equal, even when they are not) has improperly blinded most theologians to miss the complimentary yet different intentions/functions between Luke's and Paul's words about the Holy Spirit.

> In spite of this self-evident diversity of divine revelation, however, on the principle of the analogy of faith in the history of the Protestant interpretation of Scripture there has always been a tendency to emphasize the unity of the message at the expense of diversity. Thus, whether we are speaking of the entire Canon of Scripture, or of either the Old Testament or the New Testament, the unity and diversity is often reduced to mere uniformity. This uniformity is often the expression of some "pet" center, a Canon within a Canon, such as the Deuteronomic history for the Old Testament or the Pauline Epistles for the New Testament. This problem is particularly acute for the would-be interpreter of Luke-Acts. Wherever he turns in the literature on the subject, he encounters a hermeneutical strategy which presses Luke into the Pauline mold.[17]

Stronstad's writings, and later those of William and Robert Menzies,[18] will be very significant for our study of how the interpretation of God's Word (yes, the very structure of that interpretation) may have influenced humankind's "masking" of God's oral nature, as well as His directing individuals to write down certain things.

Explosion of Information

Many authors write of the phenomenal explosion of information in the modern era. Notions about the growth of knowledge estimate man has discovered and recorded as much knowledge (data) in the last 25 years as in all the recorded history of previous centuries. Man is indeed a "communicating being." There are occasions when men and women are psychologically compelled by the need to speak, or they become delusional or physically ill if they cannot. One of the most severe forms of punishment, and even torture, is separation from other human beings. Serious mental illness often results. For those of us who hold to a religious creed that says God made man to be a living soul for His pleasure believe the Bible teaches He did this, among other reasons, so they would be able to communicate with Him. The earliest biblical record shows the first couple walking and talking with the Creator. God has chosen only a few others with whom to speak directly since then, as recorded in the Old and New Testaments.

Many scholars and Bible believers hold that the creation account is largely symbolic, even though the veracity of the fact of creation may be affirmed by them. Others hold to the creation theory, but discount Bishop Usher's chronology of events—especially that the earth is only 6000 years old. Wherever the reader stands on this issue, I would solicit your consideration of God's desire to dialogue and communicate with the creatures He made when He said: *"Let us make human beings in our image, in our likeness"* (Gen. 1:26-27, NIV). If you hold to the idea that God made humankind as described in the Psalms ("crowning them with glory and honor" and "making them rulers" over the rest of His creation—Psa. 8:4-8), then you may be willing to permit yourself to try to understand my thesis concerning language, no matter what you believe about the first chapter of Genesis.

Permission to Understand

Carl Rogers, in his book *Becoming a Person*, makes an important point about one of the great barriers to good understanding. Anyone thinking about how people communicate should consider it: "I have found it of enormous value when I can permit myself to understand another person. For a person who is even partially involved in real communication, just trying to understand a different point of view may become threatening. We are afraid to permit ourselves to understand: if I let myself really understand another person, I might be changed by that understanding."[19]

It is difficult to allow this "permission" with any degree of sincerity. You will note in other chapters when I speak of my target audience for this book, I hold little hope for most theologians who have already made up their minds about why God may have chosen glossolalia at all. There is no question about their permitting themselves to understand. It would be about as easy as a traditional medical doctor, a member of the AMA, permitting him/herself to understand/consider the science of chiropractics!

AUTHOR'S INTENT INSIDE THE MATRIX OF COMMUNICATIONS

So much has been written about the subject of the gifts of the Spirit and especially "tongues" that I have chosen:

- Not to attempt this task from the scholastic methodology of opposing the Reformed tradition (which largely denies the necessity of the gifts of the Spirit once the Canon of Scripture was fixed);[20]
- Not to debate the traditional hermeneutical procedures of some Pentecostals who hold that the narrative of Acts is sufficient evidence for doctrinal justification;
- Not to enter into the argument as to whether tongues is the only initial, physical evidence of the baptism in the Holy Spirit, even though the vast majority of Pentecostals and a good percentage of Charismatics DO hold to that doctrinal position. There is a growing number who see this emphasis as an oversimplification and unjustified from a biblical standpoint. Though I have an opinion on that controversy, my contention is to discuss the reason why God chose this sign and experience, whether or not it is *normal* or *normative* (whether it is normal and generally expected or is obligatory as evidence). I have witnessed over 3000 people baptized in the Holy Spirit in 30 countries and, without exception, they spoke in tongues. (However, some prophesied first and then spoke in tongues.)

May the reader see something new by unhitching the "blinders of the habitual" that allow only the familiar to be seen.

- Not to insist that my personal experience and belief be the major matrix from which this thesis will be advanced. Rather, from the social sciences and especially Speech Communications and Cultural Anthropology—where my academic pursuit has led me—will I present my thesis for the reader's consideration.

To the point: **I am a social scientist, a confirmed Pentecostal, requesting the reader to observe with me this great worldwide revival from a different vantage point. My hope is that the reader may see something new, by observing familiar things in a wider perspective, and thus unhitch the "blinders of the habitual" that allow only the familiar to be seen. To quote N. R.**

Hanson, "The paradigm observer is not the man who sees and reports what all normal observers see and report, but the man who sees in familiar objects what no one else has seen before."[21]

THE COMPLEXITY OF "MEANING"

"Life is not an illogicality, yet it is a trap for the logician. It looks just a little more mathematical and regular than it is; its exactitude is obvious, but its inexactitude is hidden; its wildness lies in wait."[22] Communication, even with those we know well, is not easy.

You may have heard of the two old men who met after a 40-year separation. They had been very close friends in their youth. After the usual pleasantries and exclamations of how good it was to see each other after this long interval of time, one man asked about the other man's wife: "How's Mary?" His friend responded, "Oh, don't you know, Mary's in heaven." To this his longtime friend said, "Oh, I'm so sorry!" Then he realized it didn't sound right to say he was sorry Mary was in heaven. So he tried to recover with, "I guess I should say I'm glad!" Now, flushing with embarrassment to think it sounded as if he were happy Mary was dead, he tried one more shot: "What I really mean is I'm surprised!"

Language learning is perhaps the highest, most complex skill we learn as humans during the first few years of life. It is so complex that those who wish to become "experts" in communication, whether written or oral, must spend years of both formal and informal training to master (if that's possible) the language of even one culture's mother tongue.

In this section, I will explain, in as non-technical language as possible, the complexity of human speech and how its use is deeply connected to every person's self-esteem, pride, and sense of accomplishment. No one practices good communication naturally. We have to work very hard to communicate well, and even then misunderstanding is inevitable. We will first look at why misunderstandings occur, because in the process of exploring Communications Theory we will come to see how language skill is tied subconsciously to a person's deep psyche. If we can unfold, like an onion, the layers of sub-consciousness about language, the basic thesis of this book will be better understood. **Why did God choose "tongues" to be the sign of His Holy Spirit's fullness** for the believer who wishes to obey Christ's mandate made at His ascension? In Matthew's account He said: "Go and make disciples of all nations. ...Do not leave Jerusalem, but wait for the gift my Father promised...you will receive power when the Holy Spirit comes on you; and you will be my witnesses...to the ends of the earth" (Matt. 28:19; Acts 1:4, 8).

Much has been written about *glossolalia* (the original Greek word for "tongues speech") from a purely theological vantage point. Many books have been published by those opposing the stance purported in this book (i.e., the stance that Christ's words did not have a short shelf life, but are valid in our day). Much has also been written by those whose lives have been transformed by Holy Spirit power and who basically agree with the overall tenet of this book and author. But hardly anything has been written from the discipline of the communicologist—like this one.

I do not pretend to write from the professional theologian's vantage point. (However, this author probably knows more about theology than most theologians know of Communications Theory.) In this search, for you the reader and for me the writer, I hope to add one more small piece of evidence about the mysterious and unfathomable quest to know God's mind about "tongues" and why He chose this physical sign—that over 650 million people living today have experienced. Statisticians say that number is one third of Christendom. So let's "jump into" the vast arena of Communications Theory. I promise to try to keep from sounding like a "professional" and to give some examples to help the process be more understandable.

A LOOK AT COMMUNICATIONS THEORY

Why are we misunderstood? Who hasn't wondered why it is so easy to be misunderstood? We find ourselves almost shouting "I **told** you"—as if there is no way a misunderstanding could have occurred. (I want to **tell you** how the study of communications is related to glossolalia.) All physiologically normal people communicate "normally" to some degree. Anyone in any culture who can speak or write is a "communicator." For this reason, perhaps, some readers feel one need not formally study communications, since everyone does it! Then there are gifted people in all societies, who though they do not have degrees in Communications are better communicators than the professionals! But one needs the very basic tools about Communications Theory to better profit from the thesis of the book. I shall try not to frighten off the individual whose formal education has not included the "jargon" of the discipline of Communications and its theories. However, the whole thesis of the study is related to Communications Theory as the "raison d'etre" of the book. So I beg your indulgence! I will try to make this section clearly related to the issue of glossolalia (as promised in the book's title) with interesting elements not so professional sounding *and, at the same time, I will stay true to the discipline of Communications.*

Up to 90 distinct meanings have been assigned by our society for the word "run" in American English. People who learn our language as their second language are sometimes astonished to find such a wide spectrum of choices for one word. Most languages, like English, have some variety of word usage that may cause misunderstanding. In order to track this complexity of meanings some simple communication models seem called for.

Communication models have proliferated in rapid order during the past 30 years. These models provide a way for Westerners, in particular, to visualize the linear mode of "meaning making." (Yes, I said *linear* for the West, as this is not universally followed in great portions of the world's cultures.)

Communication Models

Shannon and Weaver's Mathematical Theory of Communications is widely accepted as one of the first and often quoted seeds out of which the study of Communications Theory has sprung in the second half of the last century.[23] Its linear simplicity has been much modified since then (the early 1950s) to one we will examine here from the 1960s and 1970s (that of Raymond Ross). It will be more adequate for our purposes and represents a distinct evolution from the earlier models. Two other examples of later models which may be useful to the reader would be those of Fiske[24] and Schramm.[25]

Sources and Theses

A smaller segment of the readers of this study may well be interested in the finer details of how Communications Theory, in its detailed history and influence, affects the thesis of this study on glossolalia and communications. I direct this segment of potential readers to a brief appendix (1) at the end of the study. The constant addition of new theories and electronic sophistication has constantly modified how people look at this mystery of human interaction with environment and persons. Consider, for example, the almost esoteric presentation of communications of virtual realities and the media. Here sources are listed on the development of the brain, the origins of intelligence in children, the nature of speech relative to predictability, egocentric speech and self-esteem, and such information that over time was seen as vital to reach an organized theory of human speech and communication ability.

It is not my intention, or in my training, to discuss the physiological nature of human speech (i.e., I will not be discussing the Broca's and Wernicke's areas in the left hemisphere of the brain and the role they play in the production of human speech). But I will note here the nineteenth century assumption that states people not advanced in technology and industrial/mechanical sophistication are biologically inferior has been totally discredited. The African languages I use in teaching were used by indigenous peoples hundreds of years before colonization from the West occurred. The Western nations (England, France, Germany, Spain, Portugal, and Italy) all injected their "superior" languages and marginalized the local vernaculars. "The phonology, morphology and syntax of exotic languages have proved to be every bit as rich and complex as (often more complex than) those of any Indo-European language."[26]

In English, the jigsaw puzzle of the world around me is broken into pieces that do not fit exactly with the pieces obtained when broken into French pieces.

An interesting analogy about language, cognition, knowledge, and worldview comes from J. Samuel Bois. He speaks of language as a "thinking tool." As automobiles and airplanes are transportation tools, so language is a thinking tool. He then describes how differently the function of speech is configured when using French instead of English. Because I speak and teach in both of these languages, I became very interested in his theory. I have often said I prefer to teach in French, rather than English, even though the latter is my mother tongue. When asked why, I often say it's because French is more precise, but I'm not really satisfied with that response. Here is a better one: I don't see the same things, I don't observe the same events, when I change my English for my French thinking tool. Changing my language changes me as an observer. It changes my world at the same time. I cannot dissociate my senses and my brain from the tool I am using. For example, the French take two hours to eat the noon meal in leisure—the average American, less than 20 minutes. So the word "lunch" represents quite different things as measured by the important reference of time, besides the actual food consumed! In English I break the jigsaw puzzle of the world around me into pieces that do not fit exactly with the pieces I obtain when I break it into French pieces. The frames of reference are different; the pieces are not interchangeable in all cases.[27]

If there is a change in frame of reference from English to French, imagine the change to the gift of tongues, where the human speech apparatus of the mind is not active to the same degree. God must have a reason for this! Might one not say that in surrender to the language of the Spirit of God, the frame of reference is changed from our human skill as communicators to become participants in the frame of reference of what is beyond human? "But isn't that risky?" some may ask. Sure thing! God would always have us step in faith towards Him, knowing full well there are those who will never do it simply because they will not surrender the free WILL God gave all mankind. This is part of the wonder of His words: *"Let us make human beings in our image."* In so doing He gave us the authority to disobey Him, to scorn Him and to distrust Him, OR to accept Him. Amazing! His justice must allow all the choices. The advantages of becoming a son or daughter by acceptance would be meaningless without that risky prerogative of choice.

Phenomenology

God has made us with a wonderful "awareness" capacity. The following will give the Communications Theory focus on an old philosophical concept called *Phenomenology* (the scientific investigation of experience). We will look at this concept in relation to the communications chart of Ross (to follow) and to human perception. William Howell says *meaning is perception.* (See below in the Ross Communication Model presented in this chapter.) Human consciousness, its definition, its impact on cognition, and its relation to the way we come to understand objects and events is related primarily to personal experience. Much debated and described, personal experience is ever present, but few philosophers agree on its parameters and even fewer trust it. Yet personal experience, through the physical senses, is the basic element of *phenomenology,* which in turn is one of the theories we all study when seeking to know about human perception. "All my knowledge of the world, even my scientific knowledge, is gained from my own particular point of view, or from some experience of the world without which the symbols of science would be meaningless."[28]

Insisting on Our Own "Categories"

How can we refrain from this habitual behavior of perceiving based on our experience? Is it possible? Stephen Littlejohn affirms "phenomenology makes actual lived experience the basic data of reality. All you can know, it claims, is what you experience."[29] (Here *meaning* comes from the *perception* gained only by direct experience with *phenomena.*) He further quotes Richard Palmer: "Phenomenology means letting things become manifest as what they are without forcing our own categories on them."[30] Husserl (credited by Littlejohn as founder of phenomenology) believed that only direct experience could uncover truth about any "phenomenon." By direct experience he meant focused conscious attention, careful examination with an unbiased mind.[31] These concepts are important here as they relate to the way a person approaches experiencing the Spirit of God and the way she or he forms an understanding of the "truth" about phenomena associated with being filled with the Spirit.

Whoa! It's getting pretty thick now! Let's let that simmer for a while. OK? Now something easier to capture.

Northrup and Cognitive Systems

There is an overriding cultural determining factor in the way we view the world. Where one is born on this globe is a strong "determinate" on how one perceives the world. F. S. C. Northrup contends that the West is overbalanced on the side of perception through cognitive thinking. Human experience and the subject of phenomenology are inseparable because consciousness is how one comes to understand objects and events.

Palmer's theory (the science of phenomenology) would allow the conclusion that anything a person decides to believe or conclude in life's experiences is clearly and simply *what it is*—without forcing one's own meaning or perception on it. Fat chance! Postman and Weingartner's humorous dictum, "There is no such thing as history, only histories,"[32] fits this figment of imagination by phenomenologists. I don't question the truth of *wanting* to "let things in life's experience become manifest as what they are," I just believe it naïve to hold to the chance of that actually happening—unless it is agreed that the end result is not a universally accepted given. Let me illustrate with a diagram, which for me is a seminal explanation of how human cognition is affected by the cultural matrix in which one is raised and begins the process of knowledge as a person.

Phenomenology's basic principles are valuable and instructive, but without the element of culture and social differentiation, how can it attempt universal application? My goal in what follows is to give yet another perspective to the perception of glossolalia by diverse peoples. This philosophical battle, of which phenomenology is a small part, brings me to want to expose a cross-cultural element about human perception—always inside the broad goal of how glossolalia is viewed by those who experience it and by those who don't.

I will now touch on the basic theme of phenomenology (known by experience) in the important work by Edmund Perry.[33] The reason I wish to conduct the reader to the difference in methods of thinking of Africa and China and India contrasted with the West is because the mystical and ambiguous nature of much of God's dealing with humanity is seen very differently by folks who have *not* been inoculated with Western, Greco-Roman, Aristotelian grid thinking. **In no way, however, do I intend by what follows**

to denigrate any people's thought processes or to imply that one area of the world's cognitive process is superior to another. I wish only to illustrate, in the diagram below, how only a slight shift in *sequential priority* of the same elements of cognition (the way we know, which is common to all cultures), can account for significant variation in understanding and conclusions. I am much indebted to David Hesselgrave, who shows Perry's diagram, reproduced here.[34]

A Warm-up for the Diagram

Since the Industrial Revolution, the West has aimed at imposing man's will on society and natural forces. The "Method of Science"[35] leads us to aggressively form a theory about what is not evident, then empirically testing that hypothesis with a systematic formula based on measurable consequences that *are* visible. (I know that sounds like gobbledygook—maybe read it again!) The West has the ability to prove that atoms exist, that electricity is a substance, and other such mysteries, even when these elements are not visibly evident themselves. The West's priority of thinking is called *conceptual.* For us to know something, it generally relates to a concept of some theoretical system or idea.

> **The West has the ability to prove the substance of such things as atoms and electricity, even when these elements are not visibly evident!**

The East is much less willing to base "reality" on these externals that the West points to with empirical certitude. Much of Western theory is dominated by a vision of individualism. The West criticizes the East as lacking verification for its reality, because the East is willing to focus on a deeper "reality" *that lies behind* the apparent speculative hypothesis that has only been confirmed indirectly. The East believes the West is fixated on mastering only what is the *external.* The East stresses emotional and spiritual convergence as communication outcomes. For the Oriental, reality lies behind the transitory data of the senses and is found in the unchanging eternal nature of the universe which can only be reached by intuition and psychic search. Of course, all these philosophical differences are reflected in speech/communication.

The West is dominated by language itself, which is distrusted in the East. What counts for the East is intuitive insight gained by direct experience. And that experience is not individualistic as in the West, but communally based on folks' social positions of role and status inside the community. "Eastern theories tend to focus on wholeness and unity, whereas Western perspectives are preoccupied with measuring parts and do not integrate these parts into a unified process." [36]

Obviously, in so speaking, one must allow a broad generalization concerning East and West. Neither one is an invariable unity, but allow variations within each differentiated area. This will be evident below, as the diagram will show that the East, in particular, is both *intuitional/psychical* AND *concrete-relational* as a first priority way of perceiving reality.

The significant element to be noted here (relating to spiritual matters) is that the East trusts human experience more than the West AND has a greater tolerance for ambiguity: "Orientals are extremely earthy, practical, and matter-of-fact because their knowledge of the divine is linked more directly with the immediately sensed data of human experience. Succinctly put, the Oriental constitutes the nature of the divine directly from the aesthetic as simply as analogical symbol while defining the divine in a postulational way."[37]

Three Basic Cognitive Approaches to Reality

In explaining cognitive differentiation, F. S. C. Northrup compares the sociologist/anthropologist's view of differentiation of the world's people group's cognitive processes with a chart of concentric circles that illustrate for him why so much misunderstanding occurs cross-culturally in communications.[38] The three elements that follow are descriptions of ways of thinking and capacities possessed by all peoples, but arranged in different priority of use/importance. Most phenomenologists today would find this stance too subjective, though subjectivity has value in its own right.

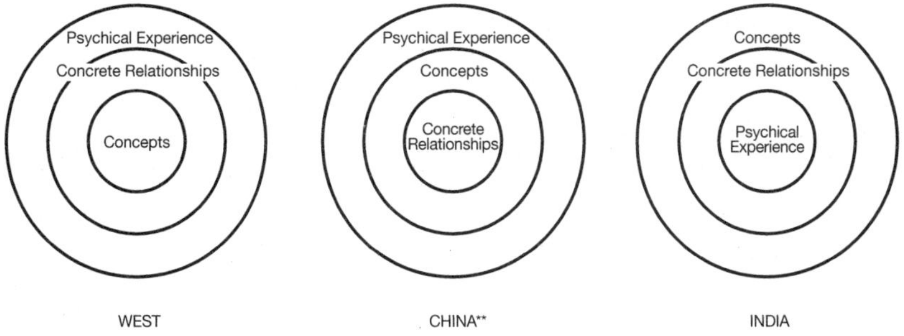

Figure 1[39]

To briefly summarize the three categories (in reality, there are many more, of course), represented by Perry's circles:

Conceptual. An idea or hypothesis based on a "tested" process of logical, practical, and sequential propositions that, for the West, lead us to say "we know" by critical thinking and analysis.

Concrete-Relational. An idea or event is "real" when *pictured* to an actual situation by symbols, stories, narrative, parables, etc. (e.g., the sayings of Confucius, African parables, drama and ritual, great portions of the words of Jesus, and the non-verbal arts). Much more of the Bible falls in this category than the West cares to admit or, even perhaps, understands.

Psychical/Intuitional. The knowledge/data prized by the West is transitory, mundane and "lower." Psychical knowledge is beyond and "higher." It lies behind the apparent.

So What's the Point of the Last Two Pages?

When Jesus talked of the Holy Spirit, He often used an allegory or metaphor or description of the Spirit's work and role in the lives of His disciples using unusual words.

- In Luke 1, the Holy Spirit is depicted as a descending *dove* at Jesus' baptism.
- In John 3, when Jesus spoke to Nicodemus He likened the Holy Spirit to *wind.*
- In John 14, when Jesus promised the Spirit's coming to the disciples He called Him the *Counselor* (or more perfectly the *Counsel for the Defense*) and the *Spirit of Truth* who now is *with* you but will be *in* you.
- In Acts 2 the Spirit is seen as *tongues of fire* (as promised by John the Baptist). *Here is speech much more concrete and relating to actual elements or ideas, more than conceptual and sometimes mystical.*

I submit we should not expect the nature of the Holy Spirit to *change* to meet the natural evolution from the Hebrew world of concrete relational thinking into the Greco-Roman world of conceptualizations as primary mode. The Holy Spirit is less understood from the rationalized, intellectualized Western world of our times than in the Eastern concrete-relational or psychical world of the 2/3rd World today. There the Charismatic message of the gifts of the Spirit resonates with a worldview much more receptive, and is both received and practiced by those with that worldview. In that world today the Church is growing so fast missiologists can hardly keep up with the numbers. Isn't it possible there is a relationship?

If the West holds *conceptual* thinking as first priority, it naturally leads to the weakening of the importance of *concrete-relational* and *psychical-intu-*

itional as modes to be utilized. The significance of this is that our monocultural Western understanding of the gospel has usually been overbalanced on the side of conceptual thinking and the cognitive power of reason, while fearing and neglecting (from spiritual ignorance) the aspects of power and conflict in the biblical message. This is partly because Western Christianity struggles with the dichotomy of the sacred and the secular.[40] This is not so with much of the 2/3rd World which lives in the unity of the reality of the material and the spiritual, the seen and the unseen.

> **Meanings are not in words... meanings are in people -David Berlo.**

Praying in tongues is much like this. It reaches to the unseen in the sense that it is not cognitive, but rather bridges the seen and the unseen, that the biblical record shows so clearly and which is so hidden from the rational mind of modern Western man. In the same sense, when the Asian Indian mind (Psychical-Intuitional) reaches behind the obvious external world of material facts (observable/verifiable) to look beyond the scientific symptoms to deeper related "truths," his world is closer to the cultural matrix of the Scriptures. Science has not blinded him to spiritual sensitivity, and when he becomes a Christian he is ready to be "owned" by the Spirit of God. In African nations, after I learned their languages, I found the believers in Africa could accept the duality of the Incarnation (God and man in Christ) and that both God's Spirit and man's personality are joined in the Canon of the Scriptures. It was the Greek-influenced mind that struggled with this for hundreds of years in historical Christianity!

COMMUNICATIONS THEORY AND PERCEPTUAL FIELD

It has often been said that words do not mean the same to all people. It is much more accurate to say that words do not mean at all! Only people mean, and people do not mean the same thing by all words. Thankfully, a number of years ago expert communicators realized the word "meaning" needed to be redefined. In the 1960s, David Berlo had a dramatic influence on the world of speech communications with his thesis that meanings are not in messages. Berlo stated meaning is not something which is discoverable; words do not really mean anything at all; and dictionaries do not and cannot provide us with meanings. *He maintained that meanings are in people.*[41] Meanings are learned; they are personal, our own property. We learn meanings, we add to them, we distort them, forget them, change them. We cannot find them. They are in us, not in messages. Everyone tends to be egocentric.

Individuals interpret the world from their own set of assumptions, past knowledge, past experiences, cultural background, and personal intellectual capacities. These human characteristics make it difficult to communicate with someone else. Fortunately, we usually surround ourselves with other people who have meanings that are similar to ours. "The elements and structure of a language do not themselves have meaning. They are only symbols, sets of symbols, cues that cause us to bring our own meanings into play, to think about them, and to rearrange them. Communication does not consist of the transmission of meaning. Meanings are not transmittable, not transferable. Only messages are transmittable, and meanings are not in the message, they are in message-users."[42]

Berlo believes those who continue to hold that meaning is in words almost always develop a common communications problem. He has labeled it the "I told them" fallacy. If one believes that meaning is in words, then one generally behaves as if the use of words will ensure the understanding on the part of the receiver. These individuals are constantly being misunderstood and subsequently, whether in the church or in the business world, we hear them exclaim, "I can't understand what's wrong with these people—I **told** them."[43]

Postman and Weingartner, in their controversial book *Teaching as a Subversive Activity,* remind us that the meaning of a perception is how it causes us to act. If rain is falling from the sky, some people will head for shelter; others will enjoy walking in it. Their perceptions of "what is happening" are different as reflected in the fact that they "do" different things. The fact that both groups will agree to the sentence "it is raining" does not mean they perceive the event in the same way.[44]

As in the old joke mentioned above of two old friends meeting after many years, they had many different meanings in their minds for the words *death, sad, happy,* and *surprised.* Though neither of them would need to look in a dictionary for a definition, the fact is *true meaning resides in the mind or perceptual field of people* (word users).

Human perception is extremely individual. When we dialogue with another person, we both *encode* and *decode* from the mass of memory banks retained from knowledge, past experience, feelings, attitudes, emotions and values that make up millions of electronic slots in the "storage disk" of the mind. From this mass of information, we both compose a message to be sent and interpret others' messages sent to us by verbal symbols or nonverbal symbols (and often both working together at the same time). This will be illustrated clearly below.

In the chapter "Meaning Making," by the above authors, three important points are made which will help us to understand the communication process illustrated in the schematic reproduced in Figure 2 below. *A word of caution: Conceptual models, diagrams, and verbal expressions of how God may wish to communicate with man and through man can probably never capture the totality of this process, even though they are helpful to our understanding. God is infinite and language is finite. One can't contain Him in words.* This point, as philosophical and abstract as it may seem, is closely related to the very heart of the thesis of this treatise. Here Edmund Rybarczyk's research helps me to help the reader. Quoting Vladimir Lossky, he says: "Eastern theology refuses to ascribe to the divine nature the character of an essence locked within itself. God—one essence in three persons—is more than an essence ... God overflows His essence."[45]

In like manner, the following communications model, one must admit, is inadequate to fully explain the complexity of human communication. In the same way, human attempts to explain glossolalia (mine included) will fall short of the majesty, the mystery, the power available to witness to the gospel, and the self-edification properties—all which accompany this gift of the Holy Spirit that God has clothed with an aura of that which seems foolish and undesirable for the uninitiated.

ROSS TRANSACTIONAL MODEL OF COMMUNICATIONS

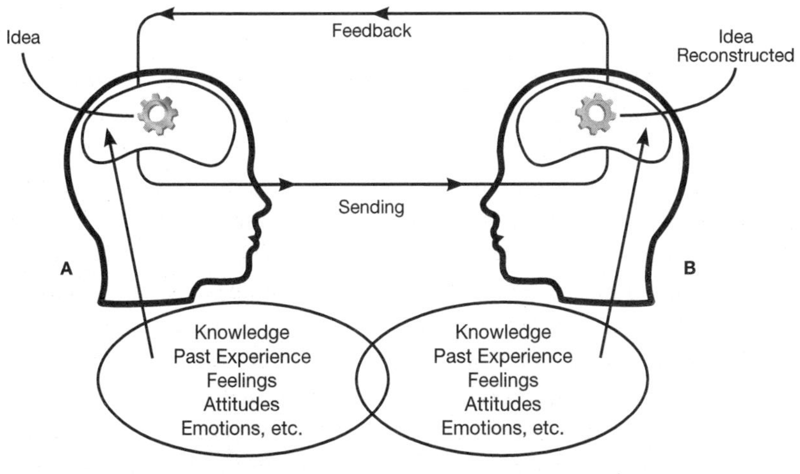

Figure 2[46]

First, when listeners from any part of the globe hear the Word of God, they tend to perceive what they want and need to perceive and what their past experience, knowledge, attitudes, etc., has led them to assume will work for them.

Second, because "learning" necessitates making a new category in one's perception, the ability to learn can be seen as the capacity to relinquish inappropriate perceptions (or to modify them as part of existing information) and to develop new—and more workable—ones.

Third, since the listener's perception allowing cognition results from one's "storage disk" already on file, it is obvious that each individual will perceive "reality" in a unique way. We have no completely common world with other individuals, and communication is possible only to the extent that two persons possess somewhat similar "data files" which allows them at least a minimum common ground of past experience, knowledge, attitudes, etc. The process of becoming an effective communicator is contingent upon seeing the other's point of view and *encoding* a message into his/her perceptual field. God saw that good communication is hard for us, even though He made humans with their superior capacity for interpersonal communications. So He sent His son Jesus as a special messenger to explain (encode) His message into our "database" of information. Since humans don't understand God's database easily, He adopted ours! This is the great wonder of the Incarnation of Christ. The great wonder of "God with us" was/is God's willingness to accommodate Himself, to come to our level; and in turn, Jesus made Himself easier to be understood. He was born a Jewish baby and grew up in human form so He could *encode* into the auditorium of His hearers! (Phil. 2:5-11)[47]

No One Practices Good Communication Naturally

We have to work very hard to communicate well, and even then misunderstandings still occur. We utilize words of our own thinking to which we have "fixed meanings" representing the way we internalized them. These assigned "meanings" were only assigned for ourselves—not the target person(s) to which we direct these words/messages and expect them to *decode* them the way we *encoded* them. The container holding these different assigned meanings (like a hard drive database—in humans, about 13 billion brain cells) that exist in a person's mind is called an individual's *fan of perception* in Figure 3 below.

What are the component parts of a person's fan of perception? We have already started to speak of it, but will here attempt to enlarge on the definition since the above model can now, perhaps, aid in the reader's *decoding* process. The hundreds of thousands of meanings and concepts are converted to electrical neurons intricately held together in the complexity of the human brain. Linguistic systems have assigned symbols (words, gestures, sounds, etc.) to these interconnected cognitive concepts. Since all new learning is related to previously acquired information, the fan of perception is replete

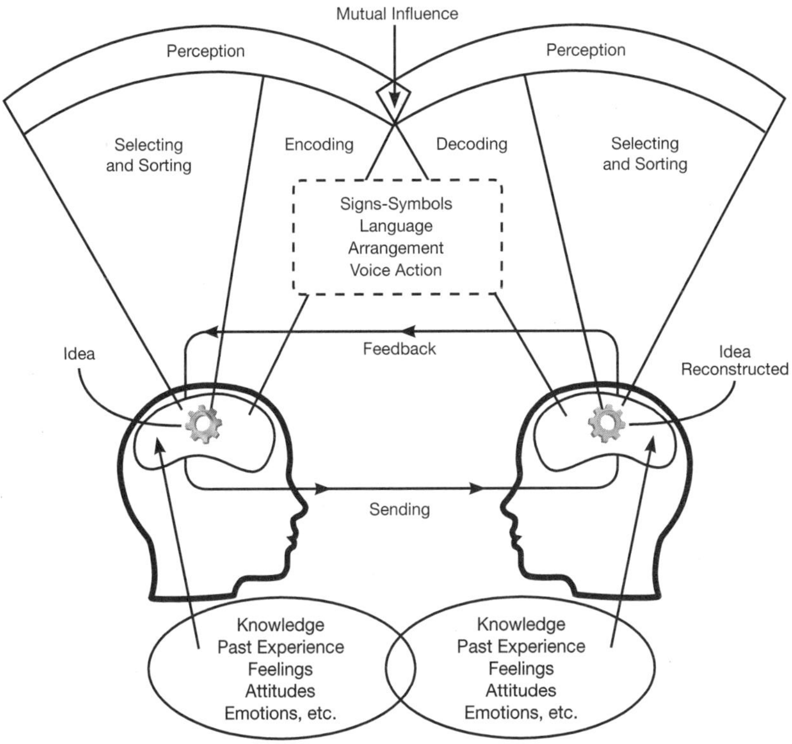

Figure 3

with meaning separated into thousands of specific groupings. Every society has designated linguistic constructs, which its members use to identify meaning in their cognitive processes. (The model before us shows that the "pool" of raw material for one's perception is knowledge, past experience, feelings, attitudes, emotions, values, etc.) These modes of perception act as filters by which information is put into proper categories and culturally accepted assigned meanings. What this implies is that all learning is metaphorical (i.e., not restricted to mere definitions of words). A person who seeks to communicate meaning encodes a message from his or her personal fan of perception by literally scanning a "database" for the information necessary to give the outgoing message a meaning. (This whole operation could take only a second or two.) Only when shared meaning occurs between the speaker and hearer can we say that real communication occurred. (Note the slight overlap of source and receiver's fans of perception in the model.)

Feedback in the figures above also relates to one's *perception.* Although we think by using words we are only communicating one message, in reality we are communicating MANY MORE. We think we are communicating only ideas, BUT by *facial expressions, gestures, tone of voice, body posture, the distance between people, use of time, and so on*, we are communicating feelings, values (such as distrust, concern, disdain, agreement, etc.), and more. A person recalls these more vividly than the words themselves!

From this writer's African experience, let's use a hypothetical event in the communication between a male missionary witness and an African audience to illustrate the above process. Let's *work* the model through a real-life communication event.

Communicating to an African Individual

Suppose the witness wants to discuss the topic: "God is love." The witness, having experienced the love of God through salvation, has no difficulty understanding the relationship of the symbol "love" and the symbol "God." His African audience has many symbols for the word "God." For proper encoding the witness must first have as part of his *fan of perception* knowledge about the correct symbol to use to express (*encode*) the "High God" or the "Creator God" that would most correctly identify Yahweh. That is not the only problem. Even the choice of the correct symbol for "Creator God" does not evoke the witness' meaning for God—who loved enough to send His own Son to die to redeem humankind back to the Father—nor that the Father's ultimate intention for humankind was for creatures with volition to *choose* to love Him. The animists from West African culture may believe in a High or Creator God, but do not possess in their *fan of perception* the understanding that this God is personal or loving or accessible. If the witness ignores these facts and simply delivers the words "God is love" (*Wennam ya nonglem* in the Mori language), assuming his audience will follow *his* understanding of God and love, they may hear his words but certainly not reconstruct (*decode)* the idea he intended.

The communication model states "Meaning is Perception." If the Mossi's concept of God, in contrast, evokes feelings of powerlessness or fear because God is viewed as judgmental and inaccessible, then the perceived meaning for both the words "God" and "love" for the African audience is obviously quite different from that of the witness. Thus the witness must either take the time to find out what the audience has in their "meaning box" for the words "God" and "love" or he must try to influence the audience to comprehend his categories for these words before *comm-uni-cation* (making the meaning common) can transpire.

Feedback

The model under consideration clearly articulates that both verbal and nonverbal feedback is present in all communication events. To obtain this feedback, the thoughtful witness must acquire further information about the African group's fan of perception through encounters in informal settings. During a communication event, feedback may involve a frown, a questioning look, a shaking of the head positively or negatively, open dialogue asking questions, or even gestures of rejection.[48] This will potentially lead to the realization that the speaker must *re-encode* the gospel message using alternative symbols and words to ensure his concept of God is understood.

SPACE FOR THE HOLY SPIRIT IN ROSS'S MODEL

The person who is "walking in the Spirit" may find "supernatural" guidance in the communication exchange identified in this model, if the communicator seeks it. It almost appears that the apostle Paul integrated the work of the Spirit into this communications paradigm when he made the following instruction to the Christians at Corinth: *"No one can really know what anyone else is thinking, or what he is really like, except that person himself. And no one can know God's thoughts except God's own Spirit. And God has actually given us His Spirit (not the world's spirit) to tell us about the wonderful free gifts of grace and blessing that God has given us. In telling you about these gifts we have even used the very words given to us by the Holy Spirit, not words that we as men might choose. So we use the Holy Spirit's words to explain the Holy Spirit's facts"* (1 Cor. 2:11-12, *The Living Bible*).

Pentecostals or Charismatics are not better people or better communicators naturally, but they have learned and experienced—through tongues speech—the submission of their own mental and verbal skills to the Holy Spirit. Thus, they have been empowered to believe (greatly enhancing their courage) that God wants them to be useful vessels, as humble servants, for the proclamation of His gospel. Added to this is the fact that speaking in tongues (as the initial physical evidence of Jesus' words in Acts 1:5: *"John baptized with water, but in a few days you will be baptized with the Holy Spirit,"*) is like a new door through which the recipient can believe God and "seek" other gifts of the Spirit such as *Faith, Miracles, Prophecy, Healings, Word of Wisdom and Knowledge.* All these are not signs of holiness but tools to work in the field to produce fruit.

Note! This does not mean that non-Pentecostals are inferior witnesses. History proves they can be very powerful witnesses. My contention is that they can be **even more useful and effective** after having been "clothed" by the mighty Baptism in the Holy Spirit.[49] Might not Christ's words to His disciples in Acts 1:8 have relevance here? *"But you will receive power when the Holy Spirit comes on you; and you will be my witnesses in Jerusalem, and in all Judea and Samaria, and to the ends of the earth."*

Special Note

The writer does not intend to suggest that Holy Spirit empowerment, as understood by Pentecostals, is a substitute for language learning for someone ministering cross-culturally. Early Pentecostals made that mistake. They found out they didn't get off the boat speaking Chinese![50] Nor should one conclude this author's intention here to be that one should interpret Paul's words to mean that words spoken in prophecy or interpretation of tongues or words of wisdom are to replace the Canon of Scripture or be the primary medium of preaching.

In his admonition in the above biblical reference, however, Paul claims the Holy Spirit can guide the word choice of the person bearing Christian witness, so the Good News is more focused and understandable within the audience's fan of perception. Given the anointing of the Holy Spirit in preaching the gospel, Paul concludes this passage to the Corinthians with this expectation: *"But strange as it seems, we Christians actually do have within us a portion of the very thoughts and mind of Christ"* (1 Cor. 2:16, *The Living Bible*).

I wish to submit here this can be accomplished **both** in the utilization of scripture and that which is **not necessarily** a direct quote or an exact idea contained in the body of Scripture. I don't hold to the "textualizers" model, that if the Holy Spirit inspires speech, in the interest of gospel witness, one speaking in this way must be restricted to the exact words as found in, for instance, the King James Version of the Bible. And unless it is a quotation, it's not the Spirit guiding the conversation or instruction or counsel. But, neither would I suggest we should be adding pages or books to the Sacred Writ.

Communication "Outside the Fan of Perception"

For the individual who has submitted one's cerebral language or "mother tongue" to the control of the Holy Spirit (evidenced by "foolish" glossolalia), that person now has the capacity to be used, at the Spirit's direction, to speak a word of wisdom, a word of knowledge, or a prophetic utterance into the fan of perception of the receiver. That would not have been possible if one holds to the notion *that the miraculous was past once the Canon was complete.* This is so, simply because he/she has no cognitive understanding or faith for such an experience. Such individuals, many of whom are good communicators of the gospel, do not believe the Holy Spirit can go beyond one's **knowledge, past experience, attitudes, feelings, emotions and values** that we call the "database" or fan of perception. I am suggesting that the "incarnational" option and power of the Holy Spirit enables believers, by faith, to appropriate more fully 1 Corinthians 2:16. (The term "incarnational model" will be amplified below.)

Two Witnesses from Outside Traditional Pentecostalism

Let me suggest that anyone who has experienced the baptism in the Holy Spirit has a decided advantage in communication if he/she truly walks in the Spirit and exercises faith in the Holy Spirit's willingness to help penetrate the auditorium of the target audience. Again, this is no substitute for perfecting the human brain through hard application, but for the diligent person, hard work and natural talents can be greatly enhanced by God's supernatural works in ordinary folks as well as professionals. Consider this unusual true happening related by Dennis Bennett, an Anglican minister:

> In a Full Gospel church in Oregon, there was a young man who had married a Japanese girl while stationed in Japan with the armed forces. The young couple returned to the United States, and were doing well, except that the young lady flatly resisted her husband's Christian faith and held steadfastly to her Buddhism. One night, after the evening service, the couple was at the altar, he praying to God through Jesus Christ, and she praying her Buddhist prayers. Next to them was kneeling a middle aged woman, a housewife from the community. As this woman began to pray out loud in tongues, suddenly the Japanese bride seized her husband's arm; "Listen!" she whispered in excitement. "This woman speak to me in Japanese! She say to me: 'You have tried Buddha, and he does you no good, why don't you try Jesus Christ?' She does not speak to me in ordinary Japanese language, she speak temple language, and use my whole name which no one in this country knows!" It is not surprising that the young lady became a Christian![51]

The Limitations of the Intellect

Can a skillful communicator find an advantage by relying on the Holy Spirit in preparation for a communicative event? Larry Christensen of the Evangelical Lutheran Church makes a poignant comment on this topic:

> "What possible value can speaking in tongues have, if I have no idea

> what I am saying?" According to the Bible, even though you do not understand what you are saying, your spirit is in a state of prayer (1 Cor. 14:14). But it is a praying with the spirit rather than the mind. It is neither an emotional nor intellectual act (although both emotion and intellect may be affected), but *an act of spiritual worship.*
>
> It would seem that prayer in which the mind is unfruitful would have little value. What blessing can it be to pray when you have no idea what you are praying about? Actually, this is one of its greatest blessings—the fact that it is not subject to the limitations of your human intellect. The human mind, wonderful as it is from the hand of the Creator, has limited knowledge, limited linguistic ability, limited understanding, and furthermore is inhibited with all manner of prejudice, little and large. Speaking in tongues is a God-appointed manner of praying which can bypass the limitations of the intellect. One may picture the difference something like this: A prayer with the mind comes upward from the heart, and must then pass through a maze of linguistic, theological, rational, emotional, and personal check-points before it is released upward. By the time it 'gets out,' it may be little more than a slender trickle. An utterance in tongues comes upward from the depths, but instead of being channeled through the mind, it bypasses the mind and flows, directly to God in a stream of Spirit-prompted prayer, praise and thanksgiving."[52]

Christenson helps us move to the well-studied and recorded issue of prayer.

Prayer Fits on the Communication Model—and Beyond

We know much about God from studying His word, but there's more about God we don't know than what we do. One can learn another culture and its language systems and do an improved job of social interaction because of that effort. Can we even approach a meaningful knowledge of God's "fan of perception"? Are we not intimidated by His vastness? Yet He invites us to pray and repeatedly the psalmist articulates for us God's wishes and our need to reach out to Him. Abraham Heschel remarks that prayer is not speech, for "the purpose of speech is to inform; the purpose of prayer is to partake."[53] If God is sometimes unknowable, inexpressible in our feeble attempts, yet our yearning for Him pleases Him, how do we attempt dialogue from the understanding of a communication model that requires some "mutual overlap" (Ross chart) for cognition to take place? Is not what the Evangelical world calls the "salvation experience" a big move in the direction of mutuality? Does the word mutuality sound presumptuous? Yet Isaiah (chapter 55, verse 6) speaks God's mind with "Seek me and you'll find me." Is this reasonable? May one of the functions of glossolalia be to jump to another realm/frequency of communication that escapes these fears and feelings of inadequacy to try to touch the Creator? Would not prayer in a personal prayer language free one from the "encoding/decoding" task for a dimension of openness to Divine reality? The time/space dimension of encoding (message preparation in Speech Communication jargon) heightens the consciousness of all the thousands of hours of learning to speak, being corrected/coached/evaluated—even disciplined or punished for poor performance by parents and the educational system during the period of "growing up." Can glossolalia convey one's inner being past the struggle of the rational mind to correctly articulate, transposing the soul to an awakened consciousness which ordinary language cannot touch? Would not glossolalia allow one to sneak

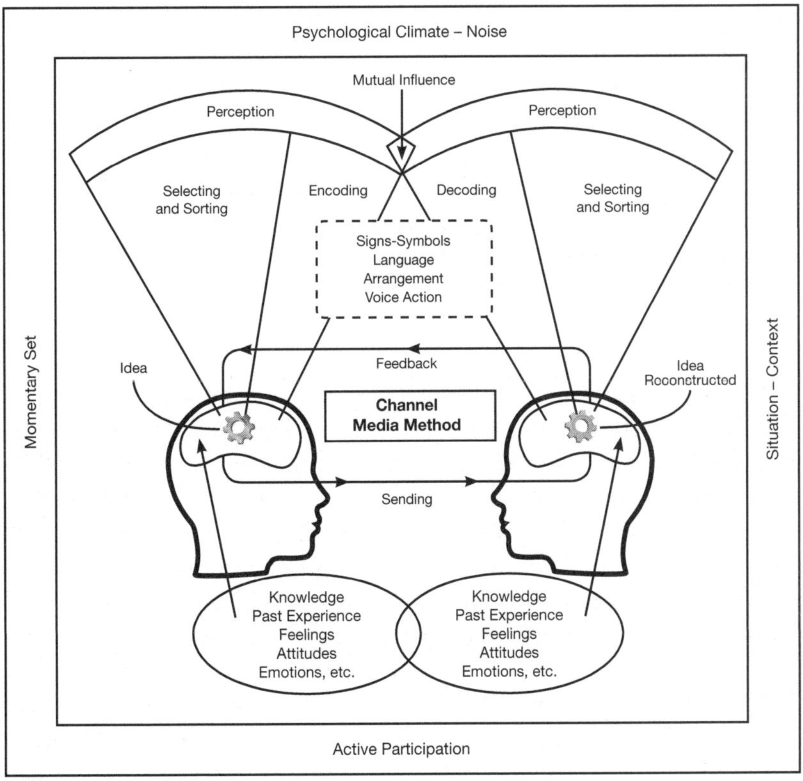

Figure 4

past the watchful dragon of consciousness? Might not one explain this much-misunderstood phenomenon as omitting the above struggle in pure soul expression? Macchia links the anthropologist Samarin's comment that "tongues says 'God is here,' in the same way that a Gothic cathedral says 'God is majestic'— to Hollenweger's oft repeated and quoted statement that glossolalia represents 'the cathedral of the poor.'"[54]

The Issue of Context

All communication takes place in a CONTEXT.

Imagine an isolation ward in a prison, alone with all the walls padded and the person incarcerated in a straight jacket. Obviously an extreme example. There, the relative absence of normal contextual objects are *screaming* at the one incarcerated. When a guard later comes to the door to feed the prisoner, his/her words will be in direct focused context to the environment. In more normal conditions in life, think of how one's location, the emotional state of one's temperament who is near or far, the temperature, the time of day—almost anything (and everything) one can think of—is relevant to the idea of how context affects communication and, consequently, how those elements influence how one speaks or writes or thinks.

Now let us consider how the CONTEXT elements in our model apply to the thesis of this effort to understand glossolalia from a communicologist's perspective. We'll look at the four elements on the sides of the model called: *Momentary Set—Psychological Climate/ Noise—Situation/Context, and Active Participation.*

Momentary Set

If you are taking a final test and have a pounding headache (perhaps the anticipation of the test brought it on), you have experienced the influence of momentary set on the process of communication. Even if you are feeling fine while taking the test, the sudden sound of fire engines and the smell of smoke in the building could be quite disconcerting; this is illustrative of how context affects us. The first time you may have heard an utterance in "tongues" in a public service may have been quite shocking or electrifying and confusing—or somehow attractive. All these illustrate "momentary set.

Psychological Climate—Noise

If your religious background contained many wild stories about folks who show much emotion in church and you were warned about those who speak in strange languages as part of the liturgy and perhaps hold up their hands while singing or praying or who all pray out-loud and all together in church, because of your previous "programming" about Charismatics, you might find this environment offensive. This could lead to confusion and a sense of psychological *noise* in such a religious setting. If you were raised in an Evangelical church and held an unconscious bias against Roman Catholics, the first time you participated in a Catholic Mass and experienced the "smells and bells" of the proceedings (the not knowing when to kneel or stand, the vaulted ceiling and the statues of saints and the sight of many candles) would create the same sort of confusion and wonder. You might not have "heard" the homily of the priest, even if it had been presented well and were biblically correct. In both cases the *psychological noise* might have drastically altered your perception of speech or behavior.

Situation—Context

Think of how differently you pray out loud at table grace when only the family is present as compared to how you pray with "significant others" present! Our reference groups represent a strong influence on our communication style and content. Young teenagers especially are ultra sensitive to peer and reference groups. If you are not a Pentecostal or Charismatic but you have a very good friend who is and with whom you have free dialogue when alone, think of how differently you may converse with him/her when your own pastor/priest is present.

Active Participation

This aspect of context that encircles any communication event is crucial to our understanding. Much has been written about *selective exposure*. At the introduction of this work, I referred to my doubt that many theologians who are opposed to glossolalia would be influenced at all by this thesis and that they were not included in my "target audience." I referred to "beating on cold iron." The issue is *selecting* what we will even consider as a possibility to influence our decisions. The element of *active participation* is the gatekeeper of permission to consider an idea or a new bit of information. Habitual smokers are almost impervious to the warnings on cigarette packages or opinions of health care specialists. Selective exposure allows many American taxpayers to cheat on their income tax because it is perceived to be outside of ethical integrity constraints. When the saying "love is blind" is examined, it contains the truth that in screening out the faults of the intended loved one, only perfection is seen.

PERCEPTION—COMMUNICATION—HOLY SPIRIT

All models (like the figures above) have weaknesses because they are inadequate to explain fully all of the elements of a given communication event. This is true for the models here, including the most recent one we have been considering in some detail. However, even our imperfect model (Ross) will be sufficient to illustrate how the Holy Spirit can be a true Paraclete (one called alongside to help). I draw your attention to four specific words: *perception, encoding, decoding,* and *feedback.*

I grew up in a preacher's home. During my youth, my parents pastored three different churches. My father never had a church split (a term from the religious world describing a disagreement in a church where part of the congregation departs); Dad had a way of heading off trouble before it grew to the extent that it needed massive surgery. He would head off trouble not by ignoring it, but by lovingly confronting people. He would discern an individual's source of dissatisfaction and minister to him/her before that person could talk to others and marshal a third of the congregation. I have often wondered if my father's perception was not a gift in the Holy Spirit, because Dad believed the Holy Spirit would be available for just such a role. I think of times in the Gospel record where it says: "and Jesus perceived their thoughts." I would not want to suggest any of us are as skilled as the Master Communicator. Nonetheless, Jesus did promise us the Holy Spirit, and He said we could do what He did with the Spirit's help.

Fan of Perception/Faith

If, when encoding messages while preaching or witnessing to another person, I employ a measure of faith to the process of *selecting* and *sorting* a verbal message, I am not only choosing from my *fan of perception,* but I have made room for *His* supernatural assistance. So actually, I have a *fan of perception/faith.* Doesn't 1 Corinthians 2:11-12 really mean, "So we use the Holy Spirit's words to explain the Holy Spirit's facts"? The reader should not mistake this reference to the role of the Spirit as a cop-out from preparation and research. I acknowledge that many Pentecostals and Evangelicals have the sad reputation of always seeking a "short cut" to accomplishment. They look for a way to avoid personal perseverance or the rigors of higher education and attainment of professional skills. (However, no one should lump all Pentecostals/Evangelicals in that mode.) I personally believe one of the best expressions of the Spirit's work for His prophetic influence is at the moment of preparation of the sermon or lecture and its outline. Now, add to this the willingness to leave Him *space* during the presentation, yes, the extemporaneous moment while speaking so the manuscript can even be improved. God, by His Holy Spirit, can supernaturally take good preparation and make it more fitting to the audience than whatever would have been possible for human communication skills alone if one had *not sought or allowed "space" for His in-breaking presence.*

Is it possible for a minister/communicator to be "over-prepared"? Of course. If the preacher or lecturer has a great investment in the preparation of the outline or manuscript, he tends to use every "jot and tittle" (Jesus' expression describing the tiny brush marks of writing Hebrew) to justify the hours of preparation and anguish in its organization. I'm suggesting that even the best preparation needs "spaces" for illumination *while the presentation is made.* If my fan of perception is related to faith (perception/faith), then when encoding during preparation or while sending a message I need also to leave *space* to decode what the Spirit is saying for faith to bear fruit.

Who better to make room for this "faith space" than the person who has already learned to sacrifice his/her intricate and highly valued speech mechanism at the occasion of the Baptism in the Holy Spirit? That experience has then been both empowering and instructive in function. The form of public communication in this case would rarely be glossolalia, but prophecy or word of wisdom or word of knowledge. Glossolalia at a person's baptism in the Spirit *opens the door to the full consummation of growth in the Spirit allowing maturation in the Gifts of the Spirit, so the best one for the occasion is possible.*

Summary

From the wise words of G. K. Chesterton,[55] this section has suggested Western logic related to mathematical regularity is good but does not lend itself sometimes to the unpredictable nature of God's Holy Spirit who, if allowed the time/space, will aid a person's communication skills and thus the effectiveness of the event. The writer suggests also the elements in the Ross communications chart **do** lend themselves to examine the inner workings of how anyone who has yielded himself to the empowering baptism in the Holy Spirit has an advantage (as the consequence of yielding/submission) in communication. In addition, by allowing "faith space" in both preparation of a manuscript or speech outline AND the actual presentation of that preparation, one can better allow/expect the "inbreaking" of the Spirit's prompting inside the extemporaneous moment. This follows such a communicator's understanding of the apostle Paul's words in 1 Cor.2:11,12,16.[56]

MORE ABOUT "MEANING IS PERCEPTION"

In 1967 this author began his graduate studies in the Speech Communications and Cultural Anthropology Departments in the

University of Minnesota. In courses on Persuasion my esteemed professor was the eminent communicologist Wm. S. Howell. He advanced the idea for the first time for me that meaning and perception are vitally linked. In fact, in his classes we learned that *meaning is perception.*[57]

Jesus, the Master Communicator, showed a new idea in the "perceptual field" of a member of the high religious body of His time, a man called Nicodemus. "You must be born again," said Jesus. This Pharisee's response shows us he really missed what Jesus was intending.[58]

From the most-often quoted chapter in the New Testament (John 3), a ruler (Pharisee) of the Jews called Nicodemus must have been shocked to hear even Jews would need to be "born again" to get into the Kingdom about which Jesus and John the Baptist prophesied. Nicodemus had a centuries' long mind-set about membership in the Kingdom. Participation in the Messianic Kingdom, for the Jew of that era, meant conformity to a moral code and ritual system. It was based on a way to escape penalty and secure a reward. Duty was a complex code. It was *perceived* less as an inward consequence of the action of the will or a personal disposition than an inherited right. By his own code and its merits that heredity claims as a child of Abraham, Nicodemus believed the kingdom was his. Pentecost says Nicodemus knew about the phrase "born again" from how the Jews treated proselytes who when baptized from heathenism were said to be "as a child newly born."[59] Did Jesus **mean** the Jews must enter by that door of humiliation John the Baptist seemed to require? To this all the Pharisees would object. As sons of Abraham they would never submit to such humiliation. I submit to you the symbol of the second baptism (of Jesus, with the Holy Ghost and fire, about which John spoke) requires a similar humiliation for the same kind of religious pride. The Pharisees of that day said they didn't need it. The same argument is being used today of the baptism of Jesus by many good believers. For many, a false **perception** is the cause of misunderstanding on this issue and reaches across the centuries.

The reception of salvation is a function of a person's FAITH. The Christian Church has so many expressions of how and when this Divine act occurs in the human heart that volumes have been written. However, rare is the "model" adapted by any church body but what it is based on faith (whether the faith of the parents presenting an infant child or the older child's faith in "confirmation" rituals or a grown person's own faith in action). The reformation of Luther made famous the formula of Sola Fide (along with Sola Scriptura and Sola Gratia). The immediate observable "sign" of salvation is generally an inward witness (Romans 8:16) that a work of grace has been accomplished. Many times the inward witness is manifested externally, but not always observable by others. Some adults (but surely not all) manifest great joy, relief, emotional weeping, etc., when the release of confession and repentance is expressed or after the moment of salvation is internalized. But the Church does not have a universal formula because it recognizes that anything "observable" is so culturally and individually determined, thus so varied, that any attempt to "systematize" the experience would be discouraged and probably rejected on a universal scope.

So, the individual believer's *perception* of the experience is highly internal and generally only recognized by an observer when the individual proclaims (testifies) to the inner work the result of faith. This study, however, will attempt to demonstrate from Scripture and human testimony that the baptism in the Holy Spirit event *does* seem to have a common sign/symbol that both the recipient and observer alike can affirm. That said, there is, however, no formula apart from glossolalia and there are as many variations of expression of that phenomenon as there are personalities.

QUESTIONS

The third chapter of Genesis relates how God came into the garden at the cool of the day to commune with Adam and Eve. I have often wondered what those walking talks consisted of. Did Adam and God discuss together Adam's naming of all the animals (2:19-20)? How did they communicate? What was the language used? Did God teach Adam and Eve a language system similar to one of the over 6000 languages in the world today? If so, was that language the one language extended to all peoples until Babel, when the record says God implanted other languages into people's minds so as to divide them—force them to come together in smaller groups of linguistic comprehension—in order to separate them from their unacceptable behavior when all mankind was using the same tongue (Gen. 11:1-9)? I have many questions, but answers would be mainly supposition. That about which I am convinced, however, is God's desire to make a creature enough like Himself so social interaction would be possible as was evident in the Garden of Eden before what is known as the Fall of Man.

What is God's "thing" with language? Is there a relationship between God's communication in the garden that was interrupted by the first couple's disobedience and God's prohibition of a common language at Babel and what God did in a strange way with language at Pentecost? Was Pentecost supposed to be "a way out of the woods" from the confusion at Babel? If yes, why did He still do something quite confusing for so many—or, both clear and confusing, both understood and so misunderstood? Why does He like riddles? Is He always going to do that with us? Is He hiding something so the "wrong ones won't find it"—like in Matthew 13—won't attempt it, manipulate it, and pollute it by their analytical minds?

What is God expecting of humans, the only creatures seemingly given unique ability to talk to Him in prayer and meditation? What is there so powerfully divisive about language, whether at Babel or Pentecost? If He wanted to give us a special prayer language that the apostle Paul spoke about to the Corinthians, why did He make the reasons for His choice so ambiguous in nature that it has been the source of much division in the Church since the third century after the resurrection? Oh my, such questions. I want to explore them.

My graduate studies in Minnesota allowed me the privilege to have been challenged by great professors such as Wm. Howell in Persuasion; by Ernest Bormann in Group Dynamics and Rhetoric; by George Shapiro in Communications Theory and the Psychological Dimension of Human Speech. It was then I first understood how the study of persuasion is an evaluative tool to study the Bible. But I soon took warning that the secular world of a great university is set against both the concepts and experiences of the Scriptures.[60] I agree with L. T. Johnson that such studies have little appreciation for the biblical text or insight into the language of that era.[61]

So, we have begun to expose the goal of this study for quest of this author to probe the relationship of some of the elements in the relatively new academic discipline of Communications Theory to one of the most divisive issues in Evangelical Christianity—the issue of what *Pentecostals* call the "gift of tongues." That quest, however, in and of itself, cannot as a method of inquiry abide by all the expectations of Western understood boundaries of cognition like Bloom's Taxonomy of Learning in the Cognitive Domain or the almost sacrosanct Method of Science with which every Western educated child is inoculated—and which gave us the mind-set of Rationalism.[62]

The complexity of the issue is related to epistemology, the grounds of our knowing. One of the reasons for this is related to what some theologians call *Apophatic Theology*, or the way of "unknowing" or the *via negativa*.[63] "Apophatic theologians have long clarified that whereas God is infinite, human language is finite. Thus all attempts to define God fall short of capturing or seizing upon God as He is. Conceptual models, diagrams, and verbal descriptors may indeed help us understand something about God, but even the most brilliant of those expressions in no way exhausts the great "I Am," the timeless "Alpha and Omega." Simply put, God is utterly transcendent.[64]

Ah, but there's hope of some penetration! Perhaps not for complete understanding, but for certain progress toward **knowing** Him. I submit this journey is more Eastern than Western in many respects because the Bible is not a Western book but an Eastern one. (Most of the communication concepts here are Western, because my target audience is more probably from that part of this "global village.") The reader has already noted I will often refer to Africa and Asia in illustration and insight for added perspective. Communications Theory from the East is more communally based and less individually focused. Along with less emphasis on the individual in the Eastern tradition, verbal symbols (especially speech) is viewed with skepticism in favor of intuitive insight gained from direct experience. Note the contrast here; in the West, experience is generally suspect.[65]

The Bible makes clear that "tongues speech" was so common in the Early Church that no explanation of the term was necessary – Christenson

The issue is complex and some effort must be expended to make even modest gains in understanding. To understand the topic of glossolalia, to show God has intentionally chosen it because it seems foolish, will involve bridge building to anyone who has not experienced it. I am reminded, however, that bridge building is an honorable task for this was the plan of God in sending Jesus the Son in the Incarnation. Crossing the bridge is still a walk of faith, not by sight as the West so longs to do, but about which the East has less qualms.[66]

GOD COMMUNICATES IN MANY LITERARY AND ORAL FORMS

Gordon Fee says one of the important things about the human side of the Bible is the wide range of literary forms God uses to speak to us.

This is a reflection of the breadth of God's revelation and His readiness to use nearly every kind of human speech and literature in order to communicate His love and purposes to us. Thus we have narrative, histories, chronicles, law codes, dramas, poems (of all kinds), proverbs, prophetic oracles, parables, stories, letters, Gospels, and apocalypses...But look how God chose to speak His living Word—by Himself becoming man and living out a truly human life on planet earth in order to let us see what He is really like. So also He chose to speak His written Word through all the ordinary human channels in order to let us hear Him in our language.[67]

Language Related to Feelings and Thought

The Charismatic Lutheran pastor Christenson helps us here.[68] The Bible makes clear, from many passages, that "tongues speech" was so common and widely shared in the Early Church that no explanation of the term was necessary, says Christenson. It was as Bauer's Greek lexicon points out, a 'technical term': the original readers of Mark, Acts, and First Corinthians would know at once what was meant, from their own experience.

He continues:

> The essence of the phenomenon is this: The Holy Spirit gives the believer the power to speak a tongue or language which he has never before learned ...It is not enough simply to refute the misconceptions that speaking in tongues is 'gibberish' or 'ecstatic utterance.' The whole question of language should be looked at from another point of view.[69]

Christenson then gives Webster's standard definitions of "language." He notes the second definition of language is more closely related to our subject.

> "Any means, vocal or other, of expressing or communicating feeling or thought" (Webster). When we look at the second definition, however, we find a highly accurate definition of speaking in tongues. It defines language in terms of the speaker: Language is an expression of meaning in terms of feeling or thought. If speaking in tongues expresses the meaning of the speaker, then it is a language, according to this accepted definition.[70]

In our Western language courses, we only allow poets to use language so "loosely."

Semanticists and communicologists have for decades spoken of the relative little knowledge the average person has of the portion of common language that is not related to words, rather beyond words. J. Ruesch, R. Birdwhistle, A. Mehrabian, and E. T. Hall, all non-verbal specialists,[71] state language is composed of about 35 percent words (verbal) and 65 percent non-verbal (gestures, facial expression, vocal emphasis, pauses, etc.). Almost all our schooling is focused on the 35 percent and almost nothing is learned about the non-verbal, except in professional acting classes, etc. Christenson here quotes from Agnes Sanford's book, *The Healing Gifts of the Spirit*,[72] where she quotes a psychiatrist, when speaking of the gift of the Spirit, who said, "It can be a spiritual power entering into a person with such force that it reaches and touches something in the deep unconscious; whereupon the person speaks a language which the conscious mind does not know, but which this deep area of the unconscious does know."

Christenson then quotes Paul Tournier, the well-read Swiss author, from his book *The Meaning of Persons*.[73]

> Glossolalia, or speaking in tongues, which played such an important part then, and which is still found in some modern communities, appears to answer the need of the spirit to *express the inexpressible* (emphasis his), to carry the dialogue with God beyond the narrow limits of clearly intelligible language.

Christenson suggests tongues speech is a new band of "meaning."

> Purely intellectual utterances are only one band of the spectrum of meaning, as we have suggested. It is altogether reasonable that something as deep and intimate as our relationship with God should find expression in supra-rational utterance—utterance which would express shades of feeling and thought beyond the capability of ordinary speech. Yet to God, who can discern our innermost thoughts, these utterances would be perfectly understandable.[74]

Christenson then sums up the Greek term "glossa" that is either translated "tongue or language" (as in English we speak of one's mother tongue when we mean language): "Speaking in tongues is therefore speaking in a language—a language which expresses the deep feelings and thoughts of the speaker, in a language which God hears and understands."[75]

Language Learning Related to "Becoming a Child"

For an adult to learn another language well enough to be able to converse naturally and competently is very punishing on the human ego and requires a certain amount of "psychic cost" or payment. In my own experience, learning French as a 25-year old living away from America for the first time was a humbling experience. Leaving my culture where my position as a pastor of a small church gave me a considerable amount of psychic income, spending the first few weeks in an environment where American English was not understood left me feeling like an idiot. This experience was frankly shocking. A pastor generally gets to be one because he/she has a certain skill in communication. (There are some exceptions.) Signs and wonders were evident those first few weeks of language study. I made the signs and the French-speaking folks did the wondering! My verbal skills upon which I had been judged favorably in high school (even all the way to the state finals in memorized oratory, plus top grades in homiletics and speech in college) only made my total lack of public verbal skills in the new environment to let me crash the harder. To top it all off, my wife Dolly did better in grammar and writing skills in French than I did. Ego crisis! Jesus talked about this:

"The disciples of Jesus were again wondering who was the greatest in the

Kingdom of heaven. He called a little child and had him stand among them. And He said: *I tell you the truth, unless you change and become like little children, you will never enter the kingdom of heaven. Therefore, whoever humbles himself like this child is the greatest in the kingdom of heaven"* (Matt. 18:2-3).

PhDs are probably the last to easily learn to speak a new language as adults. Language learning has less to do with cognitive/cerebral skills as it does with affective attitudes. And the largest of these is the attitude about making mistakes. A child can say a word incorrectly, be corrected scores of times, and not suffer embarrassment. One might easily paraphrase the Scripture above with: " *I tell you the truth, unless you change and become like little children, you will never gain verbal linguistic proficiency in a new language."*

The work is really a matter of drills, learning to be flexible with the tongue, teeth, voice, nasal cavity, a habit of mimicry and a sharpness of hearing. There is very little intellectual content in language study. Everyone in the class is on the same level. The MA in English or the taxi driver with a sixth grade education are finally equal! In this unfamiliar setting some folks go into deep culture shock. Theologians who would much rather discuss the philosophy of language find they can't roll their tongues for the Spanish "r" or gargle the French "r." Professional teachers always criticize the pedagogical system of the school when they can't articulate the vowels they need to make. PhDs find fault with everything when they can't move the back of the tongue the way other people do. Doctors write letters home questioning their missionary call when the tones of pitch in the new language just don't come.

If language learners cannot learn to laugh at themselves, they'll never do well in a new language. Instead they'll disparage the culture, the language itself, or their instructors. Anything but the one saving ingredient. Jesus said it: "*whoever humbles himself, like this child..."* Are there not direct similarities to that which must be "given up" to abandon the tongue (mental agility, cognitive competence, communication skills) to the Spirit of God, so He can express praises to the Lord of heaven in an "unknown tongue"? "No way!" says the human spirit. "No way!" says the one whose adult identity is fixated on rewarded verbal skills in business or titled position. I am becoming increasingly convinced God loves/enjoys setting up a whole series of conditions that force us to abandon our logical means to know Him. Why? Because He made us with not only the capacity to reject Him but with the mental acuity to create, to improvise, to reason *and to reason ourselves right past the way to know Him simply.* Sounds like He's taking quite a risk with us, doesn't it! But without that risk, our eventual choice to submit, love and follow would be worthless. This is part of the "foolishness of God" we grapple with in this book.

From Oralness to Literacy

Some readers of the passage in Genesis chapter one, repeated in the first chapter of the Gospel of John, know from past studies or experience that the words "*In the beginning was the Word*" refer to God himself and to what He speaks, and178 *not* the written word. (It, of course, over time became written.) We have no record Jesus ever wrote anything except when He stooped to write in the sand when the Pharisees brought the adulterous woman to His classroom for their own brand of "show and tell." People living in either the Old or New Testament did not possess literacy by the masses as we know it today in North America, Europe, or in many Asian nations. The "scribe" was not only someone who was literate but was employed by many scores of people who were not, so he could write out the literary requirements or certain social functions for them. Yet today, in 60 percent of the world, its population would be classed as "illiterate" by our standards of print literacy. For these people getting the message across in writing is a big hurdle. Before the marvels of communicating by electrical means, the available channels of communication were drums, smoke signals, reflecting mirrors, cannon shots and lantern signals and were subject to severe limitations. In the *The Responsive Chord* Tony Schwartz speaks of the problem of communications by a pre-technological society as we know it today. Napoleon established a network of 224 line-of-sight semaphore stations spanning over 1000 miles. The coded message had to be repeated accurately at each station for the correct message to get through. The chance of an error was quite high.[76] In pre-Napoleon times writing was in manuscript form. Then came printing, then the telegraph, the telephone, and now the electronic communication revolution. It's hard for us to imagine a time when oral communication was the mode of exchange for over 90 percent of a given population.

The West Ignores Oral Literacy

Today we assume literacy (by that we mean print literacy—not oral literacy) is the highest form of communication. We invest heavily in schools, books and written records. We marginalize the non-literate. Great effort in missions activity is focused on literacy. Some confuse it with the Gospel, even though no one would minimize the value of literacy for its propagation. Some missionaries are guilty of bibliolatry—they know the Word better than they know its author. People do not need to be literate before they can become Christian.[77] Because knowledge is power, great emphasis is placed on getting knowledge. We prize the accumulation of knowledge, and the computer age often rewards sheer recall.

In a chapter on "Cultural Assumptions of Western Missionaries," Anthropologist Paul Heibert[78] describes how hundreds of years of print literacy makes us unconscious of how the other half of the world communicates. We assume they are like us. When we do our studies of the Word of God:

> We think that our studies of the Bible are unbiased, that our own interpretations of the Scriptures are the only true ones. It disturbs us, therefore, when we begin to discover that theologies are also influenced by culture...All human theologies are only partial understandings of Theology as God sees it. We see through a glass darkly.[79]

Emphasis on Knowledge Over Wisdom

Given an efficient writing system to store and retrieve information, it is not surprising that North Americans highly value knowledge... Often, however, this knowledge is divorced from life. University professors do not always live the best of lives. And in the church, faith is generally defined in terms of knowledge, not discipleship. To many of us, the lordship of Christ usually means giving mental and verbal assent to his deity, rather than living our lives in obedience to His commandments. Oral cultures, on the other hand, prize wisdom—the ability to deal with everyday issues for the good of the society and the individuals involved, the skill of making knowledge relevant to life.[80]

While Hiebert emphasizes that "sight" is preferred over sound in the West, author Schwartz describes our fixation on print literacy in terms of a focus on *lines.* For hundreds of years anyone who was not "literate" according to this definition was the object of discrimination. This increased the way our society valued the linear process. Our language, Schwartz says, shows a marked dependence on linearity in word choice that signifies clear thinking and even proper behavior. We teach our children to "toe the line ... keep in line... walk the straight and narrow." We also say someone who "follows a clear line of thought" is a good thinker. And if someone really understands another person, we say he can "read him like a book." Our logic has been the logic of print where one idea follows another. "Circular reasoning" is synonymous with unacceptable logic, and everyone knows the futility of "running around in circles."[81] Our linear bias, I contend, makes it difficult to understand people from preliterate auditory cultures where the spoken word is still the only word. As mentioned above, some biblical literalists are confused when they discover in John's gospel that *"In the beginning was the Word,"* was not the written Word as we now know it. This is an issue few Bible scholars address. Naturally, unless they have had the capacity for communicative dialogue with preliterate peoples or learn a "preliterate" language, they would be limited to comprehend its essence.

PRINT FOSTERS SYSTEMS

Print literacy encourages an emphasis on systems. To organize (systematize, create retrieval engines and databases) requires systems. This in turn fosters rational thought by divorcing ideas from feelings! Oral societies live with a constant direct tie to information and the feelings of those they interact with. No printed page carries the emotional impact of an oral presentation because of the lack of the non-verbal elements of communication, which accompanies the oral medium (such as **vocalics**—the impact of the voice on meaning; **kinesics**—the part that gestures and facial expression play on the total package; **occulesics**—the vivid effect of the use of the eyes in face-to-face dialogue; **haptics**—the communication of touch; **proxemics**—the communication of the use and abuse of personal space, etc, etc.).[82]

What Is Oralness?

Paul Hiebert (above) joins Tony Schwartz[83] and a more recent Canadian author, James K. A. Smith[84] (on whom I will draw on heavily below) concerning North Americans' preference to sight over sound, touch, taste, or smell as a fundamental issue of our world-view. You SEE, even "worldview" means the way we think, based on the word "see" and other similar phrases such as "I see" (meaning I understand), "Let's look at the situation," even "I read you loud and clear" (for hearing on the two-way radio), etc. Hiebert quotes Walter Ong who sees this Western emphasis on a visual world which had its roots in Greek philosophy:

> Plato's ideas launched the new world, the opposite of the old, which his attacks on the poets proscribed. The old [oral] world had made much of man's activities and of human struggle as the focus or axis of all reality. Where the old world had been warm and human, Plato's "ideas" or "forms"... were cold and abstract. The world had been mobile, and event-full, and its oral narrative was a swirl of exciting activity. In contrast, Plato's new ideas were motionless, a-historical; where the old view had held all knowledge in a concrete human setting, the new traced everything to the abstract, the other-worldly, the totally objective, the fixed, modeled on an immobile figure visualized on a motionless field.[85]

The crowning achievement of this predisposition was print literacy and, consequently, the attachment to the written word—whether in education, politics, law, or the religious world. Schwartz [86] claims North Americans have a 500-year literary bias. Soon after Gutenberg's printing press changed the world, orality became suspect by the industrialized world. However, the majority of the world's population, even in the twenty-first century, is "illiterate" and live in oral societies where what happens (real events) are the grist of cognition and social communicative interaction. This fact is hidden from North Americans and, in my experience in teaching communications for four decades, almost no one in my classes can describe or imagine the consequences of an oral/aural society and the significance of a complete language system in all its complexity and artistic dynamic that is not written. (In spite of the fact the students in class represent a minority in the world on this issue, they don't bother to attempt to understand people labeled "illiterate.") As a people, we have 'bought into' the myth that literacy makes us superior people—a part of our extreme ethnocentricity.

> **As a people we have bought into the myth that literacy makes us a superior people– a part of our extreme ethnocentricity.**

Oral societies are highly organized (surprise!) but in ways we can hardly fathom with the textual/literate mind. All peoples have similar building blocks to cognition, but they prioritize those blocks differently. Recall figure #1 above with the three concentric circles on this topic.[87] The mode is highly interactive between speaker and listener. One can't talk to a book (and expect a response) but one can interact with concrete human experiences told verbally and in his "hearing." Communication in oral societies is not in abstractions, or in a monologue between reader and the printed page, but in dialogue form—consequentially so much more personal. *Writing divorces a message from the messenger.*[88] We read and trust even if we know nothing about the author/writer. We thus use abstractions to form ideas and formulate dogma, independent of whether he/she who wrote the words is worthy of our trust. This happens rarely in orality where what is uttered is compared with the speaker's known personality and reputation. North Americans value print and assume it is the highest form of literacy.

And here lies one of the problems with "tongues" and prophecy and other charisms. They are not literate! They are oral expressions in communication under the inspiration of the Holy Spirit. A modern society fixated on literacy has great difficulty accepting their legitimacy. A literate society encourages rational thought even at the expense of feelings—in fact, feelings are generally seen as suspect and should be divorced from ideas.

Look what Plato and Aristotle, and subsequently Thomas Aquinas, have done to the New Testament model of life in the Spirit which was almost totally oral/aural oriented.

"Tongues" are a product of the oral/aural world, cannot be written down/systematized, or repeated. Like the manna of the OT, it cannot be stored; a "new" infusion is always needed! It cannot be predicted or "put in the bulletin or litany," thus they are perceived dangerous! The apostle Paul says when speaking in tongues, the mind is "unfruitful" (I Cor. 14:2) and tongues are often related to feelings. Biblically, glossolalia must be controlled by the community and its leaders. Sadly, those same leaders, in turn, often fear God's "inbreaking" unless that event can be *scheduled!* Glossolalia has been marginalized/prohibited by the ultra "literate" conservative modern Pharisees who have completely internalized words like "inerrant," "authorized," "systematized." (All those concepts are good in correct context, but when overemphasized in the context of the Holy Spirit, they quench the Spirit.) Paul the apostle said "*not to put out the Spirit's fire*" (I Thess. 5:19). Interesting this "fire" metaphor and how often it is repeated in the New Testament.

Harvey Cox shows a good diversification between Evangelical Fundamentalists and Pentecostals relating to the issue of the "literate" mind:

> I also learned that it is a serious mistake to equate Pentecostals with Fundamentalists. They are not the same. Fundamentalists attach such unique authority to the letter of the verbally inspired Scripture that they are suspicious of the Pentecostals' stress on the immediate experience of the Spirit of God. This should not be surprising. Text-oriented believers in any religion tend to be wary of mystics. However, this does not mean that Pentecostalism does not embody a complex of religious ideas and insights. It does. The difference is that while the beliefs of the Fundamentalists, and of many other religious groups, are enshrined in formal theological systems, those of Pentecostalism are imbedded in testimonies, ecstatic speech, and bodily movement. But it is a theology, a full-blown religious cosmos, an intricate system of symbols that respond to the perennial questions of human meaning and value. The difference is that, historically, Pentecostals have felt more at home singing their theology, or putting it in pamphlets for distribution on street corners. Only recently have they begun writing books about it."[89]

Pentecostals and Charismatics believe the renewal of the gifts of the Spirit in religious worship and mission is a return to the oralness of the original New Testament model (though most would not use this communication paradigm). Most of the early practitioners of this oralness (early twentieth century) were hoping to renew the religious medium where they already worshiped (like Martin Luther had hoped to do in the Roman Church), but instead were rejected and put out of the community. One must ask: How much of that earlier rejection is related to the same rejection and marginalization by traditional "literate and linear" Christian communities *now* (where only written creeds, liturgy and litanies are trusted) and are only too quick to reject any oral or spontaneous-oriented worship? What part of that rejection is related to a misunderstanding about oralness by literate minded churchmen and women?

A Plea to Re-examine

No one would question the value of "fixating" communication in written form where it can be stored, compared unchanged after hundreds of years, while oralness may quite easily be redefined or shifted in content. (But let's be serious—written accounts of anything can and are often changed by political [read religious]"editors.") Yes, literacy is extremely valuable—we can't go back. But we can examine what it has done to a valuable system, part of human communication still used by the majority of the world's peoples. And we might look at how our literary predisposition may have produced a built-in bias against spontaneous prayer language found in Acts 2 and 9 and 11, and I Corinthians 12-14, plus many other accounts in the New Testament record. Below, we will again pick up this vital topic with the contribution of James K.A. Smith. But first, think with me about the words non-rational and non-linear.

NON-RATIONAL, NON-LINEAR

In a paper given to the Society of Pentecostal Studies in its annual meeting (2002 - Lakeland, FL) Edmund Rybarczyk (quoted above) devotes his paper to the Romans 8:26 passage, "Expressing the Inexpressible: Tongues as Apophatic Speech," where he notes the paradoxical nature of glossolalia and believes God so intended it.

> ...Pentecostals might do better to simply embrace the paradoxical nature of tongues-speech. Praying with tongues and travailing (groaning) in prayer are both very non-rational and non-linear. This non-rational paradoxical charism is not only something given to the

Church for its edification, it is something by its very symbolic character ought to be tapped into for its depth and Spirit-driven impulse. To no small extent, the Pentecostal movement flourished because of—not in spite of— its non-linear and non-rational qualities.

Here Rybarczyk makes a rather poignant point:

Something vibrant, authentic, and Spirit-inspired has been sacrificed over the near-century long attempt to explain and define the paradox of tongues as a rational and indeed "normal" Christian phenomenon. It is not normal, anymore than was Jesus' death on a cross. And we should add, that is a good thing!...In their rabid rush to become rational Evangelicals, Pentecostals have forsaken the implications that a theology of tongues could have for the Church universal. In their historical debates with other Christians, Pentecostals have processed and re-processed glossalalia mostly as a lone element in Christian spirituality.[90]

"Right on!" says James Smith:

In this essay, I will argue that the early Christian community was a charismatic community which placed emphasis on *hearing* not reading. As such, early Christianity was not a religion of the Book, though it was certainly a religion of the Word. It was a community centered, not around scribes but prophets. In the history of the Christian community, a shift occurred whereby text received a privileged status and the original oral/aural and charismatic way of being was suppressed and oppressed and gradually declared to be defunct. This emphasis on writing(s) (or the privileged status of writings) confined revelation to a past epoch; 'scribalism'—the emphasis on the letter—planted the seeds which killed and quenched the ongoing revelatory ministry of the Spirit by silencing the prophets with the Canon... realized nearly two thousand years later in Protestant fundamentalism and conservative evangelicalism—textual communities *par excellence* (emphasis Smith's). [91]

Smith continues his insights about the *prophetic* role in the New Testament Church which was also a predominantly oral/aural community. He quotes Thomas Gillespie's work[92] who has observed that with the publication of the *Didache (1883),* a reassessment was required about the oral role of the prophet in the Early Church and not on the traditional offices of bishop, elder, and deacon that became so prominent from about the year 300 AD on. In the Early Church, the prophets were the 'hermeneuts of the Gospel interpreters of the kerygma –which was not textual but rather oral (even though certain texts were quoted).[93]

The early Apostolic Church was a prophetic community. It was also a predominately oral/aural community. "Faith, Paul would insist, comes by hearing (Rom. 10:17). He also asks: How shall they call upon this one whom they have not believed? And how can they believe without hearing?" (Note, he didn't say **reading**). "Nor did he say 'How can they preach without a **text**?'"[94]

During the 15 years we lived in West Africa, we saw the destructive forces of French colonialization and their language on the rich oralness of the Mossi and Ewe of Burkina Faso and Togo. In I Cor. 1 Paul asks: "Where is the scribe? Evidently not in the Church, as time and again the early Christians were reviled for being illiterate (agammatos) and ignorant (idiotes, Acts 4:13) as was Jesus Himself (Jn 7:15)." But this lack of scribes only signaled the fact that for the Christian community, faith was *hearing* the Word, which is not only **about** Christ but **is** Christ. "*It is precisely this oral way of being which I would propose, has been recaptured in the contemporary charismatic communities...Perhaps the oral nature of Pentecostalism is best captured in the emphasis on glossolalia, which cannot be written nor can it be repeated.*"[95]

LITERACY AS KNOWN TODAY WAS RARE IN BIBLE TIMES

It is vital that we establish the significance of oralness as the condition of normal communication as practiced in the culture in which our Bible, both Old and New Testaments, was written. **Once this becomes clear, my thesis and that of James Smith as it relates to the prophetic (glossolalia and other Holy Spirit gifts) in today's church will take on enormous proportions.** So let's see how we got to where we are in contrast to the Early Church and what determined its communication climate.

Print Literacy

Electronic technology today leads us away from dependency on "print" and simultaneously towards an increased fixation on how the "printing revolution" of the fifteenth century impacted us as communicators. Print has dominated our communication environment for the past 550 years. Beginning with Johannes Gutenberg (1440) the information most valued by Western societies has been communicated in a fixed form. Where once a person's "word" (meaning his spoken word) was his badge of honor, we now don't tend to believe anything until we see it in writing. Schwartz says, "All preserved knowledge, as well as those pieces of information that achieved high status throughout the society (e.g., laws) were recorded in print. The linear process, by which information was translated into print, took on a status unto itself. Oralness is now of much less value and often called 'hearsay.' If 'seeing is believing' then listening and speaking are of much less value."[96]

Much of current missionary work is centered in cultures where oral/aural communication still predominates. Actually, less than half of the world's population is "print literate" by our standards. Good Christian witnesses must find a way to organize their "fan of perception" in a very different mode from that of mono-cultural North Americans if they wish to be effective in those contexts.

THE TEXTUALIZATION OF OUR FAITH

In this section of Communications Theory and its relation to God's mode of communication with believers today, it is important, I submit, that we pursue this issue farther. Let us now examine James Smith's thesis from above in the light of the Ross chart.

James K.A. Smith, a POAC scholar from Canada, asks the following pertinent question: "Is Christianity a religion of the book? That is, were the early Christians a people of the book or rather a people of the Spirit? Was the early Christian community a literate/textual/book community or rather an oral/aural community?"[97] Smith argues that the early Christian community was a Charismatic community, which placed emphasis on **hearing** not reading. It was a community centered not on scribes but on prophets. He argues that our literary bias has facilitated our acceptance of Fundamentalism and Evangelicalism's predisposition to consider the text and Canon of the Scriptures so important that it crowds out the necessity (or possibility) for God to supernaturally talk to us by His in-breaking gifts of the Spirit. He calls this exaggerated emphasis on **what is in print** the **textualization of our faith.**[98]

What Difference Does It Make? Who Cares—Oral or Textual?

Both oral communications and written communications activate about the same response and result in the human communication system, no? Both involve encoding the message by the source and decoding the message by the receiver. So why the fuss? This writer, with the help of good sources, will attempt to show the result is not entirely the same as will be seen. Hint: the difference has less to do with the actual physics of human speech (written or oral) as with **how each is valued by a given community.** James Smith proposes that an "oral" way of being (the horizon or worldview of a people) has been recaptured by contemporary Charismatic communities. He credits Steven Land also for his seminal work on Pentecostal Spirituality.[99]

> 'Speaking in Tongues'...is a practice which paradigmatically and dramatically underscores the oral-narrative character of Pentecostalism. Glossolalia became an integral element of Pentecostal 'oral-narrative liturgy' because that which is most characteristically human and constitutive of human community (i.e., language) required a new speech incapable of being co-opted by the routinizing of church bureaucracies or worldly regimes. [100]

This writer sees this element as a question of control and power, an idea developed in other chapters. Smith hints at this concept when he says 'tongues' is incapable of being co-opted precisely because it refuses to be written or repeated. Pentecostal communities, he says, mistrust theology and have a hesitancy to keep historical records. "There is a sense of the faithful which feels that by recording and articulating, something of the freshness of the Spirit—the *rhema* (as opposed to *logos*) word is lost by being domesticated. Writing is akin to hoarding the manna, which will only rot if one attempts to retain it. (See Exodus 16) Instead, one ought to wait for fresh rain from heaven each morning."[101]

In my youth, I can recall speakers and leaders of the church referring to King David's numbering of the soldiers in II Samuel 24, which displeased God, as an example of how too much reliance on "what can be counted" is against the "spirit of one who walks in the Spirit of God's leading and trust."

Smith draws on what he calls the "ground breaking work" of Brian Stock to help answer the question posed by this section: What difference does it make?[102] Stock's focus is on the paradigm shift in worldview impacted by a change from orality to literacy as a social value, which brought about momentous implications. "Texts thereby emerged as a reference system both for everyday activities and for giving shape to many larger vehicles of explanation."[103] These authors clearly show that it's not the presence of texts in a given society (whether they exist or not) but the *status* of those texts within the community as it goes about the task of government and legal issues. In the historical study of how folks communicated a thousand years ago, Latin words like *capitulate* (written laws and ordinances) and *bannum* (the spoken word of the king) are significant. (I know this sounds pedantic, but this is significant, as I believe you will agree.) Stock and Smith believe it was the case in the Middle Ages that texts existed (still rare—remember, no printing press yet), but their mere existence didn't make them powerful at first. The *capitulate* were the laws handed down by the rulers of Europe and were in manuscript form. They were **not** authoritative texts because the authority rested with the oral word (*bannum)* of the emperor or sovereign. Even though texts existed, their status was derivative. Texts were reminders of the power of the presence of the king. About the eleventh century, states Smith, communities became "textualized" (Smith's term to describe what occurs in the shift from an oral/aural worldview to a literate/textual mode).[104]

Again—What Difference Does It Make?

This difference totally gutted the power of the Moro Naba (emperor) of the Mossi in Burkina Faso, West Africa. There had been a continual line of emperors since the thirteenth century for this noble people. Witness the power of one's conceptualization of speech that can be total and can become totalitarian! The French colonialists came to Burkina (at that time the country was called "La Haute Cote d'Ivoire) about 1910. With them came the French insistence of the superiority of their language to all others. (This exists to this day.) With them also came the Catholic priesthood and began the first educational systems in both the fundamentals of literacy and Catholic doctrine and Christianization. By the time I personally witnessed the power of "l'alphabetisation" it was 1960. By this time the European system of literacy was well established. Although only six percent of the whole population was "literate" in writing and texts, they had all the political power and had systematically deposed the real power structure of 700 years of emperor, paramount chiefs, sub-chiefs and a great amount of the social place of elders.

From an American mission agency, our understanding of language was somewhat different than the French, but still heavily tilted toward the value of "our" definition of "literacy." We wanted the Mossi to be print literate, in *their language* as well as French. So we learned Mori, the Mossi language. Our early missionaries learned it, translated the Bible in it and taught reading and writing to thousands of Nationals so they could also read God's Word. The French totally disavowed the vernacular's value. ("Ces langages vont disparaitre"—These languages will disappear.) They haven't. In these more than 40 years, I only know one or two French Protestant missionaries who could (or would) minister in Mori. In my opinion, this difference between French and American missionaries has less to do with linguistic ability than *attitude* about language and writing and grammar.

Dr. Jack Deere, a former professor at Dallas Theological Seminary and one time proponent of ultra-dispensationalism, speaks of his own discovery of this "textualization" in his own life.

> In the process of getting theologically trained and becoming a seminary professor, I developed an intense passion for studying God's

> Word. I found myself loving the Bible more than I loved the author of the Bible. I was caught in this trap for more years than I would like to remember...It took me too long to learn that knowing the Bible is not the same thing as knowing God, loving the Bible is not the same thing as loving God, and reading the Bible is not the same thing as hearing God.[105]

Is it possible to hear from God apart from His Word? Many say no. An even larger percentage of believers today say yes. However, those who say yes quickly affirm that when God speaks today, He speaks to confirm Scripture or gives inspiration that agrees with, but never contradicts the Word of God as known in the Canon. We have very few accounts in the New Testament, which enlighten us about the actual "order of service" as practiced by the Early Church. One of the most complete is the account in 1 Corinthians 12-14. Here is a description of the expectations of a normal worship service in Corinth. In that context, the role of prophets was a part of that expectation, an important part. Those with verbal gifts (tongues, interpretation of tongues, prophecy, words of wisdom and knowledge) played an essential role in the community, which waited to hear the Lord speak (all under the examination and judgment of the body of believers—see 1 Cor. 14:26-33). Orality, then, as in much of the world today, was what the New Testament community practiced. This oral culture in which our Scriptures were first given by word of mouth and. subsequently, written down (sometimes scores of years later) is a world unknown to us and has been for hundreds of years—except for the five percent of our population in North America that we term illiterate.[106]

In my experience with two preliterate peoples and languages (Mori and Ewe of West Africa), I've found while they are underdeveloped with print literacy (only 10 to 20 percent "literate" in the 60s and 70s), they were masters at non-verbal communication which augments the effectiveness of their oral communication.

I invite you to think of Ross's chart and the feedback line of signs, symbols, etc. Our print literacy fixation causes us to be almost "illiterate" to the non-verbals everyone gives off in all cultures, but few in our society know how to effectively interpret them—even if aware of their existence! Think of the last time you endured a speaker who never looked at the audience, as if you didn't exist, and paid no mind to audience feedback, to what you were "giving off" during the speech, message or address. Too many Christian pulpits are great examples of this travesty of communication skills.

In the history of the Christian community, a shift occurred whereby texts (reading/writing/literature) received a privileged status and the original oral/aural and Charismatic way of being was suppressed and oppressed and gradually became untrustworthy. (The Princetonian Cessationists have well documented their arguments on this premise.) This emphasis on writing and the privileged status of writing confined Revelation to a past epoch where the emphasis was on the letter. Carthage and Smith believe the seeds of literalism were the seeds that killed and quenched the ongoing revelatory ministry of the Spirit by silencing the prophets with the Canon. "Protestant fundamentalism and conservative evangelicalism are textual communities *par excellence*."[107]

The authors go even farther when they state: "It is precisely this textualism of evangelical theology which undermines the Pentecostal experience of continuing revelation."[108]

The more textual a society, the less its people can tolerate ambiguity with which the Bible is so replete. I had to learn a "non-textual" vernacular language to discover this truth.

NAMING—LIFE FORCE

One of the reasons for the West's misunderstanding about much of the 2/3rd World's use of ambiguity instead of open frank communication is their reluctance to *name or noun* something. Let's look at the linguistic etymology of the power of words from the chief or emperor in traditional Mossi culture.[109]

An elder or chief has "mouth" (*Nore* in the Mori language). "Mouth" means authority/power that refers to the power of his oral speech—not written language because the first 36 emperors couldn't read or write in French or Mori. The words "naaba" (chief) and "naam" (ritual and supernatural power) are related. The "power" of a simple knife is determined if it has "mouth" or not. A sharp knife has "mouth"! A sharp knife has more power than a dull one. The traditional West African ascribes an awesome and even religious significance to the power of words. The African divides the world into categories of forces. The highest force would be the force of *nommo* (the special "word" which is significant to this explanation). On a lower level are forces that cannot act of themselves, but are activated only by the command of *nommo* (a word of power). Here we have plants, animals, minerals, tools, furnishings, etc. Many of these objects are seen to be magically imbued with a life-force that is "congealed" and waiting for a command of the magic word of a thinking person (the person who has command over *nommo*). The congealed forces can do nothing of themselves; they have no will of their own. Even a poison is not potent until it receives the oral command.[110]

Important: In the hierarchy of forces, *nommo* (spoken word) holds the highest place. Even procreation is not accomplished merely by sperm, but by sperm and word. For the Mossi, a baby is not a "real person" until he/she is officially "named." (For many West African tribes I know, a baby will not be named definitively until it can speak.) By "naming," a tooth becomes an amulet, a carved piece of wood becomes an image. Thus in all Africa, all sorcery is *word*. Since the word has all power, everything one says is binding. There is no "harmless" or casual word. (Think of the added significance to Africans the words of Jesus on this theme: "For by your words you will be acquitted, and by your words you will be condemned" [Matt. 12:37] and also the creation account where the words—"And God said...let there be..." [Gen. 1].)

The French changed all that in Burkina Faso. Only now, those who had power of *word* were those who had understanding of knowledge as pieces of information in a printed fixed form with squiggles of ink following one another, left to right, on lines that proceed down a page.[111] In so doing, they have robbed the Mossi culture of its vast pool of ancient knowledge encapsulated in proverbs, aphorisms, and legends. James Smith, drawing on Brian Stock, avows that our "literal" world and its high priority on print literacy has "stolen" much of the authority ("mouth") that exists in the Bible and transferred it all to the written text of the Bible which he defines as "textualization."

This textualism, started by the Early Church (after the year 300 AD) and more recently by the Evangelical (and increasingly Pentecostal) world is detrimental to the gifts of the Holy Spirit given by the words of Jesus, with the intent to empower the believer for the task of evangelization of the world.

I wish to make bold the essence of Smith's thesis with my own experience of watching the insidious power of transferring the focus of speech's power from orality to text-literate. I would not hold that a society can return to an earlier state and become "illiterate," but that consideration be given to the damage occasioned by the all too prevalent "black or white," two-valued orientation that Western society inherited from Aristotle and strive to recognize the value of embracing not an "either-or" mentality but a "both-and" frame of reference. Both can live together in peace and mutual benefit.

Let us now review in the light of the lesson from Africa:

In this **shift:**

Texts are no longer understood as records but as 'sites' where facts are 'embodied' rather than simply recorded.[112]

The written is no longer merely recorded but now has dictated the principles of coherence and inner meaning.[113]

As in West Africa and over 50 percent of the world, when textualization happens, the non-literate become *illiterate*; and as literacy becomes identical with rationality, the illiterate become the irrational.[114]

All of life becomes a text, the oral/aural is pressed into service of writing...viewed through the lens of a *text*.[115]

A Shift in Source of Power

Now, **texts** become the authority instead of the words of the king. The people love the written 'laws' more than the earlier authoritative words of the ruler. Smith, quoting Stock, makes a final clarification:

> Texuality, then is something different than literacy; that is, a community may possess and use texts but not yet be a textual community...the issue is not one of *use* but one of *status*. A textual community is one that accords primary status to texts and the lens through which all of life is viewed.[116]

I have argued in other chapters how the effect of Aristotelian philosophy on Western society was a major influence on our linearity and conceptual mode of thought. Smith here submits that evangelicalism (via evangelical theology) is a textual community and, as such, marginalizes and suppresses the orality of the Pentecostal tradition. "A Pentecostal evangelical theology is a house divided against itself."[117] He next steps on a virtual "land mine" of controversy: For many reasons God's revelation should not stop just because the "Canon" was decided. He claims the Bible is a testimony that the King is alive and is a magnificent reminder of the imperial presence, **not** a substitute for it.[118]

Without professing to be a professional student of Communication Theory, Smith none-the-less strikes a vital nerve to the whole issue of tongues, prophecy and the supernatural nature of revelation. In my focus on the seeming 'foolish' choice of God, for glossolalia, so evident in Scripture (like Jack Hayford puts it: "Jesus prophesied it, the Father intended it, the Holy Spirit enabled it, and the church received it,"[119] I am impressed Smith believes the prophetic role of God's intention is that revelation should not stop; that the evangelical world's need for "textualization" has frozen God's revelation in time. (This process started very early in the apostolic church, long before the word Evangelical was known.) Smith would encourage one to believe that the same God who miraculously guarded the compilation of the Canon would continue, through the editing and control of the Body of Christ (which the Pauline Epistles exemplify) and thus continues to empower and infuse His Church with continuing revelation.

Looking through the lens of Communications Theory: I submit God still wants to use humankind in the *incarnational model of His part/Our part* and *that* not only in our part of interpretation of what the Christian world calls the Canon of Scripture. I specifically focus on that which refers to the duet (God and Man) of seeking those who will "risk" the chance of error (the requirement of faith) to hear from Him in prophetic utterance **as an extension of His Word—as an amplification of His Word, and using the local congregation of Spirit empowered believers as the "editing committee" of this glorious and fresh in-breaking of His power and direction and encouragement and healing and growth.** The worlds of Christendom and secular alike may call this foolishness, but it is a wonderfully crafted system of avoiding the trap of "literalism and legalism of print" that is so ubiquitous in our modern world that we don't even know, or wish to know, of the ancient matrix of communication in which our Scriptures were spoken and recorded.

When Will We Trust the Holy Spirit?

It looks to me like the cessationists put the cork in the bottle of the supernatural (the Reformers, and later B. B. Warfield and the Princeton gang among others), so the textualizers of inspiration made the Canon to be more than a model to emphasize faith and truth in the guidance of the Spirit! Why would God stop miracles any more than stop revelation *in accord* with what is already written? It's His nature to continue both in response to "risky faith" and obedience to the Ascension Mandate of Jesus—the Living Word. Can we trust the Jesus who sent the Holy Spirit? Evidently not yet!

My individual world has been impacted by two preliterate languages (called vernaculars). If revelation can only come from a 'text,' then a whole people (in particular the Mossi and the Ewe—and untold hundreds of others) are excluded from revelation until they can read in their own mother tongue (or heaven forbid—they are taught a "sacred language" like Latin or Arabic or Ge'ez or *English*). Think how parochial is that thought! Yes, we do translate the Holy Scriptures and teach believers to read and write—so they **can** have this miraculous revelation. But, couldn't the same Holy Spirit which we believe protected and preserved the words, allowing the Canon of Scripture, give revelation *before literacy AND after literacy?* I will continue this subject below after we have explored more on Communications Theory itself.

Let's Be Honest!

One would argue—"Oh think of the error the 'oralists' would fall into without being able to read the written text."

Response: would they stray **any farther** from unity of belief than the

20,780 distinct Christian denominations[120] who compete (and some hate each other), who do not agree on Scripture, all having *interpreted the written Word?* I've fellowshipped with the different Independent African Church group leaders—with the Independents in Indonesia, with the underground church Movements in both China and Ethiopia. Conclusion: There are brothers and sisters in Christ's Body with whom I can't totally agree but, none-the-less, prove to me The Lord of the Harvest is not nearly as concerned about orthodoxy as we are! The Scriptures teach me that God says anyone who seeks Him will find Him. I don't understand it all; I too have perplexing questions; I wish everyone believed like I do, but I only know I want less and less to do with the "fighting fundies" (whether Pentecostal or Evangelical or Roman Catholic) who are content to be modern Pharisees tied up in bibliolatry and hypocritical piety. They are stuck on an **evolved print-literacy bias and hyper textuality.** They don't want any part of a Holy Spirit they can't *predict and control.* They are just like the branch of psychology known as the "Behaviorists." They say: "Show me the reinforcement schedule and I can predict and control human behavior."

The Lord of the harvest is not nearly as concerned about orthodoxy as we are!

My Prayer: *Dear God, deliver me from the false piety of the professional religious that have somehow morphed in every age and seemingly on every continent. And yet, it's only their ideas from which I want separation. Many of them are my brothers and sisters, not my enemies. Give me a generous heart, not one of superiority or triumphalism. May I believe they too have a role to play in your Kingdom. Amen.*

Orality Is Not Linearity

I want to further illustrate to the reader this topic about which few Westerners can even perceive—due to a lack of experience to comprehend an oral/aural society. I don't intend by that to be pejorative about someone not having this privilege. The honor of having learned the Mori language (of Burkina Faso) and Ewe (of Togo) has given insight into the preliterate mind and social organization of these honorable people, their great intelligence and ethical morality. Many of these noble tribesmen have since entered into the "literate" world of the French language the West prizes so highly.

Many tribes on the West African savannah use a special round drum made from the hollowed out, gourd-like plant called a calabash. These drums (called a **bendere** in Mori) vary in size from 12 to 18 inches. The circular hole cut in the top of the round gourd is covered with a goatskin held on by leather straps, which are fastened at the bottom with an iron ring. The drum requires much skill to play it properly. A particular "finger slap" must be employed using the full hand and action of the wrist and arm. This gives the proper percussive energy necessary to maximize the excellent auditory potential from the dimensions of a round sphere. Traditionally, only the members of the drummer's clan were allowed to play these instruments. A second style of drum (a **lunga**) was also used all over West Africa. It is a two-headed drum strung with rawhide strings over a hollowed-out hourglass-shaped narrow wooden log and held under the arm to vary the drum's pitch of over an octave. Most Westerners are amazed to discover that African peoples can use the drums to talk to each other, send messages over long distances (their own telegraph system), drum out a code understandable to the average citizen yet, when desired, drum out a more secret code understood only by the chief and the members of his court. The writer has spent many hours conversing with drummers about their craft. Electronic recordings were made of actual cadences while employing a simultaneous oral translation by another drummer who put into an African vernacular language (Mori) the "content" of what the drummer was sounding.

I came to an amazing and disturbing discovery. I could not understand "drum talk" until I could shift my mind away from the literal, linear, print organized orientation of my European languages (English and French). I had been so programmed by the ABCs, whose letters make up words which must be placed in the correct syntax (word order) and predictability that I chafed at the drummer's inability to drum according to *my* rules. Thus I discovered my capacity to misunderstand drum talk was phenomenal. I found myself trying to twist and turn and "literalize" segments of auditory symbols (drum speech) to my system of cognition—of which I was a prisoner. Now for the local folks, drum speech *does* have order and symmetry and makes sense. I found it *non-precise* in the extreme. The message is more a general impression whose essence (content) must be "filled in" by the receiver. It is not that the specifics are withheld from the listener, but simply that *the specifics are not the only essence of the message.*

All this reminds me that as a communicator, I make the same mistake of the disciples of Jesus when they took too literally the words of Jesus (Mark 8:14-21). In this passage Jesus accuses them of having eyes and ears but not using them. L. M. Hussey describes the disciples' fault and, at the same time, defines much of Western man's weakness in understanding the realm of the Spirit of God. "The disciples set about to torture a literal significance from phrases first coined to blast utterly a literal intent."[121]

Drum talk is a lot like speaking a language under the inspiration of the Spirit of God. And both are like using a piece of smoked glass to view an eclipse of the sun. *It conceals in order to reveal.*

This "tongues speaking" branch of the modern church, worldwide, is the fastest growing segment inside Christianity. From an obscure and much maligned beginning less than one hundred years ago, it has become the largest theological branch of Protestant Christianity (650,000,000). In spite of its imperfections and sometimes excesses, it has become a theological block second only in size to the Roman Catholic Church. Even inside the "mother" church has come an energizing renewal, marked by tongues and other gifts of the Spirit which, until now, is still growing inside the Catholic Church. These folk, loyal to their roots, call themselves Charismatic Catholics.[122]

They would be an even larger group but for the opposition to their "excesses" as judged by certain regional bishops and some local parish priests. Those members who are harshly opposed most often join a local Charismatic church inside Protestantism.[123]

"The Bible is so Unscientific"

I sometimes like to "rattle the cage" of students and/or congregations in my country by the statement: "The Bible is not a Western book; it is an Eastern book." So much of Christian theology has come from the West and is of great benefit to Christendom in all areas of the world. But in my opinion, the West often ignores the fact that Christianity springs from the same geographical and thus cultural matrix as do most of the world's great religions. The Bible is replete with dreams and visions and inclinations expressed by very "unscientific" people who have a much greater trust in man's spiritual/emotional side. The West is quite ignorant of how it rejects the outside-of-awareness, mystical/intuitional character of early Christianity as we see it in the Gospels and Epistles of the New Testament.

The reason this area of consideration is relevant to the thesis of the book should be obvious, but for most in the Western mind-set, it is not. This segment will explore why the Western mind, a product of Greco-Roman thought processes (meaning making), has often so violently rejected what now a over half a billion Christians have accepted.

VISUAL IMAGERY VS CONCEPTS: THE TYRANNY OF ARISTOTLE[124]

The Bible is a product of the Holy Spirit filtered through the Eastern mind. As a consequence, the Bible continues to speak in practical, everyday (many time earthy) terms and illustrations.[125] God's Word is full of narration, poetry and historical events. Actually, it contains precious little conceptual thinking and abstractions that are so highly praised in the industrialized world. When Hellenistic thinking began to invade Europe, from which our culture springs, its love of philosophical contemplation was highly influenced by Plato, Aristotle, and later Greek philosophers. This created in Western speakers and writers a great authority for precision deduced from logical propositions. The deductions were then placed in logical order and systematized. An example would be how A. L. Drummond describes the European mind as loving deep conceptual precision in thought "because they cannot tolerate not receiving definite, precise and conclusive answers to all questions."[126] Here is the point of departure between East and West and the intersection at which Western communicators have traditionally encountered much cross-cultural static with a great portion of the 2/3rd World. For Westerners life is logical and all their training runs towards "exactitude." This is poor preparation indeed for the truth of life about which G. K. Chesterton wrote in 1924. Many authors have written about "grid thinking" which has so influenced the Western mind and American Protestantism. Where does this communication bent toward precision originate?

Communicologists cannot talk about where we are and where we came from without referring to Aristotle. Many philosophers, linguists, and semanticists[127] postulate that the beginnings of a great portion of the way Westerns think and communicate are traceable to Aristotle's three basic laws of logic that are detailed elsewhere. The critical one is the second: *The law of the excluded middle:* Everything is either A or non A.[128]

Don Wardlaw states:

> Church fathers from Origen to Chrysostom while imbued with the mind of Christ exegeted and preached with the mind of Plato and Aristotle reflecting Greek philosophy and rhetorical style. This sermonic form persisted through the Western European advance of Christendom continuing on to the American continent and becoming the homeletical style so typically symbolized by 'three points and a poem.' Sounding like a debate, preaching in the West has for centuries sounded as if the preacher were making a case in court. As if *logos* were apologia. Preaching, per se, has meant marshalling an argument in logical sequence, coordinating and subordinating points by the canons of logic, all in a careful appeal to the reasonable hearer.[129]

The "canons" of Western logic, however, are ill-equipped to penetrate the cognitive expectations of non-Western countries where the majority of missions activity takes place. In his seminal work on Cross-Cultural Communications and the Christian faith, professor David Hesselgrave provides a caveat for those who would simply overthrow the tyranny of Aristotle.[130] He argues we should not be disparaging of the method of critical thinking and analysis that has so benefited the West in its contribution to the world. What is regrettable is this very critical thinking often hinders a missionary from easily transmitting the message of the gospel in the 2/3rd World.

We can mistake theology for revelation... and insist on our conclusions even where the Bible does not speak plainly... we can communicate our theological systems and communicate in the manner of our theologizing rather than communicate the message of the Bible itself and in the manner of Biblical revelation. When we do so, missionary communication becomes foreign in the third world—not foreign because it is Christian, but foreign because it is western. In other words, missionary communication seems lifeless, and altogether too theoretical not because it is Biblical, but because it is not Biblical enough. The Bible itself is alive and speaks in practical, down-to-earth terms.[131]

Wardlaw, warning about the same domination from our Greco-Roman heritage, states:

> In the 20th century—most American preachers of Aryan decent have modeled their preaching on the sermon as argument... Narration itself is allowed to work only within the carefully defined limits of the anecdote, the historical allusion, or the illustration enlisted to make a point or to win the argument—...The Greeks have stolen into homiletical Troy and still reign.[132]

Wardlaw continues his plea that preaching needs new shapes and that these should follow the shape found in the scriptural passage from which the message is inspired. He quotes the poignant comment of James Thurber who once said, "The trouble with books about humor is that they get it down and break its arm." Too many sermons get scriptural texts down and break their arm rather than allowing the text, like humor, to be itself in its own medium.[133]

COLLIDING WORLDS (UNSCIENTIFIC, CONTINUED)

The scene is West Africa, the days are enormously hot and hostile. Dust from the Sahara desert filters down through the air everywhere. The evenings are beautiful as the burning yellow ball in the sky descends, casting delicate pastel colors on the landscape. Suddenly, it is night. The dry air cools rather quickly and those of us accustomed to more temperate climates find this a good time to work and study and visit.

On one such full moonlit night my short-wave radio told me of the escapades of the US astronauts as they actually (real time) walked and cavorted on the moon. I had been reading for weeks about this important space shot which most of the modern world was watching via television. A large portion of what we call the preliterate world had also been listening to their transistor radios and had been contemplating it, even if not clearly understanding. And such it was on the night of one of the early moon landings. Gathered around me in the darkness were many African friends and neighbors I had come to know and love. We sat with our backs against the warm mud bricks, which had retained the heat of the day's horrible sun. We sat looking at the full moon. In the distance drumming and dancing could be heard. Our conversation drifted from the usual topics to what I had recently heard on the radio from a short-wave station in Europe. It described strangely clad men walking on the surface of the bright ball we could all see from where we were sitting.

I began to explain about the force of gravity (no easy task in an African vernacular, which does not contain much sophisticated scientific jargon). I tried to tell about the special car created at great cost so the astronauts could cover a great distance on the moon. The Africans were amazed at what mankind has been able to do. They shook their heads. Two-thirds world people often wonder how other nations can be so advanced technologically while they seem to be left so far behind, yet, were not these people around me human beings just like those walking on the moon? If one of them would say to me: "You told us that man can go to the moon. I am a man; send me." How could I explain to him all he would need to do and learn to prepare for a moonwalk? How could I tell him that while he has a head, two feet, two hands, two eyes and a nose, just like the men walking on the moon, he is lacking many things, which would take a long, long time for him to learn? Would he be willing to persevere, even if someone were willing to finance it for him? Would he have the capacity to learn all that was needed? Could he accomplish the enormous task of someday walking on the moon? In comparison to the sophisticated, competent moonwalker, isn't my African friend, who has never attended "formal" school, really like someone from another philosophical world? Not less a person and possessing as much potential for learning and growth, perhaps as the moonwalker. Not inferior, but drastically disadvantaged by being deprived of the educational system in early youth that was a prerequisite for the astronaut.

One is reminded of the words of the Apostle Paul where he talked about the natural human being not receiving the things of the Spirit of God, for they are spiritually discerned and in its natural state humanity cannot really perceive correctly what is a "God Thing" (I Cor. 2:14).

How do you explain the relationship of experience and belief to any given believer, or even a theologian, that there is a realm of reality—a consciousness that he/she may have never touched? His specialization has itself excluded him from easily perceiving it—because it is **outside** his "fan of perception." He may have habitually (and accidentally?) attenuated a part of his own God-given capacity by the very nature of his learning and experience. Could the education, which led him through linearity (Western cognitive processes), have excluded another way of "knowing"?

Now, let me tell *such* a person that there exists a realm of "knowing" by the help of God's Spirit, where it is possible to "unhitch" the usual way of *understanding*. This task may be akin to telling the African sitting near me in the dark that, though his is physically like the moonwalker, he lacks many learned skills. He is not an inferior being, like Apartheid told the world for decades. In the world of the Spirit, he may even have an advantage! He has never been "inoculated" with the world of Aristotle and Thomas Aquinas, the matrix of so much of what is Western. Let no one despair, however. Christ said, "He that seeks, finds" (Luke 11:10). Increasing knowledge of the Spirit (it's a progression) comes to those who are first born of Him, then seek to learn to "walk in Him." If one is forced to conform solely to the paradigms of the intellect that filter experience only through the gatekeepers of past experience, knowledge, attitudes, values, etc. (as in the Ross chart above) of one's perceptual field, then coming to a new and growing cognitive world of the Spirit, would be limited to traditional equations—as beneficial as they might be in the secular contexts.

Increasing knowledge of the Spirit (it's a progression) comes to those who are first born of Him, then seek to learn to "walk in Him".

Upside-Down Wisdom

The Apostle Paul, the one writer in the New Testament responsible for more books than any other, makes a decided contribution to this section on Communications by writing to the new Christians in the Roman city of Corinth. (Corinth was known for its commerce, its vice, and its love of "Sophia" from the Greeks.) The apostle is being criticized by the sophists in the congregation for not speaking 'sophisticated' enough for their fine minds. Here are his words in defense of his choice of communication style: "Christ did not send me to baptize, but to preach the gospel—not with words of human wisdom, lest the cross of Christ be emptied of its power." Gordon Fee says that almost certainly all the language in this 18-verse passage having to do with eloquence and persuasive **words** is also related to this theme.[134] The wisdom of speech, encoding from a superior rhetorical skill, chooses eloquent self-attracting complicated words that demonstrate excellency so admired by the few intellectuals who like to "dis" the unlearned and, in so doing, they empty the cross of its power. How is that? Because the message of the cross of Christ is upside-down with the world's wisdom and logic. Paul rejects wisdom (Sophia) as a rhetorical device because in its presentation it overshadows the essence of the whole plan of the universe which makes an upside-down, impossible joke (in the eyes of the worldly wise) of Christ's death. Man's perceptual fan—from his database of knowledge, past experience, values, attitudes, etc.—makes the cross look like a foolish error. [135]

The Holy Spirit seeks, through glossolalia, to make human weaknesses miraculously strong in an act of perceived foolishness resulting in the power of the cross to have preeminence in discipleship and servanthood.

In like manner, hyper-linearity and literalism—the mastery of reason and analysis—the intimidating force of skillful oratory that makes an icon of human speech skills, would displace the role of the Holy Spirit who seeks, through glossolalia, to make human weakness miraculously strong in an act of perceived foolishness, so the true power of the cross may have preeminence in salvation as well as discipleship and servanthood.

The Curse of Aristotle—Again!

Jackie David Johns gives a cogent treatise on how far afield the Greek world of Aristotle has led our concept of "knowing" from the Hebrew world of "knowing" in his article "Yielding to the Spirit: The Dynamics of a Pentecostal Model of Praxis."[136] He speaks of Aristotle's "Ways of Knowing" as Praxis, Theoria and Poesis. **Sorry—this looks like heavy stuff, but I think you'll agree it will be worth it!** I'll let J. Johns explain.

> Aristotle treated *praxis* as one of three principle ways of knowing, the other two being *theoria* and *poesis. Theoria* was a property of the

> intellect alone and was the highest form of knowledge. Only through *theoria* could an individual attain unto *Sophia*, the highest level of wisdom. *Praxis* merged thought with doing, primarily in the sense of interaction with society. *Poesis* merged thought with making in the sense of shaping material objects, for example, the artisan's work. Because it focused on interaction with society, *praxis* was beneficial for moral training, but could not bring an individual to *Sophia*.[137]

In other chapters, I have suggested the Greek world, through Aristotle and others, have negatively affected the Western Church's willingness to see that experience is also a valid way of knowing God. In fact, for the Hebrew world, the world of almost all the Bible's writers, experience was a necessity to know Him. While *praxis* is understood somewhat differently by philosophers and theologians down through the ages, it generally is agreed that its primary meaning is *knowledge gained through experience merged with thought*. But for those who still hold to Aristotle's position that "Only through theoria could one attain sophia, the highest level of wisdom," *praxis* takes a minor role. Jackie Johns contends 'knowing' related to experiencing is Hebrew and not Greek. The Hebrew word (Yada) is not standing back and contemplating, but feeling with a dynamic relational, experimental association. The Greeks stood back and contemplated to know. The Hebrews touched, interrelated. Drawing from Thomas Groome[138] Johns shows how the Hebrews believed that to know God, one must *do* His will. Bultman even stated that knowledge in the Hebraic sense was 'possessed only in its exercise or actualization.'[139] It is significant that *yada* (Hebrew for to know) is used as a euphemism for lovemaking (and Adam *knew* Eve and she conceived...KJV) and the past participle of *yada* is used for a good friend or confidant.[140]

One might consider that glossolalia may be related to the Hebrew word YADA from the standpoint of actualization of God's presence. It was emotional and actualized enough for the observers in Jerusalem to think the 120 were drunk in Acts 1. In this sense, speaking in tongues is a visceral encounter with the Holy Spirit! Jesus said it: "Streams of living water will flow from within him" (NOT from the cortex of the cerebellum shall flow...). "By this He meant the Spirit, whom those who believed in Him were later to receive..."(John 7:38, 39).

It's not logical, was not meant to be and only suffers damage to its essence in trying to force it through Aristotelian linear Euclidian constructs. Forcing Hebrew thought through a Greek paradigm does the former great harm. (Greek language specialists tend to disavow that statement, but Hebrew scholars believe it's true). In the same sense, the indirect speech style of much of the narrative portions of the Bible are less appreciated by the West, because truth is offered ambiguously (for the Westerner) who prefers almost all communication "straight from the shoulder, give me the bottom line, lay all the cards on the table" mode of speaking.[141]

Only after learning African language vernaculars has my understanding of the old Evangelical argument, "narrative passages in the Bible cannot be used for building theological understanding," been enlarged. Some of our own Pentecostal scholars support the fundamentalist's view. It is obvious these authors/scholars are generally more skillful in Greek than in Hebrew (about an eight to one ratio of theological students who major in biblical languages) nor have they often learned or internalized a current living language from a developing preliterate culture. The precision of language usage in single agendum of open, clear, straight-forward thinking (from the Greco-Roman world of Aristotle) blinds them to the ancient Hebrew world's use of indirection, ambiguity and innuendo that so characterized Bible speech in its original matrix. What is even more serious is the marginalization of parts of the 2/3rd religious world by the Aristotelian influenced West concerning the people of the developing nations use of narrative to understand theological truths AND to preach in a mode readily understandable by their audiences. In my experience, the West believes the use of narrative by the people of the developing nations is just an alternate style, when in truth it is an axiomatic element of huge proportions that the West continues to ignore out of ignorance and neglect.

Jappie LaPorta sees this almost total misunderstanding as a major reason for much of the religious racism and schism between Black and White in Pentecostal churches today (and especially traces the sad history of Pentecostal divisions in South Africa as well as what happened after the Azusa revival in the USA).[142]

> My first affirmation is that Pentecostal theology is narrative in form and structure. Our point of theological departure is not from a specific doctrine, but from a particular paradigmatic experience. This experiential approach is a legitimate and essential way of doing theology...in this theological process experience becomes more important than in traditional, rational western theology...The memory of these experiences gives *identity*...the advantage of narrative theology is that it makes possible contact and dialogue between different people...is reciprocal, because both parties involved in the contact and dialogue are engaged in the telling of and listening to stories...narrative

> theology is a rhetorically powerful and liberative instrument in the lives of individuals and communities...Narrative theology does not separate Systematic Theology and Ethics.[143]

In case I've caused you to lose the·"train of thought" (you see—on a straight track!), allow me to return to the point. Different cultural and worldviews affect the way Westerners and Africans interpret the Bible, and we can learn from each other as well as gain insight to the nature of how human speech and emotions are interrelated. In many ways the less industrial and more agrarian world of 2/3rd World countries renders its peoples closer to the original speakers and hearers of the biblical period. In this same sense, and for this reason, the "oralness" of Pentecostal worship and the employ of the Gifts of the Spirit is misunderstood by literalists. Are you "tracking" now? Think of how communication styles, differences, really do affect our theological thinking and attitudes.

> **Communication differences and styles really do affect our theological thinking and attitudes.**

Coming Close to the Thesis

Just like God hid the power of the cross behind its apparent foolishness—so He has hidden the power of the Holy Spirit for the most effective witness behind the symbol of total submission and the foolishness of glossolalia! God chose the foolishness of the cross (a Messiah killed, an ignominious death—what an oxymoron!) to redeem us. I submit, He chose the foolishness of tongues as the symbol, the required "getting lost" enough, to empower us for witness so we'd be motivated to "lose our lives to find them" (Matt. 10:39).

Contextualization vs. Syncretism (Imposing our Fan of Perception Instead of God's)

Contextualization is a relatively new word in missiology referring to the process of learning/knowing the cultural and social footprint of another society well enough to effectively find a dynamic equivalent in word or words from one's own perception, then into the target audience's language system. This would enable the speaker to be able to communicate one's intent into the language/symbol system of the receptor's understanding. (Like using a "picketing peg" that tethers a camel, to substitute for the word "anchor" that holds a ship—the desert's people never having seen a body of water. Here one has found an insight into a language where using the word "anchor" would be meaningless.) This is a good example of the proper use of *contextualization.* On the same search towards finding a meaningful word equivalent, but unlike "picketing peg for anchor," and this time in an inappropriate way, would be the use of the word "pig" to substitute for "lamb or sheep." This was attempted for a while in a remote area of Papau New Guinea of the Pacific Islands where sheep were not found and not known. It seemed viable because pigs had many of the same functions in the islands as sheep did for the Hebrews (for sacrifice, used as the favored meat consumption and many other similar functions that sheep had in Palestine). Thus missionaries experimented with this substitution in early attempts to translate the Bible. It was abandoned, however, once it was scrutinized more thoroughly because the nature of the two animals is too dissimilar.

Good theology (man's words about God) translates God's intent into our fan of perception without damaging His intend – but He often shocks our comfortable data base.

Just consider this from the Isaiah passage: "Like a *pig* led to the slaughter is dumb, so he opened not his mouth"—just didn't fit the nature of the squealing pig! Nor did the words of John the Baptist: "behold the *pig* of God that takes away the sins of the world"- when talking of the Messiah. The substitution goes too far and illustrates the danger of *syncretism,* when the essential nature of the meaning is distorted. The intent was just, but the consequences were too distorting. This is the nature of a gospel of Christ where the price of the cross is left out, where a follower no longer needs to heed the words of Jesus—"he who would come after me, let him take up his cross and follow me." *Contextualization* gets into the auditorium of the hearer—with a correct and meaningful concept. *Syncretism* also aims for cognition, but in "mixing" the new with the old (like a synthesis) for the sake of cognition, transforms the meaning into something that distorts the author's intention.

Good theology (man's words about God) translates God's intent into our fan of perception without changing or damaging His intent. None-theless, He often shocks us by doing the unexpected even in our comfortable database:

> *"Therefore once more I will astound these people with wonder upon wonder: the wisdom of the wise will perish, the intelligence of the intelligent will vanish"* (Isaiah 29:14).

Man doesn't like God to act that way. We want Him to honor our intelligence. We want Him to say:

"I will not surprise this people—I will act and speak totally inside their expectations—just like they want me to and just the way they have organized their religious world." **Not!**

Why has the church turned the 'foolishness of God' (oxymoron of Calvary—lose to win—die to live—become humble to be exalted—submit your speech power to Him in weakness to be empowered, etc.) into a "Sophia" to which the unregenerate world can better relate? Why have we tried to thwart God's wisdom with our own? We tend to guild the cross with gold and make it an icon, not a symbol of what we must lose to win. This is a tough balance to find. One MUST get into the fan of perception of the audience for the sake of cognition but, at the same time, **not distort the intent of the source (God's intention) for the sake of expedient cognition.** When we turn the upside-down wisdom of God right-side-up for the sake of acceptability, haven't we gone from the need to contextualize for cognition—to *syncretism* at the price of the pure gospel? Has not that process made something false of the nature of the gospel itself? Don't we who pray in tongues do the same when we flee the stigma of Pentecost, when we flee the accusation that we are less than acceptable (Acts 2:13-15). There is a place where contextualization must also include *confrontation* **for the sake of the preservation of God's foolishness.** Without confrontation, when essential, we simply make the essence of God's plan conform to the fan of perception of the receiver regardless of what damage that does to the integrity or intent of the source (God's Word) and the essence of the cross. *What a fine line of distinction with which we must constantly struggle!* Preserve the integrity of God's foolishness, yet be communicatively cogent/relevant. When God does precisely the opposite of what He's expected to do, instead of seeing this as wisdom we try to make it worldly reasonable. The cross, salvation, glossolalia, the gifts of the Spirit, the fruit of the Spirit are simply not reasonable (for the secular world and sometimes for us), and this is all by God's design!

REASON TO COMMUNICATE

One of the characteristics of a good communicator is the ability to influence the cognitive and effective aspects of the audience. Professional marketing research analysts boldly tell us how to sell a product or idea to the American market by using psychological persuasion. (The word persuasion also has a *positive* sense [like in Acts 28:23 KJV and II Cor. 5:11 NIV] and must not be confused with coercion.) These analysts sell their findings to media producers, some of whom make the television commercials that flood our screens. Research presented by these professionals is sometimes frightening—it can be manipulative because the human thinking processes have become well known in the last few decades. Commercials that *sell* find a way to *resonate* with the beliefs and value structures of a high percentage of their target audience.

Schwartz[144] illustrated modern communication methods related to the media on this topic. Schwartz stated when the string of a guitar is plucked in the vicinity of a piano, the particular wave-length vibration of the string "sounding" will create a sympathetic dynamic vibration on the piano string tuned to the same tone of the guitar. This is known as *resonance*. The reader may know of people who are skilled in communicating and who, it seems, are able to "affect," invisibly and unconsciously, the interest and motivation of those listening. This analogy of resonance enhances the previous analogies of Spirit-related interpersonal relationships and the potential effectiveness the Holy Spirit wishes to give as an empowerment for witness (Acts 1:8).

I believe God created mankind for His purpose and intention. He wants to communicate and reestablish fellowship with His creation. In that pursuit, He has chosen to use other "created beings" (not angels) as instruments of His divine power. As a Spirit-filled believer, I accept His command to be a witness for Him. I also can expect that the Holy Spirit will help me to "resonate," to reach out and touch the need in someone's life! I see this avenue as a direct possibility of how God's Spirit in the life of a witness or counselor or minister can lead a needy soul to growth and conflict resolution in a way not possible in the natural or professional way. How comforting to know the Spirit is available for a simple witness or a professional counselor working with those needing behavior modification. This is true for a housewife talking to a friend over the back fence or to a teenager seeking to share the positive nature of the Kingdom with school friends. The Holy Spirit will take our abilities, studied skills, and accumulated wisdom and add His own enablement that will utilize—but go beyond our own natural talents and learned abilities. He thus gives us an added edge so we can touch and minister and bless (to resonate and contaminate).[145]

THEOLOGIANS ALSO HAVE FANS OF PERCEPTION

I should not be amazed at the sincere attempt by exemplary scholars to struggle with the reasons for this contemporary Pentecostal revival burgeoning around the world. I must in all candor raise the issue of "Perceptual Field" of those who seem to know almost nothing of the issues at hand in this church growth. Often on this issue, Pentecostals have in their "fan of perception" the knowledge of intense research and personal experience instructed by the reality of glossolalia. Our opponents and "spectators" offer no perception on this truth and hence no "mutual influence" for cognition. Words fly back and forth, but because MEANING IS NOT IN WORDS BUT IN PEOPLE (David Berlo, 1960), common words "listed" in each other's mental "disks" (reservoirs of knowledge, past experience, values, attitudes, etc.) SOUND as if they are recognizable, but the mutual understanding is absent because we don't have enough mutual overlap of our fans of perception to understand each other. The following is an example that, hopefully, will help clarify the above contention. It is related to the on-going International Roman Catholic/Traditional Pentecostal Dialogue for more than 20 years running.

A spiritual experience of glossolalia can be a unifying element between two individual people or communities that at one time hardly communicated and where myths about each other was intense and extensive. I speak of the rather recent event of the Charismatic renewal in the Roman Catholic Church. Pentecostals and Catholics have never been known to cooperate in ecumenical events. They were too distrustful of one another and too far apart theologically and ideologically (they both assumed)—until the 1960s outbreak of speaking in tongues in Notre Dame and Duquesne Universities and the resultant proliferation of this phenomenon throughout the Catholic world, first in isolated places and later quite extensively. I have been a participant in the International Roman Catholic/ Traditional Pentecostal Dialogue over a ten-year period. Suddenly, the "perceptual fans of mutual influence" (Ross chart) overlapped on an experience and theology that allowed, for the first time on a grand scale, a dialogue whose intention was never to merge the churches in question. The dialogue made an honest inquiry into the truly held beliefs and practices of this one ancient and mother church and the new upstart, which is the fastest growing wing of Chistendom and perhaps somewhat of a threat to the oldest Christian Church. The common denominator was the Charismatic renewal in the Catholic Church, recognized by Pentecostals (but few others) as a common element in here-to-for ecclesiastical groups willing to remain in their mutually exclusive camps of non-communication. All at once the Catholic Charismatic communities and Pentecostals have "mutual influence" because of the glossolalic experience. Even though church liturgy and certain doctrinal beliefs remain far apart, the unifying understanding of "tongues speech" unlocks old closed doors! In this instance, the Foolishness of God finds substance.[146]

DISCRETIONARY HEARING

Good friend Bob Kilpatrick, musician and composer of contemporary gospel music, sent me an email in which he told of a new song he had just written and was producing: Title—"If You Want To Hear From God—You've Got to Listen For His Voice." Telling of the inspiration of this work he wrote:

> If we want to hear from God, we must develop two skills. First, we must be able to distinguish His voice from all the other voices. Second, we must develop our discretionary hearing—the ability to mentally block out other sounds and focus on the one sound we most want to hear.

Bob says it's like trying to identify the "professional" voices that speak the parts of the different fish in the movie "Finding Nemo." If you haven't spent much time listening to these performers before, you'll have a hard time with the "identity game." Bob used the illustration of the sound studio when he is recording a CD: "In a mix session in the studio, we can single out the tambourine that's losing the beat with this same ability. Mothers use it to hear their children stirring. Christians use this in their spirits when listening for God's voice."[147]

At first I was reminded of stepping into a "radio shack" of a ham radio operator and hearing the cacophony of all the stations coming into the shack, plus all the static noises that for the untrained ear, is total confusion. The ham operator will be listening to only one voice and he may ask you, "Can you hear that?"—referring to the station or person he's concentrating on at the moment. When this first happened to me, I remember saying, "Do you really expect me to know which one to listen to?" A ham operator will explain that it's a matter of learning which voices to block out—like Bob was saying. Discretionary hearing is the term used to describe our ability to block out certain sounds when we're trying to focus in on one in particular. Here is a little understood or taught truth about praying in our prayer language.

"If You Want to Hear From God – You've Got to Listen For His Voice".

> He will speak through other voices or writings as well. When this happens, the discretionary hearing—discernment—you have developed in the stillness will help you to distinguish His voice from the many. Just like in "Finding Nemo," sometimes God doesn't seem like

> God. Sometimes He speaks through another person, song, book, article or movie character. Even though He may appear to you in disguise, He will still sound the same—if you've learned to recognize His voice, you will know it is Him. There are times in our lives when we are in desperate or bewildering circumstances. There will be times when we need divine direction. At times, the choices before us are not between obvious Good and obvious Bad. Sometimes we must choose between one Good and another Good. It is in these times that the time in the stillness, listening, pays off. It is just like the wise virgins in the Bible who prepared for a long vigil by stocking up on oil for their lamps. We must develop our ability to hear and understand God by listening in the stillness of our private time with Him. This is not a test you can cram for. It takes time, stillness, listening. Sing it with me; "If you want to hear from God, you have got to listen for His voice."[148]

When we have practiced to listen to His voice and then act on it, we are His partners. This too is His design.

Amazing Partnership and Teacher!

In another section we speak of the incarnational method of all the gifts of the Spirit. God has chosen to use us in a partnership with Him in all of His special empowering to humans for the sake of announcing the Gospel—at some considerable risk. He might have chosen angels and, consequently, had team members much less subject to error or excess; but no, He chose to team up with all who submit and become available for this partnership.

Speaking in a private tongues/prayer language allows the Spirit to speak to our souls because we have chosen to "shut off"—attenuate but not eliminate (I Cor. 14:14)—our "learned fan of perception" of cognition (our natural speech and thinking mechanism). While worshiping Him in this mode, He impresses our deep sub-conscious with His will and His ways. We then mysteriously discern a "better way" which is communicated back to our normal cognitive processes (fan of perception), often described as "inspiration." Could not this be one of the ways Jesus comforted His disciples just before His death while talking about the role the Comforter would have?

> *"If you love me, you will obey what I command. And I will ask the Father, and He will give you another Counselor to be with you forever—the Spirit of truth. The world cannot accept Him, because it neither sees Him nor knows Him. But you know Him, for He lives with you and will*

> *be in you...But the Counselor, the Holy Spirit, whom the Father will send in my name, will teach you all things...*(John 14:15-17, 26).

WORD PICTURE TO EXPLAIN 1 CORINTHIANS 14:14

How can it happen that "shutting off" our normal fan of perception (Ross model) will help one to tune-in to the Spirit's teaching? *Here's a word picture that may seem sacrilegious to some, but poignant none-the-less*: Have you ever noticed the crazy way professional models walk down the gang-way while modeling the newest creations of "Haute Couture"? They swagger and walk with exaggeration in an unnatural, almost laughable manner! I'm sure I know why. They have "shut off" their individuality. If they walked in their natural gate, their individual female carriage and personal distinctive would be noticed and evaluated—and the observers (who have come to buy clothes) would be distracted by the personal charm (or lack of it) of the models. By insisting on an *unnatural* but uniform walk to which all models must comply, the normal distraction of their personal charms can be ignored and the new clothes can be the focus of the demonstration. In like manner, by an exercise of worship or prayer or singing in the Spirit, the normal cognitive mechanism of speech (cerebral neurons firing from the memory banks of past experience, knowledge, attitudes, values, etc.) are suppressed in favor of a mysterious speech of which the Holy Spirit gives utterance (Acts 2:4) and during which time when the intellect is "unfruitful," the Holy Spirit can impress us with His knowledge and insight. This, then, is a form of discretionary hearing that remains the domain of the submitted and empowered. The apostle Paul really had it right when he said, "he who speaks in a tongue edifies himself..." (I Cor. 14:4).

When we pray in a known language from our rational database (Knowledge, Past Experiences, Attitudes,Values, etc.), our minds are full of things we have learned. This is both normal and unavoidable. But when we pray in tongues (or seek to be filled with the Spirit initially), we must somehow release this habitual way of communication and trust the *giver* (Jesus) and not the method or formulas others may seek to instruct us about. Smith Wigglesworth simply says it in answer to a question:

> Q. I have been waiting for the baptism of the Holy Spirit for a long time. I have been told that if I will say "glory" or "Hallelujah" until I have lost myself, I will receive, but so far I have not received.
>
> A. You have had a great deal of things in your mind as to what ought to bring the baptism, and you are forgetting what will bring it, and

> that is Jesus. Jesus is the Baptizer. As soon as you are ready, He will fill you.[149]

This simple "question and answer" chapter of the above source can be useful in Communications Theory terms to advantage. No doubt well-meaning folks, without using communication "jargon," have hit on a truth perhaps by accident. Repeating the words "glory or Hallelujah" to chase away the normal encoding—decoding process (here described as "lost myself") may indeed help some to abandon rational controllable speech mechanisms (which are totally normal) to the surrender of the human need to *compose* speech, and thus allow the Holy Spirit to "give utterance" as described in the second chapter of Acts. Wigglesworth in his answer is trying, in my opinion, to dislodge any formula or idea of "sacred words" and direct the questioner to the same thing. *Don't focus on words or formulas but focus on the Baptizer.* Either way, the focus on Jesus, or focus on specific words to bring the mind to surrender and disassociation from the need to *compose* or *encode* speech, is perhaps a useful way of referring to this difficult physiological phenomenon. Also, Wigglesworth is right in suggesting God is sovereign.

> **Meanings always flit mockingly beyond the reach of men with nets and measuring sticks"**
> **–Wheelwright**

THE MEETING OF EAST AND WEST

"Meanings always flit mockingly beyond the reach of men with nets and measuring sticks."[150]

Learning a "foreign" language forces one to better learn the grammar of one's own mother tongue. In similar manner, looking at Communications Theory through the lens of another culture can facilitate cognition concerning the complexity of human speech.

How does the West communicate to the East? Rudyard Kipling spent a great period of his life in India. He is one of the earliest sources of philosophizing about differences between the East and West. He is credited with the oft-repeated ditty: "Oh East is East and West is West and ne'er the twain shall meet."[151] Understandably, it takes a great amount of abstraction to divide the world into East and West, as if there were a line on the map that one might draw, or as if there were inside of each of these global areas great homogeneity of thought, culture, and language systems. The truth is, of course, that there is great variation within what writers and philosophers normally call East and

West. Yet, we can find useful these broad categories because of the obvious divergence of worldviews represented by East and West.

Earlier we referred to "Germanic grid thinking" as characterized by a need for logic and inductive/deductive methods of observing what is visible and external. In that system ambiguity is feared. Kipling, and a host of writers after him, has attempted to capture from the Westerner's point of view how differently the Eastern mind conceptualizes and how seemingly the East is much more at ease with what the West calls ambiguity. One of the most quoted of these is F.S.C. Northrop[152] who sees the Eastern mind as mythological, introspective, and searching for inner significance. I was amazed as a young teacher in Africa to talk with well-educated Africans—some of them political ministers in the administration of a West African nation—who had been educated in France. They were able to speak with me as Westerner to Westerner, but they also retained the ability to speak in their national language in a total "unscientific" manner. The West believes it has arrived at a higher level of truth through the *method of science*. Anyone educated in the West or by Western pedagogical systems has come under the spell and philosophical assumption that the scientific method is a superior instrument in establishing knowledge and/or truth. We in the West believe this method saves us from superstition and ignorance. The method has at least five features.

Observation. What can be seen, measured, palpitated or compared is infinitely better than that which can only be conceived.

Categorization. That which is observable can be put into categories. The categorization process is a culturally valued decision process, whereby similar things or dissimilar things are sorted according to the worldview of the sorter.

Analysis. The West feels it can understand any concept if its component parts can be examined for their interrelationships. The analysis stage includes experimentation: this will result in truth if you "work it" through a system of externally visible empirical consequences.

Verification. Reliable theories can pass the test of repeatability, preferably conducted by a different set of experimenters. Verification, in the strictest sense of understanding in the West, allows someone else to repeat the experiment and arrive at the same or very similar results.

Hypothesis. Based on the first four steps, the scientific method forms a hypothesis of "truth." Truth is seen ideally as a process more than a product. A hypothesis is only good on a temporal scale. The hypothesis says: "This is what I believe, here is the way I arrived at that conclusion. Please test it and prove me wrong if you can."

Now a French-trained African official, like the ones cited above, has the capacity to talk this jargon just like it is explained here, but he is able to unhitch himself from this whole process and lapse into the thought processes of his ancestors, where "reality" and "truth" are givens related to their cosmology—the way it has always been. This type of "knowing" is assumed to be related to how the world works and is based on a much deeper reality than visible things that can be measured and weighed and counted and categorized. My African friend finds no great dissonance in being able to speak from one theoretical standpoint or the other with no seeming contradiction. Perhaps he knows instinctively the wisdom of Philip Wheelwright's statement that "meanings always flit mockingly beyond the reach of men with nets and measuring sticks."[153] Maybe it is because the African administrator was never injected as a child with the Aristotelian disease of the "undifferentiated middle."

It is not my intention here to evaluate or repeat our exposure to this topic above (Fig. #1) on the intrinsic merits of conceptual thinking compared with concrete/relational thinking.[154] Rather it is to suggest that a cross-cultural communicator who would announce the truths of God's word in a foreign culture must not assume that all people perceive "reality" alike. In the same manner, as Western man is quite deaf to the world of dreams and visions in the modern world, could it be God has more than one way of impacting man's field of perception from His world? Isn't it possible God wants to communicate to His Church using some of the same charismata of the apostles and the early primitive Church? Must Western man insist that God speak to him ONLY through his Aristotelian grid? Is that latter insistence one of the reasons some have tried to relegate the supernatural to a dispensational epoch in history that is deemed inappropriate today? Is it possible God wants to communicate to Western modern man from His heavenly "radio station" in Greco-Roman cultural terms AND from an even older model dating from the time of the disciples in Jerusalem? (Think about the science of the emission of radio waves and *frequency* related to the tuning of a receptor/radio—to receive said emission.)

I want here to illustrate the intrinsic barriers in understanding between peoples of differing worldviews because in so doing, I hope to shed light, by analogy, on the focused thesis of this book. Cross-cultural misunderstanding is the perennial problem of businessmen and women who work overseas (or even in the subcultures of America) and of missionaries from any place to any other place where the goal is to announce the Gospel of Christ. My contention is that this conflict of cross-cultural understanding is analogous to the problem of Christians from non-glossolalic confessions attempting to understand the pneumatology of other Christians who have experienced the overshadowing presence of the Holy Spirit, like one reads about in Acts 2. To do this, I will illustrate with an African proverb/legend of the Mossi of West Africa, which is a communication tool of great antiquity used by them to teach their young.

Suggestion. Now, try on a new set of mental spectacles.

> The hyena had loaned some money to the crow (a pied-crow with a white-feathered pattern on his chest looking like an apron). The crow said he would pay the hyena back in a couple of weeks. After many weeks had transpired and the hyena had not seen any money, he decided to go to the crow's house and confront him and ask him for the money. Upon entering the courtyard of the crow's house, he saw many crows, all with the same white apron on their chest. They asked him, "Mr. hyena, why have you come?" The hyena answered that he had just come to pay a visit. So they invited him to sit down and he visited and visited, all the while waiting to see if he could determine which one of these look-alikes had borrowed his money. He finally ended his stay by asking for permission to leave, but without having identified the crow in question. Weeks passed and still no money came. The hyena decided to go back and try again. And so the same formalities were observed as he claimed to have come for only a visit but was not able to identify the crow. The hyena went home very discouraged. He finally went to the rabbit. (For the Mossi, the rabbit is all-wise.) He explained the story and of his double visit to the crow's house without success in identification. The rabbit said, "It is very simple. Just announce a dance and feast at your house and we'll invite all the animals to come." So the hyena set the date, called all the animals and they came in great droves. The elephants came and ate and began to dance. The giraffes came and ate and danced. The lions came and ate and danced. As it happened, the drummer was very good. The drum went "kung—k-kung-kung—kung—k-kung-kung". The hyena and the rabbit watched as the animals came in a herd, in their own separate groups and danced and left. Finally, it was time for the crows to come and the rabbit said to the drummer, "Give me the drum." Now for the crow's dancing, the rabbit really beat out a rhythm. The rabbit stepped out in the middle of the dancing crows and danced himself as he beat out a complicated and exhilarating cadence. The crows loved it, all the animals watching loved it. As the rhythm accelerated, and as the crows abandoned

> themselves to the beat, they began to ask the rabbit, "Who dances the best?"—"Who dances the best?"—The rabbit hollered out above his drumming, "You all dance well—you all dance well—But the one with the debt dances best—but the one with the debt dances best." Now to the scintillating rhythm, one crow stepped out from the pack and danced over to the drum, and squawked as he danced, "So you said it's me, ahah—so you said it's me, hoho—so you said it's me ahah –." The rabbit turned to the hyena and said, "Grab him!"[155]

Some readers will not need the following explanation of the above story, but most of us from the Western world need some help. Not because the words of the story are in a language other than English, but because there is an *inexperienced* element related to how cognition is structured for preliterate peoples. Our mental radio frequencies are poorly tuned.

This story highlights the point that the Mossi of Burkina Faso, West Africa, used to live in a world greatly influenced by hundreds of years of past culture and social structure. They had a highly developed aural/oral symbolization code, but a relatively low level of print literacy or technological sophistication. (About 50 percent of the population is still preliterate.) One should not confuse pre-literacy with intelligence! These skillful preliterate people have a worldview with a high tolerance for non-precision in speech.[156] This cultural characteristic represents a different frequency in conceptualization. (Remember, by frequency I intend to convey the idea of how each radio station on the dial has a different numerical "address"—even though the content may be similar to another station broadcasting simultaneously—but on its own frequency.) Speaking in tongues is communicating with God on a different frequency. I Cor. 14:2 says: "For anyone who speaks in a tongue does not speak to men but to God. Indeed, no one understands him; he utters mysteries with his spirit." This is a new, and many believe higher, level of communication because it bypasses (but does not ignore) the usual "fan of perception" where selecting and sorting takes place by the person's intellect. (Many corollary issues and arguments on this topic are advanced throughout this work.)

In the story, animals represent people with their different characters and personalities. Just like in live theatre or in a dramatic presentation in the West, one suspends the necessity for literalness, thus it is *assumed* that the whole (African) audience has followed the intention of the speaker and that the hyena's unwillingness to broach the topic of debt while in the crow's house corresponds to 2/3rd World people's hesitation to come to the point as is so typically different from the open and frank mannerism of Western speech. So let me come quickly to a Western point: the rabbit is the Mossi's symbol of the wise, wily survivor possessing few natural defenses much like these tribesmen living on the edge of the Sahara who live by their wits. The great lesson of the story—*though never talked about literally and to the point*—is that pride and flattery will get you into trouble. The crow could not resist an exhibition of his dancing in front of others. So by his failure to control the temptation to flaunt his skill, he was trapped.

Why would God choose a speech form that seems so illogical and "foreign"? Try to view this issue like viewing the facets of a diamond in good light.

The differential in speech mannerism (indirection vs. to-the-point) is but one more example this writer wishes to advance in the quest of the sincere seeker about the question: Why would God choose a speech form that seems so illogical and "foreign" to common usage? **Please stay with me**. We go one step further. It's another in a series of steps this writer had to learn to effectively communicate the Gospel to preliterate but developing people in West Africa. Try to suspend your learned tendency to come to the point NOW (quickly). If I gave you the point up front, it might be meaningless. I wish you to be able to say: "Perhaps we are now better able to continue our journey to understand the basic workings of the mind in human communication." A better understanding of others often helps us understand ourselves. I want the reader to see the "tongues" potential through the eyes of one of the behavioral sciences by approaching it from similar but varied facets, like viewing a diamond in a good light.

COMMUNICATIONS THEORY RELATED TO THE BEHAVIORAL SCIENCES

Communications Theory used to be subsumed largely under the ancient topic of *rhetoric,* which was more concerned with the composition of the text or manuscript or the skills of the source/speaker than the recipients who were to decode the message. Great change came about in this discipline starting with World War I and during and after the Second World War. At that time military propaganda was recognized as an effective weapon to be used on the enemy. Political influence of society was a new interest. Thus a greater emphasis was placed on the audience than here-to-for. Now, the psychological element became an important aspect in the preparation of the text. This meant the particular mental frame of reference of the receiver took on new and more important significance for the communicator. Public education was interested on the effect the media had on children and the topic of persuasion grew in importance. Enter the Behavioral Sciences (who themselves were at the same time in a great growth period of acceptance and utility in western societies). Some, however, could not "see" what was apparent to others.[157]

The experienced archeologist seems to be able to find arrowheads lying on top of the ground that the average archeological student would overlook because he doesn't yet know what to ignore. Yet, the archeologist might not be able to tell him the exact cues that made the image of the arrowhead stand out so clearly. In this case, visual perception is tied to learning and the will to learn new ways of seeing and knowing.[158] The difference in the use of the eyes (by the professor and the student) probably cannot be attributed to physical acuity. In the psychological realm of the behavioral sciences, we can gain many insights to how people think and perceive differently, just like we have discussed above how each person's "database" of perception predetermines what is "seen" and "known." The following author, an Anglican pastor, raised an argument against those who "see" differently and who would dismiss the psychological aspect of glossolalia as an aberration or neurosis. What one does not understand, or want to understand, is often pathologized. Kelsey compares speaking in tongues to dreams or visions. The 2/3rd World peoples still consider dreams and visions as an important window on the world, much like the people of Bible times. Of course, because of the influence of Freudian psychoanalysis and Jung's input on the West (some of which is still operative and some dismissed as excessive), we in the technological world have largely disavowed the medium of dreams or visions as valid systems to influence our lives.

Kelsey Compares Tongues Speech to Dreams or (Even Better) to Visions

> I have observed no case in which the individual was more neurotic after experiencing tongues, nor have I had any medical or psychological reports suggesting this...Speaking in tongues is similar to the dreams in all of these characteristics. In order to have the experience of glossolalia one must empty himself and give up conscious control, yielding himself to the experience. As in sleep the individual does not give up control to another person as he does in hypnosis or suggestion, but to something unknown (which he does in hypnosis or suggestion), which he seems to contact through the depth of himself...The tongue speaker recognizes that control of his body is not being exerted by any known outer, physical force, but by an inner,

> spiritual one...In tongues a portion of the conscious mind, as it were, goes to sleep and permits unconscious contents to flow through the physical apparatus which is normally subject to consciousness...Most tongues speakers testify to the numinous quality of their experience and they believe that this experience expresses some aspect of the spiritual realm in the same way that the dream, as Jung suggests, expresses the reality of the collective unconscious.[159]

Kelsey believes if the religious world could/would re-establish the significance of dreams and visions as in the Bible, where God spoke to people through dreams and visions, then the experience of tongues would be more easily accepted.

A religion which values the dream can equally value tongue-speech. And a psychology which sees the dream as meaningful contact with the realm of the unknown will see tongue-speech in the same light... Far more common than is ordinarily realized, the true vision is like tongue-speech in that it appears to an individual who is perfectly conscious, knows that something beyond his ego is invading his field of consciousness.[160]

Because 2/3rd World people still do believe dreams are significant, the Holy Spirit will use that medium because it is in their perceptual field. There are now literally hundreds of Muslim mullahs who have seen a vision of Jesus at the foot of their beds inviting them to follow Him. One would think Kelsey had studied the Ross Chart above and was using its configuration to help any true seeker to understand this perplexing phenomenon by referring to human speech and the fan of perception.

FREEZING COMMUNICATION MODES

Meaning is not in words—meaning is in people (as mentioned above, David Berlo, 1960). People have always tried to make both the meaning and the mode of conveying it to "stop" in time. This phenomenon of "freezing" a holy language for revelation and liturgy at a given "holy" epoch in time and space is a reoccurring one. Latin was the only language deemed fit for the Roman Catholic mass for 14 centuries. Arabic is still the only language fit for the Koran as any other translation is judged spurious. More recently, in 1846 the creation of Conservative Judaism for the defense of "Standard Hebrew," which was under attack by Reformed Judaism's attempt to employ modern Hebrew, is a case in point. Ismer Schorsch's research quotes a line from this resistance to modern Hebrew: "Words vibrate with religious meaning, moral values and literary associations...and become a symbol of historical continuity and national unity."[161] Many conservative religious movements' resistance to modern translations of the Bible testify to the same resistance. Many individuals in my own movement fighting to retain the King James Version (KJV) translation of the English Bible as the only "inspired version" is a case in point. Even now, many years after a large portion of the movement embraced the NIV (New International Version), many publications are required to have parallel KJV and NIV scriptures in printed materials.

I can personally attest that in French speaking West Africa, where print literacy has been introduced for less than 100 years, those who have become "literate" consider themselves an elite class which then creates an illiterate marginalized group that didn't exist when the whole tribe was "preliterate." The new literate folks can then exploit the non-readers, which makes literacy a weapon of colonization and oppression. James K.A. Smith agrees that in the same sense "Evangelicalism" (via Evangelical theology) is a textual community and as such marginalizes and suppresses the orality of Pentecostal tradition.[162]

Evangelicalism (via its theology) is a textual community which marginalizes and suppresses the orality of Pentecostal tradition.

TAKE NOTE. This position is not a refutation of the authority of the Canon of Scripture, nor a weakening of the absolute belief in the authority and infallibility of Scripture.

But this is a call asking that a re-examination be held on how Evangelical theology (that we have perhaps too easily accepted) **distorted the importance of textualism which undermines our determined belief in the supernatural gifts—including Prophecy, Words of Wisdom and Knowledge, Tongues and Interpretation of Tongues.** These gifts by their nature are tightly related to oral communications. Some can be analyzed as a God-inspired use of a person's data storage in the fan of perception from which conscious communication stems. However, one (tongues) operates in a different mode. Here the usual path of encoding a message is subordinated to a deeper level of an incarnational type partnership with the Holy Spirit. We must reject the teaching that once the Canon of Scripture was complete we no longer needed the gifts such as tongues. Just as we must also reject, on the other hand, the teaching of a few that current public prophecy is equal to Scripture.

Can Westerners Overemphasize the Written Word?

Much of the non-Western world does not share the Westerner's emphasis on the written word. In fact, much of the un-evangelized world (what the secular world calls the developing world) is composed of oral societies. As Heibert states, whereas written ideas are fixed, oral ideas (stories, proverbs, aphorisms, etc.) are more fluid and may be reinterpreted over time.[163] The Western mindset is vastly different due to literacy.

Interesting it is that though dogmas, creeds, and fundamental truths are all written, this has not solidified the *interpretation* of what is written.

THE FAN OF PERCEPTION'S DIVERSITY

Above, while discussing Ross's Chart on the Theory of Communications, the element of each individual's *fan of perception* was introduced. Because we purported that one communicates (encodes and decodes relating to perception) from one's unique fan of perception, and the database in the mind so related, the question arises: What is the eventual result or final outcome of a broad diversity concerning the words glossolalia, tongues as held by a speaker using those words, or a listener hearing those words?

Consider the same words relating to "past experience or knowledge" (from the database) of a Westerner with a literary/linearity bias as compared to a person from the Eastern oriented developing world with an oral-aural/preliterate bias. Have the thousands of treatises and books written on this controversial subject considered the phenomenon of Communications Theory as a variable in their judgments? Do well-meaning theologians from diverse convictions look at the socio-linguistic backgrounds of their own ranks when discussing the phenomenon of the Charismatic revival sweeping the world? I submit here is a variable worth exploring. Can we pause and compare the "meaning is perception" factor between a Fundamentalist Evangelical (whose theology and interpretation methods have been much influenced by Reformed Theology, rationalistic and scholastic priorities, who believes God is first reasonable—whatever that means) and a Charismatic (who sees God as much less rational and more mystical—whatever that means—and more supernatural in His actions)? But wait! What about a Roman Catholic writer whose mindset has been much influenced by the Aristotle/Aquinas syndrome OR an Eastern Orthodox influenced by a well-advanced pneumatology?[165] Is this not a variable often overlooked in the scientific and social/religious academy?

In my experience, the connotative/denotative issue will serve the questions raised above.

Just like the word "chalupa" for an Anglo North American means (denotes) an item of food from the fast food chain Taco Bell, it means (denotes) a small canoe for a Spanish- speaking Latin American who has never eaten at such an establishment (or probably doesn't want to!). Once he has (probably with disgust at the Americanization of good food!), he will have both a denotation and connotation for the word "chalupa." For the average Evangelical the word "glossolalia" has negative connotations denoting the physical act of speaking in a language by which some folks with the same denotation affix to a word that connotes an experience they treasure and of which they seek to proclaim its value in obeying the great commission of Jesus the Savior.

ATTENTION! The issue here is not the correctness or incorrectness of the word *glossolalia* as denoted or connoted by the differing parties. The issue is *meaning is perception.*[166] Example: Anyone who seriously talks about God from the Scriptures is doing theology. These people are in truth exegetes—even if they have not studied the art and science of exegesis. In like manner, all professional (and non-professional) exegetes communicate—even though few have studied the art and science of Communications Theory! I remind the reader, this is the matrix of this author's intention, to look at this worldwide phenomenon from the lens of a student of communications.

We must believe the God of the New Testament wishes to empower believers to confront the evils of this secular culture. To thunder out with passion, with love and tenderness, with tact and wisdom, with all the rigor of scholarship, yet with the boldness of an apostle! And with an effectiveness of a modern communicator who studies human behavior and shapes the message with skill and understanding of how the cognitive learning system operates. He or she can thus be a most effective instrument in the hand of the Holy Spirit for a dynamic poignant message. We embrace the evangelism of the greatest evangelist of our era, a Billy Graham (Charismatics are among his greatest church resource) and cooperate with such community meetings. We must also see what the Holy Spirit is doing in the streets of the inner cities of this land away from the super meeting in the sports arena. I speak of the ministry of deliverance engaging the very powers of the devil that demand a different level of power encounter where the average Evangelical will not tread (there are a few exceptions). It is generally people of the Spirit who dare to pray for and confront the demon possessed and see the homosexual and drug addict delivered. I speak also of the mighty army of Holy Ghost baptized national preachers and laymen in over 200 countries (320,000 just in our own Movement) who every day are winning ground *"against the rulers, against the authorities, against the powers of this dark world and against the spiritual forces of evil in the heavenly realm* (Rom. 6:12). They are not all good communicators—but many of them are very skillful.

The center of their message **is not tongues!**

The Baptism in the Holy Spirit has empowered them to preach the centrality of the cross of Christ and the deliverance power of the prayer of faith. They are learning the relationship of the Spirit and the Word. Few of them have a musical team to attract the crowds or the organizational or financial enablements of the West. The best of them augment their natural skills with a dependency on the "breath of God" to help them do what they could not do in the natural. Even the lesser skilled have the Holy Spirit's availability as He doesn't only help the "favored" ones.

HOW DID THE PRIMITIVE CHURCH COMMUNICATE?

Let us consider two words—**Power** and **Process**. Note the definition of how I intend to employ the words as symbols of ideas to follow. Let's suppose these words represent a system or model of communication style and type of ministry.

Power = Revivalist, personal experience, intense interaction and confrontation. People of this mode emphasize evangelism, encourage power encounters with Holy Spirit demonstration of signs and wonders; a prophetic voice of God encouraged.

> **The power people throw stones at the process people calling them powerless Christians. The process folks attack the power folks and call them fanatics.**
> **–Creps**

Process = Organization, predictability, conservative order and preservation. People of this mode focus on training, discipling and maturing of the believers. They will sometimes sacrifice renewal and revival for the sake of tradition.

Consider how these two concepts were used the first few months after the "earth shaking" events in Jerusalem when the advent of "tongues" attracted the crowds—some of whom were impressed and listened and obeyed the preacher (Peter) and others who mocked and rejected this phenomenon. I want to look at these two words and relate them to these events as recorded in Acts concerning the communication choices of the Apostles and the thousands of new converts, some who accepted Jesus as Messiah on the occasion of Acts 2:4 and others who were being added to the church daily after that event (Acts 2:47). I will use the two words "power" and "process" as Earl Creps suggested them[167] as a means of study for examining the integration of two seemingly contradictory ideas or methods employed by the new, mostly Jewish Christians in Jerusalem. The **process model** and the **power model** both relate to the "how to communicate" methods of the Early church and still today are the cause of much of the traumatic dilemma between prophetic revivalist churches/individuals and nurturing conserving churches/individuals in many cultures.

Contrasting Fans of Perception

Creps doesn't believe one can split the difference between power and process and be a healthy witnessing communicating church. A trade off was not beneficial for the early church and it isn't today. THE ANSWER IS NOT A BALANCE OF POWER AND PROCESS BUT AN INTERGRATION OR MARRIAGE of these two seemingly irreconcilable forces. Reason and emotion need less to be balanced than integrated. In his chart, Ross would call this "mutual influence," a must, or no communication.

Power and **Process** have the same friends and the same enemies. Power and Process are friends in the book of Acts. In chapter two the Spirit came and disturbed everybody's paradigm. Tongues, wind, demonstrations—followed by Peter's smash-mouth sermon. A powerful noise and a disturbing behavior pattern. Then he preaches with power. There's the power side; there's the experiential side; and when God leads (this is the key) in this event, huge numbers of people were converted. Now, we drop down immediately after the crises experience. Do the people say, "We should have Peter preach again"? No—they develop a process for building people and making disciples. "We'll meet at the temple for public meetings, but we'll also meet in our homes and break bread together and listen to the disciples' teaching." This is the **process** side. (See Acts 2:42-47.)

The primitive church instinctively MARRIED the **process** side and the **power** side. This is also true in the ministry of the Apostle Paul to the gentiles.

POWER SIDE. In 1 Cor. 2 the apostle talks about how he came in the demonstration of the power of the Spirit. Much of this letter, however, is on the process side to correct and help mature the believers. More:

PROCESS SIDE. In Ephesians 4 he stayed two years and spoke about how God gave apostles, prophets, evangelists, teachers, and pastors to perfect the saints to do the work of the ministry. So from the same apostle we see the marriage of power and process. His goal was to deliver from the power of the enemy and then develop in the delivered ones: "the whole measure of the fullness of God" (Eph. 3:19). The same man who was saved in two seconds on the road to Damascus is now spending two years maturing the saints in Ephesus. He takes the power side in 1 Cor. 2 and marries it to the process side in Ephesians 4.

What a shame the Church of Jesus Christ has always struggled with these needed elements!

The **power** people throw stones at the **process** people and call them morbid or powerless Christians. The **process** people throw stones at the **power** people and call them fanatics or unbalanced. That marriage will always require a constant struggle to maintain. It's the nature of humans to prefer one side or the other. Like people who have differing predispositions to the left and right hemispheres of the brain, they seldom recognize the legitimacy of the other. These are not enemies of the cross of Christ; these are brothers and sisters in the Body of Christ who will be **proponents of only one of these elements to the exclusion of the other.**[168] Both sides require good communication methods to be successful. Both sides *desperately need each other for completeness.*[169]

We have discussed the necessity of a vital marriage between two seemingly opposing forces—one revivalist (communicating orally, dynamically) typified by power encounter and the other process oriented (communicating with reasoned discourse, literally, conservatively) based on tradition and order. We see the model for this marriage in both the Acts of the Apostles and the Epistles of the apostle Paul.[170]

THE WORLD'S WISDOM AND ELOQUENCE (PAUL'S WORDS) DEFEATS THE VALUE OF THE CROSS

Can a philosophy of speech affect receptivity of God's salvation/revelation?

If one charted Paul's declared speech style (the purposeful encoding of the message) on Ross's chart, one would see a deliberate "dumbing down" of word choice to his target audience **so as not to bring attention to himself and his skill as an orator. That recognized superior speech mannerism (which he had the skill to use) would have taken away from the power of God's design in hiding the message of the cross in a cloak of foolishness as the best mode to communicate the grace of God to mankind.**

When we turn the "upside-down" wisdom of God "right-side-up" (for the sake of acceptability), don't we risk the same result as the literalization of rationalism advanced by some theologies seeking conclusions that God's plan of salvation must be "world-reasonable"?[171] Didn't God say early in Isaiah:

> *"These people come near to me with their mouth and honor me with their lips, but their hearts are for from me. Their worship of me is made up only of rules taught by men. Therefore once more I will astound these*

people with wonder upon wonder, the wisdom of the wise will perish, the intelligence of the intelligent will vanish" (Isaiah 29:13-14).

Don't we as Pentecostals and Charismatics do the same when we flee the stigma of Pentecost—when we flee criticism and mockery (Acts 2:13-15)? Yes, we must, like Peter, try to give an answer for our faith as he did before the accusers when he countered their jesting, that it was too early in the day to be inebriated; but we must not subsequently go to those "speaking in tongues" and say: "Hey guys, stop it, you're being misunderstood!" No—we must also say like Peter—"This is that spoken by your own prophets." There is a place where contextualization must also become confrontation **for the sake of preservation of God's foolishness!!** Otherwise we simply make the essence of God's plan conform to the unspiritual person's fan of perception to the point where we do damage to the nature of it.

What a fine line of distinction we must constantly struggle with!! Don't we wish it was easier and less energy consuming! How to communicate with cogency and still preserve the essence of God's 'foolishness'? When God does just the opposite of what He's expected to do, instead of seeing this as wisdom, we try to make it worldly-reasonable. The cross, salvation, and Spirit baptism are simply not reasonable—by God's design. We've simply got to get over it!!

OLD PARADIGMS—NEW PARADIGMS

France would "limit/prohibit" any new words into the stream of vocabulary of the French language. There is an official, empowered board of control, "L'Academie Francaise," which works under the assumption that all the words anyone ever needs is now contained in the current French language. (They do allow some new technical words of modern invention—but only after they have "renamed" them or "christened" them with French equivalent spelling and morphological significance.) Anything else is dubbed "spurious" and undesirable. The motto is " LET'S KEEP FRENCH PURE." The academy tries to purge from written and spoken French, words borrowed from other languages (especially English—the chief rival) words such as "le drugstore," or "le hotdog" or "le weekend." Friends of ours, studying French in France preparing to later go to Francophone, Africa (former French colonies), as missionaries were shocked to discover at the birth of a child while in language study they had to officially name the baby from a list of "accepted names." They were not free to use some names commonly used in the USA because they weren't on the list! I don't mean to imply that France has no right to so act or that this action is wrong. I want to cite an example of a certain held belief about the role and nature of language.

As above, the Muslim world holds that when Allah used the medium of Arabic to dictate the Koran to Muhammad, only Arabic of the seventh century was the standard for reading and understanding the Koran. God can only be understood in Arabic of the seventh century. Purists among them deny that the Arabic language has evolved or changed in the last 13 hundred years.

We've stated before that for hundreds of years the Roman Catholic Church said: "God can best be understood in Latin." And: "Only the Latin mass is worthy of God's presence through the Eucharist." At Vatican II God changed His mind for most Roman Catholics.

The Ethiopian Orthodox Church dates from AD 362 with the first Christian Church was built in the small city of what is today Axum. The sacred scriptures are written and preserved in the language of Ge'ez. Hardly anyone still speaks it except the high priesthood, a clear case of language veneration for its own sake.

The best minds in linguistics and semantics affirm that language cannot be stopped in its evolution. It must be living and changing or it becomes an icon. But even many who accept change as the desired mode for language resist the idea of the total fluidity of glossolalia. Tongues speech cannot be written or repeated. It's like the manna of the wilderness—one always needs a fresh supply. Its existence is on a different frequency than cerebral language. The supervision of an "academy of pure tongues" would be an oxymoron! Cessationists say: "After the Canon—no more supernatural!" God has always said, "Ha!—watch me!"

The chapter to follow will give the CASE FOR GLOSSOLALIA in the Bible and will continue to inject Communications Insights tied to the issues we have just seen.

ENDNOTES:

1. I've always been fascinated by communications, hence my attempt to link this discipline to a theological concept. This information about the march of technology can be found in any good current encyclopedia.

2. Aristotle, Rhetoric, Book I, chapter 2 (about 300 BC).

3. National Geographic Channel 58, Sacramento, CA, Sunday, July 27, 2003,
8:00 a.m.

4. Tim Friend, Animal Talk (2003), iv.

5. International Encyclopedia of Communications, Vol. 1, 360.

6. Ibid.

7. Frank Dance and Carl Larson, The Function of Human Communication: A Theoretical Approach (1976).

8. Robert T. Craig, "Communication as a Field," Communication Theory 9 (1999):119-161.

9. Raymond S. Ross, Persuasion: Communication and Interpersonal Relations (1974).
10. See Stephen W. Littlejohn. Theories of Human Communication, 7th ed. (2002). This text is the most widely used source of classic and contemporary Communications Theory available.
11. Ross, 57.
12. Littlejohn, 332. See also David Hesselgrave, Communicating Christ Cross-Culturally, 2nd ed. (1991), 27.
13. Sara Sanderson King, ed. Human Communication as a Field of Study: Selected Contemporary Views (1989), 1.
14. George A. Miller, Language and Speech (1981), 1.
15. Charles Schwab, as quoted in Jo Condril and Benne Bough, 101 Ways to Improve Your Communication Skills Instantly (1998), 17.
16. Tony Schwartz, The Responsive Chord (1973).
17. Roger Stronstad, Spirit, Scripture & Theology: A Pentecostal Perspective (1995), 169-170.
18. William W. Menzies and Robert P. Menzies, Spirit and Power: Foundations of Pentecostal Experience (2000.)
19. Carl Rogers, Becoming a Person (1961), 18.
20. See Jon Ruthven, On The Cessation of the Charismata: The Protestant Polemic on Postbiblical Miracles (1993).
21. N. R. Hanson, Patterns of Discovery (1961), 30.
22. Robert K. Greenleaf, Servant Leadership (1977), 186, quoting G. K. Chesterton.
23. For the source of the oldest model see: Claude Shannon and Warren Weaver, The Mathematical Theory of Communication (1949), 4-6.
24. John Fiske, Introduction to Communication Studies (1992), 7.
25. W. Schramm, "How Communication Works" in The Process and Effects of Mass Communication, ed. W. Schramm and D. F Parks (1971).
26. George A. Miller, Language and Speech (1981), 31.
27. J. Samuel Bois, Explorations in Awareness (1957), 25.
28. Maurice Merloau-Ponty, The Phenomenology of Perception, trans. by C. Smith (1974), viii.
29. Littlejohn, 185.
30. Richard E. Palmer, Hermeneutics: Interpretation Theory in Schleiermacher, Dilthey, Heidegger, and Gadamer (1969), 128.
31. Edmund Husserl, Ideas: General Introduction to Pure Phenomenology, trans. W.R.B. Gibson (New York: Collier, 1962) and Phenomenology and the Crisis of Philosophy, trans. Q. Lauer (1965).
32. Neil Postman and Charles Weingartner, Teaching as a Subversive Activity (1969), vii.
33. Edmund Perry, The Gospel in Dispute (1958), 99-106.
34. Hesselgrave, 301-304. Perry's diagram was a synthesis of the theories of F. H. Smith and F. C. S. Northrup.
35. A process of "proving" reality by observation, categorization, analysis, hypothesis, and verification, etc.
36. Littlejohn, 5.
37. Hesselgrave, 301 (from Northrup).
38. Ibid., 301-304.
39. As modified by Perry, p. 100, and as seen in Hesselgrave, p. 303 (used by permission).

Tarr would suggest that Sub-Saharan Africa and many animist oriented cultures also are included with China as being Concrete Relational as first priority.

40. This concept was first advanced in Emile Durkheim's work in the early twentieth century with his sociological insight into the sacred and the profane.
41. David K. Berlo, The Process of Communication (1960).
42. Ibid., 175.
43. Ibid., 177.
44. Postman and Weingartner, 82.
45. Edmund Rybarczyk, "Expressing the Inexpressible: Tongues as Apophatic Speech" (paper presented at the 31st annual meeting of the Society of Pentecostal Studies, Lakeland, FL, 2002), 5; quoting Vladimir Lossky, The Mystical Theology of the Eastern Church, trans. by The Fellowship of St. Alban and St. Sergius (1976), 43.
46. Figures 2, 3 and 4 are adapted by permission from Raymond S. Ross, Persuasion: Communication and Interpersonal Relations (1974), and W. Brembeck and W.S. Howell, Persuasion: A Means of Social Influence, 2nd ed. (1976), used with permission.
47. For a good explanation of this principle, see Gayle D. Irwin, The Jesus Style, (1983).
48. Ross, 59.
49. Smith Wigglesworth, Smith Wigglesworth On the Holy Spirit (1998), 216.
50. For a reference to Parham's mistake in Topeka, 1901, see Vinson Synan, The Century of the Holy Spirit (2001), 3.
51. Dennis and Rita Bennett, The Holy Spirit and You (1971), 86.
52. Larry Christenson, Speaking in Tongues: Its Significance for the Church (1968), 73.
53. A. Heschel, Quest for God (1982), 3-4.
54. W. Samarin, Tongues of Men and Angels (1972), esp. 154, 232, and W.J. Hollenweger, Geist und Materie, Interkulturell Theologie, III (1988) 314-15, cited in Frank Macchia, "Sighs too Deep for Words," JPT 1, 1992, 52-53.
55. Chesterton, G. K., in Robert Greenleaf, Servant Leadership (1977), 186.
56. For more on this subject see Del Tarr, "Preaching the Word in the Power of the Spirit: A Cross Cultural Analysis" in Called and Empowered: Global Mission in Pentecostal Perspective; Murray Dempster, Byron Klaus, and Douglas Peterson, eds. (1991), 121-136.
57. See Appendix 1. A model from class was one evolved from the mathematically based model of Shannon and Weaver. For the source of one of the oldest models see: Claude Shannon and Warren Weaver, The Mathematical Theory of Communication (1949), 4-6.
58. J. W. Shepherd, The Christ of the Gospels (1946), 100.
59. J.D. Pentecost, The Words and Works of Jesus Christ (1981) 124.
60. For example, see the studies of Rhetoric and Persuasion by B.I. Mack, and G.A. Kennedy; B.I. Mack, Rhetoric and the New Testament (1990), G.A. Kennedy, New Testament Interpretation Through Rhetorical Criticism (1984).
61. L.T. Johnson, Religious Experiences in Early Christianity (1999), 24.
62. Benjamin S. Bloom, Taxomony of Educational Objectives: Handbook I: Cognitive Domain (1967).
63. Edmund J. Rybarczyk, "Expressing the Inexpressible: Tongues as Apophatic Speech" (paper presented at the Annual Meeting of the Society of Pentecostal Studies, 2002), 2.
64. Ibid, 3.
65. More detail on these differences between East and West are available in Lawrence Kincaid, Communication Theory: Eastern and Western Perspectives (1987).

66. Rybarczyk cites Lossky in this vein, 43.
67. Gordon D. Fee, Corinthians: A Study Guide 3rd Edition, (1997), 18.
68. Larry Christenson, Speaking in Tongues, Its Significance for the Church (1968).
69. Ibid., 27.
70. Ibid.
71. See Appendix 1 for some rather mature sources, as the discipline of Non-verbal Communication was a "new" emphasis about 30 years ago.
72. Agnes Sanford, The Healing Gifts of the Spirit (1966).
73. Paul Tournier, The Meaning of Persons (1957).
74. Christenson, 27.
75. Ibid., 27.
76. Tony Schwartz, The Responsive Chord (1973), 3.
77. Paul Hiebert, Anthropological Insights for Missionaries (1985), 135.
78. Ibid., 134-5.
79. Ibid., Hiebert (1985), 198. See also Del Tarr, Double Image: Biblical Insights from African Parables (1994).
80. Hiebert, 136.
81. Schwartz, 10.
82. For an interesting and much neglected study in the West of 65 percent of human communication see: Edward T. Hall, The Hidden Dimension (on proxemics) AND The Silent Language (general non-verbal communications) (1966); also Robert G. Harper, et. al. Nonverbal Communications: The State of the Art (1978); Mark L. Knapp, Non-Verbal Communication in Human Interaction (1972); Dale G. Leathers, Non-Verbal Communication Systems (1976).
83. Tony Schwartz, The Responsive Chord (1973).
84. James K.A. Smith, "The Closing of the Book: Pentecostals, Evangelicals, and the Sacred Writings," JPT 11 (1997), 49-71.
85. Walter Ong, "World as View and World as Event," American Anthropologist 71, (1969), 642.
86. Tony Schwartz (1973), 6-10.
87. For an interesting and informative exposé of this theory, see: F.S.C. Northrup, The Meeting of East and West (1953) and F. H. Smith in Edmund Perry, The Gospel in Dispute (1958), 99-106. Oralness leads to concrete relational thinking as a first order. Plato and Aristotle set the West on a course of conceptual thinking as a priority. Oral thinkers organize their world of communications on proverbs, aphorisms, allegory and memories, which they repeat in narrative form. Dance, songs, drama, dilemma and folk tales are used. See Del Tarr, Double Image: Biblical Insights from African Parables (1994), 11-15.
88. Paul Hiebert, 135.
89. Harvey Cox, 1995, 15.
90. Rybarczyk, 15.
91. James K. A. Smith, "The Closing of the Book: Pentecostals, Evangelicals, and the Sacred Writings," JPT 11 (1997), 50.
92. T.W. Gillespie, The First Theologians: A Study in Early Christian Prophecy (1994).
93. Ibid.
94. James K. A. Smith, 53ff. I am greatly indebted to James Smith's article and his research.
95. M. H. Cartledge, "Charismatic Prophecy: A Definition and Description," JPT 5, (1994), 100. Emphasis mine.

96. Schwartz, 6.
97. Smith, 49.
98. Ibid., 6. Smith gives credit to Brian Stock. For a thorough exposition of the cultural impact of print literacy on an oral society see Brian Stock, The Implications of Literacy: Written Language and Models of Interpretation in the Eleventh and Twelfth Centuries (1983). Especially significant is the chapter on Cultural Implications, 59-87.
99. Steven J. Land, Pentecostal Spirituality: A Passion for the Kingdom (1993), 26.
101. Ibid., 111.
101. Smith, 55.
102. Stock.
103. Ibid., 3.
104. Smith.
105. Jack Deere, Surprised by the Power of the Spirit (1993), 187.
106. See Del Tarr (1994), 151-152, for an example of how oral speech, like drum talk, can instruct us on this vital issue.
107. M. H. Cartledge, "Charismatic Prophecy: A Definition and Description," JPT 5 (1994), 62.
108. Smith, 58.
109. For a more detailed exposé of this principle see: Del Tarr, Double Image (1994), chapter 6. Remember, the Mossi were totally "orally literate" before the arrival of the French colonialists. I also know that for the purist, to say one is "orally literate" is an oxymoron. I use it here in the connotative sense of speech as a social skill highly valued, just like reading and writing is in a text-literate society. One must not naively believe that all who can speak are equal in an oral society, anymore than all who can read and write are equal.
110. Jahn Janheinz, "Value Conceptions in Sub-Saharan Africa," Epistemology in Anthropology (1964), chapter 4.
111. Tony Schwartz, The Responsive Chord (1973), 6-10.
112. Smith, 56.
113. Stock, 62.
114. Ibid., 31.
115. Ibid., 36.
116. Smith, 57.
117. Ibid., 58-59.
118. Ibid., 67.
119. Jack Hayford, The Beauty of Spiritual Language (1992).
120. David Barrett, World Christian Encyclopedia: A Comparative Study of Churches and World Religions in the Modern World AD 1900-2000 (1982), 17.
121. L.M. Hussey, "The Wit of the Carpenter," The American Mercury, Vol. 5: 329-336.
122. Killian McDonnell, Charismatic Renewal and the Churches (1976).
123. Throughout the history of the Christian Church there have always been occasional outbreakings of the phenomenon known as the spiritual gifts described by the apostle Paul in his letters to the Corinthians. Some developed into sizable movements; others were soon extinguished by the Roman Church hierarchy and most often branded as heretics. None of these "exceptions" developed into a worldwide force is presently seen. For a study of this phenomenon in Church history see Gary McGee, ed. Initial Evidence, Historical and Biblical Perspectives on the Pentecostal Doctrine of Spirit

Baptism (1991), and Eddie L. Hyatt, 2000 Years of Charismatic Christianity, A 21st Century Look at Church History from a Pentecostal/Charismatic Perspective (2002).

124. Some of the following three pages were first published in Called and Empowered: Global Mission in Pentecostal Perspective edited by Dempster et. al. (1991), 120.

125. See Olando Costas, Church and its Mission: A Shattering Critique From the Third World (1974).

126. Alfred Korzybski, Science and Sanity, 2nd Edition (1958), See: Introduction to the 2nd Edition.

127. A. L. Drummond, German Protestantism Since Luther (1951), 276.

128. For an account of Aristotle's work on informal logic, of Sophistical Refutations and its impact on later thought, see C.L. Hamblin, Fallacies (1972). This form of logic has affected Westerners, including North Americans. Aristotle made his way into the Christian world through Roman Catholic theologians such Thomas Aquinas, as well as later Lutheran and Reformed theologians.

129. Don Wardlaw, Preaching Biblically: Creating Sermons in the Shape of Scripture (1983), 12.

130. Hesselgrave (1991), 210-213.

131. Ibid., 212.

132. Wardlaw, 13.

133. Ibid., 15.

134. Gordon Fee. Corinthians: A Study Guide. (1997), 63.

135. For a brilliant exposé on how upside down are the Beatitudes of Matt. 5 in relation to the world's thinking, see: Paul Bretscher, The World Upside-Down or Right-Side Up? (1964).

136. Jackie David Johns, In Globalization of Pentecostalism, A Religion Made to Travel, "Yielding to the Spirit: The Dynamics of a Pentecostal Model of Praxis (1999), 70-84.

137. Ibid., 72.

138. Thomas Groome, "In Search of a Way of Knowing," Christian Religious Education (1981), chapter 7.

139. Rudolf Bultman, Theological Dictionary of the New Testament, Vol. 1: 698.

140. Johns, 78.

141. Del Tarr, "Indirection and Ambiguity as a Mode of Communication in West Africa" (Unpublished Ph.D. diss., University of Minnesota, 1980), Universal Microfilm # 80-19577.

142. See Japie LaPoorta's chapter 7 in Globalization of Pentecostalism, Murray Dempster, et. al. (1999), 151-169.

143. Ibid., 158-159.

144. T. Schwartz, The Responsive Chord (1973).

145. To pursue the topic of resonance in interpersonal relations, see W. Lamb, Posture and Gesture (1965), 137ff. He introduced the word "contaminator" to describe individuals who have special natural powers, usually described as someone with a magnetic personality. Lamb felt probably the biggest "contaminator" of all time was Jesus Christ.

146. For a rather comprehensive overview of many years of this dialogue, see: Pneuma: The Journal of the Society for Pentecostal Studies, Fall 1990.

147. Email from Bob Kilpatrick, June 6, 2003.

148. Ibid., Kilpatrick.

149. Smith Wigglesworth, Smith Wigglesworth On The Holy Spirit (1998), 219.

150. Philip Wheelwright, Metaphor and Reality (1962), 39.
151. Rudyard Kipling, "The Ballad of East and West," Rudyard Kipling's Verse: Inclusive Edition 1885-191 (1924), 268-72.
152. F.S.C. Northrop, The Meeting of East and West (1953).
153. Philip Wheelwright, 39.
154. For good insight into what written speech does to make us linear in orientation, see Tony Schwartz, The Responsive Chord (1973), 6, for an explanation of linearity.
155. Del Tarr, "Indirection and Ambiguity as a Mode of Communication in West Africa" (1980).
156. For a detailed explanation of this concept, see: Frank Boas, The Mind of Primitive Man (1965) and Benjamin Lee Whorf, Language, Thought and Reality: Selected Writings of B.L. Whorf, ed. John B. Carrol (1956).
157. Steven Littlejohn (2002), 3-5, gives excellent source material for those interested in the evolution of Communication Theory and the forces that formed it. For a study of diverse theories, see: Robert T. Craig, "Communication Theory as a Field" Communication Theory 9 (1999): 119-161.
158. E. T. Hall, The Hidden Dimension (1966), 105.
159. Morton Kelsey (1968), 213.
160. Ibid., 213.
161. Ismer Schorsch, The Sacred Cluster (n.d.).
162. Smith (1997).
163. Hiebert (1985), 134.
165. See Stanley M. Burgess, The Holy Spirit: Eastern Christian Traditions (1989).
166. Wm. S. Howell and Winston Brembeck (1952).
167. Earl Creps (sermon preached at AGTS Chapel in Springfield, MO on November 3, 1998).
168. For a good discussion on this topic of integration of communication methods and theological differences, see Ray S. Anderson, Ministry on the Fireline (1993) 197-209. Anderson clearly highlights both the method of communication and its content when he discusses the same conflict that emerged in the first century Church. "For thousands of pastors and church leaders who are on the fireline of God's mission in the world we need a theology that sings, even as it stings, igniting the mind and stirring the heart. I submit that a Pentecostal seminary must teach a theology that indeed sings and stings but also dances and celebrates the power of God, as well as heals and mends and matures." He points out in his epilogue that, like the concept explained by Creps, there are seemingly opposing forces of power and process. Anderson describes these as the tradition of the twelve vs. the tradition of the power of Pentecost.
169. For an explanation of the two hemispheres of the brain and their mutual dependency and differentiation, see Robert Ornstein, The Psychology of Consciousness (1977).
170. For another excellent source on the topic at hand, see Steven J. Land, Pentecostal Spirituality, A Passion for the Kingdom (1993), 44-45. He quotes J. W. Jones from The Spirit and the World (1975), for an insightful exposure to how some parts of the Church subjugate or domesticate the Holy Spirit and, in so doing, misunderstand the relationship of the Spirit and the Word.
171. See Paul Bretscher, The World Upside-Down or Right-Side Up? (1964).

CHAPTER 5

THE CASE FOR TONGUES IN THE BIBLE

But we have this treasure in jars of clay to show that this all-surpassing power is from God and not from us (2 Cor. 4:7).

1. Together we have examined in the introduction, my goals for where we are going.
2. We have considered the critics who disavow glossolalia for a wide range of reasons. (You noted, hopefully, that this writer believes an argument is more persuasive if its antithesis is also presented and especially if more than one side is presented.) We are not afraid to look at the critics, including those from inside the family itself.
3. A short recent and early history was given especially to benefit the readers who have newly come to explore the phenomenon.
4. A small chapter quoted the early leaders and laity giving us some interesting perspectives because they paid a high price for their stand on the new awakening.
5. Then came the important chapter of *communications theory*, setting the matrix (background) for the whole study.

Now a brief time will be spent considering the *case* made in the Bible for tongues (glossolalia). I am interested now in using a "close-up lens" to consider what we have been looking at from a distance.

Confusing Essence and Function

One of the most misunderstood aspects about glossolalia from the uninitiated or those who reject this experience relates to their quick reductionism of the essence of the gift. Many don't see the varied *functions* of the gift believing, from their ignorance of the subject, that all the instances of tongues are the same in Scripture. In my understanding there are six distinct, but sometimes overlapping, expressions that "are the same in essence but different in function."[1]

1. For initial evidence of the Baptism in the Holy Spirit—Acts 2:4; 10:46; 19:6.
2. For personal edification (private prayer language)—I Cor. 14:4,18.
3. For personal edification in church/public (private but communal) —I Cor. 14:2, 4, 15-17; sometimes singing in the Spirit.
4. For acceleration of prayer—Rom. 8:26 (overlaps with #2, but different function).
5. For a "sign" (understood by some spectator—not the speaker) —Acts 2:8; I Cor. 14:22-24.
6. For a "manifestation of the gift" in the church (needing interpretation)—I Cor. 14:5, 13-19).

Let's elaborate on some of the above.

TONGUES AS A SIGN

Pentecostals generally use three main biblical sources to substantiate doctrinal positions about the role of tongues (glossolalia) as a **sign** that the Holy Spirit baptism has occurred: Acts chapters 2, 10, and 19, where glossolalia is mentioned explicitly with the phenomenon of the baptism in the Holy Spirit.

Jerusalem

2:4 *All of them were filled with the Holy Spirit and began to speak in other tongues as the Spirit enabled them.*

Caesarea

10:45-46 *The circumcised believers who had come with Peter were astonished that the gift of the Holy Spirit had been poured out even on the Gentiles. For they heard them speaking in tongues and praising God.*

Ephesus

19:6 *When Paul placed his hands on them, the Holy Spirit came on them, and they spoke in tongues and prophesied.*

Tongues speech has other specific as well as implicated references in the epistles of the New Testament.

> Tongues drew the multitude's attention and glorified Christ; the phenomenon did not, however, supplant preaching in the winning of the lost. Peter's sermon was necessary for that. The suggestion of some scholars that tongues were given for evangelizing the lost is

incorrect. Tongues were given for a sign of the Spirit's indwelling, a sign of the presence of God with man.[2]

Morton T. Kelsey,[3] an Episcopalian rector, describes himself as having interacted with many friends and parishioners who have spoken in tongues.

> I speak, therefore, with some assurance in saying that, even apart from Biblical consideration, this phenomenon cannot be dismissed as just fraud or meaningless irrationality!
>
> After the time of Paul there were occasional references to speaking in tongues by the writers of the early church. This evidence is important for the person who wishes to understand and assess the significance of tongue speaking. If the practice had been confined to Biblical times and had not occurred again, it would be far easier to dismiss the matter there. If, however, glossolalia continued among those who established the foundation of the church, amid the most adverse circumstances, it deserves our careful attention...the church fathers are little known to readers today. It is significant that among those intellectually sophisticated writers glossolalia was known and accepted as one of the gifts which are given to Christians.[4] [a]

It is significant that among those intellectually sophisticated writers [early fathers after Paul] glossolalia was known and accepted...it deserves our careful attention.
– Kelsey

PRAYER AND INTERCESSION

There are many Scriptures for the use of tongues. We will start with *praying* and *singing*, but there are many more: Pray in tongues—I Cor. 14:14; then to sing in tongues—I Cor. 14:15; related to giving thanksgiving and blessing in tongues—I Cor. 14:16. Brandt and Bickett speak of **intercession in prayer** in both Old and New Testaments using the words *paga* in Hebrew and *entugchano* in Greek to explain the sense of "to appeal to" and "to plead for." A familiar Scripture includes this term.

---

[a] For the argument that tongues were so common in the NT era, see Harvey Conn in Wade Horton, 1966: "What this reveals is that glossolalia was so much a part of the apostolic scene that its presence was assumed in the gospel record. The miracle of tongues was simply an accepted and expected attendant to the Holy Spirit in the lives of the believers" (page 47). See also the works of Ron Kydd, 1984; Mel Robeck, 1985, and Eddie Hyatt, 2002.

> *In the same way, the Spirit helps us in our weakness. We do not know what we ought to pray for, but the Spirit himself intercedes for us with groans that words cannot express. And he who searches our hearts knows the mind of the Spirit, because the Spirit intercedes for the saints in accordance with God's will* (Rom. 8:26-27).

The same authors explain how Pentecostals and Charismatics see the role of the Holy Spirit in an even broader way of general praying in tongues. The scriptural understanding for this belief is based on Jude 20 and Eph.6:18 and numerous verses in Paul's letter to the Corinthian Christians. Jude says:

> *You, dear friends, build yourselves up in your most holy faith and* ***pray in the Holy Spirit."***

Paul in Ephesians says:

> ***Pray in the Spirit*** *on all occasions with all kinds of prayers and requests.*

These Scriptures probably have their base of connection with the words of Paul in I Cor. 14:15; "I will *pray with my spirit,* but I will also pray with my mind." Even though Paul says he is praying with his spirit, it becomes clearly resolved when in the previous verse (v.14) he is praying in tongues when he says: "For if I pray in a tongue, my spirit prays." "Therefore, 'praying in the Spirit' is defined as that praying which springs from the merging of the human spirit with the Holy Spirit, issuing in a prayerful utterance in an unknown tongue."[5]

> Paul intimates in I Cor. 14:2 and in 14:4 that the gift of speaking in tongues provides a person with glorious communion with God. Most likely, however, this communion results not from understanding what the person is saying but from drawing closer to God through the power of the Spirit. Yet the person who prays that way is not expected to then be able to interpret his or her own words immediately. Paul wrote, *if I pray in tongues, my spirit is praying, but I don't understand what I am saying.* That is part of the mysterious beauty of this particular gift—it does not engage the intellect in order to use it. It is a gift filled with fervor and passion for the Lord. Yet even as a person prays, he or she does not understand his or her own words. The phrase "my spirit is praying" probably refers to both the spirit and the Spirit—the person's inner spirit prays to and praises God with words given by the Holy Spirit.[6]

PRAYING IN THE SPIRIT STRENGTHENS FAITH

****Praying in the Spirit offers a new dimension in worship of God.** *"One who speaks in a tongue speaks not to men but to God"* (I Cor. 14:2, 3).

Evangelist and author John Bevere[7] in his video series *Intimacy with the Holy Spirit* explains one of the reasons why one would want to speak in tongues is that when we "pray with the understanding" (mind—I Cor. 14:15, NIV), God is forced to come down to our level.

> If I go into the oval office of the President of the United States and dialogue with him, he must come down to my level. He knows all the secrets concerning national defense, international relations, and legislative matters that I as a citizen do not know. The president must come down to my level when speaking about any of these matters. I'm an unsophisticated lay person about these matters. So it is when we talk to God in our mother tongue. English (or French/German) limits us to our mental powers when we formulate sentences to make a point. But God has made it possible for us to come up to HIS level! When we speak in tongues, I Cor. 14:2, 3 says, we speak directly to God.

Faith to believe in prayer

Murray Brown, Sr. (now deceased) was a missionary colleague of ours. Of him it is said by the Mossi of Burkina Faso that he spoke the best "language of the heart" of any Westerner who had learned their language (Mori). West Africa still today has less than 30 percent of its rural areas under electrification. In the 1940s and 50s, Murray and his family used a kerosene stove for cooking as well as a kerosene operated refrigerator—interestingly called an "electrolux." While filling the refrigerator's kerosene tank, evidently the vapors built up and the machine exploded burning his legs badly. Medical facilities were far away and in another country, but he was taken to a bush hospital where his burns were treated. Because no pain medicine was available, treatment included tying his hands and feet to the bedposts at night so he would not injure himself because of the pain of his condition. In the middle of the night, with no doctors or nurses on duty, and nothing but a candle in the room, the driver ants found him and invaded under the bandages of his badly burned legs. Calling was to no avail as he prayed in a loud voice and hollered for help from anyone who might hear him. No one came to his aid (typically true of African bush hospitals on weekends!). But suddenly, the ants retreated and disappeared. This is unheard of behavior of these ferocious carnivorous insects. His burns healed in record time. Upon completing their term two years later, the family was doing the required deputational travels in the States. At the conclusion of a missionary service in Kansas, a lady approached and asked what were the circumstances of such and such a date and time while the Brown family served in Togo, West Africa. Days and times were checked with the time zone differences and it was discovered she had been summoned by the Holy Spirit to intercede in tongues for three hours at the exact time the ants had invaded the hospital room and began to eat on Murray's burned legs. She didn't know what she was praying for but she *heard Murray's voice* and responded. (He had the most unusual and unique pair of "leather lungs." Everyone who knew him could identify his voice as being like no one else's.) "That's Murray Brown's voice," she said as she knelt in prayer until the burden lifted.[8]

****Praying in the Spirit is totally individual, personal. God can communicate with your inner soul-man without engaging your perceptual field (Ross's fan of perception) of past learning and habitual categorization of information.** In this regard, Christenson says God can work a sanctification through the power of the Spirit that, of course, is individual.

> The edification which one receives through the exercise of speaking in tongues is on a highly individual basis. Your own program of sanctification is tailor-made by the Holy Spirit according to your individual needs, and according to the place He is preparing you for in the Body of Christ.[9]

**** One can pray in tongues silently, in the inner man, to help one "pray without ceasing" as one is *encouraged* to do in I Thess. 5:17.**

Also in Ephesians 6:18 we read, "And pray in the Spirit on all occasions with all kinds of prayers and requests..." In the light of the same author who wrote the epistles to the Corinthians where the topic of praying in the Spirit was contrasted with praying with the understanding (I Cor. 14), who can suppose Paul wasn't talking of one's private prayer language (glossolalia, a universal Christian phenomenon at that time) when he wrote "And pray in the Spirit on all occasions..."? I believe it would be a stretch of interpretation to deny it.[10]

****Praying in the Spirit overcomes our weakness of not knowing what or how to pray.** In the context of hoping and wishing for God's deliverance of creation and His creatures in it, as written in Romans chapter 8, there is an amazing avenue of power in prayer that has been "explained away" by many, and in so doing has deprived godly folk of this powerful dimension in prayer.

> *In the same way, the Spirit helps us in our weakness. We do not know what we ought to pray for, but the Spirit himself intercedes for us with groans that words cannot express. And he who searches our hearts knows the mind of the Spirit, because the Spirit intercedes for the saints in accordance with God's will* (Romans 8:26-27).

I can relate this to the wonderful benediction of Saint Paul at the close of his epistle to the Corinthian church. "May the grace of the Lord Jesus Christ, the love of God, and the fellowship of the Holy Spirit be with you all" (II Cor. 13:14). God desires intimacy of *fellowship* with us, His creatures. It was so in the beginning with the first couple when He came in the cool of the evening to talk and walk with them in the garden. The word fellowship is also translated communion (an exchange of thoughts and feelings—social intercourse). This is also related to the incarnational partnership that God insists in His dealings with us. If one prays by "groaning" (Rom. 8), one does not lose consciousness; one does not go into ecstasy by a total loss of control. One prays in a language unknown to the person praying (and sometimes even praying by groanings) *in the intention of the deep longings of the heart or burdens of the circumstantial moment.* One would wonder when and exactly how the Christian Church divorced itself from human emotion in liturgical expression in a little over 200 years after Paul wrote these words. (With few exceptions, it was generally stomped out in the name of orthodoxy.) How different must have been the Apostolic Church from the "controlled—proper" model of worship that evolved through the ages. Who decided, of the many and varied models of the worship of Yahweh seen in the Scriptures, that He could only be worshiped in a predictable and sober manner? When did a "holy hush" become piety?

When in the history of the Church did a "holy hush" become the unique demonstration of piety?

> Thus, tongues symbolize the 'groans' too deep for words (Rom. 8:26) among the people of God, bringing them into solidarity with suffering humanity—even the entire suffering creation—in order to struggle toward their redemption and liberation.... After all, tongues in Acts 2 were given prophetic significance as a proclamation of God's mighty acts to Diaspora Jews who were aliens in their own land and had known only occupation by forces who wished to strip them of their unique calling and identity. Tongues also served to provide a visible link of solidarity of the hated Gentiles with the Jews who remained faithful to

their calling by accepting God's decisive act of redemption and liberation in Jesus, the crucified and risen One (Acts 10:46).[11]

SINGING IN THE SPIRIT

The Spirit-filled life is capable of bringing much joy in everyday circumstances—even in the face of disagreeable times and events. Praying in tongues privately, in private prayer and praise ("...speak to himself and to God" I Cor. 14:28 and 18) also leads to singing in the Spirit. Harold Horton remarks:

> Speaking to *yourselves* . . .in spiritual songs, that is, songs in other tongues sung to cadences dictated also by the Spirit. Speaking to ourselves thus in the Spirit is edifying ourselves. . .If we speak with tongues we have a well within us in this barren wilderness of a world. Singing thus will start a fountain in the driest desert.[12]

Brandt and Bicket add,

> Thanksgiving is the very essence of Spirit-filled living ... and 'singing and making music in your heart to the Lord' seems to mean that psalms, hymns, and spiritual songs flow out from the private sanctuary of the inner man.[13]

Under the inspiration of the Spirit of God, it is not unusual to hear and participate into a blending of harmonious singing in tongues, adding musical cadences that sometimes sound like the Eastern singing on the pentatonic scale; high notes, low notes all sung by different voices creating very inspiring worship that may go on for some time. It's very relaxing, often quiet and so worshipful. The participants are aware of such close presence of God's Spirit and nearness. Those experiencing this phenomenon for the first time will often talk about this to their friends for some time and long to repeat it. Wise worship leaders will make room for its place in Charismatic adoration of God.[14]

Each individual using his or her own prayer language (glossolalia) in a simultaneous event to participate in communal worship may seem strange for those who habitually participate in church where verbalized prayer is coordinated in a litany or in unison of one known "mother tongue" language.

COMMUNICATIONS INSIGHT

HUMILITY = TEACHABLE

THE DISCIPLES CAME to Jesus and asked the question: Who is the greatest in the kingdom of heaven? Jesus called a young child and had him stand before the group of disciples.

And he said: I tell you the truth, unless you change and become like little children, you will never enter the kingdom of heaven. Therefore, whoever humbles himself like this child is the greatest in the kingdom of heaven.
Matt. 18:3-4.

Young children learn language without much ego-defensiveness or self-consciousness. Not fearing the sanction of criticism about their learning curve, they have an incredible capacity to learn quickly and without much effort—which totally confounds an adult attempting to learn the same new language! (Of course, there are other factors besides age.) Once the child gets to school and comes under the quantitative system of evaluation by the world of education, he/she soon becomes self-conscious and fearful of mistakes in front of peers and superiors. No doubt that's why Jesus took a "little" child for an example in front of the disciples. Having learned three languages after becoming an adult, I've made a study of why some learn easier than others. It, of course, relates to the musical ability of the ear to pick up tones and nuances, besides native intelligence and other factors. But I believe the prime variable has little to do with ability, **but rather one's attitude about making mistakes.** A young child can mispronounce a word many times, as he/she learns to say it correctly, with seemingly little self-consciousness. In fact, I believe I could paraphrase the words of Jesus in this sense by saying: *"Unless you become as a little child, you will never learn to speak a foreign language fluently."*

You can see the analogy coming, can't you! Unless you humble yourself, you'll never be able to accept "God's foolishness" of glossolalia either.

POWER TO WITNESS

In Acts 5:29ff we see the boldness of Peter and the others before the most powerful Jewish court of the land. "We must obey God rather than men!" It seems the examples of this empowering of the Spirit is duplicated in many countries across the globe where a Pentecostal outpouring has occurred. The writer can testify to the zeal and boldness to witness when in Burkina Faso a remarkable visitation of the Spirit graced the campus of a minister's training school in Nagabagre in 1965. At that time, 2000 believers who had not received the Spirit's fullness rode bicycles, walked, or came on donkeys from as far as 200 miles to see and hear and receive this New Testament gift. Over a 90-day period, for 24 hours a day, at the Bible school at Nagabagre and in the capital city of Ouagadougou at a primary school, a mighty outpouring of God's blessing and power was manifest. Classes were suspended. The conviction power of the Lord was so evident that many an onlooker (and some scoffers) was unable to stand on his/her feet but fell to the floor unable to get up until he/she had cried out to God for forgiveness. The hallmark of the revival wasn't tongues (though they all spoke in tongues) but repentance. God was preparing this church for a revival that to this date, 45 years later, has not stopped. Those recognized as having received the "baptism" in turn felt the urge to witness with new boldness. During that 90-day period alone, 3500 new converts were added to the churches all over Burkina Faso as the revival spread from the Bible school and the primary school with great zeal, led by those newly empowered in the Acts 1:8 model. *"But you will receive power when the Holy Spirit comes on you; and you will be my witnesses ..."* The church has gone from 11,000 believers in 1965 to over 800,000 at the turn of the century. Of the 3000 credentialed ministers, not one receives support from abroad. There have been no Westerners in leadership since the early 50s as the model of the Apostle Paul's missiology has been the watchword. This country, nestled up next to the great Sahara, is one of the poorest countries of the world (average annual income = US $300) but they send missionaries to 15 different countries outside their own borders, besides reaching the unreached inside Burkina Faso. Tongues-inspired power will release the laity to be witnesses, just like Jesus promised. When a church stops witnessing, it stops growing. The obvious sign tongues brings to the individual is first self-awakening, then self-confidence and boldness to a dependence on the Holy Spirit to obey the focus of Acts 1:8. These are the fruits of those totally "enrobed" by the Spirit for power to witness.

During that 90-day period alone, 3500 new converts were added to the churches all over Burkina Faso as the revival spread.

The author has personally experienced the contention of Timothy Warner.

> In many parts of the world...people are much more power conscious than they are truth conscious. We preach a very logical message by Western standards, but our hearers remain unimpressed. Let them see Christian power displayed in relation to the spirit world in

which they live with great fear, however, and they will 'hear' the message more clearly than our words alone could ever make it.[15]

Power to suffer in joy. "The apostles left the Sanhedrin, rejoicing because they had been counted worthy of suffering disgrace for the Name" (Acts 5:41).

Power to be pure without self-righteousness. But it's not automatic. The will is needed, but it helps the will to be more focused.

Power to be unpopular. It even sustains teens through the perilous peer-pressure of high school years if the prayer language is maintained.

Power to be a servant. And it all starts with the "gate" of the submission required to abandon self and step in faith, the faith it requires to speak in tongues. It seems so simple! Yet this phenomenon is one of the most misunderstood, maligned, judged, condemned and ridiculed of all religious expressions. Makes sense though. You might know God would "hide" a key to usefulness and power behind a controversial **test**. One must *lose* something to speak in tongues. (See Communications Theory—Chapter 4.) L. Thomas Holdcroft gives a powerful twelve-fold list of the various aspects of the Spirit's empowerment. [16]

ABOUT POWER

Is not part of the power that comes from speaking in tongues as the Spirit gives utterance a consciousness that God is real, that He is individual? The onlooker, or critic, may not sense this, but the "tongues talker" knows—without a shadow of a doubt—this is happening to him/her and that it's real and wonderful. Note, contrary to what some professionals who haven't "tasted the orange" have analyzed, the participant is not unconscious or in a trance. The confidence that comes from such an experience is not subject to an argument! It's as empowering as it is agreeable and consciously accepted by the recipient. It can make for a powerful witness! It is not meant for a one-time experience, but as the apostle Paul writes—"be being filled with the Spirit" (Greek verbal form in Ephesians 5:18).

Morton Kelsey can help us here again. This Episcopalian rector who has done a major work on the subject of "tongues speech" has a counseling service connected to his parish with psychiatrists on the staff who also have researched and observed the Charismatic segment of his congregation. In other passages of his seminal work, he debunks the generalization that *all* tongues speakers are either crazy or possessed by the devil. Here he reinforces the particular value of tongues **to the speaker him/herself** as to the authenticity of tongues.

> How can we be sure whether one speaking powerfully is motivated by ego prompting or is speaking from a deeper center? Actually, prophecy always remains open to doubt. But if there is any reality to glossolalia, there can be no doubt that something beyond man himself takes hold of him. It can be known for certain that something outside the human ego, beyond the human will, can and does take hold of certain men. Tongues speaking is, therefore, at least important for its evidential value, in addition to giving expression to the religious feelings of the speaker.[17]

Tongues-speech, however, because of its unusual and demonstrative character (the very reason it is often maligned and/or over-esteemed), is particularly well suited to serve as "evidence." In short, tongues speech uniquely fills the bill because of its intrinsically demonstrative character. The sign value of tongues-speech is emphasized in the Pentecost account in Jerusalem (Acts 2). It was the decisive sign of God's favor on the Gentiles at their reception of the gift of the Spirit, manifested in tongues-speech (Acts 10:46). It is this sign that astonishes Peter's circumcised companions in Jerusalem and results in his command to baptize the Gentile converts (Acts 10:45-48). Whether from the lips of a Jew in Jerusalem or a Gentile in Caesarea, the manifestation of tongues-speech marks the speaker as a member of the end-time prophetic community.

"Be like the Pentecostals—allow the Lord to use you, the laity, in ministry"

On the Baptism from Larry Christenson:

> Will the baptism with the Holy Spirit change your life? Will it make any real difference in your Christian walk? Of course it will! The baptism with the Holy Spirit is a gift of God. God does not give worthless or no-account gifts. A Presbyterian minister, James Brown, puts it succinctly thus: 'The disciples before Pentecost were living behind locked doors—for fear. After they received the baptism with the Holy Spirit, they turned the world upside down.' That same transforming experience, that same dimension of power, is available to us, for Jesus still baptizes His followers with the Holy Spirit.[18]

EMPOWERMENT OF THE LAITY

The Pentecostal revival with it emphasis on the empowerment of every believer, and the bestowal of gifts upon every member of the Body of Christ, has freed lay people for ministry. Although some Pentecostal pastors still struggle with the implications of this, the vast majority of those leading growing churches seem to practice some form of shared ministry and leadership (by non-professionals) and are actively involved in equipping lay people for the task.[19]

I do not intend to leave the impression that only Pentecostals encourage ministry by the laity. My point, as substantiated by many writers, is the belief and practice of empowerment by the Holy Spirit for *anyone* predisposes "Full Gospel people" (a term used by traditional Pentecostals—probably still "stinging" from their expulsion from the traditional churches) to expect such participation on a grand scale. One only has to read the testimonials of non-Pentecostals, who are admonishing their own laity to "be like the Pentecostals—allow the Lord to use you in ministry."

Listen to Edward L. Cleary, O.P.[20] on the topic of Validity of Experience:

> Emphasizing the gifts of the Spirit, Latin American Pentecostals are confident that these gifts are present within the church, and can be relied on, in a way Catholics and other Protestants do not emphasize...Contemporary theologians have recognized the function of affectivity.

Jean Mouroux believes spiritual affectivity (taking pleasure in the Lord is the way many Pentecostals describe it) heals and transforms through joy:

> In a profound sense, neither institution nor any other person mediates a Pentecostal person's conversion to God. No formal rite (not even [water] baptism) is required and the role of the pastor is reduced. The testimony and the fervor of the person show the faith of the Pentecostal person. The Pentecostal movement does not require more than this testimony for one to be accepted as a convert and participant in services. Unlike other denominations, neither a certain level of preparation or knowledge of Scripture is required at this entry level. Thus Pentecostalism offers an open field for personal liberty."[21]

Harvey Cox, a recent writer on the fast growing Pentecostal/Charismatic movements relates theology to praxis in this regard: "Pentecostal theology is found in the viscera of Pentecostal spirituality. It is emotional, communal, non-rational, hopeful, and radically embodied."[22]

GLOSSOLALIA IS SIGNIFICANT BECAUSE IT IS A GIFT FROM GOD

Would God appoint in the Church that which was of no value or harmful? It's doubtful (I Cor. 12:28). Let's agree that this must be *prima facie* evidence God thinks has value for us.

COMMUNICATIONS INSIGHT

THERE IS A CASE to be made that praying in the Spirit has blessings distinct from praying with the understanding (I Cor. 14:2, 14, 28). When we pray with the understanding, we are limited to our perceptual field (think the Ross chart previously discussed). My perceptual field, made up of past experience, knowledge, attitudes, values, etc., is my sum total brain and mental powers capacity to articulate any idea or feeling I may wish to communicate. I'm forced/limited to use the words at my disposal. I can't use words that are not connected to the neuron data banks of my mind. But God wants me to have a more intimate system than that with which I can communicate with him. Might not this be what Jesus was describing to the apostles just before His death and resurrection?

> *If you love me you will obey what I command. And I will ask the Father, and He will give you another Counselor to be with you forever, the Spirit of truth. The world cannot accept Him, because it neither sees Him nor knows Him. But you know Him, for He lives with you and will be in you* (John 14:15-17).

If this is true, would one say that this is evidence of a new dimension in communication?

PRAYING IN THE SPIRIT IS SELF-EDIFYING

He who speaks in a tongue edifies himself...(I Cor. 14:4)

Could this 'self-edification' also be physical? I remember while teaching at our national seminary in Springfield, MO, Randy Hurst (a student of mine who later became a missionary to Western Samoa and is now the National Director of Evangelism) had a sister who suffered from severe migraine headaches. She sought professional relief from a pain clinic in Chicago. They discovered that by attaching electrodes to her head, the specialist could find the area of the brain activated when she worshiped God in tongues. Here is her story:

> In the 1980s I was having frequent migraine headaches. I went to the Diamond Headache Clinic in Chicago, and among other things they recommended that I try biofeedback training. The only place that was available to me in our city at that time was through the office of Dr. Larry Bass, a psychologist: he just happened to be a Christian from the same denomination with which I was associated.

I went for the biofeedback training every week for several months...Electrodes were attached at different places on my neck and head to register migraine-contributing tension in the various muscles. In addition to learning how to recognize and relax the tension in specific muscles, one of the techniques used was to close one's eyes and mentally picture something that created a feeling of serenity, such as imagining oneself resting in a quiet meadow or floating in warm ocean water. I found several such images by which I learned to achieve increasing degrees of relaxation.

One day, however, the muscle tension was severe, and I could not make any progress in relaxing it. None of the techniques worked. Finally, I gave up and instead began to pray silently for a member of my family who had a specific need. As I did so, I began to pray in the Spirit, mentally speaking in tongues/using my prayer language (optional choice). When the session ended, the technician asked me urgently, "What were you doing during the session, Mrs. Mitchell?" "Why?" I asked. "Because," he replied, "at three separate times you registered almost total relaxation, a greater degree of relaxation than I've ever seen registered before." Because he had been my husband's student in our denominational college, I felt free to tell him that I had been praying in the Spirit. He shook his head, and said, "It's just amazing, I've never seen anything like it." The following week during the next session, I again experienced difficulty in relaxing the tension. Remembering the previous week's experience, again began to silently speak in tongues, and nothing happened. Almost immediately I felt an inner correction from the Holy Spirit, telling me that I should not use His gifts casually, without spiritual purpose. I once again began to pray in the Spirit for the needs of others. Again the technician told me the meter had registered unusual relaxation.

"...at three separate times you registered almost total relaxation, a greater degree of relaxation than I've ever seen registered before"
–Therapist

The gift of praying in the Spirit continues to be a realm of beauty and mystery to me, but it is a solid, unquestioned bedrock of strength and comfort in my life.

Judy Hurst Mitchell, Springfield, MO.

Judy Mitchell's husband is a very qualified voice teacher and administrator in a college where they live. His side of the story is no less spectacular, and he adds some amazing insight into why God chose the tongue to be the instrumental sign of this controversial gift. (See Appendix 1.)

Of course, we Americans, from our scientific posture believe anything reliable can be measured and verified. Not everything God does for us **can** be measured, but apparently the preceding account and this following one can. Here again is not only spiritual edification, but a physical benefit as well. From a minister and nationally-known musician:

> I had lunch with an eyewitness of an amazing story of the power of glossolalia in Tibet where a missionary from Hong Kong worked with heroin addicts. She told me that they encouraged the addicts upon receiving Jesus as Savior to immediately be baptized in the Spirit and speak in tongues. The reason she gave was that speaking in tongues would help them avoid the worst parts of breaking the heroin addiction. Her experience is that those who speak in tongues don't have the cramps, sweats and vomiting associated with going "cold turkey."[23]

More on Self-Edification

It is used by God to transfer divine secrets and mysteries from His Spirit to ours.

"Tongues for personal edification is the most basic foundational operation of God, because it is designed by God to do for you what no preacher or teacher can do. It edifies you by building into your spirit godly traits such as love, divine insight into God's Word, and wisdom to know right from wrong and truth from falsehood."[24]

Roberson explains that once a person has been "baptized" in the Holy Spirit with the accompanying glossolalia, there are different functions of tongues illustrated in the New Testament. The gifts listed by the apostle Paul in I Corinthians, including tongues for public use, are given to believers for specific times "as the Spirit determines" (I Cor. 12:11). But the one function of tongues for private prayer (needing no interpretation but for personal edification) can be operated by the will of the individual. "God has done with this simple gift what He has done with no other, because He has made me the steward of my own edification... Now, as the individual decides, with his/her own free will how much or how little. One has but to reach out in faith and the Spirit will respond with a supernatural language from deep inside our spirit-being.[25]

ON PERSONAL EDIFICATION 70 YEARS BEFORE AZUSA!

David W. Dorries writes of Edward Irving, the Scottish-born and educated pastor and theologian whose contributions to the Christian Church transcended his native Scottish Calvinism. Irving's efforts to restore Christological balance to the church of his time (1830) resulted in his deposition from the ordained ministry of the Church of Scotland. It bears very interesting reading for any current Pentecostal or Charismatic to learn that fully 70 years before the events commonly cited as the beginnings of what is known as the "Twentieth Century's Revival" occurred (1901-1906), Edward Irving influenced a revival that had all the features of the "classical" Pentecostal Movement.

Edward Irving (1830) influenced a revival in Scotland that had all the features of the "classical" Pentecostal Movement.

Irving referred to the initial baptism in the Holy Spirit by the recipient as one where he/she would speak in tongues as on the day of Pentecost. He preferred to call it a "sign" or "gift" instead of the "initial evidence" as has been adopted by most of the major Pentecostal denominations today. His special term was the "Standing Sign."[26] For Irving, the most important reason for the gift of tongues was for personal edification (I Cor. 14:4). "It is not material to the question whether these tongues were tongues of men or of angels, or whether they were in use by any creature at all."[27] Dorries believes Irving felt the deep level of personal edification enables the believer to become increasingly familiar with the supernatural realm of the Spirit and, consequently, a heightened availability to other spiritual gifts to edify the church.

> Therefore it is nothing to be doubted, that tongues are a great instrument for personal edification, however mysterious it may seem to us; and they are on that account greatly to be desired, altogether independently of their being a sign unto others. And to me it seemeth reasonable to believe, that they will be conferred in private exercises of devotion, and earnest longings after edification; and, being given, to especially to be occupied in secret actings of the soul towards God...But, withal, there is an ultimate end to be aimed at, beyond present enjoyment and personal edification, which is, that they may prophesy and edify the church when they shall themselves have been edified.[28]

COMMUNICATIONS INSIGHT

LARRY CHRISTENSON explains further about how glossolalia builds us up: "The intellect, however, has an inveterate tendency to categorize and legalize. When the intellect steps aside, the Spirit can operate through this gift with a freer hand, building us up not where we may think we need building up, nor where someone else thinks we need it, but where He, in divine wisdom, knows that we need building up. Exactly how or why it happens is difficult to explain, but both Scripture and experience bear out this truth: *Through this simple, yet supernatural and God-appointed way of praying, one's life in Christ is wonderfully built up.* (Emphasis Christenson) ...Enhancement of one's private worship is the essential blessing of speaking in tongues. The other blessings are summed up in it: As you worship God in tongues, your mind is at rest and your spirit prays, unhindered by the limitations of the human understanding, and through this act of worship the Holy Spirit builds up your life in Christ."[29]

WHEN TONGUES SPEECH DUPLICATES JERUSALEM'S PENTECOST

In other places in the book I list the many functions of glossolalia. Many believers who disallow tongues for today or believe all the supernatural gifts of God ended with the apostles find "tongues" in the Scriptures, and they have deduced that all mention of the many instances of glossolalia in the Bible have but one function. There are actually six distinct functions in all, in my opinion (as mentioned at the beginning of this chapter). But the record shows there are times when tongues are especially meant for non-believers (one of the six) as proof of the power of God and His wooing the sinner in love to come to the truth of God's eternal design for mankind.

AT TIMES—TONGUES ARE REAL FOREIGN LANGUAGES AS IN THE ACTS 2 ACCOUNT

An interesting book by Harris lists 28 occurrences when glossolalia was understood by the listener (and, of course, not by the speaker).[30]

For those who would like a more complete listing and actual testimonials of some of these events, please see the short Appendix 2.

IN SPIRIT AND TRUTH

I've learned to worship in many settings in 70 countries around the world. I'm not stuck on just one style or expression. I've even learned the deep beauty and emotion of a responsive litany during a high mass celebrated by Pope John-Paul II during a liturgical celebration in the high vaulted ceiling, powerful pipe organ and rich ornate surroundings of St. Peter's Cathedral in Rome. Contrast that with a small mud church in the bush in Africa with mud walls and floor, the distraction of sweat and flies all the while many babies are crying during communion which is being served in one tin can filled with a mixture of vinegar and water, and where the "bread" was soggy mush from millet. That's just two extremes; add every form of worship in between. (I know—many of my churchmen are condemning of the first, and the Roman Catholics are shocked by the second.) My point is simply that worship in *Spirit and in truth*, as Jesus promised the Samaritan woman at the well, is a many-splendored thing little dependant on the externals and much on the sincerity of the heart-cry that wants to *know God and communicate with Him.*

Jesus was speaking in public at one of the feasts where the "hallel" of praise was a part of the rejoicing in God's essence. And in John 7:37-39 He raises His voice and cries: "*If anyone is thirsty, let him come to me and drink. Whoever believes in me, as the Scripture has said, streams of living water will flow from within him*"(NIV). The next verse explains that Jesus was talking of the Spirit those who believed in Him were later to receive. The more "earthy" King James Version more closely translates the "from within him" as the viscera of the stomach area, or "belly" (out of his innermost being). The symbolic implication here is this is not an intellectual exercise of analysis and planning with mapped and calculated intention, but rather somewhat of a flood of energy activated by the Spirit through human instruments in response to what God is and has done inside the instrument who has "come" and slaked his "thirst" at God's well. Jesus spoke to the Samaritan woman in John 4 of a similar expression. "Indeed the water that I will give him will become in him a spring of water welling up within him" (vs. 14, NIV). Does anyone doubt these sayings and predictions of Jesus also apply to the Christian life springing from the joys of sins forgiven in salvation? The role of the Holy Spirit is well documented in many Scriptures. But, there is more here, I believe, in this John 7 passage.

Jesus was speaking to the body of believers who would be established by His witnesses; the apostles and first converts who would carry the gospel of God's reach for mankind in redemption making them His children. The primitive church He established was a missionary church. This was not a church which would decide that the day of miracles was past just because Jesus had left them. This group of believers would not accept that the baptism in the Holy Ghost was a once and for all event; nor that one would no longer need the supernatural miracles of God because the Canon of Scripture would be completed in a few years. No, this was a Spirit baptized body who we now know experienced the supernatural and the gifts of the Spirit well into the third century—until the Church hierarchy shut it off because THEY wanted control. (See the Montanist issue as one of the examples.)

The great feast (Feast of Tabernacles) was one of praise. Jesus knows when the praise comes from the understanding, one uses a well-learned, intellectual language. This is also good as St. Paul explains (I Cor. 14:15). But when the praise flows (welling up like a flood), when it comes from the viscera, it's like a flooded river. T.D. Jakes says it's when you break the box of perfume—more like an accident than carefully planned action.

The Church has always wanted to control the flood! Put limits on it. When you control the flow, it's not a flood! So it's a question of WHO'S IN CONTROL, isn't it?! I believe God has a flood that operates inside the boundaries of His injunction, "Let all things be done in a fitting and orderly way" (I Cor. 14:40). The proof of this is He ordained all the activity and even the noise on the day of Pentecost that some of those who watched called drunken behavior (Acts 2:15). Peter said what they called drunken behavior was predicted in the Old Testament and God knew about it! (2:16-21). Note the last verse. "...That anyone calling on the name of the Lord would be saved." That's missionary. The religious Jews should have been preaching this message, but they had franchised their religion. They said it ***wasn't*** for everyone except under their conditions. THEY WANTED CONTROL. And they killed Jesus so they could keep it. But God had a plan anyway! This river does not live for itself. (Beware Pentecostals / Charismatics, who would make worship a selfish endogamous ritual.) The river is for the healing of the nations. It has quiet times and gives life; it has regular flood times. (Think of the Nile and Jordan among many others.) When one pumps water from a quiet river, not much sediment comes with the water. But at flood time, the residue left on the land is rich and the best crops come from the flood times.

> **The church has always wanted to control the flood! When you control the flow, it's not a flood. So it's a question of WHO'S IN CONTROL, isn't it?**

I've seen seminarians who have come to school seeking only degrees, and not necessarily a spiritual education. They sometimes seek intellectual prowess for a good position in the pastoral or teaching clergy. This is honorable and right. But when the flood time comes at the altar, some find themselves on the carpet or on their faces in the pews. They abandon their personal goals and get off the floor submitted, changed persons. They still pursue the same classes—the same MDiv. or DMin. degrees; but now there is a new light in the eye and a new ultimate goal. Now, it's His Kingdom! Here's the energy and submission and obedience that flows. The timid become able to witness where and when they would not have done it before. It's the overflow that does it.

O spread the tidings 'round, wherever man is found
Wherever human hearts and human woes abound;
Let every Christian tongue proclaim the joyful sound
The Comforter has come.

The Comforter has come, the Comforter has come
The Holy Ghost from heav'n, The Father's promise given
O spread the tidings 'round, wherever man is found
The Comforter has come.

O boundless love divine! How shall this tongue of mine
To wond'ring mortals tell the matchless grace divine
That once a child of hell, I in His image shine!
The Comforter has come.

—James Kirkpatrick and Frank Bottome[31]

THE DOOR TO EMPOWERMENT

Traditional Pentecostals believe glossolalia is the door that allows access to the pantry of God's provision, through growth and spiritual maturity, to the inbreaking of God's wisdom and direction. Again, Pentecostals are not the only ones who can receive such direction. Then why talk about it? Because, I submit, they have an advantage. Jesus told His disciples in Luke 12 how to be prepared for unexpected circumstances He knew they would face. "*When you are brought before synagogues, rulers and authorities, do not worry about how you will defend yourselves or what you will say, for the Holy Spirit will teach you at that time what you should say*" (vss. 11-12).[32] My contention is that for the Spirit-baptized individual in such a pressured circumstance, he/she will rely much quicker in the power of the Paraclete (*the Holy Spirit will teach you at that time what you should say)* than the believer who seeks to obey and trust but doesn't have the daily practice of submission and trust that is concomitant with speaking in a prayer language as part of daily communion with the Lord.

Let me put it in the vernacular: Use a map if you must, but don't stick so closely to it you miss the surrounding territory. The map is not reality and is not "real time." Use a manuscript if you will (and after 24 years of schooling you should believe I use manuscripts), but don't first reach for and trust in its power. It's a good tool, but it probably is not **current.** Besides, and here's the kicker: **Our minds and their preparation/discipline are no match for the all-knowing Spirit of God. If you constantly defend your map and manuscript because you have an ego investment in them (sounds good in itself—after all preparation is good), you tend NOT to rely on the Holy Spirit's expertise as you should**. And you'll resent the unschooled Pentecostal (not so true as once was) who confronts evil powers, while witnessing for the Lord with much more positive results because he/she does not have the fear of the non-tongues speaker about the miraculous. (Again, I don't intend to say the Pentecostal has NO fear. We are all human.) The "Spirit baptized" person feels enabled because he/she remembers the "evidence." "God did something—He came upon me—I didn't work it up—He was real then—He'll do it again now."

IMMEDIACY, NO HUMAN INTERMEDIARY

The immediacy of the "tongues link" is a strong reason for its availability to the believer.[33] This concept relates to access to God via a consciousness that needs no human intermediary. No bishop nor creed nor committee. Anyone, regardless of race, gender, or social standing can have the "link" and get in the "zone." That's power—not for the personal profit of the recipient, but for the propagation of the gospel. Danger! When Pentecostals or Charismatics turn that power around (selfishly), it's the worst kind of abuse because it is idolatry, like Jim Jones in Guyana and the two prominent TV evangelists who lost their ministerial credentials due to unholy greed for power and worldly treasure. But when the Spirit is allowed also to maintain holiness (and good ethics) in the life of the individual, the consequence of glossolalia encourages/allows/facilitates an "ushering in" of a "hierarchy-free" community and worship of the Lord. Anyone, man, woman, low class, high class, rich or poor can stand and prophesy. No official mediation licensed by ecclesiastical committee or set apart by apostolic ordination is required. Instead, God's Spirit is present in a direct, intense, and undeniable way. A tongues-oriented church has an invisible banner (it should never be visible or be posted or painted):

> Come and celebrate what God is going to do. We are not totally sure, because He is unpredictable. We are not *just* going to celebrate the past traditions but enjoy and expect extemporaneous "inbreakings" of what God wants to say to us for this hour, now, and what our

response needs to be. What He said two or three thousand years ago in the written WORD is important and must judge any new and lesser revelation. But, here's the new dimension. Fresh, unpredictable, and done in decency and order as I Corinthians tells us.

Note: This is not unlike the format of what the original Quakers practiced, only most of them hadn't yet broken into the charismata of the Apostolic Church.

IN THE ZONE

I'm going to make an analogy in the following insight that contains some risk.

COMMUNICATIONS INSIGHT

ANALOGIES ARE OFTEN imperfect. So are most printed or drawn graphic models. Black or colored ink lines on white paper can never totally convey the whole of an idea. They are useful to most of us, however. The West, based on linear thinking, likes to use models or figures in printed materials. Television uses the graphic arts so excessively, especially in commercials, it would be difficult to imagine electronic media existing without models, graphs, and figures. Those "lines" making up the charts of figures are NOT the real thing. (The picture of a check of $1,000,000 cannot be cashed.) Politicians couldn't get elected without graphs that are illustrations of some idea or concept. For what follows, I'm going to use an analogy from the field of sports. I'm speaking of the phrase, "He's in the zone."

Right away, some may say it is not proper to use sporting lingo to speak of theological things. But, of course, the apostle Paul did just that while talking about running and gaining the prize. The apostle Peter refers to the same analogy, of a runner receiving a crown of glory that never fades—unlike the Greek winner's crown (a laurel) made of leaves. So, here we go.

"In the zone" is a relatively new phrase used to describe a star player who arrives at a level of skill in which he or she is performing beyond that which seems possible. Someone watching will use the phrase "She's unconscious." This is meant as a positive compliment! "In the zone" has less to do with the physical ability of an athlete than with his state of mind (or more correctly, un-state of mind). Barry Bonds, a baseball player with the San Francisco Giants, is "in the zone" when he hits ten or more home runs in ten successive days. Michael Jordan is "in the zone" when he scores 40 or more points on the basketball court, and the last two with one second left on the clock that wins the game. "Out of the zone" is when a player becomes analytical about his/her performance, becomes introspective and calculating—trying to force a repeat of the "in the zone times" to figure out what is wrong.

Now I have another picture, model, or metaphor of what it means to be "in the zone" with the Holy Spirit. When someone has stopped trying to explain how He works, left off needing to know the exact tracing of His ways and "steps up to the plate" in confidence and faith, it's like the player who doesn't need to explain how back and leg and arm and wrist muscles function to swing the bat and hit a ball out of the park. The more you explain and scrutinize, the less it seems to work. That does not mean, however, there has been no preparation or training. The ancients, much closer to the East in cognition (after all, Christianity is an Eastern religion) knew about this with more clarity than we today. Lancelot Whyte tells us, quoting Dionysurs Areopagiticus (AD 50), "It was an essential feature of the mystical tradition that the most important insights are not gained by the deliberate pursuit of knowledge, but by what Keats called the 'negative capability' or ability to make oneself empty and to receive."[34] In fact, "life in the Spirit," this dimension of dynamic Christian experience, is sensitivity to the presence and power of the Spirit **and is in one sense elusive**. Henry Lederle says it cannot be pinned down. He quotes the words of Jesus in John 3:8—"the wind blows where it wills."

The more you explain and scrutinize, the less it seems to work.

> No formal structure can contain it. This frustrates the efficient 'can do' mind-set of modernity. The children of the Enlightenment wish to work with empirical verification, intellectual guarantees, and linear causality. This tendency to formalize may be seen throughout the history of the church. Biblical thinking has never meshed well with this rationalistic proof-mentality, and as a result biblical ideas have sometimes been externalized, solidified, or domesticated in our theology. Donald Gelpi would speak of western man's proclivity to 'reification.'[35]

John Bertone believes, with Gordon Fee,[36] the ambiguous nature of Romans 8:26 is indeed an example of glossolalia while praying.

> "...God, who contrary to human perception, perfectly knows and is

> in sync with the mind of the Spirit. The Spirit's glossolalic groanings that are unintelligible to humans are perfectly intelligible to God..."For the one speaking in a tongue does not speak to humans but to God: for no one understands, but by the Spirit he speaks mysteries' (I Cor. 14:2)...The experience of the infusion of God's Spirit within the believer expressed through glossolalic speech has the long-range potential of positive transformative power; it has the intended goal of encouraging believers to act responsibly within their relationship to God in the wake of their circumstances.[37]

COMMUNICATIONS INSIGHT

PARABLES—HIDDEN MEANING—INEXPRESSIBLE SPEECH

ONE OF THE MOST STRIKING characteristics of parables is that they all contain something hidden. Why? Because hiding something from the audience forces the audience to discover the hidden part. In discovering, an auditor never forgets the discovery. Concomitantly, the whole speech event with its thesis or intended speaker-goals may also be remembered better. See below what follows:

THE CASE FOR TONGUES—LIKE A PARABLE

This "Foolishness of God" Is Like a Parable

All parables have something in common. They all contain something hidden. The tie to the hidden part of a parable and tongues speech is that just like some people object to the ambiguous nature of a parable (some can't stand enigmatic speech, in the West especially), so some folks can't abide the idea God could have anything to do with the ambiguity of tongues speech. To illustrate this contention, I will exegete a passage from Matthew 13 through the eyes of African communicators who have helped me understand the Bible through the lens of their culture.

In Matthew 13:10 the disciples came to Jesus and asked him why He spoke to the people in parables. He replied, *"The knowledge of the secrets of the kingdom of heaven has been given to you, but not to them"* (vs.11.). In the next verse, Jesus really states a great truth, often hidden in a democratic egalitarian society like America. *"Whosoever has will be given more, and he will have an abundance. Whoever does not have, even what he has will be taken from him."* The *ideal* of American democracy does not receive these words well.

Americans don't like discrimination (though they practice it) face on. How could Jesus say—give more to the one who already has much, and take away from the poor one even what he has? The Mossi legend that follows will explain the apparent inconsistency and its later explanation will show the link to God's "foolishness."

THE STORY OF THE TWO SONS

There was a man who had two sons: The older son did not obey his father. He sometimes even criticized his father. This made the father very sad. The younger son obeyed his dad. In fact, he would often go the second mile. The father would ask him to do something and he would say, "Yes, Father"; and he wouldn't just do what his father asked, but he would do extra.

Now in this tribal culture, it is very common for a father to make arrangements with a family outside his own endogamous (or closed) family for a "daughter" (a very young girl) to be brought into his family. He will raise this girl as his own daughter, knowing full well that this "daughter" will eventually become the wife of one of his sons. (Thus marriage in much of the world is not a contract between two people, but a contract between two families.)

So, this man made arrangements for a young girl, about eight, to be brought to the family. She didn't take the role of a wife. She began to learn the ways of the family. The sons watched this girl as she grew up and became a beautiful girl—not just beautiful to look at, but beautifully natured. Both of the young men (the obedient younger son and the disobedient older son) wanted her.

As the years passed, the girl matured emotionally and physically and was ready to be married according to African custom. Every time the father thought about giving her to the older son he felt sad—"This boy does not obey me. This boy sometimes calls me a fool." And every time he thought about giving her to the younger son, his heart was filled with joy. "This is the one who deserves her," he thought. When he would mention these thoughts to the "family" about which son would marry the daughter, he would say: "I don't want to give her to the older one. He's not a good son. I want to give her to the younger son; he's the good son." But his own brothers and uncles would say, "Oh, it is not our custom. You must never give a wife to the younger son without first giving a wife to the older son." So he let this decision wait for many months. Finally, he knew what he was going to do.

He waited until one very dark night while it was raining (no moon or stars—and, of course, no electricity in the bush). In the middle of the night he got up, went to the sleeping girl, awakened her, and took her out in the middle of this hard rain to the sleeping quarters of his sons. (In African custom, adult sons each have a separate hut or sleeping room.) So he went to the older son's hut, clapped, and said: "Is my older son there?" The older son woke up: "Father, what do you want?"

The father called in a loud voice to make certain his son would hear: "I have a young thing here and I do not want water to get in its ears that it should die. Please come and take it into your hut."

The older son called out: "Father, you old fool, what are you doing out in the rain? Take that thing back to your own hut and leave me alone—I'm sleeping."

The father went to the younger son's hut, clapped, and said: "Is my younger son there?" The younger son woke up: "Hey, father, what are you doing in this rain? Why didn't you just call me from your hut? What are you doing standing out there?" So the father said the same thing. "I have a young thing here and I do not want water to get in its ears that it should die. Please come and take it into your hut." The young son quickly opened the door, came out in the middle of the night and said, "Father, why didn't you just call me from your hut? I would have come over there and saved you the trouble."

Now in the complete darkness, the father put the hand of he beautiful young girl into the hand of the younger son. He felt around and realized that it was this girl, and he gave a whoop of joy because he knew what had happened! He'd just been given a wife! When the older son heard the commotion, he called out, "What's the commotion out there?" The younger son called back, "Dad has just given me a wife!"

The disciples asked the teacher in Matt. 13:10, "Why do you speak to the people in parables." I ask the reader—what do you think? The father in the story above now had an excuse for why he hadn't obeyed local custom. When the uncles and brothers would come and say: "Why did you do this?" he'd reply, "Oh, I offered her to my older son and he refused." Jesus is clearly indicating in this passage: "There are some people I want to exclude because they have already closed their eyes and ears. They have been practicing it." Consider verse 12:

> *Whoever has will be given more, and he will have an abundance. Whoever does not have, even what he has will be taken from him.*

Remember that poor, miserable, fearful servant in Matt. 25 who took his one talent and buried it? It was taken from him-*even that which he had.* And look to whom it was given—not the one with four talents, but the guy with ten! Now, there's no equality in that!

God has the rules fixed—***the person who is self-centered, self-destructs.***

I submit God has hidden His empowerment from those who insist on their own power and prideful self-esteem. He hides His power from those who insist on an analytical, logical formula of proper expectations. He gives it freely to those who take the risk of simple obedience and full submission. Wouldn't you know He'd do something like this?! Study it! The Scriptures are replete with just such illogical doings on His part. It's His own brand of foolishness and the apostle understood it so succinctly. God resists those who try to put Him in their bottle of predictability.

> **Jesus excluded those who had already closed their eyes and ears. They had been practicing it. *The person who is self-centered, self-destructs.***

In verse 13 Jesus gives the answer to the question in v. 10. "This is why I speak to them in parables." The power of human choice is dramatically demonstrated here. What we evangelicals don't like about this interpretation is that it seems to contradict God's ultimate intention of *whosoever will.* I submit that it's our democratic cultural coloring that causes us to put the emphasis on **WHOSOEVER will**. I believe this passage, like many others, is using the same two words but with another emphasis: **whosoever WILL.**

Just like the younger son in the above parable, hundreds of good choices allowed him to meet the conditions of his father's proverb ("I have this young thing here and I don't want water...") and receive the good gift of his father. Interesting, isn't it, that the older son who did have something (the right of seniority) lost out—by his own words. "... *even what he has will be taken from him"* (v. 12).

As plainly as I can say it, I believe God has hidden the precious gift of the fullness of the Holy Spirit baptism behind what seems foolish and even ridiculous (tongues) *so the wrong ones won't find it.* He won't cheapen salvation's grace either—but waits for whosoever **WILL.** Yes, tongues seem absurd, yet intended by God to smash the pride of the intellect, which their exercise demands! Of the 19 or 21 (depends how they are counted) gifts of the Spirit, only tongues and interpretation of tongues are not found in the Old Testament. Does not this signal God wanted to do a new thing in this era of grace? Before, only select individuals, but now even *"to those who are afar off, even as many as the Lord our God shall call."* God was sovereign at Babel—He was again at Pentecost! I submit He still is today!

After making His amazing statement in v. 12, Jesus turned to His disciples, who had asked Him why He spoke so much in parables:

> v. 16 *But blessed are your eyes and ears because you see and hear. (You have chosen to use them correctly!)*[38]

And now, are you ready for the zinger?

> v. 17 *many prophets and righteous—have chosen not to see or hear.*

Amazing how true.

Some very good friends of ours do not believe any of the gifts of the Spirit are available today. They have really closed their spiritual eyes and ears for a system that would allow the power of the gospel to deliver the drug addict or harlot or transvestite or homosexual—and in the developing world the deliverance of shamans, fetishers, and the demon possessed—locked up in their liturgy or cessationist doctrine which keeps the Holy Spirit's New Testament power hidden away in the pages of the Good Book. It's safe there! I've worked and fellowshipped with them in Africa, Europe and Asia. The comparison of the overall results of converts and maturity of the churches in these mission endeavors between those who practice New Testament *power encounters* by the Spirit of God with those who disavow the supernatural is extensive. (On balance, I do acknowledge that numbers are not always the only way to measure effectiveness.) But the comparison worldwide can no longer be ignored. I almost hesitate to mention this juxtaposition because I really don't want to sound triumphant. I'm sorry if this causes offence.

COMMUNICATIONS INSIGHT

WHILE PRESIDENT of our Movement's seminary in Missouri, I was always involved in the promotional aspect of what all seminaries do to attract new students. I often wanted to run a full page ad in the usual religious periodicals saying: "SO YOU THINK ALL WE

DO IS SPEAK IN TONGUES?"—then, in the ad explain that the primary goal of the seminary was not tongues, but the evangelization of the world. I'd then describe the thousands who had received accredited degrees from the institution and who are ministering at home and in 120 countries of the world with the fastest growing Protestant church in the world—*but I didn't think it would be too irenic!*

What role does the Holy Spirit play among those who have surrendered to be clothed by God's special provision? There are examples past and present.

The noise and unusual behavior of the 120 on the day of Pentecost attracted the 3000 souls who on that day took Jesus as their Messiah. The Holy Spirit doesn't limit Himself to just the unusual in sound and sight. As a priority He seems intentional in enabling personal soul winning.

The personal witness in the case of Philip (Acts 8) is a good example. While engaged in his work, the Holy Spirit sent him on a mission to a sole individual in Gaza. We know this episode as the story of the Ethiopian eunuch traveling home after having come to Jerusalem. Most Bible scholars agree he in turn was an instrument of witness and part of God's plan for a people far from Palestine to hear the story of the gospel. The cases of the Holy Spirit's intervention and guidance, even as to geography, in the missionary journeys of the apostle Paul are too numerous to mention. This represents personal interaction and specific direction. Many books have been written about God's personal intervention and specific events in time and space like this.

My own encounter with the voice of the Holy Spirit leading me to a life of missionary endeavor is written elsewhere in this book. (It happened at the moment of the initial Baptism in the Holy Spirit as in the Acts accounts.) One other account, about which I first heard when attending the 75th anniversary of the church in Brazil, will illustrate but one of thousands of such reports.

THE BRAZILIAN EXPLOSION

Two Swedish immigrant men, who had recently come into the current Spirit-directed revival at the turn of the last century soon after coming to America, attended a small Pentecostal prayer meeting in Wisconsin. During that prayer meeting the Holy Spirit, through tongues and prophecy, directed them to the mission field but to a country/area not recognized by them. By consulting an atlas in the local library it was determined that they should head for Brazil and to a specific area of that country. They simply obeyed.

Gunnar Vingren and Daniel Berg headed out in faith, only knowing the final destination. The story is electrifying and shows faith and its fruit. Only

God could know how their obedience and risk would result in the utilization of economic and socio-political elements inside Brazil (involving the rubber industry and displacement of people) to produce a church, now numbering over 22 million souls in 90 years. Does this only happen to Pentecostals? No, *and I must say this carefully,* but they have an advantage BECAUSE OF THE IMMEDIATE ACCESS TO SERVICE AND A REDUCTION OF THE FEAR TO CONFRONT THE ENEMY'S EVIL POWERS. Those who are clothed by the Spirit are best equipped to be the instruments of revival and blessing of a loving God. Attention! They are not better people or better missionaries. It's just that they are closer, in my opinion, to *hear/understand,* the plan of God that was given at the time of Jesus' instructing His disciples about how to be better equipped for the task. (He said: *don't leave Jerusalem without* it.) Risk? You bet! Dangerous? Right on! Does any normal church bureaucracy like losing this kind of governance? Absolutely NOT—including some Pentecostal denominations.

Even Second Best Isn't Bad

> None-the-less, while it may be easy to point out the weaknesses and failures of our brothers, and of ourselves, one must readily admit, that in spite of "second best" choices being made by so many missionary bodies and church governance, we must rejoice! For the Holy Spirit is able to use all of this hodge podge of activity, often so sincerely done but so inexpertly done. And yet, He's building His Church around the world. The phenomenal growth of the Church where the Holy Spirit is at work gives us great pleasure, gratitude and rejoicing, no matter under what "label" is it presented. This is especially true of those who believe in the Pentecostal understanding of the operation of the Gifts of the Spirit as found in Corinthians, Romans, and Ephesians. Those who are willing to confront the power of the devil and demonic oppression and spiritual warfare are those finding the greatest church growth. In that spiritual climate, multiplied thousands of young men and women are giving themselves to the same priorities of the gospel as we find in the New Testament. In our Movement alone, there are at this writing 80,000 men and women around the world (outside North America) studying for full time service in ministry (over 1000 Bible Schools) to join the already 320,000 credentialed men and women in full time ministry.[39]

Harvey Cox attempts to explain why, after nearly 100 years, people are still so attracted to the phenomenon of speaking in tongues.

> But why did it spark such an outburst in Los Angeles, and why does it continue to draw so many people today... It was understood not primarily as a supernatural tool for world mission but as a deliverance from the iron cage of grammar and a graceful provision to those who did not have the strength or the fluency to pray with their own words. Thus the practice of tongue speaking has persisted even though the interpretation has changed. It has persisted, I believe, because it represents the core of all Pentecostal conviction: that the Spirit of God needs no mediators but is available to anyone in an intense, immediate, indeed interior way.[40]

COMMUNICATIONS INSIGHT

LET'S REPEAT COX'S words relating to communications. "It was understood ... as deliverance from the iron cage of grammar and a graceful provision to those who did not have the strength or the fluency to pray with their own words, thus the practice of tongue speaking has persisted...because it represents the core of all Pentecostal conviction: that the Spirit of God needs no mediators but is available to anyone in an intense, immediate, indeed interior way."[41] For some that's too mysterious. For the practitioner it makes sense only to the deep subconscious. Bring that "knowledge" to the surface of analytical, cognitive rules of rational thought, and it will still be called "foolishness." Regrettable but true. The very fact of becoming useful in God's economy of redemption (immediacy) without ecclesiastical approval for some is tantamount of going hunting out of season with no permit!

DID GOD INTEND FOR TONGUES TO BE AN "ATTENTION GETTER"?

York brings up an important point I hadn't yet started to consider. God must have intended tongues to attract attention as it does. York seems to say this was intentional on the part of God.

> ...the matter of speaking in tongues needs to be addressed. The occurrence of speaking in tongues in Acts was "remarkable" in that it was highly noticeable and became the object of agitated discussion (Acts 2:7-12). It was also "evidential" because it was the most telling evidence Peter could appeal to in defense of his having baptized Gentiles (Acts 10:44-48; 11:15-17). Pentecostal believers worldwide notice

> the same two functions within the contemporary spread of the gospel. The supernatural, including such manifestations as healings and speaking in tongues, is still remarkable to vast numbers of people. Around the world, crowds still rush together asking, "What does this mean?" Further, speaking in tongues is still evidential as it occurs within the context of Christian worship.[42]

Here York makes a parenthesis to note that in Africa he witnessed the enemy Satan's use of tongues through his human instruments. Let's be very clear on this matter. The magicians of Egypt could duplicate some of Moses' miraculous plagues, but that didn't nullify God's power in this show of force before Pharaoh (II Tim. 3:8). This author has witnessed the same in Africa—but the Holy Spirit has given the Church a great gift in the discerning of spirits (I Cor. 12:10). York continues:

> However, when the gospel is preached and believers seek to be filled with the Holy Spirit, the entire church knows they have been filled when they begin to worship God in other tongues. This phenomenon is typical worldwide within the contexts of Pentecostal worship, and it is the primary reason why seemingly ordinary men and women become powerful witnesses of Christ.[43]

One might add, this is one of the primary reasons this Holy Spirit revival is the fastest growing arm of the Protestant Church for a number of decades until today. Mission and church statisticians now put the number between 550 and 650 million believers who are glossolalic. People of the Spirit are not the only witnesses by any means (and thank God!) but one is hard put to find, outside their ranks, whole congregations who are in the "ministry" as are many Pentecostal churches, especially in the 2/3rd World. It should be noted, that many North Atlantic Pentecostal Churches' growth has plateaued, as has the intensity for witness by their members.

York continues:

> It would appear fitting as something of an antithesis to the phenomenon at Babel, that those empowered to represent Christ among the nations of the world should receive their endowment of power with the accompanying sign of speaking in languages of the world. As Don Richardson observes, 'seen in the context of Jesus' ministry and His clearly articulated plans for the whole world, the bestowal of that miraculous outburst of *Gentile* languages could have only one main purpose...the evangelization of all peoples.[44]

For many years I was privileged to be a member of the Association of Evangelical Seminary Presidents of North America. From time to time a fellow member of that fine association would quiz me on my personal belief about tongues as the Initial Evidence (a term used by most Pentecostals and some Charismatics from the biblical record). Some asked only out of curiosity (the subject of tongues still does that) and others, like many Evangelical presidents of seminaries, are curious because they have a large and increasing percentage of their student bodies from Pentecostal and Charismatic churches. Some seemed, in full sincerity, to wish I would tell them I had accepted the belief one could receive the Act 2:4 experience without speaking in tongues, or at least it may be *normal* but not *normative*. I would often relate to this question with a story told to me, more than once, by David du Plessis (who came to be known as Mr. Pentecost).[45] While I was the president of the non-denominational California Theological Seminary in Fresno, David invited me to participate in the International Roman Catholic/Pentecostal Dialogue of which he had been one of the instigators and the Pentecostal chairman for a number of years. When the same question was asked by Pastor Criswell of the great Southern Baptist Church in Dallas, David recalls his answer.

If you object to the words 'initial evidence' you might say that speaking in tongues is the consequence of being baptized in the Holy Spirit.
–du Plessis

> Bro. Criswell, if someone came to you and asked to be baptized in water, but asked not to get wet in the process—what would you say? You wouldn't say that the reason to be baptized was to get wet, right? One could do that with the garden hose. Wouldn't you say that getting wet was the *consequence* of getting immersed in water? And if the person didn't want to get wet, they probably shouldn't ask for the experience. If you object to the words 'initial evidence' you might say that speaking in tongues is the *consequence* of being baptized in the Holy Spirit.[46]

York comments on how one should respond to the above question of friendly non-Pentecostals by linking the response to *Missio Dei*:

> What should be noted, however, is the correlation between speaking in tongues and the resulting experience of Christian witness, especially among those of diverse ethnicity and language. As long as

> there is a hurting and broken world divided primarily along lines of language and ethnicity, I hope Pentecostals will increase their emphasis upon speaking in tongues. It would be an untold tragedy to back away from that part of our heritage that most directly gives evidence of God's determination, to bless all nations through Christ, the seed of Abraham (Gal.3:16).[47]

One of the most colorful early founders of the Pentecostal Movement was a woman evangelist who founded the International Church of the Foursquare Gospel, Aimee S. McPherson. Gary McGee describes her as a flamboyant person in her description in *Word and Work* magazine in 1917. Here's one response she would give in this arena:

> Q. What is the use of this sign of tongues which accompanies the incoming Spirit?
>
> A. When you walk down the street looking for a barber, first you look for a *red and white pole,* the *sign,* in other words. When you are looking for dinner you look for a sign that says, *Restaurant.* The barber's pole can not shave you, neither can the wooden restaurant sign feed you, but they are just signs to indicate that behind those doors there is a barber who can serve you, or within the restaurant doors there is food that will satisfy your hunger. So it is with the Bible sign, the speaking in tongues. It indicates that the Comforter has come to abide within.[48]

WHERE DID THE CASE FOR TONGUES GET LOST IN HISTORY?

Protestant scholasticism represents the theological roots of the silencing of the Spirit in western missions. Western missionaries' lack of supernatural belief was the biggest cause of the great Independent Church Movement in Africa. The West lays this phenomenon onto "African" doings—as if the dark continent has distorted the "true gospel" out of its innate depravity. Sengue sees the reason as a clash of Western thinking and African thinking—not the clash of the gospel and African culture![49] Pomerville agrees: "Christianity has been both cause and catalyst of social change in Africa; and one of the most prominent features of modern Africa has been the emergence of independent churches, founded by Africans in protest at some feature of the Christianity of the missionary societies.[50] This clearly shows the loss of the belief in and perception of the supernatural in Western culture is an all-important antecedent factor in the study of the independence movements. He continues:

> The fact that Pentecostalism has such a dynamic role in contemporary missions is directly related to its experiential dimension of the Christian faith. As such, it is not only a "corrective" of post-Reformation Protestant Scholasticism, but the vehicle by which two-third world peoples satisfy their predisposition to transcendence and the supernatural to which the western mind pretends to be superior.[51]

We will come back to this important issue in the following chapters.

ENDNOTES:

1. See The Assemblies of God, "Our 16 Doctrines," *A Paraphrased Version of Statement of Fundamental Truths* (Pamphlet).
2. Harvey Conn in Wade Horton (1966), 44.
3. Kelsey (1968), 9.
4. Ibid., 32.
5. Robert L. Brandt and Zenas J. Bicket, *The Spirit Helps Us Pray; A Biblical Theology of Prayer* (1993), 25-27.
6. Grant Osborne, gen. ed. 1&2 Corinthians, Life Application Bible Commentary (1999), 202.
7. John Bevere, video series *Intimacy with the Holy Spirit,* Video 2: "Communicating with God" (2001).
8. I have corroborated this story with Brown and the sister in Kansas.
9. Christenson (1968), 79.
10. See James L. Slay, "Its Value to the Individual" in Horton, ed., *The Glossolalia Phenomenon* (1966), 236. Also see Larry Christensen's (1968) similar thoughts, 75.
11. Frank D. Macchia, "Sighs Too Deep for Words: Toward a Theology of Glossolalia," *Journal of Pentecostal Theology,* 1 (1992).
12. Harold Horton, *Gifts of the Spirit* (1934, reprint 1975), 136.
13. Brandt and Bicket (1993), 281.
14. For early references to this phenomenon see Max Wood Moorhead, "Pentecost at Calcutta," *Cloud of Witnesses to Pentecost in India,* March 1908, 7; also: Frank Bartleman, *Azusa Street: The Roots of Modern-Day Pentecost* (1980), 56-57, described its occurrence at Azusa Street as the "heavenly chorus" or the "heavenly choir."
15. C. Peter Wagner quoting Timothy Warner in Ralph Winter and Steven C. Hawthorne *Perspectives on the World Christian Movement,* Pasadena, CA: William Carey Library (1999) 537.
16. L. Holdcroft, *The Holy Spirit: A Pentecostal Interpretation* (1999), 130-131.
17. Kelsey (1968), 17.
18. Larry Christenson (1968), 40.
19. Satyavrata in *The Globalization of Pentecostalism* (1999), 211.
20. Edward L. Cleary in *The Globalization of Pentecostalism* (1999), 144.
21. See Jean Mouroux, *The Christian Experience: An Introduction to a Theology* (1954), 272.
22. Harvey Cox, *Fire From Heaven. The Rise of Pentecostal Spirituality and the Reshaping of Religion in the Twenty-First Century* (1995), 319.

23. Bob Kilpatrick, personal interview, August, 2004.
24. Dave Roberson, *The Walk of The Spirit—The Walk of Power* (1999), 88.
25. Ibid., 89.
26. David W. Dorries, "Edward Irving and the 'Standing Sign' of Spirit Baptism," *Initial Evidence* in Gary McGee, ed. (1991), 41-56.
27. "On the Gifts of the Holy Ghost, Commonly Called Supernatural" in *The Collected Writings of Edward Irving in Five Volumes,* Vol. 4, Rev. G Carlyle, ed. (1864), 523, as cited in McGee (1991).
28. Carlyle (1864), 548, in McGee (1991).
29. Christenson, 79, 81.
30. Ralph Harris, *Spoken By The Spirit: Documented Accounts of "Other Tongues" from Arabic to Zulu* (1973). Also, Stanley Frodsham, *With Signs Following.* (1946).
31. "The Comforter Has Come"; Words: Frank Bottome (1890) in *Precious Times of Reflections and Revival.* Music: William J. Kirkpatrick.
32. See also James A. Cross, *The Glossolalia Phenomena* (1966), 188.
33. See Harvey Cox (1995).
34. Lancelot Whyte, *The Unconscious Mind Before Freud* (1960), 80; quoted in Wade Horton, *The Glossolalia Phenomenon* (1966), 225.
35. Henry Lederle, "Initial Evidence and the Charismatic Movement" in McGee (1991), 134.
36. Gordon Fee, *God's Empowering Presence: The Holy Spirit in the Letters of Paul* (1994), 577.
37. John Bertone, "The Experience of Glossolalia and the Spirit's Empathy" in *Pneuma*, Vol. 25, No. 1, Spring 2003, 61, 63.
38. This African story and analysis first appeared in Del Tarr, *Double Image: Biblical Insights from African Parables* (1994), 27-31.
39. Annual report of Assemblies of God World Missions, David Lee, director, 2005.
40. Harvey Cox (1995), 86-87.
41. Ibid., 87.
42. John York (2000) 184.
43. Ibid., 185.
44. York, 185, quotes Don Richardson, *Eternity in Their Hearts* (1981), 157 (emphasis Richardson's).
45. David du Plessis, *A Man Called Mr. Pentecost* (1977). Another book of interest by du Plessis is *The Spirit Bade Me Go: An Astounding Move of God in the Denominational Churches* (1961).
46. Personal remarks, told many times while in association with du Plessis during the Roman Catholic/Pentecostal Dialogues.
47. Ibid., 185-6.
48. McGee (1991) 122.
49. Ngoni Sengue, "Identity Crises in African Church," *EMQ* 17:2 (1999), 9-99.
50. Paul Pomerville, "A Case Study in the Contextualization of the Gospel: A Critique of the Reformed View of Scripture in the Post-Reformation Period" (1980), 95.
51. Ibid., 95.

Author's note: Cox has shown great interest in glossolalia, even at one time wished he could experience it. But he hasn't at his own admission in the time frame of his book here quoted. I believe when he does speak in tongues—not for the sake of research but for the same reason Jesus described it ("You shall receive power to be my witnesses"), he'll no longer use the word ecstasy in its description because of that word's connotation in some foreign contexts. If, on the other hand he uses "ecstasy" to mean the expression of joy, rapture, intense wonder—his connotation is OK with me. Allow me one more step in this, perhaps useful, visual imagery.

CHAPTER 6

TESTIMONIALS
The Role of Testimonies

The oral nature of the phenomenon of tongues and Pentecostal movements has always allowed space for verbal, extemporaneous expression of ordinary believers—even in many public meetings. It's part of the natural ethic of what characterizes the Movement. A Roman Catholic or Anglican believer will receive great internal blessing and strength by following a litany of responsive reading in the rich liturgy of the Church. But a Pentecostal will experience a similar blessing by giving or hearing or reading the personal expression of God's sovereignty and intervention in one's daily life. This section illustrates this principle with a purposeful variety of expressions from a number of denominational sources, many of whom first opposed the idea of glossolalia.

When I heard from a good friend... that he, a Presbyterian minister had received the "gift of the Holy Spirit" and was glossolalic, I should advise him to see a psychiatrist.

Here are excerpts from the preface to Maloney and Lovekin's book, *Glossolalia: Behavioral Science Perspectives on Speaking in Tongues.* This segment written by Maloney:[1]

> This book is the result of a collaboration. On the one hand, the endeavor is an effort to understand a strange phenomenon; on the other hand, it is an attempt to deepen a treasured dimension of faith...Yale Divinity School in the 1950s was not a place known for its religious expressiveness. So it is not surprising that, when I heard from a good friend and classmate that he, a Presbyterian minister, had received the "gift of the Holy Spirit" and was glossolalic, I should advise him to see a psychiatrist. I was sincerely worried about the

> mental state of my friend and thought he had had a nervous breakdown...We had lost touch with each other for several years...We renewed our friendship and much to my surprise I found my friend soundly normal. He was a successful associate pastor at a nearby church, had a fine family, and paid his bills each month—yet he still spoke in tongues!
>
> This astounding discovery prompted me to investigate the phenomenon of glossolalia. I truly desired to understand fully this unique expression of religious fervor that had transformed the life of my friend but had left him as normal as anyone else. This began a twelve year programmatic study of speaking in tongues from the viewpoint of the social/behavioral sciences.

This introductory testimony by Newton Maloney is but an example of what is to follow. Most of the accounts are by those who at first opposed this latter movement of the Holy Spirit or, as in the case of Maloney, had serious misconceptions about it.

Pentecostals owe so much to the other churches that came before us. I know many Pentecostals and Charismatics don't like it when I say that, because they think for one to be loyal to one church, one must throw stones at all the others. That may be the way of the competitive West, but it's not the Jesus Way.[2] Besides, I am loyal to but one church. His Church. The Church Universal. I refuse to get the Assemblies of God and the Kingdom of God mixed up!—though I am pleased to be a part of the AG and owe much to its nurture. It has been the movement that allowed my personal growth and facilitated my ministry. I've been loyal to it. But my first allegiance is to the larger Kingdom.

The Holy Spirit's Flow Is Like a River

The following is a testimonial of how this *strange* flow works (in the world's and some Christians' eyes). While president of the Assemblies of God Seminary in Springfield, MO, I arranged for about 100 seminarians and their wives to caravan in buses to a great revival meeting in Florida which had been in progress for years with folks coming from all over America and many foreign counties to observe and make up their minds as to its validity. In many ways the length and universal scope of this revival paralleled the Azusa Street Revival of 1906-10. At the time of the seminarians' trip to Florida, over 100,000 people had come to confess their sins at an old-fashioned altar of repentance. The local church hosting those meetings was the Brownsville

Assembly of God in Pensacola, FL. In my mind as president, seminarians should be exposed to other experiences besides the library and lectures. My wife Dolly and I accompanied the group in one of the buses. The whole group was blessed by the meetings. I was encouraged to see many individuals seeking God on a deeper level than ever before.

On the return home, the buses each left to return on their own schedule. On one of the smaller buses, the prayer and praise, "like a residual of the services," got so intense the driver thought it not safe for him to drive and just stopped to let everyone pray individually or collectively as he/she wished. He stopped on a state hi-way (not an interstate) where there was a grassy area next to the road. The group got out of the bus and sat, knelt, or lay down on the grass to pray, sing and continue the wonderful spirit of God-consciousness that spilled over from the recent scene at the church they had just left. Soon they saw a small group of men and women approaching on foot, dressed in work clothes and looking uncertain about what to say or do. A spokesperson from the group said, "We were just passing in our 18 wheelers, felt an awesome presence or power come over us. We had to park our rigs a ways away so are on foot. What's going on here?" (They could see and hear crying, praising, speaking in tongues, singing—all from seminarians oblivious to the visitors.) It was explained to them that what they saw was what had been happening in a church up the road a few miles, and it was hoped they were not disturbing the area. The visitors made the following statement: "We don't know what this is or why you are here—but what you have, would you give it to us, too?" Five strangers were explained the way of salvation and were born into the Kingdom! And the bus passengers were soon on their way with a vivid example of "rivers flowing from within." This experience will, no doubt, stay with them in their ministries for some time to come.

"We don't know what this is or why you are here—but what you have, would you give it to us too?"

From Episcopalians

Reverend Dennis J. Bennett was the first Episcopalian priest in the 1960s Charismatic Renewal Movement to write, travel, and speak of his experience of the Spirit's fullness.

At the time of his baptism in the Spirit, he was the pastor of Saint Mark's Episcopal Church in Van Nuys, California. The following excerpts of his testimony were delivered to that parish church just prior to his leaving to become Rector of Saint Luke's Episcopal Church in Seattle, Washington. The booklet *Episcopalians and the Baptism in the Holy Spirit*, compiled by VOICE, contains the testimonies of nine prominent pastors and professional lay members who witnessed this glossolalic phenomenon during the decade of the 60s.

> For most of us, religion is a plodding thing, resting on the grim determination of man, rather than on the power of God, and yet Jesus said His yoke was easy and His burden light...I have been pondering these things for a long time, but about five months ago, I received a spiritual experience that made me realize what was missing and that is precisely: the power of God, the Holy Spirit, in our lives. We talk about Him, but we don't know Him, and recognize His work in us as we should. He does not FILL us, as the Bible says He will do, so instead of living by the power of God in us, we try to follow God's RULES by our own power. In the words of the Bible, we are still living by law, and not by faith...
>
> I met some people about five months ago, Episcopalians, who had received the fullness of the Holy Spirit. (I have since found that many Episcopalians, both clergy and laity, know about this, but have been fearful of telling about it, for exactly the reason that you see now at Saint Mark's—people just don't understand)...I had, as I am sure many of you do, associated this Gift with religious frenzy and fanaticism, and never thought that it might have spiritual importance.
>
> When I prayed for God to grant me the fullness of the Spirit, and opened my mouth to praise Him, I found to my amazement that as I repeated words of praise, the Holy Spirit did take my lips and tongue and form a new and powerful language of praise and prayer that I myself could not understand, and that as I so praised God, the Holy Spirit did fill me with joy and peace and power which has not departed!
>
> It became clear to me that the willingness to release the tongue to praise God in whatever words or language He chose to use was a vitally important key to receiving of the fullness of the Holy Spirit, for the Bible says that our tongue—our faculty of speech—is at the same time the best member of our body, and also the most wicked, a "fire," a "world of iniquity." When you consider the harm that we can do with words, and the way in which we deceive and temporize with

> words, it is not unusual that we should be asked to let our faculty of speech be used by God to His glory—in the way that He chooses—before we can have His fullness.
>
> Several people from the Parish received this Gift of the Holy Spirit at about the same time I did, and all of us were filled with joy at what we had found. We soon discovered, however, that others were not necessarily going to feel the same way, and that the question of the unknown tongue would be misunderstood...I know I am not alone in this. I know of dozens of Episcopal parishes throughout the country where the work of the Holy Spirit is known in just this same way. I know of dozens of Episcopal Clergy who know about it all, and rejoiced in their knowledge.[3]

While with the Episcopalians, let's look at the testimony of yet another vicar, the Rev. Eugene Ford, Vicar of St. Martin's Episcopal Church, Moses Lake, Washington.

> **A Change in My Goals**
>
> Since receiving the Pentecostal experience with the initial evidence of speaking in tongues, my life and ministry have been transformed beyond measure: and the process is still going on. Before entering into the deeper walk in the Spirit, what I wanted for my ministry was what most other ministers want, I suppose. I wanted to be known as a good preacher, so I spent hours each week preparing to preach. I wanted to be recognized as a good churchman, so I was a salesman for "Episcopalianism." I wanted to be known that I could run a good organization, so I worked at keeping the church (with its several organizations) running smoothly...As a result of all this I hoped to be called to a larger church and there look forward to doing more of the same, only on a larger scale...
>
> So often I wondered how what I read in the Bible and what I saw going on in the church were related. It seemed what the church was doing must be for God because the CHURCH was doing it, yet much of what the church was doing could have been done by any lodge or secular organization in the community without changing the format one iota.
>
> On the evening of May 13, 1962, I heard something which changed the whole direction of my life. Dennis Bennett, Vicar of St. Luke's Church, Seattle, spent four hours with a small group of St. Martin's

> communicants, telling what God had done in his life. He said it was the same thing that happened to the disciples on the day of Pentecost, and that the results were also the same...While hearing him tell his story, the Spirit of God created a hunger in my heart. Later, praying in the nave of my church, I asked for and received the Pentecostal experience and entered into a new way and a new walk of the Spirit. Entering this new dimension of spiritual reality several things began to happen: people for whom I prayed were frequently healed; others received the baptism with the Holy Spirit and spoke in tongues; the Bible became a living book; and I was enabled to preach without manuscript. But the most important thing that happened, without my even thinking about it, was a change in my goals. No longer did I care about being known as a good preacher, or a good organizer, or a good churchman. No longer did the thought of being rector of a large church fascinate me. Immediately, I knew what St. Paul was talking about when he wrote: "...every advantage that I gained I considered loss for Christ's sake. Yes, and I look upon everything as loss compared with the overwhelming gain of knowing Christ Jesus my Lord.
>
> ...What God wants is all that counts. And what God wants is NEVER understood by the world and FREQUENTLY misunderstood by the church, but it is still all that counts.[4]

Walter J. Hollenwager is a Dutch theologian and author who has researched and written on the Pentecostal movements perhaps more than any other contemporary European. He reports on another Anglican.

> Jean Stone, an Anglican, says this of the effect of the Baptism in the Holy Spirit. "It brought a profound understanding of the love of God, a desire to read the Bible; the experience of the Baptism in the Holy Spirit makes a person who had not before believed in the infallibility of the Scriptures a Fundamentalist Anglican, it brings a deep conviction of sin, the power to testify and to pray with the sick."[5]

From the Lutherans

We are all so indebted to the Lutherans and other early Protestant churches. Martin Luther, the father of the Reformation, along with John Knox and John Calvin (and others), broke new ground under threatening and dangerous days in Christendom. Truthfully, his *Sola Gratia, Sola Fide, and Sola Scriptura* [only grace, only faith, only Scripture], embraced by many

Protestant denominations, has even brought needed changes into the Roman Catholic Church. Let's listen to some Lutherans who have experienced glossolalia.

We'll start with Rev. A. Herbert Mjorud's testimony, who is an ordained minister with the American Lutheran Church. He had left a law practice and graduated from Lutheran Bible Institute in Minneapolis, MN, from where he took his first pastorate in the Twin Cities and later in Anchorage Alaska. Subsequent to this, he felt directed by the Lord to become an evangelist serving many churches and conferences in the ALC during which time he studied deeply the empowering gifts of the Holy Spirit, and especially he desired the gift of healing. On the occasion of attending Dennis Bennett's church in Seattle:

> ...Upon entering, one could sense the warmth of the Spirit immediately. There was joy and radiance on the faces of the people, and what thrilled me most was the sense of awe and reverence. I had preconceived ideas about the Pentecostal experience, but was delightfully surprised to hear a demonstration of speaking in tongues and the interpretation, with no more emotional content than if one were praying in the English language. My prayer was, "Lord, what these people have, I want!"...
>
> When I expressed an interest they asked, "Would you be willing to pray for this?" "My earnest desire is for the gift of healing," I answered, "but I'm afraid tongues would not be acceptable in Lutheran circles. Nevertheless I want whatever the Lord has for me, because He knows the circumstances in my church. If speaking in tongues is God's desire for me, I am willing to speak in a thousand tongues. Let Him have His way!" Yet fear kept me from receiving...It is very difficult for us pastors to give our tongue because our mind has been using it for years. It is not easy to release this instrument which is the most important aspect of our personality.

"My earnest desire is for the gift of healing." I answered, "but I'm afraid tongues would not be acceptable in Lutheran circles."

> Soon after I was called to Canada for a series of meetings. One night seven of us gathered around the altar after the congregation had been dismissed. As we stood there, I heard a terrible wind. Others listened and said that it must be a storm. We then knelt and prayed one after the other, according to our needs. Suddenly the sound of

> roaring wind come down as from heaven, closer and closer, until it filled the room. As I started to pray the pastor's wife immediately spoke in another tongue. Then we laid hands upon the first individual, a logger who was a young convert, and prayed that he might be filled with the Holy Spirit. When he began to thank the Lord, he, too, started speaking in another tongue. We prayed for each one and all were filled with the Holy Spirit that night...We went outside where several individuals were waiting in their cars for us. "Did you hear the storm out here?" I asked. "No." "Wasn't there any wind?" "Didn't you hear a terrible roar from the church?" "No, we didn't hear a thing." God had clearly visited us with a miraculous demonstration much like Pentecost. The healing ministry that I had been seeking became an evident gift from that time on.[6]

William Thorkelson, staff writer for the *Minneapolis Star*, reported in the late 60s that he knew of two dozen pastors and several hundred laymen of the American Lutheran Church who had experienced glossolalia. At first he thought this spiritual phenomenon had only been associated with Pentecostal churches. Then he heard of the renewal movement amongst the Protestant Episcopal Church. One Lutheran pastor of the ALC wrote him that within a diameter of 25 miles there are three Lutheran pastors and three Methodist pastors, besides many, many others in the denominational churches far and wide who minister through the gifts of the Spirit, including "speaking in tongues." The pastor wrote, "It is quite evident in our day that God is trying to reveal to us that "Pentecost is not a denomination—it is an experience."[7]

"It is quite evident in our day that God is trying to reveal to us that Pentecost is not a denomination— it is an experience."

The Lutheran minister, Reverend Allen Blegen gave testimony to his Pentecostal experience while pastoring the Emanuel Lutheran Church of Chicago. He stated he had longed for greater spiritual attainment and began to seek deeper truth about the Holy Spirit. "I read all the books about the Holy Spirit I could secure, but still was not satisfied. It hadn't occurred to me to read anything written by a Pentecostal because I had been taught that they were a fringe sect, made up of highly emotional and predominantly ignorant people."

He had asked several people to pray for him after he became convinced the Acts 2:4 experience was for him. But he did not receive the blessing. It was several months later while in his own home, while reading a magazine about the Holy Spirit, while all the members of his family were asleep he knelt by his bed and asked the Father to "please reach forth your hand and lay it on my head and say to me 'Receive the Holy Ghost.'"

> I knew He was answering my prayer for the joy of the Lord came upon me. Words of a new language I had never learned flowed from my tongue, followed by a burst of holy laughter which I could scarcely control. Never since have I experienced such holy laughter, although daily I speak to God in tongues, in prayer, praise and thanksgiving...First Corinthians chapters 12,13 and 14 have become increasingly precious in my life. When I was president of the Lutheran Bible Institute, in Chicago, I did not fully face these chapters, nor did I realize the depth of meaning that has now been revealed to me...In my ministry at Immanuel Lutheran Church, Chicago, I teach these things. Several of our members are Spirit-filled...It seems to me that the only hope for the church is a fresh baptism in the Holy Spirit.[8]

The Lutheran pastor/author Larry Christenson illustrates how tongues is not the gift some folk desire from God because they feel they deserve something better, especially something that demonstrates/highlights a possession they already have.

Here is an excerpt from a lady writing to her pastor:

> During the past year my husband and I have felt a deepening in our spiritual lives....We found ourselves searching for the truth of God and His will for us. I prayed that He would reveal His presence and give me a closer walk with Christ and fill me with the Holy Spirit. In January of this year, God started answering this prayer, but not in the way I would have expected....He gave me a real sense of His presence but with it came this strange gift of spiritual speaking. Believe me, it was a very humbling experience. After all, I'm a college graduate and have always been grateful that I was given a good mind and a keen intellect. Instead of giving me great wisdom or understanding, which I felt I was capable of, He gave me this seemingly useless language. How could a language be useful if nobody understands it? Yet, I knew of others who had received this and were rejoicing about it.[9]

From the Spanish-speaking World

Edmond Cleary speaks of the experience of tongues as "tomada del

Espíritu" (being taken over by God). He relates this "foundational experience" as just the beginning. "The rest of the journey involves a moral reformation. The guide here is a strict moral code. Humility results as Latin American Pentecostals hope for progress, if not perfection." Cleary goes on to explain how "being taken over by God" affects women members: "Scholars are taking a new look at the implication of Pentecostal gender relations. Building on the work of Elizabeth Brusco[10] "...new roles open to women in the life of the church, and the equalization of work traditionally relegated to 'women's sphere' all serve to undermine hegemonic ideologies of *machisomo and marianismo.*" Cleary cites others also who substantiate the notion that Pentecostalism can dismantle traditional moral and social codes. "The believer sees herself as an individual responsible for her own liberation from the oppression of evil, defined as natural passions and instincts...as a primary responsibility to God (rather than one's spouse or family) that transforms women into active, responsible agents in their own and their families' lives."[11]

On another personal level Cleary says: Pentecostals center their lives on experience of the Holy Spirit. This is better described as individual rather than subjective or illusory experience, an event radiating throughout one's body and evident to others. It is a vividly felt contact with God. Pentecostals' experience of God is a primary and constant part of their religion. The structures of their worship are designed to enhance these experiences on a routine basis through expressive, intense, and performance-oriented liturgies...Emphasizing the gifts of the Holy Spirit, Latin American Pentecostals are confident that these gifts are present within the church and can be relied on, in a way that Catholics and other Protestants do not emphasize."[12]

The Powerless Become Powerful Because of Pentecost

Mike Peterson advances the thesis he wishes to submit surrounding the question of social influence in Latin America. He believes that the macro-social level is little affected by Pentecostals, but the micro-social level is.

> The new churches are alienating...they do not transform the system at the macro-level, at the systematic level. However, at the micro-social level, on a small scale, at the local level, they are useful, they are reformist, they are ameliorist.[13]

Peterson speaks of those "excluded" from society (outcasts) created by unemployment and civil rights. They are excluded from the official social system so they are exposed, vulnerable groups that have no social security whatsoever. Many of these are becoming Pentecostals. Pentecostalism helps the outcasts in their daily struggle for survival by strengthening their subjectivity, building their self-esteem, giving them a sense of dignity.

> A poor man said to me: 'What kills is not hunger, it is humiliation, contempt." Pentecostals give them the sense of dignity. They are born again, they become aware they are the children of God; they have been chosen, saved. And the outcasts lift up their heads and fight to survive. This occurs especially with Blacks who are the most outcast, who are often lumped with the marginalized drug pushers, thieves, prostitutes, etc. But when they become Pentecostals they say: "We are good people, we are worthy people" ...they are new people, they are different, they have experienced a personal revolution. It may seem like an illusion, and perhaps it is, but it does have a social effect.[14]

The other important aspect is they all carry the Holy Spirit; everyone can speak in tongues. It does not matter if the unbelievers think it is an illusion; such a conviction gives them strength to have control over their lives. They especially are able to overcome their sense of powerlessness in a society that excludes them.[14]

A second aspect is the moralization of private life, family life...a popular alternative to the drug culture is Pentecostalism because it challenges the drug culture and recovers substance abusers, especially alcoholics. Quoting a Catholic priest from Brazil, "I once had an effective catechist in the faveles; her father was an alcoholic and we prayed with him, went to see him, etc. But we could not get him away from alcohol. During a Pentecostal worship session he converted, he handed himself to Jesus, he received the Holy Spirit, he spoke in tongues and gave up alcohol. I have lost the catechist, but she has recovered her father.[15]

Peterson continues by stating that the strict ethics of most Pentecostals is economical; it leads to parsimony. No longer are they spending money on drugs, anti-depression drugs, vain perfumes, or on fashion. To the poor this is important. The society recognizes this and often one can see the job market advertising for them. In a leading Brazilian newspaper: "Wanted; housekeeper, preferably Pentecostal." In fact, they are honest, they do not steal and they accept the salary they are offered.[16]

From a Historical Evangelist

The following is an account from the diary of Charles Finney, the great revivalist of the nineteenth century, of his encounter with what he calls the baptism in the Holy Spirit.

> I returned to the front office, and found that the fire that I had made of large wood was nearly burned out. But as I turned and was about to take a seat by the fire, I received a mighty Baptism of the Holy Ghost. Without any expectation of it, without ever having the thought in my mind that there was any such thing for me, without my recollection that I had ever heard the thing mentioned by any person in the world, the Holy Spirit descended upon me in a manner that seemed to go through me, body and soul. I could feel the impression, like a wave of electricity, going through and through me. Indeed, it seemed to come in waves and waves of liquid love; for I could not express it in any other way. And yet it did not seem like water but rather the breath of God. I can recollect distinctly that it seemed to fan me, like immense wings; and it seemed to me, as these waves passed over me, that they literally moved my hair like a passing breeze.
>
> No words can express the wonderful love that was shed abroad in my heart. I wept aloud with joy and love; and I do not know but I should say, I literally bellowed out the unutterable gushings of my heart. These waves came over me, and over me, and over me, one after another, until I recollect I cried out, "I shall die if these waves continue to pass over me." ...How long I continued in this state, with this baptism continuing to roll over me and going through me, I do not know.[17]

**"The Holy Spirit descended on me...it seemed to come in waves and waves of liquid love; for I should say, I literally bellowed out unutterable gushings of my heart"
– Charles Finney**

Another example of how those who reject the Pentecostal experience have manipulated history is shown by Harvey Cox's account of John Wesley's evaluation of the Montanists.

> Once the church historians began to pay attention, they noticed, sometimes to their chagrin, some very respectable predecessors of those who hold to the "Latter Rain" theory. One was none other than John Wesley (1703-1791), the revered founder of Methodism. Like the increasing number of Pentecostals who study the history of Christianity today, Wesley knew that although speaking in tongues virtually disappeared as a general practice a century after Christ's death, reports of its recurrence among Christians have cropped up

here and there in nearly every century. He also wanted to understand both facts. Why had it disappeared? And why did it pop up now and then? One important instance of this recurrence of tongue speaking happened under the leadership of Montanus, the leader of a vigorous Christian movement that appeared in the latter part of the second century. Montanus's followers also preached that the Spirit had a higher authority than the bishops. Wesley described him as "real scriptural Christian" and extolled him as "one of the best men then upon earth." The reason why tongue speaking and similar gifts had disappeared, Wesley said, in a sentence that presages the "latter rain" theory, was that "dry, formal, orthodox men" had begun to "ridicule" such gifts because they themselves did not possess them. Worse, they decried them as "either madness or impostors."[18]

More on Testimonials—From Kelsey

Morton Kelsey recounts the Pentecostal experience in 1962 at Yale University.

> One of the young men wrote of this: I was stunned by this combination. I discovered that a Baptist minister plus an Episcopalian church plus healing = the Holy Spirit. Others had been led to groups in which they heard tongues and prophecy. Within a month students from several denominations were being drawn to the movement...It may have been the remark of a man who had first spoken in tongues while listening to the pastor talk that did it; he told the chaplain that the Bible was now a living thing to him, that words seemed to jump off the pages and "this fellow Jesus suddenly became real and living." The pastor of a Presbyterian church in San Diego, CA, recently discussed the gift of tongues from the pulpit. While he acknowledged that there were dangers, and also that there is real opposition to the movement, he concluded that, "This wonderful experience of the Holy Spirit is for more than a matter of speaking in tongues. It can mean a new flood of Christian love in the heart of a man. It can mean a better stewardship and better disciplined Christian life...There is good evidence that many lives have been transformed and blessed by it."[19]

Kelsey speaks of Lutheran pastor Egertson who expressed what the baptism in the Spirit meant to his church:

> A dozen of the finest people of our congregation experienced "tongues" with other manifestations of the Holy Spirit's power.

> Though the novelty of tongues has since gone, many experience the edification of tongues mainly in private devotions, and this has seemingly opened the door to other gifts of the Spirit...At first it was a startling experience. The expected reaction against such an un-Lutheran experience was there. However, peoples' minds soon came to rest...There seemed to be no "holier-than-thou" spirit noticeable. A gift of the Holy Spirit is not a sign of having arrived, but a tool to be used in building up the church.[20]

This section of the book might go on for hundreds of pages as the dynamic nature of receiving the Baptism in the Holy Spirit causes many varied experiences, but almost always an impression folks want/need to write about.

Does the reader get the impression that inviting the Holy Spirit baptism is often a surprising experience, both for the receiver and the observer? Even more assuredly, speaking in tongues (glossolalia) almost always invites controversy by others, and especially on the part of the recipient's personal risk or a leap of faith. Let's look at this phenomenon of risk (potential for loss) in the next chapter.

ENDNOTES:

1. H. Newton Maloney and A. Adams Lovekin, *Glossolalia: Behavioral Science Perspectives on Speaking in Tongues* (1985).
2. Note Gayle Irwin's work, *The Jesus Style* (1983).
3. Jerry Jensen, ed., *Episcopalians and the Baptism in the Holy Spirit* (1964), 7-9.
4. Ibid., 11-12.
5. Walter J. Hollenwager, *The Pentecostal* (1976), 5.
6. Jerry Jensen, ed., *Lutherans and the Baptism in the Holy Spirit* (1996), 6-9.
7. Willmar Thorkelson, as reported in *Lutherans and the Holy Spirit* (1964), 32.
8. Jensen (1996), 19, 20 and 31.
9. Christenson (1968), 75.
10. Elizabeth Brusco, "The Reformation of Machismo: Asceticism and Masculinity Among Colombian Evangelicals" in *Rethinking Protestantism in Latin America* (1903), 143-158.
11. In Murray W. Dempster, Byron D. Klaus, Douglas Peterson, eds: *The Globalization of Pentecostalism, A Religion Made to Travel* (1999), 138.
12. Edmond Cleary quoting Mouroux, *The Christian Experience: An Introduction to a Theology* (1954), in Murray W. Dempster, Byron D. Klaus, Douglas Peterson, eds: *The Globalization of Pentecostalism, A Religion Made to Travel* (1999), 144.
13. Mike Peterson, D. Min candidate at Asbury (Unpublished Thesis Manuscript), "The New Churches and Social Action" (nd), 137.
14. Ibid., Peterson, 137.
15. Ibid., Peterson, 137.
16. Ibid., Peterson, 138.

17. Bonnie C. Harvey, *Charles Finney: The Great Revivalist* (1999), 41, 42. Author's note: It is interesting how these words "I literally bellowed out the unutterable gushings of my heart..." have been excised and absent from years of quotes of Finney by Evangelical historians and reporters.
18. Cox (1995), 91. For an instructive piece relative to the rejection of Montanism by the early Roman church see Eddie Hyatt, *2000 Years of Charismatic Christianity* (2002), 28-29, and Kilian McDonnel, *The Baptism in the Holy Spirit* (1972), 44, where he (a Benedictine and chairman of the Catholic team of the International Roman Catholic/Pentecostal dialogue) says: "The Church never really recovered its balance after it rejected Montanism."
19. Kelsey (1968), 111.
20. Ibid., 114.

CHAPTER 7

RISK TAKING/LOSS—GOD'S MODEL The Risk God Takes With Humanity

When contemplating J. R. Flower's excellent verbalization of this thesis (1920, see chapter 8), it occurred to me God is/was always taking a risk with something as fragile or controversial as tongues! **But then, God has always taken risks!** He took a risk with Noah who might have refused to build his boat; with the man Abraham with whom He made a covenant and who might have failed the almost impossible task of being sent to a place he'd never seen. The God by whom he was being led, Yahweh/Elohim, wasn't even known by his Sumerian kin. In this chapter we will illustrate the risk God took by intrusting His plan of redemption with many biblical personalities, most of whom were ordinary folk. *The topic of risk in God's plans for humanity is eventually focused on the chance God takes with the sign called glossolalia.*

One of the most repeated warnings of critics of glossolalia is: "Be careful the devil doesn't give you something you didn't want."

The Risk of Counterfeit or Failure

When God selected tongues as a sign and tool, He took the risk of counterfeit and of being accused of using (ordaining, installing) an evidence or test that can be duplicated in external form by the enemy. Those who oppose glossolalia like to cite the magical powers of Jannes and Jambres of Pharaoh's court (II Tim. 3:8) who were able to duplicate some of the miraculous signs performed by the power of God through Moses, or the "tongues speech" of shamans in Africa or other ecstatic manifestations.

One of the most repeated warnings of these critics of glossolalia is: "be careful the devil doesn't give you something you didn't want." They ignore the truth that the power of Satan and his duplication in front of Pharaoh, which was real, didn't nullify or disprove God's power working through Moses for any of the ten plagues.

The risk of counterfeit is small, however, in comparison with the risks God takes with mankind throughout the Scriptures, and especially with the coming of the Messiah, our Savior, first with an unmarried, unknown virgin, probably no more than16 or17 years old, from a backwater town. (One could ask—why didn't God go to some pious, well- known and socially positioned young Jewess?)

Then, what if Joseph (Mary's husband) hadn't believed the angel in the dream and had proceeded to "put her away privately"? The fragile story then steps to the subsequent escape to Egypt in the face of Herod's murderous plans. The Father could have lost Him in the desert (40 days) at His temptation. He might have lost Him at Gethsemane or while on the cross. It seems to us He is a risk taker. Jesus' closest followers, the 12 disciples, never could understand the Kingdom—until after Pentecost. Notice that not one of them believed His words: "After three days I'll rise from the dead." The angel's words to the women at the tomb were; "He is risen*, just as he said, remember how he told you?"* (Luke 24:6).

Jesus probably would have lost the disciples and close followers if He had not shown Himself to them after the resurrection. The resurrection changed his brother James from a reluctant follower to the leader of the church at Jerusalem and, according to Josephus, one of the early Christian martyrs. Showing Himself, now alive, to above 500 followers after the seeming crushing defeat on Calvary certainly was indispensable. They were already secluding themselves behind closed and locked doors. But there was yet another event without which it is doubtful the religion of Jesus the Messiah would have survived. What was it that would loose a force powerful enough to overcome Jerusalem's violent opposition to the early Christian movement, not to mention the brutal slaughter of the Lord's followers later in Rome? It was Pentecost. (Interesting that on reading those words, many Christians today would say, "You're putting too much emphasis on Pentecost," while I'm saying, "Why won't you agree that the members of the Church's first 200 years were Charismatic?") And so, while the resurrection (the centerpiece of our faith) was vital, so was the indisputable experience of God speaking through the mouths of the 120 as recorded in Acts. What else can explain the transformation of cowards to martyrs for the sake of the gospel? Who can, to this day, fully explain the inner strength and witness of the Spirit-baptized individual who says: *God knows my name; I'm important to Him. If He can do this with my speech apparatus, He must be able to make me a useful disciple. There's hope for me. I can be His instrument. I will use this power to witness.* "Just as He said" (Acts 1:8).

Jesus didn't leave us without a "sign"—but He hid it in something so "intellectually ugly" and risky that many would reject it and even justify their decisions with pride! God is so awesome!

Jesus didn't leave us without a "sign"—but He hid in something so "intellectually ugly" and risky that many would reject it and justify that decision with pride.

Each of the above "steps of risk" involved vital people in God's ultimate plan. Should we expect Him to change His ways now—concerning His intention to empower believers with the potential of supernatural faith to confront the evil powers of this age? Should we be surprised if He continues to demand the unreasonable from man's viewpoint? I submit it's the doorway to a walk of faith that releases God's power *just as he said.* It's all part of His interaction with us that seems foolish.

> *For my thoughts are not your thoughts,*
> *Neither are your ways my ways, declares the Lord.*
> *As the heavens are higher than the earth,*
> *so are my ways higher than your ways and*
> *my thoughts than your thoughts (Isaiah 55:8-9).*

ON THE TOPIC OF THE RISK GOD EXPECTS US TO TAKE

When the institutionalization of the Church becomes more important than growth through proclamation by powerful witnesses for Christ, the stigma of Pentecostal charismata—by the world AND the Church world—will weaken the resolve to "keep the way clear" for the Holy Spirit. The results have been catastrophic throughout history.[1] The reluctance to accept God's "higher ways" occurring in the first 250 years of the Apostolic Era were subsequently repeated in almost every renewal movement in the last 1800 years. Churchmen and women are still questioning, even after the greatest Charismatic renewal in history and fewer than 100 years after the Azusa Street awakening at the turn of last century. From the West especially, and many other points of theological reflection, come voices of skepticism, wondering if God *really chose* this distasteful sign and humbling experience.

> Institutionalism is an emphasis on organization at the expense of other factors. In the church, such an emphasis, or overemphasis, on

> organization always comes at the expense of the life and freedom of the Spirit... virtually all historians of Christianity agree that the institutionalization of the early church was accomplished by the demise of the charismatic gifts.[2]

Why should we expect God to have changed His mind about the risk/faith factor involved in speaking in tongues, since it is so seemingly evident in all His interaction with mankind? Should one expect it to be incongruous with accepting God's salvation? "By faith you are saved...The just shall live by faith...Without faith it is impossible to please God...Blessed are they who mourn (their loss/weakness) for they will be comforted." All these and more require the risk of faith. "Sola Fide" was the great discovery of Martin Luther and embraced by most of the reformers.

God is building His church with half-people because that's all there are.

Just as God demands "risk" of the recipient to establish the ambiguous "tongues link" with the believer, He in turn takes a risk that this "power for witness" might be distorted and turned inside-out. This is the dark side of the abuse of spiritual gifts. We should not be shocked that God permits it even if He does not approve of it. His grace is extensive. *He is building His church with half-people because that's all there are.* Witness the gross abuse of "servants of the Lord" down through the ages of the Church (see chapter 2).

GOD'S UNEXPECTED EXPECTATIONS: SURPRISING CIRCUMSTANCES

God's ways seem weird! If a human administrator relating to the secular or religious world related to the personnel under his supervision like God relates to those He has committed responsibility, such a natural "boss" would probably be seen as a **rebel**.

When Jesus talked about the Kingdom (He was always talking about it), He constantly surprised His listeners. Good guys turn into bad guys. Those believing to be rewarded are punished instead. Things are reversed. The last are first and vice versa.

> Paradox, irony, and surprise permeate the teaching of Jesus. They flip our expectations upside down. The least are the greatest. The immoral receive forgiveness and blessing. Adults become like children. The religious miss the heavenly banquet. The pious receive curses. Things aren't like we think they should be. We're baffled and perplexed.[3]

Let's make a short list—poignant crisp accounts—of how God delights in hiding things in parables OR in unexpected ways that force those who seek Him to REACH for Him, not unlike a parable which always has something hidden, that forces the audience to try to find the hidden part. Maybe God does this not only to retain our attention, but because it leads us to discovery. One especially retains that which one discovers. In pedagogical terms it's called "Guided Discovery" which the best teachers use for the greatest effect. The Scriptures show how God surprised the following people (or their family members). No doubt they wondered what God was up to!

ABRAHAM. (His name was first Abram before God renamed him in Genesis 12.) God called him to do the extraordinary: leave his people, his country, his family and go to a place "where God would show him." He didn't have an AAA map to quickly look up the place. What a risk God took. Abram had to trust a God he hardly knew. This was not the God of his culture. This God made great promises, but He didn't come through very fast. He kept repeating the promises and Abram had to take this all by faith. Sure, God rewarded him for it "and counted it for righteousness," but not until Abram had stuck his neck out many times. God kept talking about a great posterity, so big Abram couldn't count them. All he knew was Sarah his wife couldn't even get pregnant! How many years did he wait for the promise? Abraham looked at Sarah and said, "No way!" God said, "Just watch me!" Then, when all hope was gone, wow, two sons! But the one that counted (Isaac) was requested to be slain at the hand of Abram himself. You talk about tests!! You can't predict this God. It seems He will simply not provide what is comfortable or what is attractive as easy steppingstones for man to find His Way. How many ways can we say it? God is not reasonable! Why do we continually try to make Him acceptable to our comfort zone? God's ways are exciting and made up of ambiguous surprises. We literalists hate ambiguity.

God is not reasonable! His ways are exciting and made up of ambiguous surprises. We literalists hate ambiguity.

JACOB AND ESAU (Gen. 25ff). God ran against tribal custom and put the younger, Jacob, ahead of his older brother. Father Isaac was confounded and tricked. Jacob lived up to his name as "heel catcher—one who struggles with man and overcomes." Yet, God says He loved him—this rascal! No one would have expected this. Many years later, Jacob struggles with God's messenger and gets a permanent limp to remind him of his weaknesses. God must know something about this "cheater" that is valuable. Maybe Jacob really has a heart for God, an attribute not too apparent at first blush. If I listen carefully, I can hear Jacob (this rascal) say: "God talked to grandfather Abraham, and God has a special relationship with father. I want Him to be with me too." Was that heart cry for God in the soul of Jacob the element that made him preferred to his brother?

JOSEPH, son of Jacob. Look at the pressing test God put to this young man! What a risk God took with him. When all his brothers mistreated him, did Joseph wonder, "Where is the God of my father?" He might have given up and turned his back on God down in the dry well in the pasture or while all alone in the Egyptian prison, after having been sold, betrayed, threatened by his very flesh and blood. It's amazing he held up under the mental anguish and consternation. We admire him. So did the Egyptians. Then, falsely accused, imprisoned, forgotten and finally justified. After about a dozen years of trial he saved his people, because God prepared him for such a task. What would God have done if he'd bombed out with despair? Wonderful story, but so much responsibility riding on one young man's shoulders.

MOSES. Now here's a story! This potential tool for God is seen floating alone as a wee baby in the Nile River. What a "cheeky" mother—good for her! We'd say today, watching her set her baby off afloat in a small boat: "Ma'am, aren't you afraid of being charged with child abuse?" (He might have drowned in the Nile—or just drifted on to dehydration.) Had God prepared Pharaoh's daughter for a baby? *(There's a cute riddle for young people about this: Who was the greatest financier in the Bible? Pharaoh's daughter; she went to the bank and drew out a little prophet!)* Moses was made a prince of Egypt and then educated like one. But from an Egyptian point of view, he blew it! He was a murderer on the run. God couldn't have scripted it better. Forty years in obscurity and life as a shepherd had prepared him for the great task. (He must have learned something not taught him in the university of Egypt!) But look how God uses some ordinary thing (an old staff) to be a symbol of God's power as well as symbolic of Moses' submission. So God has to position this "symbol" under His control, not Moses' control. *Naturally, God is simply going to do what He always does: No test, no gain.* "Moses, I will own this symbol," says God, as it becomes known as the "Rod of God." Whether it becomes a snake or is used to change the Nile to blood or bring the rest of the plagues in Egypt later, Yahweh tells Moses to throw down his "symbol" and it becomes a snake from which he runs. God then says, "Pick it up by the tail." That's risky business! (When we see snake handlers on TV's National Geographic, they always pick up a snake right behind its head.) This rod will always show God is in control. What a great analogy for other symbols in our lives that require us to "lay down the staff," like the trust and risk it requires to lay down our language skills to allow the Spirit to pray through us. When we pretend to "own" our speech skills (our better way), what we are really doing is refusing to "throw down the staff"—human language being our proof of superiority in all of God's creation.

Then, God sends him back to deliver Jacob's family after 400 years in Egypt. What a task. Six hundred thousand complaining Jews! How many times did he want to quit? And how many times did God test him? And, think of the two times in this drama that God tempted him to take the place of Abraham and be the founder of a new remade nation? A story full of the unexpected and potential failure. God loves it! We read and wonder!

GIDEON. God couldn't get him to think he was somebody. He was so scared, he put God to the test twice. Must have had low self-esteem—but then, he was asked to leave his farming and become a soldier. Why didn't God choose a REAL soldier? One that would say, "Hey, this is right up my alley—let's go for it God!" No—God chooses a nobody whose linage has never had an important person in it. Then God devises a plan to route a whole army with only 300 men and—get this—with some torches and water pitchers! Gideon might have said, "Whoa! That's not for me. I need all the soldiers I can get, even the ones who don't correctly drink water from the brook like You said, God." I wonder what Gideon's blood pressure was while holding his torch that night? I wonder if the Apostle Paul thought of these things when he wrote:

> *Oh, the depth of the riches of the wisdom and knowledge of God! How unsearchable his judgments, and his paths beyond tracing out! Who has known the mind of the Lord? Or who has been his counselor?* (Romans 11:33-34.)

Of course, he was quoting David the psalmist.

Now **he** knew something about God's unpredictability and His "strange ways."

DAVID. What a surprise for the prophet Samuel! He thought he could spot a good man at first sight when he saw him. God said: " ...*The Lord does not look at the things man looks at...*" (1 Sam. 16:7). He had to settle for the one the family of Jesse was keeping out of sight. Didn't even invite David to the prophet's party! But, oh, that oil poured on his head that signaled the coming of the presence of God's Spirit. "*...and from that day on the Spirit of the Lord came upon David in power...*" (16:13). Unpredictable from man's standard.

God has been doing this for thousands of years. You'd think we'd stop being surprised, but we never learn. We're still caught up in our own perceptual thinking grid, the way our culture and family has taught us. God said to David: *"I took you from the pasture and following the flocks to be ruler over my people Israel"* (2 Sam. 9:8). Jesus did the same in choosing the disciples! Would we have chosen **that** bunch of fellows to whom to give the keys to the kingdom? Mighty risky, Jesus! Did you see personal character in those plain workers, unknown laborers, even unsophisticated men, or did they have potential, something like the Father saw in David? "*...the Lord has sought out a man after his own heart and appointed him leader of his people...*" (I Sam. 13:14).

We will look hard in the Scriptures to find a person more honored (by many writers and God's own words) than David. But he couldn't hold any office of responsibility in the church where I hold ministerial papers!

RUTH. After all the warnings about marrying foreign women stated in the Torah, God ordains Ruth to be in the linage of the Messiah. Wonderful story, none-the-less. Ruth risked much, but she did what she knew to do (in seeking food for her mother-in-law) and God intersected her life with a divine appointment—just like he did in the life of Rebecca, who had no idea that in accepting her role in the family as "water girl," doing what she knew to do, God's divine appointment was waiting at the well—but only after she agreed to water the stranger's camels! God was **testing** both of these women.

The reader will remember I'm seeking to show the myriad examples of God's dealings with us in strange, abrupt, unexpected, weird (?) ways to serve as analogies of what for me is God's unusually personal and deeply subjective **test** for every person who would seek the baptism in the Holy Spirit; to be clothed with His power to serve Him more effectively in His Kingdom. Many complain what the biblical record shows to be the "norm" is so unreasonable! I'm often surprised by the diverse tests and unusual circumstances in so many of those He calls to service as I review in my mind the story line in the Scriptures. Have you, like me, wondered at God's treatment of Job? Of what God allowed Satan to do to him—the loss he had to suffer at God's permissive hand? In this book, man's wisdom and reason are seen in all their weaknesses—even though sometimes in reading this oldest of books one is tempted to agree with Job's tormentors! It's a hard book for some to read. Its deep meaning is rather hidden: Why does God allow the "righteous" to suffer pain and loss? Why doesn't God simply "put a hedge around us" (Satan's words) to justify our faith in Him and set us apart as winners in the culture in which we live? I once saw these words on a church sign: *If all Christians were rich and had no pimples—everybody would be a Christian.* It seems God's justice won't allow such a utopian state because folks would serve Him for the wrong reasons!

JESUS THE MESSIAH

Let's terminate this review of some of God's "paths beyond tracing out" by examining in more detail the incarnation of Jesus with the same human reasoning's "natural eye." When God sent the Son, He utilized many extraordinary events that baffle the mind. Greek mythology has some strange behavior concerning their gods who interacted with mankind. But the complexity and wisdom of Jesus' first coming demonstrates God's love in sending a Redeemer to live, interact and give His life to redeem mankind back to God. The Greeks don't even come close to the power of Jehovah's incarnation event. Yet, He does it all in such an unexpected manner. The idea of a **redeemer** is the single most unorthodox thing God could have done. This is the event that sets Christianity apart from all the other world's major religions. Not even Judaism could accept it. They *should* have, since they had prophecies in many of the books of the Old Testament foretelling God's eventual plan. They even had sacred animal sin offerings that typed the coming Redeemer. Buddhism doesn't even hint of such a thing. Islam criticizes even the thought that Allah could have pain or suffer concern. Yes, he's the merciful, the all-knowing and compassionate one but Allah, as Muslims see him, would have to do something contrary to his nature to buy back, redeem sinful man. Unthinkable! It's no wonder they reject Jesus as Messiah.

God has the power to destroy and punish, but he is a God of restraint. To give us free will, God had to foreswear the use of force against us. This is "God is Love."

–S. Peck

Can you imagine asking the religious rulers of Israel of that epoch: "To what social level family will the Messiah be born?" Wouldn't they have answered, "To a well-known family of great reputation and standing"? Or, "With whom will the Messiah associate when he comes?"[4] They would probably have answered that He would associate with the power brokers of the day—and especially the religious elite who had the nation's conscience in their hands. And wouldn't they have expected Him to dress, speak and behave according to all the minute observances of at least one of the recognized religious orders of the day? Jesus seemed to come and be completely out of the frame of reference of these "keepers of the throne of David"! And when He challenged them to get to know the Father, they tried to kill him. Then they finally did, and the world has never been the same *nor can most people really understand how unreasonable is God's RESTRAINT.*

> God has the power to destroy and punish, but he is a God of restraint. To give us free will, God had to foreswear the use of force against us. This is "God is Love." In agony He must stand by and let us be. He has no recourse but, weeping, to watch us punish ourselves. Jesus showed us this characteristic in the New Testament—Christ impotently suffered death at the hands of human evil. He did not raise a finger against His persecutors. What about holocausts? It is a brutal bleeding question! Having forsaken force (during this time of grace) God is impotent to prevent the atrocities that we commit upon one another. This strange God reigns in weakness and He will win the battle against evil.[5]

Peck said that as well as I've ever seen it, and I resonate with his eloquence. The particular state of the USA you come from (or if you live in any other country in the world), there is probably a city or region that is looked down on by others in your area. Like Fresno is (unjustifiably) seen by Californians as the worst place to live in the state, or to be from Detroit, by most Midwesterners is seen as a disadvantage. Well, the region of Galilee, in Israel, was seen as inferior and materialistic by the Jerusalem "high-hats" (like New Yorkers from the "city" look down on the rest of the country in America). The town of Nazareth, in Galilee was seen as a place of vice because near there, a large Roman garrison that policed the country was located and it was associated with all the accompanying sin and corruption of the "uncircumcised" military. Yet it was to this village Gabriel came to a virgin pledged to be married to a man named Joseph. Imagine the "disadvantage" of how the Jewish leaders looked down on the rural people of Galilee and the inferior *patoi* unlearned language they spoke.[6]

One begins to wonder if God does anything in a conventional manner. Ah, that's a good word—conventional! We have so "sanitized" Christmas and the birth of Jesus. Yancey, in his special style, so poignantly explains:

In contrast to what the cards would have us believe, Christmas did not sentimentally simplify life on planet earth...Christmas art depicts Jesus' family as icons stamped in gold foil, with a calm Mary receiving the tidings of the Annunciation as a kind of benediction. But that is not at all how Luke tells the story. Mary was "greatly troubled" and "afraid" at the angel's appearance, and when the angel pronounced the sublime words about the Son of the Most High...Mary had something far more mundane on her mind: *But I'm a virgin!*...In modern United States, where each year a million teenage girls get pregnant out of wedlock, Mary's predicament has undoubtedly lost some of its force, but in a closely knit Jewish community in the first century, the news an angel brought could not have been entirely welcome. The law regarded a betrothed woman who became pregnant as an adulteress, subject to death by stoning...Luke tells of a tremulous Mary hurrying off to the one person who could possibly understand what she was going through: her relative Elizabeth, who miraculously got pregnant in old age after another angelic annunciation. Elizabeth believes Mary and shares her joy, and yet the scene poignantly highlights the contrast between the two women: the whole countryside is talking about Elizabeth's healed womb even as Mary must hide the shame of her own miracle. Nine months of awkward explanations, the lingering scent of scandal—it seems that God arranged the most humiliating circumstances possible for his entrance, as if to avoid any charge of favoritism...Mary's pregnancy, in poor circumstances, and with the father unknown, would have been an obvious case for an abortion (in our day with family planning clinics offering convenient ways to correct "mistakes")...I am impressed that when the Son of God became a human being he played by the rules, harsh rules: small towns do not treat kindly young boys who grow up with questionable paternity.[7]

The author continues with one more powerful thought about the quality of this young girl when she said, "I am the Lord's servant; may it be to me as you have said" (Luke 1:38). "Often a work of God comes with two edges, great joy and great pain, and in the matter-of-fact response Mary embraced both."[8]

COMMUNICATIONS INSIGHT

I REMEMBER so vividly these two emotions when in 1945 I tried to explain to my sixth grade teacher the "mechanics" of speaking in tongues only a few weeks after having received this blessing. (I only know a little bit more now than then!) Miss Erickson was a wonderful Lutheran Christian. I told how I was so overjoyed at having received the baptism in the Holy Spirit that summer, with the evidence of glossolalia and singing in the Spirit—and then to see the incredulous look of skepticism and doubt on her face and in her remarks. She was interested to hear about "speech and tongues" and wondered openly if I had "manufactured" this experience. Then she dismissed the whole episode with: "Well, my church tells me that Pentecostals are too emotional and are certainly a cult." I was eleven and that was painful, even if I didn't yet know what a cult really was.

Can you imagine how Joseph, Mary's intended husband, must have asked that question? "God, why couldn't you have waited until we were married, so the town's folk wouldn't think we'd lost self-control?" For an unmarried girl to be pregnant in that society, as in Arab society today, means all the males in her family have failed to protect her and they lose face (wajh).[9] She might have been thrown down a well, or more normally stoned. Joseph saved her! He believed the angel's report in the dream.

Joseph again: "God, you told me the Messiah is to be born; that's the fetus my Mary is carrying. But Lord, since you've arranged so much up until now, why do we have to go to a cave with the animals for His birth? How about arranging for a room in the best inn in Bethlehem for the Son of God?" But Jesus, the Redeemer of the world, came in the absolute poorest way, wrapped in a large cloth, then re-wrapped in narrow strips of cloth around the first. No signs of royalty or position or wealth, even though this baby was indeed the King of kings and Lord of lords. What irony! Surely this must have pleased the Father in heaven, for His own reasons. The fact of the birth of the Messiah would not be announced to the rulers or powerbrokers of the religious world, but to the most unlikely people—shepherds.

Shepherds were despised as a clan by the then-current hierarchical social strata. Even though the Jewish people as a race came from pastoralists like Abraham, Isaac and Jacob, they were considered "unclean" because of their work and couldn't even observe the ceremonial laws of purification. They were uneducated in the Torah, and thus were considered ignorant. The visual presence of God was absent in Israel for more than 500 years (since before king Josiah and the disappearance of the Ark of the Covenant).[10] But these humble shepherds saw the "glory" of God and they witnessed the birth of Christ—chosen by the heavenly hosts! Wonderful—unusual—shocking. Why, why, why so unreasonable and unpredictable?

Have you ever wondered "what if" Joseph hadn't believed the dream about this pregnancy's origin? Or later the dream to flee to Egypt? Wasn't that quite a risk thinking this young man, one would assume, with normal expectations and goals for married life would accept **the plan** with all that travel—and on foot at that?

God, You surely chose the right dude! We need to honor him more than we do, perhaps. But please be patient, Lord. We're trying to "hold on" to this strange ride as we follow Your plan that has such unexpected turns. Please be patient, Lord, we're trying to hold on the notion that the gospel message is ***reasonable*** *like even some honored theologians of our day would suppose.*

To have this new religion start with the scandal of Jesus being called a bastard would have been a strong barrier to overcome—but the gospel writers record it anyway! Amazing! Why not just leave it out? Think of the risk

God took when he stretched Himself out on the dissection table—a risk he seemed to enjoy. "Examine me, test me." You decide. "Today as I read the accounts of Jesus' birth I tremble to think of the fate of the world resting on the responses of two rural teenagers."[11] Modern science can look at the virgin birth with mockery. They can name insects and some reptiles where this may happen, but the leap from insects to humans? In the non-human realm, where this may be possible, all the offspring are female—but Mary birthed a male child. *Now that we are listing some of Your many surprises, God, I guess we shouldn't be shocked that You have made it so unreasonable*—***was it so a believer would have to look beyond science into the arena of faith?***

Because Jesus was also man, I am amazed at the success He had in the face of the risks along the way. I don't suppose we'll ever know, on this side, just when the realization came that He was the Son of Almighty God. Did it precede age 12 in the temple, did He wonder how Joseph and Mary would ever really understand when He stayed behind those three days, discussing the things of the Father with the scholars and teachers? Unusual. No wonder Luke says: *"But they did not understand what He was saying to them...but His mother treasured all these things in her heart"* (Luke 2:50-51).

Wow! The way He chose His closest buddies/associates is amazing in light of today's managerial and leadership manuals. Instead of recruiting hardened revolutionaries, He chose ordinary workmen. Nondescript, like the four fishermen and the tax collector. And then, as if that were not enough to get our attention (not to mention the social climate of His day), Jesus chose women in His membership of close associates, unheard of. They were considered inferior—much like today in many church circles.[12]

Can we imagine the consternation on the part of John the Baptist when asked by Jesus to be baptized—instead of the other way around like John at first argued? (Matt. 3:14)

Does it seem unusual, even odd, for Jesus to be tempted **40 days,** without food, in the desert by the devil? Couldn't He have blown the whole thing there? And if you argue that Jesus **could not** have failed—why the experience in the first place! Risky, no?

COMMUNICATIONS INSIGHT

WHY DID JESUS use so much indirection of speech? Was His speech style complex?

Have you wondered about the temptation of Jesus to go to Greece and really "wow them," as requested in John 12 after those Greeks had heard His unusual way of speaking? The Greeks, as the world's greatest sophists, might have treated Him much better than His own "House of Israel." And while on this subject of style of speech: What about the 33.7% of the words of Jesus in parabolic form? Of course, the Jews were used to parables much more than today's expectations in the West, but think of the contradiction of "whosoever will" and speech as in Matt. 13, set expressly to exclude folks who miss the parabolic indirection. Then there's the "Upside Down" speech of the Beatitudes in Matt. 5.[13]

THE RISK OF INCARNATION

We can only wonder at the risk of telling the 12 disciples He would be killed and leave them—and to be killed by the most despicable death Romans reserved for rank criminals. They must have been electrified at His words. It was unthinkable the Messiah would be put to death and leave them. Unreasonable that the group of believers He wished to create would be deprived of its founder. Risky—no? As if He were saying: "Go into all the world and make disciples—you'll be hated, mocked, and even those who kill you will think they are doing God a favor. Don't worry, Guys; I've overcome the world—it's up to you now. I'm going to send you a Comforter to help you; go wait for Him—but I'm out of here!"

> **First stage – God "out there", second stage – God "with us", and finally, third stage – God "in them". Astonishing!**

Lord, we marvel at the willingness to "empty yourself" of heaven's splendor and power in the beautiful passage of Philippians 2: "Who, being in very nature God, did not consider equality with God something to be grasped, but ***made himself nothing...*** *How hard was that? Is that even a just question to ask? Is not this "risk" and "loss" theme a major one that we mortals resist, reject, distort, and analyze away? I want to say that making Yourself nothing in the incarnation is somehow related to the issue of submission required to be clothed with the Comforter You promised the disciples before You left. Is this why some find it so hard to let Your Spirit "speak" through them—because it requires a sort of "emptying" of self, of relinquishing the god-likeness of the power of speech and meaning making? Was Your "putting on flesh" in the incarnation a symbol, a picture, a microcosm of what You require for the empowerment promised? For questions I don't lack! Will I ever really know what a risk You took, God, to see Your son born with blood smeared on His tiny frame,* *sucking air for the first time in never-before-used lungs? Lungs that, as the Creator in the beginning, had breathed life's breath into the dust-doll You called Adam in the garden. Wonderful!*

The Ministry of Jesus—So Unexpected, So Unpredictable

Yancey:

> The more I studied Jesus, the more difficult it became to pigeonhole him...He urged obedience to the Mosaic law while acquiring the reputation as a lawbreaker...He had uncompromising views on rich men and loose women, yet both types enjoyed his company...He spoke eloquently about peacemaking, then told his disciples to procure swords. His extravagant claims about himself kept him at the center of controversy, but when he did something truly miraculous he tended to hush it up. As Walter Wink has said, if Jesus had never lived, we would not have been able to invent him.[14]

Rulers Rather Than Witnesses

There is an astonishing event just prior to the ascension of Jesus into heaven. Jesus had just reinstated His fearful band who all abandoned Him at the crucifixion. Remember? They were still interested in *power* and asked if this was the moment He was going to restore the kingdom to Israel (Acts 1:6). Jesus wanted to talk about another kind of power, the result of which would mean the physical death of most of those in His tight little group. "*But you will receive power when the Holy Spirit comes on you; and you will be my witnesses in Jerusalem, and in all Judea and Samaria, and to the ends of the earth*" (v. 8). Amazing! We read and criticize the disciples. But we are no different. We are like them. We'd rather be *rulers* than *witnesses*! How often has the Church, down through the centuries, gone after verse six (political kingdom) when His heart cry for us is to have verse eight (self-effacing witnessing) kind of power? And He **hides it in a seeming ridiculous mannerism** that frankly many have rejected. Wouldn't it have been better to have the sign of the Spirit's coming to be an oral/aural visible demonstration of the recipient's giftedness? Something culturally accepted and admired? Something any observer might have understood and desired for him/herself? Of course, such a thing would have run counter to the above list, and many more things He does seems unreasonable to us. *I'm starting to get it, Lord.*

Why Take a Chance?

"It would be difficult to find two more diverse attitudes than we find expressed toward the experience of tongues. On the one hand it is valued as the fountainhead of meaning and vitality, a direct contact with God. On the other, is viewed as a dangerous experience giving the individual over to the unknown and hostile forces of reality, one which results in personal and social disaster."[15] "But isn't it dangerous?" one might rightfully ask. Yes—birth is dangerous, and for this reason many couples have no children. They look at not just the danger of parturition but of raising a child in today's world.

Kelsey again, in answer to the question—isn't it dangerous? "Yes, but isn't a dead church more dangerous than a dangerous one? As the New Testament has tried to teach us, the real danger is in being half alive. When death is right in the center of things, inside oneself and society, its deadness can be disastrous. And so perhaps we are better off to live and face dangers, those of tongues included...Ananias and Sapphira found dealing with God a deadly dangerous business."[16]

How interesting that God risks the potential weakness of human vessels as the delivery system—when He could have eliminated man's potential faults and manipulation for personal power needs. No wonder the Church, through the ages, has eliminated this potential by non-maintenance of the gifts. So the clergy has grabbed power from the "sons and daughters, the old and the young" (Joel's prophecy and Peter's quote in Acts 2) and thus institutionalized a "safer, better" way. In that process the Church deprived itself of so much of God's power and guidance, not to mention the chance to partake of the incarnational nature of the gifts. Because there is a "human" part of any gift, it must be managed by the loving (I Cor. 13) examination and approval in public settings. So if I'm to be an instrument of the Holy Spirit in the Church with any prophetic form of utterance, I must have the maturity to allow the body of prophets to "consider, weigh carefully" what has been uttered so it may accord with Scripture AND be profitable for the whole church (I Cor. 14:26, 29). God could have chosen another way, you know.

We want a Messiah who flies like Superman and a personage of fantasy like a video game. We don't want a hero that loses every time!

Instead of constructing Christendom on the reality of paradox and that which appears unreasonable and risky, He could have based it on solid behavioral and sociological principles, not on the cross and its demands, and certainly not on the risky business of a partnership with humans and their potential weaknesses. Like Muggeridge suggests in the temptation of Christ: "Satan was offering Jesus the chance to be the thundering Messiah we think we want."[17] We want a Messiah who flies like Superman and a personage we can dial in like a video game with all its fantasy! We don't want a video game where the hero loses every time! The Church has always sought to evict that which is ambiguous and enigmatic. In so doing it has opted for what can be predicted and controlled (prediction and control—the mantra of Behaviorism, a school of psychology). "Did not Jesus realize that people want more than anything else to worship what is established beyond dispute?"[18]

The Watershed

This is the great watershed of philosophy and theology as it contemplates God's dealings with mankind, His creatures. We cherish freedom, but we shrink from His *incarnational* principle of risking the whole ballgame with us as partners. In this arena, we want less freedom to think independently and more of His absolute control—so we don't have the uncertainty of making a mistake. Or, if we do falter, we can blame Him for His system. So we've opted not to accept the New Testament way and simply taken control while pretending it's His way. Again, we really don't like His way which gives us so much responsibility; because it demands too much maturity. Yancey quotes Dostoevsky on this topic of Christ's temptation, likening it to the Inquisition of the sixteenth century, when he states that in rejecting Satan's offer, Jesus surrendered His greatest advantage: the power to control belief. Karamazov (in poetic form) says the Church corrected this mistake of Jesus and retook the authority to compel belief—executing thousands who refused this falsely assumed power.[19]

ISLAM AND CHRISTIANITY COLLIDE HERE

So too has Islam opted to control belief—totally! The incarnation is not possible. The cross of Jesus was not necessary. First, because it is outside the nature of Allah to lose anything. A God making Himself weak to redeem us is an oxymoron. And second, mankind was not born in sin, but born good. Third, in Muslim thinking, one person cannot be responsible for the sins of another. So Islam is totally set up on a system of works, obedience, and submission to a god that takes no chance of a partnership with man. When a Christian witness gives the message of the gospel to a Muslim—"Jesus, the Son of God loves you and He died for your sins"—that testimony shows a fundamental weakness of God's character, besides the fact that God couldn't have a son.[20] Islam is a perfect antidote to the soul of God's ultimate intention to save us. The idea of a Messiah crucified is also an oxymoron for a Jew. Here is the great stumbling block. How could God lose to win?

I submit in this same line of thought that glossolalia is too uncertain/ambiguous for those who seek certainty. The temptation in the desert reveals a profound difference in the way the tempter operates and the way God interacts with mankind. I can force Dolly, my wife, to love me by wielding a bullwhip. This is much like Satan who has the power to force, dazzle, even destroy. God chooses a more subtle system, one that allows choice—because as in my relationship with Dolly, her love is only valuable to me when she has the choice to reject my love. So when she doesn't refuse and loves me, I have a prize beyond anything, except God's love.

Earlier I spoke of this free choice of submitting my mother tongue as an indispensable element in God's scheme. Yancey speaks of God's ways in contrast to Satan's as internal and non-coercive—a kind of *abdication*.[21] Perfect, I say! One abdicates one's speech apparatus (so linked to a person's God-given humanity and superiority on God's continuum of created beings), so as to allow the Spirit to speak as the Scriptures describe.

> **The Pharisees wouldn't have liked our era of grace…Grace is ambiguous, slippery, full of restraint. Priests never did like prophets.**

Try to hold this thought: We have again come full circle to why God does not overpower us in salvation through the illogical way of the cross and uses the same unbelievable system for our empowerment to be more effective witnesses.

We want certainty and final proofs so we can use them as weapons on others and bedrock unshakeable anchors for our own security of belief. Given enough time, it seems every historical renewal in the Church tries to improve on God's best plan of restraint. He limits Himself and offers us an uncertainty that requires our faith and risk which leads to partnership with the same risk of failure that faced Jesus the Son and our Master. For the believer who wishes something far less ambiguous (a logical wish), one can embrace an extreme position of God's sovereignty, free from human volition, where a believer's faith is greatly inactive, where all is predestined by God so one's present and future state is totally fixed (like Islam in the extreme, and many Christians in our world). What has been abdicated in that position is something else, far less "foolish" than the potential of His partnership in ministry. One can still be His child, but that "security" has become a prison—not New Testament empowerment. The

Pharisees wouldn't have liked our era of grace either. Law is concrete, predictable, clear—it's comfortable. Grace is ambiguous, slippery, full of restraint. The priest never did like the prophet. The priest had predictable power, while the prophet even dared correct the priest. Heaven forbid! Let's not have any of that in the Church.

One of the weaknesses of much of the Pentecostal movement's teaching has been a relative lack of understanding about the "incarnational" nature of spiritual gifts. Jesus was both God and man—by the Father's ingenious design. (Of course, that took 600 years for the Church to come up with that difficult word, and some excommunications, before settling on the "Filioque"!) The Bible is both divine (inspired) and written by some 40-plus human authors, each contributing his own culture and language usage. Jesus could have come as only God (and not have been called Emmanuel—"God with us") but would very likely not have related as well to humankind if He had been only divine. The Bible could have been written by angels taking dictation from God (like the Muslims say about the Koran—or the Morman's belief about their book). It's the same with the gifts of the Spirit. God wants a partnership. He doesn't speak very often with a voice from heaven like He did with Jesus at His water baptism, or when the apostle Paul fell to the ground on his way to Damascus! No, God has chosen that *sharing system* again.

ERROR OF TWO EXTREMES

This idea of God *sharing* (in partnership) His power and presence with mankind has always plagued the Church's understanding. A goodly number of Pentecostals/Charismatics don't really understand it either. That misunderstanding has led to acceptance of extreme positions about the operation of the gifts of the Spirit. On the one hand are those who think the gifts of the Spirit are purely *natural abilities*—like medical doctors, skilled scientists, professional musicians, computer programmer specialists, etc. This group accepts that God uses special people, but the supernatural element is minimized. The opposite view is that the operation of the gifts of the Spirit are *totally supernatural.* In this view, the gifts are infallible and cannot be corrected or judged. God's Word teaches otherwise, that the gifts to the Church are to be evaluated for their benefit to the Church by the corporate Body of Christ.[22] Donald Gee suggests it's not correct to accept either of these two extremes.[23] As Lim states so clearly, the gifts are **incarnational**! This is God's way. Just as God chose to use man's cultural attributes in the composition of His Word (with identifiable personality traits and writing styles), so He wants to *use* us. In like manner, Jesus the Messiah was both God and man when He came to be crucified and move His followers from the Old Covenant to the New by His death and resurrection. It's risky, it's spectacular, it's humbling and very hard for many to accept. We fail to accept that though carnal and imperfect, God desires to employ these vessels of clay so He can seek slowly to move us to the image of Christ in us. I believe there is a tie to all this and glossolalia. God uses our speech apparatus and, if we let Him, He'll speak from our "inner most being" by our submerging (not annihilating) our speech capacity so the supernatural aspect can have preeminence. Here, the natural meets the supernatural in an incarnational mode. Yes, it's wonderful—in the true generic understanding of the word.

Wouldn't it be less risky, God, if You used a safer system—we ask. *Why did You allow the personality of Luke in Luke-Acts to come through? How come we can so readily identify Paul's style of writing? Lord, if You'd have just used one "scribe" and dictated the whole thing—like You wrote in the stone tables on Sinai—all this argumentation in form criticism would be obsolete! But because You chose, again, to involve humans in Your involvement with us when the gifts of the Spirit are being employed, it's like Dr. Lim says:* "In any utterance the messenger is an inseparable part of the message. A person's background, personality, vocabulary, level of maturity, strengths and weaknesses, and relationships all become part of the message."[24]

ANY FIRE IN THE HOUSE IS DANGEROUS

I found this out when discovering that six of seven insurance companies would not insure our cabin when I admitted to having installed a wood stove to heat it! Fire in the stove is beneficial; but in the attic fire is disastrous! One is not safer by doubting the existence of the atom just because we've not seen one yet. What is the Church losing by proclaiming that God's "foolishness" is **not** wisdom, as the apostle Paul states (I Cor. 1:25) but indeed folly? Tongues, no doubt, represent both risk and loss—but can there be growth and development without conflict? The early witnesses of Christ stirred up so much conflict they were stoned, burned, and fed to wild beasts. If tradition is correct, only one of the original apostles lived out his natural life, and even he suffered banishment—hardly free of conflict. In fact, Jesus promised it. Have we stopped teaching/preaching the words of the Master in Luke 12:49-51?

> *I have come to bring fire on the earth, and how I wish it were already kindled. But I have a baptism to undergo, and how distressed I am until it is completed! Do you think I came to bring peace on earth? No, I tell you, but division.*

This is a forgotten Scripture in most of the pulpits in North America. The Church, including mine, is too concerned about being accepted, having a political influence, making an impression of concession and political correctness. I affirm the Christ is expecting a more "prophetic" role for the Church of Christ, a role that looks more like the warnings of Jesus about the world hating His true followers. I don't suggest that seeking peace is never *also* our task. Nor should believers seek to be hated by exhibiting belligerent behavior. The church militant I know overseas is closer to the New Testament record than our soft life of relative ease in North America. This year we ministered to dozens of preachers in a West African nation where in one city alone, six of our churches were burned, 25 Christian believers killed by explosives (scores more wounded), and three of our pastors killed by rifle fire—not counting members of their families who were raped and then decapitated. One pastor and his young son hid in the human excrement of a latrine for 16 hours while the terrorists sought them. Though rescued, they were completely infested with worms, but thankful for life. (Some readers may even be repulsed by such an account. Does this sound like Hebrews 11?) My intent is not to be sensational. But how should one report such an event? How should one react to a fellow Christian writer who says God has always been "reasonable"?

> *Lord, You must not be worried about what mankind says about You. You didn't react to the mockery of the crowd in any stage of Your life. From Your birth before wedlock, to the unconventional teaching style, to the accusations of breaking the law (especially the Sabbath law) to subjecting yourself as the Messiah to the unthinkable—crucifixion! We read these accounts, we hear Your warnings, but we run from the persecution You outlined in the Beatitudes* (Matt. 5:11-12).

At this writing the Muslim world, almost impossible to reach with the gospel for so long, takes umbrage at the idea that God would need to suffer to accomplish anything. It's not part of the Islamic world's concept of Allah's nature. Kenneth Bailey has an insightful answer here for us who have a Western Christian orientation.[25] How foolish the cross seems to the perishing (I Cor. 1:18).

Muslims all over the world find Jesus a prophet, but He is not esteemed to be divine. There is no way He could have suffered such and been anything but a normal man—not special as Christianity makes Him. Jews believe He was a traitor and that's why God smote Him by such a shameful death—"stricken by God." They are still waiting for the Messiah, but he must be properly born of a "correct family" and act in the political best interest of the nation of Israel. Ah yes, man will have a savior, but man will make him in the shape and image they want and can understand. Let's put him in OUR box. But this is not the plan of God. Never has been! Isaiah 53:10: "*Yet it was the LORD'S will to crush him and cause him to suffer...*"

We see it, Lord! We praise Your name, Your ways are surely past finding out and Your paths are hidden, yet so sweet and enlightening. We still ask why? But we accept it and say You must have so designed this illogical plan so the design itself would be an instrument of sifting and choosing after Your will.

> Hallelujah! How shall I tell it? Words on paper cannot express one hundredth part of the blessings God has brought to my soul since He gave, even me, the Baptism in the Holy Ghost. How I have longed for God to have complete possession of body, soul, and spirit, yet I feared to let Him take that possession. Oh the long, weary tempest-tossed years of waiting! But He has come, and my soul delights itself in fatness.

If we make God rational from our own worldview, can we then justify ignoring some of His ways?

> It is not popular, nor honorable, nor dignified, oh no! It makes one appear little and foolish and despicable in the eyes of the people, but oh how rich one feels towards God. This blessing is the true riches, the beaten gold, the pearl of great price, the white stone with the new name, the everlasting joy. The blessed Holy Spirit must take hold of the organs of speech Himself and sing and speak in new and strange tongues to give vent to the eternal weight of glory. After such an outburst of praise, how calmly the soul sits at the feet of this adorable Lord, and drinks of the river of His pleasures.[26]

The Hebrew world had built up some traditions about the Messiah when He came. Much of it was built on political need and desire for Israel to be an important power in the region. My Jewish friends, both Christians and followers of Judaism, are astounded at the unthinkable contemplation that the champion would have to lose, and so ignominiously (a stumbling block to the Jews and foolishness to the Gentiles—I Cor. 1:23). In the face of all this comes the words of Jesus and the radical and revolting image to ask Jews who have hundreds of laws about abstaining from blood—to "eat my flesh and drink my blood" (John 6:53-56). After this pronouncement by the Master, many of those following left Him over those words. There are many more items too numerous for our space here. Finally, back to the thesis of this book. What seems foolish is, in truth, *wisdom*. Some of the great and current theologians still are stumbling.[27] John Stott suggests God is a *rational* God and does not delight in *irrationality*. Tongues are not for today, he says. It was a unique one-time historical event—finished. The weight of the historical, ancient and modern theological accounts discredited by such a stance is astounding. **If we make God *rational* from our own worldview, can we then justify ignoring some of His ways?**

I'm reminded of South African Jappie LaPoorta's chapter, "Unity or Division"[28] on the issue of what's *rational,* quoting Walter Hollenweger on the role of narration to theology who suggests all our theology came at one time from narrative we've forgotten.[29] Behind all dogmas and celebrations of the West are myths (narrative in his usage) and they have been "sanitized" by rationality! Modern Western man seems to need the glue of rationality/reason to bind together their history, folktales, novels and even autobiographies. LaPoorta then quotes James Cone[30] who explains why African-Americans are so good at narrative because it has liberating power for both the teller and the recipient. The real "literalists" in the Greco-Roman mode of speech don't like "Black Preaching" either. It's not "sanitized like a lawyer making his brief." LaPoorta ends by stating five reasons why for South African Pentecostals he has opted for Narrative Theology.[31]

COMMUNICATIONS INSIGHT

FOR THE WEST, *rational speech* must be discursive, straightforward and direct. South African Narrative Theology is non-Western. It is based on archetype stories of human experience. It identifies people of experience. It is liberating because it leads to greater understanding. It does not separate Systematic Theology from Ethics.[32]

As mentioned above, the experts say up to 65% of the human communications event is non-verbal. On our Ross chart (chapter 4) find the rectangle of dotted lines around the words: Symbols—Signs—Voice Action—Language Arrangement. This represents the part of speech we practice but don't teach or encourage. Is there something here we are missing in our search for literalism? There are those who state the Spirit of God is better expressed in some form of body language rather than mind language.

Lord, why didn't You conform to the expectations and "comfort level" of all those potential followers, including us in this century? (Of course, the question is rhetorical.) *You have always surprised us and when we can grow up in our faith to have simply accepted the unusual we see Your unconventional ways are not only unique, but genius, wise and essential to the ultimate intention of wooing us by Your infinite love and grace. You are awesome! But You sure "mess us up" along the way! We've got this fixation on being "Number One," haven't we! Of caring too much what others think. Even in the Church, we don't want to have the stigma of any of the things You were accused of. Yet we want to bear Your name, but we surely don't want to pay anything near what You paid. Oh God, forgive our ignorance—even worse, forgive our pride and stubbornness. We are a lot like the Corinthians, aren't we:*

> *But God chose the foolish things of world to shame the wise; God chose the weak things of the world to shame the strong. He chose the lowly things of this world and the despised things—and the things that are not—to nullify the things that are, so that no one may boast before Him* (I Cor. 1:27-29).

The words hit with sledgehammer blows. "He chose the...despised things...so that no one may boast before Him." I've got to think about that one some more!

This verse provides the key to the thinking of the apostle Paul in 1 Corinthians chapters 1-3. God says man's wisdom would never suffice to bring humankind to salvation. So He chose a whole series of paradoxes to accomplish this. Included in this list would be:

1. A simple message that was best announced by fallible humans many would judge as weak and unfit as prophets.
2. The message itself would be judged as absurd by the "high and mighty" of both the secular and much of the religious world (the foolishness of what was preached 1:21). The wise of the world fabricate a message that doesn't save them *by* the cross of Christ—but saves them *from* the cross.
3. God deliberately chose a symbol so controversial that His own people would stumble over it—so believers would qualify as the called ones (both Jews and Gentiles) and, consequently, receive the power and wisdom of God (1:22-24).
4. The Messiah crucified! No way! The Messiah must, by very nature and definition, be a conquering presence that would finally vindicate the Jewish ethos and ethic—all in one fell swoop! Crucifixion made Him the "stricken/smitten one of God"—like a criminal (Isaiah 53:4). Even the miracles He did were unconvincing for many and they refused to believe (Matt. 12:38-39; John 6:30). No reputable person would be crucified, even for Gentile thinking.

5. If Jesus would have had a "handler" like some of today's politicians, he would have marched Jesus back to the Temple Mount after the resurrection and confronted the religious rulers with their unbelief and blasphemy: *"Look, I did just like I predicted. Here I am, you stiff-necked mockers!"* It would have been reasonable! It would have been powerful! But He didn't. In fact, we find no record that any unbeliever saw His resurrected body. What blessed divine (and for us) unreasonable restraint.

Yet this "foolishness" is wiser that any one might have orchestrated. **Jesus conquered death by dying!** Who but God could have conceived of such a plan? Accept this foolishness and live forever. Would the Father and Son have sent the Spirit with a reasonable, acceptable, logical plan to manifest Himself after all this immaculate plan of seeming folly? *Yet we want Him to be reasonable and not insist on tongues!* Don't do this, Lord! Give us something else![33]

CHOOSE YOUR TOOL

I often think of the apostle Paul's words to Timothy, warning him of people who were known as "having a form of godliness but denying its power" (II Tim. 3:5). It's like the actions of folk who have a fireplace in their homes. Fire is both dangerous and helpful. Fire is useful but must be governed by *risk management.* Among the items at a fireplace are two elements of note: a pair of tongs and a fire extinguisher. As mentioned above, quoting David du Plesis, one can choose the tongs or the fire extinguisher. It's "safer" to put out the fire completely! It's cleaner and neater. Of course, all that's left are *cold wet ashes* and a lot of cold and little heat (an analogy often told me by David du Plessis). The Old Testament also speaks of this principle of overreacting to the nature of things that often are judged as imperfection. "Where there are no oxen, the manger is clean, but from the strength of an ox comes an abundant harvest" (Proverbs 14:4). It's true. Every revival is a combination of divinity and dirt. The "priests" don't like cleaning the manger, or picking up hot coals. They either kill the ox or douse the fire. It's reasonable! But God isn't! Why does He seem to consistently require *risk management* or the exercise of faith to please Him? The reader must decide if that question is even relevant for personal consideration. Interesting words are instructive from James L. Slay:

Yet this foolishness is wiser than anyone might have orchestrated. Jesus conquered death by dying.

> Many books have been written concerning the ministry of the Spirit and Pentecost. Nearly all are in accord in asserting that we need apostolic and Pentecostal power. At the same time, however, very few seem to realize that Pentecostal and apostolic power calls for dedication and consecration and that it may produce manifestations that would prove distasteful to many. More than thirty-five years ago E. Stanley Jones, said, "Had the Christian church followed out the intimations and implications of what took place at Pentecost, we would have been saved from the narrow contentious centuries and from the grave-clothes that still bind religion today."[34]

This author spent 18 years as president of two "Charismatic" seminaries. Before coming to these administrative posts, I was impacted by the beginnings of a mighty spiritual Holy Ghost renewal/revival in West Africa (reported above), the fruits of which are still ongoing with unprecedented growth (from 11,000 to nearly one million believers in one country alone and in the space of 45 years). As CEO of these graduate level institutions of theological training in the USA, my perceived task was to combine both a high level of academic rigor needed by Christian scholarship (with full national and regional accreditation) *with* ministerial effectiveness demonstrated by spiritual power in the graduates' ministries. This is almost an impossible task. Note the words "almost impossible." Some would delete the word "almost."[35] Though I agree with the "almost impossible" task of integration needed between "heat and light," I submit it is in God's plan that these seeming opposing elements be kept in dynamic tension. I've come to believe He loves to watch us struggle with such issues.

Imagine the struggle with the Academic Affairs Committee as I repeatedly attempted to "modify" the 300-plus year old Master of Divinity degree! (Until about mid-1960, it was traditionally called a BD, Bachelor of Divinity.) I wanted to include course offerings in this traditional pastoral degree that better mirrored the real world of New Testament ministry that is so evident in reading of the Gospels, Acts and Epistles. It still seems reasonable to me that training *for* ministry means *doing* ministry. The Pentecostal seminary in which I was the CEO had early in its existence received Regional Accreditation and was already provisionally accredited with the "Cadillac" of theological schools/seminaries (ATS—Association of Theological Schools—whose full accreditation it achieved during my residence). Accrediting associations have traditionally been slow to approve Pentecostal schools, sometimes with reason of academic weakness, sometimes because of a lingering bias about non-traditional religious expression and their perception of a Pentecostal's overemphasis on the experiential side of faith. So, the "guardians" of the accreditation process resisted any "modification" for fear of jeopardizing the hard fought process. I didn't then, nor do I now, feel it's an either/or dilemma. But it may be easier to forgo the struggle of integration of praxis and theory, of heat and light for surrender to the "powers" that be.

Pentecostal and charismatic seminaries are modeled explicitly (via the unchallenged dicta of ATS) on a profile of Protestant theology, which denies the explicit pattern of ministry training and commissions in the NT. (See" The 'Imitation of Christ' in Christian Tradition; Its Missing Charismatic Emphasis" *JPT* 16:1, 60-77). This highly-evolved and truncated theology is further distorted by the teaching modalities of Berlin and Athens into a state of affairs unrecognizable in the normative New Testament patterns. But we have already eaten of the fruit. Is it too late to spit it out? Or has it been digested and become a very part of who we are with all of its consequences? Can the new wine of a biblical, Pentecostal/charismatic ministry formation be poured into the Berlin-Athens wineskins? In any case the Spirit of God will realize His goals, either with or without us. So to answer our question: Are Pentecostal/charismatic seminaries a good idea? Perhaps, but only with the most radical biblically based reform.[36]

THE ELEMENT OF PERSONAL LOSS (THAT WHICH IS UNREASONABLE)

The great paradox in Scripture: God's expectation about our attitude concerning loss. The list is long: lose to win; total change needed to be born again—born once won't suffice; the first will be last; humble yourself to be exalted; AND one must turn (after all the effort it takes to grow up) and become a little child again. Strange words, no? There is a great parallel here in all God's dealings with us, His creatures. Robert Greenleaf's seminal work on Servant Leadership exegetes Robert Frost's poem "Directive."[37] Frost says for Greenleaf that one can find direction in life to find inner peace and self-actualization only after one has been willing to LOSE. And on this journey, if you haven't lost enough, you won't find your way. This loss is not an accidental loss—as what is subject to fate or circumstances. **It is loss one is willing to make—even though it's painful and frightening!** AND you must follow the guide "who only has at heart your getting lost." Greenleaf suggests most of us don't want such a guide. Listen to the words of Jesus from this perspective:

> *"Whoever will save his life will lose it, and he who would lose his life for my sake will find it."*

> *"Unless one is born again, he cannot enter into the kingdom of God."*
>
> *"Unless you turn and become as little children, you will never enter the Kingdom of heaven."*
>
> *"It is easier for a camel to go through the eye of a needle than for a rich man to enter the kingdom of heaven."*
>
> *"He who would be my disciple must deny himself, take up his cross and follow me."*

Loss, loss, loss. We hate it. We want God's way without it. We seek those who will scratch our itching ears and promise us we can have it all without the cost of loss. We are just like many in the West who sequentially go from one medical doctor or counselor to another until they finally find one who will tell them what they want to hear, rather than prescribe a course of action that may cost them (loss—acceptance and acknowledgment of truth) what they don't want to pay!

There can be no salvation without repentance. That involves **loss** and freely admitting we must lose something. Any other road to God is bogus. Of course, God's best promises are waiting those who make that decision—yet any manipulative ruse to pretend real repentance (to get the prize cheaply) will be frustrated. This is the essence of Matt. 13:10-18. This is the central theme of Frost's poem about the hidden goblet for drinking the pure water that brings you "beyond confusion." **This is the thing hidden so the wrong ones won't find it!**[38]

People who will not mourn their sinful state cannot be forgiven. They refuse to admit weakness and *loss* so they can now have the capacity to be comforted (Matt. 5:4).

For me, one of the most insightful passages in the very popular book by Scott Peck *The People of the Lie*[39] was the case of a client who wanted control of him, the therapist.

> She wanted the reins in her hands every moment. The process of deep healing within the psychoanalytic framework, requires the patient to regress on some level to some degree. It is a difficult and frightening requirement. It is no easy thing for adults, accustomed to independence and the psychologic trappings of maturity, to allow themselves to become like young children again, dependent and so very vulnerable...It is like a death. Yet it can be accomplished. When it is, healing will result. When it does not, the foundation cannot be reconstructed. No regression, no healing; it is a simple as that.[40]

The Master Jesus said it too: "*Unless you change and become as little children, you cannot enter the kingdom of heaven*" (Matt. 18:4).

The psychiatrist Peck (above) working with the patient who *would not be healed* because she would not yield to the counselor/patient role of needing help, of allowing a dependant attitude:

> Throughout all the four years she worked with me...Charlene insisted on controlling the show...she would have had to give me the reins, to let me care for her... She wanted the reins in her hands every moment...But the issue of pure power was more important...she did not want to relinquish any power for any reason. She wanted healing, but she was not willing to lose anything, give up anything in the process. It was as if she demanded of me, "Heal me, but don't change me."[41]

...God has so designed it so the intellectually proud and powerful won't find it; are glad they don't have it; proud they are superior to it.

True Holy Spirit speech is as lofty and original as it is confusing and illogical. It is symbolic speech beyond the range of verbal communication. I'm convinced God has so designed it so the intellectual, proud, and powerful **won't find it; can't find it; are glad they don't have it; proud they are superior to it.**

Yet one can hear the gentle echo of the words of Jesus saying to the disciples, "Don't leave Jerusalem without it. You need it so you can be without confusion. You must turn the world upside down and you're not ready. You need this power to be my witnesses." Frost says it well:

> *I have kept hidden in the instep arch*
> *Of an old cedar at the waterside*
> *A broken drinking goblet like the Grail*
> *Under a spell so the wrong ones can't find it,*
> *So can't get saved, as Saint Mark says they mustn't.*[42]

You can't get "saved" (Presbyterians say "come to faith") without this submission and willingness to lose, and in like manner one cannot receive the Holy Spirit baptism without the same attitude about loss and being lost. God says (I believe) the act of this submissive loss creates a place (a capacity) for His creative gifts and revelations. Fuller knowledge of himself, an amplification and the discovery of new territory in God's Word, is what awaits the seeker. But the steps are painful and self-effacing! Greenleaf, if alive today, may not have agreed to the specific application herein of the fullness of the Spirit (however he was an old-time Quaker). But from the one meeting I had with him before his death (as a member for many years of the Greenleaf Foundation), I believe he'd approve of the power of the symbolism and why this thesis may have merit.

> The source of this attitude towards loss and being lost is *faith*...By these means mortals are raised above the possibility of hurt. They will suffer, but they will not be hurt because each loss grants them the opportunity to be greater than before. Loss by itself is not tragic. What is tragic is the failure to grasp the opportunity which loss presents...[43]

What one purposefully discards is as important as what one decides to accept and keep. God has purposefully set the rules thusly. Those who totally focus on the rational and reasonable will miss God's heart. Repeat—He has so set the rules: "So the wrong ones won't find it." *And He does this from the matrix of godly restraint.*

In God's dealings with mankind, He repeatedly confronts man with the unusual and the unpleasant. The Roman cross Jesus had to experience is such an interruption of inconvenience. We see this mirrored in the speech of the apostle Peter in Matt. 16. *"Peter took him aside and began to rebuke him. 'Never, Lord!' he said. 'This shall never happen to you!'"* (v. 22). It was an interruption of His ministry, of His miracles, of His teaching. Besides, Peter and the other disciples of Jesus were expecting Him to set up the Messianic Kingdom, and they'd been promised prominent positions in it. The cross was as contradictory as anything humans can imagine. It represented a *loss* Peter couldn't face at that juncture in his spiritual maturity. (Later he did face it and accepted it.) Funny how we don't seem to understand the words of Jesus (so oft repeated), *"He that would lose his life will find it."* Hear those incredible, majestic, prophetic words of Isaiah 53 that astound us in their depth of accuracy and poignancy.

> Vss. 1 & 2: *Who has believed our message and to whom has the arm of the LORD been revealed? ...He had no beauty or majesty to attract us to him, nothing in his appearance that we should desire him.*

So strange and unbelievable—so outside the box that Isaiah prophetically announced the preaching of the cross is foolishness to some (like the apostle Paul in I Cor. 1:18). The Messiah simply could not be so treated in the minds of those waiting for Him. As to the next verse (two) about His lack of beauty—how gauche to think the Christ would not be one of the "beautiful people" as is the fixation of the West with **image** (back lighting, makeup, wigs, false or augmented body parts, implanted perfect teeth, permanent pasted-on smile, steroid pumped up muscles or voluptuous curves and Botox when you get older). A complete psuedo package of fake. God is strange indeed—He evidently doesn't buy Hollywood's values. A Hollywood movie set is all front door: go through that and you're in the back yard!

Vs. 3: ...*He was despised, and we esteemed him not.*
Vs. 4: ... *We considered Him stricken by God, smitten by Him, and afflicted.*

For the Core of "Submission" as It Relates to the Topic

In the novel *Song of Abraham* by Ellen Gunderson Traylor,[44] the author details the nomadic life that Abraham undertook to obey God when He called him from Ur of the Chaldeans. The first chapters show the pain of leaving his family, his religious beliefs, his language and culture—in short, his worldview. The struggle to trust in this new God (of whom he didn't even know His name) and to learn to step out into the vagueness of nothing was constantly being asked by this "new" God. He left Ur and then Haran and then even his brother Nahor—with no destination: "By faith Abraham, when called...obeyed and went...he did not know where he was going" (Heb. 11:8). Imagining what Abram said, author Traylor says it so well: **"How strange, that we must be all brought to nothing before we hear You speak to us, my God."** And so it was with Noah—stepping out in faith, never having seen rain. So with Joseph, in a 13-year ordeal he had to lose all and wait in despair for years—in faith—to do God's will. And with Moses, who had to be brought to nothing (for 40 years) to be able to respond to the burning bush and become God's deliverer. He then obeyed God who proceeded to shatter the culture the Israelites had "artificially" built up after 400 years in Egypt. God had to utterly smash it, including their eating habits, work habits, entire world of expectations, and bring them to a "nothing desert experience" so He could get their attention at Sinai and the new law. When the nation finally got to Canaan, they didn't obey Him and He had to bring them again to nothing in two captivities, so they would again listen to Him. **Will it never end?**

To the New Testament, so it was also with the disciples—their whole world shattered by the cross and their champion not only killed but humiliated and crushed—brought to zero! They were left with no future, after having "left all and followed Him." What about Paul, the greatest of the apostles, one "born out of a due season," who had to be rejected by the first disciples and isolated for how many years until he was ready to take the message to the Gentiles, because most of the Jerusalem Christian crowd wouldn't, nor were they culturally flexible enough, to take it themselves. What a formula! Who wants it? Who NEEDS it? *"We must all be brought to nothing before we hear You speak to us, my God."*

In LIKE MANNER, this humanly undesirable walk of faith in order to be clothed of the Holy Spirit, this leap of faith—and belief the Spirit will use my lungs, diaphragm, larynx, tongue and mouth to praise Him in a void of linguistic trust, why would that please Him? Why would that "edify" the speaker? (I Cor. 14:40). WHAT IN GOD'S NAME DOES HE WANT? Why will He absolutely insist I exercise faith—to please Him? (Hebrews 11:6).

What in God's name does He want? Why will He absolutely insist I exercise faith—to please Him?

WOULDN'T IT HAVE BEEN BETTER TO HAVE COMPROMISED WITH THE JEWS? A LITTLE SOFTER, MORE GENTLE?

In Christ's ministry in Israel before those who held religious/social power, He was always "in their face." Even today, doesn't He intentionally insight the suspicions of the modern Pharisees by choosing the "upside-down" ways of the Kingdom? When Jesus walked the streets of Jerusalem, He sought the very people the Mishnah kept from the temple. That made Him dangerous! The sick, the infirmed, the imperfect, the injured or maimed—none of them were allowed into the temple in Jerusalem. Jesus championed these same outcasts. Jesus used healing to defy the local authorities! The man born lame who could now go to the temple, in fact, was told to report there. ("In your face," Jesus is saying). He associated with prostitutes, and He shared meals with them and others deemed the trash of society. Even the tax collectors (in your face). He publicly forgave the sins of the paralytic in Luke 2 (which was a blasphemous act), knowing it would insight criticism. In Luke 7, a party was set to trap Him on the issue that He was upstaging the temple! (That is like offering a passport without using the official offices of government.) Doesn't it seem many times Jesus purposefully made people mad?

Did He do this to unmask their pious legalism—their false pride in "knowing all about God" but totally missing Him in their hypocritical literalism. If you doubt this, go count the times!

Jesus told stories that insulted the priesthood (like The Good Samaritan).

Today we often explain this story (the most popular of all the parables) to apply to helping of the needy or, as an example of the servanthood of Christ. This is good. But in Jesus' day the story had connotations of damning consequences! Besides shooting at the pride of the officials of religion, it meant loving their enemies (and the archenemy, the Samaritan). He was on a collision course with the religious authorities and His own execution. Today, the way Jesus spoke would be outside what is considered "politically correct" and would be a prime target of the American Civil Liberties Union. No leader, no prophet in Jewish history had spoken in such terms (and there had been some gutsy prophets). He was defiant with healings and parables. Speaking like this in the countryside would be one thing. But under the nose of the Jewish authorities was another. What an affront to the local authorities when He came as a man of peace riding on a donkey through the Eastern gate. Zechariah and other prophets so hinted of the Messiah's role here. Then He chased out the moneychangers and animal sellers (who many think were giving kickbacks to the priests) all the while the imperfect, His preferred ones, were prohibited from the worship of His Father by the temple guards. Confrontation big time. He reminded the authorities their ideologues/fundamentalists had killed Isaiah, Jeremiah, and now John the Baptist. But he was preparing the most shocking miracle yet—His resurrection. Not a rational claim the disciples had to make—but a claim of faith. No Christian doctrine is so challenged today as this one. There is no room in the rational world for this belief. Folks look for a rational reason for it. (His body was eaten by animals; stolen by the disciples; He never died but took mandrake to feign death, etc.) *Faith cannot be reduced to its minimum—reason.*

THE POWER OF ETHNOCENTRISM

Can we learn something in this regard from Jonah? Jonah as an example of the inability to break out of his own ethnocentrism (that God could only bless the Jewish people) to minister in truth and expansive, effusive love and faith of the Father to the heathen of Nineveh. Jonah, like many of us, had the audacity to lecture God. Jonah got in God's face with what he didn't like about His inclusive love of all humanity. Many in the Protestant world of faith do the same by holding to cessationism (that the Bible's record of the supernatural is no longer valid today, that the miraculous is finished because miracles only happened in "boxes of past time" which are gone—allegedly they have "ceased"). But God has chosen a spiritual phenomenon foolish enough to knock down the idol of religiosity and the icon of egocentrism to which man is focused. No small wonder, this characteristic of Yahweh! Why do we tend to resist Him at every turn? Is this tendency related to His wisdom? Ah—yes, no doubt related to the Pauline passage where he puts this issue very subtlely: "*For Christ* (who knocked him [Paul] down to get his attention—not subtle) *did not send me to baptize, but to preach the Gospel* (ah yes, after all, words ARE important—man's greatest gift is speech)—*not with words of human wisdom* (what a shame, man's gift of speech with no chance to be exhibited) *lest the cross of Christ* (here is subtle) ***be emptied of its power.***" Paul continues: "*For the message of the cross* (No! Let's not go there—too costly) *is foolishness to those who are perishing.* (Doesn't he want to win the lost? Isn't that the ultimate intention?) *But to those who are being saved, it is the power of God*" (I Cor. 1:17-18). What?? Do that again! **What** is powerful? *The foolishness of the message of the cross.* (I give up. Why not make it wise and desirable—why foolish? I would have made it something shiny and irresistible, like a new model Sports Utility Vehicle—or a sizzling T-bone steak.)

Now here is Paul's peroration (climatic point) where he quotes from the prophet Isaiah. "*For it is written: I will destroy the wisdom of the wise; the intelligence of the intelligent I will frustrate*" (vs.19). The ultimate "foolishness of God" was to send a Messiah who would be crucified instead of being a triumphant political power. No one of that day would have believed that a reputable person would be crucified, much less be the blessed Savior. So, why would we expect this God and Savior to have chosen anything but the unusual, or even seen as foolish, to be the sign of the indwelling Holy Spirit? Tongues—what blessed liberating foolishness!! What confounding unthinkable human choice. What distasteful logic. BUT, OH GOD, YOU ARE CONSISTENT!! God must be after something. He must want me to choose what my psychological "ID" would never desire. In fact, He must want me to DENY a part of the way He made me.

Gordon Fee, in *Listening to the Spirit in the Text*, agrees loss and weakness is the state God seems to demand for the fullness of His Spirit to best operate in humans. "It is because of our 'between the times' existence that we desperately need the Spirit's help in our present frailty...This 'spirit amid weakness' phenomenon is consistent with Paul's over-arching theology. It is when we are totally dependent upon God, when we allow God to work through our weaknesses, our shortcomings, and our sufferings that we can be freely used in power."[45]

COMMUNICATIONS INSIGHT

"IF YOU ARE LOST ENOUGH TO FIND YOURSELF"

IN A PERSON'S SEARCH for the heart of God, there is meaning that language cannot contain. The person who is glossolalic (unlike the literalist) knows this—even if he/she can't verbalize it! Because "Meaning is Perception" the person who has found meaning in the symbolic exercise of tongues speech does not need to, probably cannot, articulate this overwhelming perception of God's presence in everyday language. When forced to try to explain it, somehow, it rather ruins or diminishes the wonder of it all. Believers in the literal word also know what terms like salvation, kingdom of God, eternal life mean—they are obliged to know. The reputation of the professionals in that field depends on it.

"But seekers who are responding to symbols don't know, don't have to know, wouldn't be helped by knowing. They are not too interested in *meaning as bounded by the vagaries of language.* Rather, they seek a guide who only has at heart their getting lost."[46]

For them perhaps the test is: If you *can* "find yourself," you're not lost enough!

What must be lost here, is the belief that meaning can only be achieved by external "literalness." What must be lost here is the security of total predictability. You must be lost enough to find yourself. What must be lost here, is one's total resistance to a "tolerance for ambiguity" (see below).

LIVING ON THE EDGE

On the edge of danger, on the edge of failure, on the edge of faith! Serve Him in integrity and you'll find yourself in a God-orchestrated place of danger to do His will.

Man says—foolishness!
Man says—danger, don't go there.
Man says—illogical, can't, shouldn't be done.

God Says: "Get Moving, and Don't Ask Where You're Going!" (Abraham)

There is a safe place to do God's work. It's logical and predictable and controllable by man's bureaucracy and planning. You can do good work here.

The "administration" will approve. The world will even tolerate it. This is where most of the "work" of God is done. God even blesses it or, maybe better said, He permits it.

There is another place to do God's work that He allows—for a short time, it seems. It's the unethical, fanatical, carnal egocentric trip certain naturally Charismatic folks follow to their eventual ruin and shame. Some didn't start out on this road but "fell" into its prideful trap while on the way to do God's will. Some have even started on this trip with the gifts of the Holy Spirit! We are all poorer for their folly and all suffer from their shame. Some of these folk had national attention because of their natural talents. This only exacerbated the magnitude of our shame and sadness.

Moses didn't expect the burning bush; Nor Joseph prison; Nor Abraham Sarah's bareness; David didn't foresee Saul's anger; Nor the disciples Jesus' suffering and crucifixion.

There is a better place than either of the other two above. It's a stretching place of ministry. It's a challenging place where resources are required that one did not learn or were not given by birth. This is the exciting walk of trust on which weaker, more conservative folk fear to venture. Like offered to artists, the crowds applaud but don't comprehend the cost or the prize garnered by this path. This path is closer to God's heart. If one allows Him, He will place us on the edge of danger that requires faith to endure the ride. So it was with Abraham, Joseph, Daniel, Gideon, Moses, Paul (shall I go on?), Joshua, Elijah, and many more.

Moses didn't expect the burning bush; Joseph didn't expect the prison experience; Abraham didn't expect Sarah's bareness; David didn't foresee King Saul's anger and jealousy; the disciples didn't foresee Jesus' suffering and crucifixion; Paul didn't expect rejection by the 12 disciples; it wasn't reasonable or predictable to think the Savior Jesus would defeat death by dying. The Father placed Jesus on this path which He accomplished perfectly and challenged the disciples to follow—even down to us. On this path it looks like it demands "foolish abandon" (but not presumption) which is the *faith walk* that pleases Him, The Way Maker. Is it any wonder He places the gifts of the Holy Spirit on the "faith shelf" so the wrong ones don't get them; so the logical ones disparage them; so the willfully carnal ones will put up with cheap forgeries. HOW WONDERFUL HIS WAYS AND HIS PATHS PAST FINDING OUT!!

Harvey Cox describes how unreasonable is this spiritual movement: "Pentecostal theology is found in the viscera of Pentecostal spirituality. It is emotional, communal, non-rational, hopeful, and radically embodied." He admits to being able to stop being the usual skeptic; and once he was liberated from this bias, new insights developed.

> I quickly found that my new attitude allowed me to follow the spectacular spread of Pentecostal-ism better than either credulity or skepticism could. As I pored over these archaic accounts, it became clear to me that for those early converts, the baptism of the Spirit did not just change their religious affiliation or their way of worship. It changed everything. They literally saw the whole world in a new light. Spirit baptism was not just an initiation rite, it was a mystical encounter.[47]

Those who insist "God is a reasonable God" have evaluated too shallowly. He's NOT reasonable as the general understanding of this word is used. He is only "reasonable" if one's definition of that term includes how contrary to human reasoning are the real important ways God interacts with us and leads us to risk His plan. **Jesus couldn't have saved His life if He was going to save mine!** *If you can say* ***that*** *is reasonable, then I'll accept your definition.*

God allowed real skeletons 'out of the closet' in the biblical record (unlike King Herod of Jesus' time, who abolished the listing of the names of his ancestors so no one could trace the debauchery in that family). Matthew's list of Jesus' ancestors showed that God relates in unvarnished reality to the ones "He so loved" and include a daughter-in-law who seduces her father-in-law to become pregnant, a prostitute named Rahab who lied freely, and Bathsheba (another woman), the wife of Uriah and the object of King David's lust. The very use of women's names in any genealogy of the period was unusual enough, but to show raw humanity related to the Master and Messiah is unthinkable!

Reasonable? No way! Look at the unconventional way the Lord Himself broke with tradition when leaving the task the Father gave Him to His followers. It included socially inferior folks and ignored the gender bias of the times. Jesus illustrated the unconventional "organizational chart" in John 13 where He dramatized the idea of a leader being a servant. Unthinkable! Yancey says in the garb of a slave, He bent over and washed the grime of Jerusalem from the disciples' feet:

> What incomprehensible behavior from a ruler who would momentarily announce, "I confer on you a kingdom." In those days foot

> washing was considered so degrading that a master could not require it of a Jewish slave. Peter blanched at the provocation...author Scott Peck describes it as one of the most significant events in Jesus' life: "until that moment the whole point of things had been for someone to get on top, and once he had gotten on top to stay on top or else attempt to get farther up. But here this man already on top—who was rabbi, teacher, master—suddenly got down on the bottom and began to wash the feet of his followers. In that one act, Jesus overturned the whole social order."[48]

Jesus warned His disciples against seeking positions over others (Mark 10:35-45). In the meetings of the Early Church, all were free to exercise their gifts (I Cor. 14:26ff)—even women who were not supposed to interrupt the services with questions with their new-found freedom, but were encouraged to prophecy in public. Thus, no ranking among members of the group was predicted.[49] Tenney makes clear this was done for the sake of building up the members of the body, "God has so composed the body, giving the greater honor to the inferior part," in order that members may have the same care for one another. What a departure from Hebrew culture. What a departure from most ecclesiastical organizational structures of our day! This 2000-year-old structure would stretch many relatively new church organizations in an era when management systems pride themselves on innovative plans. Again Yancey stretches us with this paradox:

> It never ceases to amaze me that Christian hope rests on a man whose message was rejected and whose love was spurned, who was condemned as a criminal and given a sentence of capital punishment.[50]

Now tell me that's reasonable! The very fact that Jesus did what He did and then as much as said: "Hey guys, here's what the plan is. You'll go to the ends of the world and die in the process. But you'll have to do it without seeing me." If Jesus really wanted to make a Kingdom last, be profitable, stand on its own, He'd have stayed and administrated it Himself, incorporating all of Covey's three books on the subject, no? (Don't misunderstand, these are good books! Most of us need them.)

COULD GOD SUFFER?

The Christian belief that Yahweh could suffer is totally unacceptable in the Muslim world. In their criticism and rejection of God even having a son, then the idea that Allah/Jehovah/Yahweh could conceive of a plan wherein God could suffer—is unimaginable and totally rejected.

Kenneth Bailey, author and authority on the Mid-East, has written of this dilemma in his book, *The Cross and the Prodigal*.[51] From Luke 15, the part the West has called the Prodigal Son, Bailey correctly shows the younger son was not the main character of this second-best known parable of Jesus. Bailey shows the main character of this parable to be the father. As a background to understanding this parable, Jesus was demonstrating to the listening "long bearded" scoffers of Luke 15:1-2 who, by their legalism and for their own power needs, had misrepresented the Father (God) and changed Him to a severe and legalistic judge. Jesus needed to show Him as a loving, forgiving, merciful Patriarch! Bailey wants to show the pain the Father was willing to bear to redeem His wayward son—as well as the older son who was not lost in a far country but lost at home. The cross is as unreasonable for many who operate in the natural world today as it was in the times of the New Testament. *"The man without the Spirit does not accept the things that come from the Spirit of God, for they are foolishness to him, because they are spiritually discerned"* (1 Cor. 2:14).

ECCLESIAL LOSS OF CONTROL—SURRENDER

Though some oversight of subordinates is surely necessary in the Body of Christ (Church), much of the ecclesiastical *control* of pastors and priests in the church is a carnal exercise and nearly always is done in the name of God! The same goes for teachers/professors in ecclesiastical circles. For years I have instructed students about many subjects related to communications and ministry, as well as how to live the Christian life. Any skills I may possess at expressing an opinion or to inspire others has given me, and give me still, a sense of control. I feel much safer "having control" of a situation than in taking the risk of letting the situation control me. *Loss of control* is naturally resisted but is related to the attitudinal position the Holy Spirit wants me to accept for the empowering I need for ministry. Specifically, this relates to the surrendering of most highly valued skills to Him in an utterance of the soul. Henry Nouwen characterizes this for me, as he is a professor *extraordinaire*. When he moved from the classroom after 20-plus years as professor to living with mentally handicapped people in Toronto, he related the profound change that took place in himself and talks about it in relation to contemplating Rembrandt's famous picture *The Return of the Prodigal Son*.[52]

> Moving from teaching university students to living with mentally handicapped people was, for me at least, a step toward the platform where the father embraces his kneeling son. It is a place of light, the place of truth, the place of love. It is the place where I much want to

> be, but am so fearful of being. It is the place where I will receive all I desire, all that I ever hoped for, all that I will ever need, but it is also the place where I have to let go of all I most want to hold on to. It is the place that confronts me with the fact that truly accepting love, forgiveness, and healing is often much harder than giving it. It is the place beyond earning, deserving, and rewarding. It is the place of surrender and complete trust.[53]

How quickly the Early Church got away from the practice of priesthood of the believer. Interesting! God keeps bringing the Church back to that model with every renewal in history.

Why didn't God choose something for me to give up that was easy, like giving up swimming in Minnesota in January? Why did He relate glossolalia to my willingness to lose something I most want to hang on to? Is it related to Nouwen's words: "accepting love, forgiveness, healing is often much harder than giving it"?

Is not rigid predictability of liturgy often really an exercise in control—in the name of "decency and order" a rational, seemingly God-honoring exercise! Is not "decency and order" good? Can it be overdone? Would not His "in-breaking" be resisted because one can't control it easily? (Like the pastor whose soul is yearning for spiritual growth:—"Oh God, let something happen in church today that's not in the bulletin.") The gifts of the Spirit are too dangerous, even for many "Pentecostals." And they shouldn't be. Look at the beginning of the Church by the event at Pentecost.

> Tongues of fire sat upon not only the twelve or the seventy chosen evangelists, but upon the ordinary believers as well, including the women. Instantly all became active witnesses for Christ. The fire did not fall on the twelve to be communicated by them to others. It did not leave the ordinary men to be mere spectators, while the work of the Lord was committed to the selected ministry. It swept away the priesthood and made a way whereby every man and woman might enter into the heavenlies. True, all were not apostles or evangelists, but all were priests and had equal access to the throne of God. From now on no man was to be a depository or storehouse wherein spiritual favors might be stored for the use of those who might purchase or otherwise secure them.[54]

How quickly the Early Church got away from the practice of priesthood of the believer! Interesting, isn't it? God keeps bringing the Church back to that model with every renewal movement in history only to have the leaders of those churches born out of the renewal, to **take back the power and access to themselves in an act of franchising the power and blessing of God's intention—and in the name of God!** J. D. Pentecost speaks of this perennial model in his chapter "The Deterioration of Israel's Religion," while lauding the opportunity God gave the Jewish nation to influence the whole world with a religion of such transcendent truth and ethical power that the world had, never up-to-then, seen:[55]

> The notion of religion was sublimer than the people had mind to appreciate or will to incorporate and adequately actualize. Worship is easier than obedience. Men are ever readier to serve the priest than to obey the prophet, and sacerdotalism flourished in Israel while prophecy decayed and died.

"There is always tension between those who stand for individual experience and those who stand for ecclesiastical authority...This same tension accounts for much of the modern rejection of tongues."[56]

GOD IS A HARD BARGAINER

In order to be a true disciple, one must submit him/herself completely to the will of Jesus Christ. Such a one must deny himself, that is, set aside his own will and his own rights to his own life; he must then submit himself completely to the will of Christ. The cross in the life of Jesus was the supreme test of His obedience to the Father's will. It was to Him like the forbidden tree in the Garden for Adam and Eve. To be the disciple of Jesus entails willing submission, whatever that brings. Why then, should one expect God to make an exception to the difficult series of steps to spiritual maturity and be empowered by the Spirit and skip a step of submission? That step includes one of the hardest things for God's "top of the communications chain" creatures to surrender.

In the wilderness, the devil tempted Jesus to find a shortcut to power. "Go against the Father's will" which was the same temptation in Gethsemane as the temptation of Adam and Eve in the original Garden of Eden. The reason the enemy is still using this same old pitch is that it still works. I want strongly to advance the idea that being endowed with the power to witness cannot come without loss and submission. There is no salvation from sin without "Forgive me!" There is not a true "baptism in the Holy Spirit" without a personal confrontation with His will against my will: a power play deep in the subconscious. It's not easy for us to release this instrument (meaning making/speech) which is the most important aspect of our personality!

COMMUNICATIONS INSIGHT

SLAVE MODEL OF COMMUNICATION

THE FOLLOWING SIMPLE model, called the "slave model," is used in classes of administrative structure. I use it here to show this sad *"taking back"* activity of the real miracle of Pentecost. At Pentecost God set up a new *accelerated* access to Him—here-to-for not available—A to C directly. The slave model says—"'A' can only have access to 'C' by passing through 'B.'" The Church of priests and pastors loves the slave model.

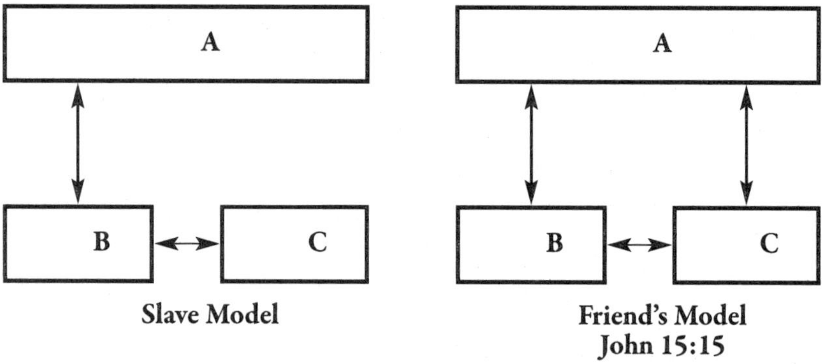

FIGURE 5

Men and women keep thwarting God's plan by some "organizational priesthood" that says—NO WAY! You can only get to God through me. The idea of the above model is not original with either the author or the secular world of administrative theory. It had early expression in the words of Jesus to His disciples in some of His closing words to His beloved twelve just before His betrayal and crucifixion.

> *I no longer call you servants, because a servant does not know his master's business. Instead, I have called you friends, for everything that I learned from my Father I have made known to you* (John 15:15).

There is a place for leadership in the Body of Christ, but there is no biblical precedent for playing "keep away" with access to truth and power for witness (Acts 1:8) by hierarchical ordinances and legalism that insists on the slave model of communication.

The more entrenched the religious authority, the more hostile towards haphazard inspiration.[57]

How sad many Pentecostals today love this model almost as much as those who originally gave the early Pentecostal founders the "right foot of fellowship" at the turn of last century. What temptation power is! The leaders of those denominations who basically rejected the gifts of the Spirit as being operative then or now would seek the same control of the faithful as the Pharisees in Jesus' day. In spite of man's reluctance to allow the Comforter His place, God keeps taking the risk of encouraging man's capacity to partnership with Him—even when men generally show their unwillingness to trust the Holy Spirit. For God so loved... that He gave...and gave...

> Let the Holy Spirit therefore be paid lip service, but for all practical purposes be shut up in the Bible where he can do no harm. Let His presence attend the confessional statement of our particular brand of Protestantism. Let the bizarre and miraculous elements which the NT documents narrate about his activity be relegated to those far-off apostolic days: It would be very embarrassing and doctrinally untidy if the Holy Spirit were to speak to men today, or to enable miracles to be performed and men to speak in tongues not their own. The Bible, accordingly is the safest place for the Spirit. That's where he belongs, not in the hurly burly of real life.[58]

AMBIGUITY...RELATED TO LOSS OF CONTROL

You can't make a creed out of tongues speech. It can't be repeated or written down. You can do this with intellectualized spoken, written language. The "oralness" of tongues speech is a form of "tolerance for ambiguity" the hyper-literalist fundamentalist cannot, will not accept (see Harvey Fox). Fundamentalists oppose it so solidly. If accepted, their whole house would fall down. Just like the Pharisees of Jesus' day and the reason they killed Him, theirs is the impetus to "inerrancy" which at its best is honoring Scripture, but at its worse is bibliolatry. The Church has always dogmatized God's dealings with man (too often for their own power and control needs). Oddly enough, this is the greatest danger for Pentecostals today. There is increasing pressure in our movements to "fundamentalize" our theology away from the oralness of Pentecost to the literalness of fundamentalism. This author's contention is the "foolishness of God" in this regard would recommend God's dealings with man on a deeper internal (non-analytical) level. As soon as it is "written" on tablets of stone, it is diminished and soon to be fossilized into man-manipulated dogma. We write it and "frame" it for protection from heresy (in itself not bad). But God is not nearly as afraid of heresy as man. (I don't say He doesn't oppose it—just that it is we who go ballistic.) The Apostle Paul's missiology, too, shows the ambiguity of letting the churches mature through their own weakness and self learning, by letting them make mistakes and fall and learn and mature and endure.[59] He chose this method of maturing the churches in the Gentile world instead of "Jerusalem Law." Paul in Galatians 3 harshly thunders against the fundamentalists of his day (the Judaizers): "Foolish Galatians! Who has bewitched you?" All who rely on observing the law are under a curse (because no one can do everything the law says). Clearly, no one is justified before God by the law because the "righteous shall live by faith." Faith is the road of ambiguity. Is this why God has "hidden" this experience in the cloak of foolishness?—I ask repeatedly.

Gordon Fee says: "Paul and the early church had not been tampered with by the mind-set of rationalism, and he found great value in prayer from the heart, from within, but which did not necessarily need approval from the mind to be uttered before God." They are little interested in meaning bounded by the rigidity of language "needing the approval from the mind to be uttered before God."[60]

The Battleground

Here lies the battleground between the rational mind and the mind of the Spirit for those seeking the "Baptizer" in the Holy Spirit. (Notice I didn't say seeking tongues. That's always a mistake.) Let's go back to Robert Frost's insightful but ambiguous poem *Directive,* which speaks of a guide who seeks to get you lost so you can find enlightenment and peace.[61] "You must be *lost* enough before you can find yourself." The house, the temporary, is gone; but the water is here. Cold, clear, lofty and original—new and fresh. Not in doctrines and creeds, not in the control of the local water company adding chlorine, fluoride, and other foreign elements!

THE ALABASTER JAR (OR BOX)

In Luke 7 there is the story of the town prostitute who Jesus had forgiven the day before at some sermon he preached or some public occasion. Simon the Pharisee invited Jesus to a banquet at his house so he and others could inquire for themselves if Jesus was indeed a prophet who assumed He could forgive sins. In the Oriental custom, uninvited persons were able to come and observe but not eat. A prostitute also came with other uninvited people and stood behind His feet while He was reclining at a table. She was forgiven much and thus loved much (Luke 7:47). To show this great appreciation, she wept on His dirty feet, wiped His feet with her hair (grounds for divorce in Jewish law to expose your long hair to any man not your husband), and then reached in her garment and took out an alabaster box or jar of this expensive perfume, often saved for one's own burial. This infuriated Simon who looked on and criticized Jesus in his heart.

An alabaster jar of perfume is permanently sealed. It didn't have a screw top so she could measure a few spoonfuls, dispense what she wanted, and then re-cap the precious liquid. She had to break the seal and part of the jar to do it. She couldn't have **controlled** the precious ointment that came out once the jar was broken.

- The following points are significant for this analogy:
- The woman brought an alabaster box.
- She didn't open it and dispense what she **wanted** to control. She didn't measure it out a few ounces at a time with an eyedropper.
- When you break it—you **can't control how it comes out!**
- You haven't really worshiped until you've broken the box!
- At Pentecost in Acts 2—Why the demonstrations? Why tongues? (You speak but you've lost cognition).
- The real power isn't what can be **seen—it's the perfume aroma (of worship!).** Don't just look at a test with your eyes—but with your nose too! Deeper than visible.
- The **invisible,** not seen or felt or weighed or measured **or analyzed or scrutinized.**
- You can change the atmosphere with praise and worship in the Spirit.

COMMUNICATIONS INSIGHT

TONGUES ARE LIKE THAT. You haven't really worshiped until you've broken the jar! And when you do the normal control of the intellect, the selecting and sorting process of intentional speech (of communication theory) is "unfruitful" as explained in 1 Cor 14:14. It's a direct loss of control of the speech mechanism in the normal cognitive sense. And I'm sure that's what God intends. I'm very sure of it. You speak, but you've lost cognition. Dangerous? Absolutely! Ambiguous? Assuredly! The real power isn't what can be seen or heard; it's the perfume aroma (of worship) either in personal prayer language or to be interpreted to give edification to the believers in a public meeting. This is the invisible, not seen or weighed or measured. Can't put it in the liturgy or list it in the bulletin (both which are valid in their own context—but not fitting for the Holy Spirit's insistence to be in control).

There is a watershed between the Eastern Church and the Western Church on this issue of how each one differed, historically, relative to the extent that individual expression of the experiential in belief and worship was allowed.[62]

Kelsey looks at the administrative difference relative to the authority and administrative power of these two early divisions of the Christian Church.

> The West of necessity developed a practical, authoritative, extroverted, Latin Christianity. In such a tradition individual experience of the gifts of the Spirit was soft-pedaled...The Greek church remained far more other-worldly and mystical...In this tradition the individual gifts of the Spirit flourished...Early in the development of the traditions of Western Christianity, tongue speaking came to be looked upon with grave suspicion.[63]

It seems to fit, so exactly, that Thomas Aquinas—the architect of much of Roman Catholic theology—was also the epitome of Aristotelian two-valued grid thinking would classify the gifts of the Spirit in one of two categories in Summa Theologica (1274). Either they were once given by God for a time period—and then ended—OR if someone claimed that God had given him the gift now, it was clearly an impossibility. It had only one source—the realm of demons. Kelsey says:

> It did not seem to have occurred to Aquinas that the events in Acts had any relation to the experiences of the Corinthians, and just as well for Aquinas, for even he would have trouble reconciling the church's point of view with this connection...and so, his thinking must proceed from the purely rational side, rather than experience...there was simply no place for such notation in the world view of Aristotle to which Aquinas was committed.[64]

COMUNICATIONS INSIGHT

COMMUNICATIONS / THE REGULATION OF "PROPHETIC" SPEECH IN PUBLIC

THE INSPIRED WRITINGS of the apostle Paul about the proper use of the gifts of the Spirit clearly demonstrate how maturity is needed for the correct and safe employ of the gifts for the edification of the whole Church. Simply stated, one has to "grow up" and think as an adult, not as a child. There has always been those immature folk who have used the gifts of the Spirit improperly—for their own carnal power or ego needs. And often the leadership has failed to regulate them from a biblical perspective. First Corinthians 14:20 shows the way. *"Brothers, stop thinking like children. In regard to evil be infants, but in your thinking be adults."* The Corinthian believers were abusing the vocal gifts, especially tongues (communication gifts that get the attention of the whole Church) especially in the case of public tongues that require the gift of interpretation to accompany glossolalia, but also prophecy or the words of wisdom or knowledge or the gift of discernment of spirits. All but tongues sound similar to the extent they are spoken in the local vernacular for edification through cognition by a locally understood language. The term *prophecy* has its own distinction, but is often used as a blanket word for all the gifts that *sound* like prophecy. And here Paul gives clear communication directives to the Church: *"Two or three prophets should speak, and the others should weigh carefully what is said"* (I Cor. 14:12).

All public gifts that are (or sound like prophecy—the umbrella word) are to be examined/evaluated/judged. It takes a mature individual to stand corrected –especially when first learning how to use the gift. It also takes much tender love and courage to publicly correct such a gift when used improperly. If the leader does not have the capacity or faith to use the gifts, how will he/she be able to regulate them? It is my suspicion that this single lack by leadership was a major cause in the Early Church of the discouraging of the gifts, and in the Church today the cause of much of the dearth of spiritual gifts in certain regions of the church. *It requires a mature individual to either regulate the gifts or be regulated by the body in their use. This is the God-intended "safety net."*

ENDNOTES:

1. Eddie L. Hyatt, *2000 Years of Charismatic Christianity* (2002).
2. James L. Ash, Jr., "The Decline of Ecstatic Prophecy in the Early Church," *Theological Studies* 37 (1976), 227, in Hyatt (2002), 24.
3. Donald B. Kraybill, *The Upside-Down Kingdom* (1990), 24.

4. See Charles Kraft, "Communicating Within Culture," *Christianity in Culture* (1981), 147-165.
5. M. Scott Peck, *The People of the Lie* (1983), 206-207.
6. See Dwight Pentecost, *The Words and Works of Jesus Christ* (1981), 43-44 (much like the speech of Marsailles, France, as seen by those in Paris).
7. Philip Yancey, *The Jesus I Never Knew* (1995), 30-32.
8. Ibid., 32.
9. See Raphael Patai, *The Arab Mind* (1973), 101-106.
10. Robert Cornuke and David Halbrook, *In Search of the Lost Ark of the Covenant* (2002).
11. Yancey, 21, 32.
12. I'm reminded of a recent message by an Ethiopian student preacher in Addis Ababa Bible College whose words included this phrase: "God doesn't call the qualified—He qualifies the called." (Maybe a bit of an overstatement—but often true in history and in Scripture.) His remarks reminded me of the saying attributed to Don Basham relating to the role of God and the role of man concerning the gift of the Holy Spirit and glossolalia: "Without the Holy Spirit you can't; but without you, the Holy Spirit won't!" Don Basham, *A Handbook on Holy Spirit Baptism* (1969), 82.
13. Paul Bretschner, *The World Upside-Down or Right-Side Up* (1964).
14. Yancey (1995), 23.
15. Morton Kelsey (1968), 227.
16. Ibid., 227.
17. Malcom Muggeridge, *Jesus: The Man Who Lives* (1975), 55ff.
18. Yancey (1995), 74.
19. Fyodor Dostoevsky, *The Brothers Karamazov* (n.d.), 229-39, in Yancey (1995), 74-75.
20. Dale Fagerland, "The Cross and the Crescent: Understanding the Islamic World," in *The Eleventh Hour Institute* (2001), 234-5.
21. Yancey (1995), 76.
22. David Lim, *Spiritual Gifts, A Fresh Look* (1999), 43-46.
23. Donald Gee, *Spiritual Gifts in the Work of the Ministry Today* (1963), 10.
24. Lim (1999), 247.
25. Kenneth Bailey, *The Cross and the Prodigal* (1973).
26. M. Chapman, "A Personal Testimony," *Bombay Guardian Press,* September, 1907, 36.
27. John R.W. Stott, *Baptism and Fullness: The Work of the Holy Spirit Today* (1975), 113.
28. Jappie LaPoorta, "Unity or Division" in *The Globalization of Pentecostalism, A Religion Made to Travel,* Dempster et. al. (1999), 151-169.
29. Walter Hollenweger, *Umgang mit Mythen: Interkulturelle Theologie* (1982), 78-79.
30. James H. Cone, *God of the Oppressed* (1975), 17-18.
31. LaPoorta, 157-158.
32. Ibid., 158.
33. Grant Osborne, gen. ed., 1 & 2 Corinthians, *Life Application Bible Commentary* (1999), 32-33.
34. E. Stanley Jones, *The Christ of Every Road* (1930), 97, in James L. Slay, *The Glossolalia Phenomenon* (1966), 240.
35. See David Kelsey: *To Understand God Truly: What's Theological about Theological Education?* (1992) and *Between Athens and Berlin: The Theological Education Debate* (1993).

36. Jon Mark Ruthven, "Are Pentecostal Seminaries a Good Idea?" *Pneuma:* Fall 2004, 344-345.
37. Robert Greenleaf, *Servant Leadership: A Journey into the Nature of Legitimate Power and Greatness* (1977), 313ff.
38. Ibid., 323. Again, Luke 4 and Matt. 13.
39. M. Scott Peck, *The People of the Lie, Hope for Healing Human Evil* (1983).
40. Ibid., 158.
41. Ibid., 159-160.
42. Frost in Greenleaf, 323.
43. Ibid., 327. *"Whoever will lose his life for me, will find it"* (Matt 16:25).
44. Ellen G. Gunderson, *Song of Abraham* (2003).
45. Ibid., 119. Quoted in Rybarczyk, "Expressing the Inexpressible: Tongues as Apophatic Speech" (2002), 13.
46. Robert Greenleaf explaining Robert Frost's poem "Directive," *Servant Leadership: A Journey into the Nature of Legitimate Power and Greatness* (1977), 319 (Emphasis mine).
47. Harvey Cox, *Fire From Heaven, The Rise of Pentecostal Spirituality and the Reshaping of Religion in the Twenty-First Century* (1995), 17 and 319.
48. Yancey (1995), 191.
49. Merrill C. Tenney, *Survey of The New Testament* (1985), 124.
50. Yancey (1995), 246.
51. Bailey, *The Cross and the Prodigal, A Commentary and Play on the Parable of the Prodigal Son* (1973).
52. Henry Nouwen, *The Return of the Prodigal Son: A Story of Homecoming* (1992).
53. Ibid., 12-13.
54. Daniel N. Buntain, *The Holy Spirit and Fire* (1956), 33, quoted in McGee (1991), 123-4.
55. J.D. Pentecost, *The Words and Works of Jesus Christ* (1981), 538.
56. Kelsey (1968), 159.
57. I.M. Lewis, *Ecstatic Religion* (1971), 34.
58. Michael Green, *I Believe In The Holy Spirit* (1975), 12.
59. See Rolland Allen, *Missionary Methods, St. Paul's or Ours?* (1962, 1993).
60. Gordon Fee, *Listening to the Spirit in the Text.* See especially his chapter, "Toward a Pauline Theology of Glossolalia" (2000) 105-120.
61. Ibid.
62. Robert Greenleaf (1977), 321.
63. See S.M. Burgess, *The Holy Spirit: Eastern Christian Traditions* (1989) and *The Spirit and the Church: Antiquity* (1984). See also: Peter A. Botsis, *What is Orthodoxy?*(1987).
64. Kelsey (1968), 42, 46.
65. Ibid., 49.

CHAPTER 8

THESIS—NO SHORTCUTS

We've looked at the risk God has always taken to bring us redemption. We've also considered the loss factor in our obedience to His plan; a loss factor little desired but seemingly required to please Him. It's obviously related to the essence of faith. Now, we have the background for the heart of the matter in the thesis I want to advance.

The temptation of Jesus in the wilderness by Satan, directly after John the Baptist baptized Him in water in the Jordan River, is thought to be a pivotal event in the life of the Messiah. Many Bible scholars believe Satan tempted Jesus to shortcut the longer process and change the rules, thus avoiding the cross. To wear a crown instead of a cross would have tempted any lesser man. Later, the apostle Peter tempted Him with the same thought (Matt. 16:21-23). The enemy tempted Eve and Adam with the same idea of shortcut (Gen. 3:4).

In refusing Satan's three-pronged temptation, Jesus forfeited the three greatest powers at His disposal: miracle, mystery and authority. So the Church has taken them over and formalized them in liturgy.[1] And the Church of the Inquisition took over what Jesus refused—*the power to force belief.* They did this with their distorted interpretation of Luke 14:23, where the giver of a banquet instructed his servants to invite any who could come and "Make them come in." When God created man in His image, He gave us the power to reject Him because He wanted to woo us by love and entice us to follow Him with the wondrous free will we received. Rarely down the halls of time has the Church understood this well. That's why, in the "foolishness of God," He places a "cross" in our path for salvation and "tongues" in our path for the endowment of power to witness as a provision. Both are illogical/unreasonable/scandalous and unintelligent. We

To wear a crown instead of a cross would have tempted any lesser man.

want a God without ambiguity, one we can show our friends as the "Superman" of our and their expectations.

> "Doesn't Jesus know that what the people want more than anything else is to worship what is established beyond dispute?"—Philip Yancey[2]

All the while, God's way is one of abdication and seeming weakness. His restraint allows His enemies to oppose Him. His great plan will allow no other. Abdication of our prideful "meaning making" gift is the key to allow the Spirit to speak through us. It's not the only way He speaks. He uses "mother tongues" (over 6000 in the world's cultures), but He longs to see the surrender of our prideful "mother tongue" as symbol of our trust in response to His enticement.

The whole creation waited for an articulate expression of its praise to the Creator. To man, this distinctive privilege was given. Made in the image of God, man alone received the power to coordinate thought and tongue into intelligent speech. In a sense, as he audibly worshiped and communed with God, he became the high priest for every living thing.

And what tremendous power there is in speech! Its power as an evil influence, resulting from man's fall, is shown very emphatically by James: "Behold, how great a matter a little fire kindleth!" On the other hand, the tongue possesses great power for good. Especially is this true in the experience of the children of God. With the mouth confession is made unto salvation; angelic praise is not comparable with that which ascends from the lips of redeemed men: the salvation of a lost world is dependent upon the tongue, for God has decreed that by man shall the unsearchable riches of Christ be "proclaimed." (See also Matthew 12:37.)

Surely, speech is representative of all the privileges and powers which are man's prerogative. How fitting it is, then, that the Holy Spirit should single out this most important faculty as the initial, physical evidence of the infilling with the Spirit. It is a marvelous tribute to man that God is mindful of him and desires to converse with him.

Brembeck continues:

> But how much more marvelous is it that at the filling with the Spirit He actually takes control of man's unworthy tongue and speaks through him. This significant act most certainly shows His esteem of this highest accomplishment of His highest creature.[3]

Some reject the miracle of glossolalia because they say all the supernatural signs are no longer needed once the Canon of Scriptures was complete.[4] Others say unless the language of the Spirit is an actual language spoken and understood by someone who happens to be near, then anything else is spurious. Others resist the idea of needing this "submissive test" of giving up the mother tongue. "Do we need it?" they ask. It so seems. We accept it, but we regret the fact that it has been so divisive in the Body of Christ. Paul Hiebert, an Evangelical Anthropologist (that title is seen as an oxymoron by the secular discipline of Cultural Anthropology) speaks of the tender nature of stating theology. I like it because it is so irenic:

> We need a humble and open spirit that is sensitive to the leading of God in our study of Scripture. As one writer put it, we must do theology on our knees. We need also to recognize that the same Holy Spirit at work in us is also at work in the lives of other believers. If we do so, we will not take a stance of militant confrontation against those who disagree with us. Rather we will seek to examine with them our differences in the light of Scripture...As priests in the kingdom of God, we have the right to interpret God's Word. As members of the body of Christ, we are responsible for listening to one another...the interpretation of the gospel is ultimately not the task of individuals or of leaders, but of the church as a "discerning community"...We must, however, speak the truth in love, seeking not to conquer those who disagree, but to win them.[5]

I intend to keep Hiebert's words close because I need to stay "on my knees" with what follows in this section about the reasons you may have chosen the foolishness of glossolalia. I have to fight, very often, the seeming need to "defend myself" against my Fundamentalist (and some Evangelical) brethren in the Body of Christ, who have consistently marginalized me and others of us who hold to the doctrines/beliefs that the gifts of the Spirit evident in the New Testament Scriptures and during the first 250 years of the Apostolic Church are valid for today's task of world evangelization—as instructed by our Lord at His ascension. Here's my prayer:

> *Dear Lord, might my feelings of needing to ardently "defend the faith of my experience" mean I care too much about what others think? Have I forgotten the warnings You gave Your disciples in John 15 and 16 concerning others' attitudes about anyone who would follow you? Like the disciples, we still want the part where You restore the Kingdom and we can escape persecution and struggle and reign with You! That would give us positions of power and we could tell everyone—"see we were right all along." We'd rather say: Lord, let Your kingdom come without too much effort, and certainly we don't want persecution and hard-*

ship—it's too costly or to risky or too dangerous! Help me, Oh Lord! I need not to "conquer" those who disagree or are on a genuine search for you. I need rather to "win" those who are seeking, and just love and esteem those in the family who are firmly committed to resistance and doubt. Amen.

CHRIST'S MODEL OF SELF-EMPTYING

Killian McDonnell, a Benedictine monk, in his pamphlet *Fanning the Flame*[6] so poignantly focuses on the thesis of why God may have chosen this "foolish" sign of the Spirit's baptism when Jesus gives this gift of power.

> " ...since giving also involves receiving, a conscious act of the will, accepting the gift, is required on the part of the recipient, if he is to experience properly the benefits that result from the gift. This acceptance involves the self-emptying that Christ himself underwent (Phil. 2:7). Only once the ego has been stripped away can the gift of the Spirit be fully experienced."

You've got it, Father McDonnell! The ego of mankind is a potent force. God gave us the capacity to be egocentric, and then delights when we give that prideful temptation back to Him! He gave us the ability to reject His love, and then makes us His children when we choose **not** to reject but accept His gift of eternal life by the sacrifice of the Son on the cross. What seeming folly! Why give us the power, Lord, to be "rejecters" when You could have hard-wired us to accept only You? What ego involvement we have in our rational mind and its highest expression in the genius capacity of "meaning making" of human speech; of critical analysis; of rationalistic pride; of pedantic exuberant word choice. What persuasive rhetoric; what self-flattering verbal concoctions! But you've said it, Bro Kilian. *"When Christ Himself did not consider equality with God something to be grasped (His right, His status as the begotten) but made Himself nothing (choice), taking the very nature of a servant, being made in human likeness"* (Phil. 2)—**"Only once the ego has been stripped away can the gift of the Spirit be fully experienced."** There it is! He hides the secret behind something so seemingly foolish, only the "right ones" find it!

"Only once the ego has been stripped away can the gift of the Spirit be fully experienced"
–K. McDonnell

John R. Stott adds to this concept:

> We hold on desperately to our own cultural inheritance in the mistaken notion that it is an indispensable part of our identity. We are unwilling to let it go. Not only do we maintain our own cultural practices with fierce tenacity, but we treat the cultural inheritance of the land of our adoption without the respect it deserves. We thus practice a double kind of cultural imperialism, imposing our own culture on others and despising theirs. But this was not the way of Christ, who emptied himself of his glory and humbled himself to serve.[7]

In the same analogy, we hold on to our native language like we do culture. We refuse to be seen as childish and agree to let the Holy Spirit speak through us, when He has specifically designed the issue with both humbling ourselves and emptying of ourselves to receive His empowerment for service to deliver folks from the power of the enemy. Repeat; God has, in my opinion, deliberately so designed the equation with humbling and emptying attributes as a required prerequisite!

Early seekers of this gift of glossolalia so desired the presence of God as newly defined at the turn of the last century that it was often compared to the parable of the Pearl of Great Price in the gospels and the surrender of all else for its procurement (Matthew 13:45-46).

Everett Wilson speaks of just such an analogy[8] and of the physical/psychological (subjective) experience of self-denial in the initial "tongues" event.

> Pentecostal experience began accordingly, at the moment when the seeker, like the procurer of the New Testament 'pearl of great price' determined that what he or she wanted above all else was available only at the devastatingly high cost of relinquishing all consideration to one's own claims and merits... Many researchers of the growing Pentecostal/Charismatic movements have noted the sociological elements by mapping its spread, documenting its composition and demonstrating the range and activities of its participants. Good and useful data. But it provides little insight into the subjective and personal experience that for most adherents appears to be the movement's essence.[9]

Playing on this theme is Bonino's response to Macchia's "sacramental" understanding of tongues as a dynamic sign used by God representing a work of the Spirit has occurred.[10] It is a recognition of the 'presence' of God that cannot be expressed in human words, nor does it remain hidden away in subjective consciousness of the convert but finds a audible 'material' expression. "Because it can be heard...it communicates to others."

Pentecostal experience begins, for many, only at a high psychical cost. At least on occasion these men and women may have felt an inexpressible joy, but whether or not exuberance was necessary, in order to have a climactic spiritual experience, some kind of abandonment was...From that point many Pentecostals found deepening spiritual resources that provided them with previously absent initiative, daring vision and persistence...The intensity and motivation of such an experience was not easy to maintain. It demanded an extreme focus, an ongoing willingness to forfeit the claims to one's being that were relinquished at the outset, to open the wounds of self-denial, repeatedly, again and again.[11]

COMMUNICATIONS INSIGHT

NOT JUST AN ADD-ON

JESUS OFTEN SPOKE of the power of words and that which proceeds from the mouth as highly significant in communication. (In Matthew 12:37 he says a person's words will either convict or acquit the individual.) In Matthew 7:21 Jesus says: *"Not everyone who says to me, 'Lord, Lord' will enter the kingdom of heaven, but only he who does the will of my Father who is in heaven."* Some folks want to say the right words to be called a Christian, and just add that title to their résumé without changing their lifestyle (fraudulent and useless). But in this instance, words alone won't do it unless the human will is added and points towards *obedience*. "He who *does* the will of my Father"—this is the essential key. There is no obedience without surrender of one's own will. Here is again the tie between becoming a true Christian and becoming a powerful witness as Christ's *communicating* disciple. There is surrender in the act of salvation, there is surrender in the act of the baptism by Jesus into the Spirit's domain. To *say* "I'm a Spirit-filled believer" and just add that to one's résumé is powerless unless that individual has been obedient to the psychic humiliation of surrendering the speech/mind process to the mind of the Spirit which will be witnessed by glossolalia. Glossolalia is humiliating and "foolish." But it's the 'pearl of great price,' which is total submersion into God's will and purpose. Will we ever understand completely the 'bottom line' of the role that submission plays where God has "fixed" the rules so the unrepentant will not be saved; nor the unyielding receive the fullness of the Spirit?

The Supremacy of the Human Intellect

"The gift of tongues humbles the pride of intellect, revealing that a person is more than a community of reason." Thus David Dorries describes a point that the Scottish Presbyterian Edward Irving made in 1830 concerning the "Standing Sign" of speaking in tongues when baptized in the Holy Spirit. Quoting from the writings of Edward Irving,[12] Dorries voices Irving's deep understanding of the Spirit.

> What a deep subject of meditation where a man thus employed in secret converse with and enjoyment of God, although his reason be utterly dead. Far from being anti-theological, however, Irving simply is asserting the priority of the deeper communion of the human spirit with God's Spirit in relation to the rational dimension. While the pride of mankind boasts of the supremacy of the intellect, the childlike and unintelligible utterances of tongues makes "void and empty the eloquence and arguments, and other natural ornaments of human speech." In order "to show that God edifies the soul, in a manner wholly independent thereof, by direct communications of the Holy Ghost, which is the milk of our babyhood, the power in the word to nourish any soul..." This inner dialogue between Spirit and spirit, transpiring on a level beyond rational comprehension, provides the Spirit-baptized believer with an increasingly maturing grasp of spiritual reality that eventually gives expression to rationally comprehended revelations for the edification of others.[13]

"The gift of tongues humbles the pride of intellect, revealing that a person is more than a community of reason"
–Edward Irving, 1830

Gordon Fee picks up on this partnership of God's Spirit and man's spirit by suggesting the apostle Paul's use of *pneuma* refers to both God's and man's spirit (14 instances in his writings), leading Fee to express this partnership as S/spirit. So there is a dynamic interaction between the Spirit of God and man's spirit, not unlike the above information of Edward Irving's understanding many decades before the Azusa revival.[14]

Fee also aptly explains one of his many attempts to describe tongues thusly: "God, for His own loving and mysterious reasons, re-creates us to be vehicles for unintelligible and non-rational modes of communication.....This non-rational dimension of Christian spirituality is also given in light of our own plight as sojourners in a fallen and sin-infected world. As members of God's kingdom and the kingdom of this world, we live between the ages."[15]

> It has been repeatedly said by interpreters of this passage (I Cor. 14) that here Paul is trying "to damn tongues with faint praise." But any careful analysis of the structure of these verses will show that this is simply not true. Eventually he will *prohibit* tongues—when it occurs in *the community and without interpretation.* What Paul does here is not to "damn tongues"; rather he gives the valid reasons for tongues. First, the person speaking in tongues "speaks to God." Paul can hardly be against that. Second, such a person also "edifies himself." That may sound self-serving, and in community it is. But Paul does not speak negatively here. There is a place in the Christian life for one's own person to be built up. This is made perfectly clear in verses 14-15. God can bypass the mind of the individual and thereby build him up by his own speaking "mysteries to God *in the Spirit.*" Uninterpreted tongues, therefore is inspired speech in the vertical dimension. As such it belongs to the life of private prayer, not in gathered community. But the minds of others cannot be bypassed, if they are to be built up in community worship. Therefore Paul says, "especially (desire) the gift of prophecy"(v. 1). [16]

COMMUNICATIONS INSIGHT

ALLOW ME TO RESTATE it in the context of the above excellent scholars: Tongues is the only "demonstrable gift" that requires the speaker to surrender normal cognitive processes of cerebral speech. (Speech is the 'highest' of all human characteristics that separates mankind from other creatures—about which man has often been the most proud and least likely to abrogate.) It seems to please the Lord when we submit or surrender this most prideful human skill. It's not easy for us to release our tongues (human speech) which is the most important instrument of our personality. I'm coming to believe it is highly symbolic to Him and highly difficult for us, especially those whose "literary or oral communication skills" bring them power and attention. James, the half-brother of Jesus, speaks of the power and importance of the tongue among all the members of the human body. He graphically illustrates the relationship of the tongue (human speech related to attitudes and intentions) by the analogy of a bit in the mouth of a horse and a rudder that can guide a ship.

> *Likewise the tongue is a small part of the body, but it makes great boasts. Consider what a great forest is set on fire by a small spark. The tongue also is a fire, a world of evil among the parts of the body. It corrupts the whole person, sets the whole course of his life on fire, and is itself set on fire by hell...but no man can tame the tongue. It is a restless evil, full of deadly poison* (James 3:5, 6-7).

Dennis Bennett, one of the first Episcopalian pastors to write and teach about this glossolalic experience further explains:

> It became clear to me that the willingness to release the tongue to praise God in whatever words or language He chose to use was a vitally important key to receiving of the fullness of the Holy Spirit, for the Bible says that our tongue—our faculty of speech—is at the same time the best member of our body, and also the most wicked, a "fire, a "world of iniquity." When you consider the harm that we can do with words, and the way in which we deceive and temporize with words, it is not unusual that we should be asked to let our faculty of speech be used by God to His glory—in the way that He chooses—before we can have His fullness.[17]

As advanced above, tongues speaking (especially initially) represents loss, the ingredient God often (perhaps always) demands from the one who would follow Him in faith. There is a part of "tongues" that relates to the prophetic role of the ultimate design of God through the ages. It related to the people of God, the Jews, who were expected to be a prophetic people with a salvific influence on the nations of the world. Starting with Gen. 3:16, the promise of God through Abraham has always been an expectation that His chosen people would be "missionary," reaching the nations. They largely failed in this task, instead becoming an ethnocentric and insular people who protected their heritage—not accomplishing God's calling given to them. It took the tongues of Pentecost (Acts 2) to again "restate" God's intention by dramatically illustrating the universality of His intention that He wants a prophetic people to **announce, predict His ways, and confront the world with its resistance to His love.** To do this, "tongues" symbolized they must abandon their own intellectual prowess and allow the Holy Spirit to "come from their gut" with words and intensity needed for the task. I can hear Jesus saying to His disciples: "Don't leave Jerusalem without it."

> The words and noises do not immediately define God or His purposes, nevertheless they move the believer's heart and spirit toward

God and His purposes. Because these noises are non-rational and unintelligible they stand in contrast to direct and descriptive statements to and about God. *Glossolalia* and groaning are, in Paul's mind, exercised from a position of weakness before God, but they nevertheless allow the Spirit of God to pray and work through the believer. Perhaps these apophatic practices more immediately allow the Spirit to work in harmony with the foolishness of the word of the cross (I Cor. 1-2), the revelation that is God's wisdom to a world that highly valued (and still values) power, knowledge, and the genius of intellect. The world naturally longs for brute power that comes in and rectifies wrongful deeds and circumstances. The world loves clarity and genius. In contrast, the incarnation (whereby God humbled himself) and the cross (where God really humbled himself) stand as two symbolic expressions of the very nature of God as one who does not always fit the satisfying categories of power and genius. God righted the wrongs in the universe through lowliness, weakness and suffering...Mysteries of mysteries, Christ defeated death by dying.

Rybarczyk concludes:

Similarly, Paul's theology is open to and seizes upon something of the brokenness of life as something God delights in using for His glory and creation's benefit. This is not expected. This is not linear. This in not rational. It is none of that, but it is apophatic.[18]

COMMUNICATIONS INSIGHT

WRITER RYBARCZYK[19] uses the term "apophatic" to describe the historical Eastern Orthodox Church's concept of knowing by "unknowing." Since God is infinite, and human language is finite, all attempts to define or understand fall short of capturing or seizing upon God as He is. Apothatic theologians reason that the human mind is in itself incapable of fully comprehending God. Here Rybarczyk resources John D. Zizioulas[20] *(Being As Communication: Studies in Personhood and the Church)* and John Meyendoff[21] *(Christ in Eastern Christian Thought).*

I shall return often to this "upside down" logic that is represented in paradox and unexpected ways that God seems to insist as a mode of dealing with humanity—for His reasons—certainly not mankind's. Frank Macchia believes Jacques Ellul has expressed that prayer in tongues is a meaningful response to God, since it symbolizes the essentially non-communicative nature of all prayer.[22]

COMMUNICATIONS INSIGHT

ELLUL SAYS that prayer is not verbal communication, which includes an agreement between persons about the meaning of the verbal signs used. (See Chapter 4 and the Ross Communications Chart.) Prayer consists rather of a response to the total self to the prior and ineffable self-disclosure of God. Ellul views prayer as a way of 'being' with God that transcends words and may be expressed in tongues, bells, dance, and incense... Prayer is striving 'with the One who is unknowable, beyond our grasp, unapproachable and inexpressible, asking that he be *hic et nunc,* the One he promised to be.[23]

THE ELEMENT OF WEAKNESS EQUALS STRENGTH

Second Corinthians in the New Testament is the most personal of the apostle Paul's letters. We see inside the man in this book. I am almost embarrassed at times, reading his self-offered vulnerability to a church that owed so much to him, but abused him so easily. Yet, he dramatically uses this personal painful injustice to clearly bring into vivid relief the paradox of God's words to him in this humiliating exposure. *"My grace is sufficient for you, for my power is made perfect in weakness"* (II Cor. 12:9). Tongues is certainly seen as "weakness" by the onlooker and inexperienced. (It's described as much worse by many.) It is tied directly, I submit, to the message of the cross—the ultimate upside-down paradox. Rybarczyk (above) also makes this connection, as do many of the early pioneers in Pentecost. The paradox of the cross underlines Paul's description of apostolic ministry and, as such, gives the model for every believer, whether in Corinth 2000 years ago or in our age when the Movement of the Spirit is accelerating at breakneck speed. Our human vessel is weak and still subject to the life of the cross; and amazingly, God likes it that way! The modern world loves heroes who can dribble a football (soccer) half the length of the field through the best opposition and score with power and cunning; or hit a baseball out of the park in the last inning to win the game! Hero worship seeks that these same "macho" characteristics should exist in the leaders of the Church so the members can justify mimicking that model. Corinth did—and we still do, too often.

And what does the fool boast in? Weaknesses! Paul is indeed what his opponents claim—even more so! He has been in more weaknesses than even they know about (II Cor. 11:21-29). Instead of being like the soldier who was highly honored for being the first to scale the wall, in battle, Paul had to escape down the wall—and in a basket! (II Cor. 11:30-33). Instead of being able to give the content of great visions and revelations, he must speak about a physical weakness! (12:1-10). Why this irony? Why this defense that is not a defense? The answer lies in the failure of the Corinthians to understand the true nature of the gospel. God redeemed man not with cosmic displays of power, not with armies marching to free the oppressed. He redeemed man through the humiliation of an incarnation in the life of a Jewish baby and death on the cross. But in that humiliation He revealed His true nature, and in that cross God Himself suffered for man's sins. That weakness is power. And those who follow Him must truly follow Him.[24]

...in that cross God Himself suffered for man's sins. That weakness is power. And those who follow Him must truly follow Him.
–G. Fee

What incredibly wise foolishness! There are striking similarities between the attitudes of the world concerning the message of the cross of Christ and the attitudes of the biblical record of those whose physical evidence marked the baptism in the Holy Spirit.

- *"For the foolishness of God is wiser than man's wisdom..."* (I Cor. 1:25—an almost irreverent statement by the apostle Paul—and title of this book.)
- *"For the message of the cross is foolishness to those who are perishing, but to us who are being saved it is the power of God."* (I Cor. 1:18—Salvation by Christ's cross.)
- *"Some of them, however, made fun of them and said, 'they have had too much wine.'"* (Evaluation by some in the Acts 2 account of tongues speech at Pentecost in Jerusalem.)
- *"But God chose the foolish things of the world to shame the wise: God chose the weak things of the world to shame the strong."* (Paul's introduction to the paradox of God's wisdom in I Corinthians, chapter 1.)
- *"So if the whole church comes together and everyone speaks in tongues, and some who do not understand or some unbelievers come in, will they*

not say that you are out of your mind?" (Unbelievers' impression of tongues speech in I Cor. 14:23.)

How can Weakness be Powerful?

For me, one of the all-time examples of the many paradoxes of God's dealings with mankind is the Beatitudes of Matthew 5. These are very hard words for even pious Christians. They seem so upside-down with the world's values. All of them take a "weak" position: the characteristic of a pacifist; behold the Omnipotent God who chooses to lay such a light touch on humanity as to give us independence!

Blessed are the poor in spirit. *The world says the opposite—blessed are those who spirits are high.*
Blessed are those who mourn. *No, say secular people—blessed are those who refuse to mourn.*
Jesus said, **"Blessed are the peacemakers."** *How can that be? Blessed are those who* ***dictate*** *the peace.*
The Master even said the **meek are blessed**. *Utter foolishness—blessed are the aggressive. We're number one!*
Blessed are the merciful. *Wait a minute—blessed are those who* **insist** *on getting justice.*
Blessed are the persecuted for Christ's name. *No—come off it! Blessed are those who are accepted for being so agreeable.*[25]

Word Picture

Strength from weakness was illustrated by Deborah Gill,[26] **during a teaching message to a Sunday morning worship service at a summer family camp. I here relate this image from the Greek word *akrogoniaios* which the apostle Paul uses to describe Jesus' role in the Kingdom**

(Ephesians 2:19-22). The difficult-to-pronounce Greek word has three meanings in Scripture: cornerstone, a keystone, and a capstone. Dr. Debbie showed how all three perfectly illuminate the matchless characteristics of the Master's place in the mature Christian life and without which the "structure" of our faith would be a shambles. The only one of the three I wish to repeat here is the *keystone* which best relates to the Roman arch that enriched the architectural world then, and even today. Until the keystone is placed during the construction of an arch, the structure is inherently weak. In fact, a centering device must be used to keep its forming sides from falling in on each other until the keystone can be carefully placed. Leonardo da Vinci, the amazing

Italian inventor and visionary called the arch: "A strength developed from weakness." The Roman arch is one of the strongest structures in the construction industry. It didn't require pre-stressed concrete and steel so common today; in fact, when properly engineered, it didn't even require mortar.

Take glossolalia out of the baptism in the Holy Spirit, and that doctrine's house would fall down too! Some have removed it, and all that's left is weakness and the need for a continuous scaffolding centering device holding up a ridiculous proposition. Good analogy? I'd say yes.

Why does God expect me always to abdicate the freedom He gave me so I can please Him? Yancey depicts God's power that way when He (the Father) is interacting with us.[27] He says he sometimes wishes God would use a heavier hand: "My faith suffers from too much freedom...At times I want God to overwhelm me, to overcome my doubts with certainty, to give final proofs of his existence and his concern."[28] When I try to interact with colleagues as an administrator, using patience and ambiguity to *allow* them to have time/space and their own prerogatives, I look so weak and incompetent. Yancey says he sometimes wants a God without ambiguity.[29] I can relate to that and conclude that *glossolalia is too ambiguous for the seekers of certainty*. M. Scott Peck writes,

> The healing of evil—scientifically or otherwise—can be accomplished only by the love of individuals. A willing sacrifice is required...I do not know how this occurs. But I know that it does...Whenever this happens there is a slight shift in the balance of power in the world.[30]

Building on this thought of the strange strength of weakness, and a willing sacrifice,

Yancey articulates the meaning of the cross of Christ:

> Jesus' death on the cross made a decisive case against his Messiahship for the Jews: crucifixion had fulfilled the curse of the law...What changed history was the disciples' dawning awareness (it took the Resurrection to convince them) that God himself had chosen the way of weakness. The cross redefines God as One who was willing to relinquish power for the sake of love. Jesus became, in Dorothy Solle's phrase, "God's unilateral disarmament."[31]

I have so much yet to learn of this principle. In retrospect I can see how the Lord wanted me to learn more about this strange "upside-down" paradox early in my life.

I grew up wishing my high school classmates in Slayton, Minnesota, USA would understand how much I wanted to be a "regular guy" and be accepted and that they not think I was so weird. Most of them interpreted my unwillingness to approve of the secular world's lifestyle as if I felt I were better than they. They felt I was excluding myself from their group by self-righteousness, so they excluded me every chance they could, even though I excelled in most activities of the school. It was a lonely road and I felt persecuted for my faith and my church's stand about nicotine, alcohol, and the debauchery of Hollywood. I remember one especially hurtful comment on the team bus returning from an out-of-town basketball game (which we had won!): "Don't expect Tarr to do that; he's one of the last of the Mohicans." It took me a long time to glory in the cross of Christ—to accept that I needed to become more like God, not less. It took even longer for me to learn that His justice forces Him to limit Himself to His rules that allow many to miss His ways, even when He doesn't want them to, as if He doesn't care about the verdict of those who don't quite understand His paradoxes. He's willing to take that risk—He's forced Himself to take that risk, so the wrong ones don't understand His ways. In the straightforward presentation of the gospel, it seems so clear and easy; but in closer examination, it's like Christ is hiding His path, concealing the way, so one must struggle to find it and in the struggle give up the greatest creative power—the power of choice—the power to accept Him or reject Him. *He's set the rules so our choosing Him goes against our God-given right to reject Him.* Give up sin by admitting to a rebellious nature with the words "God forgive me," to then find salvation. Give up the compass of earthly rationality to see His wisdom. Give up the pride of human speech mechanisms to allow the Spirit to speak "mysteries" back to God. It's too much. Why, this blessed, incomprehensibly genius idea that is so easy for our God-created ability to reject and so hard, instead, to accept? It's wonderfully terrible! Smith Wigglesworth describes this process in a chapter "Unconditional Surrender" as "repent, repent, repent." Maybe that's a clue.[32]

> **He's set the rules so our choosing Him goes against our God-given right to choose to reject Him.**

COMMUNICATIONS INSIGHT

LANGUAGE AS A WEAPON

PEOPLE OF ALL COUNTRIES and even subcultures in any one nation perceive their own dialect or accent as superior to any variant.

This perception is often used as a weapon against others who speak differently. Think of how the Northeast of the US deprecates the Southeast's use of American English and vice versa. In fact, the whole Midwest of the US also pokes fun at the "drawl" from Alabama, Mississippi or Texas. In our own United States, this teasing/criticism has been exacerbated by the expression "NBC Standard" as the speech most desired for radio and television announcers. Because Chicago was the origination of network radio broadcasting in the early part of the last century, an announcer who may have come from Texas or South Carolina would never get an "anchor" position without first learning to speak the local accent of Chicago or the Midwest American English. You may be an announcer from some small local station in Tyler, Texas, and use the local dialect with your friends, but you'll learn another accent if you want to be on CNN's national network.

This is not just a USA phenomenon. Parisians scoff at the use of French in Marseilles. Sicilian Spanish users have a certain disdain for Spanish speakers from Latin America. There is no end to this discussion. In the time of Jesus, language was an issue in many biblical references. Galilee, where Jesus grew up, got little respect from the rest of the country and was seen as the most culturally backward. Yancey, on this topic, tells how Galileans who learned Hebrew pronounced it so crudely they were not called on to read the Torah in other synagogues. Simon Peter's use of Aramaic betrayed him in the courtyard by his rural accent when Jesus was being interrogated. Aramaic words preserved in the Gospels show Jesus, too, spoke in the Northern dialect which, no doubt, encouraged skepticism about Him. *"How can the Christ come from Galilee? Nazareth! Can anything good come from there?"* (John 7:41)[33] I find it interesting God was so confident about the eventual outcome of His great experiment, that He seemed delighted to put this message at a disadvantage and area of weakness from so many aspects: geography, genealogy, social class, economics, etc. God could have chosen a power base for the birth of the Gospel of His Son. He purposely chose weakness and self-restraint.

Deep Roots of Philosophy = Divergence of Thought in Our Worldview

If we are to make sense of this current worldwide revival of the Holy Spirit, whose agents are most actively those who have been "filled with the Spirit" and speak in tongues (which simply gives them the power and inner confidence that God can and will use them as witnesses, for tongues are not the magic bullet, just the physical sign), we must bypass the world of Aristotle who gave us the philosophical matrix of our developed science and the paradigm for our technological sophistication. In fact, Aristotle's mentor Plato believed man has knowledge of the world through not only reason (rationality) but by a combination of reason and direct experience of the non-physical world. According to Morton Kelsey, "man's subjective experiences are just as real and important as his experience of the outer world, in Plato's view. This was basically rejected by Aristotle. While philosophers give Plato credit for setting us on the course of the Method of Science few, according to Kelsey, "realize that Plato accepted without question the value of religious experience, of what the Greeks called 'divine madness.'" Plato wrote, "Our greatest blessings come to us by way of madness; provided the madness is given us by divine gift."[34]

> Plato did not believe, as moderns do, that we get all of our knowledge and feelings through sense experience and reason. He believed that men had contact with a realm of non-physical reality...clearly the man who paid such reverence to the oracle of Delphi would have seen nothing inherently absurd in tongues.[35]

Kelsey then suggests that the Aristotelian West was embarrassed by tongues of the Montanists, thus it was first condemned and then ignored for centuries. But not so the Eastern Orthodox tradition whose contact of the individual with the spiritual world is still a concrete reality.[36]

Kelsey mentions an experience with a Russian priest that parallels my personal contact with an Orthodox monk at one of the monasteries at the Meteori rock formations in central Greece (where the Orthodox monks retreated and built monasteries on top of the massive rock formations to escape the Turkish invasions of the seventeenth century). In that monastery our discussion centered on the Holy Spirit and how their view differs with the Roman Church, which is similar to Kelsey's experience.

> No wonder my Russian priest friend had so little trouble discussing the subject of tongues with openness and warmth. He did not have to be defensive. He stands within a philosophical tradition in which it is possible for tongues to be meaningful.[37]

Working for years with Africans (who are Orientals, culturally) and learning their languages has given me a perspective on Eastern theology in contrast to Western theology learned in American institutions. Spending some time in Orthodox monasteries in Greece has reaffirmed my earlier suspicions that

African theological students can relate easier to Orthodox thought, in many ways, as opposed to Western Greco-Roman thought through the grid of Aristotelian rationalism. Orthodox theology seems to have never needed to suppress the mysterious role of the Spirit of God like the West, and maintain that we humans have the innate capacity to be mystically encountered by God. Rybarczyk says Gregory Palmas reasoned that:

There is an organ of vision on our souls...something in us that experientially-ontologically corresponds to God Himself. This something is not simply our moral capacity, our rationale, or our aesthetic sense. Those characteristics are emphasized in Western discussions, but the East goes further by suggesting that there is a spiritual *something* constitutive of mankind that was created in order to apprehend God... that man is capable of *transcending his own nature,* that being created according to the image of God, he possesses 'an organ of vision' that is neither the senses, nor the intellect.[38]

The Transition from Plato to Aristotle and the Scourge of Thomas Aquinas

Let's stay with Kelsey who says it best:

> Aristotle believed that we have knowledge only through sense experience...Since this truth is applied to knowledge of God as well as anything else, therefore man's knowledge of God must also be inferred from some experience. And this belief, then casts doubt upon most direct religious experience of the non-physical realm.[39]
>
> By the middle of the 13th century Thomas Aquinas was facing the fact that Christian thinking based on Plato...could not be sold to a world that was being swept by a new thought [Aristotle]. It could not have been done without his genius, for there is a deep cleavage between the world view of apostolic Christianity and that of Aristotle...Thus there is little emphasis in Aquinas upon direct experience of the Holy Spirit, on revelation through dreams, and visions and spiritual intuition, on angels, and demons, or on speaking in tongues...Together the senses and our reason not only bring all our knowledge to us: they make *absolute* available to us. The direct contact with God does not exist at all except as mediated through matter and thus through our sense experience... Aquinas' influence comes close to being determinative...Aquinas was conferred as **the** theologian (Kelsey's emphasis) of the Catholic church through the encyclical letter of Pope Leo XIII , *Astern Patris,* in 1879...Protestant theology

> simply broke up a train on the same track and got up a new head of steam, using for fuel the revolt against authoritarian limits on experience...Protestant thought which attempts to deal with the actual experiences of the New Testament, follows the track of the basic rationalism of Aristotle and Aquinas, and so has little place for any direct experience of the spiritual, tongues included.[40]

COMMUNICATIONS INSIGHT

IF ONE ALLOWS the only source of conscious speech to be the Fan of Perception as in Ross's Communications Model (see chapter 4), one can easily see how Aristotelian logic disallows many elements of the mysterious. Pentecostals and Charismatics hold that "Tongues Speaking" makes room for the direct contact of man with the spiritual realm which modern Communications Theories would disallow. In like manner, there is no place for FAITH in the Method of Science that has acted like an inoculation of educational theory for all of the developed world and, in increasing measure, the developing world as well. Both of these useful and valued taxonomies of the West are a direct result of Aristotle's "excluded middle." The Law of Identity: **A is A.**

The Law of the Excluded Middle: **Everything is either A or non-A.**

The Law of Non-contradiction: Nothing is both A and non-A.

Vast regions of the global population, especially the Orient and Mid-East, believe the West in embracing Aristotelian theory has excluded much of reality and that the above formula does not contain all of reality. They say Westerners have become "masters of the external."

In a chapter, "The Flaw of the Excluded Middle"[41] Paul Heibert too shows what Aristotle has done to Western thinking. Though taking a different tack about the role of Plato, he comes to the same conclusion:

> Many missionaries trained in the West had no answers to the problems of the middle level—they often did not even see it...When tribal people spoke of fear of evil spirits, they denied the existence of spirits rather than claim the power of Christ over them...[effective missionaries] must include a theology of divine guidance, provision and healing, of ancestors, spirits and invisible powers of this world...On this level, some sections of the church have turned to

> doctrines of saints as intermediaries between God and humans. *Others have turned to doctrines of the Holy Spirit to show God's active involvement in the events of human history. It is no coincidence that many of the most successful missions have provided some form of Christian answer to the middle level questions.* (Emphasis mine.)

The baptism in water in its many varied forms practiced by hundreds of different denominations hardly requires the element of the excluded middle, but baptism in the Holy Spirit obviously does. Let's turn to the vast differences between the two.

Baptisms: Similarities and Differences

This chapter, THESIS, has many facets as is evident by its complexity. I will now move one step further on the topic of *baptism*:

This "baptism" Jesus promised (Acts 1:4-8) just before His ascension back to the Father was different than the water baptism of John the Baptist. Jesus said it was. Any priest, pastor, rector, or bishop can administer water baptism. (And in some circles no "official" minister is needed.) Only Christ is the agent of this mighty immersion of the Spirit. John the Baptist said He would be (John 3:11). Since the essential meaning of "baptism" is to be "covered, to be enveloped," it signifies a total submergence within the reality of the Holy Spirit so whoever is so baptized has a vivid sense of the Spirit's presence and power. Another expression to describe this life-changing experience is the "infilling" of God, which must refer to the full penetration of the indwelling Spirit. When one is fully "submerged," which only follows after full "submission" of the will and release of the human ego, even man's speech mechanism, of which we are so distinctively proud, must also become subjected to the Spirit's loving control.[42] When one looks at the combined descriptions in Scripture for this event, one gets a clear picture of its importance and impact on the life of the believer. More on the element of loving control.

The Spirit's Loving Control

Sounds simple, and for some it is. Just relax in the secure arms of the Holy Spirit—no? **NOT!** For some folks, "baptism" or "submersion" means too much loss of perceived personal control. Jesus makes it clear that the way to God is the same as the way to a *new childhood.* (You know, that "born again" stuff.) One may ask—do I trust myself and such a radical transformation? Do I trust God that much? Can't I be "baptized in the Holy Spirit" and not have to trust the Holy Spirit to such an extent? Receiving this "baptism" requires a total willingness to let God be God, to do all the cleansing and renewing that each individual's needs, which may not be the same as one's neighbor needs. One may ask: "Can't I just have part of this gift and keep my Ross Chart perceptual field (knowledge, cognition, and understanding) active?" Fear of complete surrender is the enemy's oldest and most effective tool to keep us from the full potential in Christ—the Giver of this "other" baptism.

The VISIBLE Issue of Evidence—Other Views on a Theme

Both of these baptisms, in water and in the Holy Spirit, are intended to be able to be witnessed. Why, one may ask? When the Pharisees and the teachers of the law accused Jesus of blasphemy on the occasions when He said to those to whom He ministered, "Your sins are forgiven," He was treading on dangerous grounds according to Levitical law. One who usurped the prerogatives of Deity was to be killed. To answer His critics in Luke 5:32 Jesus said: *"Which is easier: to say, 'Your sins are forgiven,' or to say, 'Get up and walk'?"* It was easier to say one's sins are forgiven because it required no visible proof. To say "Get up and walk" required a demonstration. If when Jesus told the lame man to get up and walk nothing had happened, He would have been seen as an impostor. Anyone present can witness either water baptism or Spirit baptism! Both are valid as testimonials for any observer, but even more important is the interior conformation for the person being baptized. I believe this is especially true of Spirit baptism because it is easier to get wet than to speak a new language. You'll know it when you get wet. That's not too hard. But you'll also know it when you speak in tongues, and it's an indisputable witness to the recipient because he/she knows he/she is not doing it him/herself. *Perhaps God knew we humans would need this demonstration to prove to the recipient God's power and approval.*

Fear of complete surrender is the enemy's oldest and most effective tool to keep us from the full potential in Christ—the giver of the "other" baptism.

J. R. Hall[43] gives two reasons why God chose tongues as the evidence of the Holy Spirit.

1. The power of speech itself. The power to express thought is the power of personality and reveals character. Jesus said, *"Out of the abundance of the heart the mouth speaketh"* (Matt. 12:34). Since the ability of speech sets humanity apart from other creatures, how a person uses this gift of words identifies that person's moral and religious character...Therefore, speaking in tongues by the Spirit

reveals that the Holy Ghost has "sealed" the individual—both identifying that person with Christ and signifying that the person now belongs to Christ (I Cor. 6:19-20; Eph. 1:13-14; 4:30).

2. A second possible reason why God chose speaking in tongues is that it may be the only universal evidence possible...If a person merely speaks in a known language, no supernatural evidence is present, but if a person speaks in an unknown language, then this miraculous happening testifies to the inner presence and work of the Spirit.

In this instance, Hall agrees with J. R. Flower's writing in 1920. (See below.)

In the African languages I have learned, I have perhaps a new cognition of the general essence of what the Holy Spirit seeks with us as His vessels of service related to the issue of glossolalia. I believe a more profound enlightenment has come to me than is possible in a European language. To express thirst or hunger, I say in French—I *have* hunger (J'ai faim) or in English—I *am* hungry. (Note the power words of HAVE and AM.) But in Mori, of the Mossi, one says "kom n tara mam"—**Hunger has me.** (Note, the power is not possessed by the person but resident in what is sought or needed.) Williams says, "When Pentecostals use words like 'outpouring or infilling,' it does not mean one has more of the Holy Spirit. Rather the Spirit who is totally present now totally claims the person. In popular Pentecostal language: 'You may have the Spirit, but now the Spirit has you!'"[44] I wish to reiterate here: You cannot be clothed, endowed by, filled with, or have the Spirit of God fall on you as an event **without your submission and permission, both involved in faith—of course.** It's His requirement. But remember, it is a gift. Paradoxically, it's costly: to the human ego and prideful accomplishments and titles. It may even be costly to some of your theology.

Williams summarizes well: "All this terminology—baptizing, filling, outpouring, falling, coming on—suggests a total experience of the presence of the Holy Spirit. In one sense it is an immersion, a submergence within (baptized); in still another it is an invasion from without (outpouring, falling upon, coming on). Such terminology is variously used by Pentecostals to describe their own experience."[45] **Some would say, how can it be possible that so many words (filling—outpouring—falling—coming on—flood—immersion, etc.) describe this event? Is not that proof it is spurious, because more than one word is used to express it? If it were genuine, it wouldn't need this ambiguous search for definition!** My response would be twofold. First, the Bible itself uses many different terms describing this single event. Second, in the mode of the word "transcendent," human language simply cannot *contain* even a part of God's nature and revelation. Of course, "literalists" would say no. I've found you can't reason with them.

Donald A. Johns adds to our attempt to understand the phenomenon of Spirit baptism.

> It seems to me that speaking in tongues is essentially one kind of experience, produced by a certain kind of contact with the divine Spirit. The first time this kind of contact occurs is the initiatory event of being baptized in the Spirit, but the same kind of inspired speech can be the result of subsequent contacts as well. Whether *baptizo* means "immerse" or "flood," there is an overwhelming of the human psyche by the person and power of the Spirit of God. As to why God chose to produce tongues as a manifestation of this divine "coming upon," I use a hint supplied by Robert Capon in his *Parables of Grace* that "[Jesus] (and the Spirit as well) *prays in us.* Prayer is not really our work at all. [46] If so, then to initiate a believer into a charismatic ministry that is completely powered and directed by the Spirit, the Spirit must do all the work, at least in the speech content. The result is prayer and praise that is itself the total work of the Holy Spirit.[47]

One might differ with this slightly if one supports the idea of God expressly *sharing* the experience with mankind in the analogy of the incarnational aspect of the partnership God has so designed. Perhaps it's going too far to suggest that God "overpowers" the speech apparatus where "the Spirit does all the work, at least in the speech content." But to say the "Spirit prays in us" would allow both interpretations.

Mankind, without the Lordship of God in a life, is very proud and self-centered and individualistic. More than all others in God's creation, humans are proud of their ability to express their desires and comm-uni-cate their uniqueness and independence and self-achieved value. When a believer surrenders this highest of all attributes, which sets him or her apart, to be dominated by the Holy Spirit and speak in "tongues," all that pride disappears by a willing "giving it up." That which seems so ridiculous to many is a strong and valid evidence of self-abnegation. (Of course, one can, in turn, use this gift incorrectly in a prideful manner as when the apostle Paul needed to correct the Corinthian Church in his letter to them.)

COMMUNICATIONS INSIGHT

"THE CAPACITY for speech distinguishes human nature among living beings,—it likewise differentiates—in OT theology—God from the many other gods. It is not to be wondered at that one of the finest varieties of religious experience links divine and human speech. Nor is it surprising the result of that mix transcends rational thought."[48]

Glossolalia frees the individual from the constraints of editorial scrutiny of the mind and all its self-consciousness and self-restraint. In that mode, it allows the soul to speak mysteries to God, which is self-edifying (I Cor. 14:2). I suggest strongly the concept "links divine and human speech" fits closer to my conviction of the mechanics of glossolalia than it being the "total work of the Holy Spirit."

Robert Culpepper describes what he thinks most Charismatics would agree to as a definition of glossolalia: "They appeal to Acts 2:4 and I Cor. 14:13-14 for the basic ingredients of this definition...to mean that the believer does the speaking while the Holy Spirit supplies the words. In this process there is disengagement of the mind and the speech apparatus so that the speaker's mind neither chooses the words that are spoken nor understands what is said."[49]

Brandt and Bicket, while speaking of *prayer*, speak squarely to the subject of submission/self-abnegation.

> Submission is to praying what blood is to the human body. Apart from submission, prayer is only a cold and lifeless form. The Greek word used by Paul, *hupotasso,* means to "subordinate," "subject oneself," "yield voluntarily," "submit oneself." Submission under girds all effective prayer. It is essential to the initial infilling of the Holy Spirit. Apart from its continued practice there can be no Spirit-filled life-style. . . Submission is always the initiative of the one who submits, for it emanates from the core of a person's being, the central will. If imposed or forced, it is not submission at all. Jesus was the epitome of submission. He could say without equivocation, "'I always do what pleases the Father'" (Matt. 11:29)...All lack of submission within the household of faith is traceable to a fundamental rebellion against God.[50]

No Merit System by Self Effort

The Spirit of God active in salvation requires repentance. "Forgive me—I'm in need of you—I am wrong." Why should we come to believe the role of the Spirit in the promise of Jesus about the Holy Spirit's help (*"He shall be IN you"* [John 14:17] regarding Spirit empowerment) would allow anything different than *subordination* (the active initiative of the one who submits)? Never! God always demands that we relinquish to Him the gift of volition He gave man at the creation. "Repentance finally turns out to be the capacity to forego pride and accept graciousness."[51] Herein lies the secret mankind stumbles over. We'd rather "work it out" in a system of merit that does not require *beholdenness*. Oh, how we hate that word! We try hard to find a system to position God into a debit posture—so He **owes** us, while all along He tries to get us to exercise our creative right to choose to submit: our puny efforts at righteousness, our prideful attempts at self-justification, our avid insistence on bookkeeping of good deeds so we can present them like a gift package of merit. All this in the name of avoiding grace. God's foolishness is **so wise!** He must have our will to choose Him—otherwise our efforts are worthless to Him. We don't get it, do we?

COMMUNICATIONS INSIGHT

AS RELATED to the coming of the promised "Comforter," He chose something that would **cost** the recipient the loss of his/her prideful superior asset called "meaning making," or languaging ability. Humans are at the top of the "communications chain" in this aspect relative to all the other creatures in God's world. The submission of language from the cerebral realm to the visceral (from where the Holy Spirit can speak and inspire) is **symbolic** of the many ways God and mankind interact. We will see, later, how this is related to the oft-repeated phrase of Jesus, *"Lose your life so you can find it."* (This idea appears seven times in the gospels.) It's also a sign to the recipient (who is speaking in tongues) that "this is no joke; I'm not making this up. God is bathing me in love and power." So the individual says inside, "Wow! That's empowerment. God CAN use me. He knows where I am. I DO have worth—hey, there's something to this after all!" Never mind that some will **still** think (Acts 2:13) that you are excessive or defective. Until you can stand that stigma, that criticism, you won't "get it" because your pride will prevent the submission that God in His wisdom, and maybe His humor, demands. It's part of the package. This **too** is His design.

John W. Welch spoke of this secret before the student body of future ministers in 1939:

Some people question tongues as the evidence of the Baptism. Here is the philosophy of tongues: The Baptism is the submerging of the whole being, including the mind, and tongue proves the submerging of the mind. Speaking a language unknown to the mind shows that the mind and the whole being are, at that moment, subjected to God. What physical phenomenon would better prove the submerging of the mind than tongues?

Without the baptism in the Holy Spirit our ministry is limited. We are limited to preaching things we have learned from books of men or testifying of past experiences. But with the Spirit's indwelling, our minds are illuminated, giving us a fresh revelation of Jesus and His Word and enabling us to bring forth the thoughts of God with expedience and power. Besides illuminating the mind for service, the Spirit's indwelling helps one surrender his will and emotions to God. This in turn, facilitates spiritual introspection and cleansing.[52]

The Superior—Unique Sign

For who among men knows the thoughts of a man except the man's spirit within him? In the same way no one knows the thoughts of God except the Spirit of God (I Cor. 2:11).

This is why tongues is no doubt the superior sign (given in Acts 2, 10, 19) over any of the other gifts of the Spirit (listed in 1 Cor. 12, 14; Rom. 12; and Ephesians 4) to signal the human organism that He is active. This is the point of the argument that only the person him/herself knows that glossolalia is not self-created. Why not prophecy? Is this good? Yes, of course. Do we need it? Yes, Paul makes it clear; we need prophecy, and in some contexts it is more desirable. Why not Word of Wisdom or Knowledge as signs to the individual the Spirit is resident? Because those gifts of the Spirit are operated in the medium of the "understood language" of both the hearers and the speaker of the gift. The speaker/user of any of those gifts may always doubt part or the whole of its source as being supernatural **because the human mind is active in selecting and sorting (process of meaning making—see chapter 4) with proper syntax, sentence structure, etc., for the sake of cognition.** The "spirit within him—man's own spirit" knows he/she is not the source of glossolalia—if it is genuine. Cannot it be memorized? Cannot it be just gibberish—or made up to impress or trick? Of course, but the "thoughts of a man **know** this." And when it is genuine, a person also knows this deep within; there's no doubt, contrary to the element of doubt that may exist with any gift operated in the person's cognitive **personally known** language potential. The Scripture says it well:

> *No one can really know what anyone else is thinking or what he is really like, except that person himself. And no one can know God's thoughts except God's own Spirit. And God has actually given us His Spirit (not the world's spirit) to tell us about the wonderful, free gifts of grace and blessing that God has given to us by the Holy Spirit, in words that we as men might choose. So we use the Holy Spirit's words to explain the Holy Spirit's facts* (I Cor. 2:11-12, *The Living Bible*).

Yes, our cessationist and doubting siblings in the Body of Christ are certainly right to compare this powerful truth to Romans 8:16 (the Spirit Himself testifies with our spirit that we are God's children), but they don't have the capacity, through their own choosing or ignorance—like a veil—to see this does not **only** concern salvation, a work of the Spirit. But *in the context of a New Testament Charismatic church where glossolalia was normal and everywhere pervasive* this passage ALSO speaks to the Charismatic world of the building up of the confidence of the speaker. In private prayer and intercession or in public edification of the worshiping believing church, **the believer comes to know he/she can be His instrument to fulfill the Ascension Mandate of Acts 1:8 (to be His witnesses).**

No man in his right mind would have chosen glossolalia—any more than any Jew would have chosen a Messiah to be so weak to let himself get killed by the ignominious death of the Roman cross.

It's idolatry to make a system of salvation that omits God's plan of the cross. Man says: "If I'm to believe in you, you must do it my way, in a way that's less costly, in a way whereby I can merit or earn my way. I refuse to be beholden; I'll accept no grace." So also, it's idolatrous to say: "I will have the fullness of the Holy Spirit indwelt—but on my terms. And my terms will omit any 'foolishness' and especially any stigma of "these men are drunk" (Acts 2:13). By insisting on tongues, God insured that man, in his pride, would stumble over the true source of power that only comes by submission and "weakness." We want power and miraculous signs and wisdom, all admirable commodities, but without cost, just like the Jews and Greeks of Paul's day in the New Testament.

> By demanding signs and wisdom man proved himself to be an idolater. In this way man set himself up as the authority who passed judgment upon God by insisting: 1) God must validate Himself to man; 2) He must submit himself to man's criteria as to how God must act; 3) He must act in power, meaning our view of power; 4)

> He must act in wisdom, meaning our view of wisdom... But wait, if Jews will believe in signs, and Greeks will respond to wisdom, then let's give them signs and wisdom. God has plenty of both. No, Paul says, we give them the cross, an act designed by God to be a scandal to the sign-seeker and folly to the wisdom-seeker.
>
> Consider their reasoning on this. A God who is so weak as to get Himself killed by His enemies, who didn't cause the earth to open up and swallow them, who wouldn't come down from the cross and act like God—who needs a God like that? Such weakness in God is scandalous...How could a God of wisdom be involved in such foolishness?[53]

A 1700-Year-Old Danger!

Most Pentecostal movements in North America who began in the early 1900s are now facing pressure from some of their younger, often better educated scholars and ministers to modify the long held belief that tongues are **not** optional for the New Testament pattern of the doctrine of Holy Spirit baptism. Some of this criticism is welcome, in my opinion, if it questions the "idol complex" that speaking in tongues can become (a misplaced emphasis on the external sign to the weakening of the central essence of Spirit baptism). But too often, I believe, this internal pressure coincides with an affluent society of an "upwardly mobile" social and economic structure and status consciousness, where the price of accepting God's "foolishness" is too high. When we kept our old Ford V8s together with baling wire and held meetings in tents and storefronts (in the 1940s), the stigma of Pentecost was much more tolerable than while meeting in multi-million dollar cathedrals with stainless steel kitchens. Now, I don't believe these are mutually exclusive—but might not there be some relationship? The great test of about six traditional Pentecostal denominations in North America will be: can they remain viable instruments of witness and deliverance from the power of Satan inside this current wave of affluence and relative acceptance by the community and Church world? Be warned! The reformers made that mistake before us. Not just about the power of the unpredictable, surprising, unorthodox ways of Spirit control, but to the very bedrock of salvation through the demands of repentance and forgiveness the cross of Christ requires. What God has done in Christ crucified and in the New Testament model of the fullness of the Spirit both are a direct contradiction of man's conception of wisdom, rationality, and power. Let's tamper with them at our own risk and demise as a witnessing community.

Church history is full of examples of this carnal evolution. Man's demands on God to accommodate man's wisdom and need for selfish power is reflected in religious man's reluctance to pay the price of being called foolish in the eyes of the world. The apostle Paul again repeats his earlier upsetting "upside-down words" about folly:

> *Let no one deceive himself. If anyone among you supposes that he is wise by the standards of this age, let him become foolish by the standards of this age, in order that he may become truly wise. For the wisdom of the world is foolishness with God* (I Cor. 3:18-19).

And the Lord Himself prays this powerful thanks to His and our Father:

> *I praise you Father, Lord of heaven and earth, because you have hidden these things from the wise and learned, and revealed them to little children. Yes, Father, for this was your good pleasure* (Matt. 11:25-26).

Now we adults don't like that! So we seek to change the "hidden wisdom—that children can understand" and make it more palatable. Sometimes may it be easier to deny that wisdom than to lower our selfish pride and conform to the Father's "good pleasure"?

While penning these lines, I've been teaching in a Bible College in Addis Ababa to a class of 27 men and women, from ten different denominations, all with ministerial experience in Ethiopia. A few years ago, under the Communist regime called the "Dirge," a devastating Atheistic curse on the whole country from 1974 to 1991, many of these students suffered persecution. Some of them fled to neighboring countries for safety. Most of their churches were outlawed by the regime. However, the Holy Spirit was mightily active in the "underground" meetings with an explosion of Pentecostal experience and commitment to evangelism. Today 90 percent of all Evangelicals are called "Pentes" due to this Charismatic revival that cannot be traced to any denomination or orchestrated source. They now send missionaries from all their churches touched by the renewal to all parts of Ethiopia and beyond. This is typical of all Pentecostal revivals—empower the laity! Since coming a month ago I've learned of the following two incredible happenings, from a student here at Addis Bible College and from the lady who works in the apartment we are renting.

Muslim Funeral Cortege

(*From one of our students, who pastors in the area of the miracle.*) Two Ethiopian evangelists, working in the southern part of the country were invited by their Muslim neighbors to attend the burial of a six-year-old girl. While the men passed the body (wrapped in a sleeping-mat) from shoulder to shoulder as they walked to the cemetery, the evangelists took their turn in friendly gesture. While carrying the body, one of the evangelists heard the voice of the Spirit say: "Now's the time to pray out loud for deliverance." He hesitated. The impression came again. He shared this with his colleague who became afraid and left off carrying and walking with the group. The first man took courage and prayed out loud for the deliverance of God. Under the Spirit's power in prayer, he fell to the ground, dropping the girl's body! The family and friends became angry and shouted their displeasure—until they saw not only the preacher get up, but the girl too, who began unwrapping herself (to the disbelief of the procession). Now four months later, she's well and over 600 new believers have formed a new congregation.

(*From the "house helper" in the apartment complex.*) A young man studying for the Orthodox priesthood of the Ethiopian Coptic Church received the baptism in the Holy Spirit and was put out of the church and his studies. He began to train for the ministry of an independent movement of Charismatic churches. His mother, a pious Orthodox believer, was much opposed to her son's change of direction as the priesthood is a position of pride for any Ethiopian mother. Soon after this, the mother died. At the traditional wake in the living room at home, the son felt impressed to lay his hands on the coffin and pray for his deceased mother. She revived and began knocking on the inside of the wooden coffin! People vacated the house from all the openings! He had to search for the person who had the key to free his mother from the beautiful box! She now no longer opposes her son's decision and many family and friends have come to a personal experience with the risen Lord. She sits on the front pew of her "new church."

Some will read the above accounts and ask: "Tarr, did you verify these testimonies?" My answer is yes. That, however, will not suffice for some who, as in the account in John 11:45-47, wouldn't believe the resurrection of Lazarus even after witnessing it. Jesus also said in John 9:39 in answer to the skeptics: *"For judgment I have come into the world, so that the blind may see and those who see will become blind."* Tough words.

COMMUNICATIONS INSIGHT

A CEREBRAL APPROACH TO RELIGION

IN THIS WESTERN CULTURE of Greco-Roman philosophical matrix or mindset, we are afraid of any proposition that might suggest the experiential could replace or even be equal to the rational.

Our speech habits mirror the model of rhetorical style. Our cognition prides itself on the syllogism and the Venn diagram of plotting an idea to be advanced.

"The Eastern mindset, on the other hand, has no problem with the experiential as a way of perceiving reality. In fact, the Eastern mind perceives supernatural things more readily than the Western mind."[54]

> "In an era when great stress is placed on a more cerebral approach to religion, it is conceivable that Paul's counsel might easily stress the need for more 'praying in the Spirit' rather than less."[55]

How hard is it for Westerners, in particular, to give up our cerebral approach to religion? Why would Jesus repeatedly speak of all the things one must give up to be His disciple if there was no cost? Start to make a list. It's going to cost you to follow Him. It will cost you to speak in tongues. A momentary surrender of a portion of the total dominance of one's mental capacity and cognitive control, for some, will be harder than for others. But even for the predisposed, it will demand abnegation on some level.

THE UNEXPECTED AND THE UNCOMFORTABLE

I submit sometimes God demands the unexpected and the uncomfortable. In John 6, many disciples *"turned back and no longer followed Him"* when His words about Himself as the "bread of life" actually freaked them out because of the strict dietary laws the Jews observed. Jesus then added the words: *"Whosoever eats my flesh and drinks my blood has eternal life, and I will raise him up at the last day"* (John 6:54). They had been taught strictly to refrain from blood by the most rigorous and meticulous methods of the slaughter and preparation of meat. *Kashrut* is the Hebrew word that refers to the Jewish dietary laws. It is a variation of this word from which the commonly understood word *kosher* is derived. It means fit, proper, or in accordance with the religious laws. All food preparation (especially meat) not prepared properly is called *trefah.* The Torah forbids the eating of blood, even when it comes from kosher animals and birds (Lev. 7:26-27, also 17:10-14). Two methods are permitted to eradicate all the blood. The method of "soaking and salting" consisting of 16 steps or instructions and the method of broiling where five steps are required. Not even a trace of blood could be consumed.[56]

Why would Jesus institute the ordinance of Holy Communion (the Eucharist for some) that would be so contrary and so repulsive to Old Testament teaching and the understanding of Kashrut? Would not this new "covenant" cause some to refuse to even consider this observance? Was that part of His design? Would not some be unwilling to "give up" one of the most stringent and tightly held rules? Jesus must have had His reasons.

Abandon the Struggle

As a boy, I once knew a lifeguard who demonstrated to me, coincidentally as I stood talking to him by the poolside, a graphic picture I have never forgotten. An older man, very obese, was seen to struggle wildly in the water. He was obviously in trouble. Joe, my friend the lifeguard, sat motionless on his high chair. "Joe, aren't you going to help him?" I shouted. "Not yet," said Joe. Other swimmers at the pool also began to holler to Joe for action. Someone hollered his suggestion Joe was scared because the man was so heavy. Joe stood, held up his hand, and shouted, "Just a minute, and I'll get him." We wondered WHY? in dumbfounded anxiety. When the drowning man had almost ceased to struggle, Joe dove off his perch, swam swiftly to the big man and with his hand under the drowning man's chin, and sometimes pulling him by the hair, "towed" him to safety. "You have to wait until they stop struggling when they are that big," said Joe, "or he may have taken us both down." Is it possible God has so designed the reception of the Holy Spirit so one must give up the struggle (of the power of speech from cognitive learning) in order to be empowered by the mysterious workings of the Holy Spirit? Can we think about it?

COMMUNITY OF THE SPIRIT

Janet Powers[57] speaks to us today about the words of Jesus to His disciples in Acts 1:8: "But you shall receive power when the Holy Spirit comes on you; and you will be my witnesses..." "Acts 2 is really the story of a new prophetic community being created, and tongues is the sign that this community has indeed received the spirit of prophecy...glossolalia is seen as the sign of a new charismatic community and is closely related to other types of inspired speech: praise, prophecy, proclamation and prayer... a sign that all who belong to this charismatic community have been empowered for ministry."[58]

> When the meaning of tongues is grounded in the verbal proclamation of the gospel, the importance of the community in bearing witness to the gospel is ignored. But when tongues is understood as the new spiritual language of the new community created by the Spirit, the nature of this new community becomes part of the proclamation of the kingdom. In Acts, whenever glossolalia is experienced, social and cultural barriers are broken down and new communities which witness to the transforming power of God are created."[59]

Byron Klaus (at this writing the president of the Assemblies of God Theological Seminary in his monthly "Prez Release" to the constituency and supporters) writes of the impact of Harvard sociologist Robert Putnam's book, *Bowling Alone*. Putnam's thesis is that Americans are living in a society of "disconnectedness" and paying a huge price because of the alienation from one another. Individual needs and concerns have crowded out the human need to be in community for mental and physical health. Klaus comments:

> Reading Putnam has been a source of serious spiritual conviction for me...While Evangelical and Pentecostal traditions offer a spiritual bond that is significant, the cultural tendency toward privatized faith and individualist piety blunts the fullest potential development of social capital by these traditions. This tendency to value individual concerns over the needs of the family and local community is increasingly interwoven with the post-modern affirmation that "truth" is naïve or even worse than that...that it is oppressive. Exclusive claims to "truth" are not in vogue these days. Jesus is the Way, the Truth and the Life is considered "narrowness" and often categorized as bigotry.[60]

Surely God knew this when 2000 years ago He made a way for a prophetic community to know they were a part of something He thought. This being that man's cerebral capacity to render Him irrelevant by mental gymnastics would have an answer in the time when this absurdity would have popular currency. So He woos us to the "frequency of the Spirit" where we join the mystical and also exhilarating moment of surrender to His utterance—His immersion into a spiritual community that defies the traditional barriers between Charismatic and Roman Catholic, Episcopalian, Presbyterian, Baptist, etc. It's the common denominator of glossolalia that allows immediate bonding between these otherwise suspicious doctrinal camps. Note, the doctrinal differences are still there, but are not the issue they once were. But when a Baptist becomes a Bapticostal, the Pentecostal is quick to allow the Baptist's Calvinism to melt into a less significant difference. So also the Roman Catholic, who formerly considered the Pentecostal the most radical of the "Separated Brethren," now remembers his/her baptism with speaking in tongues and jumps great barriers to embrace the former heretic. Amazing! Klaus again:

> We survive in a western culture that is starving for relationship, but addicted to countless forms of self-centeredness. Post-modern militancy against exclusive truth claims may very well replace the Inquisition and the McCarthy era as the historical examples of the destructiveness of human zeal "religiously" applied.[61]

I wish I could say that Charismatics, Pentecostals and the Third Wave of Spirit-baptized folk had completely solved the problem of being alienated from community and have formed spiritual families working together. Though great inroads have been made toward true ecumenism, great distances are yet to be accomplished. The medium of Spirit baptism, however, is there and needs to be fully actionized. The last chapter to follow will develop this potential of what I believe is one of the great intentions of God's Spirit in our fragmented age. God wants a relationship with us, the process of which can best be begun by His empowering presence. One needs only to listen to the attempts of people who talk of the closeness of the inner reality of glossolalia. They know this tainted *mother tongue* can't possibly make the grade! It's from another world!

The Community of God so Needs the "Inbreaking" of the Spirit

I was twelve years old when I first observed the power of communal witness of the Spirit. It was in a church service in Duluth, Minnesota. The church was not of our family's denomination, but an independent Swedish movement of a group of Pentecostal churches of Scandinavian decent in northern Minnesota and the Dakotas. A couple (I assumed a man and wife) were singing a duet. After a verse or two (I can't remember the song) the Holy Spirit came on the husband and he stopped singing, quietly wept for a few seconds, then spoke in tongues before the whole congregation in a calm but forceful voice. The wife, also deeply moved, immediately gave the interpretation in English. The interpretation was an amplification of the song and the morning message, which was yet to come. Though only a young boy, I was very impacted by the powerful presence of God in the meeting and doubly impressed when the pastor later gave the Bible lesson, which had been introduced by the exercise of spiritual gifts. First time events are often vividly recalled and impressive. The whole tenor of the meeting was not contradicted or changed, but rather accelerated by the "demonstration" of the Spirit. The church was galvanized by a feeling of community, having collectively participated in the event.

My plea is to consider to seek a level/frequency of communion with the Paraclete which would accelerate God's revelation through His Word, plus release the "extemporaneous moment" when the written Word can find incarnate amplification to the immediate circumstance of the scene. The door of "tongues," in the life of the believer, allows the prophetic role of the Spirit (in the language of the meeting) to zoom in on the hearer's need just like I Cor. 14 clearly illustrates.

Question: Can one assess the loss of God's "inbreaking" by those who judge the above account spurious or *no longer biblically viable—finished—from another era but not for today?* Is it possible those who hold the cessationist view are limiting Christ's promise of the multiple roles of the Holy Spirit (John 16:13-15)? In Phil. 3:10ff Paul strains to know God on a deeper level and makes himself very vulnerable before his readers. What a heart cry!

> *I want to know Christ and the power of His resurrection and the fellowship of sharing in His sufferings, becoming like Him in His death, and so somehow, to attain to the resurrection from the dead.*

He continues, fearing he may be misunderstood, to discount any taint of boasting about the past ministry or victories won in his apostleship. Can you hear him still launching a challenge today? "Plug into the 'foolishness of God!' Believer, don't get hung up on God's seeming foolish way if you are hungry for Him in His holiness, power, and intimate presence. Don't analyze it to death! God is calling you to the New Testament community of faith. It's *not* a denomination. Come walk with him. Release your potential in Him and His Spirit."

Experience has taught us this prophetic role is not automatically renewed with each generation. Those tired of "loss" and "stigma," as we are describing it, even from others in the Body of Christ, invite the believer to seek approval of the world and shake off the stigma of the prophet. (Inside the Church, over the centuries, priests have never liked prophets.) Many yearn to seek an accepted place in the "priesthood/clergy" and "wearers of the cloth." Traditional Pentecostal denominations, now nearly 100 years old, will need to fight hard to maintain what the Early Primitive Church of the apostles lost soon after the first 200 years! But we should rather be encouraged to remember and exemplify; after Pentecost, the disciples went from a cowering, fearful, enclosed and defeated bunch to a band of Spirit-inspired proclaimers of the good news who made a lasting mark on their world.

COMMUNICATIONS INSIGHT

INVISIBLE TO SEE / IMPOSSIBLE TO SAY

SAINT EXUPERY'S book *Le Petit Prince* has a line that is simple yet profound: "L'essentiel est invisible pour les yeux"(that which is essential is invisible to the eye). The closer we get to living and feeling and knowing that, the closer to real wisdom and knowing God we'll have traveled. Generally, the problem with speech is that once we've "said" it with our cognitive mind, it's finished. Like the child's game of "Captain, May I?" or the fairytale story of Rumplestiltskin. You remember—the princess could only escape from her coerced promise if she could "say" the elf's name. Speech: its power is the woof and warp of our conscious and subconscious minds.

Saint Exupery, in his poetic, artful genius, knew that often the greatest truth is not attainable from the window accesses of the external. So glossolalia! One reaches a level of *knowing* that the eyes and ears and tongues, governed by the obvious, miss. It's not "tongues" that do this. It's the submission to the Great Creator God, which tongues represent that opens this invisible "past knowing" arena.[62]

THE HOLY SPIRIT PRAYS FOR US—UNDERSTANDING OUR WEAKNESS

In the same way, the Spirit helps us in our weakness. We do not know what we should pray, but the Spirit Himself intercedes for us with groans that words cannot express. And He who searches our hearts knows what the mind of the Spirit is, because the Spirit intercedes for the saints in accordance with God's will (Romans 8:26-27).

I have often referred to Gordon Fee as one of my best examples of "knowledge on fire" which became the by-word of my wish for the products of the seminary I was privileged to lead for nearly a decade. Fee is an exegete and textual critic par excellence, and also one who communicates with passion and effective intensity. Few have this enviable integration of intellectual and emotional strength. He taught for us at California Theological Seminary in the 1980s where I witnessed times during a lecture when the gift of prophecy was evident—not something necessarily in his notes! Against the majority of New Testament scholars, and some of his own brethren, he speaks to the thesis of this work about his conclusion that Paul is indeed speaking of praying in tongues in this Romans passage.

Giving fair shrift to all the critics, as is his style, I here will give highlights to show Fee's position about the special frequency/mode of tongues speech—in this case praying from the deep feelings of the heart—rather than from the mind of understanding. Excerpts follow from *God's Empowering Presence.*[63]

> ...our "not knowing what to pray for as we ought" first of all does not refer to our not knowing *how* to pray...Rather, these words imply that

> over and again in times of prayer...our lack of knowledge has to do with the larger picture, as it were, thus "*what* to pray." What is not implied is that we do not know how to intercede *for others*, hence the Spirit helps us make intercession on their behalf. To the contrary, the appeal is before God on *our* behalf, the Spirit's appealing to God for us because in our weakness we do not know how to pray in our own behalf.
>
> Much of the discussion about this language has taken place within the context of a Western culture in which the majority of people who, when praying privately, do so silently, without either speaking aloud or "mouthing words." It remains doubtful whether this was often the case in the ancient world. Praying was very much like reading, where even in private one read "aloud"...The casual evidence for this in the NT, of course, is Philip's "hearing" the Ethiopian eunuch as he is "reading" from Isaiah (Acts 8:30). So also with praying...Daniel prayed "aloud" when praying alone, but so does the parable of Jesus in Luke 18:9-14, as does Luke's narrative about Jesus' praying in 11:1 as well as the Synoptic narrative about his prayer in the Garden. In all of these cases the narrator assumes a culture where people prayed "aloud," that is, articulated for themselves as they prayed.
>
> The present sentences, in fact, correspond remarkably with what Paul elsewhere calls "praying with/in the Spirit" (1 Cor 14:14-15; Eph 6:18). These correspondences occur at two crucial points; (a) the Spirit is subject of the verb "interceding," that is, the Spirit himself is seen as praying from within us and (b) the persons involved do not understand what the Spirit is saying—or not saying, as the case may be...we have especially the description of his own prayer life in 1 Cor 14:14-15, that is of two kinds: praying with his mind and praying with his S/spirit. Although this text is too allusive for us to know for sure what "praying with his mind" meant, the context suggests that it does not mean "prayer without words," that is, inaudible, but basically *generated from within his own mind...*" praying in the Spirit" in that context can refer only to the praying in tongues about which he speaks in vv 2, 19, and 28—private, articulated but "inarticulate" with regard to his mind (that is, the Spirit prays and the mind itself is unfruitful in this case).[64]

Next Fee zeros in even closer to the issue of how speaking in tongues does not proceed by way of the mind, nor is the mind totally obviated in tongues speech (I Cor. 14).

> Even though there is still some mystery here—for all of us—several features about that second form of praying are noteworthy for our present purposes: (a) On the one hand, Paul himself distinguishes between the uninterpreted tongue in private prayer and that which is public and therefore needs interpretation (v. 19). (b) On the other hand, Paul indicates (14:14-15) that private "praying in tongues" requires no interpretation; rather, one's prayer is "by him/herself" and "to God" (vv. 2,28); thus in such praying "the mind" does not enter into the prayer as such (v. 13). (c) Such prayer is specifically said to be "by the Spirit" (v. 2); and in vv. 14-15 he says my S/spirit prays, "i.e., the Spirit prays in tongues through me." (d) In such prayer by the Spirit one *speaks "mysteries"* to God. (e) That such praying is "vocalized" almost goes without saying; how does one "speak" in a "tongue" and not do so "aloud"? And (f) even though such prayer does not proceed by way of the mind, Paul is nonetheless adamant that he will engage in it (vv. 14-15) and that those so praying are "edified" (v. 4)...Rather than seeing praying in the Spirit ("tongues speech if you will") as some sort of mindless activity, Paul sees it as a highly significant expression of prayer. In it the believer can take special encouragement even in the midst of recent exigencies (weaknesses, suffering, endurance), for the Spirit is praying in keeping with God's will and with "inarticulate groanings" that God himself will understand, since he knows the mind of the Spirit. One may not know how all this works out in practice, but Paul at least sees it as a powerful encouragement from the "firstfruits" of the Spirit.[65]

The Spirit as a Wall Breaker

When tongues are recognized as the chosen "sign" of God which distinguishes the recipient as a member of the new community of New Testament covenant to be the heralders of the Kingdom, it portends *the barriers God wants to break down*, in turn, to the walls of ethnocentricity which will be an impediment to the building of the Church. The old nation of Israel largely failed here. Even the Jewish apostles didn't want to abandon the old ways. It took the Romans to force them away from the "familiar" and "traditional" so they could plant the Church. God had to use Paul, a Jew but raised in Gentile Tarsus, to get the job done. Paul had the capacity the other Jewish apostles didn't for the **culture free** message of redemption so Jewish customs would not be made a part of the "good news." Perhaps only Paul could have done that as was needed in the Gentile world.

Four examples come quickly to mind that show the cross-cultural nature of the Holy Spirit—to help avoid insular thinking. For starters: Nazareth, Jerusalem, Caesarea, and Los Angeles:

1. In Luke 4 and the words of Jesus in the synagogue at Nazareth, his 'home town' (in quoting Isaiah 61):

"The Spirit of the Lord is upon me, because he has anointed me to preach good news to the poor. He has sent me to proclaim freedom for the prisoners and recovery of sight for the blind, to release the oppressed, to proclaim the year of the Lord's favor."

Jesus was announcing the very folk that local culture had marginalized was His target for blessing and deliverance.

2. In Jerusalem, after Jesus went back to the Father and sent the Comforter, He showed anyone with "ears to hear" the broad non-sectarian appeal of the new age of the Spirit. In at least 15 languages spoken to the expatriates attending the feast, they heard the "tongues" the apostles hadn't learned, but the strangers heard them magnify God in their mother tongue.

3. The apostle Peter was summoned in a vision to break from his xenophobic upbringing and travel to the hated city of Caesarea, to a "pagan Gentile" home and bring the gospel of Jesus to a large gathering in the home of a soldier. The convicting Spirit of God both saved and baptized in the Holy Spirit a receptive crowd of non-Jews. When the Jewish Christians in Jerusalem heard of this unthinkable event (to enter the house of a Gentile and even eat with them), Peter recounted that God indeed accepted this event because they spoke in tongues just like in the Jerusalem account (Acts 2).

4. Again, when the Spirit was poured out at Azusa Street in Los Angeles in 1906, the services for three years were multi-cultural (in an age when racial discrimination was "politically correct" in America). "The blood of Jesus has washed away the color barrier" was the expression for the breakdown of cultural racism. In the announcement of Jesus in the synagogue of Nazareth—*away the exclusivity of Judaism, and suppression of the poor*. In Caesarea, *erase the old 'unclean' titles so indelibly imprinted in Jewish minds.* At Azusa, *gone the parochial attitudes of denominationalism, racism and suppression of those who are "different."* Welcome, the ways of

> the Spirit creating an international, multi-ethnic, multi-cultural Church on earth that will reflect the image of the throng John the Revelator saw gathered around the throne of God.

Can glossolalia do THAT, you ask? In response: It was not the FACT of tongues, but the EFFECT of the surrender/submission necessary for the Spirit of God to break through **the threshold of a life in the Spirit when, if pursued, will bring the recipient to a posture pleasing to the design of the Spirit.** The word to be emphasized is **threshold.** Too many have only sought "tongues" for show or to be accepted in a circle of believers (like a union card). Failing to grow and "bear fruit, fruit that remains," they have never passed the threshold into the bounty of God's provision. Many Pentecostals have made this "distinctive" their "idol." Gordon Fee argues against putting too much emphasis on the sign. This to guard against those who do not really receive the gift of the Spirit but, nonetheless, because of pressure, speak in some sort of gibberish of their own doing.[66]

> **The word to be emphasized is *threshold.* Submitting to the "scandal" of tongues is a "positioning" before God which he uses in Missio Dei.**

An unnamed "sacramentalist" minister and professionally trained leader gives testimony after praying in "tongues":

> I have found that once received, the 'gift of tongues' is mine. I can speak in tongues at any time. I am in control of the gift and its steward so to speak... The tongue, however, by-passes my rational mind. I do not know what it says; I only know that it is primarily praising God, and for me any praise opens me more and more to God.[67]

The testimony of Episcopal priest Dennis Bennett:

> I realized what I was doing. It became clear, perfectly clear. I knew that God the Holy Spirit, whom I had never directly experienced in my life before, was putting these words on my lips. He was guiding, and I was letting Him. He was not taking over; I had to *let* the 'words' come and I could stop at any time. But I was letting God guide my voice, and these words were being formed in a language I had never heard, saying and expressing to God the Father, through Christ, all of the things that I had always wanted to say to God but had never been able to say. I had not known how to say them in my own language. Somehow this new language was more eloquent![68]

I repeat: Submitting to the "scandal" of speaking in tongues is a humble "positioning" before God making the available ingredient He uses in Missio Dei (God's intention to woo mankind to Himself). Too simple? Even if true, surely, this is but one small part of a much more comprehensive search for more enlightenment on the subject. This we know. That internal, personal witness to the individual is the same empowering boldness that turned the disciples of Jesus from cowering "fraidy cats" to dynamic witnesses who turned the world upside down. It's happening again as modern Pentecostals (in all their diversity, imperfections, weaknesses and even sometimes excesses) are doing today in the world. It's quite amazing to me that God is using the same kind of imperfect folks as He always has. I'd sure rather say the people of the Spirit are better, more intelligent, more pious, stronger, less carnal and all-around superior folk. Sorry. I've been in administration too long to make such a wishful claim. I can say those who have genuinely been "filled with the Spirit" bear more fruit of the Spirit and are much better folk than they used to be.

God has called thousands of missionaries (some very successful) who had never spoken in tongues, some who have been schooled against this New Testament charism. Others have submitted their lives to the ascension mandate without knowing of such availability of the Spirit's power. Pentecostals are indebted to so many of them for blazing the trail. This is especially true of those from America and Europe of the nineteenth century when initial great strides were made in missionary endeavor. But there is a new wave of missionaries from the old North Atlantic system, as well as from the 2/3rd World—from the churches raised up by the former, the latter far surpassing the "First World's" numbers.

In my sending body alone, there are now 2400 regular missionaries under appointment from the US churches. But from the overseas churches (that the USA church planted in the last 90 years) has come an army of over 8000, which are totally supported by their sponsoring countries as full-time missionaries. They are going across boarders to other countries and continents, many in places Americans and Europeans are not welcome. Another low estimate of 10,000 ministers are crossing cultural boundaries inside their own countries in an effort to evangelize "other kinds" of people. This missions endeavor is not paid for by the home churches or individuals in America. In Brazil, over 3500 new churches are planted each year in this movement. In Nigeria 500 new churches are planted annually by the National Church. This is duplicated on a smaller scale in at least 50 of the 204 countries where the US church has raised up a fraternally related church. There are less than five percent of expatriates in administrative positions in any of their organizations. Most have none.

MISSIOLOGICAL EVIDENCE

Does the element of glossolalia make a difference in the task of world evangelism? On Sunday, September 15, 2002, at Capitol Christian Center, Sacramento, California, the special speaker, Rev. David Brickner (a Jewish Christian and president of Jews for Jesus) recounted how the first Christians were Jews. "They were the first 'Jews for Jesus!'" These Jews at Jerusalem were confronted with a problem. Gentiles wanted to accept Jesus too! God had to give Peter three recurring visions of a sheet full of "unclean" animals to be eaten before he was willing to go to Ephesus in obedience to God's call. We read of this journey and revival among the Gentile household of the centurion Cornelius in Acts 10. When the Jews in Jerusalem heard Peter had gone into a Gentile house and eaten with them, plus that the Gentiles had received Jesus as Lord, they were apprehensive. They had to be convinced it was all right to have "Gentiles for Jesus"! Here Brickner made a gross omission in recounting the story because he skipped the vital element that allowed the apostle Peter to convince his brethren this was a work of God. Just like most Evangelicals today, he omitted the important element. When Peter stated that the Gentiles in Cornelius' house had accepted salvation *and spoke in tongues* (as the Spirit fell on them), only then did the Jerusalem Jewish Christians accept the validity of Peter's mission.

> *"For we heard them 'speak in tongues' and praising God . . . as He came on us at the beginning"* (Acts 10:46 and 11:15).

Let's ask the question: Would the Jews in Jerusalem, who had just seen thousands of mostly Jewish nationals join their ranks, have approved the conversion of the Gentiles in Ephesus if there had not been the testimony of the physical sign of tongues as proof of the genuine article to which Peter and his band could refer? I doubt it, for they were all choked up with the Jewish law and their own ethnicity. These new and foreign ones didn't keep the dietary law. They didn't keep the Sabbath, and probably not many of the other 612 major Jewish laws. So too, the Church through the ages, and not long after the time of the apostles and first patriarchs of the Church, found it easier to "legalize" the element of conversion. The role of prophetic ministry was all too dangerous. The Church turned to the "predictable" and the "safe" and that which they could control. Not this unruly Holy Spirit whose influence is too risky and whose influence can't be put into the bulletin! "Let's keep

Him safely locked up in the age and time of the biblical record. Keep Him safely in the Bible, not in our times and in our liturgical worship. He must be predictable. WE must be in control. This is a realm of POWER which the Church is willing to legitimize for the sake of 'decency and order.'"

THE SOCIOLOGICAL FACTOR

Wilson gives us some good copy about the intensity and abandonment necessary for the Spirit to 'speak' through us for empowerment. The Social Sciences have always been attracted by any emotion attached to prayer or the worship of God (just like the 'watchers' in Jerusalem at the Acts 2 event). He first rather debunks the social scientists' past attempts to find a specific social, ethnic, economic, class predisposition or motivation for those who became Pentecostal as does Killian McDonnell.[69]

> There were enough upwardly mobile or better-situated adherents among the Pentecostals to question deprivation or other social explanations as a primary reason for the members' inclusion. And the assumption that association with Pentecostals *ipso facto* points to an emotionally volatile or mystical personality type, for reasons discussed here, is also dubious. ...What does become the recurrent theme, the motif, of Pentecostalism is personal crisis. The use of tongues, as well as uninhibited emotional and physical displays, are best explained by disengagement from the prevailing rationality brought on by a need for existential confirmation. Prayer, at least at these climactic moments, was hardly perfunctory; taking rather the form of a consuming sigh, a sincere plea for confidence, wholeness and enlightenment, an audacious pursuit of the divine.[70]

COMMUNICATIONS INSIGHT

SUCH A PERSON using the prayer language of other tongues and praising God is surely at a loss for words to express his feelings and joyfully finds the Holy Spirit compensating for that deficiency. Glossolalia is an energizing by the Holy Spirit through the human instrument that does not depend on the intellectual process of "meaning making" using *encoding* and *decoding* so often spoken of in communications theory.

> J. Rodman Williams states: "Hence glossolalia was for Paul a vehicle of prayer. It was also spiritual prayer, not mental; thus praying in a tongue was utterance transcending the limits of human conceptualization."[71]

For mankind to really "worship in Spirit and in truth" (John 4:23) James Slay says human knowledge does not suffice. The apostles knew more about the Master than any who have lived before or since. They had knowledge but needed the "quickening and clothing" of the Spirit to best communicate that knowledge, a *communication not adulterated by human limitations.*[72] The question is not that Spirit-baptized folk are the only ones who can know something of the mind of Christ (that's obvious), but the question becomes—can one afford to MISS the closer link to the Holy Spirit's truth, His power and guidance by rejecting this "humiliating act of surrender" He has designed?

"Not adulterated by human limitations"—what a concept! I submit this is the "hoop" to jump through; the barrier of proof; the test God has so designed. So you think you are competent enough without the baptism of empowerment? Get over it! You need Him! If you *can* "get over it," He'll take your skills, your learning, your best natural gifts and make them into so much more than they would be with your own cunning and abilities. And even if you don't have any skills, He'll still use you in your incompetent state of weakness, in some appropriate way according to your faith and availability. (And that is what so many professionally trained theologians and clergy can't tolerate—"What audacity these bumpkins have to think they can replace us professionals!"—which was the major envy and judgment of the Pharisees concerning the disciples of Jesus.) In this sense, here is *The Foolishness of God*: Lose to win, humble yourself to be exalted. Serve to have influence. I believe God has to require a "humbling" choice to overcome man's natural tendency to need to rule and dominate. And this system of His is hardest on those who have the most to lose to be humbled! So what else is new about this God?

Slay again: "Why did the infilling of the Spirit elicit glossolalia in this public and spectacular manner? The answer is seen in the miracle's lasting effect on all who were filled and those who were willing to believe. Barton says:

> The ecstasy and "speaking in tongues" was to them ocular evidence that the days of Samuel, Elijah, and Elisha had returned. Joel's prophecy was now in process of fulfillment. Here was ocular and audible evidence that Jesus was the Messiah and the Messianic Age had actually begun.[73]

"When He comes in His fullness He gives vocal evidence. The human or natural man will surrender all before giving up the power of self-expression.

When this happens, it is evident that His presence prevails and predominates."[74]

A Remembered Scene

The scene: Lome, Togo, May, 2002. Pentecost Sunday with 1500 in attendance in the "chapel" of West Africa Advanced School of Theology, founded in 1970.[75]

While this great congregation sings in joy and rhythm "Gloire a Mon Seigneur," this thought came to me: Tongues is yet another cornerstone the builders have neglected/abandoned/rejected. It is not the building! It may be the least of the gifts on God's list (say the critics), but it is the symbol of the humility God seeks for those he would call to the paradox of Matthew 16:25. It is the foolish door God has chosen to give entrance into the Holy of Holies of the sumptuous feast of His love! It's the dangerous room of commitment and submission to the paradox of losing in order to obtain. It's as if He says: "Can you do this strange thing for me? Can you get foolish in the eyes of the world?" John 7:37-8: *"On the last and greatest day of the Feast, Jesus stood and said in a loud voice, 'If anyone is thirsty, let him come unto me and drink. Whoever believes in me, as the Scripture has said, streams of living water will flow from within him.' By this He meant the Spirit, whom those who believed in Him were later to receive."* When that stream flows, people are attracted, people are blessed, people come to God.

Tongues is yet another cornerstone the builders have neglected/abandoned/rejected. It is not the building… but it is the symbol of the humility God seeks…

Glossolalia Is Both a Shield and a Focus

From a Presbyterian revivalist nearly two centuries ago:

> When I am praying in my native tongue, however fixed my soul be on God, and Him alone, I am conscious of other thoughts and desires, *which the very words I use force in before me.* I am like a man holding straight forward to his home full in view, who, though he diverge neither to the right hand nor to the left, is ever solicited by many well-known objects on every hand of him. But the moment I am visited with the Spirit, and carried out to God in a tongue which I know not, it is as if a deep covering of snow had fallen on the country round, and I saw nothing but the object of my desire and the

> road which leadeth to it. I am more conscious than ever of the presence of God. He and He alone is in my soul. *I am filled with some form of the mind of God,* be it joy or grief, desire, love, pity, compassion or indignation; and I am made to utter it in words which are full of *power* over my spirit, but not being accessible to my understanding, my devotion is not interrupted by *association or suggestions from the visible or intellectual world:* I feel myself, as it were, shut in with God into His won pavilion, and hidden close from the invasions of the world, the devil, and the flesh. (Emphasis by Drummond)[76]

Edward Irving is so articulate in this paragraph. He speaks for my own soul.

COMMUNICATIONS INSIGHT

LIMITATIONS OF THE RATIONAL MIND

LUTHER SPEAKS to the limitations of the rational mind with the shocking and earthy expression: "Reason is the devil's whore." In discussing the advantage of the Eastern mind, specifically of the subcontinent of India and Sri Lanka, David Hesselgrave explains: "That which the west values so highly (and the reason we defend it so vehemently) is seen by East Indians as 'lower' or relative knowledge. Dogmas, creeds, philosophical systems and ceremonial rituals are but shadows and pointers to absolute truth."[77] If viewed as primary "higher" truth, as we do in the West, they are seducers of the mind. No doubt, it was to this point Luther slaps us awake with his poignant sentence in some almost inexplicable sense (for we Westerners are not used to speaking on this level), to allow the Holy Spirit to give utterance is when the pure mind "sees."

One should not wonder at the repeated attempts to explain this mystery of glossolalia from so many different angles. David Lim, a Chinese theologian from Singapore, relates to the word "sublimation" in this regard with thoughts from F.D. Bruner:

> The Spirit does not exhibit himself supremely in sublimating the ego, in emptying it, removing it, or in ecstasy overpowering it, extinguishing or thrilling it, but in intelligently, intelligibly, christocentrically using it.[78]

David Lim agrees with this non-Pentecostal only in some ways, but sees his point as valid. Others attempting to understand the internal mechanics of glossolalia feel the word "sublimation" useful. But Lim adds his insight from the Eastern perspective:

> The mind is not blanked out and put into neutral, as may be the case in some Eastern religions. That being so, the mind should not be wandering around in the world of politics, sports, and schedules when worshipping God. True worship requires the mind, as well as the spirit and the body...One should at least sense whether one is praising God for His greatness, love, care, or holiness.[79]

COMMUNICATIONS INSIGHT

THIS FOR David Lim is part of his expression, noted elsewhere, that the operation of all the gifts, including tongues, is an *incarnational* joint exercise between man and the Spirit of God. This view is **complimentary**, not mutually exclusive. That is, while the cognitive speech mechanism, that which in its complexity is uniquely human, is surrendered as to forming the syllables of understandable speech, the mind is not in neutral or totally passive as if in a trance. But rather, in partnership with the Spirit of God as He gives utterance, using the lungs, larynx, mouth, teeth and tongue used in normal cerebral originated speech of the participant/worshiper.[80]

SHOCKING DISCOVERY (FOR ME!)

In this study and writing project, working now with many hundreds of sources and the years involved striving to be cogent and relevant (I'm a slow writer), I had first exhilarating joy, then disappointment, to discover that some of the first thinkers and writers about the "new" Pentecostal revival at the turn of the last century were also struggling with how to give an adequate answer to the question of WHY TONGUES? One of them had a better explanation than I was striving to give, and it was written 85 years ago! My joy in substantiation; my sadness that I was a "Johnny-come- lately!" Listen to this! It is so powerful. It is so *good* that I have given up any prideful temptation to think I might have a *new* idea to bring to the Movement for which I am so grateful. (And J. R. Flower wasn't even a Communicologist—nor had the word been coined!)

> **From J. R. Flower over 80 years ago:** (I present it in bold type to give it its due.)

The question of the speaking in tongues as the sign of the baptism in the Holy Spirit is quite vital...The very life of the Pentecostal Movement hinges on this point. We have gone deeply into the subject. No immature conclusions were reached. Men and women of the most careful, conscientious deliberative nature, who have been in the old view that sanctification and the baptism in the Holy Spirit were equivalent, have examined the evidence on both sides of the subject and have been compelled to agree by the evidence before them that the speaking in tongues as the Spirit gives utterance is the one sign of the baptism in the Holy Spirit having been received.

Flower continues:

There is one point in favor of this view that is incontrovertible. What is the meaning of the word 'baptism'? By referring to the text in Acts 2 it is found that it means a filling, a submergence, an inundating, an overflowing. It was not merely an impartation of gifts, but the taking possession of the faculties of the human being so that every function of the body was under divine control. There is one faculty of our being which it is very difficult to bring into subjection and that is the mind. The baptism in the Holy Ghost must include the mind as well as the body in order for it to be a 'baptism.' What proof have we that the mind is under the control of the Holy Spirit? Would miracles or healings prove it? Would discernment prove it? Would faith, or knowledge or wisdom prove it? No! For any one of these signs might be manifested and the one performing the sign could have his own mind under perfect control. But we have a tongue which is in very close relationship to the mind. It is quite difficult to yield over the control of this member to another influence, and a careful observance of those seeking and receiving the baptism in the Spirit will demonstrate this. It is the last human member to be brought under control. When it is finally yielded and overwhelmed with the Holy

> **...there may be a question about prophecy as to whether or not the mind was laying passive under the operation of the Spirit. With the speaking in tongues there is no such question.**
> **–J.R.Flower**

> **Ghost, the inevitable result is speaking in tongues as the Spirit gives utterance, where the mind can lie passive and listen and wonder as another force apart from itself uses and manipulates the tongue. Then and then only can be demonstrated that the entire being has been under control of the Holy Spirit. Can you find any other test that is as severe as this? But you say, 'would not prophecy be a similar test of the subjection of the mind?' Yes, the test is similar, but far inferior. In Acts 19:6 they spoke in tongues first and then prophesied. There is no mistake regarding the speaking in other tongues, but there may be a question about prophecy, as to whether or not it is real prophecy or the individual speaking out of his own heart while the blessing of the Lord is on him. The Spirit's presence would be manifested in the energizing of the individual, but there might be a question as to whether or not the mind of the one exercised was lying passive under the operation of the Spirit. With the speaking in tongues there is no such question.**[81]

I wish to amplify the importance of the inspired writing of J. R. Flower, written only a few years after vital meetings of all credentialed ministers (men and women) in the fledgling Pentecostal Movements wrestled with the question of tongues. Consider the words of the apostle Paul in I Corinthians 2:11-12.

> *"For who among men knows the thoughts of a man except the man's spirit within him? In the same way no one knows the thoughts of God except the Spirit of God. We have not received the spirit of the world but the Spirit who is from God, that we may understand what God has freely given us."*

Flower said above that no other test proves a person is under the control of the Holy Spirit (including the hardest member of the body to tame—the tongue) than the test of glossolalia. Prophecy, as a coveted gift of the Spirit—the one preferred for public expression—is far inferior as a test of whether or not the whole person is "lying passive under the Spirit's control." Flower says, correctly in my opinion, the reason for this is that one may speak in prophecy out of his own heart while the blessing of the Lord is on him or her. I'd add, *the person him/herself may even question if what was just uttered in prophecy was not partly or in whole from his/her own intellect.* But when speaking in tongues, the speaker knows **for sure—no doubt** that he/she didn't manufacture those words. See above in the Scripture quoted: "who knows the thoughts of a man except the man's spirit (mind) within him"? Here the source of edification that springs from the realization that God the Holy Spirit is using the individual to bring boldness and courage that will lead that person to be a stronger witness and RISK where no action would have otherwise been ventured. This is: "...that we may understand what God has freely given us." Speaking in tongues, at this exact juncture, gives strength because we understand what was given was from God. This is like the inner witness of Romans 8:16: *"The Spirit Himself testifies with our spirit that we are God's children."*

A Filter of Exclusion

The ancient popular hymn The Old Rugged Cross has the words "To the old rugged cross I will ever be true, Its shame and reproach gladly bear."[82] Gordon Fee says it is idolatry to make a system of salvation that omits God's plan of the cross just because we find it inconvenient.[83] We can't have salvation OR the Holy Spirit's power "on our terms."

> All who are stirred up to seek the baptism in the Holy Ghost should know that the path of the Pentecostal life is identical with the way of the Cross...for the life of one who has really received the Spirit's baptism is inseparably connected with the shame and the reproach of the Cross.[84]

Another contemporary scholar who agrees with Gordon Fee on the relation of glossolalia to the cross, is M. Duggan[85] who, however, chastises Pentecostals for conceiving the power of the Spirit in triumphalistic domination of the natural order rather than as Paul, who saw it in Christological terms and as strength through weakness related to the cross of Christ. This is no doubt well taken for those among us who perhaps from a defensive posture of repression go too far in self-justification. On the other hand, what's a person to do who speaks in tongues? Change the message to suit a more rational explanation? Take away the stigma and marginalization by others and be "real" clergy or member of a "high-class prestigious church" and never share this blessed reality with anyone for fear of being misunderstood? I say no. But I agree that many who find it hard to forgive those who called us demon possessed should be more irenic in nature, forgiving those who have in the past and still do marginalize Pentecostals and Charismatics.

DANGER—THIS STRETCH OF ROAD HAS SEEN MANY ACCIDENTS

(I saw such a road sign while driving through a narrow winding road in Pennsylvania.)

Most contemporary Pentecostal Movements which were started in North America in the early 1900s are facing pressure from the younger, better educated scholars to modify this "foolishness." Some of the criticism from the ranks is well placed if it questions the "idol" tongues can become. I speak of a misplaced overemphasis on the external sign to the weakening of its central essence. But too often these internal pressures coincide with older ministers and laypersons who were once part of a quite powerless, small, despised group of believers (in the earlier years) who are now sitting on a new plateau of upward mobility in economic and social status—AND younger equally affluent well educated believers under the influence of seminaries and clergy who love their positions of influence and social respect in society (by itself not an undesirable attribute but where the price of accepting God's "foolishness" is too great). Be warned! Some of the reformers of Martin Luther's vintage made that mistake concerning *all* the supernatural gifts of the Spirit. And not just about the power of the unpredictable, surprising, unorthodox ways of the Spirit of God—but to the very bedrock of salvation through the demands of repentance and forgiveness the cross of Christ requires. What God did in Christ crucified and in the New Testament model of the baptism in the Holy Spirit is in direct contradiction to the natural, secular man's conception of wisdom, rationality, and power. May we not tamper with the concept of loss and submission to human pride; this is the price of God's plan lest we risk our demise as a witnessing community. Church history is filled with examples of this carnal evolution—man's demand on God to accommodate man's wisdom and need for selfish power. Let me argue for a better way—an irrational, paradoxical way of sweet surrender that brings precious quiet strength to make war on the enemy and the up-building confirming strength to the participant. Surrender of self in the spirit of the cross is a real price! God comes close when complete surrender is present. This is the penetrating consciousness of tongues as a "God Thing." Who can understand it but one who has tasted it? Serious inquirer: Is the Spirit stirring your soul and mind to seek the giver of this New Testament approved gift? Oh, let Him sweep in with His unfathomable love!

FIVE VIEWS ON THE THESIS FROM OTHERS

I. First, Larry Christenson:

> Webster lists two basic meanings for the word 'language'...When we look at the second definition...we find a highly accurate definition of speaking in tongues. It defines language in terms of the speaker: *Language is an expression of meaning in terms of feeling or thought.* If

speaking in tongues expresses the meaning of the speaker, then it is a language, according to this accepted definition...A semanticist told a friend of mine, 'No sound is without meaning.' A sigh has meaning. A grunt has meaning...In *The Healing Gifts of the Spirit,* Agnes Sanford takes it a step further; she quotes a psychiatrist who said, 'It can be a spiritual power entering into a person with such force that it reaches and touches something in the deep unconscious; whereupon the person speaks a language which the conscious mind does not know, but which this deep area of the unconscious does know.' Paul Tournier suggests much the same thing in his book, *The Meaning of Persons:* 'Glossolalia, or speaking in tongues, which played such an important part then, and which is still found in some modern communities, appears to answer the need of the Spirit to *express the inexpressible,* to carry the dialogue with God beyond the narrow limits of clearly intelligible language.'"[86]

II. Another contemporary scholar French Arrington, on the SYMBOL OF THE SPIRIT'S COMPLETE CONTROL OF THE BELIEVER

The wild, untamable nature of the human tongue is vividly portrayed by James in the third chapter (James 3:7, 8). James also tells us that the tongue is a valuable indicator of the quality of a man's religion; for let a man seem ever so religious, yet if he bridleth not his tongue, his religion is vain (James 1:26 KJV). Whereas, the control of the tongue by means of true religion, manifests mastery over man's entire nature: "In many things we offend all. If any man offend not in word, the same is a perfect man, and able also to bridle the whole body" (James 3:2 KJV). Not only is the tongue the last thing to yield to man's dominion, but it is also the last thing to yield to the Holy Spirit. Hence it is an accurate recorder of the extent to which the believer has submitted to the control of the Spirit. At the very entrance of the Spirit-filled life, then, the believer is given a remarkable illustration of the submission of his tongue, a submission which is to characterize that whole life.[87]

III.

COMMUNICATIONS INSIGHT

CHRISTENSON ON this topic of bypassing the limitations of the intellect:

What blessing can it be to pray when you have no idea what you are praying about? Actually, this is one of its greatest blessings—the fact that it is not subject to the limitations of your human intellect. The human mind, wonderful as it is from the hand of the Creator, has limited knowledge, limited linguistic ability, limited understanding, and furthermore is inhibited with all manner of prejudice, little and large. Speaking in tongues is a God-appointed manner of praying which can bypass the limitations of the intellect. One may picture the difference something like this: A prayer with the mind comes upward from the heart, and must then pass through a maize of linguistic, theological, rational, emotional, and personal checkpoints before it is released upward. By the time it 'gets out,' it may be little more than a slender trickle. An utterance in tongues comes upward from the depths, but instead of being channeled through the mind, it bypasses the mind and flows, directly to God in a stream of Spirit-prompted prayer, praise and thanksgiving.[88]

IV. John Bertone:

The result of this phenomenon of glossolalia is not benefit received through intelligible speech, which requires human rationality and reasoning (1 Cor. 14:14). Therefore, it must be the experience of the Spirit connecting with the human spirit, where the individual senses emotional alignment between himself or herself and the Spirit in communication with God. In our present age cognitive learning takes precedence over the nurturing of the emotive side of the human personality. Fostering and expressing emotions is part of healthy human experience, however, especially when it finds impetus from alignment with the Spirit of God in the experience of speaking in other tongues. Even though it is unintelligible speech, the benefits of this contact with the Spirit communing with God brings edification to the speaker.[89]

V. Dave Robertson on "Divine Transfer"

Robertson speaks of a "divine transfer" that enables us as individuals in the Body of Christ to pray in tongues. If this "transfer" (s/Spirit) never took place, it would be the Holy Spirit alone praying, without the individual's participation. But with this transfer it is ... "literally our human spirit praying as the Holy Spirit creates the prayer."[90] This incarnational nature can perhaps be best explained by Romans 8:26-27: *"In the same way, the Spirit helps us in our weakness. We do not know what we ought to pray for, but the Spirit Himself intercedes for us with groans that words cannot express. And He who searches our hearts knows the mind of the Spirit, because the Spirit intercedes for the saints in accordance with God's will."*

TONGUES AND AMBIGUITY

Playing by heart—not the sum of perfect parts.

We understand the term "playing by heart" in gospel music as the difference between the skill of "playing from memory extemporarily and from performing by reading the musical score with notes." The latter doesn't allow improvisation. We see the two systems as quite different. Pentecostal music is often criticized as being unsophisticated, and it is true if you were to compare Pentecostal worship services with a liturgical worship service where what is expected is classical music of the golden age of the Middle Ages.

In the article "Playing by Heart," taken from the *New York Times* magazine, Paul Irvin tells how he makes harpsichords for a living and that he is a martial arts specialist. Surprisingly, he links what he has learned in Tai Kwon Do to how to make the best harpsichords. Listen to him.

> In Tai Kwon Do I came to absorb one of its underlying principles: understand the larger perspective and all the details will fall into place. At the upper levels of Tai Kwon Do, a person can take on several attackers at once because he has learned to react to the bigger picture, not to its individual parts. If he were to take the time to contemplate the perfection of his punch or the intentions of his opponent he would be mincemeat.
>
> It struck me that the method I had been using to design my instruments was somewhat artificial, that harpsichords were not meant to follow such strict formulas. I decided to rely on my gut, to make decisions as I made them. Rather than obsess over tiny fractions of an inch I began to place my faith in what looked right, to trust my years of playing. From the first note I played, on harpsichord number 26, it sang in a way that none of my previous instruments ever had. The sound was warm and free and alive, a work of art more than just the sum of perfect parts.[91]

All of this is related to a tolerance for ambiguity. When we speak in tongues, we don't know what we are saying as described before. When I speak my mother tongue or any learned language subsequent to my mother tongue, I am using the amazing facility of speech and the precise exact operation of its intricacy under my total control. This process is exacting—like playing a perfect, precise, and predictable harpsichord with no tolerance for error. When I submit myself to the Holy Spirit, being clothed in the Spirit, I am launching myself into the space or "free fall"—like jumping off a cliff. Somehow God approves and appreciates this because I have given Him control of humanity's most precious gift—speech. I am not speaking uniquely from my brain, but I am speaking from my visceral regions. (Jesus said, *"From your innermost beings will flow rivers of living water."*) As Paul Irvin has learned, his best harpsichords (there is a two- or three-year wait to buy one) come from a system of seeing the bigger perspective and the ambiguity of abandoning the precision of his first harpsichords, the broader perspective of making them from his gut is what gives warmth and freedom and life to his instrument.

In like manner the Pentecostal, from a perspective almost indescribable, has learned he can tune the instrument of his soul to a mode of communication the Apostle Paul describes by saying, *"He that speaks in an unknown tongue edifieth himself"* (1 Cor. 14:30).

Jesus refers to the Spirit of God in a very ambiguous way in John 3:8. He upbraids Nicodemus for being a spiritual leader in Israel and not understanding how mysterious and "un-programmable" the Spirit of God is. He used the wind as an analogy to show that God's actions are mysterious and free. Should we wonder why God chose this mysterious, non-rational way for a symbol of His very nature? This is so much like Him! In this vein, Frank Macchia says (while quoting Buber, Ellul, Kasemann and White), that glossolalia is an unclassifiable, free speech in response to an unclassifiable, free God; it is the language of the *imago Dei.*

> Language as rational communication cannot follow one into the depths of the encounter between the mystery of God and the mystery of the self before God. Nor is language adequate in expressing the depths of our encounter with God to others. This insight relates to the role of the theophanic imagery in describing our encounter with the divine...Helen White said of the poet, "He is from the beginning haunted by the paradox that, while he cannot resist the urge to expression, what he has to say is ultimately beyond expression."[92]

Macchia helps us to see deeper by comparing glossolalia to an art form as an expression in relation to the inexpressible. To this he goes to Abraham Heschel who states about prayer:

In no other act does humanity experience so often the disparity between the desire for expression and the means of expression.[93]

Macchia continues:

The closer one draws to the divine mystery, the more urgent it becomes to express oneself and, concomitantly, the less able one is to find adequate expression. This is the crisis out of which tongues breaks forth. Any attempt rationally to communicate the experience ends it, for to reflect upon and rationally communicate an experience is to distance oneself from it already. Tongues is a way of expressing the experience without ending it. This does not mean that rational and literate theology and worship is thereby made insignificant...As Heschel has pointed out, an abandonment of the language game in our encounter with God does not imply unfaithfulness to the mind, for the struggle to express the inexpressible is at the root of all creativity in art and scholarship; "for the world of the unutterable meanings is the nursery of the soul, and the cradle of all our ideas."[94]

COMMUNICATIONS INSIGHT

THE BURDEN OF THE INEXPRESSIBLE

"I BELIEVE THAT THE inner significance of speaking in tongues or praying in the Spirit can be found in something virtually every spiritual tradition in human history teaches in one way or another: that the reality religious symbols strive to express ultimately defies even the most exalted human language. Virtually all the mystics of every faith have indicated that the vision they have glimpsed, though they try desperately to describe it, finally eludes them. As The Preacher in the biblical book of Ecclesiastes puts it:

All words wear themselves out; a man cannot utter it;
the eye is not satisfied with seeing, nor the ear with hearing.

Confronted with this verbal paralysis, what can people do? They sing, they rhapsodize, they invent Metaphors; they soar into canticles and doxologies. But ultimately, words fail them and they lapse into silence. Or they speak in tongues."[95]

Macchia's expression, "*...for to reflect upon and rationally communicate an experience is to distance oneself from it already*" ... forces me to add some Mossi wisdom on this truth by the little proverb:

"*Wiougou manegeda doogo ne a nore n youlen samda ne a zoure.*"

There is a three-foot long lizard who lives in the riverbank. To make its nest to lay eggs, it will spend hours *smoothing the entrance to this den with its long snout, then goes in and spoils it with its tail* (the translation of the above proverb). Speaking to God in tongues obviates the inadequacies of learned and planned language expression. Macchia's quote of Heschel above bears repetition.

...for the struggle to express the inexpressible is at the root of all creativity in art and scholarship. Again, I wish I'd said that! How better to declare the deep longing in humankind, for those who search for God with total abandon. In reading many of the testimonies of early believers who broke forth in glossolalia and paid a high price for acknowledging it, many of them speak of a life-threatening, groaning, and rushing toward God until the wave of love and blessing and sense of acceptance flooded their souls. Speaking in tongues was not the goal; it was the consequence of this longing *to express the inexpressible.* For the accountant mentality, the mathematician's world, the physicist type, all who deal in exact quantums compared to the artist or poet—of course, it is ambiguous, equivocal, and maddening!

Any attempt rationally to communicate the experience ends it...Tongues is a way of expressing the experience without ending it.
–Macchia

Once experienced, it's a realm of *being* that is felt better than described. But I'm trying! Some would say, yes—very trying! Others might take hope in their search and let the Holy Spirit "own" them.

How different we are as a group of Homo Sapiens. How opposite some of us are from each other. Some go to the Louvre in Paris and look endlessly for the Coke machine. Others run out of time just looking at one or two magnificent paintings or sculptures. (I don't intend to deprecate either of these opposites.) Victor Turner and Edward Bruner's edited volume, *The Anthropology of Experience*[96] speak of experience as not just sense data, cognition, or products of reason, but also feelings and expectations. From this perspective lived experience, as thought and desire, as word and image, is the primary reality. Ronald Bueno illustrates this truth "as one of the secrets of why the experience of 'tongues' is seldom transcient but generally enduring" –often sought to be repeated and reexperienced, so as to repeat the awe and sense of mystery! Bueno describes it as intimate—visceral—and not cerebral! But neither must it be sought or perceived as magical, as in the sense of magic being an ethereal power dependent on a formula or source other than Jehovah God. It is probably HERE the Early Church, and the later reformers, so often erred.

The person who has not **submitted** his intellectual faculty to be able to experience this gift of 'edification' (1 Cor. 14:4—personal prayer language) would, only naturally, be apt to confuse this mystery with the rational mind and thus falsely categorize it as magic, or even worse.[97] So the mathematician-type criticizes "emotionalism/fanaticism" and the artist-type accuses the technocrat of "insensitivity and esthetic blindness."

DOES GOD KNOW ABOUT PUBLIC RELATIONS?

John York quotes Don Richardson's *Eternity In Their Hearts* when he speaks of the day of Pentecost in Acts 2. This signaled the worldwide expansion of the gospel witness that followed the initial outpouring of the Holy Spirit on the disciples and the rest of the 120 persons in attendance. Don Richardson analyzes the significance of the miracle of Pentecost as follows:

> But wait—regarding that bestowal of the Holy Spirit's power—suppose God had hired you as a public relations expert to plan the event for Him! Suppose He had given you just one specification—it must happen in a manner which will make absolutely clear to even the dullest disciple that the power about to be bestowed is not merely for the personal blessing or exaltation of the recipients, but rather to enable them to take the gospel across the world to all peoples.
>
> Even if you were the most ingenious public relations consultant of all time, you probably would not have fantasized a clearer way to get that point across than the following...
>
> The power of the Holy Spirit coming upon the apostles and other faithful followers of Jesus caused them to speak miraculously in the many Gentile languages represented by the throng of diaspora Jews and Gentile converts then gathered in Jerusalem. Why? Seen in the context of Jesus' ministry and His clearly articulated plans for the whole world, the bestowal of that miraculous outburst of Gentile languages could have only one main purpose: to make crystal clear that the Holy Spirit's power was and is bestowed with the specific goal of the evangelization of all peoples in view.[98]

York continues:

> If, as Richardson suggests, Pentecostal tongues provided a significant object lesson for the Early Church, perhaps there may be a correlation between the practice of speaking in tongues and the growth of churches among modern Pentecostals. In any case, Pentecostal

> churches are notable for emphasizing the Spirit's empowerment of all believers so that they may bring in the last-day harvest.[99]

I do not wish to suggest the passage above from Richardson signals his endorsement or practice of private or public tongues. I don't personally know his position here. We are all aware of the many fine Evangelical missionaries who, when confronted with the enemy's power of which the apostle Paul spoke (Ephesians 6:12), have sought the New Testament endowment of power to combat these forces of which they learned little in seminary. Many of them have talked to me privately while overseas, rejoicing in this newfound dimension to witness. Some have asked that this not be expressed to their constituencies at home, because of the political realities and the stance some mission boards have taken on the issue of tongues. I rejoice with them and accept their request of silence. York notes about this issue of sensitivity to the tongues question:

> Many have argued that changed lives are the best recommendation to Christianity to a watching non-Christian world. In the same way, Spirit-empowered Christian witness may be the best recommendation of Pentecostal experience to watching Christians of non-Pentecostal tradition...Joel's prophesied Pentecostal experience has resulted in churches that win the lost in country after country around the world.[100]

COMMUNICATIONS INSIGHT

SHATTERING THE COGNITIVE PACKAGING

"AS A THEOLOGIAN I had grown accustomed to studying religious movements by reading what their theologians wrote and trying to grasp their central ideas and most salient doctrines. But I soon found out that with Pentecostalism this approach does not help much. As one Pentecostal scholar puts it, in his faith 'the experience of God has absolute primacy over dogma and doctrine.' Therefore the only theology that can give an account of this experience, he says, 'is a narrative theology whose central expression is the testimony.' I think that he is right, and it may well be that the reason for the kind of magical realism imbuing many Pentecostal testimonies is the same one that pushes people toward dancing and jumping and praising in strange tongues: the experience is so total it shatters the cognitive packaging."[101]

South Asian View

Satyavrata cites some of the reasons Pentecostalism has currency in South Asia and speaks of an experience-focused spirituality.[102]

"A personal experience of the Spirit is undeniably the central focus of Pentecostal spirituality." This is an integral part of South Asian Pentecostalism and, in fact, resonates deeply with the dominant religious tradition in the region in which an authentic experience of the divine is at the heart of religion and must be the mark of any true spirituality. Satyavrata also speaks of 'expressive worship' that affirms the 'Asian-ness' of his countrymen with their emphasis on concert prayer, exercise of spiritual gifts, signs and wonders and acceptance, in general, of the supernatural. About this issue, he quotes Spittler.[103] "They also need to demonstrate with their fellow Pentecostals throughout the world, that biblical truth must be released from its intellectual captivity and certified in practical experience."

COMMUNICATIONS INSIGHT

GLOSSOLALIA IS NOT ECSTATIC SPEECH

LET'S LOOK at Spittler's phrase, *"Released from its intellectual captivity."*

It's vital here to make a clear point of distinction, as exact as possible, of my intention and understanding about the extent to which the mind is and is not "unfruitful." Speaking in tongues, from this communicologist's stance, is not an ecstatic state of subconsciousness, nor a trance, nor an involuntary suspension of the function of the mind as is commonly understood by animistic peoples who most often are drug induced when in a trance-like state. Speaking in tongues is not something that happens to the speaker. It is a conscious yielding of one's speech apparatus, relating to the choosing of words (encoding) from one's perceptual field of words/thoughts stored in the data bank of memory. In this sense speech is *released from its intellectual captivity*. Pentecostals/Charismatics who call "tongues" ecstatic speech have probably never done ethnographic studies in the field, like a cultural anthropologist who has come in contact with folk religion practices, thus not understanding the cultural anthropological significance of that term. (For more on **"what tongues speech is not,"** see Appendix 1. Also, continued below.)

But glossolalia **is** speaking a "prayer language" that the Bible describes "as the Spirit gives utterance." In that sense alone the mind is "unfruitful." The mind does not *decide* what words to use or what thought to convey *for another person's cognition* when "speaking in tongues." The mind **is** fruitful during "tongues speaking" as to the overall intention of the soul. For example, suppose an individual is burdened about the health of his sick child. He prays in earnest for the child (in a mother tongue or another learned language), and while praying he is inspired to pray in tongues while thinking about the needs of the fevered child. At this juncture, his mind is "unfruitful" about the process of word choice (selecting and sorting from his word data bank in the composition of his prayer), but the mind is still active about the overall subject of his intention, the sick child. It's unfortunate even some Pentecostals and Charismatics use the word "ecstatic utterance" to describe tongues. That phrase is often used by anthropologists to describe the incantations of a shaman from an animistic society who falls under a trance during a folk-religious ritual. **This is not the same thing**. Yet they both have the similarity that the language used may not be understood by an observer. (The enemies of Pentecost like to use that small similarity to lump them together as being demonically influenced.) However, like the old saying in logic class: *All cows have four legs but not all animals with four legs are cows.*

Now, in the above sense of "being released from intellectual captivity": When we exercise our speech skills in a known/learned language, we are the rulers, the governors of what is expressed. (Communications Theory teaches us, however, that we do not control what the hearer perceives!) This is true even when we wish we could express ourselves better or more perfectly. We make our words "captive" to our wills and intentions by the very act of speaking. The person praying about the sick child has learned he can be "edified" (I Cor. 14:2) by "speaking mysteries with his spirit" (14:4) and believes (because of Rom. 8:26-27) that in spite of the ambiguity of not knowing what the words mean, can **better** express his/her true heart's desire, even though the mind is "unfruitful" about the words themselves. Let's continue farther on this theme.

A FRESH LOOK FROM ASIA (AND AN "A-HA" EXPERIENCE FOR THE AUTHOR)

Subordination of the Mind and the Incarnational Principle

In a recent well-received book by a Chinese scholar and pastor in Singapore, David Lim,[104] four basic views of Spiritual Gifts/Charismata are cited. I list them to give context to the fourth view: **God's** Incarnational **Plan.**

1. The gifts are no longer needed because we have a completed Bible (typical cessationist view).
2. The gifts are optional, and some are more important than others. A wide variety of beliefs in this category—all the way from seeing the baptism in the Holy Spirit as legitimate but not for everyone, to regarding "tongues" as only inspired of the devil. Still others, that tongues are the "least" of the gifts and one should seek the "better gifts."
3. The baptism in the Holy Spirit is a badge of holiness. *This is the most dangerous*, as Lim explains, because it led to the "sacerdotalism" of the second century Church and this author believes has led many of the Evangelicals of our day to reject the whole Pentecostal/Charismatic movement. Briefly, this stance makes experience an authority as valid as scripture itself. It still exists in some Pentecostal churches today, with much the same disastrous results. Then, it led to the sanction by the ecclesiastical body of the hierarchy declaring the belief as heretical. Gifts disappeared under the strong excommunication of the young Church. If one believes that gifts equal holiness, then those who possess them have great power to see demons in others, to direct their lives, to have visions and dreams on behalf of others' lives. "The less spiritual stand in awe at the overwhelming demonstrations of gifts manifested by them."[105] CAN ANYONE WONDER WHY 1 CORINTHIANS 13 STANDS POSITIONED FRONT AND CENTER, in the middle of this potentially powerful issue? Lim quotes Donald Gee:

   > A view of the gifts of the Spirit contained in a slogan that they are "a hundred percent miraculous" has obtained considerable acceptance in some quarters. We are told that "there is no element of the natural in them at all." This is the pardonable language of enthusiasm for enforcing the truth that a supernatural element in spiritual gifts does exist, and we can respect the statement as such. But it will not do as a statement covering all the facts. We need a more balanced view. If we do not achieve it, we shall perpetuate the extremes that have marred the Pentecostal testimony from its beginnings. Indeed, in that way lies considerable danger.[106]

4. The fourth position appears to be the biblical one: **The Incarnational Nature of the Gifts.** *My personal note is that Lim's*

input, for me, IS ONE OF THE GREATEST "GESTALT" events in my research. (*Reading Lim's words suddenly brought together in clear form the way to say what my subconscious has been working on for months in relation to this book.)* This view allows each believer to be led by the Spirit and walk in the Spirit. It's a collective way of allowing decision making to be a humble task for the individual with the safety of the whole body of believers rather than to any one person alone. Here are some of its other biblical elements:

A. When Paul allows the churches he is establishing across Asia to **participate** in their own discipline problems (like Corinth), he was *suborning knowledge to love.*[107] Here, in my opinion, is one of the most dynamic, yet little understood missiological principles ever written: Allen states for everyone to plainly see, but SADLY, with little acceptance because its principles are too costly for the power hungry. The same balance, God's part—Man's part, He used in the composition of the scriptures and in His Son's incarnation, is the same formula for proper use and control of the gifts of the Spirit!

> **Lim's input for me is one of the greatest "Gestalt" events in my research.**

B. When God chose Jesus to come and be ALL God and ALL man (an idea the First Church struggled with for 600 years ending, among other things, in the concept of the Filioque), he was demonstrating this concept: "God so loved—that He gave..." He might have used an angel or a creature from another planet with no human component. But no, he chose to RISK the weak, failing, imperfect shell of man. He chose this less-than-perfect medium to engage man's **participation** as his instrumentation. Amazing. This is too much for most of us historically. It forces us to live in this risky balance. We want it neater than that—so we legislate it to a controllable entity. Of course, when we do that, we kill it. The historical, traditional Church always has. Many Pentecostal churches, begun almost 100 years ago, are facing the same choice. There is and always will be a stigma connected to the role of the Holy Spirit and human partnership with Him. **It has been so divinely designed.**

C. The establishment of the Canon of Scripture involved this principle. He used man. God didn't write it in His handwriting in heaven and drop it down in perfect form (either like the Book of Mormon or the Koran purport), but he RISKED the weakness of mankind to give us this precious treasure, both a divine book and of human instrumentation. Men wrote it with their own vocabularies, their own personalities, employing culturally-influenced use of speech inside the historical moment of their lives.

D. Speaking in tongues (*personal mode*—devotional—edification of the speaker, or for the edification of the body—*public mode*) is a constant reminder of this **incarnational model.** His part—our part. He says: go ahead, **participate. You are part of the message.** Struggle with that—find the balance. Do it, but let the others judge. Find the right timing, the correct attitude/spirit in which to participate, let all be done with the rule of love and in decency and order. "Don't quench the Spirit"(I Thess. 5:19). "Don't forbid to speak in tongues" (I Cor. 14:39). Can you stand that scrutiny? Can you grow up enough, be mature enough to accept the loving judgment of the Body? You don't like that? Get over it! If you can't, you'll be doomed either to put out the fire and restrict all gifts of the Spirit, or go into fanaticism by your lack of submission to the mature control by the Body of Christ.

Can you stand the scrutiny? Can you grow up enough, be mature enough to accept the loving judgment of the Body? You don't like that? Get over it!

But think of the empowering inner testimony of individuals who, using their prayer languages, **know** it's real, **know** God sees where they are and that He wants to use them; He loves them; He's leading them. That's powerful! Lim says it is illustrative of Col. 1:27: *"Christ in you, the hope of glory."* [108]

The Church has always struggled with this ambiguous, risky, less-than-predictable, less-than-cleanly-controllable concept. We think we need to improve on God! He's foolish, you know! If God would only let us run His church, we'd do it better. The fact is, God does let us run His church and we'd do a better job of it if we'd learn the incarnational secret of this powerful model: **Trust Him, and BE under subordination.**

In I Cor. 12:2 we have a glimpse into the marvel of why God chose the incarnation as a model for His interaction with mankind. Jesus the God-man.

Neither one to the exclusion of the other. In the same "partnership" the Scriptures were not dictated in a heavenly language, nor from man's intellect and knowledge, but BOTH. Equally true of the spiritual gifts to the Church and especially relevant for the gift of tongues in its initial evidence of the baptism in the Holy Spirit. Any imbalance here leads to schism and excess. David Lim, quoting Godet[109]gives enlightenment to this "precise ambiguity." Here we have a clear picture of Paul's words: *"You know that when you were pagans, somehow or other you were influenced and led astray to mute idols"* (v. 2). Paul contrasts their lives before with their lives as Spirit-filled Christians. They had worshiped mute idols and were used to ecstatic frenzies and utterances. I have witnessed this among the shaman of West Africa. "They had felt that the more the divine spirit moved upon a person, the less became his self-control; the less self-control, the more he possessed of the divine spirit."[110] Godet explains:

> Their rule was: the more pneuma (spirit) the less *nous* (intelligence). The judgment accorded with Greek and even Jewish prejudices. Plato said in *Phaedrus:* "It is madness (the exaltation due to inspiration) that the greatest of blessings comes to us." And in the *Timaeus* he says: "No one in possession of his understanding has reached Divine and true exaltation."[111]

Might not this explain why Paul needed to correct a segment of the Corinthian Church that evidently was emphasizing the same kind of excesses based on an incomplete knowledge of the balanced incarnational view of how the gifts were to work and how they were to be understood? Let me quickly come to the point.

If one believes that total loss of control of the intellect in ecstatic speech is what the gift of tongues involves, then one is making the same kind of mistake the Gnostics made about the nature of the Son of God. The dualism fallacy of Plato plagued the Early Church and still plagues us today. Like with the Son of God (Divine and human) and the composition of the Bible (divine inspiration and human instrumentality), God desires a partnership WITH mankind. It's risky—too risky for the conservatives who want less/no risk (so they can be in control) and not wild enough for those who want to have total control by playing God and His authority without the constraints of the evaluation of anyone. I submit that it's a matter of CONTROL for both extremes. Some want more human control and others want to claim more control by God. The middle position is one of considerable ambiguity but seems to be the model God keeps giving us over and over. Lim says Paul's problem in Corinth was how to answer those who would say "God told me" or "God made me do it," so you can't correct me or disagree.

Paul emphasizes that we are now more in control as new creatures in Christ than when we were pagans. A contrast is made between speechless idols and the God who speaks to and through us as new creations in Christ than when we were pagan without Christ...God does not violate, attack, or destroy one's personality, but brings a person to his potential...(The Corinthians) had zeal coupled with ignorance.[112]

Carl Bremback agrees, though he wrote before WWII! He uses the word used by the critics current in that era saying those practicing glossolalia had abandoned human control and were "passive."

> ... After coming into deepest union with Christ, so that like Paul we say: "I am crucified with Christ," "Christ liveth in me," we do not become passive. We do not give up self-control. As never before we live.[113]

COMMUNICATIONS INSIGHT

Bremback and Horton relate to COMMUNICATIONS THEORY AND THE MIND

> But some may ask, "When is there ever an occasion for the mental passivity which you Pentecostalists advocate?" We have discovered that our critics object most to passivity when it relates to the intellect. They insist that any practice which requires the intellect or mind to be even partially inactive is bound to be harmful to the whole man.

Bremback's answer:

> For example, consider the manner in which the prophecy of Scripture came to holy men of old. Peter tells us (2 Peter 1:20, 21): "Knowing this first; that no prophecy of the Scripture is of any private interpretation. For the prophecy came not in old time by the will of Man: but holy men of God spake as they were moved by the Holy Ghost." (KJV) Certainly this is a description of yielding one's will to another, receiving truths and speaking them forth at the behest of another. Moreover, at times these men were caused to utter prophecies which were foreign to their own thoughts, and even incomprehensible to them except through a special revelation.

Here one must ask, did not this revelation require some passivity before the Spirit of God, or did this come by the intellectual genius of man?[114]

> Harold Horton gives this splendid note on the nature of tongues: "It is a supernatural utterance by the Holy Spirit in languages never learned by the speaker—not understood by the mind of the speaker—seldom understood by the hearer. It has nothing whatever to do with linguistic ability, nor with the mind or intellect of man. It is a manifestation of the mind of the Spirit of God employing human speech organs. When man is speaking with tongues, his mind, intellect, understanding are quiescent. It is the faculty of God that is active. Man's will, certainly, is active, and his spirit, and his speech organs: but the mind that is operating is the mind of God through the Holy Spirit."[115]

THE INCARNATIONAL DUET! IS IT RELATED TO WILL AND CONTROL?

The devil tried to get Jesus to leave his "incarnational" position and operate solely in His Deity. *("Turn these stones to bread.")* If He had, He would have jeopardized the whole plan of God's restraint relative to our volition as His great plan. Jesus has always refused this paradigm shift from the God/Man to the all-powerful deity position. He refused to come off the cross. He refused to heal when asked for a sign. He refused to jump off the pinnacle of the temple. The enemy succeeded in moving Adam and Eve from their God-ordained position "in His image" by the paradigm shift pictured in the LIE. "In His image" included a partnership of **like** God but **not** God, one step below that of Jesus who was *like* God *and* God too. We have a similar continuing partnership that pleases Him if we accept it and not try to modify it. That partnership is related to His Incarnation, *but is only a model of it.* Yet, the model He has offered requires both parts to be functional in **our model** just as in His model (the one He refused to change at Satan's temptation).

God has left so much up to us in this great test we are engaged in!

I was pleasantly surprised to find a book by this same title, *The Foolishness of God,* written by John A. Baker.[116] It is not about tongues, but about this dilemma of how a powerful God can leave so much up to us!

> "What kind of a God must he be—if he be—who stands behind the moral order as we see it? Our answer is clear. He will not be a God

who thinks of perfection in terms of precisely defined acts and words and thoughts. The world which he has made will not admit this...He will be a God who lays upon us the necessity of living in relationship...of mutual forgiveness... And above all he will be a God who makes it impossible to achieve any of these things except in freedom, creating them out of our own inner resources, assenting to them by a voluntary loyalty, realizing even through our necessary rules an environment of liberty; and thus he shows himself a God who requires not slaves, not machines, but partners. [117]

That's good stuff!

A CONTINUUM OF CONTROL

A:	B:	C:
(Evil spiritual control)	**(Delicate balance, God/mankind)**	**(Human control)**
I———	**———**	**———I**
Pagan ecstasy	**Tongues speech**	**No tongues allowed**
(absence of intellect)	**(subordination of intellect)**	**(intellectual dominance)**

Do we have any scriptural basis for the balanced incarnational understanding? I believe so. Consider the first epistle of John. In I John chapter 4, that apostle gives the same type of test for examining the Spirits as Paul used in I Cor. 12:3:

> *Dear friends, do not believe every spirit, but test the spirits to see whether they are from God, because many false prophets have gone out into the world. This is how you can recognize the Spirit of God: Every spirit that acknowledges that Jesus Christ has come in the flesh is from God, but every spirit that does not acknowledge Jesus is of the antichrist, which you have heard is coming and even now is already in the world* (I John 4:1-3).

True, this portion of Scripture may well address the particular philosophical and religious problems of that day, but I know they are still around today. Please notice the incarnational requisite. The God partnering with mankind concept is front and center.

The spirit that says:

> **A: False or Evil Spiritual Control** –"I'm speaking *from* God and you'd better listen-up because this is out of my control; God is forcing me to say this!" This **false spiritual control** does not acknowledge this special, surprising, disturbing *partnership/balance* needed to stay on track,

nor does it conform to I Cor. 12:7 plainly stating that each manifestation of the Spirit is for the common good. The **"pagan ecstasy"** mode is generally seeking personal power and/or profit, not the good of others.

On the opposite end of the continuum is:

C: Human Control —Intellectual Dominance—"There is no supernatural element to this: it's all human (or worse) and in the name of 'decency and order' we reject and rule out any such element of God working in you or your pronouncement." It's plain to see who is in control here and God would have to use a baseball bat to even get some folks' attention. Both extremes here are operating in the name of God, but by purposeful distortion or ignorance or resistance to New Testament teaching are distorting the mystery of God's presence.

B: Delicate Balance, *Partnership*—of the subordination of human intellect and the encoding/decoding mystery of glossolalia that conforms to what seems foolish and so risky on God's part but what seems so clear when seen in the light of so many elements of God's interaction with us. We don't *lose* our intellect, but we subordinate it to the *utterance of God's Holy Spirit.* It sounds almost too wonderful, and maybe that's one of the reasons folks find it so hard to accept or even desire.

Can you hear the innermost thoughts of those who would not open themselves to God, to the fullness of the baptism in the Holy Ghost? "Lord, you can't really have chosen this shameful thing that I must do to be yielded to you! I will praise you with grammatically correct phrases. I will extol your name in testimony to the neighbors. I will write excellent thoughts that will inspire my readers. I will form words of prayer in public which will lift the spirits of my brethren and show what a God of love and mercy and grace you are." **And they continue:** "But short-circuit all that learned, polished professionalism for 'baby talk'—I can't do that. Think of the years of hard study and grueling exercises in sentence construction I went through to earn the respect of my teachers. My position has depended on my mastery of my mother tongue; surely you appreciate this, Lord. I've been taught argumentation and forensics. I present ideas in logically powerful rhetorical symmetry."

Some Have Been Programmed Against this Experience

"What would I do in front of my friends who have heard me criticize this nonsense of speaking in tongues? Surely you can fill me with your blessed Spirit without this humiliation!"

It is very difficult for us pastors to give our tongue because our mind has been using it for years. It is not easy to release this instrument which is the most important aspect of our personality.[118]

COMMUNICATIONS INSIGHT

HERE'S A REFRESHINGLY different idea: Contrary to most modern communication theories that seemingly correctly propose that to really understand someone, enough of a common world of meaning needs to be established to get into the other person's " fan of perception." Gurevitch suggests the need to "make the other person strange" to be able to recognize her foreignness and encounter her reality as a wonderful way to experience new things and to grow intellectually and spiritually. "In order to have real dialogue, we need the ability *not* to understand them. We must see them as strange before we can really see them at all."[119] This theory suggests we too often just go to the comfortable categories too quickly and miss the hidden riches of diversity. Most of the time we hide from reality by judging the person in abstract pigeonholes too quickly, because it's easier to recognize what we think we know than take the effort to make a new category.

To follow the above insight, I turn to Adeney who says:

When you become a stranger and enter another culture, the result is a radical "defamiliarization" of all you know. You are forced to open your eyes and really look... In a similar way, your strangeness shocks your hosts into recognizing a broader reality than before. Of course the host may just stereotype you into whatever image he has picked up about American Christians, Berkeley radicals or Cambridge intellectuals (pick your stereotype). But if dialogue really takes place he will soon be surprised to find that you are stranger than you seem. And the shock in his eyes may be God's gift, through you to him...Real conversation is a treasure that seems all too rare these days. When such opening of the heart occurs between people from radically different cultures, it is a miracle of grace. This may be one of the highest aims for which we were created. Each person, and each culture, has a unique secret. Each is capable of knowing something of God which no one else knows. In the meeting of strangers we have the opportunity to share that treasure with each other."[120]

Adeney then quotes George MacDonald: "There is a chamber also (Oh

God, humble and accept my speech)—a chamber in God's own heart, into which none can enter but the one, the individual, the peculiar person—out of which chamber that person has to bring revelation and strength for his brothers and sisters. This is that for which a person was made—to reveal the secret things of the Father."[121]

Now I have an answer for a repeated phenomenon of which I have always hesitated to speak and, even now like MacDonald above (Oh God, humble and accept my speech), wish not to be misunderstood or seem pompous. There have been critical moments in ministry when while speaking in tongues in private worship and petition, a revelation of *what to do* has subsequently come into my conscious mind which has blessed many people. I don't refer to the acquisition of personal gain or position; rather, the establishment of a curriculum for seminary education or the plan to raise the significant sums of money for a new building complex which would be beneficial to the Body of Christ. Is it possible that the exercise of the private prayer language spoken of by the apostle Paul (praying and singing in the Spirit), which edifies the speaker would also be a part of the secret chamber in God's heart? To go from knowing God to KNOWING God, with specific divine insight that might entail? In a mysterious way this dimension is past/beyond explanation for the literalist or the skeptic or the modern Pharisee—and even beyond explanation for the practitioner of this glorious prayer language. This process has allowed the river of subconscious intention to flow from one's "whole being" and not just from the intellect. What wonder!

COMMUNICATIONS INSIGHT

DIFFERENT FREQUENCY

SINGING OR PLAYING music on an instrument is a different communication path than speaking. Many musicians feel through music they can come closer to pure *communication* than through the rules of syntax and grammar of human speech. Music does wonderful things to the "climate" of the mind/soul. In like manner, glossolalia is on a different level/frequency than normal speech. (See chapter 5 for research of brain waves during glossolalia AND appendix 1 for more on music and the human tongue and its relationship to glossolalia.) We are multidimensional. God wants to activate us on all levels. Denying this is the myopia of people who insist on the "super literate tyranny of words."

ENDNOTES:

1. Yancey, 74.
2. Ibid.
3. Carl Bremback, *What Meaneth This?* (1947), 245.
4. We noted the major critics in a previous section.
5. Paul Hiebert, *Anthropological Insights for Missionaries* (1985), 202-203.
6. Killian McDonnell and George T. Montague (1991), 21.
7. John R. Stott, "The Bible in World Evangelism" in *Perspectives on the World Christian Movement: A Reader* (1999), 24.
8. Everett Wilson, "They Crossed the Red Sea, Didn't They?" in *The Globalization of Pentecostalism, A Religion Made to Travel*, Murray W. Dempster, Byron D. Klaus, Douglas Peterson, eds. (1999), chapter 5.
9. Ibid., 87.
10. Bonino in *Globalization,* 121.
11. Ibid., 88.
12. "The Church with Her Endowment of Holiness and Power" in *The Collected Writings of Edward Irving in Five Volumes,* Vol. 4, G. Carlyle, ed., 505.
13. David W. Dorries, "Edward Irving and the 'Standing Sign' of Spirit Baptism" in *Initial Evidence, Historical and Biblical Perspective on the Pentecostal Doctrine of Spirit Baptism,* McGee Gary, ed. (1991), 51.
14. Rybarczyk, quoting Fee in "Expressing the Inexpressible: Tongues as Apophatic Speech" (2002), 11, from Fee's *God's Empowering Presence: The Holy Spirit in the Letters of Paul* (1994).
15. Gordon Fee, *Listening to the Spirit in the Text* (2000), 46 and 117-120. Fee further elaborates this difficult arena of definition.
16. Gordon Fee, *Corinthians: A Study Guide, 3rd Edition* (1997) 257.
17. Jerry Jensen, ed., *Episcopalians and the Baptism in the Holy Spirit* (1964).
18. Edmund Rybarczyk, "Expressing the Inexpressible: Tongues as Apophatic Speech" (paper presented at the 31st Annual Meeting of the Society for Pentecostal Studies, Lakeland, FL. 2002), 3, 14.
19. Ibid.
20. John D. Zizioulas, *Being As Communication: Studies in Personhood and the Church* (1985), 89-90.
21. John Meyendoff, *Christ in Eastern Christian Thought,* 2nd ed. (1987), 93.
22. Frank D. Macchia, "Sighs Too Deep For Words," *Journal of Pentecostal Theology* 1 (1992), 51.
23. J. Ellul, *Prayer and Modern Man* (1970), 58.
24. Fee, *God's Empowering Presence* (1994), 288.
25. My all-time favorite author on the Beatitudes is a Lutheran professor who gives an unusual explanation and these stark contrasting ideas: Paul Bretscher, *The World Upside-Down or Right-Side Up?* (1964).
26. Deborah Gill, Spencer Lake Christian Center, Waupaca, WS, July 13, 2005. Dr. Gill is the National Director of Christian Education of our church, is a great teacher of Greek and an excellent exegete in her own right. She is married to an architect and brings a good analogy from that discipline to the subject of *strength from weakness.*
27. Yancey, (1995), 76.

28. Ibid., 77.
29. Ibid., 77.
30. Scott M. Peck, *The People of the Lie* (1983), 269.
31. Yancey, 204.
32. Smith Wiggelsworth, *Smith Wigglesworth On The Holy Spirit* (1998), 205.
33. Yancey, 60.
34. Phaedus, 244, quoted in M. Kelsey (1968), 173.
35. Ibid., 173.
36. Ibid., 181.
37. Ibid., 181.
38. Rybarczyk, (2002), 9.
39. M. Kelsey (1968), 184.
40. Ibid., 186. Kelsey draws from two works discussing the psychological approach to knowledge about God: Geddes MacGregor, *Introduction to Religious Philosophy* (1959), 173, and Henry Van Duson, *Spirit, Son and Father* (1958), 80ff.
41. Paul G. Heibert, "The Flaw of the Excluded Middle," in *Missiology 10* (January 1982) 35-47.
42. For more on this truth, see J. R. Williams in " Baptism in the Holy Spirit" in *Dictionary of Pentecostal and Charismatic Movements,* Stanley M. Burgess, Gary B. McGee, and Patrick H. Alexander, eds. (1988), 40-48. J. R. Williams speaks of other expressions used in Acts as the "falling" of the Holy Spirit (Acts 8:16; 10:44); also "come on" as used by Jesus in Acts 1:8, "you will receive power when the Holy Spirit *comes on* you"; also, Luke's gospel uses the words of Jesus "clothed with" as in Luke 24:49: "Stay in the city until you are *clothed with* power from on high." These last two speak of an **investiture** of/by the Holy Spirit.
43. "A Oneness Pentecostal Looks at Initial Evidence" in McGee (1991), 181-182.
44. J. R. Williams, 42.
45. Ibid.
46. Robert F. Capon, *The Parables of Grace* (1988), 70.
47. Donald A. Johns, "New Directions in Hermeneutics" in McGee (1991), 164.
48. R.P. Spittler in *Dictionary of Pentecostal and Charismatic Movements* (1992), 341.
49. Robert Culpepper, *Evaluating The Charismatic Movement: A Theological and Biblical Appraisal* (1977), 88.
50. Robert L. Brandt and Zenas J. Bicket, *The Spirit Helps Us Pray: A Biblical Theology of Prayer* (1993), 282.
51. Kenneth Bailey, *Poet and Peasant and Through Peasants' Eyes* (1976), 183.
52. John W. Welch, "What the Baptism Really Is," *Advance (*August 26, 1939), 6.
53. Gordon Fee (1997), 71.
54. David Lim (1999), 161. (Lim quotes and footnotes William Richardson in "Liturgical Order and Glossalalia," *New Testament Studies* 32 (January 1986), 148.
55. Ibid.
56. For a complete explanation of these processes, see: Hayim H. Dorin, *To Be a Jew: A Guide to Jewish Observance in Contemporary Life* (1972), 97-120.
57. Janet Evert Powers, "Missionary Tongues?" *Journal of Pentecostal Theology* 17 (2000), 51.
58. She also quoted Roger Stronstad, *Charismatic Theology of St. Luke* (1984), 68-69.
59. Powers, 54, quoting Frank D. Macchia, "Sighs Too Deep For Words: Towards a Theology of Glossolalia," *Journal of Pentecostal Theology* 1 (1992), 47-73.

60. Byron Klaus, "Prez Release" (a monthly commentary from the President of the Assemblies of God Theological Seminary, February 2003).

61. Ibid.

62. Saint Exupery, *The Little Prince*, trans. by Katerine Woods (1943).

63. Gordon D. Fee, *God's Empowering Presence: The Holy Spirit in the Letters of Paul* (1994).

64. Ibid., 580-582.

65. Ibid., 582.

66. Fee quoted by Benny C. Aker in *Dictionary of Pentecostal and Charismatic Movements* (1988), 456.

67. Cited in Kelsey (1968), 123.

68. Ibid., 100.

69. For an anthropologist's work showing earlier social scientist's error on this finding, see: Luther P. Gerlack and Virginia H. Hine, *People, Power, and Change: Movements of Social Transformation* (1970). For a Roman Catholic's very detailed research on glossolalia and how the Social Sciences are prejudiced against those who speak in tongues, see: Killian McDonnell, *Charismatic Renewal and the Churches* (1976).

70. Everett L. Wilson, "They Crossed the Red Sea, Didn't They?" in Murray Dempster, et. al., *Globalization* (1999), 86.

J. Rodman Williams, *Renewal Theology II* (1990) 218.

James Slay in *The Glossolalia Phenomenon,* Wade Horton, ed. (1966), 234.

73. James Slay quoting George A. Barton, *The Apostolic Age and the New Testament* (1936), 14.

74. Ibid., 226.

75. What an emotional "space" for us. It was here over 30 years ago the opinions of a jealous missionary wouldn't allow the use of these grounds to plant a new church for the immediate community around the school. This school was eight klm from there, the only AG church in this town of 250,000. (It's triple that now.) So we started a youth meeting at our house with a football team (the Jupiters) every Friday night. Many were saved and many more of their siblings and family members also left their world of fear and animism/fetishism for the light of the gospel. There is another church of 800, about two klm from here, also related to the first converts of that football team. It was due to the healing of some family members that the real attraction to Christianity took root.

76. Andrew L. Drummond, *Edward Irving and His Circle* (1934), 135.

77. David Hesselgrave, *Communicating Christ Cross-Culturally* (1991), 312.

78. In Lim (1991, 1999), 149, Frederick Dale Bruner, *A Theology of The Holy Spirit: The Pentecostal Experience and the New Testament Witness* (1970), 287.

79. Ibid.

80. Ibid., 149-150.

81. J. R. Flower, *Pentecostal Evangel* (April 17, 1920), 4.

82: Lyrics and Music by George Bennard

83. Gordon Fee (1997), 71.

84. Max Wood Moorhead, ed., "Pentecost in Calcutta," *Cloud of Witnesses II* (1907), 10-11.

85. M. Duggan, "The Cross and the Holy Spirit in Paul: Implications for the Baptism with the Holy Spirit," *Pneuma* 7 (1985), 135-46. See also F. Macchia in "Sighs Too Deep for Words," *JPT* 1, 1992, 68-69.

86. Larry Christenson, *Speaking in Tongues: Its significance for the Church* (1968), 26. (Christenson quotes Sanford and Tournier without biographical precision.)

87. French Arrington, *The Acts of the Apostles* (1986), 242.
88. Larry Christenson, *Speaking in Tongues* (1968), 73.
89. From John Bertone, "The Experience of Glossolalia and the Spirit's Empathy: Romans 8:26 Revisited" in *Pneuma*, Vol. 25, No. 1 (Spring 2003), 60.
90. Dave Roberson, *The Walk of the Spirit—The Walk of Power* (1999), 16.
91. Paul Irwin, "Playing by Heart," *Reader's Digest* (March 2000).
92. Frank D. Macchia, "Sighs Too Deep For Words," *JPT* 1 (1992), 62-3.
93. A. Heschel, *Quest for God* (1982), 39.
94. Ibid.
95. Harvey Cox (1995), 9.
96. Victor Turner and Edward Bruner (1986), see introduction.
97. Ronald Bueno (citing Turner and Bruner) in *The Globalization of Pentecostalism,* Dempster, et. al., eds.(1999), 281.
98. Don Richardson, *Eternity In Their Hearts* (1981), 156-7.
99. John V. York, *Missions in the Age of the Spirit* (2000), 81.
100. Ibid.
101. Harvey Cox (1995), 71.
102. Ivan M. Satyavrata, "Contextual Perspectives on Pentecostalism as a Global Culture: A South Asian View" in *The Globalization of Pentecostalism: A Religion Made to Travel* (1999), 211.
103. Russell Spittler, "Pentecostal Theology: A Classical Viewpoint" in *Perspectives on the New Pentecostalism,* Russell P. Spittler, ed. (1976), 61-61.
104. David Lim, *Spiritual Gifts: A Fresh Look* (1991, 1999).
105. Ibid., 42.
106. Lim, 42-43.
107. See Roland Allen, *Missionary Methods: St. Paul's or Ours* (1962, 1993), 117.
108. Lim, 45.
109. Fredrick L. Godet, *Commentary on First Corinthians,* Vol. 2 (1886), 173.
110. Lim, 55.
111. Godet, *First Corinthians,* 174.
112. Lim, 56.
113. Carl Bremback, *What Meaneth This?* (1947), 125, quoting F. J. Huegel in *Bone of His Bone* (n.d.), 79, 84,85.
114. Ibid., Brembeck 128.
115. Ibid., 129.
116. John A. Baker, *The Foolishness of God* (1970).
117. Ibid., 127.
118. Herbert A. Mjorud in *Lutherans and the Baptism in the Holy Spirit,* Jerry Jensen, ed. (1996) 6-9.
119. D. Gurevitch, "The Other Side of Dialogue: On Making the Other Strange and the Experience of Otherness," *American Journal of Sociology* 93 (March 1988), 79-99, quoted in B.T. Adeney, *Strange Virtues: Ethicsin a Multicultural World* (1995), 139-141.
120. Ibid., Adeney, 140-141.
121. *George MacDonald Anthology,* ed. C. S. Lewis (1946), 29. (Emphasis MacDonald.)

CHAPTER 9

INTENTION OF THE HOLY SPIRIT RE: UNITY IN THE BODY

I believe implicitly that one of the Holy Spirit's primary functions in the world is one of the most neglected by most Pentecostals, the very folks who claim to be the closest to His will and design for the kingdom of our Lord and Christ. They have embraced His "foolishness," as it relates to glossolalia as this work is trying to define, yet have only rarely attempted to plumb the seriousness of another part of God's design in desiring a deeper submission and faith in the supernatural and gifts of the Spirit. That other part is the topic of this chapter. It relates to the prayer of Christ in John 17 where a clear glimpse of His heart on the matter of unity is heavy with emotion and longing.

There should always be a relationship between Pentecostal power and reconciliation.

I am attracted to the idea that the Holy Spirit's coming in Acts 2, in direct promise and instruction of Jesus prior to His ascension, is often suggested to be a unifying act of God in response to the divisive force of Babel, (that Pentecost was a reversal of the language confusion of the Genesis 11 account of Babel). But this is not the place and I'm not the one to pursue this thesis. I agree with Arrington that it would not be easy to strongly support it.[1]

It does seem appropriate, however, to insist that every biblical account of the coming of the Holy Spirit in the New Testament had a clear "mantra" about unity and reconciliation and empowerment of those who were disenfranchised by the current system, be it religious or secular, and was a direct reflection of the Joel prophecy as stated by Peter on the day of Pentecost.

Jesus Speaks of His Anointing

In the synagogue in His hometown of Nazareth, Jesus proclaimed the Spirit of the Lord was upon Him and anointed Him to preach the gospel to the poor, bring deliverance to the captive, to release the oppressed (Luke 4). These are the disadvantaged, the powerless of the society. This suggests the power of reconciliation from the normal forces that divide humanity into economic strata, racial compartmentalization and ethnocentricity. There should always be a relationship between Pentecostal power and reconciliation.

Peter Breaks the Barriers

Peter addressed the crowds gathered to hear the wonders of God proclaimed in their own languages in Jerusalem as recounted in Acts 2. He said God would pour out His Spirit on all people: sons and daughters included—young and old included—servants, both men and women included. What a different idea from the carefully guarded classification of the Hebrew world! He was cutting across the strata of gender, age, and social levels.

Now in quick succession:

Frank Macchia often writes about this neglected effect of true Pentecostal experience:

"Hence, spiritual fullness is only realized in conjunction with koinonia. Glossolalia is then a corporate as well as an individual experience. Along with interpretation, it is a shared experience revealing that the mystery and freedom of our being *coram Deo* is not only a freedom for God, but a freedom for one another...After the Spirit fell at Pentecost, Peter described the meaning of the speech miracle evidenced there by stating that young and old, free and slave, male and female now have equal right to minister for God (Acts 2:17-18). Wherever glossolalia is experienced in Acts barriers are broken down between people: between rich and poor (ch. 2), between Jew and Gentile (ch. 10), and between Christians and the followers of John the Baptist (ch.19)...It is the lowest common denominator between people who might be very different from one another, revealing a deep sense of equality that cannot be denied and that challenges any discrimination based on gender, class, or race.[2]"

COMMUNICATIONS INSIGHT

MACCHIA SUMS UP the breaking down of social and religious barriers when the Holy Spirit comes with a word (for my focus on communications) with this poignant sentence: "Tongues protest the tyranny of words in worship, allowing other forms of self expression to have equal importance."[3]

The Naming of a Chapel Highlights the Issue of the Forgotten/Ignored Element of the Coming of the Holy Spirit in an Individual's Life

While president of the Assemblies of God Seminary in Springfield, MO, a new building was designed and constructed. Because many in the church felt William J. Seymour, the founding pastor of the Apostolic Mission on Azusa Street in Los Angeles, never received the honor due this apostle of renewal, I proposed to the Board of Directors the new chapel be named in his honor, including one of the stained glass windows to show his likness and that of the humble old building where the Pentecostal revival started in 1906. This was sensitive enough to need the approval of the executive presbyters of the church. There was general informal approval around the table as I presented the consent of the seminary's board, but one of the three executive presbyters who opposed the idea stated, "According to Parham, William J. Seymour renounced tongues in his later ministry." I objected and said Parham was a racist and is implicated in an act of thievery. Parham was so blinded by the segregationist's poison of his day, he did not see that speaking in tongues was not *all* the evidence needed in his case. Parham was the one who caused the initial split on racial lines, no doubt over worship style, and probably was party to the theft of Seymour's 50,000 name mailing list of Apostolic Faith Magazine by two white women, Lumm and Crawford.[4]

Thank God for Charles Hackett (Executive Director of Home Missions) who, when Thomas Trask, the General Superintendent was willing to put this issue to a vote, said: "If we really want to send a message to our African American brethren that we are serious about including them in our fellowship, this is the type of symbol they would appreciate and admire." The vote was taken and passed with only three dissenters.

Here's why I feel so strongly about the "Anglo" church's weak position on the issue the Holy Spirit so strongly desires for the Church of Christ:

While participating in the International Pentecostal/Roman Catholic dialogue referred to above, I was pleased for the acquaintance of a fellow Pentecostal from the Apostolic Faith Mission of South Africa where the Holy Spirit's outpouring occurred not long after the Azusa happening. Jappie LaPoorta believes the ultimate intention of the coming of the Spirit is unity in the body of believers as was evidenced in both Azusa Street in Los Angeles and in Doornfontein, Johannesburg, South Africa.[5]

The Focus of the Issue Is This, According to LaPoorta

> The emphasis of tongues as initial evidence, without a change of heart and attitude is unacceptable for blacks. They assert that when

> the Spirit's baptism takes place racism is removed. They further maintain that the Spirit's baptism has political and socio-economic implications, because it does not stand aloof from the biblical injunction of Gal. 3:28 'In Christ there is no male nor female, slave nor free, Jew nor Gentile, but all are one.'"[6]

That particular dissenting presbyter to the naming of the chapel above is mistaken when he asserts Seymour rejected tongues. What Seymour rejected was the narrow limits of that presbyter's understanding about tongues as being only *one item* of many, isolated from the Spirit's broader intention. Seymour came to believe "tongues as initial evidence" was not true "evidence" until it was *also evidenced* by a whole cluster of accompanying related ones. "When only the mouth speaks but the heart remains in darkness and carnality tongues are valid but not yet complete!"[7] Daniels relates this issue to the doctrine of sanctification and the difference between the two branches of Pentecostalism: Wesleyan and Reformed.

I submit this emphasis on ethics could have been embraced even by the "progressive sanctification" crowd. —C. Robeck

> The Church of God in Christ and Pentecostal Holiness Church, reflecting a Wesleyan perspective, teach the doctrine of entire sanctification, while the Pentecostal Assemblies of the World and Assemblies of God, reflecting a Reformed or Keswick perspective, teach the doctrine of progressive sanctification. At least for William Seymour and Charles Harrison Mason the holiness doctrine of sanctification was integral to the doctrine of the Baptism of the Holy Spirit because it made ethics central to Pentecostal teaching rather than glossolalia as initial evidence.[8]

I agree with Robeck when he projects to the future, from the historical perspective of the past. Think of what might have been the outcome, had the whole Pentecostal movement adapted this centrality of **ethics** instead of only the too often misunderstood "overemphasis" of tongues (as stated by our critics). **NOTE**: Placing the emphasis on ethical and moral issues like the "entire sanctification" crowd, **without denying or excluding tongues from the evidence of the baptism of the Spirit,** much of the misunderstandings and accusations concerning the "lunatic fringe" (for which we all have suffered) might have been avoided from the outset of this great revival. I submit this emphasis on ethics could have been embraced even by the "progressive sanctification" crowd.[9]

In my experience, unity has more to do with the emotions than cognition; more with feelings than analysis. One feels drawn to another person on a visceral level more than cerebral. (Of course, this move towards greater empathy, understanding and acceptance is both from the mind and the emotions, and this effect is not mutually exclusive as to the two elements.) Yet, being stirred emotionally allows more easily the old barriers of antipathy and estrangement to be overcome. If two people share a common life-threatening event, even antagonists will forget their animosity and join together in a common life-saving protecting mode. They will even share the same personal space that normally would never be ventured. (Witness the coming together of political foes in the USA immediately after the twin towers were knocked down by Islamic extremists in 2001.) Just so is the experience of hungering after God and His Spirit. When the results of that search bring physical and emotional blessing, it can cause people from normally diverse and often antagonistic or territorial cliques and divisions to suddenly find themselves enjoying mutual company. At that moment of time, the old barriers and elements of division are lost in a new dimension of God's blessing. This was the case of Azusa. William Seymour said, "The blood has washed away the color line."[10] This is a powerful statement when one considers the highly acceptable segregationist view of race relations in America at the time.

Justice and Reconciliation

"Tongues also symbolize the need for justice and reconciliation within the body of Christ. Tongues thus represents 'a broken speech for the broken body of Christ until perfection arrives.'"[11]

> Tongues resist a complacent sectarianism that rests secure in its safe haven free from any accountability to the injustices and divisions within and outside the churches. Tongues also resist a complacent catholicism that rests secure in its possession of the fullness of catholicity, having therefore no responsibility to reach out in acts of justice and reconciliation to everyone, including the sectarians. Tongues allow the poor, uneducated, and illiterate among the people of God to have an equal voice with the educated and the literate.[12]

COMMUNICATIONS INSIGHT

TONGUES AS A SIGN for the powerless in society: Whether the prophecy of Joel in the Old Testament; the words of Jesus in Nazareth; the words of Peter in Jerusalem; the revival in Azusa; the revival in Johannesburg – no one needs to 'authenticate' the experience for someone "overcome by God." Not a judge, not a priest, not a pastor, not anyone else, necessarily. Each individual is so conscious that God the Spirit has moved on him/her, that the 'power' factor is self-evident (Acts 1:8). What the Christian church so pointedly needs to hear is ministry empowered by the Holy Spirit is for men and women equally, gender reconciliation.

Janet Evert Powers:

> The Pentecostal understanding of glossolalia was crucial to their understanding of the qualifications of women ministers. Glossolalia was a supernatural gift, and the actions of one who had been baptized in the Spirit were considered the actions of God rather than the actions of a human speaker. Because a woman minister preached under the control of the Holy Spirit, early Pentecostals were able to ignore the traditional qualifications for ministry. They saw authority vested in the manifestations of the Spirit, rather than in the human speaker.[13]

She continues: "If God is the speaker, then anyone can be used as God's vessel. Since the same Holy Spirit is in the woman as in the man, the experience of Pentecost means that the new age, in which women can be the mouthpiece of the Lord, has arrived. ...This Pentecostal argument depends...on the Pentecostal understanding of baptism in the Holy Spirit."[14]

Pentecostals, both as individuals and as a group, look back into history and retrieve the stories of the archetypal Azusa Street Mission that stimulated a non-racial, non-sexist, spirit-filled, tongue-speaking, united movement. Hear the heart cry of LaPoorta, a "Black" (his word) church leader from South Africa who recounts the schism along racial lines in both the Pentecostal revival at Azusa in the USA and the same division in South Africa:

> Racism in both Azusa and Doornfontein was responsible for the building up of the broken wall of separation. Racism was ideologically justified by the misuse of scripture. This misuse of scripture blurred the biblical imperatives, such as love for the neighbors, who happened to be Black... Racism has caused serious physical damage to both Black and White. Both groups are in dire need of liberation. The Blacks need to be liberated from inferiority, shame, complacency that the apartheid system has instilled in them. Whites on the other hand need to be liberated from a false sense of superiority.

Both groups need to re-orientate their minds about blackness in particular. This will enable Blacks to boldly affirm their human dignity. This will enable Whites to acknowledge the black roots of the movement and accept black leadership in the movement. Finally, Pentecostalism needs to be liberated from the ideological baggage it carries. This will enable it to be relevant and prophetic. These experiences will expedite the process of unity between Black and White. The fragmentation of the Pentecostal movement on race in general and AFM of SA in particular, is a deviation from the divine intention. Therefore, the unity struggle in which the black churches were engaged was a noble struggle. This struggle is in line with the biblical imperatives and the divine paradigm of Azusa.[15]

HAS THE CHURCH UNDERESTIMATED THE HOLY SPIRIT'S POWER FOR UNITY?

This sub-chapter title almost seems an oxymoron in the light of the thousands of divisions in church circles because of glossolalia! Yet we rejoice to see this day upon us now, at this writing. "Glossolalia is a sign that cuts through differences of gender, class, culture and language to reveal the new community of the Spirit which is characterized by transformed relationships and empowered to bear witness to the world."[16] Because of this, glossolalia is an important part of the Christian witness to the gospel in a torn and broken world. This is a new creation in which the social and cultural barriers which create hostility between people are broken down by the power of the Spirit. Glossolalia is more than a sign that the Church has been empowered for mission; it is also a sign that the eschatological community of the Spirit is a present reality and that God is at work in the world.[17]

This same phenomenon occurs in many places in history, as well as currently. It was true at Azusa Street and before that in India. It was true in my experience in Burkina Faso in 1965, as reported previously. Note, however, I observed that the force of unity related to the outpouring of the baptism in the Spirit in Africa was visible in praxis only where the choice of the fruit of the Spirit called LOVE was evidenced by a conscious choice to engage the will to that end. In Burkina Faso, the colleagues who resisted this renewal also continued in old ways of discrimination and parochialism. Often outside forces, and some internal as well, divide and confuse some of the unifying relationships. Obedience to the commands of Jesus to love one another must be one of the most difficult to maintain for some folks—even after a "baptism in love" has swept away old animosities and competitive spirits.

How can the commonality of experience of the baptism in the Holy Spirit bring Catholics, Episcopalians, Lutherans, Baptists, and Pentecostals together in a united meeting? Is it that they have found a common thread in the manifestation of the Spirit of God in their lives? Look how this blessing has changed the individual member's attitudes about each other. Shouldn't we be talking about reconciliation in those terms? It would seem evident that 1 Corinthians 13 would be better called the "lubrication of love for the operation of unity in true ecumenicity in Christ's body, the Church." It is painfully interesting that along with the good "feelings" that facilitate rapprochement, love is **not** a gift, but a fruit related to conscious decision of the will. In previous paragraphs I suggested a higher consciousness and practice of Christian ethics in the matter of tolerance across racial lines may have set the new "tongues" movement on a trajectory closer to the prayer of Jesus in John 17; yet what extreme effort and perseverance would have been required, and still is. How sad the Master must be to see our continued failures here. Not because the realm of Spirit baptism is not a great vehicle for such a godly rapprochement, *but because it requires our volition inside that potential.*

Unity in Social Justice

Not enough significance has been given to the power the Holy Spirit makes available to break the spirit of prejudice and ethnocentrism that so plagues the human race. Hardly any major conflict between countries or peoples in history lacks the element of racism. The incidence of exclusion and marginalization (that doesn't necessarily result in open warfare) stemming from this curse probably cannot be numbered even in today's world.

Example: When the Holy Spirit was poured out in Caesarea (Acts 10), violently prejudiced Jewish Christians in Jerusalem (still playing the old mental tapes of Judaism) rejected and criticized Peter for having eaten in the house of Gentiles (whom Jews called dogs). But when Peter told of the experience of tongues spoken by these Cesareans, he said, "...the Holy Spirit came on them like on us at the beginning" (Acts 11:15). The Spirit baptized Jewish Christians backed off, changed their tune and even rejoiced. It is very significant that tongues were important enough to displace even hardened Jewish laws. This experience gave evidence which overturned Jewish particularism and opened the Church to the Gentiles. "Glossolalia is the new language of the Spirit which shows the believers' participation in the new community of the Spirit."[18]

Jesus established a "new order" of social justice in Luke 4 while witnessing to His own people in Nazareth with the oft quoted words: "The Spirit of the Lord is upon me." He addressed the plight of the poor, the prisoners, the blind, the oppressed to whom the time of the Lord's favor had come. As stated above, whenever the Spirit is poured out in a new anointing, whether in Jerusalem in Acts 2 or at Azusa Street in 1906 or in Dornfontein, South Africa, it seems the Holy Spirit is again and again opening the door for the Church to step forward into a world that lifts the bar of ethnic tolerance and unity that is decidedly contrary to mankind's natural inclination based on language, culture, and ethnocentricity. God the Holy Spirit never seems to stop trying to accomplish His great unifying project. I want so desperately to express my heart's desire to see a greater fulfillment of what I believe is the Spirit's intent:

We must go back to the constraints of Pentecost, which cannot be separated from a prophetic voice that cries out against the injustices of a sinful society.

I see a day when Pentecostals no longer can be classified as Evangelical-plus on the issues of social justice. When sociologists chart us on issues of racism and intolerance today, they can chart us along with the worst of them. I believe the Holy Spirit is moving us back to the path we left in the '20s when this Movement chose preservation over the prophetic.[19] We must go back to the constraints of Pentecost, which cannot be separated from a prophetic voice that cries out against the injustices of a sinful society. We seem many times to have lost our way on this issue. We cannot be both Pentecostal and **non-prophetic!** I believe Maachia agrees and gets proscriptive for the future of the movement:

> The challenge is to broaden and deepen the theological understanding of how tongues symbolize an experience with God that continually urges the people of God to move beyond the confines of private piety or even church fellowship to the global issues of justice, peace, and the redemption of the world... Contemporary Pentecostals must rediscover that sense of urgency, believing that tongues connect individual Christians and churches with the need for global justice, reconciliation, and redemption...Such insights must be further developed if tongues are to guide a Pentecostal theology that is contextual and open to urgent social issues of global significance.[20]

Does this not relate to the "ultimate intention" of the Spirit about unity and liberation from carnal behavior so antithetical to the Spirit of Christ? Harvey Cox suggests African-Americans can show us the way to reconciliation: while white Pentecostals, he says, almost always see tongue speaking itself as the principal distinguishing mark of their faith, blacks understand tongues to be a mark of the divine power "which brings people together in reconciliation . . . creating a new community in Christian brotherhood."[21]

Unity in Dialogue with Those of Differing Opinions

I see a day when we don't hang our heads in embarrassment in an ecumenical meeting. Nor will we carnally project a powerful air of "in your face" when our inner city churches thrive and attract the wounded world to its front doors, or when soon we are acclaimed the largest Protestant church in the world. I see a day when defensiveness and suspicion about dialogue in our community will give way to the examination of a subject to be held at arm's length and scrutinized in the clear light of current scholarship. "By what process was this conclusion reached?" one would ask. "Was the information forced through a certain epistemological grid to arrive at a forced conclusion?" "What data was ignored in the process?" I believe the pristine truth of Pentecost will not only stand up under such scrutiny, but gain strength and glimmer by the rigor of the exercise! (But the participants will neither seek nor tolerate the plaudits of men or church in so doing.)

Unity in Scholarship

I see a day when some of our present instruction won't limit students to the controlling sphere of pseudo-Bible restricting, mind choking, "narrow" dogma. I speak of boundaries built of fear and weakness of experience that hedge in the largest "diameter" an issue could span, the smallest "degree of arc" of diversity to be considered relevant, the absolute length of the "radius" of truth. I see a day when we as a greater Pentecostal movement will shed our inferiority complex and finally square our shoulders in humility, not pride or triumphalism, to affirm "this is that spoken by the prophets." This is the biblically-based truth that delivers mankind's captives by attacking the roots of satanic power. Why? Because it's the genuine article Jesus promised.

Unity With the Poor—In Obedience to Jesus' Words

I see a day when God again calls us to a *conversion* to the poor. Our job (in the Spirit of Jesus) is not done when we simply build them a chapel or give food and clothing. This we must continue also to do. When I read my Bible, it suggests I get more involved than just the United Way of non-involvement. Yes, Jesus also reached the rich, but look at the context and content of His sharp words (Matt. 19:16ff). He always insisted the strongest expression of faith in Him would be best demonstrated by releasing the poor from their bondage by a change of our own attitude (Luke 4). IT GETS EVEN WORSE! God loves it when I get so close to the object of His love that I smell like them! I call it **The Smell of Sheep.** When I get close enough and really relate to God's sheep (think of Peter after the resurrection—"feed my sheep" times three), I'll even be in the position to receive ministry **from** them. There is a blessing by the poor of this world (the Charismata of the poor).

Unity of Repentance

I see a day when a spirit of repentance settles on us like a cloud. There has never been a true revival in history without deep repentance. We could start by asking forgiveness about our glib conclusion that God has "cut a covenant" with us Pentecostals (in particular) like He did with Abraham. (Of course, we are a part of the grafted-in covenant.) We could continue by seeking forgiveness about accusing God of "poor aim" when the Holy Spirit is poured out on any group **over which we have no control** (as if the first decade of last century was the only model God has). No one can hide behind corporate repentance. I, as an individual, must seek forgiveness in all areas where I have offended Him.

Unity Through Ecumenical Witness

He was known as "Mr. Pentecost." I speak of David du Plesis, born in South Africa, who became an American and was mightily used to bring the Charismatic experience to hundreds of leaders in many of the main-line churches over a 50-year period. My church defrocked him in the 1960s but then sensibly reinstated him in the 80s after recognizing its sectarian error and the singular hand of the Spirit on his ministry. It was David who invited me to be a member of the International Roman Catholic/Pentecostal dialogue in 1984.

Maachia believes a Pentecostal theology will be a force of ecumenical witness. "Does not Pentecost symbolize a fragmented people struggling through encounters with the Spirit of God to realize more and more of the ecumenical witness to which Christ has called them? Does not the book of Acts narrate the story of just such an ongoing struggle?"[22] Robeck has shown the early Pentecostals viewed their movement as a witness to the work of the Spirit to create a unified witness to the gospel among the people of God."[23] Hollenweger (quoted in Maachia) shares some of this thinking, though with a different approach. "I am convinced that there is a theology hidden in this spirituality. A description of these theologies cannot start with their concepts. I have rather to choose another way and describe how they are conceived, carried, and might finally be born. I am not sure whether the moment of birth has come yet, but that something is growing, is in travail and will finally break forth with elemental strength is all too clear."[24]

Robeck himself joins in: "Pentecostalism is ecumenical and multicultural, though much of the movement does not yet realize it."[25]

Undefined Certainty! Feelings About Dialogue and John 17

I struggle to express how often I feel an intimacy with God and a blessing from the Lord during the times when I have been a participant in the International Roman Catholic/Pentecostal dialogue over a 12-year period (eight times in that period.) I don't know exactly how to express this. Many people in my church believe all dialogue is compromise, as if it's OK to hate a Catholic but not OK to love one. They are confused when I explain that the act of dialogue (we argue Scripture for eight hours a day for six days running—but no *argumentum ad homonym* allowed) is not to find points of merger or union but to destroy myths of misunderstanding. I try to communicate an inexplicable peace and "rightness" that is sensed during this time; a sense of closeness to God, like when preaching or inviting folks to seek God at the altar. I have voiced this many times, when in the midst of differing ideas inside the mutual respect of esteem and even love at those dialogues. As yet, I don't have the reason of why participation with the nine permanent members appointed from Rome gives such an inner blessing. Is it because the Lord of the harvest has an intense interest in this vast expansive church, the church that makes such claims to be the original Apostolic Church? Is it because the Holy Spirit is seeking to renew this monolith of nearly 1700 years? Is it because there are genuine "seekers" in both camps who sincerely seek to worship Him in Spirit and in truth—and that Spirit is stronger than the doctrinal differences that so easily divide us? Would that common desire move folks who seem to be far apart on the surface to a mystical place of unity with the Holy Spirit where organizational unity isn't even an issue?

> **Here is our death to the pride of *meaning making with cerebral power;* here is the defeat of the dominance with words ...and the surrender of our *living computer.***

Harvey Cox, again so articulate, reminds us that the founder of the Four Square Gospel Movement, Aimee S. McPherson, believed in the special role of the Holy Spirit to unify the children of God.

At Azusa street literally any person who came in could stand and

> prophesy. There were no official mediators, licensed by an ecclesiastical hierarchy or set apart by apostolic ordination. Instead, God's spirit was present in a direct, intense, and undeniable way. ...Aimee Semple McPherson's commitment to transcending the color line was no doubt one of the main reasons why the Azusa Street pioneers had sought her out for the anniversary. From the earliest days of her barnstorming, Sister Aimee had always insisted that the coming together of the races was one of the surest signs of the presence of the Spirit.[26]

"Let the Holy Ghost Come In"

God has given us a way to obey the essence of Philippians chapter 2.

> *Your attitude should be the same as that of Christ Jesus.*
> *...made himself nothing.*
> *...taking the very nature of a servant*
> *...He humbled himself*
> *...and became obedient to death—even the death on a cross!*

Here is our death to the pride of "meaning making with cerebral power"; here is the defeat of the dominance with words that only humans, God's top communicators, can invent and wield so pridefully. He bids us leave behind this potential power in worship to Him; to surrender our *living computer.* God has "hard wired" us to *need* Him in the incarnational (shared) partnership where the spiritual element has priority as He uses this vessel of clay—not by coercion, but by our choice. Amazingly, He has given us the capacity to reject all of this! But why should we?

There is an old hymn of the revivalist churches of the 1890s, "Let The Holy Ghost Come In," long lost to our present musical needs. But it fits this moment. The last verse and refrain go like this:

> Do you want the "pow'r" to make you true and brave,
> So that you can rescue those that Christ would save?
> Make the consecration, trust in God, and then,
> Let the Holy Ghost come in.
> *Refrain*
> Let the Holy Ghost come in.
> Let the Holy Ghost come in.
> Make the consecration, trust in God and then,
> Let the Holy Ghost come in.
>
> —Words: R. F. Reynolds.; Music: C. E. Rowley

ENDNOTES:

1. French Arrington, *The Acts of the Apostles* (1986).
2. Frank Macchia, "Sighs to Deep For Words, *JPT* I (1992), 65-66.
3. Maachia quotes Harvey Cox here in *Fire From Heaven* (1995), 93.
4. For a report on this issue, see Ian MacRobert, *The Black Roots and White Racism of the Early Pentecostalism in the USA* (1988), 9, 60.
5. Jappie LaPoorta, "Unity or Division" in *The Globalization of Pentecostalism* (1999), 151-169.
6. Ibid., 166.
7. David Daniels in "Everybody Bids You Welcome," *The Globalization of Pentecostalism: A Religion Made to Travel,* Dempster, Klaus, Petersen, eds. (1999), 238.
8. See also Cecil Robeck, "William J. Seymour and Bible Evidence" in *Initial Evidence: Historical and Biblical Perspectives on the Pentecostal Doctrine of Spirit Baptism,* ed. Gary B. McGee (1991), 81. See also S. David Moore, "William J. Seymour" *Ministries Today*, May/June, 2005, 48.
9. Robeck, 81.
10. Harvey Cox, *Fire From Heaven, The Rise of Pentecostal Spirituality and the Reshaping of Religion in the Twenty-first Century* (1995), 195.
11. See Spittler, "Glossolalia" in *Dictionary of Pentecostal and Charismatic Movements,* eds. Stanley M. Burgess and Gary B. McGee (1992), 341.
12. Ibid.
13. See Janet Evert Powers, "Your Daughters Shall Prophesy" in *The Globalization of Pentecostalism* (1999), 318.
14. Ibid., 320.
15. Jappie LaPoorta, "Unity or Division" in *The Globalization of Pentecostalism* (1999), 157-166. AFM stands for Apostolic Faith Mission, which is one of the largest and earliest Pentecostal denominations in South Africa.
16. Maachia, "Sighs Too Deep For Words" (1992), 65.
17. J.E. Powers, 55.
18. Johannes Behm Kaivoc, *TDNT III*, 447-454, as in Janet Powers, "Missionary Tongues? *JPT* 17 (2000), 51.
19. Howard Kenyan, "An Analysis of Ethical Issues in the History of the Assemblies of God" (Ph. D. diss. Baylor University, 1988), 401-403.
20. Maachia, *Sighs,* 18.
21. Cox (1995), 72.
22. Maachia, *JPT*, 1992.
23. Cecil M. Robeck, "A Pentecostal Looks at the World Council of Churches," *The Ecumenical Review 47* (1995) 60-62.
24. Walter J. Holllenweger, "Theology of the New World," *The Expository Times 87* (May 1976), 229.
25. Cecil M. Robeck, Jr., "Taking Stock of Pentecostalism: The Personal Reflections of a Retiring Editor," *PNEUMA*: *The Journal of the Society for Pentecostal Studies 15* (Spring 1993), 39ff.
26. Ibid., 113 and 126.
27. Adapted from Ken Gire, *Moments With the Savior: A Devotional Life of Christ* (1988).

APPENDIX 1

COMMUNICATION SOURCES AND COMMUNICATION POTPOURI

Theologians get bored with Communications Theories. Others not in the discipline of the social sciences are worse than bored. The following "bits and pieces" is some of the technical information the author sees as pertinent to the larger scope of the thesis, but perhaps not interesting to a large segment of the readers. Some of this specialized information may prove to be useful for those seeking input on Communications Theory in general.

1. EARLY EXAMPLE OF COMMUNICATIONS THEORY

The following communications model was referenced in chapter 4 as an example of one of the earliest communication models available in the new emerging discipline after World War II.

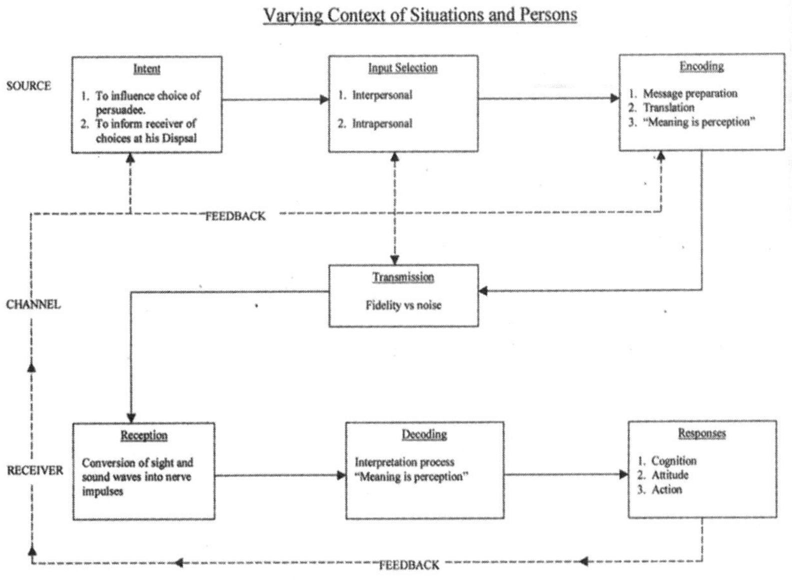

Model of the Communication Process
--from Wm. S. Howell

This model, by Wm. S. Howell of University of Minnesota, is from a class on Persuasion in 1967. Though slightly modified from its original elements, its contents are found in "How Communication Works" in The *Process and Effects of Mass Communication,* W. Schramm and D. F Parks, eds. Urbana, Ill.: University of Illinois Press, 1971. See also: Fiske, John. *Introduction to Communication Studies*, London: Routledge, 1992.

There is a big chasm between this model in the 1950s and the leap of theories in current technological jargon! The constant addition of new theories and electronic sophistication has continually modified how people look at this mystery of human interaction with environment and persons. Consider, for example, the almost esoteric presentation of communications of virtual realities and the media. See: Biocca, Frank and Mark Levy. *Communication in the Age of Virtual Reality*, Hillsdale, NJ: Lawrence Erlbaum Associates, Inc. Publishers, 1998. See also: Steuer, J. "Defining Virtual Reality: Dimensions Determining Telepresence," *Journal of Communication*, 42 (4). They represent the constant progression of communications theory in the age of electronic realities. Even new words are being coined, such as *informatics* to describe the combination of telecommunications; the processing power of computers; the memory capability of CD-ROM, optical disk and other storage technology, etc.

See also: Woods, Bernard. *Communication, Technology and the Development of People*, London: Routledge Publishing, Inc., 1993.

2. OTHER MODERN RESEARCH

The modern study of language draws on the social and behavioral sciences—on semantics, linguistics, anthropology and psychology especially—and on the preoccupation with symbolic systems that characterizes much of twentieth century philosophy. It also incorporates parts of the biological sciences and especially the neuro-physiological mechanisms involved in producing and hearing speech. Here is an examplefrom the *Scientific American*, Feb. 2002 (p. 28) under subtitle "Parts of Speech":

We humans may recite Shakespeare while our ape cousins merely grunt their approval of "iambic pentameter." But the part of the brain required for our chatter has a longer evolutionary history than previously suspected. A region with Brocda's area known as Brodmann's area 44, critical for the power of speech, is larger in the left hemisphere of humans than in the right. A study has now found that the same asymmetry exists in other great ape species: chimpanzees, bonobos and gorillas. Reporting in the Nov. 29, 2001, *Nature*, the Emory University researchers conjecture that the area may have originally been associated with the production of gestures used by apes for communication. This area eventually became used as a source of speech in modern humans.

Much earlier research on the same topic probably would have made a notation that such conclusions are only permitted by persons who have abandoned "Creative Design" theories which are today so opposed by many scientists.

Recent Brain Scan Research Regarding Tongues

As referenced in chapters above, modern technology has found interest in identifying electronic impulses inside the brain's vast neurological networks while someone practices glossolalia. For those interested, see the work of Cari Peterson from Oral Roberts University in an article accessible in French at http://franternite-chretienne.ch/fraterinfo.php?menu=427. See also studies from the University of Pennsylvania in a study soon to be published in the journal *Psychiatry: Neuroimaging*, and this is fully described in Andrew Newberg's new book *Why We Believe What We Believe*, Un. of Penn: Free Press/Simon and Schuster, 2007.

Development of the Brain

"We know that the growth of the brain, especially primary tissue, occurs very rapidly. After birth, motor maturity appears to come first, followed by sensory, visual, and auditory maturity." See in: Brophy, Jere, Shari Nedler, and Thomas Good. *Teaching in the Preschool*, NY: Harper and Row, 1975. See Tanner, J. "Human Growth and Constitution" in Harrison, J. Weiner; J. Tanner and N. Barnicot, eds. *Human Biology: An Introduction to Human Evolution, Variation, and Growth,* NY: Oxford University Press, 1964; as well as Piaget, J. *The Origins of Intelligence in Children,* NY: Basic Books, 1969. The ways children learn to speak, in his theory, is related to sensorimotor experience and interaction, not just by looking and hearing, but by exploring the external world.

On Predictability

Diggory suggests that if a child is to organize his world and to speak about it, his world must be organized into a basic consistency. All cultures teach, explicitly and implicitly, that certain things go certain places, and other things happen at prescribed times. Without this structure, the child is confused and speech is retarded. Important here. Speech is orderly and related to an accepted worldview—order—predictability.

The child's ability to respond to and benefit from language is a key to his conceptual attainment. Indeed, sophisticated language is one basic ability that separates man from other animals. In: Fraser, C. U., and R. Brown.

"Control of Grammar in Imitation, Comprehension, and Production," *Journal of Verbal Learning and Verbal Behavior, 2* 1963.

"We are the only animals who can haggle about the definition of ourselves and therefore can be, within limits, whatever we choose to define ourselves as being." See: King, Sara Sanderson, ed. *Human Communication as a Field of Study: Selected Contemporary Views*, State University of New York Press, 1989.

There is a great topic on how our presuppositions or assumptions are the determinants of our perception of experience. See: Gadamer, Hans-Georg. *Truth and Method,* New York: Seabury, 1975. See also: Deetz, Stanley on Gadamer's work: Deetz, Stanley. "Conceptualizing Human Understanding Gadamer's Hermeneutics and American Communication Studies" *Communication Quarterly 26*, 1978.

Egocentric Speech

This one I find very interesting, especially watching our grandchildren! Some research shows that children who talk to themselves talk more to other people. Bright children's egocentric speech (talking aloud to oneself) leads them to use verbal mediators for thinking and problem solving. In: Kolberg, L., J. Yaeger, and E. Hjertholm, E., eds. "Private Speech: Four Studies and a Review of Theories," *Child Development, 39,* 1968. In the human species, the important role of speech is learned early and becomes an inseparable part of self-esteem. From the child's "social birth" in school for the next 12 to 16 years in the Western world, verbal skills will be perhaps the primordial element on which the person will be evaluated by parents and society and certainly the educational system.

Speech Codes

Some of our grandchildren can speak American English (well, ——like——, you know——cool!—— totally——) in a code we hear them use when talking on the phone or with close friends. Some other of our grandchildren attend a British school in Africa and have parts of their vocabulary distinctly different than their cousins in California. How do teenagers in America know what to say and say what they mean? Their group's speech code determines this. Speech codes are powerful and can actually guide what the communicator "hears and sees." See: Philipsen, Gerry. "A Theory of Speech Codes," in *Developing Communication Theories,* Gerry Philipsen and Terrance L. Albrecht, eds., Albany, NY: Suny Press, 1997.

In this sense, glossolalia was a speech code for the Apostolic New Testament Church. The apostle Paul asked the Samaritans: "Do you speak the new "speech code" since you believed?" (Acts 10).

3. A STUDY NEEDS TO BE DEVELOPED ON THE SIGNIFANCE OF W O R D AS RELATED TO THE MOUTH (The symbol of power and authority in the old world)

One only needs to do the engine search in good database of the Bible under the relationships between these two words: Word and Mouth. Astounding! Here are two or three examples:

"In the beginning was the Word, and the Word was with God, and the Word was God. He was with God in the beginning (John 1:1-2). "The Word became flesh and made his dwelling among us. We have seen His glory, the glory of the One and Only, who came from the Father, full of grace and truth" (v.14).

"*...Out of His mouth came a sharp double-edged sword.*" This was the vision John saw of Jesus in heaven while writing the Apocalypse. Strange? Not for the Mossi (and many other West African tribes where *mouth* and *power/authority* are the same word!) A knife has a "mouth" if it is sharp. A dull knife (like a table knife) doesn't even have a "mouth."

The creation story in Genesis 1 starts every act of creation with: "And God said..." **Not** God wrote or painted or depicted, but SAID.

What does man know, innately, about himself, a creature of God, and the attribute he possesses that is related to "made in His image"? Even in the Hindu search for God and inner meaning (from in the *Rig Veda* hymn) is the phrase "His mouth became Brahmin." Find in: Wright, Paul. *People and Their Beliefs*, Bruxelles: International Correspondence Institute, 1987.

The Mossi concept of "Nori" (mouth) also means *authority/sharpness/power.* When a chief is "clothed," he is given "mouth/authority" in the same sense that Jesus is described as the Word of God. This existed before any written word. There is an oralness to God that our literalness fails to grasp. Pentecostal tongues reaches back to the oral period of God, the oral attribute of God, the oral kind of ambiguity that has a texture, weight, palpability, and essence of non-precision that helps us fathom, or attempt to Know Him. There is much in animism and other Eastern religions that strive to reach past the literal and external world of materialism that in some strange way keeps up the search for the Creator—which our literalism of the materialistic world has dampened. Our literalness is like giving a label to something. Once it is labeled, the search for meaning ceases. Hinduism, Buddhism, Shinto, Taoism, and even parts of Islam have all retained an intuitive nature that modern Christianity denies by its literalism. Most Evangelicals are literalists par excellence. Much of Protestant Christianity today has been influenced by the Method of Science that leaves no room for the path of faith. Pentecostalism harks back to a more primitive era in Christianity where the immanence and transcendence of God are again allowed to be a part of the Christian ethic and experience. (See David Hesselgrave, *Communicating Christ Cross-Culturally* [1991], 311ff. And also Paul Wright, *People and Their Beliefs* (1987), 112. both give a glimpse into how Taoism views itself relative to language. "It's beyond words...according to its followers, Taoism cannot be described...if it could be explained, it would no longer be Tao. It can only be understood intuitively, that is, in one's spirit, not by rational thought." That's far from the tenets of the B.B.Warfield's ethic of the supremacy of human reason. (Warfield, Benjamin B. *Counterfeit Miracles*, 1918; reprint, Carlisle, PA: Banner of Truth, 1976.)

4. WORDS WEAR THEMSELVES OUT!

Harvey Cox sees this dimension: "I believe that the inner significance of speaking in tongues or praying in the Spirit can be found in something virtually every spiritual tradition in human history teaches in one way or another: that the reality religious symbols strive to express ultimately defies even the most exalted human language. Virtually all the mystics of every faith have indicated that the vision they have glimpsed, though they try desperately to describe it, finally eludes them. As the preacher in the biblical book of Ecclesiastes puts it:

All words wear themselves out; a man cannot utter it; the eye is not satisfied with seeing, nor the ear with hearing.

Confronted with this verbal paralysis, what can people do? They sing, they rhapsodize, they invent Metaphors; they soar into canticles and doxologies. But ultimately, words fail them and they lapse into silence. Or they speak in tongues. Harvey Cox, *Fire From Heaven: The Rise of Pentecostal Spirituality and the Reshaping of Religion in the Twenty-first Century* (1995), 92. (Emphasis mine.)

5. NON-VERBAL COMMUNICATION

Africans taught me early and late that we Westerners are non-verbal illiterates. Discovering this, I began teaching potential missionaries the rudiments of this almost unknown science in North America (relative to our advance in other sciences). Here is a list of works I've found useful for me in teaching pastors and evangelists the need to begin to open up their "fans of perception" to this neglected issue.

Bauml, Betty J. *A Dictionary of Gestures,* Metuchen, NY: Scarecrow Press, 1975.

Birdwhistle, Ray, L. *Introduction to Kinesics*, Washington, DC: Foreign Service Institute, Department of State, 1962.

Hall, Edward T. *The Hidden Dimension,* Garden City, NY: Doubleday and Company, 1966.

__________ *The Silent Language*, Garden City, NY: Doubleday and Company, 1966.

Harper, Robert G., et. al. *Nonverbal Communications: The State of the Art,* New York: Wiley, 1978.

Knapp, Mark L. *Non-verbal Communication in Human Interaction,* New York: Holt, Rinehart, and Winston, 1972.

Koneya, Male. *Louder Than Words...Nonverbal Communications,* Columbus, OH: Merril, 1976.

Leathers, Dale G. *Non-Verbal Communications Systems,* Boston: Allyn and Bacon, 1976.

Mehrabian, Albert. *Non-Verbal Communication*, Chicago: Moody Press, 1975.

____________ *Silent Messages,* Belmont, CA: Wadsworth Publishing, 1974.

Reusch, Jurgen and Welson Kess. *Non-Verbal Communication: Notes on Visual Perception of Human Relations*, Berkeley, CA: University of California Press, 1956.

6. ON THE TONGUE ITSELF (Merlin Mitchell)

While writing and speaking to my friends about the subject of The Foolishness of God, I have repeatedly been asked if I was aware of the rather recent common occurrence of how modern technology can now detect glossolalia with electronic instruments. The following is very interesting and relates to a small segment in the main text of the book.

I am a voice teacher, with a Master's degree in music from the University of Missouri at Kansas City. When my wife Judy, suffered from migraine headaches she consulted Dr. Diamond of the renowned Diamond Headache Clinic in Chicago. Among other things he recommended several changes in her diet, sleep patterns, and trying biofeedback treatments. Dr. Larry Bass of Springfield, MO became our source of help with the biofeedback treatments.

Dr. Bass immediately found that Judy's tongue and jaw muscles were filled with tension. He said that the tongue and jaw muscles are the strongest muscles of the body. They are stubborn and are the last muscles to respond to relaxation treatments. This was of real interest to me in my study of the voice.

As voice teachers, we have also found that getting students to relax their tongues and jaws is one of our major challenges. It is interesting to see how the spiritual laws of God and the physical laws (which I believe are of God) run parallel and intertwine with each other. The Bible tells us in James 3 that the tongue is the most unruly member of the body. This is true spiritually and physically. The tongue is stubborn and unruly as an instrument of gossip, back-biting, and bad language. It is also stubborn and unruly physically. The tongue is a very complicated structure of opposing sets of muscles. It can be (and most of the time) is physically stubborn as it responds to our range of feelings of fear, anger, pride, insecurity and self-consciousness. It is physically unruly in many seasoned, as well as beginning, singers. There are muscles in the tongue that raise it, lower it, widen it, narrow it, push it forward, pull it back, turn it over both ways, retroflex it both up-back-and over and also down and under. God designed it so that it can reach forward out over the lower and upper lips to lick off the ice cream, as well as reach in and up and around every tooth in your mouth. Every swallow of food or liquid is forced back and down from the lips and teeth back through the oral cavity, down through the oropharynx, past the epiglottis and down into the esophagus by the tongue. It is the major instrument for speech and singing, as well as whistling. Its action can be comparable to that of a snake. If the brain is allowed to work with a tongue that is not encumbered with stiffness in the opposing set of muscles (e.g. the muscles that raise the tongue are not stiffened against the ones that lower it, and the muscles that widen it are not in isometric tension against those that move it backward, etc., etc.) the voice can then have a chance to function freely and beautifully.

The tongue sits directly above the voice box. Its musculature is connected to the jaw, the back of the throat, and the hyoid bone from above. The hyoid bone is the only bone in the throat. The musculature of the larynx or voice box is connected to the hyoid bone from below. If there is tension in the muscles of the tongue; the jaw will also be tense, and there will "chain reaction" from the tongue down through the jaw and then on down through the hyoid bone and on downward into the vocal cords. If the voice is going to function freely, there must not be any negative isometric tension (e.g. unwanted muscle against opposing muscle tension) in the lips, tongue, jaw, and throat. We want a feeling of effortlessness in the vocal anatomy. We're designed for "muscular equilibrium" in the vocal anatomy when we sing and speak. If the musculature of the tongue, jaw and throat is free as we phonate (make vocal sound), the brain will have freedom to move the tongue, epiglottis, lips, soft-palate, vocal cords, mouth opening, nasal passages through all of the complex range of motion that is called for in human vocal expression. These movements are from micro-millimeter in distance up to as much as the width of three fingers between the upper and lower front teeth. Some of the fine tunings of the epiglottis and tongue are hundredths of a millimeter. If the throat and tongue are stiff, these fine tunings will not be possible and the singer or speaker will experience fatigue, with the resultant tone lacking in resonance and beauty.

In the old hymn, "O For a Thousand Tongues," by Charles Wesley, we find the verse: "Hear Him, ye deaf; His praise, ye dumb, *your loosened tongues employ.*" The Holy Spirit is our Comforter and Helper (Paraclete). He helps us to relax with His peace and power. I've had many Pentecostal voice students in my 42 years of college teaching tell me that they find it much easier to sing when they are singing in the Spirit. They are able to sing with wider range and greater freedom, when they sing in the Spirit. In special meetings that my wife and I attended at the First Assembly of God church in Santa Cruz, CA, the evangelist preached on having a "song in the Spirit." After delivering a beautiful message on this theme, he gave the altar call. There was a special awareness of God's presence that all of us had as we prayed. Perhaps fifteen to twenty minutes into this season of prayer and worship, the evangelist went to the microphone and said that he felt that someone was in the service who had a song in the Spirit, but they were afraid to sing. As he encouraged this person to sing out, a most beautiful high soprano voice (which seemed to be in surround sound) filled the room. She was singing short sections of melody from well-known sacred songs. The rest of us in the congregation were able to sing along with her. The most unusual thing about my personal experience with her was that I found myself singing in the same unknown tongue that she was singing. The congregation was also able to sing in harmony with her. We had total musical freedom. We could do scales or arpeggios. Everything fit together in what was like a heavenly musical wind.

In the meeting the next night, the evangelist reported that the girl who sang in the Spirit the night before was a student from Bethany Bible College. She was so tone deaf that her dorm mates asked her not to sing when they were having devotions, because her singing was so off-pitch and distracting that they were not able to worship. The Bible encourages us to keep being "filled with the Spirit" (Ephesians 5:18). The Old Testament Hebrew word for Spirit is *ruach*, which also means wind and breath. The New Testament Greek word for the Holy Spirit is *pneuma*. We use this in words such as pneumonia, or pneumatic tires. Obviously this is a way for God to say that the Holy Spirit is the breath of God. We also find in the dictionary that the Latin work *spirare* is the root of our words *respiration* (a synonym for breathing), *inspiration* (a synonym for inhalation), *expiration* (a synonym for exhalation). Spirare is also the root word for Spirit.

As I said earlier, the spiritual laws of God and the physical laws run parallel and interact with each other. The Bible tells us that Christ (the Living Word) was and continues to be revealed to us by the Holy Spirit. In our natural world, it is impossible for us to phonate any word without the flow of breath. We singers, preachers, and teachers will find that we can speak and sing best when we "fill up" with natural breath, every time we inhale. I tell students to fill up from the lower abdomen all the way to their vocal cords. When we fill up with breath, we will have the capacity to sing long phrases with control over range, volume, duration, flexibility, vibrato, and style. When we learn to sing "on the breath," we can be much more relaxed and effective in our vocal delivery. Being physically filled with breath and properly suspending the breath, the tongue and the rest of the vocal anatomy will be able to function with freedom. I believe this is paralleled with the breath of the Spirit. We need to *keep on being filled with natural breath*, but more importantly, we need to *keep on being filled with the breath of God*. (Emphasis Mitchell.)

Merlin Mitchell, MA
Springfield, MO

APPENDIX 2

EXAMPLE OF DUPLICATION OF ACTS 2

(Where the incidence of hearing one's own language spoken, and not understood by the speaker, resulted in the coming to faith of the hearer or hearers)

Wade Horton[1] gives a list of people recognizable in the greater Pentecostal Movement who witnessed or participated in events where the "tongues" spoken were understood by someone present: Stanley Frodsham tells of an incident where several Russians were present; Vessie D. Hargrave remembers an incident where many people came to Jesus because of a young girl speaking Spanish—a language she didn't know;

Dr. Bob O'Bannon recounts hearing an illiterate camel driver in Egypt who spoke English while receiving the baptism in the Holy Spirit; Rev. E. J. Boehmer relates being present when perfect German was spoken by a non-German speaker which resulted in a change of attitude and experience.

Another source noted earlier is Ralph Harris' small book *Spoken By The Spirit: Documented Accounts of "Other Tongues" from Arabic to Zulu.*[2] This small book lists over 20 such occasions of this phenomenon.

This author, during the great Holy Spirit revival in Burkina Faso in 1965 where 2000 people received the initial infilling of the Holy Spirit manifested by glossolalia in a 90-day period, heard a Burkinabe speak perfect English while being baptized in the Spirit. The young man did not live in a country where English was spoken, had never been over 50 miles from his home and upon being quizzed, could not understand or speak one word of English after the experience. His family members present were as amazed as I. A witness to this event was Pasteur Zabre, Sidibe, the Director of the Ecole Biblique a Nagabare, Burkina Faso.

F. Bartleman, an early minister from the Azusa Street revival and often quoted in subsequent literature writes of similar experiences where the "unknown tongue" for the speaker has an impact on the hearer who understood the glossolalic utterance: (The following is unedited as found)

At one time Sister Prince, a coloured lady, well-known and reverenced among us...spoke in the most perfect German, of which she knew nothing in the natural. Two brethren who were German born, in different parts of the house, interpreted to those around them, and a few minutes afterwards notes were compared, and it was proven to be genuine.

Let me say, the messages, as far as I have interpreted, have always been proper messages; praises to God, exhortations, warnings etc. Never anything of an irreverent or foolish character, but very often of a very highly exalted and intensely practical import, often of tremendous meaning especially for the individual for whom the message was intended...Rev. S. J. Mead—well-known in church circles, and highly respected, lately returned from Africa, where, while actively engaged in the mission field, God spoke to him and bade him come at once to Los Angeles, for what reason he did not then understand—arose to his feet, he readily interpreted the message just spoken by the girl, giving the name and dialect of the tribe in Africa to which the language belonged, and then immediately proceeded to speak the very same message in the very same tongue which he himself had become familiar with, while in the field in Africa. Bro Mead is now on his way back to his field in Africa with other workers called to go with him from these meetings. Glory.

Brother Berg, well known in the churches here, a returned missionary from India, while at the altar seeking power from on high, and rather doubting, was spoken to by a white man, who was all unconscious of the language in which he was speaking, that of Gujerat. The message was so assuring to our brother that he opened his heart wide, without reserve, and the fire went through him in a most wonderful way. He now longs to get back to dear India especially to tell the good news to his fellow missionaries, who he declares must have just this experienced...Rev. Joseph H. Kelly, ex-soldier from the Philippines was converted later in St. Louis and returned for missionary work in the Island of Mindanao. Lately he felt called to return to this country to gather up a band of workers to return with him. After making strenuous efforts in that direction, he seemed only to fail, and finally to be discouraged. The devil so taunted him, that pressed beyond endurance he finally declared to himself that if God did not care for the Philippines, he need not either, and determined to return without making any further efforts towards interesting any one else in that direction. He has spoken in many churches in this country on the subject. Having heard of the work in Los Angeles, however, and of the "Tongue" business, he, like Saul of old, began to breathe out threatenings and headed this way, declaring that before he returned to his field, he would do the Lord one more good turn and expose the Tongue deception proper. By the time he reached the place he was just about furious as so many others have been. In fact, as he confesses freely, he was simply an unvarnished backslider. But God had mercy on his soul. The saints realized his condition quickly and began to pray for him openly. This he resented. His Irish blood got the better of him, and he confesses he even harbouored a desire to whip the preacher soundly. But soon after, while sitting in his chair a delicate, quiet little white sister spoke to him in a tongue which he understood—that of a hostile tribe in the interior, where he had been labouring. He knew that language was altogether unknown in this part of the world, and he nearly fell off his chair. There was something more than "nigger religion" in this. He went upstairs to the private room, quite in serious trouble, but still resisting. But there the Lord slew him properly—stretched him on the floor until he was glad to ask for quarter.

The next day after having asked to be forgiven, he knelt at the penitent form and sought his Pentecost. And then another white sister, just as ignorant of the Filipino, spoke a message to him in another tongue he had become familiar with in those Islands. It was sufficient, and he swept into the experience. And now the Lord is giving him his band of workers after all. But best of all, instead of going back a plain backslidden preacher, he goes filled with the Holy Ghost. Oh glory! And the "tongues" have played their part already.[3]

ENDNOTES:

1. James Cross, "Its Value to the Church," in *The Glossolalia Phenomenon,* W. Horton, ed. (1966), 210-212.
2. Ralph Harris, *Spoken By The Spirit: Documented Accounts of "Other Tongues" from Arabic to Zulu* (1973).
3. Frank Bartleman in *Triumphs of Faith,* early periodical, n.d. (Probably written before 1910 as found with other articles of that era) no page.

APPENDIX 3

WHAT "TONGUES" IS NOT

It would be difficult to find an issue in religious circles that has been more controversial and divisive through the centuries than glossolalia. (Perhaps the modes of water baptism would come close.) As in most such religious debates, the element of myth surrounding one side's opinion is at times substantial. The following is the author's attempt to list the misunderstandings and/or misrepresentations expressed by those who oppose today's worldwide renewal. Most of these misunderstandings stem from ignorance and others from intentional distortion or bias. Obviously, the opinions expressed here are those of the author, a recipient and user of the gifts. Relevant scripture will be applied where pertinent.

GOD'S POWER HELD NOT ONLY BY GLOSSOLALIC PEOPLE

1. Those who speak in tongues don't have a corner on the Holy Spirit's power!

I believe what is proposed here is important for any true seeker of the glossolalia phenomenon because of the many godly people who oppose the baptism in the Holy Spirit but who are participants in many significant spiritual activities that are available in the life of any believer. Pentecostals and Charismatics are often guilty of claiming more than can be demonstrated from scripture or experience. Gordon Anderson has written, in my opinion, the most coherent article explaining some of the reasons people of the Spirit are misunderstood. He explains that it's often related to their own lack of teaching while trying to teach others or fully explain their beliefs.

The argument is: If the evidence for the baptism in the Holy Spirit is a supernaturally gifted life and a significant ministry, then Hudson Taylor, Chuck Swindoll, Charles Stanley, Billy Graham, and many others must have been baptized in the Holy Spirit, even though they have never spoken in tongues...This argument is perfectly coherent and has been found to be compelling to many in the charismatic, Third Wave, and non-Pentecostal world.[1]

Anderson suggests Pentecostals need to learn to explain that not *all* the gifts for ministry and deliverance from the power of Satan are reserved only for those who are glossolalic. The historical record and Scripture show that many who have not experienced the baptism in the Holy Spirit can and have experienced "signs following."

All that is needed to clarify the Pentecostal understanding of the baptism in the Holy Spirit and its relationship to other schools of thought is the fact that Pentecostals do not believe *all* power and gifting for ministry occur only after the baptism in the Holy Spirit...But the baptism in the Holy Spirit confers dramatically more power for ministry, especially in the supernatural realm of miracles, signs, and wonders; ministries that promote the apostolic or missionary call to plant the church and minister in the supernatural.

For Pentecostals—tongues is only a small part of the "Endowment of Power" for witness (Acts 1:8), like the tongue of a shoe is only a small part of a unit made up of sole, heel, upper part, inner sole, glue, stitches, tacks, color, and adornment, etc. To study tongues alone, like many who have never experienced them but feel expert to write about them, is to miss the wider *whole* for only a *part,* a part they woefully cannot and will not understand. Both those who write defending tongues in a narrow sectarian way AND those who denounce or disparage the tongues phenomenon[2] but who fail to see the bigger picture; *are they not guilty of eisegesis*?

THE MESSAGE OF PENTECOST IS NOT TONGUES

The message of Pentecost is not its Pentecostal 'distinctive' alone.

The true message of Pentecost is not its methods or style.

The message of Pentecost is not the spectacular, though it seems to attract the secular and religious media.

The message of Pentecost **IS** the working out of the ascension mandate of Jesus, the Christ of God, centered in His cross, a belief and practice of the supernatural "signs following" accompanying that message as described and registered in the New Testament.

2. Tongues is not the goal.

Speaking in tongues is the evidence or consequence of receiving the baptism in the Holy Spirit, not the gift itself.

The baptism in the Holy Spirit is not just tongues. THE BAPTISM IN THE HOLY SPIRIT IS THE BEGINNING OF A RELATIONSHIP that only total submission of one's being (of which tongues is a sign) is like the entry point/door. Pentecostals who make tongues the "goal" are shortchanging themselves and other believers. They just get in the door of this big room full of gifts and fruit and growth and maturity and sanctification—and just stand there! The Baptists are right when they say the Holy Spirit would lead us to sanctification and growth. Our own early recipients of the gift said the same.[3]

3. Tongues are not simply to be equated with emotionalism.

Morton Kelsey says:

Most of us who have never witnessed tongues speaking or happen to have seen it only in emotionally charged surroundings, hold to a general belief that an uncorked emotionalism is necessary to the experience. I can testify this is simply not true. Tongues speaking occurs just as readily in a quiet devotional atmosphere. This truth cannot be emphasized enough. One who has once spoken spontaneously in tongues can open himself to the experience at will and without any particular stimulus or emotional effect.[4]

John York has a subchapter under "Further Concerns" in which he states:

...The Baptism in the Holy Spirit is not to be equated with either emotionalism or some other human reaction to the Spirit's presence. Human personalities are different, and learned responses vary. What is essential is the reality of the impartation of divine power focused in witness and service. There are those who equate Pentecostalism with exuberance in worship or emotional behavior. While it would be unwise to belittle the significance of human emotions or lively worship patterns, these are not the essence of Pentecostalism. The heart of Pentecostalism is the supernatural empowerment of believers so that they may, in word and deed, adequately bear witness to the nations of the world.[5]

4. Tongues are not short memorized phrases.

Some short memorized phrase like "ouppa, uppa—ouppa, uppa" repeated over and over to fake the real gift of God is not true glossolalia. Sometimes teachers can so emphasize "tongues" as the goal of the deeper search for God that to receive the approval and approbation of a group of believers, someone is tempted to "manufacture" the experience. Caution! No one should seek a manifestation. Seek the presence of God and His holiness. One does not speak in tongues for the sake of tongues. This does not magnify God; it magnifies the speaker. Great words come from Minnie Abrams of the Holy Ghost revival in India. This teaching comes from the "Latter Rain" *(Evangel,* 1906), and plainly shows what one should expect after the baptism in the Holy Spirit.

What kind of results? Results that help in the kingdom of God; that tend toward the salvation of souls and the upbuilding of believers. You will see that, and if you do not see it, I hope you will begin to doubt your baptism, because that is what the baptism of the Holy Ghost is given for, that we may be witnesses to the power of the Lord Jesus Christ through His death and resurrection, so as to bring people under the power of repentance, in order that they may receive the remission of sins. Now that is the Word of God...[6]

5. Tongues are not a prerequisite to salvation.

This stance is rare, but sadly still held by a small minority of Pentecostals.

Some Pentecostals have made extravagant claims for the baptism in the Holy Spirit. Some have argued that a person must speak in tongues to be saved. Using the lamp oil obtained by the wise virgins in preparation for the bridegroom as a symbol for the Holy Spirit (Matthew 25), they claim that a person must have the Holy Spirit to be ready or saved. Since in this camp, the baptism in the Holy Spirit is always accompanied by speaking in tongues, one must speak in tongues to be saved. This is preposterous and can be dismissed.[7]

6. Tongues are not for public show to demonstrate "holiness."

Gifts are never a proof of holiness. Rather, holiness is demonstrated by the fruit of the Spirit which is "grown" by the believer to attract the onlooker or inquirer to the Savior. Jesus said that by one's "fruit" one's character is known, one's value is determined—not by one's gifts. (Matt. 12:33, Luke 6:44). Tongues outside the context of intense prayer and worship are never meant for prideful display or analysis by others. Just like Jesus always turned down requests for a demonstration of miracles to impress a crowd or important people,[8] neither should "tongues" be used for such purposes. Prayer in the Spirit is not for public show! This was one of the errors of the Corinthian believers. The apostle Paul, writing to correct the excesses of tongues in public worship (I Cor. 12- 14) was concerned that the Body of Believers would be edified by the gifts of the Spirit, not hindered by their improper use. It is clear, by the context of these chapters, that the gift of tongues, very evident in the church at Corinth, was falling short of its God-intended purpose. "Tongues were front and center. Tongues were spoken simply for drama and display. Edification of the Body was disregarded."[9] The apostle seeks to remedy this excess by the following admonition:

For this reason anyone who speaks in a tongue should pray that he may interpret what he says. For if I pray in a tongue, my spirit prays, but my mind is unfruitful. So what shall I do? I will pray with my spirit, but I will also pray with my mind; I will sing with my spirit, but I will also sing with my mind. If you are praising God with your spirit, how can one who finds himself among those who do not understand say "Amen" to your thanksgiving, since he does not know what you are saying? You may be giving thanks well enough, but the other man is not edified (1 Cor. 14:13-17).

Let us not, however, make the mistake of so many who, seeing Paul's need for correction of tongues, conclude he meant to disallow them. The very next verse from the above passage is: *"I thank God that I speak in tongues more than all of you"* (v. 18). And at the end of chapter 14 are these words. *"Therefore, my brothers, be eager to prophesy, and do not forbid speaking in tongues."*

Tongues are no substitute for:

Perseverance in prayer that waits before God in patience and faith.

Desperation in intensity of prayer that is willing to pay the price in personal self-denial, such as fasting.

Repentance before the Lord in humble contrition and sorrow for sin.

Commitment to a lifestyle of godliness and holiness.

Glossolalia in private prayer can be a part of the above (in fact, a great aid). But the fault with some Pentecostals and Charismatics is the mistaken belief that tongues is a shortcut to the acquisition of selfish desires; that somehow God will reward them because they are the believers in the *Full Gospel.* Tongues, and all the other charismata, are **tools**. Tools are not for blessing. Tools are for hard work, to work the field that results in fruit, fruit that remains and blesses the Father. He's the fruit inspector (John 15:8).

How many times did the Savior refuse to "show a sign" to the religious of His day, or to Satan at the Lord's great temptation at the start of His ministry? Speaking with "tongues" has no meaning, unless the Spirit gives utterance.[10]

7. Tongues are not ecstatic utterance (rather they are the expression of the incarnational model).

Tongues are not ecstasy where the speaker loses control of consciousness and goes into a trance. As earlier mentioned, rather like the Bible was written by 44 different authors *inspired* by the Spirit of God using human instrumentality, AND like the Christ was the Messiah both God and man, so the Holy Spirit uses human instrumentation in the gifts of the Holy Spirit, including and especially "tongues." The "unfruitful" passage in I Cor. 14 doesn't mean "unconscious" or in an ecstatic state. There is a cooperation/coordination because it's God's way. The view is complementary, not mutually exclusive.

There is a sublimation of native human speech, but not exclusion of the mind/understanding capacity. David Lim says: "Spiritual gifts do not cause a person to lose control of his faculties. Rather, as the person yields himself fully to the control of the Holy Spirit he finds he can most effectively exercise spiritual gifts as well as the full range of his natural abilities."[11] The mind is not blanked out and put into neutral, as may be the case in some Eastern religions. That being so, the mind should not be wandering around the world of politics, sports, and schedules when worshiping God. True worship requires the mind, as well as the spirit and body.

Larry Christianson says:

Another misconception is that speaking in tongues is a highly emotional or "ecstatic" utterance. The terms "ecstatic utterance" or "tongues of ecstasy" are *never* used in the Bible in reference to a speaker in tongues. Those who hear a speaker in tongues are sometimes described as "ecstatic" or "amazed" (*existanto*, Acts 2:7; *exestasan*, Acts 10:45) but the speaker himself is *never* described in this way. These misleading terms occur frequently in commentaries, and even turn up in translations of the Bible. The original text of the Bible gives no basis for such a translation. It seems to stem from an assumption on the part of the commentators and translators, who perhaps have not experienced the gift.[12]

8. Not all "tongues" are equal.

Too easily one can assume that anytime the word "tongues" is used to connote the Pentecostal practice of the gift of the Holy Spirit, that it's always of the same quality or definition. This can be illustrated by the following. A close friend of mine recounted that the first time he heard a colleague speak French was when he arrived at the city where his friend was studying that language in Europe. My friend spoke no French, had never had a French lesson. When his host spoke French to a citizen of that country, he thought he spoke beautifully. He wrote in his journal for that day, "So and so speaks beautiful French—I wonder if I'll ever speak this language as well?" He and his friend's paths diverged at this juncture, and he was not able to evaluate his friend's linguistic ability in French until about a year latter. In the meantime he himself had studied French for eight to ten hours a day for a year and had benefited from local friendships for conversational language acquisition. When he heard this friend again use French (he asked me to forgive him please), "he murdered the language!" In fact, he added, after using French for 30 years, his friend's proficiency in vocabulary and pronunciation was not admirable!

My purpose in recounting the above is not to flatter anyone, nor to unjustly criticize anyone, but to illustrate the obvious. There is more than one reason why the private or public use of tongues in prayer or worship are not equal. Some may ask if an evaluation of this supernatural enablement is even subject to evaluation. Allow me to explain. I recognize that any attempt to evaluate tongues may seem unspiritual! Others might say: "If one believes that 'the Holy Spirit gives the utterance,' how can some 'tongues' be better than others?" I'll risk it in this: **In a partnership, the partners may not be equal.**

9. Pentecostals should not be stereotyped.

All people are not necessarily "torch bearers for the gift." One need not be known as a one-subject persuader simply because he/she has benefited from this gift. One can be a dynamic New Testament witness without being a "tongues" apologist. In fact, in some circles one should be able to let the power of Pentecost be present without talking about being Pentecostal. Just like one should not start a conversation with a Muslim by saying: "Why don't you believe Jesus is the Son of God?" Tongues does not need to be and should not be a dominant topic unless one is asked to speak about it, or the circumstances are conducive for it, or one feels a direct leading from the Holy Spirit to broach the subject in conversation. One should not feel obligated, in some circles, to make oneself obnoxious. In the African bush we have "hammer mechanics"—because the only tool they have is a hammer. They'll even tighten or loosen a nut on a bolt by "hammering" on it. Some Pentecostals are like that!

10. The baptism in the Spirit is not baptism in water or the salvation experience.

However, one may be baptized in the Spirit at the same experience [in time] as salvation floods the soul with the regenerating power of God as one appropriates the sacrifice of Calvary; but even then, speaking in tongues will follow the regeneration of the soul by the Spirit. This happened in Acts 10. Note: baptism in water is visible and very humid, and the manifestation of the Spirit baptism will be visible and oral/aural. (See Acts 10.) The Bible shows clearly that baptism in water and baptism in the Spirit are distinguishable. John the Baptist makes this as clear as anyone in the New Testament. All four gospels report his words as to this distinction, as if the Holy Spirit wanted to make sure no one missed it. *"I baptize you with water for repentance. But after me will come one more powerful than I, whose sandals I am not fit to carry. He will baptize you with the Holy Spirit and with fire"* (Matthew 3:11; Mark 1:8; Luke 3:16; John 1:31-33). Yet, many still think one receives the baptism of the Spirit WHEN one is saved/converted and deny the existence or need of the subsequent blessing and endowment of power for witnessing (Acts 1:8).

Jesus himself makes it clear there is a distinction. Here are His words in Acts 1:5: *"John baptized with water, but before many days you shall be baptized with the Holy Spirit."* These are not the only Scriptures for such understanding. Acts 19 shows us St. Paul expected there to be a differentiation between being baptized in the name of the Lord and baptism in the Holy Spirit with evidence: *"On hearing this they were baptized into the name of the Lord Jesus. When Paul placed his hands on them, the Holy Spirit came upon them and they spoke in tongues and prophesied"* (vss. 5-6).

In the Acts 10 account, where St. Peter was in the house of the Gentile Cornelius, the order was reversed but the distinction was still clear. Those assembled to hear Peter were suddenly filled with the Holy Spirit and "...*The circumcised believers who had come with Peter were astonished that the gift of the Holy Spirit had been poured out even on the Gentiles. For they heard them speaking in tongues and praising the Lord"* (Acts 10: 45-46). Seeing this, Peter asked if there was any reason why these should not be baptized in water—*"They have received the Holy Spirit just as we have"* (v. 47). So they were baptized in water.

Christenson on the Distinctions

Larry Christenson helps with this clear distinction by showing that the SOURCE, or the agent baptizing, is different:

> Water baptism is a rite or sacrament administered by the Church, on the authority of Christ. Jesus himself never baptized with water (John 4:2). Baptism with the Holy Spirit is administered by Jesus himself. No human being has ever received the commission to baptize with the Holy Spirit. This is an office which Jesus has reserved for Himself alone. He is the only baptizer with the Holy Spirit. Thus baptism with the Holy Spirit also has two distinguishing features: It is with the Holy Spirit, and the One who baptizes is Jesus himself.[13]

11. Tongues are not spiritualized sacerdotalism.

Some Pentecostals and Charismatics use the phenomenon of speaking in tongues as a badge of holiness to form an elitist separatist hierarchy like the Second and Third Churches. These folks believe they can impart the gifts of the Spirit to another person at will. They claim to have special powers through dreams and impressions to control the lives of other sincere believers who fall prey to their persuasive powers and personal magnetism. They refuse to "test everything" by the Scriptures (I Thess. 5:21-22) and believe experience, sanctioned by themselves, is equal to the Bible itself. Like organizational sacerdotalism, this is spiritual sacerdotalism and leads to excessive and sometimes disastrous behavior as at Jonestown in Guyana, South America.

"In like manner, any experience of God's blessing, without a commitment to fulfill the mission of God will lead to excess. Those who experience glossolalia cannot afford to be encapsulated in a celebration of blessing."[14]

12. The gifts of the Spirit are not owned.

David Lim (1991) helps us here:

> Because of the teaching that one may *possess* gifts, people of low self-esteem may infer that they do not and could not possess the gifts. By making maturity and holiness prerequisites to ministering gifts, the immature and 'not so holy' have been left out.[15]

On the other hand, some other emotionally immature individuals try to use tongues and other gifts for personal "psychic income" and ego power by the improper employ of the gifts. This has not led to the good of the Body of Christ but to the selfish ends of the individual. Only privately used tongues (one's prayer language) does not need to be evaluated by the Body of Believers. Once glossolalia is used as a public manifestation of that gift (ideally in a group of believers), it is a gift given to the community of faith and must be evaluated by the Body collectively (I Cor. 14).

13. Tongues are not spiritual pride or arrogance.

The most unattractive aspect of the tongue speaking movement is the spiritual pride and arrogance which is found among many who practice it...most mature Pentecostal leaders emphasize this very point and speak against this excess: Tongues is not the end-all, far from it. From their point of view it is an entrance into a new life of great possibilities and vistas. Speaking in tongues is the *rite d'entrée* to the deeper levels of the psyche...But since it gives no more than entrance, its values lie not so much in what it is, as in what it brings and what results follow it.[16]

I don't intend by the above list to claim the list is exhaustive. But in my experience these represent some of the most often misunderstood or misapplied concepts.

ENDNOTES:

1. Gordon Anderson, "Baptism in the Holy Spirit, Initial Evidence, and a New Model," *Enrichment Journal* (Winter 2005): 73, 77.
2. See Jimmy Jividen, *Glossalalia, from God or Men?* (1971).
3. See Ray Hughes in *The Glossolalia Phenomenon* (1966), 170.
4. Morton Kelsey (1968), 13.
5. John V. York, *Missions in the Age of the Spirit* (2000), 184.
6. Minnie Abrams, *The Latter Rain Evangel* (1909).
7. Gordon Anderson (2005), 72.
8. Philip Yancy, *The Jesus I Never Knew* (1995), 166. Yancy reminds us that people rarely found it easy to believe in miracles; they were quick to find alternative explanations for them, like magic or the devil's power. Then, as now, miracles aroused suspicion, contempt, and only occasionally faith.
9. Robert L. Brandt and Zenas J. Bicket, *The Spirit Helps Us Pray; A Biblical Theology of Prayer* (1993), 275.
10. For a good explanation of this see Ray H. Hughes *The Glossolalia Phenomenon* (1966), 172.
11. David Lim, *Spiritual Gifts: A Fresh Look* (1999), 187, 191.
12. Larry Christenson, *Speaking in Tongues, Its Significance for the Church* (1968), 87.
13. Ibid. (1968), 41. See also "Glossolalia and the Scriptures," Harvey Conn, *The Glossolalia Phenomenon* (1966), 26.
14. John York, *Missions in the Age of the Spirit* (2000), 163.
15. David Lim (1999), 19.
16. M. Kelsey (1968), 231. (Emphasis Mine.)

GLOSSARY of Specialized Words

Every academic discipline or specialized subject, whether in education, or theology, and especially in the social sciences possesses a "jargon" of words that are meaningful for a restricted number of people inside its rather closed subject area. Hoping not to patronize on the one hand or to seem "affected" on the other, I offer this limited glossary of words that for some are not too common.

AAA: If the reader is not from North America, you may not understand this symbol. It stands for American Automobile Association and is the source of the best road maps for travel in North America.

Abnegation: A self-denial or renunciation of something. Used here as a surrender of some of the total domination, or a weakening of the exclusive dominance of human reason.

Allegory: To speak figuratively by means of symbolic truths or generalizations.

Amilliennialist: One who denies there will be a 1000 year reign of Christ on earth.

Animism: A belief that immaterial spirit is the origin of much of reality—attributes life to objects in nature or to *inanimate* objects

Apologetics: A systematic argumentative defense of a doctrine. A branch of theology defending the authority of Scripture or divine origin of Christianity.

***Argumentum ad homonym*:** Latin for "attack the person" instead of his/her ideas.

Arminian: One whose doctrine is influenced by Arminius, a leader during the Great Reformation. In opposition to absolute predestination believing salvation is open to all.

Ascension Mandate: Another term for the Great Commission of Jesus (as in Matt. 28) to "Go into all the world and preach the gospel to every creature."

Behaviorism: A branch of psychology pioneered by John Watson. It interprets measured observable responses to stimuli as the only concern of its research.

Calvinist: One whose doctrine is influenced by that of John Calvin, the early Suisse reformer. Often related to the doctrines of predestination and eternal security.

Cessationist: One who holds that the charismata (gifts of the Spirit) *ceased* with the apostles of the finalization of the Bible.

Charismata: Greek based word for gifts—used here for the Gifts of the Spirit.

Confessionalism: The practice of doing theology within the context of a particular confession of faith, which is usually denominationally specific.

Contextualization: Putting a message, idea, concept into the cultural *context* of the target audience (those listening, reading, or to whom the message is intended).

Didache: The teaching of the twelve apostles, an anonymous Christian treatise of the early second century.

Dispensational: A rather rigid theological position (system) regarding time periods of God's dealings with mankind through the ages past and projected to the future.

Ecclesiastical: That which is related to the organized church of believers.

Egocentric: A psychological term indication a limited outlook or concern to one's own activities or needs.

Eisegesis: The opposite of "drawing meaning out" (exegesis) by "reading meaning into" and generally a derogatory term. Imposing a foreign meaning into a text.

Empirical: Capable of being verified or disproved by observation or experience.

Enigma: Obscure speech or writing—hard to understand.

Epistemology: The study and theory of knowledge and "how we know."

Erudition: Extensive knowledge acquired chiefly from books.

Eschatology: A division of Systematic Theology dealing with the doctrine of the end times and the second coming of Christ.

Esoteric: Knowledge rather limited to a small circle or group.

Ethnocentric: Based on a belief that one's own group is superior.

Exegete: A verb (the noun in exegesis) meaning to explain, interpret the critical comprehension of a text by drawing out the intention of the author.

Fan of Perception: A communication term referring to an individual's data base of "knowing" (as shown in the Ross model of communications in chapter 4).

***Faveles*:** Spanish for the slums of large Latin American cities.

Gestalt: A school of psychology that coined the phrase: "The whole is more than the sum of its parts." A unified whole or configuration.

Hermeneutics: The study of the methodological principles of interpretation of the Bible especially concerned with the original Bible culture and its languages.

Incarnational: A recent theological concept based on the incarnation of Jesus as the Son of God, but here used as a metaphor for the partnership God desires with mankind.

Litany: A lengthy prayer or recitation by a leader with alternate responses by the congregation.

Matrix: A multifaceted word of many definitions. In communications it refers to something from which something else originates, develops, or takes form.

Metaphor: A figure of speech in which a word or phrase used literally for one thing is used in place of another. (i.e. figurative language like *drowning in money*)

Missiology: The study and theory of missionary endeavors and their results.

Montanism: An early revival of charismatic nature of the second and fifth centuries characterized by "new prophecy" seen to be perpetual in the Church. Though Tertullian was the most renowned proponent of a conservative branch of Montanism, the doctrine and movement was eventually rejected by the Roman Catholic Church as heretical partly due to excesses, and partly because women were permitted ministry. It has more recently come to be understood in a more positive light.

Morphology: (In this book) The study and description of word formation in language.

Ontological: A philosophical term: Relating to or based on *being* or existence.

Oxymoron: A combination of contradictory words (like *cruel kindness*).

Paraclete: An anglicized Greek word for the Holy Spirit meaning "one called alongside to help."

Paradigm: A pattern or example; a theoretical framework of an idea supported by other ideas believed to be true based on experience.

Paralanguage: From Greek, *para* (beside or alongside). The broad term for many forms of non-verbal language systems.

Parturition: The process of giving birth to offspring.

***Patois*:** (French) Uneducated or provincial speech—a jargon.

Pedantic: The act of making a show of knowledge.

Pentatonic scale: A musical scale consisting of only five tones arranged like a major scale with the fourth and seventh tones omitted. (Many Orthodox Christians sing with this scale)

Phonology: The science of speech sounds.

Pneumatology: The study of the Holy Spirit—Pneuma=breath.

Postmillennialist: One who believes Christ will return after the millennium.

Postulate: A hypothesis advanced as an assumption or essential condition.

Premillennialist: One who believes Christ's second coming will preced His 1000 year reign on earth.

Prima facie: From the Latin or French meaning: "At first view or appearance." Legally sufficient evidence to establish a fact.

Pro forma: Made or carried out as a formality.

Psychical: The which lies outside the sphere of physical science or knowledge—often spiritual in origin or force.

Quiescent: To be at rest, quiet; inactive or motionless.

***Raison d'etre*:** Commonly used French term for "reason for being."

Reasoned discourse: A communication concept of attempting persuasion by well-planned and sequenced argumentation as practiced in the west.

Reductionism: A procedure that reduces all complex data or phenomena to simple terms. This action is sometimes called oversimplification.

Reification: The act of regarding something abstract as if it were concrete or real.

Rhema: (Greek for the Hebrew *dabar*) Like *logos*, translated as "the word of the Lord." Many modern scholars prefer this word for the spoken Word of the Lord.

Sacerdotalism: The system, methods, or spirit of the priesthood—generally used in a negative sense.

Salvific: Relating to the word *salvation*, pertaining to the power or effect of the work accomplished in the plan of God through the cross of Christ.

Semantics: Often used in popular thought

as being worthless—"Oh, that's just semantics"—but here almost always used in the generic sense of the study of meanings.

Shamanism: Early folk religion of animistic origin. A shaman is known in the West as a "witchdoctor."

Sine qua non: Latin for "without which not."

***Sola gratia, sola fidei, sola scriptura*:** Latin for only grace, only faith, only scripture. These concepts came out of the Protestant Reformation as foundation stones for its existence.

Syncretism: The combination of differing forms of belief or practice. For our purposes, this generally is seen in a negative light—like diluting the Scriptural norm with secular ideas.

Syntax: The study of the way linguistic elements (words) are arranged to have meaning in a given language system.

Taxonomy: An orderly classification of ideas, things, etc. and the study of same.

Triumphalism: The attitude of superiority or of meriting the advantage.

Waldenses: A Christian movement (judged a sect by Rom) of the 12th century.

Worldview: From the German *Weltanschauung*: Any culture's perception of making sense of the world (its world).

Yahweh: Transcribed from a Hebrew name for the God of the Bible.

BIBLIOGRAPHY

Abrams, Minnie F. "How the Recent Revival Was Brought About in India." In *The Latter Rain Evangel* (July 1909).

——"The Object of the Baptism in the Holy Spirit," *The Latter Rain Evangel,* (May 1911). Quoted in Gary B. McGee *Initial Evidence, Historical and Biblical Perspectives on the Pentecostal Doctrine of Spirit Baptism.* Peabody MA: Hendrickson Publishing, 1991.

Adeney, B. T. *Strange Virtues: Ethics in a Multicultural World.* Downer's Grove, IL: Intervarsity Press, 1995.

Aker, B. C. In *Dictionary of Pentecostal and Charismatic Movements,* ed. S. M. Burgess, Gary McGee, and P. H. Alexander P. H., Grand Rapids: Zondervan, 1988.

Allen, Roland. *Missionary Methods, Saint Paul or Ours?* Grand Rapids, MI: Eerdmans Publishing Co. 1962, 1993.

Anderson, Gordon. "Baptism in the Holy Spirit, Initial Evidence, and a New Model." In *Enrichment Journal* (Winter 2005).

Anderson, Ray, S. *Ministry on the Fireline.* Downer's Grove, IL: Intervarsity Press, 1993.

Ardrey, Robert. *The Territorial Imperative.* New York, NY: Atheneum Press, 1966. Reprint, New York: Kodansha International, 1997.

Arrington, French. *The Acts of the Apostles.* Peabody, MA: Hendrickson Publishers, Inc, 1986.

Ash, James L. "The Decline of Ecstatic Prophecy in The Early Church." *Theological Studies* 37 (1976).

Bailey, Kenneth. *Poet and Peasant and Through Peasants' Eyes.* Grand Rapids, MI: William B. Eerdmans Publishing Company, 1976.

——*The Cross and the Prodigal, A Commentary and Play on the Parable of the Prodigal Son.* Saint Louis: Concordia Publishing House, 1973.

Baker, David. *Sigmund Freud and the Jewish Mystical Tradition.* Princeton, NJ: D Van Norstrand Co., Inc., 1958.

Baker, John, A. *The Foolishness of God.* Atlanta: John Knox Press, 1970.

Barker, Larry, L. *Communications,* 4th ed. Englewood Cliffs, NJ: Prentice-Hall, 1987.

Barnouw, Erik, ed. *International Encyclopedia of Communications,* Vol. 1. Oxford University Press, 1989.

Barrett, C. K. *The First Epistle to the Corinthians.* Peabody, MA: Hendrickson Publishers, 2000.

Barrett, David B. *The Encyclopedia of Christianity.* New York: Oxford University Press, 2002.

——*World Christian Encyclopedia: A Comparative Study of Churches and World Religions in the Modern World AD 1900-2000.* Oxford: Oxford University Press, 1982.

Bartleman, Frank. *Azusa Street: The Roots of Modern-Day Pentecost.* Plainfield, NJ: Bridge Publishing, 1980.

——*Triumphs of Faith,* n.d. (probably written before 1910 as found with other articles of that era).

Barton, George A. *The Apostolic Age and the New Testament.* Philadelphia: University of Pennsylvania Press, 1936.

Basham, Don. *A Handbook on Holy Spirit Baptism.* Springdale, PA: Whitaker House, 1969.

Bauml, Betty J. *A Dictionary of Gestures.* Metuchen, NY: Scarecrow Press, 1975.

Bennett, Dennis and Rita. *The Holy Spirit and You.* Plainfield, NJ: Logos International, 1971.

Berkoff, H. *The Doctrine of the Holy Spirit.* Atlanta, GA: John Knox Press, 1964.

Berlo, David, K. *The Process of Communication.* New York: Holt, Rienhart and Winston, Inc., 1960.

Bertone, John. "The Experience of Glossolalia and the Spirit's Empathy." In *Pneuma*, Vol. 25, No. 1 (Spring 2003).

Bevere, John. "Communicating with God." *Intimacy with the Holy Spirit,* Video 2. Palmer Lake, CO: John Bevere Ministries, 2001.

Biocca, Frank, and Mark Levy. *Communication in the Age of Virtual Reality.* Hillsdale, NJ: Lawrence Erlbaum Associates, Inc. Publishers, 1998.

Birdwhistle, Ray, L. *Introduction to Kinesics.* Washington, DC: Foreign Service Institute, Department of State, 1962.

Blackstock, Terri. *Evidence of Mercy.* Grand Rapids: Zondervan, 1995.

Bloesh, Donald. *The Holy Spirit Works and Gifts.* Downer's Grove, Il: Intervarsity Press, 2000.

Bloom, Benjamin S. *Taxonomy of Educational Objectives: Handbook I: Cognitive Domain.* New York: David Mckay, 1967.

Blumhofer, Edith. *Restoring the Faith: The Assemblies of God, Pentecostalism, and American Culture.* Urbana: University of IL Press, 1993.

Boas, Frank. *The Mind of Primitive Man.* New York: Free Press, 1965.

Boddy, A. A. *Confidence*, Vol. IV, No. 8 (August 1911).

Bois, J. Samuel. *Explorations in Awareness.* NY: Harper and Row, 1957.

Bonino, Jose Miguez. "Changing Paradigms: A Response." In Dempster, Murray W., Byron D. Klaus, and Douglas Petersen, eds. *The Globalization of Pentecostalism, A Religion Made to Travel.* Carlisle, UK: Regnum Books International, 1999.

Bosch, David Jacobus. *Transforming Mission;Paradigm Shifts in Theology of Mission.* Maryknoll, NY: Orbis Books, 1991.

Botsis, Peter A. *What is Orthodoxy? A Short Explanation of the Essence of Orthodoxy and the Differences between the Churches.* Pellis Str. Attiki: Frangoccleia, 1987.

Brandt, Robert L., and Zenas J. Bicket. *The Spirit Helps Us Pray; A Biblical Theology of Prayer.* Springfield, MO: Logion Press, 1993.

Bremback, Carl. *What Meaneth This?* Springfield, MO: Gospel Publishing House, 1947.

Brembeck, W., and W. S. Howell. *Persuasion: A Means of Social Influence,* 2nd ed. Englewood Cliffs: Prentice-Hall, 1976.

Bretschner, Paul. *The World Upside-Down or Right-Side Up?* St. Louis, MO: Concordia Publishing House, 1964.

Brophy, Jere, Shari Nedler and Thomas Good. *Teaching in the Preschool.* New York, NY: Harper and Row Publishers, 1975.

Bruner, Fredrick Dale. *A Theology of The Holy Spirit: The Pentecostal Experience and the New Testament Witness.* Grand Rapids: William B. Eerdmans, 1970.

Brunner, E. *Misverstandnis der Kirch.* Trans. by Harold Knight, *Misunderstanding of the Church.* Philadelphia: Westminster Press, 1953.

Brusco, Elizabeth. "The Reformation of Machismo: Asceticism and Masculinity Among

Colombian Evangelicals." In *Rethinking Protestantism in Latin America*. Virginia Garrand-Burnett and David Stoll, eds. Philadelphia, PA: Temple University Press, 1993.

Bueno, Ronald. "Listening to the Margins: Re-Historicizing Pentecostal Experiences and Identities." In Dempster, Murray W., Byron D. Klaus, and Douglas Petersen, eds. *The Globalization of Pentecostalism, A Religion Made to Travel.* Carlisle, UK: Regnum Books International, 1999.

Bultmann, Rudolf. *Theological Dictionary of the New Testament,* Vol. 1.

Buntain, Daniel, N. *The Holy Spirit and Fire.* Springfield, MO: Gospel Publishing House, 1956. Quoted in Gary B. McGee *Initial Evidence, Historical and Biblical Perspectives on the Pentecostal Doctrine of Spirit Baptism.* Peabody MA: Hendrickson Publishing, 1991.

Burgess, S. M., Gary McGee, and P. H. Alexander, eds. *Dictionary of Pentecostal and Charismatic Movements.* Grand Rapids: Zondervan, 1988.

Burgess, S. M. *The Holy Spirit: Eastern Christian Traditions.* Peabody, MA: Hendrickson Publishers, 1989.

———"Medieval Examples of Charismatic Piety in the Roman Catholic Church."

R. Spittler, ed. In *Perspectives on the New Pentecostalism.* Grand Rapids: Baker Book House, 1976.

——— *The Spirit and the Church: Antiquity.* Peabody, Mass: Hendrickson Publishers, 1984.

Canales, Isaac. Plenary Address, Lay Leadership Conference, Sacramento, CA: Oct 1, 2005.

Capon, Robert F. *The Parables of Grace.* Grand Rapids: Eerdmans, 1988.

Carlyle, G., ed. rev. "On the Gifts of the Holy Ghost, Commonly Called Supernatural." In *The Collective Writings of Edward Irving in Five Volumes,* Vol.4. London: Alexander Strahan, 1864.

Cartledge, M. H. "Charismatic Prophecy: A Definition and Description," *JPT* 5 (1994).

Cavaness, Barbara Liddle. "Factors Influencing Decrease in the Number of Single Women In Assemblies of God World Missions." Ph. D. diss., Fuller Seminary, 2002.

Chan, Simon. *Pentecostal Theology and the Christian Spiritual Tradition.* Sheffield, UK: Sheffield Academic Press, 2000.

Chapman, M. "A Personal Testimony." *Bombay Guardian Press* (September 1907).

Chesterton, G. K. Quoted in Robert Greenleaf. *Servant Leadership: A Journey into the Nature of Legitimate Power and Greatness.* New York: Paulist Press, 1977.

Christian, Kenneth W. *Your Own Worst Enemy.* New York, NY: Harper Collins, 2002.

Christenson, Larry. *Speaking in Tongues, Its Significance for the Church.* Minneapolis, MN: Dimension Books, Bethany Fellowship, 1968.

Cleary, Edward L. O.P. In Dempster, Murray W., Byron D. Klaus, and Douglas Petersen, eds. *The Globalization of Pentecostalism, A Religion Made to Travel.* Carlisle, UK: Regnum Books International, 1999.

Comfort, Philip. gen. ed. *Life Application Bible Commentary: Galatians.* Wheaton, IL: Tyndale House Publishers, Inc., 1994.

Condril, Jo and Benne Bough. *101 Ways to Improve Your Communication Skills Instantly.* Alexandria, VA, Goal/Minds, 1998.

Cone, James H. *God of the Oppressed.* New York, NY: The Seaburg Press, 1975.

Conn, Harvey. "Glossolalia and the Scriptures." Edited by Wade Horton. *The Glossolalia Phenomenon.* Cleveland, TN: Pathway Press, 1966.

Cook, Jerry. "Why I'm a Pentecostal." *Foursquare World Advance* (July-August 2002).

Cornuke, Robert, and David Halbrook. *In Search of the Lost Ark of the Covenant.* Nashville, TN: Broadman and Holdman Publishers, 2002.

Costellow, Etta. "After Two Years." *Cloud of Witnesses to Pentecost in India* (August 1909).

Cox, Harvey. *Fire From Heaven: The Rise of Pentecostal Spirituality and the Reshaping of Religion in the Twenty-First Century.* Reading MS: Persus Books, 1995.

Craig, Robert, T. "Communication Theory as a Field." *Communication Theory* 9 (1999).

Creps, Earl. An Address to the AG Seminary Chapel, November 3, 1998.

Cross, James A. "Its Value to the Church." Edited by Wade Horton. *The Glossolalia Phenomenon.* Cleveland, TN: Pathway Press, 1966.

Culpepper, Robert. *Evaluating The Charismatic Movement: A Theological and Biblical Appraisal.* Valley Forge, PA: Judson Press, 1977.

Cutten, George B. *Speaking in Tongues: Historically and Psychologically Considered.* Newhaven: Yale Univ. Press, 1927.

Dance, Frank and Carl Larson. *The Function of Human Communication: A Theoretical Approach.* Appendix A. New York: Holt, Rienhart & Winston, 1976.

———"The Concept of Communication." *Journal of Communication* 20 (1970).

Daniels, David. "Everybody Bids You Welcome." In Dempster, Murray W., Byron D. Klaus, and Douglas Petersen, eds. *The Globalization of Pentecostalism, A Religion Made to Travel.* Carlisle, UK: Regnum Books International, 1999.

Deere, Jack. *Surprised by the Power of the Spirit.* Grand Rapids, MI: Zondervan, 1993.

———*Surprised by the Voice of the Spirit.* Grand Rapids, MI: Zondervan, 1996.

Dempster, Murray W., Byron D. Klaus, and Douglas Petersen, eds. *The Globalization of Pentecostalism, A Religion Made to Travel.* Carlisle, UK: Regnum Books International, 1999.

Dorin, Hayim H. *To Be a Jew: A Guide to Jewish Observance in Contemporary Life.* New York: Harper Collins Publishers, 1972.

Dorries, David W. "The Church with Her Endowment of Holiness and Power." In *The Collected Writings of Edward Irving in Five Volumes,* Vol. 5. ed. Rev. G. Carlyle.
London: Alexander Strahan, 1864.

———"Edward Irving and the 'Standing Sign' of Spirit Baptism." In *Initial*
Evidence, Historical and Biblical Perspective on the Pentecostal Doctrine of Spirit Baptism, ed. Gary McGee. Peabody, MA: Hendrickson Publishing, 1991.

Dostoevsky, Fyodor. *The Brothers Karamazov.* Garden City, NY: Nelson Doubleday, Inc., publication date missing in book.

Douglas, J. D. ed. *The New International Dictionary of the Christian Church.* Grand Rapids, MI: Zondervan, 1974.

Drummond, Andrew, L. *Edward Irving and His Circle.* London: James Clarke and Company, Ltd., 1934.

———*German Protestantism Since Luther.* London, Epworth Press, 1951.

Duggan, M. "The Cross and the Holy Spirit in Paul: Implications for the Baptism with the Holy Spirit" *Pneuma* 7 (1985).

Dunn, James D. *Baptism in the Holy Spirit.* Philadelphia: Westminster Press, 1970. du Plessis, David. *A Man Called Mr. Pentecost.* Plainfield, NJ: Logos International, 1977.

——— *The Spirit Bade Me Go: An Astounding Move of God in the Denominational Churches* (Self published), 1961.

Edman, V. Raymond. *The Light in Dark Ages.* Wheaton, IL: Van Kampen Press, 1949.

Ellul, Jacques. *Prayer and Modern Man.* New York: Seabury Press, 1970.

Fagerland, Dale. "The Cross and the Crescent: Understanding the Islamic World." In *The Eleventh Hour Institute.* Springfield, MO: African Service of Theological Formation, 2001.

Fee, Gordon. *Corinthians: A Study Guide,* 3rd ed. Springfield, MO: Global University, 1997.

———"The Epistle to the First Corinthians." In *The New International Commentary on the New Testament.* Grand Rapids: William B. Eerdmans, 1987.

———*God's Empowering Presence: The Holy Spirit in the Letters of Paul.* Peabody, MA: Hendrickson, 1994.

———*Gospel and Spirit: Issues in N.T. Hermeneutics.* Peabody, MA: Hendrickson, 1991.

———*Listening to the Spirit in the Text.* Grand Rapids, MI: Eerdmans, 2000.

———"To What End Exegesis?" *Bulletin for Biblical Research* 8 (1998): 75-88.

Fiske, John. *Introducion to Communication Studies.* London: Routledge, 1992.

Flower, J. R. *Pentecostal Evangel,* April 17, 1920.

Fraser, C. U., and R. Brown. "Control of Grammar in Imitation, Comprehension, and Production." *Journal of Verbal Learning and Verbal Behavior* 2 (1963).

Friend, Tim. *Animal Talk* (New York: Free Press), 2003.

Frodsham, Stanley. *With Signs Following.* Springfield, MO: GPH, 1946.

Garr, A. G. *Cloud of Witnesses to Pentecost in India.* No publisher (1907).

———"Tongues: The Bible Evidence to the Baptism with the Holy Ghost." *Pentecostal Power* (March 1907).

Gaston, W. T. (no title). *Word and Witness,* March 20, 1913.

Gee, Donald. "Don't Spill the Wine." *Pentecost,* No. 61 (September-November, 1962).

———"Editorial." In *Pentecost.* London: No. 58 (December 1961).

———*Spiritual Gifts in the Work of the Ministry Today.* Springfield, MO: Gospel Publishing House, 1963.

Gentile, Ernest B. *The Glorious Disturbance.* Grand Rapids, MI: Chosen Books, 2004.

George, A. C. "Pentecostal Beginnings in Travancore, South India." *Asian Journal of Pentecostal Studies* 4 (July 2001).

Gerlach, Luther P. and Virginia H. Hine. *People, Power, and Change: Movements of Social Transformation.* Indianapolis, IN: Bobbs-Merrill, 1970.

Gill, Deborah. "Cornerstone, Keystone, Capstone." Message on July 3, 2005, at Spencer Lake Christian Center, Waupaca, WS.

Gillespie, T. W. *The First Theologians: A Study in Early Christian Prophecy.* Grand Rapids: Eerdmans, 1994.

Gire, Ken. *Moments With the Savior: A Devotional Life of Christ.* Grand Rapids, MI: Zondervan Publishing House, 1998.

Godet, Fredrick L. *Commentary on First Corinthians,* Vol. 2. Edinburgh: T and T. Clark, 1886.

Goff, James R. Jr. *Fields White Unto Harvest: Charles Parham and the Missionary Origins of Pentecostalism.* Fayetteville: University of Arkansas Press, 1988.

Goodall, Wade and Rosalyn, eds. *By My Spirit; The Assemblies of God, 1914 to 2000.* Springfield, MO: Gospel Publishing House, 2000.

Goodman, F. *Speaking in Tongues: A Cross-Cultural Study of Glossolalia.* Chicago: University of Chicago Press, 1972.

Gordon, A. J. *Ministry of the Spirit.* Philadelphia: The Judson Press, 1950.

Green, Michael. *I Believe In The Holy Spirit.* Grand Rapids: Eerdmans Publishers Company, 1975.

Greenleaf, Robert. *Servant Leadership: A Journey into the Nature of Legitimate Power and Greatness.* New York: Paulist Press, 1977.

Gromacki, Robert G. *The Modern Tongues Movement.* Phillipsberg, NJ: Presbyterian and Reformed Pub. Co., 1967.

Gulshan, Esther. *The Torn Veil.* Basingstoke, UK: Marshall Pickering, 1984.

Gumprez, John J. and Hymes, Dell. *Directions in Sociolinguistics.* New York: Holt, Rienhart and Winston, Inc., 1972.

Gunkel, H. *The Influence of the Holy Spirit.* Philadelphia, PA: Fortress Press, 1979.

Gurevitch, Z. D. "The Other Side of Dialogue: On Making the Other Strange and the Experience of Otherness." *American Journal of Sociology* 93 (March 1988).

Hall, Edward T. *The Hidden Dimension.* Garden City, NY: Doubleday and Company, 1966.

——— *The Silent Language.* Garden City, NY: Doubleday and Company, 1966.

Hall, J. R. "A Oneness Pentecostal Looks at Initial Evidence." In *Initial Evidence, Historical and Biblical Perspective on the Pentecostal Doctrine of Spirit Baptism,* ed. Gary McGee. Peabody, MA: Hendrickson Publishing, 1991.

Hanson, N. R. *Patterns of Discovery.* Cambridge: Cambridge University Press, 1961.

Harper, Robert G. et. al. *Nonverbal Communications: The State of the Art.* New York, NY: Wiley, 1978.

Harris, Ralph. *Spoken By The Spirit: Documented Accounts of "Other Tongues" from Arabic to Zulu.* Springfield, MO: Gospel Publishing House, 1973.

Harvey, Bonnie C. *Charles Finney: The Great Revivalist.* Uhrichsville, OH: Barbour Publishing, Inc., 1999.

Hasel, Gerhard F. *Speaking in Tongues.* Berrien Springs, MI: Adventist Theological Society Publications, 1986.

Hayford, Jack. *The Beauty of Spiritual Language: A Journey Toward the Heart of God.* Dallas, TX: Word Publishing, 1992.

Hernando, James D. *Dictionary of Hermeneutics.* Springfield, MO: Gospel Publishing House, 2005.

Heschel, A. *Quest for God.* New York: Crossroad, 1982.

Hesselgrave, David. *Communicating Christ Cross-Culturally*, 2nd ed. Grand Rapids: Zondervan, 1991.

Hiebert, Paul, G. *Anthropological Insights for Missionaries.* Grand Rapids: Baker Book House, 1985.

——— "The Flaw of the Excluded Middle." *Missiology* 10 (January 1982).

Hill, D. *Greek Words and Hebrew Meanings.* Cambridge: Univ. Press, 1967.

Hine, Virginia. "Pentecostal Glossolalia: Toward a Functional Interpretation." *Journal for the Scientific Study of Religion* 8 (1969).

Hirschmann, Maria Anne. *Hansi: The Girl Who Left the Swastika.* Wheaton, IL: Tyndale House Publishers, 1977.

Hodges, Melvin L. *The Indigenous Church* Springfield, MO: Gospel Publishing House, 1976.

Hodges, Melvin L. *Build My Church* Springfield, MO: Gospel Publishing House, 1957.

Hoffer, Eric. *The True Believer: Thoughts on the Nature of Mass Movements.* New York: Harper and Row, 1951.

Hollenwager, Walter, J. "The Black Roots of Pentecostalism." In *Pentecostals After a Century,* ed. Allen Anderson and Walter J. Hollenweger. Sheffield, UK: Sheffield Academic Press, 1999.

——— *Geist und Materie, Interkulturell Theologie, III.* Munich: Chr. Kaiser Verlag, 1988.

———*The Pentecostal.* London: SCM Press, 1976.

——— "Theology of the New World." *The Expository Times* 87 (May 1976).

——— *Umgang mit Mythen: Interkulturelle Theologie.* Munchen: Kaiser- Tassenbucher, 1982.

Horton, Harold. *Gifts of the Spirit.* Nottingham, England: Assemblies of God Publishing House, 1934. Reprint GPH, 1975.

Horton, Stanley. *The Ultimate Victory: An Exposition of the Book of Revelation.* Springfield, MO: GPH, 1991.

Horton, Wade, ed. *The Glossolalia Phenomenon.* Cleveland, TN: Pathway Press, 1966.

Howell, William and Winston Brembeck. *Persuasion a Means of Social Control.* Englewood Cliffs, NJ: Prentice-Hall, Inc., 1952.

———*Persuasion a Means of Social Influence.* Englewood Cliffs, NJ: Prentice-Hall, Inc., 1969.

Huegel F. J. *Bone of His Bone.* Grand Rapids, MI: Zondervan, 1959.

Hughes, Philip E. *International Commentary of the New Testament: The Second Epistle of Corinthians.* Grand Rapids, MI: Eerdmans Publishing Co., 1962.

Hughes, Ray H. "Glossolalia in Contemporary Times." In *The Glossolalia Phenomenon,* ed. Wade Horton. Cleveland, TN: Pathway Press, 1966.

Hunter, Charles and Francis. *Why Should "I" Speak in Tongues?* Houston, TX: Hunter Ministries Pub. Co., 1976.

Husserl, Edmund. *Ideas: General Introduction to Pure Phenomenology.* New York: Collier, 1962.

———*Phenomenology and the Crisis of Philosophy.* New York: Harper & Row, 1965.

Hussey, L. M. "The Wit of the Carpenter." *The American Mercury,* Vol. 5.

Hyatt, Eddie, L. *2000 Years of Charismatic Christianity.* Lake Mary, FL. Charisma House Publishers, 2002.

Hymes, Dell G. Introduction: "Toward Ethnographies of Communication." In *The Ethnography of Communications*, ed. John Gumperz and Dell H. Hymes. *The American Anthropologist*, Vol. 68 (1966).

The Interpreter's Bible, Vol. X. NY: Abington Press, 1951-55.

Ironside, H. A. *Holiness, the False and the True.* Treasury of Truth, Vol. 79. Published by Loizeaux Brothers

Irwin, Gayle, D. *The Jesus Style.* Palm Springs, CA: Ronald Haynes Publishers, Inc., 1983.

Irwin, Paul. "Playing by Heart." *Reader's Digest* (March 2000).

———*Spirit Style.* Cathedral City, CA: YAHSHUA Publishing, 1994.

———*YHWU Style.* Cathedral City, CA: YAHSHUA Publishing, 1991.

Jahn Janheinz. "Value Conceptions in Sub-Saharan Africa." *Epistemology in Anthropology.* New York: Harper and Row, 1964.

Jensen, Jerry, ed. *Episcopalians and the Baptism in the Holy Spirit.* Los Angeles, CA: Full Gospel Businessmen's Fellowship International, 1964.

———*Lutherans and the Baptism in the Holy Spirit.* Los Angeles, CA: Full Gospel Businessmen's Fellowship International, 1996.

Jividen, Jimmy. *Glossalalia, From God or Men?* Fort Worth, TX: Star Bible Publishers, 1971.

Johns, Donald, A. "New Directions in Hermeneutics." In *Initial Evidence, Historical and Biblical Perspective on the Pentecostal Doctrine of Spirit Baptism,* ed. Gary McGee. Peabody, MA: Hendrickson Publishing, 1991.

Johns, Jackie David. "Yielding to the Spirit: The Dynamics of a Pentecostal Model of Praxis." In Dempster, Murray W., Byron D. Klaus, and Douglas Petersen, eds. *The Globalization of Pentecostalism, A Religion Made to Travel.* Carlisle, UK: Regnum Books International, 1999.

Johnson, L. T. *Religious Experiences in Early Christianity.* Minneapolis: Fortress Press, 1999.

———"Towards a Theology of Speaking in Tongues." *Theological Studies* 32 (1972).

Jones, C. E. "The Journey Towards God was a Journey Into God." In Burgess, S.M. and Gary McGee. *Dictionary of Charismatic and Pentecostal Movements.* Grand Rapids, MI: Zondervan Publishers, 1988.

Jones, Charles, J. *Guide to Study of Pentecostal Movement,* 2 vols. Metuchen, NJ: Scarecrow Press, 1983.

Jones, E. Stanley. *The Christ of Every Road.* New York: The Abingdon Press, 1930. In James L. Slay, "Glossolalia, Its Value to the Individual," *The Glossolalia Phenomenon,* ed. Wade Horton, Cleveland TN: Pathway Press, 1966.

Jones, J. W. *The Spirit and the World.* New York, NY: Hawthorne Books, 1975.

Jung, C.G. *Collective Works,* Vol. 9. NY: Pantheon Books, Inc., 1951.

———*Collective Works,* Vol. 12. NY: Pantheon Books, Inc., 1953.

Kaivoc, Johannes Behm. *TDNT III.* Quoted in Janet Powers, *Missionary Tongues, Journal of Pentecostal Theology* 17 (2000).

Kelsey, David. *Between Athens and Berlin: The Theological Education Debate.* Grand Rapids, MI: Eerdmans, 1993.

——— *To Understand God Truly: What's Theological about Theological Education?* Louisville, KY: Westminster John Knox, 1992.

Kelsey, Morton T. *Tongues Speaking an Experiment in Spiritual Experience.* New York: Doubleday, 1968.

Kennedy, G. A. *New Testament Interpretation Through Rhetorical Criticism.* Chapel Hill: Univ. of North Carolina Press, 1984.

Kenyan, Howard. "An Analysis of Ethical Issues in the History of the Assemblies of God." Ph.D. diss., Baylor University, 1988.

Kildahl, John P. *The Psychology of Speaking in Tongues.* San Francisco, CA, 1972.

Kincaid, Lawrence. *Communication Theory: Eastern and Western Perspectives.* San Diego: Academic, 1987.

King, Sara Sanderson, ed. *Human Communication as a Field of Study: Selected Contemporary Views.* State University of New York Press, 1989.

Kipling, Rudyard. "The Ballad of East and West." *Rudyard Kipling's Verse: Inclusive Edition 1885-1918.* New York: Doubleday, 1924.

Kirkpatrick, William J. and Bottome, Frank. "The Comforter Has Come." In *Precious Times of Refreshing and Revival,* 1890.

Klaus, Byron."Prez Release." A monthly commentary from the President of the Assemblies of God Theological Seminary (February 2003).

——— "Prez Report." An eNewsletter to AGTS friends (April, 2006).

Klug, Eugene F. and Otto F. Stahlke. *Getting into the Formula of Concord: A History and Digest of the Formula.* St. Louis: Concordia Pub. House, 1977.

Knapp, Mark L. *Non-Verbal Communication in Human Interaction.* New York: Holt, Rinehart, and Winston, 1972.

Koenig, John. *Charismata: God's Gifts For God's People.* Philadelphia: Westminister Press, 1978.

Kolberg, L., J. Yaeger, and E. Hjertholm, eds. "Private Speech: Four Studies and a Review of Theories" *Child Development* 39 (1968).

Koneya, Male. *Louder Than Words...Nonverbal Communications.* Columbus, OH: Merril, 1976.

Korzybski, Alfred. *Science and Sanity,* 2nd ed. Lakeville, International Non-Aristotelian Library Pub. Co., 1958.

Kraft, Charles. *Christianity in Culture.* Maryknoll, New York: Orbis Books, 1981.

Kraybill, Donald B. *The Upside-Down Kingdom.* Scottdale, PA: Herald Press, 1990.

Kuyper, Abraham. *The Work of the Holy Spirit.* Grand Rapids: Wm. B. Eerdmans, 1941.

Kydd, Ronald A. *Charismatic Gifts in the Early Church.* Peabody, MA: Hendrickson Pub., 1984.

Lamb, Warren. "Interpersonal Communication." In *Posture and Gesture.* London: Gerald Duckworth and Co., 1965.

Land, Steve J. *Pentecostal Spirituality, A Passion for the Kingdom.* Sheffield: Sheffield Academic Press, 1993.

LaPoorta, Jappie. "Unity or Division." In Dempster, Murray W., Byron D. Klaus, and Douglas Petersen, eds. *The Globalization of Pentecostalism, A Religion Made to Travel.* Carlisle, UK: Regnum Books International, 1999.

Leathers, Dale G. *Non-Verbal Communication Systems.* Boston: Allyn and Bacon, 1976.

LeBaron, Albert. "A Case of Psychic Automatism, Including 'Speaking in Tongues.'" *Proceedings of the Society for Psychical Research* 12 (1896-1897).

Lederle, Henry. "Initial Evidence and the Charismatic Movement." In *Initial Evidence, Historical andBiblical Perspective on the Pentecostal Doctrine of Spirit Baptism,* ed. Gary McGee. Peabody, MA: Hendrickson Publishing, 1991.

Lee, David (director). Annual Assemblies of God World Missions Report (2005).

Lewis, C. S. ed. *George MacDonald Anthology.* London: Geoffrey Bles, 1946.

Lewis, I. M. *Ecstatic Religion.* Baltimore: Penguin Books, 1971.

Lim, David. *Spiritual Gifts: A Fresh Look.* Springfield, MO: GPH, 1991. Reprint, GPH, 1999.

Littlejohn, Stephen, W. *Theories of Human Communication,* 7th ed. Belmont, CA: Wadsworth Publishing, 2002.

Lossky, Vladimir. *The Mystical Theology of the Eastern Church.* Translated by The Fellowship of St. Alban and St. Sergius. Crestwood: SVS, 1976.

MacArthur, John. *Charismatic Chaos.* Grand Rapids, MI: Zondervan, 1992.

Macchia, Frank D. "Sighs Too Deep for Words: Toward a Theology of Glossolalia" *Journal of Pentecostal Theology* 1 (1992).

———"The Struggle For Global Witness: Shifting Paradigms in Pentecostal Theology." In *The Globalization of Pentecostalism*, eds. Murray Dempster, Byron Klaus, Douglas Petersen Irving, CA: Regnum Books International, 1999.

———"Tongues as a Sign: Towards a Sacramental Understanding of Pentecostal Experience." *Pneuma* (Spring 1993).

MacGregor, Geddes. *Introduction to Religious Philosophy.* Boston: Houghton Mifflin, Co., 1959.

Mack, B. I. *Rhetoric and the New Testament.* Minneapolis: Fortress Press, 1990.

Mackie, Alexander. *The Gift of Tongues: A Study in Pathological Aspects of Christianity.*
New York: George H. Doran, 1921.

MacRobert, Ian. *The Black Roots and White Racism of the Early Pentecostalism in the USA.* New York: St. Martin's Press, 1988.

Maloney, H. Newton, and A. Adams Lovekin. *Glossolalia: Behavioral Science Perspectives on Speaking in Tongues.* NY: Oxford Un. Press, 1985.

Matheius, Johann. *Luthers Leben in Predigten.* Prague, Czech Republic: Herausgegeven von G. Loesche, 1906.

May, L. C. "A Survey of Glossolalia and Related Phenomena in Non-Christian Religions." In Watson E. Mills. *Speaking in Tongues: A Guide to Research on Glossolalia.* Grand Rapids: Eerdmans, 1986.

McClung, Grant L. *Azusa Street and Beyond: Pentecostal Missions and Church Growth in the Twentieth Century.* South Plainfield, NJ: Bridge Publishing, Inc., 1986.

McDonnell, Killian. *Charismatic Renewal and the Churches.* New York: Seabury Press, 1976.

McDonnell, Killian, and George T. Montague, eds. *Fanning the Flame.* Collegeville, MN: Liturgical Press, 1991.

McGee, Gary. "The Calcutta Revival of 1907 and the Reformation of Charles Parham's 'Bible Evidence Doctrine." *AJPS* 6:1 (2003)

———ed. *Initial Evidence, Historical and Biblical Perspectives on the Pentecostal Doctrine of Spirit Baptism.* Peabody MA: Hendrickson Publishing, 1991.

———"Minnie F. Abrams. Another Context, Another Founder." In *Portraits of the First Generation,* eds. James R. Goff and Grant Wacker. Fayetteville: Un. of Ark. Press, 2002.

———"Taking the Logic 'A Little Farther': Late 19th Century References to the Gift of Tongues in Mission-Related Literature and Their Influence on Early Pentecostalism." *Asian Journal of Pentecostal Studies* (in production, 2006).

———and Burgess, S. M., and P. H. Alexander P. H. eds. *Dictionary of Pentecostal and Charismatic Movements.* Grand Rapids: Zondervan, 1988.

Meeter, John E., ed. *Selected Shorter Works of B.B. Warfield.* Nutley, NJ: Presbyterian and Reformed, 1973.

Mehrabian, Albert. *Non-Verbal Communication.* Chicago: Moody Press, 1975.

———*Silent Messages.* Belmont, CA: Wadsworth Publishing, 1974.

Menzies, Robert P., and William Menzies. *Spirit and Power.* Grand Rapids, MI: Zondervan Publishing House, 2000.

Merleau-Ponty, Maurice. *The Phenomenology of Perception.* Translated by C. Smith. London: Routledge Kegan Paul, 1974.

Meyendoff, John. *Christ in Eastern Christian Thought,* 2nd ed. Crestwood: SVS, 1987.

Miller, George, A. *Language and Speech.* San Francisco: W. H. Freeman and Co., 1981.

Mills, Watson E. *Glossolalia: A Bibliography.* Grand Rapids, MI: Eerdmans, 1985.

———*A Guide to Research on Glossolalia.* Grand Rapids: Eerdmans, 1986.

Mitchell, Merlin. "The Amazing Tongue." Interview by the author, 2005.

Mitchell, Judy Hurst. "Biofeedback" Interview by the author, 2005.

Mjorud, Herbert A. In Jensen, Jerry, ed. *Lutherans and the Baptism in the Holy Spirit.* Los Angeles, CA: Full Gospel Businessmen's Fellowship International, 1996.

Moore, S. David. "William J. Seymour." *Ministries Today* (May/June, 2005).

Moorhead, Max Wood, ed. *Cloud of Witnesses II.* Colombo: Ceylon, 1907.

———"The Latter Rain in Calcutta, India." *Pentecostal Evangel* (April 17, 1920).

———"Pentecost at Calcutta." *Cloud of Witnesses to Pentecost in India* (March 1908).

Morton T. Kelsey. *Tongue-Speaking: An Experiment in Spiritual Experience.* New York: Doubleday, 1968.

Mouroux, Jean. *The Christian Experience: An Introduction to a Theology.* New York: NY: Sheed and Ward, 1954.

Muggeridge, Malcom. *Jesus: The Man Who Lives.* New York: Harper and Row, 1975.

Nanez, Rick M. *Full Gospel, Fractured Minds?* Grand Rapids, MI: Zondervan Publishers, 2005.

Newberg, Andrew. *Why We Believe What We Believe.* Un. of Penn. Free Press/Simon and Schuster, 2007.

Newman, Barclay, M. and Eugene A. Nida. *A Translator's Handbook on the Acts of the Apostles.* NY: United Bible Societies, 1972.

Northrup, F.S.C. *The Meeting of East and West.* New York: Macmillan, 1953.

Nouwen, Henry. *The Return of the Prodigal Son: A Story of Homecoming.* (New York, NY: Doubleday Dell Pub., 1994.

Olson, Bruce. *For This Cross I'll Kill You.* Carol Stream, IL: Creation House, 1973.

Ong, Walter. "World as View and World as Event." *American Anthropologist* 71 (1969).

Ornstein, Robert. *The Psychology of Consciousness.* New York: Harcourt Brace Jovanovich, Inc., 1977.

Osborne, Grant, gen. ed. "1&2 Corinthians." *Life Application Bible Commentary.* Wheaton, IL: Tyndale House Publishers, 1999.

Oyer, John S. *Lutheran Reformers Against the Anabaptists.* The Hague, Netherlands: Martinus Nijhoff, 1964.

Palma, Anthony D. "Spirit Baptism: Before and After." *Enrichment Journal* (Winter 2005).

Palmer, Richard, E. *Hermeneutics: Interpretation Theory in Schleiermacher, Dilthey, Heidegger, and Gadamer.* Evanston, IL: Northwestern University Press, 1969.

Parham, Charles F. "The Pentecostal Baptism Restored." *Apostolic Faith* (October 1906).

———*A Voice Crying in the Wilderness,* 2nd ed. Baxter Springs, Kansas: Apostolic Faith Bible College, n.d.

Patai, Raphael. *The Arab Mind.* New York, Charles Scribner's Sons, 1973.

Patterson, E. M. "Behavioral Science Research on the Nature of Glossolalia." *Journal of American Scientific Affiliation* (1968).

Peck, Scott M. *The People of the Lie, Hope for Healing Human Evil.* New York: Simon and Schuster, 1983.

Pentecost, J. Dwight. *The Words and Works of Jesus Christ.* Grand Rapids, MI: Zondervan Publishing, 1981.

Perry, Edmund. *The Gospel in Dispute.* Garden City, NY: Doubleday, 1958.

Peterson, Mike. "The New Churches and Social Action." Asbury Theological Seminary (unpublished manuscript, n.d.).

Philipsen, Gerry. "A Theory of Speech Codes." In *Developing Communication Theories,* ed. Gerry Philipsen and Terrance L. Albrecht. Albany, NY: Suny Press, 1997.

Piaget, J. *The Origins of Intelligence in Children.* NY: Basic Books, 1969.

Pierson, Arthur T. "Speaking in Tongues." *Missionary Review of the World* XX (September 1907).

Pomerville, Paul A. *The Third Force in Missions.* Peabody, MA: Hendrickson Publishers, Inc., 1985.

———"A Case Atudy in the Contextualization of the Gospel: A Critique of the Reformed View of Scripture in the Post-Reformation Period." M.A. Thesis, Seattle Pacific University, 1980.

Postman, Neil. *Teaching as Conserving Activity.* New York: Delacorte Press, 1979.

Postman, Neil and Charles Weingartner. *Teaching as a Subversive Activity.* New York: Dell, 1969.

Potter, Charles F. *The Faiths Men Live By.* NY: Prentice Hall Pub. Co., 1954.

Powers, Janet Evert. "Missionary Tongues?" *Journal of Pentecostal Theology* 17 (2000).

———"Your Daughters Shall Prophesy." In *The Globalization of Pentecostalism,* eds. Murray Dempster, Byron Klaus, Douglas Petersen. Irving, CA: Regnum Books International, 1999.

Price, Fredrick. "Manifestations." In *Indian Witness* (1907).

Reusch, Jurgen and Welson Kess. *Non-Verbal Communication: Notes on Visual Perception of Human Relations.* Berkeley, CA: University of California Press, 1956.

Richardson, Don. *Eternity in Their Hearts.* Ventura, CA: Regal Books, 1981.

Richardson, J. T. "Psychological Interpretations of Glossolalia: A Re-examination of Research" *Journal for the Scientific Study of Religion* 12 (1973).

Robeck Cecil M. Jr. *Azusa Street, Mission and Revival, The Birth of the Pentecostal Movement.* Nashville, TN: Thomas Nelson, Inc., 2006.

———, ed. *Charismatic Experiences in History.* Peabody, MA: Hendrickson Pub. Inc., 1985.

———"A Pentecostal Looks at the World Council of Churches." *The Ecumenical Review* 47 (1995).

——— "Taking Stock of Pentecostalism: The Personal Reflections of a Retiring Editor." *Pneuma: The Journal of the Society for Pentecostal Studies* 15 (Spring 1993).

——— "William J. Seymour and the Bible Evidence" In *Initial Evidence,Historical and Biblical Perspective on the Pentecostal Doctrine of Spirit Baptism,* ed. Gary McGee. Peabody, MA: Hendrickson Publishing, 1991.

Roberson, Dave. *The Walk of The Spirit—The Walk of Power.* Tulsa, OK: Dave Roberson Ministries, 1999.

Rogers, Carl. *On Becoming a Person: A Therapist's View of Psychotherapy.* Boston: Houghton Mifflin, 1961.

Ross, Raymond S. *Persuasion: Communication and Interpersonal Relations.* Englewood Cliffs, NJ: Prentice Hall, 1974.

Ruthven, Jon. "Are Pentecostal Seminaries a Good Idea?" In *Pneuma, The Journal of the Society of Pentecostal Studies,* Vol. 26, No. 2 (Fall 2004).

——— "Back to the Future for Pentecostal/Charismatic Evangelicals in North America and World Wide: Radicalizing Evangelical Theology and Practice." Unpublished manuscript, 2003.

———*On The Cessation of the Charismata, The Protestant Polemic on Postbiblical Miracles.* Sheffield, England: Sheffield Academic Press, 1993.

Rybarczyk, Edmund. "Expressing the Inexpressible: Tongues as Apophatic Speech." Presentation at the 31st Annual Meeting of the Society for Pentecostal Studies (2002).

Saint Exupery, Antoine. *The Little Prince.* New York: Harcourt, Brace & World, 1943.

Samarin, William J. *Tongues of Men and Angels: The Religious Language of Pentecostalism.* NY: Macmillan, 1972.

Sanders, J. O. *Spiritual Leadership.* Chicago, IL: Moody Press, 1980. Rev. ed. 1989,

Sanford, Agnes. *The Healing Gifts of the Spirit.* Philadelphia: Lippincott, 1966.

Sapir, Edward. *Language, Culture, and Personality.* Berkley, CA: University of California Press, 1957.

Sargant, William, FRCP. *Proceedings of the Royal Society of Medicine.* London: Longmans, Green and Co., 1949.

Satyavrata, Ivan M. "Contextual Perspectives on Pentecostalism as a Global Culture: A South Asian View." In *The Globalization of Pentecostalism*, eds. Murray Dempster, Byron Klaus, Douglas Petersen. Irving, CA: Regnum Books International, 1999.

Schaff, Philip. *History of the Christian Church I.* Grand Rapids, MI: Eerdmans, 1955.

Schorsch, Ismer. *The Sacred Cluster.* NY: The Jewish Theo. Seminary, n.d.

Schramm, W. "How Communication Works" in *The Process and Effects of Mass Communication*, ed. W. Schramm and D. F Parks. Urbana, Il: University of Illinois Press, 1971.

Schwab, Charles. Quoted in Jo Condril and Bennie Bough. *101 Ways to Improve Your Communication Skills Instantly.* Alexandria, VA: Goalminds, 1998.

Schwartz, Tony. *The Responsive Chord.* Garden City, NY: Anchor Press/Double Day,1973.

Sengue, Ngoni. "Identity Crises in African Church." *EMQ* 17:2 (1999).

Shannon, Claude, and Warren Weaver. *The Mathematical Theory of Communication.* Urbana: University of Illinois Press, 1949.

Sheikh, Bilquis. *I Dared to Call Him Father.* Old Tappan, NJ: Chosen Books, 1978.

Shepherd, J.W. *The Christ of the Gospels.* Grand Rapids, MI: Zondervan Publishing House, 1946.

Simpson, A. B. *The Alliance Witness,* Vol. 98, No. 9 (May 1, 1963).

Slay, James L. "Its Value to the Individual." In *The Glossolalia Phenomenon,* ed. Wade Horton. Cleveland, TN: Pathway Press, 1966.

Smith, F. H. in Edmund Perry. *The Gospel in Dispute.* Garden City, NY: Doubleday, 1958.

Smith, James K.A. "The Closing of the Book: Pentecostals, Evangelicals, and the Sacred Writings." *JPT* 11 (1997).

Spittler, Russ, P. "Glossolalia" in *Dictionary of Pentecostal and Charismatic Movements,* ed. Stan Burgess and Gary McGee. Grand Rapids, MI: Zondervan Publishers, 1992.

———"Pentecostal Theology: A Classical Viewpoint." In *Perspectives on the New Pentecostalism,* ed. Russell P. Spittler. Grand Rapids, MI: Baker Book House, 1976.

Steuer, J. "Defining Virtual Reality: Dimensions Determining Telepresence." *Journal of Communication,* 42 (4).

Stock, Brian. *The Implications of Literacy: Written Language and Models of Interpretation in the Eleventh and Twelfth Centuries.* Princeton: Princeton University Press, 1983.

Stolee, H. J. *Pentecostalism: The Problem of the Modern Tongues Movement.* Minneapolis, MN: Augsburg Publishing House, 1936.

Stott, John R.W. *Baptism and Fullness: The Work of the Holy Spirit Today.* Downer's Grove: Inter-Varsity Press, 1975.

———"The Bible in World Evangelism." In *Perspectives on the World Christian Movement: A Reader.* Pasadena, CA , Wm. Carey Library, 1999.

Street, A. E. In "The Intercessory Missionary." Fort Wayne, IN: n.d. (Presumed to be 1910 from similar dated material).

Stronstad, Roger. *The Charismatic Theology of St. Luke.* Peabody, MA: Hendrickson Publishers, 1984.

———*Spirit, Scripture and Theology.* Baguio, Philippines: APTS Press, 1995.

Synan, Vinson. *The Century of the Holy Spirit.* Nashville, TN: Thomas Nelson, 2001.

———*Holiness-Pentecostal Movement.* Grand Rapids, MI: Eerdman's Publishing Co., 1971.

———*The Twentieth Century Pentecostal Explosion.* Altamonte Springs, FL: Creation House, 1987.

Tanner, J. "Human Growth and Constitution." In Harrison, J Weiner, J. Tanner, and N. Barnicot, eds. *Human Biology: an Introduction to Human Evolution, Variation, and Growth.* NY: Oxford University Press, 1964.

Tarr, Del. *Double Image: Biblical Insight from African Parables.* NY: Paulist Press, 1994.

———"Indirection and Ambiguity as a Mode of Communication in West Africa, a Descriptive Study." Ph. D. diss. University of Minnesota, 1980 (Mircofilms # 80-19577).

———"Preaching the Word in the Power of the Spirit: A Cross Cultural Analysis." In *Called and Empowered: Global Mission in Pentecostal Perspective.*

Murray Dempster, Byron Klaus, and Douglas Petersen, eds. Peabody, MA, Hendrickson Publishers, 1991.

———"Transcendence/Immanence and the Emerging Pentecostal Academy." *The 9th William Menzies Annual Lectureship, APTS.* Baguio City, Philippines: January 2001.

Tenney, Merrill. *New Testament Survey.* Grand Rapids, MI: Wm B. Eerdmans Pub. Co., 1985.

Thoburn, J. M. *The Church of Pentecost.* NY: Methodist Publishing House, 1899.

Thorkelson, William. As reported in *Lutherans and the Holy Spirit, Voice.* Los Angeles, 1964.

Toon, Peter. *The Development of Doctrine in the Church.* Grand Rapids: Eerdmans, 1979.

Traylor, Ellen Gunderson. *Song of Abraham.* Polson, MT: Port Hole Publications, 2003.

Tucker, Ruth A. *From Jerusalem to Irian Jaya.* Grand Rapids, MI: Zondervan Publishing House, 1983.

Tunks, George. "I Believe in the Holy Ghost." *The Pentecostal Evangel* (June 2, 1963).

Turner, Victor, and Edward Bruner, eds. *The Anthropology of Experience.* Urbana, IL: University of Illinois Press, 1986.

Tournier, Paul. *The Meaning of Persons.* New York: Harper, 1957.

Unger, Merrill F. *The Baptism and Gifts of the Holy Spirit.* Chicago: Moody Press, 1974.

Van Duson, Henry. *Spirit, Son and Father.* NY: Charles Scribner's Sons, 1958.

Versteeg, John M. *Perpetuating Pentecost.* Chicago: Willte, Clark, and Colby, 1930.

Wacker, Grant. "Travail of a Broken Family: Radical Evangelical Responses to the Emergence of Pentecostalism in America, 1906-16." In *Pentecostal Currents in American Protestantism,* ed. E.L. Blumhofer, et al. Chicago: University of Illinois Press, 1999.

———*Heaven Below.* Cambridge, MA: Harvard University Press, 2001.

Wagner. C. Peter. In *Perspectives on the World Christian Movement.* Winter, Ralph, and Steven C. Hawthorne. Pasadena, CA: William Carey Library, 1999.

——— *The Third Wave of the Holy Spirit.* Ann Arbor, MI: Vine Books, 1988.

——— *Your Spiritual Gifts Can Help Your Church.* Ventura, CA: Regal Books, 1979.

Wardlaw, Don. *Preaching Biblically, Creating Sermons in the Shape of Scripture.* Philadelphia: Westminster, 1983.

Warfield, Benjamin B. *Counterfeit Miracles,* 1918. Reprint, Carlisle, Pa: Banner of Truth, 1976.

Weiss, Ichamenes. *The History of Primitive Christianity.* NY: Wilson-Erickson, 1937.

Welch, John W. "What the Baptism Really Is." *Advance* 6 (August 26, 1939).

Wesley, John. In his journal, Sunday, November 25, 1759. In Bremback, Carl. *What Meaneth This?* Springfield, MO: Gospel Publishing House, 1947.

Wheelwright, Philip. *Metaphor and Reality.* Bloomington: Indiana University Press, 1962.

Whorf, Benjamin Lee. *Language, Thought and Reality: Selected Writings of B.L. Whorf,* ed. John B. Carroll. New York, NY: Wiley, 1956.

Whyte, Lancelot Law. *The Unconscious Mind Before Freud.* New York: Basic Books, Inc., 1960. Quoting Dionysurs Areopagiticus, 50 AD. In James L. Slay, "Its Value to the Individual." *The Glossolalia Phenomenon*, ed. Wade Horton. Cleveland, TN: Pathway Press, 1966.

Wiggelsworth, Smith. *Smith Wigglesworth On The Holy Spirit.* New Kensington, PA: Whitaker House, 1998.

Williams, Cyril, G. *Tongues of the Spirit: A Study of Pentecostal Glossolalia and Related Phenomena.* Cardiff: Univ of Whales Univ., 1981.

Williams, George H., and Edith Waldovoel. "A History of Speaking in Tongues and Related Gifts." In *The Charismatic Movement,* ed. Michael P. Hamilton. Grand Rapids: William B. Eerdmans Publishing Co., 1975.

———"Baptism in the Holy Spirit." *Dictionary of Pentecostal and Charismatic Movements.* Burgess, Stanley M., Gary B. McGee, and Patrick H. Alexander, eds. Grand Rapids, MI: Zondervan Publishing House, 1988.

Williams, J. Rodman. *Renewal Theology II.* Grand Rapids: Zondervan, 1990.

Willis, Lewis, J. "Glossolalia in Perspective." In *The Glossolalia Phenomenon,* ed. Wade Horton. Cleveland, TN: Pathway, 1966.

Wilson, Everett. "They Crossed the Red Sea, Didn't They?" In Dempster, Murray W., Byron D. Klaus, and Douglas Petersen, eds. *The Globalization of Pentecostalism, A Religion Made to Travel* (Carlisle, UK: Regnum Books International), 1999.

Wilson, Sarah H. In "Guest Column," *Christianity Today* (2004).

Woods, Bernard. *Communication, Technology and the Development of People.* London: Routledge Publishing, Inc., 1993.

Wright, Paul. *People and Their Beliefs.* Bruxelles: International Correspondence Institute, 1987.

Yancey, Phillip. *The Jesus I Never Knew.* Grand Rapids, MI: Zondervan Publishers, 1995.

____________ "Letters from the Borderlands." *Outreach* (September/October, 2003).

York, John, V. *Missions in the Age of the Spirit.* Springfield, MO: Gospel Publishing House, 2000.

Zizioulas, John D. *Being As Communication: Studies in Personhood and the Church.* Crestwood: SVS, 1985.

GENERAL INDEX

SCRIPTURE INDEX

AUTHOR INDEX